The Complete Adoption Book, Third Edition

Everything You Need to Know to Adopt a Child

Laura Beauvais-Godwin and Raymond Godwin, Esq.

ADAMS MEDIA
AVON, MASSACHUSETTS

Published by Adams Media, an F+W Publications Company
57 Littlefield Street
Avon, MA 02322
www.adamsmedia.com

ISBN-13: 978-1-59337-369-6
ISBN-10: 1-59337-369-4
Printed in the United States of America.

J I H G F E D C B

Library of Congress Cataloging-in-Publication Data
Beauvais-Godwin, Laura.
The complete adoption book : everything you need to know to adopt
a child / Laura Beauvais-Godwin and Raymond Godwin.— 3rd ed.
p.   cm.
Includes bibliographical references and index.
ISBN 1-59337-369-4
1. Adoption—United States. I. Godwin, Raymond. II. Title.
HV875.55.B45 2005
62.734'0973—dc22
2005019809

The authors have made every effort to ensure that the information contained in this book is current and up to date; however, matters relative to adoption often change quickly. Because adoption involves people and changing information, the authors have found that each adoption scenario is unique and different to some degree. This book, therefore, should not be a substitute for an adoption professional's involvement in your specific adoption matter.

This publication is designed to provide accurate and authoritative information with regard to the subject matter covered. It is sold with the understanding that the publisher is not engaged in rendering legal, accounting, or other professional advice. If legal advice or other expert assistance is required, the services of a competent professional person should be sought.
—From a *Declaration of Principles* jointly adopted by a Committee of the
American Bar Association and a Committee of Publishers and Associations

Many of the designations used by manufacturers and sellers to distinguish their product are claimed as trademarks. Where those designations appear in this book and Adams Media was aware of a trademark claim, the designations have been printed with initial capital letters.

This book is available at quantity discounts for bulk purchases.
For information, please call 1-800-289-0963.

We dedicate this book to our dear children, Erika and Elizabeth, who have taught us that a true family is one based on love, openness, and honesty. We also thank their birth mothers, who made this all possible.

CONTENTS

Preface

I n the United States today, there are between 200,000 and 500,000 single people or couples who want to adopt. This dream is said to be very costly and difficult to achieve. Yet, nearly everyone we know who has actively and diligently sought to adopt has had a baby or child in the home within eighteen months.

Seventeen years ago my husband Ray and I did not know this. In fact, we were not aware that there were choices in the area of adoption. We did not know that a couple could adopt and have a baby within months. When we seriously began to consider adoption, we gave little thought to independent adoption. The idea of advertising for a baby made us uncomfortable; more important, we did not know anyone who had adopted independently. We had heard that independent adoption was risky and that it usually required the assistance of an expensive attorney.

So, for a couple of years we pursued adoption through more traditional channels. Like many prospective adoptive parents, we spent years examining applications and finally completed the forms for a few adoption agencies. This was a rather complicated process since some applications were quite lengthy, and even after completing forms and sending in application fees, we had no guarantee of becoming parents. After attending a meeting conducted by an international adoption agency, we finally decided that we would adopt through an agency that placed Korean babies in a matter of months.

Then on the day that we mailed our final application to the international agency, an acquaintance called us and asked whether we would be interested in meeting with a pregnant woman who wanted to place her baby for adoption. We were stunned. In a reversal of all our expectations, we became parents in four short months through independent adoption.

Moving from that fateful telephone call to our daughter Erika's arrival was trying, despite the fact that our adoption was relatively simple and uneventful. So after we became adoptive parents, my husband decided to use his experience in family law and his personal experience as an adoptive parent to provide independent adoption services. Two and a half years after Erika was born, an agency for whom Ray worked as a consultant asked whether he would be interested in adopting a baby that was soon to be born. Three weeks later, Elizabeth was in our arms.

Later, I provided contracted services for the Department of Social Services. Then seven years ago, I was invited by David and Mary Mexcur of New Hope Christian Services, an adoption agency in New Hampshire, to start international adoption programs in South Carolina; so in 1998, Carolina Hope Christian Adoption Agency was born.

Our goal in writing this book is to provide you, the prospective adoptive parent, with a step-by-step resource to guide you through a process that can sometimes feel overwhelming. Couples often tell us that they feel bewildered—that they do not even know where to begin. We have been there, too. In fact, when we were researching the adoption laws and practices of Canada, we were reminded of what it was like to begin the adoption process for the first time. When we started to look at adoption, we were helped tremendously by adoptive parents associated with a local chapter of RESOLVE, an infertility support and referral organization. They understood adoption issues and knew how to give us good, practical advice. Simple things such as encouraging the birth mother to stay on a nonmaternity floor if she wished was invaluable information at a time when our emotions were running high. In fact, knowing people who had been through all the emotions that we were about to experience was very comforting.

Still, even with this advice we often felt unsure about how to handle certain situations. Unfortunately, we knew of no book that could help us with issues such as talking with birth mothers, meeting with obstetricians, and when to pay medical expenses. Nor did we know of a book that could prepare us for the perplexing situations that my husband and I would encounter: the obstetrician who told my daughter's birth mother that the adoption was illegal or the hospital staff who made insensitive remarks.

Our experience has taught us that nearly every adoption unfolds a little differently from what is expected. Adoption—like all other miracles—has its quirks and unpredictable moments. Nevertheless, there are some constants in the process, and preparation can alleviate a great deal of uncertainty. If you follow our advice, there's no reason pursuing adoption shouldn't be a positive experience for you and for the birth parents too, if they are involved in the process.

As with any process, the more you know about adoption at the outset, the more confident you can be. There is a lot of information contained in the following pages and a lot of choices to make. Do not become overloaded. Find what is best for you. As you will see, adoption can be broken down into manageable steps. In the chapters that follow, you will find much of the legal and practical information you will need to make you comfortable with the process. We have experienced many different adoption situations and learned a great deal about the nuances of the process. We also remember how we felt when we first got involved in adoption. We hope this book reflects that.

All information offered in this book is true to the best of our knowledge. Information, however—especially legal information—can change rapidly. Rely on an adoption attorney for updates.

Names have been changed throughout, unless otherwise stated, and certain facts altered to protect anonymity.

Attorneys, state agencies, newspapers, support groups, books, newsletters, professionals, and organizations mentioned in this book *are not* endorsed by Laura Beauvais-Godwin or Raymond Godwin. It is up to the reader to investigate the credentials of any person or organization before using its services.

ACKNOWLEDGMENTS

This book could not have been written without the many professionals who provided us with their expertise. We would like to thank the staff at the National Adoption Information Clearinghouse and the North American Council on Adoptable Children.

Thanks for all your encouragement and hard work.

Our very special thanks goes to the countless friends, adoption professionals, adoptive parents, birth parents, and adoptees whose lives have demonstrated that adoption is a loving choice and have made so many dreams come true.

Chapter One

Looking at Adoption Today

f you are reading this book, chances are you are considering adoption. This book is designed to assist you in navigating through this process, explaining how to decide if adoption is right for you and how to know which method may be the best.

Perhaps you have always wanted to adopt a child and are now at a point in your life where you can seriously proceed with such plans. You may be married; you may be single. If you are in the middle of infertility treatment or nearing the end of that treatment, you may be wondering, "Where do I turn now?" It may be some time since you ended your treatments, and now you are ready to proceed with adoption. Perhaps you have children, maybe several children, but you would like to have more children. Many families facing the "empty nest" decide that adoption is the way to have the excitement of children in the home.

Regardless of what you know about adoption and whether you even want to adopt, you probably do know that the world of adoption is far from simple. There is a lot to learn because there are so many options. For you, the good news is that also means a lot of choices.

Today's prospective adoptive parents are far more educated about adoption than those beginning the investigation just a few years ago. Chances are you have already done some research on the Internet regarding adoption. If you clicked on any search engine, you have come across Adoption.org and Adoption.com, two sites that provide an abundance of information about adoption, as well as countless adoption organization Web sites. You probably know that there are many agencies out there, there are many children available for adoption, and the children profiled are usually older or have special needs. You also have some idea of what the fees are for the various types of adoption.

Although the Internet is a great resource for information, the endless information may still not provide you with the guidance needed to make the right choice since searching is usually not systematic and detailed. Initially the process will probably seem confusing. Should you hire an attorney and adopt independently or go with an agency? Is it better to adopt internationally or simply go through the local social services department? No one can answer these questions for you. You must consider the advantages and disadvantages of each route and decide which risks and expenses you can live with and which ones you cannot.

However, no matter how much fact-gathering you may have done, you still may feel that you need a systematic way to determine the type of child that would be best for your family and what would be the best route to complete an adoption. This book is designed to help you learn about your options in a more organized manner than just searching various topics on the Internet. There are pros and cons to each type of adoption that you must consider. Each family considering adoption has various expectations and limitations. Some of these expectations may need to change if you are realistically going to adopt. On the other hand, you may know your limitations, what resources you have, and the type of child that you would like to adopt. Some people have the fortitude to deal with certain types of legal risks; others do not. Certainly income and financial resources will determine the type of an adoption you can pursue. Also the age and race of the child that you seek to adopt will determine the route taken. If you want to pursue the adoption of a child who has come from an institution or has experienced some trauma, you will need to consider the risks for the child and for your family.

Even after doing some research and perhaps even after you have decided on the method you want to pursue, approaching the adoption itself can feel overwhelming. There can be so many fees, unknown expenses, and so much paperwork. You have to think about getting through a home study, possibly meeting a birth mother, or even traveling to another country. You may create worries of your own by presuming that you must look a certain way, weigh a certain amount, and earn a certain income.

All adoptive parents go through some of these worries, and they should. After all, this is a major life decision. With so many avenues to explore, it is important to take your time and ask as many questions as you can. Emotionally, you have a lot at stake; so proceed cautiously. Get all of your facts in order and try not to let your feelings run ahead of your wallet or reality. Remember, proceeding cautiously does not mean proceeding slowly.

Many couples spend a year or two or three just "thinking about adoption," doing some research, and making a few contacts. Everyone knows that adopting a child, especially through a social services department, means there can be much uncertainty as to how the child will adjust and how you will adjust to having another person in your home.

Those going through infertility treatment may still be trying to conceive; others are just not quite ready to make the decision. Each month may hold some promise that you may conceive, making it difficult to commit wholeheartedly to the adoption process. Without the immediate promise of a real live baby, you may find it hard to put much effort into completing forms, getting the paperwork together for a home study, and writing out your life stories. The thought of talking to a birth mother may unnerve you, and when you consider traveling to another country, you remember the friend who got malaria while in Africa.

So you say to yourself, "Let's wait another couple of months and see whether anything happens." This is understandable. What we hope to do in this book is show you that the obstacles are not insurmountable. Sure, it is unfair. Biological parents do not have to go through the research, assemble documents, submit to a home study, or pay the fees. But if you are considering adoption, it is worth it. There are babies and children to adopt, and it does not take years to do it. Usually the cost of adopting an infant in the United States or a baby from overseas will cost you what a car will cost you. You do not have to be rich, and you do not have to be perfect—just stable and loving.

THERE ARE CHILDREN TO ADOPT

Many people believe that all adoptions are difficult, take years, or are so expensive that no one but the wealthy can afford to adopt. However, there are many children seeking homes, and a good percentage of adoptions cost little or no money.

How many parents are looking to adopt? You will sometimes see the figure of two million couples being bandied about. That figure, though, really relates to the number of infertile couples, not all of whom are pursuing adoption. Elizabeth Bartholet, author of *Family Bonds*, wrote that at any given time there are approximately 200,000 women looking to adopt, and now that number of women considering adoption has increased to 500,000. The latest statistics seem to indicate that there are about 100,000 nonrelative adoptions each year. That means that in any given year about one prospective family in five of those considering adoption will adopt. Those numbers may not seem like very promising numbers. This may be because there is a real lack of concrete data regarding numbers of families seriously seeking to adopt and numbers of children placed for adoption. We do know that many more families are choosing adoption, not just as a way to have children but as a way to make a difference in the lives of children. Families are choosing adoption not only because of infertility, but also because they want to have more children. These are single people as well as couples who may have older children and are in their forties and fifties and know that they would like to have the opportunity to continue parenting. Sometimes couples who have been married before want to have children together because they are still young enough to parent but perhaps a bit too old to go through childbirth.

We also know that virtually everyone who seriously seeks to adopt will have a child.

The number of adoptions by nonrelatives has fluctuated over the years. In 1951, there were 33,800; in 1961, there were 61,600. Adoptions reached a peak of 89,000 in 1970, and then fell to 47,000 in 1975. Throughout the 1990s, there were probably about 63,000 adoptions by nonrelatives every year. In 2000 and 2001, 127,000 children were adopted in the United States. According to the National Adoption Information Clearinghouse in 2004, the number of adoptions each year since 1987 has remained fairly constant. The numbers of adoptions taking place can be hard to measure because only Citizenship and Immigration Services keeps nearly exact numbers of international adoptions. These numbers are higher than ever and now account for 15 percent of adoptions. Child welfare departments usually maintain good records for each state, and the number of adoptions through publicly funded child welfare agencies has increased to more than 50,000 and now accounts for 40 percent of all adoptions. However, the number of private domestic adoptions—whether through agencies or attorneys—has not been tracked consistently outside of social service departments. It is estimated though that about 30,000 to 50,000 domestic infant adoptions took place, about 50,000 children were adopted through the foster care system, and in 2003 more than 21,000 children were adopted internationally. Therefore it could be safe to say that at least 100,000 nonrelative adoptions took place in 2003.

Intrafamily adoptions (grandparents adopting grandchildren, aunts and uncles adopting nieces and nephews) and stepparent adoptions account for about 60,000 adoptions. Because many such adoptions are private, the exact number is not known. Many other adoptions may go unrecorded as well. All that is really clear is that adoption figures vary dramatically from state to state—influenced not only by population, but also by the various state laws regulating adoption. So, hard numbers are elusive. We do know this. People are adopting. The experience of adoptive professionals and parents proves it.

WHO CAN ADOPT?

Before you even consider the best method of adopting, you may not be certain if you can adopt, and from looking at these Web sites, you may be less than certain as to who qualifies to adopt.

Nearly anyone who can provide a child with a stable, loving environment can become an adoptive parent. You do not have to be under thirty-five, have a large income, own a home, have money in the bank, or be married, childless, or infertile. Unlike any other group of parents, however, you will be required to provide information that indicates you are stable and loving; you are not too old to parent; your health is sufficient for parenting; you have enough income to provide for a child; you have adequate space for the child to live; if you are married, your marriage is healthy and you do not have an extensive divorce history; and if you do have children, they are not exhibiting problems related to poor parenting.

Each state requires that you be evaluated by a social worker or caseworker, who will then prepare a preplacement report known as a home study. Regulations as to what is included in this study are established by each state, but the basic standard is really one of common sense. What does it take to be a fit parent—basic financial wherewithal, stability, and love. The home-study process is designed to screen out those who would not make suitable parents because of serious medical problems, mental illness, insufficient income, a criminal history, record of child abuse, or current drug or alcohol addiction.

Unless you have a serious problem, chances are good that you will be able to adopt.

You may run into other restrictions, depending on what avenues you decide to explore. Some licensed agencies place restrictions as to who can adopt as a means of limiting the number of prospective adoptive parents. Public agencies have requirements that those adopting children with special needs be able to meet the challenge of raising a child who has physical, mental, or emotional disabilities or illnesses. Every foreign country has its own guidelines as to who can adopt.

HOW TO BEGIN

Many people begin investigating adoption by looking under "adoption" on the Internet. They then may e-mail the attorneys and agencies or call them. If you want to adopt an infant from the United States, contacting some agencies can be very discouraging. If you are looking to adopt a healthy infant, most social services departments have years-long waiting lists. Private agencies may also have long waiting lists, and they may have many requirements and restrictions, not to mention high fees. The next step you may then take is to call attorneys' offices, where you may be told that you will need to advertise for a possible birth mother, meet her, and possibly pay her living expenses for several months. If you then turn to an international adoption agency, you will learn that if you adopt from certain countries, you must travel to the country and stay there for at least two to three weeks. All these options seem to have a downside.

All you want is a baby or child, and suddenly you must consider what route you want to take, whether you will be accepted, whether you can afford it, and whether you are ready to take the risk. For many, it can feel overwhelming.

No matter what avenue you choose, there will be risks, whether they are financial risks, risks relating to the child's health, or risks associated with birth parents' rights. But these are calculated risks—not blind risks. For some, the risks associated with certain kinds of adoptions are enough to keep them away from these options. Others decide to go ahead. Only you can make the choice.

WHAT KIND OF CHILD DO YOU WANT?

In deciding which route to take, you may first want to consider what kind of child you want to adopt. Initially most people—especially those who have never had any children—think of adopting a healthy newborn infant or a very young baby of their own ethnic background. But as people begin to consider adoption, the categories of adoptable children they will consider can broaden. This does not mean that a couple who had their heart set on a healthy Caucasian infant but could not afford the fees decides to "settle" for a two-year-old of another ethnic background. It is far more complex than that. All adoptive parents must carefully consider their background, resources, family, neighborhood, friends, faith, community, and available schools in considering what kind of child would be best suited for their family.

WHAT ROUTE DO YOU WANT TO TAKE?

There are two broad categories of adoptions: domestic and international. Within each of those two categories there are two general types of children to be adopted: those who are healthy and those who have special needs.

When adopting domestically, most people are interested in adopting healthy infants.

There are two routes for achieving this goal. One is private, or independent, adoption. This entails hiring an attorney who will either locate a birth mother for you or instruct you on how to find one yourself through advertising or networking. The other route is to go with an agency, either public (a state agency) or private. The advantages, disadvantages, and legal issues associated with these two routes are discussed at length in the chapters that follow. For now, you may simply find it helpful to know that state agencies do have some healthy children to place for adoption and that applying to a state agency does not necessarily mean applying for a child with special needs, as many people believe.

Many couples begin as foster parents and then learn as much as possible in order to be in the right place at the right time for a permanent placement. The success of this approach depends on the state and the timing. Not many infant adoptions take place through these state agencies, but your local state agency may present an opportunity. Some attorneys specialize in representing foster parents who aggressively push for adoption.

Most state agencies and a few private ones focus on placing children with special needs in the homes of adoptive couples. The special needs category includes both physical and psychological needs, with the label "physical needs" covering a wide range of medical conditions. Special needs children often come from abusive homes. Having been surrendered voluntarily by dysfunctional birth parents or taken from such homes by court order, they have usually been placed in foster homes for a time. The state agency operating the foster care system also has an adoption unit, which attempts to place the children for adoption. Again, the severity of the "need," whether physical or psychological, varies greatly.

ADOPTING AFTER INFERTILITY

If you have been undergoing infertility treatment, you have probably felt out of control. Not only have you not achieved a successful pregnancy, but also other areas of your life have probably been very much affected. You may not have taken the vacation you wanted because it conflicted with your infertility treatment, or infertility has affected the way that you relate to others. For example, you may find it difficult to be around pregnant women, while attending a baby shower has become nearly intolerable. The self-doubt and out-of-control feelings that accompany infertility may remain with you as you approach the adoption process.

It is important to try and resolve some of the negative feelings associated with infertility and also to examine your true feelings toward adoption, both positive and negative. Infertility treatment is an exhausting, time-consuming undertaking, and you may feel that you do not have the emotional energy to pursue these issues diligently. If you choose adoption, however, now is the time to begin resolving your feelings. If you pursue a private adoption, you may be parents quickly—perhaps even before you have had time to search within yourself and feel whole again. On the other hand, couples pursuing agency adoptions may be required to attend infertility and adoption workshops for several weeks. They also may be on a waiting list for one to five years—plenty of time to explore their feelings.

Adopting a baby does not necessarily alleviate all the insecurities that accompany infertility. Join an adoption support group or an infertility support group, such as RESOLVE, to learn more about infertility and adoption issues. Read this and other books that deal with adoption after infertility. Not only will you be better prepared to be in charge of your adoption plans, but you will also be more comfortable in talking with others about your desire to adopt.

ARE YOU READY TO ACCEPT PARENTHOOD THROUGH ADOPTION?

You have probably invested much time, money, and energy in attempts to have a biological child. Somewhere in the middle of your infertility treatment, you probably began to ask yourself why you so desperately wanted to have a child. As you thought about that question and underwent more invasive procedures, you may have been more convinced than ever that you wanted a biological child. As a successful pregnancy began to seem less and less likely, however, you had to move from your dream of having a biological child to considering child-free living or adopting. Now, as you think of beginning the adoption process, you need to establish your reasons for becoming parents and to realize that an adopted child can fulfill your need to be parents. The first step then is to explore why you really want to be a parent. Even if you are not adopting after infertility, many of the same questions need to be addressed: Why do I want to have a child, and what type of a child do I want to parent?

Life is a constant series of decisions. Some are minor, such as what to have for breakfast; some are major, such as choosing a college or a partner or deciding to have children. Nearly all the decisions we make are reversible. We can change our job, get a divorce, or transfer to another college. But one decision is never considered reversible, and that is the decision to have children.

That is why it is crucial to answer the question, "Why do we want to have children?" Although your reasons do not have to be completely logical, they should be defined because of the tremendous responsibility and expense that come with being a parent. You need to establish some rational and sensible motives for having children, if you are about to adopt.

People who set out to have biological children have many reasons for doing so, some more important than others. Here are the most common reasons people give for wanting children. Each is followed by a response suggesting why an adopted child would most likely meet a couple's needs.

To have the perfect child. Many people fantasize about having the "perfect" child. They think, "He will have my nose, my hair, my husband's eyes and lashes, my family's mind, and his family's language skills."

Response: Now imagine the worst possible genetic combination and ask yourself how "perfect" such a child would be. Don't forget to consider the worst traits of your family and in-laws. In other words, the "perfect" biological child might not be so perfect. There are many genes your child could inherit.

To pass on your family's genes. Perhaps your family is one that believes "blood is thicker than water." In fact, you may feel a great responsibility to pass on certain characteristics of your family or yourself to a child.

Response: Again, children can draw from a very large gene pool. There is no guarantee of passing on any single characteristic to your child. It may be that the characteristics you want to perpetuate have more to do with your values than with your family genes, however, and these are passed on to your child through your nurturing, not your genetic role. An adopted child will have the same opportunity to develop strong, positive values that a biological child would.

To have a child with your interests, talents, and abilities. The reasons for wanting a child who shares your interests are similar to those for wanting the "perfect" child: your desire to pass on the best of the family's traits. For example, you may be a wonderful pianist. Music may always have been a great love in your family. You might fear that an adopted child would not have the same innate musical ability that a biological child would have.

Response: First, acknowledge that even a biological child will not necessarily inherit your musical abilities. Second, be aware that you can seek out and select a birth mother who is musically inclined, if you believe that musical ability is inherited. Finally, remember that even a child born without innate musical ability can be coached to play a musical instrument and to appreciate fine music.

Of course, we must accept our children for who they are, not for what we want them to be. Whether our children are born to us or adopted by us, they are ours to love for themselves, not for what they do.

To pass on the family name. When people think of perpetuating a family heritage, the "family name" is often the thing they think of first. Viewed in this light, it becomes almost an obligation to pass on the family name.

Response: If you are a Louis Johnson III, can you feel comfortable naming an adopted child Louis Johnson IV? Some people's initial response is negative. Yet, when they think further about what it means to name a child after themselves or another family member, they realize that it does not really matter whether the child is biological or adopted. The feelings that parents have for their adopted children are the same as for biological children. Feelings of love make the connection between the parent and the child; the name can just be an extension of that connection.

To have your child accepted by other family members. Many couples fear that other family members will not love and accept an adopted child, particularly one of a different ethnic background.

Response: Research indicates that even relatives who are opposed to the adoption develop very strong feelings for the child once the child is placed.

To experience pregnancy and birth. Some women believe that to feel truly feminine they must experience pregnancy, giving birth to, and breastfeeding a baby.

Response: If these reasons for having a child are very important to you, then you need to grieve the loss of these opportunities. If you cannot move past the grieving stage, then perhaps you need to continue infertility treatment.

Joining an infertility support group, such as one offered by RESOLVE, can help you through the grieving process, as well as assisting you and your spouse in deciding when to continue infertility treatment or when to end it. Knowing when "enough is enough" can help you and your spouse move toward resolving your infertility and accepting adoption or child-free living.

To control the mother's health during pregnancy. Another reason to want biological children is to have as much control as possible during your pregnancy. As a conscientious person, you would eat well, take prenatal vitamins, avoid alcohol and drugs, and seek proper medical care.

Response: Adoptive parents are right to be concerned about the birth mother's well-being and health during her pregnancy, since we know that her health can influence a child's development. Actually, depending on what route to adoption you follow, control of the birth mother's health is not entirely out of your hands. Nevertheless, for some couples considering adoption, the risks are too great. Perhaps you and your spouse need to put your fears into words. Sometimes identifying fears can help you face them. Then you can determine what risks you are willing or not willing to take.

To rear a child that you love. This should be your number one reason for wanting to be a parent: to provide a loving and stable environment for a growing child. To make this investment in a life, you want the child to be truly yours. Indeed, some people believe that the love you have for a child is a result of the biological connection and not the relationship; therefore, an adopted child can't be truly theirs.

Response: Adoptive parents, some with both biological and adopted children, unanimously say that they love all their children the same.

For most, the decision to adopt follows infertility treatment. You may take comfort in knowing that although adoption may be your second choice, it is not second best.

WHAT ARE YOUR REASONS FOR WANTING A CHILD?

Having thought about some of the things that motivate people to have children, you and your spouse need to explore your reasons for wanting to be parents. Here is an exercise designed to help you do just that.

1. Working independently, write out the reasons you want a child.
2. Identify the reasons you have in common. Are there answers that are important to both of you? Is there one answer that is very important to you but not to your spouse?
3. Write out the needs that you believe having an adopted child can fulfill.

Chapter Two

Infant Adoption

The great majority of those seeking to adopt wish to adopt a healthy newborn infant. In the United States, it is estimated that between 30,000 and 50,000 infants or young babies are placed for adoption each year. In general, about 2 to 3 percent of unmarried women place a child for adoption. The percentage among African-American and Hispanic women is estimated to be lower.

Newborn infants born in the United States are placed almost exclusively through private agencies or attorneys. Few infants are placed through social service departments. Many families find a birth mother who is expecting a child on their own and then seek the assistance of an agency or attorney.

In general, if the laws of your state permit you to conduct a private adoption—most do—and you find a birth mother on your own, then you will most likely retain the services of an adoption attorney. Most state adoption statutes are broken down into two categories—nonagency placements, which include private or independent adoptions and familial placements, and adoption agency placements. Many states add the additional category of international adoption placements which can include agency and attorney-assisted placements in the country in which the child is born. Familial or family placements are usually stepparent, grandparent, and other family-related adoptions.

If this discussion sounds confusing, it can be! Understanding the terminology, however, helps an adoptive couple ask the right questions and know what is happening step by step in their adoption plan as it unfolds, whether domestically or internationally. For example, understanding how an adoption agency works can ensure a couple makes the correct decisions as to their baby, the birth mother and the adoption plan.

When parents seek the assistance of an adoption agency to find a birth mother and then adopt her child through the agency, what does all that really mean? Of course, the easy answer is that the agency assists the birth mother in placing her baby into the adoptive couple's home. However, does "adopt her child through the agency" mean that the agency retains temporary legal custody of the child until the adoption finalization—in essence becoming the child's guardian—or does the adoptive couple take temporary legal custody immediately upon placement?

The answer to this question is important for many reasons, but we're getting ahead of ourselves; let's start from the beginning.

WHAT IS AN ADOPTION AGENCY?

An *adoption agency* is a business incorporated as either a nonprofit or a for-profit entity. It is licensed by its state to place children for adoption and to conduct home studies. Some agencies only conduct home studies and are not child-placement agencies. The director of the agency must have certain qualifications, such as a master's in social work and several years of experience in the adoption field.

The social workers or caseworkers working for the adoption agency generally have at least a college degree, if not a master's in social work or other related field. Sometimes years of experience in social work or adoption will allow someone to work for the agency without having a specialized degree. Being qualified by state standards, however, does not guarantee that the worker is knowledgeable about adoption issues or highly sympathetic to your concerns and needs.

Fortunately, there are numerous directors and social workers involved with adoption agencies who are highly qualified and professional. Many are themselves adoptive parents and so can bring a special touch of empathy to the process.

Each state has its own laws and regulations as to who can form an agency and what guidelines must be followed to maintain an agency license or certification. Remember, just because an agency is incorporated as a nonprofit entity does not mean that the owner of the agency is not profiting from the organization; the owner will profit by drawing a salary. Nor does another agency's for-profit status imply that those who operate the agency are money-hungry and unscrupulous.

Whether an agency is nonprofit or for-profit has more to do with tax and legal considerations than anything else. It is commonly believed that operating as a nonprofit organization means an agency is more ethical and caring, since almost all well-known charities and religious organizations are nonprofit entities.

It is important to question an adoption agency about its experience and professionalism, no matter under what umbrella the agency is incorporated. The agency's written policy and the way it really functions can sometimes be quite different.

For example, most agencies have a policy stating that their purpose is to provide suitable homes for children—not to find children for couples. Their focus is often on the birth mother, with the agency in essence acting as her advocate; while the couple's interests may be secondary.

To use an illustration, in one case an agency, which had been working with an adoptive couple and the birth mother for four months, informed the couple for the first time (on the weekend they were to pick up their baby) that the birth mother wanted an open adoption after placement and that the couple had no choice in the matter. In this case, "open adoption" meant visits with the birth mother on a regular basis after placement and finalization of the adoption.

The agency director informed the couple that this was the way adoptions were done, and if the couple did not consent to such an arrangement, they were not ready for adoption in general—not just this adoption. The couple declined to go forward with the placement after speaking with their attorney who informed them that not all adoptions were open after placement and that the couple did have a choice.

There is no question that birth mothers and children do need advocates. But adoptive parents also have rights and feelings. An ethical agency will be clear up front as to its role in representing the birth parents and how the expectations of the adoptive couple will be met.

PRIVATE AGENCIES THAT PLACE INFANTS

Some adoptive couples think that all they have to do is apply to an agency, and after a short time, they'll receive a phone call that a baby is waiting to be picked up at the agency offices. Other than completing paperwork, the couple does nothing else—they do not meet the birth mother beforehand, they are not present for the birth, and they do not visit with the baby at the hospital, waiting anxiously for the legal documents to be signed by the birth mother. The baby may be a few days old or several months, depending on how long it takes to sort out the birth father's rights.

This may have been how couples adopted prior to the 1970s; however, this picture no longer matches reality. Today, most birth mothers will insist on choosing the adoptive couple themselves after either reviewing pictures and information about the couple or meeting with them, or both. A couple applying for adoption will usually put together what is called a portfolio, which essentially is a scrapbook about them, complete with photographs with descriptions and a "Dear Birth Mother" letter. These books are presented to the prospective birth mothers. From there, she may select a family or ask to meet two or more families.

Thus, the decision as to placement is very often left up to the birth mother, not the agency. Of course, the agency controls which portfolios it presents to the birth mother. But placements are no longer simply made on the basis of first come, first served. A couple's background, appearance, religion, jobs, hobbies, and more are now factored in by the agency and the birth mother.

It is vital that you understand the agency's procedures and costs. Discuss what the application fee is, if any, and what the fees are when matched. If the agency charges a minimum or no fee to apply with them, then certainly give them your application and portfolio. If up-front fees are reasonable, work with several agencies to increase the likelihood of being selected.

A good agency that does not have several birth mothers every month approaching them will encourage you to actively seek a birth mother through other agencies, networking organizations, and attorneys. Many attorneys also only charge a minimum or no fee to place an application with them along with a portfolio. A minimum fee would range from $150 to $750; to provide a comparison, some agencies (and attorneys) are changing $1,000 to $4,000 just to have a couple's profile accepted!

Most agencies will not permit you to apply with them until you have completed a home study because most states require that a couple must be approved by way of a home study to take placement of a child. When a situation arises in which a birth mother is available, they do not want to present any families unless they know that the family is approved and ready to take placement.

Agency staff generally network with other adoption professionals and oftentimes learn about certain adoption situations in which a family is needed. So even if a birth mother does not come directly to the agency with which you applied, the staff members may hear about other situations in which a child is available.

For example, sometimes a birth mother may have very specific requirements as to the family she seeks, and the agency which is assisting her does not have a couple who would meet her demands. Many times a birth mother will ask for a couple who are of a particular faith or a couple who are both college educated.

Agency adoptions take several different forms. Let's begin with the traditional agency adoption.

RELIGIOUS AGENCIES

Some agencies providing adoption services have a specific religious affiliation. These include Catholic Charities, Lutheran Social Ministries, Jewish Family Services, and Bethany Christian Services. From this group, some take applicants only from certain religious affiliations, while others have more flexible policies, especially for children with special needs or minority children. This means that a couple will be considered even if they are not of that faith. One well-known example of this flexibility is Holt International Adoption Agency. After the Korean War in the early 1950s, Holt would only place children with families who espoused very conservative religious values. The demand was so great, since there were so many children available, that Holt relaxed its religious requirements in order to find homes for the number of orphans created by the post-Korean War conditions in South Korea during that time.

These agencies receive charitable donations and so can often keep their expenses lower. Moreover, they often do not charge directly or in advance for the birth mother's expenses (unlike most adoption agencies) because so many birth mothers change their minds when working with a religious adoption agency. These agencies usually have a set fee with coverage for living expenses only upon placement. If the birth mother changes her mind, you are not charged for her living expenses nor would you lose monies paid to a birth mother during her pregnancy, since the agency assisted the birth mother prior to birth pursuant to its mission statement.

To this end, services are sometimes provided to the birth mother through the agencies' own organizations. For example, they may allow or require her to live in a home for unwed mothers or with a family who will care for her during her pregnancy.

Religious agencies network with churches, crisis pregnancy centers, hospitals, private religious schools, and other organizations that often refer birth mothers to them. Because some of these agencies are well-known names, they are often the first place a birth mother will go when she learns she is pregnant.

Other religiously affiliated adoption agencies are offshoots of homes for unwed mothers. These homes may have been created as conscious alternatives to abortion, and their staffs may provide career training and counseling services. Such agencies often provide strong emotional support for choosing an adoption plan.

Adoptive couples should be aware, however, that agencies with religious ties will present to a birth mother all her alternatives to a crisis pregnancy: for example, her parenting her newborn baby will be considered with a full explanation of government and private aid for a single mother with a child. Also, she may be encouraged to seek out a relative to care for the baby while the birth mother completes her education or obtains a stable job, with the plan being that she accepts full responsibility for care of the child at a later date.

There is, of course, nothing wrong with a birth mother knowing all her choices and then making an informed decision as to the life of her child. In fact, this approach should be encouraged in order that the adoption plan is handled in an ethical manner. Some agencies, however, attempt to persuade the birth mother to parent her child and to consider adoption only as a type of second-rate choice.

When a woman places a child for adoption, the fees charged to the adoptive parents not only cover the agency's time involvement in your adoption plan, but also often will pay for the upkeep of the home and services to other pregnant women, not all of whom are considering adoption.

Like birth mothers, many adoptive couples often turn first to an organization affiliated with their religion. This can work to your advantage if the agency is selective and you meet its requirements. Some religious agencies, however, can be overly controlling in their approach to adoptive parents, insisting on significant paperwork, attendance at several workshops, a home study that can feel invasive, and excessive initial fees. These requirements can limit the number of applicants and slow down the adoption process so that it takes six months to a year just to complete all the requirements. The main reasons for putting families through these laborious tasks appear to be twofold: Older agencies are still processing adoptive couples the way an adoption agency did in the 1950s and 1960s and change is slow; and there is a philosophy that the agency must weed out the couples who are not serious about adoption and one way is to make the process involved and somewhat tedious. However, if you are willing to go through the requirements, this puts you into an "exclusive" set of prospective adoptive parents and thus increases your opportunity of being selected by a birth mother.

TRADITIONAL ADOPTION

Traditional adoption is usually a closed adoption in which the birth and adoptive parents never meet or may meet after the child is born and after the birth mother and possibly the birth father have relinquished the child to the adoption agency. Only a few agencies still adhere to this approach. The scenario is that the agency calls you to take home a baby who has been released for adoption. This often means that the child has been in foster care for a few weeks. Why? This may be because there was not family available for the child when she was born. One agency recently contacted us to determine if we had an available family for a week-old African-American baby boy. The agency was out-of-state and was charging $18,000, not including legal fees, that the family would have to pay to finalize the adoption. This means with travel costs, home study, and legal fees, the adoption could easily cost $22,000. While the reality is that some families would be able and willing to pay an agency such a fee, most families cannot afford such fees.

At other times, agencies choose foster care for the baby because the birth mother may have a set period of time after she signs a surrender of parental rights following the baby's birth in which to change her mind about placing the baby for adoption. If she does change her mind, then she can revoke her surrender of parental rights and undo the adoption plan.

This waiting period may be anywhere from seven to ninety days, depending upon state law, and some agencies will not permit a child to be placed in an adoptive home before the waiting period has elapsed. In some states, in fact, it is against the law to do so because the child is considered a "high legal risk." Other states allow the baby to go home with the adoptive parents, but they are referred to as "foster parents" until the waiting period has elapsed and the birth parents' rights are terminated. Unquestionably the worst-case scenario is for an infant to be placed in a couple's home, only to have one of the birth parents change his or her mind and remove the child. This happens only rarely, but when it does, the heartache is immense.

The waiting period for a birth mother to revoke her rights is relatively short, seven to ten days normally; however, many states have a waiting period to confirm whether a birth father steps forward and either files his name with a state birth father registry or otherwise asserts his parental rights. In some states, a legal action against the birth father must be filed to terminate his rights, and this can often take thirty to ninety days to complete.

So even if the birth mother signs a surrender and does not revoke that surrender during the waiting period, her baby may still be placed in a foster home until the whereabouts of the birth father are determined or his rights are essentially ended. Again, the agency does not want a baby to be in the adoptive parents' home, only to have a birth father show up to say that he wants to parent the child.

The U.S. Supreme Court and most state supreme courts have adopted the position that a birth father only has a limited "window of opportunity" in which to assert his rights, and the time frame to do so involves only a few months after the birth: it is not open-ended. Many agencies want to make sure the birth father is totally "out of the picture" before placing the child in the family's home, and that is why several months must go by.

In some states, the agency is not allowed to place a child into a couple's home until the parental rights have been terminated; however, most states do not have any statutes addressing this situation. The agency itself may have an internal policy that it will not make a placement of a child into an adoptive home until all birth parent rights to the child have ended. This is characteristic of agency placements only and of only some agencies. In many agency and nonagency placements, if the birth mother's rights are terminated, the child will be placed with the adoptive family, with the birth father's rights to be terminated by the time of or at the adoption finalization. The placement is still considered "at risk" or "at legal risk" until the birth father's rights are ended; however, the agency, the couple, and the couple's attorney must evaluate the level of risk.

It is imperative that an adoptive couple understand an agency's policy on placement before a waiting period has expired or before the termination of a birth father's rights. Of course, this policy is not simply to favor birth parents but to avoid the legal challenges associated with adoption. However, delaying placement with an adoptive couple can have unintended consequences.

For example, a birth mother could find herself in a dilemma. Should her child be placed in foster care or not? A birth mother usually does not want her baby in foster care; most often she very much wants the baby to go home from the hospital with the adoptive couple. Because some agencies are usually not willing to place a baby with a couple until the birth parents' rights have ended, birth mothers often end up avoiding agencies altogether. Agencies that are compelled by state law or internal policies are best able to comply with the birth mother's wishes by making the adoptive couple the foster family until the birth parents' rights are terminated.

FACILITATED AGENCY ADOPTION

With a facilitated agency adoption, the agency introduces you to a birth mother before the baby's birth. This option is much like a private adoption through an attorney (see Chapter 3). This approach is really a hybrid of an agency adoption and a private agency. Adoption agencies were forced to provide this alternative because birth mothers demanded more say and choice in their adoption plans. You take on essentially the same involvement that you would in a private adoption, and unless the agency receives outside funds, you will be paying the birth mother's legal, living, and counseling expenses in addition to the agency fee.

Agencies that match families with birth mothers in six to twelve months usually charge large up-front fees. One agency actually has a different fee structure based on how quickly you want to be matched with a birth mother. These agencies have a very large advertising budget and advertise nationwide in the Yellow Pages and elsewhere for a birth mother. The expenses associated with advertising for one birth mother who ultimately places her child for adoption can be $5,000 to $10,000. Advertising is expensive, but it works. Birth mothers often turn to the phone book to seek out adoption resources. Having the phone system and staff in place to answer and screen these calls takes additional resources.

If an agency requires you to pay a large up-front fee and essentially "guarantees" you a child within a certain period of time—usually two years—you must find out what their policy is if a birth mother changes her mind or if no birth mother selects you. Also, ask for references from several couples who have adopted through the agency.

Because advertising can be the most expensive part of an adoption with no guarantees, some agencies now require their clients to advertise for their own birth mother. Once you find a birth mother, the agency will handle her concerns, provide her with counseling, and sometimes make arrangements for her housing and medical care.

The chief difference between this type of agency adoption and private adoption has to do with cost. The up-front costs of the agency adoption and additional payment to the agency at the time of placement are much higher—several thousand dollars at the time you start with an agency and more upon placement of your child. Moreover, once you make such an investment in an agency and locate a birth mother, you and the birth mother are pretty much committed to working with this agency.

There are risks with this approach. If a birth mother changes her mind and decides to keep her child, the couple is not only heartbroken, but they may also be several thousand dollars out of pocket as well. If a child is placed with you as a result of your finding a birth mother on your own and for some reason the birth mother cannot or does not want to work with the agency, the agency usually will require that you forfeit all of your initial fees. This arrangement is usually spelled out in the agency-client contract. Be very cautious of such a contract; it means that you can lose substantially. Some agencies will allow you to put the money toward a second adoption, while others will not.

While this approach is similar to private adoption, the difference of course relates to a greater involvement of the adoption agency. In a private adoption, you will pay an attorney larger legal fees than if the attorney only finalized your adoption placement from an agency.

THE MIDDLE ROAD

With the third option, you are informed that a birth mother has chosen you after viewing your portfolio, and you will receive the baby after the birth mother has signed the documents terminating her parental rights. Like a traditional agency adoption, the fees are generally higher than if you find the birth mother yourself.

Many agencies have taken this middle road between an independent adoption, in which you meet the birth mother (and maintain contact with her before placement), and a traditional agency adoption, in which you find out about the baby to be placed with you after the baby is born and a certain time has lapsed. Taking this in-between route can protect the emotions of both the birth mother and the adoptive couple, in the event that the birth mother changes her mind.

The caveat with this method of adoption is that you must be very careful in working with an agency that requires large payments for a specific birth mother's living and counseling expenses. If she changes her mind, you will probably not be reimbursed for the monies paid to her and for her benefit. Since this middle approach may not include your meeting the birth mother, you will not have the opportunity to evaluate her sincerity and resoluteness about placement.

You will want to confer several times with the social worker assigned by the agency to work with the birth mother. An agency will often assign one social worker to work with you and another to work with the birth mother. The two social workers will confer together about the birth mother, but there may not be an opportunity for the adoptive couple to meet with the birth mother's social worker unless they insist upon it.

Even if they do, if the social worker is inexperienced, he or she may not know what to ask a birth mother in order to gauge her resolve in placing her child for adoption or to spot warning signs that certain issues have not been addressed. Unfortunately, it is too easy for an agency to charge its nonrefundable fees for matching you with a birth mother about which the agency should have had reservations.

If you do not meet with the birth mother, you will not pick up on the warning signs. Meeting you, furthermore, can force a birth mother out of denial and lead her to make a concrete decision about an adoption plan. Otherwise she may continue to draw monies from the agency as she works through certain issues about the adoption—at your expense. If you know that there is some hesitation, articulated or not, then at least you can make the decision whether to risk your money and your emotions. The same scenario can also happen with attorneys who match couples with birth parents.

Since many birth mothers are open to meeting the adoptive couple, an agency taking the middle road approach should still encourage and allow such contact between the birth mother and the couple.

IDENTIFIED AGENCY ADOPTION

Identified agency adoption, also called designated agency adoption, is essentially an independent adoption that becomes an agency adoption. Usually, the prospective adoptive parents and a pregnant woman have made some form of contact with each other before involving an agency. An identified adoption proceeds much like an independent adoption, except that the agency provides guidance and support. Also, the laws governing an agency adoption are followed, rather than those governing an independent private adoption through an attorney.

Agencies recognize that more and more people are choosing independent adoption through attorneys and are, therefore, providing more identified adoption services. Actually, this compromise can offer the best of both worlds: the personal control the birth and adoptive parents seek in an independent, private adoption and the emotional and sometimes legal advantages permitted in an agency adoption. Some agencies even counsel prospective adoptive parents on how to proceed in attempting to locate their own birth mother, just as in an independent adoption.

In the four states where private adoption is illegal, an identified adoption is one of the few options available. In a few more states it can be advantageous (see Appendix A). In most states, however, an identified adoption offers limited benefits.

Regardless of what type of agency adoption occurs, when it comes time to have the adoption finalized in court, you must use an attorney. The attorney is hired independently of the adoption agency. The fees for the attorney to go to court to finalize the adoption can vary widely.

WHY CONSIDER AN IDENTIFIED AGENCY ADOPTION?

If you are thinking about private adoption, there are a number of reasons why an identified adoption could make sense. For instance:

1. *Counseling for birth and adoptive parents.* The counseling that birth parents receive through an agency can help determine whether they are quite sure of their decision to place the baby for adoption. Counseling can also help prepare them for the feelings they will experience once the baby is born. Adoption creates many highs and lows for everyone, birth and adoptive parents alike, and it can be reassuring to have a counselor on hand to provide support and encouragement, to give the feeling that someone is "holding their hand" throughout the process. Although agency staff often provides counseling, the counseling may not always be considered "objective," since the agency's financial reward is greater if the birth mother places the child for adoption. Therefore, if a birth mother needs counseling, it may be best to also employ an outside counselor so that the birth mother can never claim that she did not receive the counseling she felt that she needed.

2. *Birth mothers' expenses.* Expenses that adoptive parents cannot legally pay for in some states in an independent adoption, such as rent, may be permitted in an agency adoption, although state laws vary considerably on this point. Paying expenses can help facilitate the adoption process and provide the necessary security for the birth mother to work with you. But be careful! You do not want to fall into the trap of paying for excessive expenses.

3. *An agency can obtain Medicaid for the baby.* If a birth mother is employed, has health insurance, and does not qualify for Medicaid, her health insurance will cover her delivery and hospital stay, but it may not cover the baby's. The adoptive couple's health insurance may not cover the baby until the baby is in their physical possession. If a baby has a health problem and must remain in the hospital, the hospital bill can be astronomical. The child may not be covered by anyone's insurance, and the baby will not qualify for Medicaid based on the birth mother's income. When an agency takes temporary legal custody of the child, Medicaid can then usually be obtained for the child.

4. *Fewer legal complications.* In some states, the birth parents' rights are terminated earlier in an agency adoption than they would be in an independent adoption. This provision usually prevents the removal of a child from a couple's home if a birth parent changes his or her mind, saving much heartache for everyone involved.

Knowing that her parental rights are terminated once the baby goes home with the adoptive couple can actually give a birth mother greater peace of mind. There is no temptation to second-guess her decision or agonize about whether to change her mind. She is also more secure knowing that the birth father's rights have been terminated and that he cannot interfere with the adoption plans.

Although placing a child for adoption can be very sad for birth parents, having the process reach closure quickly means the birth parents do not have to revisit their decision on a day-to-day basis for weeks on end.

5. *More legal options.* In states in which independent adoption is illegal, a couple can essentially pursue a private adoption and then contact an agency to make it into an identified agency adoption. An agency can also serve as an intermediary in states where intermediaries are not permitted. This means contracting with an agency so that an intermediary or a birth mother can contact the agency instead of you. For example, you may wish to write to obstetricians and enclose your adoption business cards. Instead of putting your name and telephone number on the card, you can supply the agency's name and telephone number, along with your first names.

6. *Protection of privacy.* When advertising in newspapers and through adoption business-type cards, you can use the agency's name and phone number instead of your own. By doing so, you remove some of the anxiety associated with screening phone calls, especially prank calls.

Note: This does not always work to your advantage. Many birth mothers will not want to deal with an agency. Be sure to specify in your ad that the phone number belongs to an agency. Birth mothers will hang up if they feel they are being deceived—and rightfully so. No birth mother wants to hear "Happy Land Adoption Agency" when she is expecting to reach Arlene and Peter at a private home.

7. *Support system for birth mother.* For adoptive couples who do not wish to meet and talk with the birth mother on a weekly or even a monthly basis, the agency social worker assigned to the birth mother can "hold her hand" in a positive sense, can refer her for counseling, and provide social contact to help her in her "down moments."

IDENTIFIED ADOPTION: SOME DISADVANTAGES

With an identified adoption, problems sometimes arise if you or the agency are not clear in your expectations. As identified adoptions become more common, long-established traditional agencies that primarily place babies may decide to go along with the trend and offer identified adoption services. The problem is that such agencies are historically biased against birth and adoptive parents being in control, and this strong bias can eventually show.

An example of agency bias has to do with foster care. Some agencies will encourage a birth mother to place the baby in foster care for six weeks or longer. Even if you have met the birth mother yourself and have begun to work out an arrangement, the agency may have its own agenda, insisting, for instance, on repeatedly contacting the birth father and getting him to relinquish his rights even when the birth father is completely unresponsive and the state laws provide an adequate way to terminate his parental rights without his having to formally sign them away.

Another bias of some agencies is to bar communication between birth and adoptive couples because traditional agencies have always done adoptions this way. A birth mother who felt secure and connected to the adoptive couple is now instructed to only contact the agency! She could have very negative feelings about the new arrangement.

Some state regulations require that agencies discuss alternatives to adoption with the birth mother whether she wants to or not. That's not necessarily bad. A woman seeking to place a baby for adoption has a right to consider all her options. When she does so and still chooses adoption, she is less likely to change her mind after the baby is born. However, if you have met with a birth mother who is resolute in her decision to place the baby for adoption, she may feel very uncomfortable having to discuss in detail with a stranger why she is not planning to raise the child or even why she is not considering an abortion. Repeated probing about feelings and family backgrounds can make a birth mother feel she is guilty of something. Understanding counselors will respect a woman who is very firm in her decision and not press her for an elaborate explanation. Again, it is important to meet with the caseworker who will be interacting with the birth mother to gauge her experience in working with birth mothers.

Before committing yourself to an identified adoption, find out what the expenses will be. The cost of this kind of adoption varies greatly from one agency to the next, as do the billing systems used. Some agencies charge one fee; others bill by the hour. Circumstances make a difference: If you meet a birth mother when she is nearly nine months pregnant, she will probably not receive as many hours of counseling as a woman who contacts you when she is three months pregnant.

Other factors that can increase the cost include the level of the birth father's involvement, his counseling, the distance the social worker has to travel to meet with the birth mother and father, and whether she communicates with the birth mother and father by long-distance telephone.

Watch out! If you have not personally met the birth mother, an agency may want to charge you for a direct placement instead of an identified adoption. One couple had spoken with a birth mother and then contacted an agency to conduct an identified adoption. The cost was $2,000 one day, $14,000 the next. Because the couple had not met the birth mother face to face, the agency wanted to charge them the higher rate.

In states in which private adoption is illegal, such as Massachusetts, agency fees for an identified adoption can be astronomical—$4,000 just for the home study. It may be less expensive to adopt in another state. Even if you have to live in a hotel for two weeks after the baby is born, it will still be much cheaper than an agency fee of $10,000 plus the birth mother's expenses.

Finally, find out whatever you can about an agency's reputation. Some agencies will "steal" a birth mother from you and steer her to one of its own couples. A dishonest agency would find this very profitable because when an agency finds a baby for someone, the fee is almost always more (often four times more) than for an identified adoption. Consult your attorney before making a commitment. Be aware, however, that some attorneys discourage identified adoptions, since they usually make less money when an agency takes on more responsibility. Be sure to ask the attorney what her fees are for a private adoption and what is charged for this type of adoption; it should be one-third to one-half less since the agency is doing more of the hands-on things with the birth mother.

IS AN IDENTIFIED ADOPTION FOR YOU?

Now that you know the pros and cons of an identified agency adoption, the question becomes one of individual circumstances. For some situations, an identified adoption may be the best way to go. Consider the following scenarios:

Scenario A: You live in a state in which the birth parents' rights are terminated at a later date in an independent adoption than they are in an agency adoption.

For many couples, this is the most important reason to go with an identified agency adoption. They could not bear to have a birth mother change her mind after the baby is already placed with them. In New Jersey, for example, parental rights can be terminated only two to three months after placement if the birth mother does not agree to appear in court shortly after birth. The agency's involvement, however, ensures that rights are terminated earlier without the need of a court appearance, usually within days after birth, providing security for the adoptive couple and closure for the birth mother.

Scenario B: You want to adopt a baby from another state, and the law requires an agency in an out-of-state placement.

If you adopt a baby from Florida, for example, and you are not a Florida resident, the baby must be released to an agency before he is given to you. Even in states that do not require an agency, you may want to use one as a security measure. You want to make sure everything is signed and sealed before the adoption proceeds through Interstate Compact (the branch of the state department of social services that oversees interstate adoptions). Also, having a sensitive, knowledgeable social worker in the same city as the birth mother can be a comfort to her, especially if you live miles away yourself.

Scenario C: You are unsure about a birth mother and believe that counseling will help her become more secure in her decision, but she refuses counseling.

The agency worker can just be there for support for the birth mother without the need for therapy or counseling. Of course, an agency is not necessary for a birth mother to receive counseling. If everyone agrees, a social worker or therapist not affiliated with an agency can counsel birth parents. In fact, an agency should offer outside counseling so that the birth mother can never say that the agency coerced her into her releasing her child.

Scenario D: A birth mother needs to have more expenses paid than are permitted by law in an independent adoption.

Some states restrict the expenses that a couple can pay in order to prevent the practice of "buying" babies by paying excessive expenses. For example, until recently, in North Carolina an adoptive couple could not even pay for the medical expenses of a birth mother. Such laws usually allow agencies to pay for more of the birth mother's expenses than are permitted in an independent adoption. The couple is in essence paying for the birth mother's expenses; the monies are just going through the agency first.

Additionally, an agency can represent both adoptive parents and birth parents. However, many will make it clear that they do not represent the interests of the adoptive couple; others give the appearance of regarding the concerns of the adoptive couple by assigning them a social worker separate from the one assisting the birth mother. Because of some of the financial and emotional risks discussed earlier, it is suggested that a couple hire an attorney to represent them even if they are seeking a placement through an agency. The attorney will be the couple's advocate, emphasizing the concerns of the couple and seeing to it that an inexperienced social worker does not disrupt an adoption plan. Also, the attorney will be needed to process the adoption paperwork with the court after placement.

WHEN AN AGENCY TURNS YOU DOWN

Agencies do not have an unlimited number of children for placement; therefore, some establish criteria for adoptive parents beyond what is mandated by the state. These criteria may be related to geographic area, age, marital status, educational level, and religion and must be applied equally and without bias to all applicants.

Some agencies also have a screening process separate from the mandatory home study. Remember, being refused by an agency that makes direct placements and conducts home studies is not the same thing as not having an approved home study. You may simply have failed to get through the agency screening for direct placement purposes.

If you select an agency that requires large initial fees to cover their advertising budget and states that you will be matched with a birth mother within a specific period of time, the agency may not want to have you as part of their program if they believe that a birth mother is unlikely to select you. This is only fair to you and to the agency. For example, if you and your husband are over fifty years old and have three children, it is unlikely that a birth mother is going to select you.

A reputable agency is not going to permit you to give them a large fee in the hope that a birth mother will select you if your chances are slim. Such an agency should encourage you to seek other avenues by which to adopt, such as international adoption.

Once the screening process is completed, the agency will conduct a home study, if one has not already been conducted by another agency. If an applicant is rejected, the agency should provide detailed information as to why. In New Jersey, for example, the agency must offer services to help the couple adjust to the decision, as well as give information about the agency's grievance procedure.

ADOPTIVE PARENTS' RIGHTS: GETTING ALL THE INFORMATION

As prospective adoptive parents, you do have certain rights, and one of the most important is the right to information, especially about the adoptive child. Agencies are required to provide any medical information about the child that is available, as well as any genetic and social background. Sometimes this information will be part of the placement agreement; at other times, it will be a separate document. Some states require in-depth information, including the child's diet and feeding habits. If the child has special needs, the agency may be required to provide the applicant with a list of long-term needs and available community resources for coping with them.

Remember, clients have the right to refuse a child. This is not so adoptive parents can "shop"—that is, pick and reject children; it is to encourage them to make an intelligent decision, based on full information, as to whether they can appropriately meet a child's needs.

Sometimes couples will state that they are open to adopting a toddler with certain physical disabilities, when what they really want is a healthy infant. Do not try this. There's no point in going through an agency that places many children with special needs unless you are willing to be honest about the kind of child for which you can care.

PRIVATE AGENCIES: WHAT TO LOOK OUT FOR

Although there are many excellent agencies that truly support both the birth parents and the adoptive parents, some agencies are set up in a way that makes the process difficult for everyone involved. Here are some of the problems you could find yourselves running into:

1. *The agency is not sufficiently aggressive in recruiting birth mothers.* Many adoption agencies are not even listed in the Yellow Pages. Some long-established traditional agencies do not appear to be what one might expect. We did consulting work for one agency that gave no indication that it was in the adoption business. Because the agency also provided a broad range of social services, a birth mother coming into the office would be hard-pressed to find brochures or other information that explained the advantages of adoption. This agency, like many others, simply did not emphasize adoption services.

2. *The agency expects you to find the birth mother.* Some agencies require you to pay a sum of money up front, up to $10,000 in some cases, and the couple must then find their own birth mother! The agency fee is for taking care of all the details and some of the expenses after a couple finds the birth mother.

3. *The agency has restrictions regarding who can adopt.* Agency restrictions usually relate to age, religion, weight, ethnic background, income, educational level, marital status, and an infertility diagnosis. Some agencies are so restrictive that they have two applications: one to determine whether you meet the initial standards and a second application if you met the standards in the initial screening process. Even when a couple meets all the standards, success is not automatic.

4. *The agency permits limited contact, if any, between adoptive parents and birth parents.* Some agencies still take the old-fashioned approach to arranging adoption. Many, however, are beginning to allow more communication, so that the birth mother and adoptive parents may meet in person or through pictures and biographical sketches. Most parents see this as a step in the right direction.

5. *The agency has a long waiting list.* An agency may claim that the wait is two to three years, but this may be after the home study is completed. You may wait six months to a year for the home study. One agency is listed as having a waiting time from application to homecoming as two to four years. Yet, I know couples who waited four to five years for the arrival of their baby. Not surprisingly, the waiting period for a child with special needs and non-Caucasian infants in the statistics is often much shorter than that for healthy Caucasian infants.

CONTRACTING WITH AN AGENCY: WHAT TO ASK

Before you decide to use an agency and send them a large sum of money as some agencies require, you will want to investigate it thoroughly. Talk with the staff; if you can, talk to other parents who have dealt with them. Many agencies will provide the names and telephone numbers of couples who will gladly talk with you about their experience.

Before you visit an agency, call and ask the counselor or secretary about its philosophy on adoption. What you ask will depend on what kind of child you are seeking to adopt. If you are looking for a healthy infant and the agency requires that you do at least part of the work of advertising and networking for a child, then you will want to ask questions about their relationships with birth mothers and what support systems they provide. If you want to adopt a toddler-age child with special needs, you may want to ask questions about what birth family background they usually provide and what services and subsidies are available to meet the child's special needs.

Trust your instincts. If you call an agency and feel that you are being treated as an irritant, even though you are asking the questions very politely, take it as a warning. On the other hand, do be reasonable; agency personnel have a limited time to talk on the telephone.

Some of your more in-depth questions might better wait for an initial interview or for one of the seminars that the agency gives on a regular basis.

No matter what kind of agency you are contacting, you will want to ask these questions:

1. *What are their requirements and restrictions?*
2. *What kinds of children does the agency place?*
3. *How many children did the agency place last year?*
4. *What are the agency's fees?*

If there is a standard flat fee, ask:

- What is the payment schedule?
- If the birth mother changes her mind, is any money refunded?

If the fee is based on the number of hours the parties spend in counseling and on the nature of the adoption, then ask:

- Is there a cap on the fees?
- Do the fees include the birth mother's living and medical expenses?
- How much do the home study and postsupervisory visits cost? An

agency's adoption fees may sound reasonable, until you hear that the agency requires a social worker to visit your home eight times at a cost of $2,000, when your state requires only two visits. A reasonable fee would be well under $200 for each visit.

- What is the initial fee? Some agencies charge large up-front fees and then expect you to play an active role in finding your own birth mother. Retaining an agency the way you retain an attorney is fine. However, paying $10,000 or more to an agency and still having to find your own birth mother is too risky. If an agency asks you for more than $1,000 up front, ask whether that money is returned if it turns out you do not need the agency.

5. *What is the agency's home study process like?* If you have already had a home study completed, ask whether the agency accepts home studies conducted by other agencies.
6. *Does the agency provide you with a copy of the home study?*
7. *Does it release the home study to attorneys or other agencies upon request?* If so, ask whether there is a fee. A small fee is reasonable—$100 per copy is not.

These are the questions that are appropriate to ask at the beginning of your investigation. Once you get more serious about an agency that places infants, you can schedule an interview to ask more in-depth questions. For example:

1. *What roles do the agency and the birth mother play in selecting a couple?*
2. *Do you get to meet the birth mother during her pregnancy?*
3. *How does the agency feel about dealing with an attorney or another agency, if you find a birth mother in another state?* If you find a birth mother on your own in another state, there may be no need to use the agency.
4. *Does the agency discuss all of the woman's options with her?* You want a birth mother who is firm in her decision to place the baby for adoption. You want her to feel comfortable, not pressured to make a decision or to defend her choice.
5. *How does a social worker determine whether the birth mother is sincere?* This is especially important to ask if an agency identifies a birth mother for you and then asks you to pay her living expenses and counseling fees.
6. *If the agency senses that the birth mother is uncertain about her adoption plans, how does it respond?*

    - Does it notify the adoptive parents of the apparent uncertainty?
    - Is it made clear to a birth mother that to have a couple pay for her medical

and other expenses when she has no real intention of placing the baby for adoption is fraud and that she could be prosecuted?

7. *At what hours are agency personnel available?* If you are working directly with a birth mother and the agency is involved, it is very important that you be able to reach someone at the agency during nonbusiness hours. What if the birth mother goes into labor earlier than expected? What if the hospital personnel are giving you problems about visiting the birth mother or baby?

8. *What if the birth mother wants to meet with you immediately, along with a counselor?* Many agency personnel believe that phone calls after 5:00 P.M. are an intrusion and that few emergencies warrant this invasion. For the most part, this is true. Be reasonable. But remember, you are paying for a service.

When investigating an agency that places children with special needs, other questions and concerns arise. Begin by telling them what kind of child you are interested in adopting. If you are very specific, saying you want a one- to two-year-old blind girl, the agency staff person may offer to put you on the waiting list; however, the opportunity to adopt such a child may range between limited and nonexistent. If you are very specific about the kind of child that you want to adopt, you should apply to many agencies and work with the large adoption exchanges.

Here are some important questions to ask.

1. *How many and what kinds of legally free (or almost legally free) children are in the agency's caseload?*

2. *Does the agency place children only from its county (or other geographic region), or does it place children from other parts of the state?*

3. *What is the average wait for a child?* Is this from the time of the home study or from the time the application is completed?

4. *What kinds of pre- and postadoption services does the agency provide?*

5. *If the child is in foster care, would you be allowed to visit the child there once he or she was assigned to you?*

6. *What is the agency's policy toward adoption subsidies?* Are most of the children it places eligible for federal or state subsidies?

7. *If you decline a child who is offered, what is the agency's policy about future placements?*

8. *What if a situation does not work out? How is this handled?*

9. *What level of openness is expected with the birth family?* You will want to raise this question before committing to an agency. If the agency believes that birth families and adoptive families must maintain some level of openness no matter

what the circumstances, then you will want to find out what they mean and whether they have any exceptions. You may find an agency that wants to bar all contact; this, again, is not an appropriate response.

INVESTIGATING AN AGENCY'S REPUTATION

Agencies have legal custody of the child adopted domestically until the adoption is finalized and can use this as leverage with the adoptive parents before and after placement. Expenses are one area in which they can exert control—occasionally through deception. No matter how many questions you ask the agency staff directly, one of the best ways to find out about an agency's reputation is to ask others about the agency and how it handled their adoption.

You can expect to hear from people who are somewhat disgruntled. Adoptive couples sometimes complain about costs even when they knew up front what the expenses were going to be. Couples who have sought to adopt a child with special needs may not have "heard" the agency staff tell them all the possible legal risks involved or the child's potential problems.

Chapter Three

Independent Adoption

ndependent adoption is legal in most states and is also called a private or self-directed adoption. The birth parents and the adoptive couple find each other through advertising, or through a personal referral, usually by a mutual friend or acquaintance, or through an adoption attorney. There is no agency involved.

Private agency adoptions of newborn infants and the same adoptions involving attorneys are often very similar. With the private agency adoption, it is the agency that referred you to the birth mother; whereas with the private adoption involving an attorney, it is the lawyer who has matched you up with a birth mother. You should remember that if you use the services of an agency to find a birth mother, you will also require the services of an attorney to finalize the adoption. However, if you are working with an attorney who finds a birth mother for you, most likely, you will not need the services of an agency unless the laws of your state or where the child is born require an agency to be involved.

In a private adoption, the birth parents and the couple usually meet to become acquainted and discuss the adoption. For birth parents or adoptive couples who do not wish to meet, communication can take place by telephone or letter, or it can be handled by a third party, provided this is legal in their state. From these contacts an understanding develops that the birth parents' child will be placed with the adoptive parents. The adoption statutes of various states refer to this kind of adoption as a nonagency adoption, to distinguish it from an agency or stepparent/family adoption.

To get started, contact an adoption attorney to make sure you are on the right legal track. Do not worry that you will have to fill out mountains of forms; your attorney will take care of the paperwork. While you are waiting for an appointment with your attorney, read Chapter 5 of this book and begin to follow some of the steps it outlines for getting the word out. Write your broadcast letters. Assemble your portfolio. Install a second phone line. Your adoption adventure is under way!

THE INDEPENDENT ADOPTION PROCESS

The first thing to know is that independent adoption is illegal in some states. Laws regulating adoption vary considerably from state to state; you will therefore need to find out what your rights are before proceeding.

Where independent adoption is legal, the basic steps are as follows. These same steps are usually very similar regardless of the state in which you live. A couple hires an attorney. This attorney will act as an unpaid intermediary; that is, the attorney will charge fees for legal representation but not for serving as an intermediary. The couple may give her a portfolio containing photographs of themselves, a letter, and other material that gives a picture of their lives, which their attorney can then show to birth mothers.

At this point a couple will have a special cell phone to take phone calls from prospective birth mothers. The couple may begin advertising in newspapers and networking with friends and family to try to meet a prospective birth mother.

This is also the time to arrange for a home study. Every state requires that adoptive parents undergo a home study to determine their parental fitness. In most states the task is delegated to licensed adoption agency staff and independent home study professionals, who then submit the home study to the court. To initiate this process, contact an agency or social worker who is certified to conduct home studies.

The next thing that is likely to happen is that a pregnant woman (or a parent with a child) will call in response to your advertisement or letter to discuss her intentions to place her child for adoption. If you and she are comfortable about meeting, you discuss this possibility. If one of you is not comfortable with meeting face to face, you will talk about keeping in touch by telephone, e-mail, or through your attorney, who will either meet with the birth mother, have someone from their office meet with the birth mother, or contact the birth mother by telephone.

Next, the birth mother or birth parents meet with you at a restaurant or other public place or at your attorney's office. If both of you are comfortable with each other, you and she will probably make a verbal commitment to each other. If you do not meet, this commitment will take place by telephone. This commitment, of course, is that she desires to place her soon-to-be-born child with you for adoption and that you and your spouse will take placement of that child.

Depending on the circumstances, you and the birth parents will decide whether the adoption is to be an independent or an identified agency adoption. An identified agency adoption is one in which an independent adoption is converted into an agency adoption. The agency may provide counseling for the birth parents, in addition—at least in some states—to obtaining surrenders of parental rights in a shorter time frame than with an independent adoption. Because an identified adoption is considered an agency adoption, the laws that govern agency adoptions apply. Your attorney can help you sort out the pros and cons of either choice.

Be careful not to discuss the possibility of agency involvement with a birth parent until you have built a relationship with her and she has committed to you. Many birth mothers do not want a third party, such as an agency social worker, asking them a lot of questions, and many birth mothers equate an adoption agency social worker to a child welfare or state department of social services caseworker and may not want any contact with them. If you and the birth parents agree to an identified agency adoption, contact an agency that provides such services.

Again, discuss your choice of agencies with your attorney. It is vital that the agency staff work well with birth parents. Birth parents know that they have choices; the newspapers and the telephone Yellow Pages are full of adoption advertisements. Also, many birth mothers are going online to locate prospective adoptive couples and adoption professionals. If you have not built a solid rapport with the birth parents and the agency staff are condescending or lacking in sensitivity, the birth parents may well go elsewhere. Also, the commitment you and the birth mother have to each other and your rapport with her are vital in an identified agency adoption so that an agency cannot steer her to one of its couples. Some agencies will do this because an agency can charge more for a direct placement—it finds a birth mother for a couple—as compared to the identified agency adoption scenario in which you find the birth mother.

If you do not get an agency involved, then you or your attorney should discuss with the birth parents the advantages of counseling. The benefits are twofold: (1) Some states require birth parents to have counseling or at least be offered counseling, and (2) more important, counseling may assist the birth parents in understanding adoption issues and their feelings about them.

Also, your attorney should discuss with the birth parents the opportunity to be represented by their own attorney. In some states, such as New York, a birth parent must be represented by an attorney who is not representing the adoptive couple.

Now you or the birth mother will contact an obstetrician or clinic and the hospital where the baby is to be delivered, if this has not been taken care of already. Finding a physician who is open to adoption is very important. It is also important, if possible, that your attorney become involved in choosing the hospital since some are actually hostile toward adoption; he will contact the hospital's social services department to determine its policy on adoption.

At the time of birth, depending on where you live, the birth parents will give up their parental rights by signing legal documents referred to as "surrender of parental rights." This is different from a consent-to-adoption document, which is not a surrender of rights but simply indicates the birth parents' approval of you as adoptive parents. Confusingly, some agencies and attorneys refer to the termination document as a consent form, so you must ask what purpose the consent document serves in your state. Almost all states require the birth mother to sign the surrender after birth which usually occurs either in the hospital or at the attorney's office. Some states allow the birth father to sign before birth, but most require his signing the surrender after birth. If a state allows the birth mother to sign before birth, she must still ratify or reconfirm in writing her pre-birth surrender.

Each state has different laws as to when birth parents' rights can be terminated, how long birth parents have to change their minds and revoke their surrenders, and whether the birth parents must also appear in court to have their rights terminated officially (even after signing the surrender documents). Some states also allow a choice as to appearing in court or signing out of court. Check with your attorney since these laws can change.

Now the baby is born. Your attorney may visit the birth mother in the hospital so that she can sign legal forms. Before the birth you should find out what documents are needed by your insurance company to ensure immediate coverage for the baby.

You and possibly your attorney go to the hospital, where the baby is given to you. Often a birth mother will discharge herself before the baby goes home. In this case she must sign documents allowing the baby to be placed directly with you. Many hospitals, however, require the birth mother or her relative to place the baby in your arms. If the birth mother does not wish to see the baby and the hospital requires her to be there at the baby's discharge, then your attorney can arrange legally for her to avoid this situation by filing legal documents in the county court.

Your attorney next files the adoption petition or what is sometimes called an adoption complaint with the court. Some time later, usually 60 to 180 days later, depending upon your state's regulations, your attorney is provided a court date for the hearing to terminate the parental rights of the birth parents and to finalize the adoption. Unless the parental rights of the birth parents have already been terminated, they must be provided notice of this hearing, but they are not usually required to attend unless they have changed their minds about the adoption.

If you reside in one state and the baby is born in another, then your attorney must also complete Interstate Compact forms and file them in both the "sending state" (the state that the child was born in) and in the "receiving state" (the state where you reside). There are several other forms that the birth mother and the adoptive parents must sign for interstate purposes.

As a final step, your attorney accompanies you to court for the adoption hearing and presents your testimony, including how you came in contact with the birth parents, what monies you have paid, and why you wish to adopt the baby. The adoption agency or social worker (independent investigator) who conducted your home study will have provided your home study to the court, including a favorable recommendation as to your fitness as parents. The judge hearing the adoption will generally review the home study to ensure that the agency has recommended you as adoptive parents. Each of these steps will be discussed in detail in the chapters that follow.

WHY PURSUE AN INDEPENDENT ADOPTION?

Adoption can be a wonderful experience for the birth parents who are placing the baby in a loving home, for the baby who is going there, and, of course, for the couple who has longed for the baby. With an independent adoption, the experience can be especially positive. Both sets of parents can feel more in control because they are the decision-makers. They meet and decide together what is best for the baby. A birth mother feels very secure in knowing and approving of the adoptive parents. The decision about the couple is made by her alone, not by an agency. Although she will still feel sad about placing her child for adoption, she will have seen firsthand that the child will be reared by a mother and father she has chosen and who can provide love and stability, an impression she will carry forever.

Indeed, independent adoption is usually a birth mother's first choice. Twice as many birth mothers choose independent adoption as opposed to agency adoption. Birth mothers choose this approach because they want to be in control. They do not want agency personnel questioning their motives for choosing adoption or explaining their options to them. Although many agencies are far less controlling than in years past, a birth mother may just want to feel that she is working with a couple, and the lawyer is simply there to see that all is legal.

Often they have already made an adoption decision and are ready to go ahead. They want to choose the adoptive parents themselves. In fact, the level of control a birth mother has is often what determines whether she will place the infant for adoption.

Most birth mothers select adoption because they are young, are in school, know they can provide little for themselves and the child at this point in their lives, and want a better future for everyone. They're not after a better career for themselves or a swimming pool and trips to Disney World for their child. They want the child to have a stable, loving home life. A nineteen-year-old woman with few resources in her second year of college cannot provide a home for a child if she must work full-time in a minimum wage job.

Most birth mothers care enough to make a decision that is best for themselves and the baby. A birth mother chooses adoption because of her love for her child.

Many adoptive couples start out believing a certain stereotype of the birth mother: that she is ignorant, unfeeling, on welfare, and basically a "low life." The reality is, the average birth mother is "the girl next door who got pregnant." No one kind of person is more likely than another to be a birth mother. Almost all, however, want what is best for their child and direct involvement in the decision-making.

Empirical data on private adoption is difficult to find, partly because states are not required to keep track of how many adoptions take place, and so many do not. But based on the data from the National Council for Adoption, it would appear that at least two-thirds of the infant adoptions finalized in the United States each year are independent adoptions. Some believe the figure is closer to 80 percent.

In any case, in the majority of situations that we have known, couples who pursue independent adoption have a baby in about one year or less. The process takes commitment, but once a couple commits, they become parents. If you work diligently, very likely you will have a baby in your home sooner than you thought possible. The advantage of private adoption is that it works, and it works quickly.

Here are some other advantages to think about:

The infant is placed directly with the adoptive couple. In traditional agency adoptions, an infant will often be placed in a foster home for a period of time, weeks or even months. Many birth mothers strongly oppose this arrangement. An independent adoption satisfies the birth mother's concern for her child's welfare and allows an adoptive couple to experience the first days of infancy with their child.

The adoptive parents may share in the pregnancy experience and in the baby's delivery. If a birth mother lives nearby, the adoptive mother may take her to doctor appointments and may even act as her coach during labor and delivery. A birth mother may want the adoptive parents to be a part of her life. This can often help her to see past her own difficult circumstances and focus instead on the benefits of her unplanned pregnancy.

"He was our child from the moment we took him home, if not before; it started, oddly enough, with the sonograms; you could see his face as clearly as a black-and-white picture; there was such a quick connection. We simply bonded with the baby. It just happened, and it wasn't something we made happen. Bringing him right home from the hospital was so thrilling. Then getting up in the middle of the night and taking care of this little one gave us an indescribable love for this precious child."

Independent adoption can be less expensive. Usually an attorney charges for the legal services provided and the birth mother's expenses, including medical costs. Usually such adoptions cost a family $6,000 to $20,000. Agency adoptions can be more expensive. The administrative and personnel costs involved in a single agency adoption can range from $10,000 to $15,000, and that may not cover the birth mother's medical, living, counseling, legal, and transportation expenses.

Some agencies have the adoptive parents pay a birth mother's expenses indirectly as part of the agency's fees, in which case, the fee will range from $20,000 to $30,000. In an independent adoption, it is often possible to find a birth mother who has her own medical insurance or who qualifies for Medicaid coverage and so does not need living expenses. In such cases the adoptive couple pays only for the medical expenses of the baby and any counseling requested by the birth parents, in addition to necessary living expenses. In many adoptions the couple's medical insurance will cover the baby's hospital costs.

INDEPENDENT ADOPTION: SOME DISADVANTAGES

Not every couple has a positive experience with pursuing independent adoption. Sometimes the problem is the attorney. Although most adoption attorneys are straightforward and reasonable in their fees and practices, there are some dishonest ones. Some will charge for expenses never incurred by the birth mother and engage in other illegal practices. In other cases, the attorney is honest but does not assist his client with sufficient one-on-one attention; he does not get directly involved with the birth mother or hospital or agency (if one is needed). Basically, the couple is on their own. Needless to say, this gives independent adoption a bad name.

For other couples the personal involvement in an independent adoption is simply too difficult. Many adoptive mothers feel sorry for the birth mothers and develop a real bond, The phone calls and visits with the birth mother, while enjoyable, can be also be nerve-racking; this is particularly true if you are the birth mother's main emotional support. The time at the hospital can be exhausting and all-consuming, and if the birth mother changes her mind, it is devastating.

One other potential difficulty with independent adoption is that birth parents who could really use some counseling may not get it. Even in an independent adoption a birth mother has every right to receive counseling. Of course, most adoptive parents will pay for a woman's counseling expenses if she requests it. She does not have to go to an adoption agency to receive counseling. Your attorney should be able to advise the birth mother of counselors in the area.

An attorney is not, of course, an adoption counselor. Nevertheless, a compassionate attorney should be able to discuss with a birth mother her reasons for placing the baby for adoption. This will give him a sense of whether the woman is sincere or whether she is being coerced by someone or is emotionally confused. A sensitive attorney can also determine how well she is coping with her adoption plans. These discussions help a woman verbalize her feelings, helping her further solidify her reasons for making adoption plans. Again, an attorney should never be a substitute for competent counseling. Your attorney must make sure a birth mother has access to counseling. Any attorney involved with adoption has a list of capable therapists.

Note: In nearly every state you are permitted to pay for counseling fees, but double-check to be sure it is legal before you do so.

IS A DOMESTIC INFANT ADOPTION FOR YOU?

Whether you pursue an adoption through an agency or through an attorney, you will most likely have to meet the approval of the birth mother. You must also still have an approved home study.

People who have difficult personalities or overwhelming problems are usually no better candidates for independent adoption then they are for an agency adoption. After all, in either independent or agency adoption, adoptive parents must undergo a home study conducted by a licensed adoption agency or certified social worker to determine their suitability as parents.

Some people, it is true, do pursue independent adoption because an agency will not accept them, especially when age is an issue. Others, however, never decide whether independent or agency adoption is right for them. They just happen to learn of a pregnant woman, sometimes through a mutual acquaintance, and the parties come to an agreement. In such cases they may have no contact with an agency, except perhaps during the home study.

The following is a list of some of the tasks and stresses associated with adopting a newborn infant. Discuss with your spouse how each makes you feel. If you feel negatively about one aspect of independent adoption, do you believe that you can overcome these feelings?

1. *Placing an advertisement in newspapers or circulating a letter to friends, professionals, and family telling of your desire to adopt and responding to calls the ads/letters generate.* You do not necessarily have to take this step. Agencies and attorneys advertise for birth mothers and can then match you with a birth mother.

2. *Speaking articulately and compassionately with a woman who calls in answer to an advertisement or letter.*

3. *Meeting with a birth mother.* Most couples who pursue adoption do meet with the birth mother to get to know each other and share background about each other. In some states, such as Virginia, identifying information (complete names and addresses) must also be shared between the adoptive and birth parents.

At first many couples are afraid of that initial meeting. Yet, no adoptive couple we have ever known was sorry they met with their child's birth mother. Also, we have found that a positive relationship between the adoptive couple and birth mother, even if minimal, helps the birth mother follow through with her decision to place her child for adoption. That she has chosen you and approved of you helps affirm her decision—especially right after the baby is born.

4. *Presenting yourselves as "normal" people when meeting the birth mother.* Many kinds of people meet with birth mothers and complete the adoption. However, there are special considerations to be aware of and adjustments that may have to be made if:

- *You have an obvious physical disability.* Tell the birth mother before you meet her in order to avoid any surprised reaction, though you should not mention it immediately in your first conversation.
- *The husband has long hair and earrings and dresses for shock value.* If the husband has long hair because he is, for example, a musician and your profile or your newspaper ad states "professional jazz musician" or "nature lover," a birth mother probably will not expect a couple dressed like June and Ward Cleaver. In fact, many birth mothers would be delighted by a "funky couple." In general, however, a man with shorter hair and no earring has a better chance of appealing to a birth mother—even a birth mother who likes to dress in the latest fad.
- *The husband or wife is obese.* Unless the birth mother is a real fitness or sports buff, she will probably not care if one of you is overweight. Yet, a birth mother could be turned off if you are extremely overweight. If this is your situation, you may want the birth mother to know your positive attributes before she meets you in person, and before you do meet, you may want to mention that you are working hard to lose weight.

5. *Meeting with a birth mother and making arrangements with her, knowing that she may change her mind.*
6. *Taking a limited financial risk with a birth mother, such as paying some of her medical expenses and/or living expenses.*
7. *Becoming emotionally involved with one or both birth parents.*
8. *Pursuing an adoption in which the baby may be born with medical problems; if it is, deciding whether you can go through with the adoption.*
9. *"Working" with more than one birth mother at a time.* Making arrangements with two or more birth mothers, knowing that you want only one baby, can be very emotionally taxing.

INDEPENDENT ADOPTION: ONE COUPLE'S STORY

Here is one example of a couple's experience in seeking an independent adoption.

My husband Richard and I were happy with the differences in our ages and our religious and ethnic backgrounds. We had been married for four years. I had been married before, and that marriage had ended in divorce. My marriage to Richard signaled a new beginning, a chance to have a family, even though I was now older than I would have preferred to be as a prospective mother.

Sadly, nature and the state of technology at the time of my experience were defeated by my "advanced" age. I was in my early forties. A biological child seemed an impossibility, and we were unsure about taking the step toward adoption. Even if we decided to adopt, agencies might turn us away for having an unconventional profile.

Richard felt that I needed to be absolutely sure about the decision to adopt since he would undoubtedly be content without children. This placed the responsibility for making the "right" decision on me, and I lingered for months with the possibilities, the fears, and the longing, while becoming more and more discouraged by the imagined failure ahead.

At last, after reading an article in their newsletter about independent adoption, I called RESOLVE of Central New Jersey and spoke to a woman who was planning an independent adoption information session. She spoke at length about her own experience, which seemed miraculous.

Feeling a burst of hope in spite of my misgivings, I announced tearfully to her, "We're thinking about adoption, but I'm afraid we won't qualify because I'm too old, we're of different religions, and I've been divorced."

"It only matters to the birth parents," the woman said. "If they like you and want you to be their child's parents, then you won't have any other significant barrier." My uncertainty disappeared with this new information. "I'm now sure that we should try to adopt a child," I told Richard that evening. "I don't look forward to the next twenty years without a child."

"Are you really sure?

"Yes!"

Within two weeks my friend phoned me with the news that someone knew a pregnant woman who wanted to place her baby with a nice couple.

This was too much good fortune to be believed. Yet later in the week, the young woman, Linda, called and confirmed that she hoped to find a nice couple for her baby since it was too late in the pregnancy to have an abortion.

She was nineteen. She had another child whom she relinquished to her in-laws when she and her husband divorced. Because of her pregnancy, they had a "shotgun" wedding when they were sixteen. Things had gone from bad to worse, and she did not want to repeat her mistake this time with another man.

Richard and I met Linda in person. We reviewed her health history with the aid of a questionnaire supplied by our attorney. Linda and I went to the obstetrician together. We also went to a social service agency in case Linda wanted counseling, financial support, or Medicaid.

Linda called frequently. She said she used me as her lifeline, and she was very appreciative of my time and the monies spent on her medical care. I felt that I had developed enough of a relationship with Linda that I would be alert to a difficulty or a change of heart. When she told me that she had located the address of her boyfriend's parents in New York, an alarm went off.

Would Linda actually make contact with them or with her boyfriend with the idea of reuniting and keeping the baby, perhaps even using the pregnancy as leverage (again)? While such a plan seemed foolhardy, it was entirely possible, given Linda's past experience.

Was she feeling reluctant to part with this potential bundle of love, silky skin, and gurgles that was growing inside her? Did she wish that her boyfriend would see the error of his ways and love her again?

Sure enough, with just two weeks remaining, Linda phoned to say simply, "I've decided not to give you the baby, so I won't be talking to you again." Good-bye, little love. Good-bye, hope. Good-bye to the settled situation.

Richard cried with grief, surprising me with the intensity of his feelings, since I had been the one to initiate the adoption and carry on the relationship with Linda. He said that somehow his stake in adoption had crept up on him, with its promise that he would soon be a daddy, that we would experience the joy that a new baby brings, and that this long wait would finally end. He had been unprepared emotionally to feel much one way or another. Now he could see that this unexpected disappointment could happen again and again, even if we found another birth mother.

With renewed determination, I proposed contacting the attorney about this change in plans and about placing ads in the newspaper. Using suggestions from the attorney and from people at a RESOLVE meeting, I phoned in the first of several advertisements to run in New Jersey newspapers, while Richard made arrangements to install another phone line in our home.

The ad read "Everything is ready for a baby." I didn't see any other ads like that. Maybe it would catch someone's eye.

The ad appeared the following weekend. Nothing happened. I used call forwarding during the days that I went to work. My new friend Karen from RESOLVE, who had recently adopted, had agreed to take calls during those times. She had a vibrant phone personality and was deeply sensitive and caring. She was so kind to do this for us. However, no calls came.

Three days later, when I arrived home, I phoned Karen just to check in.

"You just got a call!" Karen said. "You better call back fast before she calls someone else!"

"Hello. This is Ellen," I said. "I understand you just called about our ad in the paper. . . . Yes, we are ready to adopt a baby immediately. How wonderful! A baby girl!"

Richard and I brought home our little girl within a week. She was born the weekend our ad ran, and her birth mother, Sandy, still had the newspaper.

Sandy had made earlier adoption plans with an agency but changed her mind because of a negative experience with a social worker. Ultimately she had resolved her problem by requesting information about independent adoption. Her requirements were to have the adoptive parents pay for medical expenses, since she did not want to involve an agency of any kind, and to have the adoptive parents—us—take the baby home right away without resorting to foster care, despite the sixty to ninety days that would elapse before she could surrender her parental rights under New Jersey law.

Sandy was delighted that we resided in a certain county in New Jersey because she knew it from her childhood experiences with her family. She was going back to college and wanted no further contact. She preferred not to meet with us prior to our taking custody of the baby because she wanted to protect herself from additional involvement.

Her mother and sister wanted to speak to me on the phone. It felt like the embrace of a family.

"What a great family our daughter comes from," I said to Richard later. The miracle of adoption had happened to us too, just nine months from the start of our quest. Would it last? It did.

It was a beautiful resolution for all concerned. In fact, Richard and I are sure that the reason it took nine months was that we had to wait for our daughter to be born!

Chapter Four

Choosing an Adoption Attorney

I f you decide you want to adopt through private channels, one of the first steps is to contact an adoption attorney. Your attorney is by far the most important professional in the adoption process. He or she will guide you through your state's adoption laws and provide you with practical tips. Your attorney is also someone the birth mother can contact to discuss legal and financial matters.

Many people have a trusted attorney who has completed their wills, conducted the closings on their homes, and provided legal advice on other matters. He may be likable and competent in the areas of wills, real estate closings, and general law; he may even have assisted others with one or two agency adoptions in the past. However, this is not necessarily the same attorney you want to guide you through a private adoption. Not only must an adoption attorney be very knowledgeable about your state's adoption laws and the nuances of Interstate Compact requirements, he must also have a comfortable manner with clients and people in general. This is especially important because the attorney will be talking (and often meeting) with birth parents, social workers, and sometimes the parents of birth parents. It is better to find a good adoption specialist.

Perhaps you've had the experience of engaging a professional (a doctor, a dentist, an infertility specialist, a CPA) who was extremely competent but not very personable. You may have overlooked any boorish or rude behavior because she was "very good with numbers and gave great financial advice" or an "excellent endocrinologist." The adoption attorney must be someone you like and with whom you feel genuinely comfortable. If you like him, the birth parents will probably also like him and feel comfortable with him. This cannot be emphasized strongly enough. Adoption plans have ended because an attorney was condescending or rude to a birth mother. A birth mother wants to be treated with respect and sensitivity and will look for another couple if your attorney is lacking in these areas.

If you have friends or acquaintances who have hired adoption attorneys, ask for a recommendation. Other sources for recommendation are infertility or adoption support groups, or you could contact the American Academy of Adoption Attorneys.

SERVICES AND FEES

In states where this is legal, an attorney can serve as an intermediary, matching a prospective adoptive couple with a birth mother. In California, for example, which permits attorneys to bring birth mothers and couples together, birth mothers as well as adoptive parents often hire attorneys as intermediaries. Not surprisingly, California has one of the highest numbers of infant adoptions each year compared with other states, most through private placement.

Attorneys who work as adoption intermediaries often advertise in the Yellow Pages under "Adoption," using ads explicitly directed at birth mothers. Some advertise in states where intermediaries are permitted, even if their practice is not in that state. It is not unusual to find a California attorney placing an ad in a Louisiana newspaper.

An independent adoption always begins with finding a birth mother. In some states this task may be carried out by an adoption attorney for an additional fee, but many other states forbid the practice, regarded as too much like "baby selling." In other words, an attorney can charge for legal services connected with representing a birth mother or adoptive couple but cannot simply charge for the matching of a couple with a birth mother. Find out what the rules are in your state and make sure your attorney's fees are in accordance with them.

Establishing a relationship with your attorney is important; if at all possible, work with an attorney who is referred to you by other couples. You must be able to trust her since your heart and money will be in her hands. Sometimes you will be referred to an attorney, often out of state, by an adoption professional, and you have little or no relationship with him. You will do well to remain cautious—especially of an attorney who claims to have located a birth mother and then immediately asks for large amounts of monies related to the woman's needs, such as traveling, hotel rooms, rent, food, medical fees, and counseling.

Remember, at this point your emotions and your checkbook may not balance. At the very least, obtain documentation proving pregnancy and for all expenses before paying for anything. Not only is it unethical for an attorney to ask you to pay for a woman's gynecological visits without proof of a bill, it is also illegal. Once you have disbursed substantial expenses and lawyer's fees "up front," you may feel compelled to continue sending more money; otherwise, you will have forfeited your initial investment. Find out your attorney's total fees before committing, including the expenses you will be reimbursed if no birth mother selects you within a reasonable period of time—usually eighteen months.

THE ATTORNEY AS INTERMEDIARY

How does an attorney arrange for birth mothers and adoptive parents to select one another? An ethical attorney usually uses the same system employed by many adoption agencies, allowing a birth mother to select adoptive parents from an assortment of portfolios. A portfolio is a three-ring binder containing biographical information, pictures, a letter to the birth mother, and sometimes your home study (without last names or other identifying information). For advice about putting together a portfolio, see the end of this chapter.

Once the birth mother has decided upon the couple or couples she may be interested in, the attorney may suggest that she meet them. If she prefers not to meet with anyone, the attorney will simply contact the couple and describe the birth parents to them.

Sometimes a birth mother will want to meet more than one couple before she makes up her mind. Of course, only one couple will ultimately be selected, which can lead to disappointment.

Some attorneys are unethical. Be cautious of the following scenarios:

- An attorney places several prospective adoptive couples in one room at the same time and then allows a birth mother to pick one.
- You are at an introductory session with other prospective parents to find out about an attorney's services, and the attorney suddenly states, "A birth mother has just called, and someone will soon receive the infant." This actually happened to a friend of ours!
- The attorney claims that a birth mother is interested in you and then asks you for money for her expenses. Although this is not necessarily a sign of trouble, the couple may find themselves paying money for weeks before their attorney tells them that the birth mother has "changed her mind." The attorney gives no explanation about your money. You just lost a few thousand dollars. Unfortunately, this experience is not uncommon.

During the year after one couple first retained an attorney, for example, he "found" them two birth mothers. The first time he immediately asked the couple to send money for expenses. They sent $3,000. A few weeks later the couple received a call from the attorney's office telling them that they would not have wanted this birth mother because she was using drugs. (The couple never met the birth mother.) A few months later the couple received another phone call from their attorney about a second birth mother. Of course, they were expected to send more money, which they did. By this time, with the attorney's expenses continually rising, they were borrowing money from relatives. (Once someone spends $6,000, it is hard to say, "I do not want to go through with this adoption.") A few weeks later they were once again told, "The birth mother changed her mind." The couple is not even sure whether these birth mothers ever existed. They had only one "documented" adoption expense from their attorney—furniture for the birth mother. (Incidentally, it is usually considered illegal to pay this kind of expense, depending on the kind of furniture and amount of money expended.)

If anything like this should happen to you, call the State Bar Association or State Supreme Court immediately and file an ethics complaint against the attorney. Then call the attorney and demand your money back—all of it.

Again, we highly recommend that the adoptive couple have contact with the birth mother before you have paid out substantial sums of money. The attorney may simply be "throwing" money at pregnant women who may have "thought of adoption" so that he can charge you more attorney fees without really evaluating her motives.

If you do not really have a relationship with the attorney, then go meet the attorney and go meet the birth mother. Meeting you is a reality check for a birth mother; the meeting tests her resolve to place. Also, you can evaluate her yourself; look for consistency in her presentation. If your common sense is telling you beware, then listen; however, be sure to discuss with your attorney about your "feel for the matter." Read Chapter 7 on birth mothers, and you will learn what to look for as red flags.

One final note of caution: When an attorney is acting as an intermediary to link you up with a birth mother, the usual wait for a placement is a year to a year and a half. If the attorney says, "I can guarantee you a baby within three months," be very careful. It is nearly impossible for an attorney to do this. Remember, price does not guarantee success.

YOUR ATTORNEY'S ROLE IN A DOMESTIC OR INTERNATIONAL AGENCY ADOPTION

In an agency adoption, the attorney's role is more limited than in an independent adoption, but not less important. Normally, the attorney will not interact with the birth parents or assist you when the baby is placed in your arms at the hospital. However, your attorney is a resource person and must be aware of state laws regarding agency policy and procedure. Your attorney should review all documents that the agency has you sign, including the application, placement agreement, and especially any documents that the birth parents sign, such as the surrender documents, to ensure that they comply with your state's law. For example, you want your attorney to make sure all paperwork is filed with the local court in states where parental rights are revocable until filed. This is particularly important if you are dealing with an out-of-state agency. Also, the attorney will assist the agency in complying with Interstate Compact requirements. In addition, an attorney can often get through the bureaucracy and confirm that all necessary paperwork is filed.

Remember, an agency is usually representing the birth mother and child; you need an attorney to represent you. Therefore, share with your attorney your interactions with the birth mother and agency social worker. The attorney's goal is to determine if the agency is doing its job. For example, one agency never asked the birth mother's mom how she felt about the adoption—a critical question, especially if the unborn child will be the first grandchild.

In another case, a Nevada agency obtained the surrenders of both birth mother and birth father but never discussed with the out-of-state adoptive couple that their attorney should review the Nevada surrenders to ensure they complied with the couple's home state adoption laws. The couple was told to retain an attorney when they returned to their state with the baby since the agency attorney would be handling everything except for finalization of the adoption in the couple's home state. The problem is that the Nevada surrenders did not comply with the couple's state laws on surrenders; the agency attorney had to go back to court to terminate the rights of the birth parents—a needless expense and delay of time!

Your attorney's role in an international adoption is usually limited and may be unnecessary. In cases such as this, your attorney's duties are limited to filing the necessary legal documents in your county court to accomplish a readoption of your child. It is a readoption since your child has most likely been adopted in another country. In some county courthouses, you do not even need an attorney if you can obtain the forms.

However, if you are dealing with a small agency or with an intermediary, your attorney can ensure that the foreign translation of the Judgment of Adoption or the termination of parental rights document contains the correct legal language to satisfy the laws of your state. Also, your attorney can help you complete the various international documents and put you in touch with the right person in the United States and overseas. If you have not finalized your adoption overseas, then your attorney's role is critical in presenting your case to the family court judge in your county to ensure that your local judge will accept the wording in the foreign adoption documents which terminate the rights of the overseas birth parents.

In any adoption—domestic or international—your attorney can also guide you so that you pay only expenses that are permitted by law.

PUTTING TOGETHER A PORTFOLIO: A QUICK OVERVIEW

An attorney—as well as many agencies—will commonly ask you to provide a portfolio (also called a profile) so that birth mothers can "see" you and possibly select you. A portfolio is a picture story of your life as a couple or as a family with children; in fact, it is referred to as a "life book" in some parts of the country. It is like a scrapbook or picture album containing pictures of you, any children, close relatives and friends, pets, your home, important occasions, and favorite activities. Its purpose is to tell your "story" to a birth mother.

Even if you plan to do your own advertising and are not expecting your attorney to find a baby for you, a portfolio can be a useful thing to have. It can be shared with your birth mother at any point to give her an idea of who you are and what your lives are like. You can also present the portfolio at the your initial meeting with the birth mother; flipping through the pages and talking about the pictures you are showing her will help break the ice and make both of you less nervous.

One couple met a birth mother just after she gave birth. When they went to the hospital to meet her, they were able to present their lives very succinctly by showing her their portfolio. Once the baby is placed with you, a birth mother may want to keep the portfolio as a keepsake.

Portfolios are not beauty contests. They are not designed so that a birth mother can select the family with the largest home, nicest furnishings, or prettiest smiles. They are meant to provide a picture description of you as a couple and family. If your home is very large or elegant, try to minimize this. It may only intimidate a birth mother.

Designing Your Portfolio

Choose an album book in which pages can be rearranged and added. Avoid bulky, fabric-stuffed books, which are difficult to store and mail. We recommend using low-acid paper for the original to ensure that it will last a lifetime—or several lifetimes. Someday it will be a precious keepsake for your family.

Once you have your album, you may wish to select a theme, usually one related to childhood. For example, the cover may have motifs of Beatrix Potter, Disney, Winnie the Pooh, or other storybook characters or baby animals such as bunnies, ducks, or teddy bears. These motifs may then be sparingly placed throughout the rest of the album. Avoid motifs involving babies—booties, diaper pins, pacifiers, etc. These are not appropriate.

The next step is to place pictures of yourselves, special people in your lives, and important life events in chronological or thematic order. You might include pictures of your wedding; holidays with family and friends; vacations, outings, and picnics; your home; and favorite activities or hobbies, such as your art collection, crafts, woodworking productions, or activities like horseback riding, skiing, and gardening.

Select photographs that are homey and provide a feeling of comfort, warmth, and responsibility. Do not include pictures of the two of you in your bathing suits or in skimpy outfits or pictures that show alcoholic beverages. If your favorite cousin looks as if he belongs to a motorcycle gang, you may want to leave him out. Not all birth mothers and fathers care about issues such as smoking, drinking, or style of dress, but even if they do not, the birth mother's parents might see the portfolio and influence the birth mother to select a more "wholesome" couple. Play it safe. The birth mother may exclude you if you were pictured drinking alcohol.

Place no more than three to six pictures on most pages, with up to eight pictures on just a few pages. This may sound like a lot of pictures, but if you trim them, you can fit about eight comfortably. Using heart-shaped, round, and oval cookie cutters as stencils makes for nicely trimmed pictures. Write captions for each picture or set of pictures. It is better to write or print, if your handwriting is legible; otherwise, type your labels and attach them to the pages. When referring to yourselves, use your first names. Personalize the information as much as possible while still maintaining your anonymity. Be creative but not too cutesy. Include no more than fifteen pages of pictures in the book.

Adding Elements to Your Portfolio

The next item to prepare is a "Dear Birth Mother" letter. This letter describes your feelings toward the birth mother who is reading the letter and also how you feel about the decision she is making. It says something about the two of you, why you want to adopt, and why you will be wonderful parents to her child. The letter goes on the first page of the portfolio. A sample birth mother letter can be found on page 58.

These are the essential features of the portfolio. Many couples also include a copy of their home study. Home studies usually highlight people's positive characteristics. If yours is like this, place what is called a "sanitized" home study (with all identifying information taken out) in the back of your portfolio. Accompanying your home study are letters of reference; these add a nice touch to your portfolio as well.

If you do not include a home study, an alternative is to write a one-page "resume," or biographical sketch, that highlights your life and some of your positive assets, such as your stability, love, financial security, home, family, hobbies, and favorite activities. In fact, even if you do include a home study, a birth mother may be more likely to read a one-page outline of your life than a multipage home study. Place the biographical sketch in the front of the portfolio, after the "Dear Birth Mother" letter.

Now your portfolio is finished. But can you be sure it looks right? Have a few trusted friends look it over and give their feedback. If you can, send a copy to your agency or attorney's office for suggestions. When you are satisfied with your finished portfolio, take it to a shop that does color copying and have two copies made. Keep at least one copy at home and send one or more to your attorney.

Remember, if you or your attorney identifies a potential birth mother and a portfolio is mailed to her, you may never get that portfolio back again. Keep the original at home. Once you adopt a child, the portfolio makes a lovely beginning to a baby book! That's one reason why putting together a portfolio is never a waste of time. You can always use the original to tell your child the story of how you adopted him.

Some people like to include a video with their portfolio. If this appeals to you, the guidelines are fairly simple. Share the kind of information you included in your birth mother letter and biographical sketch. In other words, talk a little about yourselves and her. You may also want to include a special occasion that captures you at your best. Keep the video short—about five to ten minutes.

There are now agencies and adoption support consultants that will place your portfolio and video on a Web site which is accessed by birth mothers across the country. Since the Internet has become a daily item of use, more and more birth mothers are being located this way. The only drawback is that most of the birth mothers will be from another state and, in many cases, another region of the country. You will need to travel to that state and stay there until approvals are received from the offices of the Interstate Compact for the Placement of Children (ICPC) located in your state and the state in which your child is born. The approval process can take from three to fifteen business days; the average is approximately five to eight.

Make sure that you have several friends review your portfolio or video online; these friends must be honest and yes, blunt enough, to tell you what portions are unflattering!

Correct them and move forward.

Chapter Five

Finding a Birth Mother

Now that you have decided to adopt, should you share your desire to find a baby with people you know? Telling others about your decision essentially means publicizing your infertility, and that makes many people uncomfortable. Try telling a few people in your "safe zone" first—people that you trust, such as close friends or relatives. Later you may feel ready to share your plans with coworkers or acquaintances.

If you are truly serious about adoption, however, it is best to tell nearly everyone. The more people you inform, the more you will increase your chances of finding a birth mother. As you explain your situation, it is important how you present yourself. Even though deciding to start looking for a birth mother was likely a very emotional process for you, this is not the time to share those emotions. As you let people know that you and your spouse have chosen to go on to this next step in your lives, talk about your interest in adoption in a casual, matter-of-fact tone. Never sound desperate. Most couples are rewarded with sincere empathy.

Sharing your desire for children often opens the doors of people's hearts, leading them to go out of their way to pass on the word about your adoption plans. Do, however, be prepared for a few negative reactions. Some people will respond with surprising ignorance. Fortunately, this group is likely to be in the minority.

Your job is to throw the "pebble"—the news that you want to adopt—into your "pond" of friends and acquaintances and wait for the ripple effect to take place. Your friends and acquaintances will tell their friends and acquaintances— often people you do not even know—who will tell their friends and acquaintances, hopefully resulting in your contact with a birth mother. Perhaps you have had this experience when searching for a job. If you tell twenty-five people that you are interested in adoption and they each tell another twenty-five, you will have "told" 625 people. This "ripple effect" does work.

NETWORKING

Establish a network for spreading the word about your decision to adopt. Remember that a contact from a birth mother usually comes from the most unexpected sources, not necessarily from your "planned" efforts.

Here are some good places to start your networking campaign.

People in Adoption or Infertility Support Groups or Organizations

Infertility and adoption support groups can provide a strong network of people who are also pursuing adoption. At first, you may be tempted to view these couples as your competition. But sometimes they may have contact with more than one birth mother and will be able to refer one to you. We know of a couple who had contact with three birth mothers. After adopting two of the babies themselves, they referred the third birth mother to another couple, who adopted a beautiful baby boy.

In another situation, a woman named Michelle casually mentioned at a RESOLVE board meeting that she would like to adopt an older baby. A few days later, an adoptive mother named Betty, who had also attended the meeting, received a phone call from a birth mother who had an eighteen-month-old baby. Betty told the birth mother that although she was not interested, she knew of someone else who might be. Two days later the birth mother contacted Michelle and her husband. Ten days later Michelle and her husband brought home a baby girl.

Another benefit of knowing other prospective adoptive couples is being able to make referrals to them. If you are not interested in adopting a particular baby, it is comforting to be able to give the birth mother another couple's name. Betty, for example, did not just have to say "no" to the birth mother. She successfully referred her to another couple.

Friends and Relatives

Telling friends and relatives, especially those far away, that you want to adopt can extend your likelihood of locating a birth mother by tapping resources that you would otherwise not have been able to reach. One couple's friend was at her obstetrician's office for a routine visit when she struck up a conversation with a pregnant woman. The woman was experiencing a crisis pregnancy and intended to place the child with an adoption agency. The friend referred the birth mother to the couple, who successfully adopted her baby.

In another example, a couple's friend's cousin knew a nurse who knew a birth mother. The nurse referred the birth mother to the cousin's friends—the adoptive couple. The adoption was a success. Yes, it sounds confusing, but this is how you make contact with birth mothers. The moral of a complicated story? Don't overlook anyone.

Coworkers, Clients, and Customers

Telling coworkers, colleagues, and sales representatives, for example, can also provide you with a far-reaching network. However, a woman who plans to remain at home once her baby arrives should be cautious about broadcasting this information too freely. She does not want to jeopardize her job or career advancement.

If your job involves routine contact with clients or customers, mention that you are seeking to adopt when they ask, "Do you have children?" In our own case, Ray was weary of the "You've been married ten years and still no kids?" comment from those at his office. He finally told them that we were infertile and hoped to adopt soon. Not long after that disclosure, a secretary telephoned him with a birth mother contact that resulted in our adopting Erika.

Hairdressers, Manicurists, and Barbers

Consider the broad range of people you come into contact with each week. Your hairdresser probably sees hundreds of clients a month. One of these contacts just might be a pregnant woman, her mother, or her friend, who happens to share information about her adoption plans while getting her hair cut. Do you think this couldn't happen? It does.

Your Dentist or Other Health Professional

Medical forms include questions about your general health and whether you are taking any medication. These may provide an opening for you to share your situation with the health care professional.

Some people try to adopt through obstetricians, sending countless letters to every ob-gyn in the Yellow Pages. This effort is usually in vain. In some states, it is even illegal for a doctor to assist a nonfriend in meeting a birth mother. In any case, ob-gyns are inundated with letters from couples hoping to adopt. Unless you know a physician personally or are in the medical field yourself, you will seldom get a lead in this department.

If you are in the medical profession, however, you will probably have some opportunities for adopting a baby. One physician and his wife adopted a baby just three days after they first began to consider adoption seriously. This came about because the wife had casually mentioned to one of her husband's colleagues that they were now considering adopting. "That's interesting," the physician said. "I know of a baby who was just born who is going to be placed for adoption."

Clergy

If you are religiously affiliated, the network you maintain through your denomination or affiliation can be a wonderful way to find a prospective birth mother. Many birth mothers want to select a couple of a particular faith.

Talk with your pastor or clergy person. If you have been having problems conceiving or have a history that means you most likely will not be able to have a biological child, explain this and your desire to adopt. (Do not be surprised if he or she is unaware of the emotional impact of infertility.) Let the clergy person know that if he learns of a pregnant woman from another church who wishes to have her child adopted, you would be glad to be contacted. He may be able to spread the word to his colleagues and associates.

Pastors, priests, and rabbis need to know about potential adoptive parents since they are often the first to counsel a family whose daughter is experiencing a crisis pregnancy. How reassuring it would be for a pastor to tell the parents of a pregnant teenager or the teenager herself that he knows of a wonderful couple who could provide a secure and loving home for the baby.

Ask your clergy person for the names of other clergy who may be interested in talking with you or receiving a letter from you. Send them each a letter (see examples later on in this chapter) enclosing copies of letters that can be given to birth mothers.

If your faith places an emphasis on the sanctity of unborn life, let the woman know this in your letter. Emphasize the attributes of your faith that will make you a better parent. One note of caution about discussing your faith, however: Do not assume that the birth mother places a great emphasis on her religion or that she expects you to do so just because the referral was through her clergy person. A birth mother's main concern is probably that appropriate family values are taught to the child—the kinds of values that often come through religious teachings.

BROADCAST LETTERS

Sending out letters is a relatively inexpensive way to make contact with a birth mother. Although writing one takes time and forethought, once one letter is written, duplicates are the easiest things in the world to produce. Here are some likely people to send letters to:

- *Friends.* When you send out your holiday cards, you may want to share with your friends your desire to adopt. Of course, you do not have to do this at Christmastime. But the holidays are a time for children and babies, and people tend to be extra responsive.

- *Professional or volunteer associates.* If you belong to a professional or volunteer organization, you may consider sending letters to some or all of its members. There are print shops listed in the Yellow Pages that handle the whole mailing process for you. All you do is give them your letter and list of names and addresses, and they duplicate the letter and mail it for you. In one situation, two birth mothers contacted a couple who used this method. Apparently, people are very receptive to these letters.
- *Clergy.* As noted earlier, contact with clergy can be a good way to locate a birth mother. Sometimes it is better to contact a clergy person outside your own church or synagogue. You probably do not want to adopt a baby whose birth mother or birth grandparents attend your church or synagogue.

Here's a list of where not to send letters. Although sending letters to these organizations will do no harm, the likelihood of finding a birth mother this way is next to zero.

- *Crisis Pregnancy Centers (CPCs).* At first glance, CPCs might seem to be a likely source for pregnant women seeking to place their babies for adoption. However, the staff at these centers is usually not permitted to give birth mothers the names of couples who are interested in adoption. CPCs get many letters from couples who want to adopt which they have no choice but to throw away. When a woman considers adoption, they usually send her to an adoption agency of the same religious affiliation as the center.

    If you know someone who works at a CPC, you may mention to her your desire to adopt. She might be able to provide your name to a pregnant woman, if the crisis pregnancy center where she works does not view this as a conflict of interest.
- *Planned Parenthood.* Planned Parenthood and other clinics already receive many letters from prospective adoptive parents. Even if they had a policy of responding to them, they wouldn't have the resources to do so.
- *Obstetricians.* Don't waste your time sending letters. However, if you are personal friends with an obstetrician, midwife, or nurse who comes in contact with pregnant women, do let these friends know of your desire to adopt. You may feel awkward asking them about referring a pregnant woman to you. Just letting them know of your desire to adopt may be enough to keep you in mind if such a situation arises.

Writing the Letters

Separate letters should be written for friends, associates, clergy, and potential birth mothers. Examples of three letters can be found on pages 58–60.

Make sure that your letter to the birth mother includes these two things: Be sure you express your special understanding of what she is experiencing and also tell her something about yourself—your hobbies, home, talents, interests, and positive attributes. Follow these guidelines:

- *Keep it easy to read.* Remember, she may be a teenager. Keep the language simple and the sentences short. You are trying to impress her not with your command of the English language but with your genuine desire for a child and the love that you can provide to that child.

- *Be sensitive to her needs.* Let her know that you are sympathetic about her unplanned pregnancy and that you realize she does care about her unborn child. This woman did not choose abortion. Without directly saying so, let her know that you respect her for choosing to carry her pregnancy to term.

- *Mention your infertility.* You do not have to mention your specific infertility diagnosis, but telling her that you have this problem can help her feel for your situation as well. Never say, "We cannot have children of our own." Adopted children are your own.

- *Mention what you do for a living, but don't go into much detail.* If for example you are a teacher, state so, but if you are a math teacher, leave out that detail. Some professions are better to mention than others. If you are a plumber or mechanic, you may mention the type of company you work for. For example, if you are a mechanic, you may say that you work on cars and especially love restoring old cars. If your profession sounds intimidating, such as being Chief Financial Officer and Executive, for a very large company, you may want to just give part of your job description such as financial planner for a company.

- *Mention your favorite hobbies and activities, especially ones that a child may enjoy.*

- *Share the positive points of your marriage.* For example, if you enjoy long walks and talks, you may want to mention this, as it suggests a warm and communicative relationship.

- *Share your religious faith or your personal values.* If you are involved with a religious organization, talk about how this will help you to raise a child. If you are Protestant, it is usually best not to mention your denomination, unless you are targeting pregnant teenagers or women who share that denomination or belief. If you are not part of an organized religion, then you will want to share the values that will make you a good parent, such as commitment to family and community, honesty, hard work, and acceptance of others.

- *Show that you are willing to have some level of "openness" in adoption.* If you are willing to maintain an "open" relationship with the birth mother, then tell her about this. If you are not willing to see the birth mother after the baby is placed, do not mention it. Please note, however, that most birth mothers do not expect to see you or the baby after placement. Whatever degree of openness you are comfortable with, let her know. Every birth mother should at least be given the opportunity to receive pictures and progress notes about the baby. Do let her know that you will send these to her. It is very comforting to a birth mother to know that she is not just handing a baby over to someone, never to hear about the couple or the baby again.

- *Make it personable.* Do not greet the birth mother as "Dear Birth Mother." Just say hello, or use some other informal greeting. Use your first names in letters and portfolios. Do not refer to yourselves as Jane and John Doe or "The Adoptive Couple." You are two real, living human beings with feelings: Let this come through.

Sample Letter to a Birth Mother

Hello,

You and I are in very different circumstances, and yet in some ways, we are in very similar circumstances. We both find ourselves in a situation that we wish we could change. You have an unplanned pregnancy, yet love the child that you will give birth to. I cannot bear a child, but would love to have a baby for our family. My husband and I have longed for a child for three years. But I had four miscarriages, and the doctors cannot give me any treatments that will help me carry a child to term. I value unborn life and do not feel that it is right to keep trying to give birth to a baby while risking another miscarriage. My husband also cares about my health and that of the unborn child. Besides, our goal is to be parents, and through adoption, we can love and cherish a child.

Just to let you know a little about us, I will tell you about our home and our activities. We live in a lovely ranch home with four bedrooms. Outside is a large yard with apple trees. There are two parks within walking distance of our home. My husband has a management job with an oil company. He was recently promoted. I am a third-grade schoolteacher. I enjoy my job, but I would like to be home with a child. If we are blessed with a child, I plan to stay home full-time. Both my husband and I love snow skiing and take about four or five trips to Vermont each winter. During the year, we enjoy bike riding and long walks and talks together. Sometimes we take a picnic basket to the beach or park and then walk for hours. We also love to socialize with our friends. Many of our friends have small children. David and I both teach Sunday School at our church. Our lives are very full. There is only one thing missing—a child.

We would love to meet with you, if that is your desire, or if you are more comfortable, we could exchange information over the telephone or through letters and pictures. David and I are also willing to maintain a relationship with you, even after the baby is born. If you select us as parents, we would be happy to send you pictures and letters to let you know what the child is doing at each age. We would even consider a more open relationship if you are comfortable with that. Of course, we also want to respect your privacy and the life ahead of you.

We also could pay for your medical expenses if you do not have insurance. All information between you and us would remain confidential. We have an attorney so that everything is legal.

Please let our friends who have given you this letter know what you would like best. They can then contact us, or you can contact us directly at (800) 123-4567.

We wish you the best, whatever you decide. I know it is a difficult time in your life. We do care and are willing to help.

Susan and David

Sample Letter to Friends

Dear Friends,

As you may already know, David and I have longed to have children and have been unable to do so. This time of year is especially hard for us, as we would love to have presents under the Christmas tree for our child.

Recently we have decided to adopt and are letting all of our friends know in case they may know of someone who wants to place her baby for adoption.

We have everything that a child could want. Most of all, we want to provide a child with love, stability, and acceptance.

Our jobs are going well. In fact, David was recently promoted to northeast director of marketing. I do enjoy my job, but I would rather be at home with a child.

If you hear of anyone who is pregnant and knows this is not the best time in her life to raise a child, please let her know that we would be interested in meeting with her, talking with her, or making whatever arrangement she finds comfortable. We have an attorney so that everything is legal. Our number is (222) 555-1234.

Dave and I have also enclosed some "Adoption" cards. If you feel comfortable with distributing them, you could help us by placing them by public telephones and in the women's rooms at shopping centers.

We appreciate your help, and we'll keep you posted about our progress.

Wishing you all a Joyous Christmas and Happy New Year,

Sue and Dave

Sample Letter to Colleagues or Associates

Dear Fellow Rotary Member:

This may seem like an unusual appeal, but I hope you consider it seriously. As a fellow volunteer, I know that you are in contact with many people and, therefore, may know of a woman who is experiencing a crisis pregnancy and is interested in placing the baby for adoption.

If you do, my wife Gloria and I would be most interested in contacting her. For five years now we have longed to become parents but cannot. Our lives have gone well, and sometimes it seems as if we have everything—everything except a child to love.

Please contact us at (555) 123-4567 if you know of someone who is considering adoption. We have an attorney so that everything is legal. If you can, please pass the enclosed letter on to her.

Thank you.
Terry Harkins

BUSINESS CARDS AND FLIERS

Business cards are yet another way to get the word out. They can be designed so that the front of the card presents a color photograph of a baby and the word "Adoption," or you could place a picture of you and your spouse on the front of the card with the word "Adoption." On the back of the card, write a message similar to one that you would put in a newspaper advertisement (see p. 65-66). As with an ad, include your e-mail address and phone number. Place these cards in malls, rest rooms, restaurants, and other public places. You also may want to mail several to each of your friends with the letters described earlier.

Because fliers are larger and are inexpensive—you pay only for paper and photocopying—you can add more information than you would in a classified advertisement. You may not want to list your phone number, but just your e-mail address. Fliers can be placed at bus stops, college campuses, and other public places where young women may be. This takes a little more "guts" to do. The thought of going through a college campus and putting up such fliers may feel humiliating. If you feel this way, then do not do it. Perhaps you would feel better if someone else did it for you so that you are one step removed—especially if someone asked you to take down a flier.

NEWSPAPER ADVERTISEMENTS

One of the most common ways for adoptive parents and birth mothers to make contact is through newspaper advertising. Writing an advertisement for a newspaper takes a little work, but the rewards can be great. Like all ads, adoption ads should be short, convey an important message, and immediately attract the reader. You are not only presenting yourselves, but you are also seeking a most important person—your baby. Your ad should display warmth and compassion as well as your unique characteristics.

A list follows with some tips on writing an advertisement. Before you write your own, read other adoption advertisements. Which ones grab your attention? Decide why that advertisement makes a positive impression on you. If you can, fashion your ad in a similar way, yet make yours unique. You want a birth mother to see your ad and say to herself, "They sound like a nice couple who could provide a good home."

What should you include in your ad? This list includes what to cover and what not to cover.

1. *What kind of child you are interested in adopting.* How much should you say about what kind of child you would like to adopt? Most couples seeking to adopt through private channels are interested in a healthy Caucasian newborn infant. If these are the limits you are placing on the child you seek to adopt, you should not mention it in your ad. Most birth mothers who are calling you will be Caucasian and pregnant and planning to place the baby with you immediately after birth.

Here are some other issues parents have to consider in wording their ad:
   - *The child's health status.* Don't mention that you want a healthy baby. A

birth mother may think you are looking for a "doll" and not a real child who will get sick throughout his life. Most birth mothers who respond to advertisements are pregnant and believe that the baby is healthy.

- *The child's racial/ethnic background.* Many newspapers have policies that prohibit you from mentioning ethnic background or age. The best thing to do is wait until you talk with the woman on the telephone to determine her ethnic background and that of the birth father. If you are interested in adopting an African-American or biracial child, you may choose to mention this in your advertisement. Part of your ad may read, "interested in infant of any racial background."

    If you are of a specific nationality and state that you want only a child from that ethnic background, you may find yourself waiting a long time for a birth mother to respond. Instead of stating that you want, for example, a baby of Irish descent, you may say in your ad "Irish-American couple seeking to offer a child happiness." You may also want to advertise in a newspaper that targets those of your specific nationality.

    Some couples do not want to adopt a child of a certain ethnic heritage. Even if you feel strongly about this matter, do not mention it in your ad. Screen your telephone calls to find out the birth parents' ethnic backgrounds.

- *The child's age.* If you want an older baby or young child, placing an advertisement in the newspaper probably is not a good way to find such a child. Yet if you are willing to adopt a child from birth to three years of age, your ad may read like this: "Couple seeks child for adoption."

2. *Your first names.* We advise against using false names. In the first place, it is unethical and, in the second, impractical. Once you meet with the birth parents, it will be very difficult for you to keep calling your husband "Harry" if his name is "Massimo" and for him to call you "Sue" when your name is "Angelina." On the other hand, a birth mother may not respond to an ad if she has never heard of your first names before. She may feel more comfortable calling a Mary and John than a Xenia and Archibald. If your names are particularly ethnic-sounding, you may want to Anglicize them a bit. "Mordecai" could become "Mort," and "Raymondo" could become "Ray."

    If your name comes from another language, just change it to English. Instead of being "Jose," call yourself "Joe." Then if you inadvertently call your spouse by his or her more ethnic-sounding name in the presence of the birth parents, at least your spouse can honestly say, "That's what my family calls me."

    The point is not to misrepresent yourselves. If you are Jewish and your names are very ethnic, you would not want to select names traditionally Christian such as "Mary" and "Christopher."

Some adoptive parents are very concerned about retaining their anonymity and do not want a birth mother to find out their full identity. If your names are "Archibald" and "Penelope," you may fear that a birth mother will be able to figure out who you are. You may be thinking "How many couples are there named 'Archibald' and 'Penelope' in the state of Iowa?" You may fear that your specialized profession will be a dead giveaway to a birth mother intent on finding out who you are. After all, how many "Samantha and Jacks" are there in which the wife is an orthopedic specialist?

The truth is that no combination of first names is either common or unique. What you should really consider is what you could lose by using an alias. It is too easy for you or your attorney, legal secretaries, physicians, or anyone else involved in the adoption to make a mistake and call you by your "real" names. If this happens, the whole adoption could fall through if the birth mother feels that you have been lying to her.

Apart from that, it is morally wrong to try to deceive a birth mother about your names. When the truth is discovered—and it probably will be—the birth mother's trust will be diminished, even if she does not immediately change her mind about placing her baby with you. Besides, you may have an ongoing relationship with this woman for the rest of your lives, even if just through letters and pictures. If your child seeks out his birth mother when he is eighteen years old, how will everyone feel when it is discovered that you had lied about your names all these years?

3. *Your unique characteristics.* Nearly every couple who advertises claims to be "a loving, happily married couple who will provide a child with much security." You therefore want your advertisement to stand out. Emphasize some unique characteristics that make you special. For example, if you are gifted as an artist, musician, baseball player, or tennis pro, you may want to include these details in the ad. One prospective adoptive father was a mechanic and did not want to include this in his ad. It turned out he had many interesting hobbies, such as hiking and woodworking. The couple included this information in the ad instead and soon had a response from a birth mother. They are now parents.

Your profession is a unique characteristic that can serve to your advantage and sometimes disadvantage. Birth mothers seem to respond most favorably to teachers and nurses and less favorably to physicians and attorneys.

Activities that revolve around animals, beaches, mountains, and other outdoor activities are especially appealing.

Be careful not to set yourself too far apart from a birth mother. You may be very well educated, have a large home, and take many vacations, but don't call attention to it. The following will not do: "Harvard graduates who love tennis, golf, and yachting in the Caribbean seek to provide a child with much love. Call Biff and Buffy." Most birth mothers are intimidated by such a show of education and wealth.

4. *Your religion.* Again, your religion or a profession that may suggest your religion can work either for or against you. In many cases, however, mentioning a religious affiliation is seen as a positive attribute. Saying you are Presbyterian or Baptist, in most cases, will mean little; saying you are active Christians would be viewed positively by most birth mothers. Even a birth mother who has not been in a church in twenty years may still desire that her child be raised in a religious home.

   Many Jewish couples worry that they may have difficulty finding a birth mother who will work with them since very few birth mothers are Jewish. Actually, experience shows that this is usually not an obstacle. Birth mothers are typically more interested in whether you practice a religion and will make good parents.

5. *Your financial status.* If you are financially comfortable or a member of a respected profession, you may discreetly mention these facts in the ad. Birth mothers are not interested in knowing that you are a highly successful broker on Wall Street. She would rather know that you are a financially stable businessman. If you, the adopting mother, are a successful businesswoman, this could be mentioned in more nurturing terms. Yes, we are being sexist, but the truth is that a birth mother needs to identify with you and wants to know that you will be loving and nurturing. You may choose to mention little about your career.

6. *Medical expenses.* If you are willing to pay for some medical and other expenses, instead of directly stating this in your ad, simply say, "We care and want to help." Most birth mothers whose medical bills are not covered by health insurance will have Medicaid coverage.

7. *Legality of independent adoption.* Even in states where it is legal, which includes most, you will be surprised to find how many people think that independent adoption is illegal. If no other adoption ads are in the newspaper, you may want to mention that the adoption plans are legal and confidential.

8. *Your telephone number.* When you place an ad in the newspaper, you need to have a cell phone so that you can be available by phone at all times. Other phone services that can keep you available for a birth mother's phone call are a second phone line, call waiting, call forwarding from your home phone to

your cell phone, or a toll-free line that overrides your other numbers. Most birth mothers are willing to make a long-distance phone call as she will probably also have a cell phone.

9. *An e-mail address.* More and more birth mothers have access to e-mail and may actually be more comfortable e-mailing you at first.

Other Considerations for Advertising

Start your ad with the letter A or with the word "Adopt." This will put your ad at or near the beginning of the adoption ads or "Personals" column of the newspaper. One couple told me that a birth mother confessed to them, "I called you because your ad was one of the first of thirty ads, and I am not going to call all thirty ads." We do suggest that you not compete with more than four other adoption ads. Although having other adoption ads can be a good sign—it probably means this is a newspaper in which adoption ads are read and responded to by birth mothers—it is hard to make an ad stand out. Make sure yours is unique.

Be brief and to the point. Cut out extra words and phrases. Just don't go overboard! On the other hand, saying that you are a loving couple sounds unnecessary, but you must say it. Leaving it out is like not putting "attractive male/female" into a singles ad; if you do not say it, it is assumed you are unattractive.

The truly adventurous may want to experiment with a very unusual ad, testing it out in one newspaper to start. Make sure the newspaper or magazine fits your style.

Finding an 800 or 888 number is nearly impossible. Now 877 and 866 are toll-free numbers but may not be readily recognized as such. So to make it clear, you should write the words "call toll-free" at 866-ADOPT-83.

Sample Advertisements

ADOPT Manager and piano teacher want to share the love that we have for each other and our joy in music with a child. We care and want to help. Call Fred and Wilma toll-free at (877) 123-4567 or e-mail freddy9999@hotmail.com.

ADOPT Professional yet fun-loving couple desires to share our love of life with a child. We enjoy camping and horseback riding. Call Martha and Harry toll-free at (866) 333-4444 or e-mail horses7777@intel.net.

An accountant and teacher—financially secure—want to offer a child a wonderful home by the beach, but most of all—lots of love. Call Blair and Lois collect at (333) 123-4567 or e-mail beachcombers@aol.com.

A successful broker and loving at-home artist seek infant. We can provide a child with many blessings, but most important, lots of love and happiness. Call Steve and Jane collect at 1-555-123-4567 or e-mail artsyone735@yahoo.com.

Physician and nurse who cherish quiet walks, friends, and family want to share our love with a child. Call John and Karen at 1-800-123-4567 or e-mail healthyandfit@lll.com.

We want to share our large home and small farm in the country—but most of all our love and happiness with a child. Call Susan and Jim at 1-888-555-6543.

Teacher dad, loving at-home mom, and big sister long to share our love with a child. Call Tony and Sally toll-free at 1-866-123-4567 or contact our adoption agency at 866-83-ADOPT.

Adoption is a loving choice, as three-year-old brother knows. Dad, loving at-home Mom, and Grandma and Grandpa all can't wait. We care and want to help. Call Wayne and Lisa at 1-888-765-1234 or e-mail us at bigbrother@values.com.

Loving dad and mom want to provide a child with strong family values and security plus fun days at the beach with lots of cousins. Call Mark and Pam at 800-123-4567, PIN 1234, or our attorney John Smith at 800-555-1313.

WHERE SHOULD YOU ADVERTISE?

Perhaps you've been wondering how far from home it is best (and safest) to advertise for a child. Here are some options.

Out of State

As a general rule, the state where you advertise is the state where the baby will be born. (Note: Not all states that permit independent adoptions allow advertising. See Appendix A.) This means that if you live in New Jersey and advertise in Iowa, you must correspond with someone in Iowa and possibly visit the birth mother there at least once before the baby's birth, in addition to the trip to Iowa to receive the baby. Of course, many trips to another state can be expensive. Laws differ from state to state, too, resulting in possible complications. But even without complications, you will need to either retain an attorney or engage an adoption agency in each state. Before you decide to advertise in a state other than your own, therefore, ask yourselves these questions:

- Am I willing to travel there at a moment's notice?
- Can I afford to make more than one trip to that state?
- Am I willing to incur the expense of living in a hotel before and after the baby is born? (You will usually live in a hotel from one to two weeks while all the Interstate Compact on the Placement of Children paperwork is filed through your state and the state in which the baby was born.)

- Am I willing to incur the expense of maintaining a long-distance relationship by telephone?

If you decide that advertising out of state is still a good idea, then the question becomes "Where?" Some couples find that they get a better response advertising in less densely populated areas of the United States, such as the Midwest and the South, than they do in the Northeast. A couple seeking a Caucasian infant is more likely to find a birth mother in a rural area than in a cosmopolitan or urban area.

In Your Own State

If you advertise in your own state, select a small hometown newspaper about fifty miles away from where you live. Do not advertise in a newspaper that is distributed too close to your home. You or the birth mother may not want to live in the same town. Although birth mothers and adoptive parents and children are maintaining closer relationships these days, living in the same area and having mutual acquaintances may infringe on everyone's privacy.

What Kinds of Newspapers?

Once you have decided in which state(s) to advertise, decide which area of the state to target. Some say the best place is near a college campus, beach town, or military base. In other words, advertise in a community where there is a high concentration of young women.

This does not necessarily mean a college newspaper, although you might assume this would be the perfect place to advertise. Unfortunately, these young women often choose abortion over adoption. However, there are couples who have advertised in campus newspapers and received positive responses.

If you do choose a campus newspaper, select a college that is rural and, if possible, of a religious affiliation that does not condone abortion since there will likely be more pregnant young women who are considering placing their baby for adoption. If you think of this newspaper as one means of locating a birth mother but not your only means, you will have nothing to lose.

What about a large daily paper? It is true that a large newspaper goes to more homes. However, the "Personals" section of a small newspaper is more likely to be read by a birth mother or her friend or family member. Weekly newspapers are also more likely to stay in the home longer than a large, daily newspaper, and since advertising in a small newspaper is usually less expensive, you can afford to do it more often. If you advertise in a newspaper that is also available online, you will reach more people.

Call the various newspapers to determine their rates. Ask to have the papers mailed to you so that you get a "feel" for the area and so you can see how many other couples are advertising in each paper.

Remember, with a daily newspaper, it is best to place your ad every day. If this is too expensive, try placing it twice a week and once on the weekends. Similarly, if you place the ad in a weekly newspaper, plan to do so for several weeks.

Newspaper Networks

If your finances are limited, you can still get broad coverage in some states by advertising in the Newspaper Network Association in your state. Then your ad will go in both daily and weekly newspapers. For $100 to $250 per week, you can place an ad of twenty-five words or less (extra for each additional word) in all the newspapers that belong to that association. About 90 percent of the newspapers will place your ad.

For a larger sum of money, you can place your ad in several networks simultaneously, giving you multiple-state coverage. Again, this can be done with one call to a local network association. For more information, see the listings in Appendix B.

An obvious but important note: If you have invested several hundred dollars in placing ads, you should either have a cell phone and much privacy at work or stay home for a week or two to answer the phone. That's too much money to spend only to have a prospective birth mother reach an answering machine. Birth mothers are generally more comfortable talking woman-to-woman; keep this in mind when deciding who will answer the phone.

Finally, if you want to go nationwide, advertise in *USA Today*. Yes, it is expensive (about $1,500 a week), but you will probably find a birth mother in a matter of two or three weeks. Again, if you do this, stay home to answer the telephone.

Note: If you advertise in a national newspaper or in a different time zone from yours, you may receive phone calls at odd hours. For most people, this poses only a minor inconvenience.

How Long Should You Run Your Ads?

It is easy to be discouraged if you place an ad in a weekly newspaper and have not heard from a birth mother in a month. If you still have not had any calls after two or three months, you may need to advertise in a different paper.

If you have paid for a certain period of time, such as a month, keep the advertisement for that period, even if a birth mother contacts you and decides that she wants to place the baby with you. You could get a call from another birth mother. It can sometimes help to have more than one option.

INTERNET ADOPTION SERVICES

Online listings for adoptive parents and hundreds of Web sites for adoption agencies and support groups are among a number of Internet services now available. Adoption Online Connection is the first Internet listing service that offers in-depth national exposure for prospective adoptive parents. Listings go primarily to adoption agencies, hospitals, and organizations offering services for unwed mothers. The fee is about $40–$65 if a photo is included—plus a monthly fee of $25. The listing you submit resembles a portfolio and includes a birth mother letter, your 800 telephone number, and possibly your e-mail address. The Adoption Online Connection cannot serve as an intermediary, so an agency, service, or birth mother must contact you directly.

Even though the Internet reaches states where other types of adoption advertising is not permitted, it is not illegal for a woman to respond to an Internet listing; however, there is potential for prank messages and calls.

Will you find a birth mother through this method? Perhaps. As the Internet becomes more popular and user-friendly, the potential of finding a birth mother in this way increases. You may not find a birth mother directly this way, but you could find out about other people who are also looking to adopt, and by connecting with them as you would with an adoption support group, you may find a child who another couple has decided not to adopt.

Adoption.com and adoption.org probably have the largest network of placing portfolios for prospective adoptive parents. If you want to place your portfolio on a smaller scale, two Web sites dedicated to Christian couples can be found at *www.linkadoption.com* and *www.babytalkadoption.com*.

SEARCHING FOR A BIRTH MOTHER: ONE COUPLE'S STORY

The quest for a birth mother can sometimes involve a few unexpected twists and turns, as Leslie and Paul discovered. Here's the way Leslie, who eventually retained Ray as her adoption attorney, tells the story.

• • •

It seems as if a large chunk of my life was spent thinking about getting pregnant, trying to get pregnant, and then worrying about it—I'd been an infertility patient for more than eight years. At last, my husband Paul and I decided to end the treatments and focus our energies on adoption. Reaching this decision lifted a huge burden from our shoulders. Finally, we could share our secret.

Apart from our immediate families, no one was aware of our situation. We had felt it would be easier to keep our infertility under wraps. In that way there would be no pressure and no nosy questions from well-meaning friends and acquaintances.

The response to our adoption plans was wonderful. I'll never forget how immensely pleased our families were when we broke the news. Until then, they had just figured we didn't want to have children. It's funny—I went from telling no one to telling everyone. When people would casually ask, "So, do you have any children?" I'd say, "No, but we're hoping to adopt." Even on airplanes, I started asking other passengers how many kids they had. Invariably they'd turn the question around and ask me, which was the perfect entree.

We had already decided to pursue an independent adoption.

Having made this decision, we barely knew where to begin. We figured it was best to speak with an attorney first and proceed from there.

Unfortunately, the first attorney we talked to left us cold. We were uncomfortable with what we perceived as her lack of integrity. I feared that if we used her that some day down the road someone would knock on our door and demand our baby back because the adoption wasn't conducted legally. So I found another attorney who seemed much more credible and kept him on retainer. He immediately recommended that we install a separate phone line and begin our newspaper campaign. We placed ads in papers all over the country. Our ad was short, and we ran it daily for thirty days in roughly four to six papers a month.

It worked. We received calls from all twelve states in which the ads appeared. The calls ranged from the serious to the ludicrous—such as the man who guaranteed that I'd become pregnant if I spent a week with him! After all, when your phone number is appearing all over the country, you are bound to attract some weirdos. But we attracted serious callers, too. Like the Louisiana college students, newly married and shocked to discover that the young wife was pregnant. Knowing that they couldn't possibly raise a child now, they began seeking out adoptive parents. They said they were instantly drawn to our ad.

In fact, after I'd spoken to the young woman a few times, she asked for more information about us—what we were like as a married couple, our careers, and what we'd be like as parents. She also wanted to speak to our attorney. Things were looking quite promising, and I was starting to feel excited. So was Paul. With the Louisiana woman five months pregnant, we might have a baby in four months! Shortly after we sent them our biographical sketches, however, the couple called to say they could no longer work with us. They didn't like the abrupt manner with which our attorney treated them on the phone. They felt he was unsympathetic and brusque. I was stunned. They also admitted they'd been in contact with other couples, and frankly, why should they deal with a condescending attorney when plenty of other couples out there have warm and thoughtful attorneys?

At first, I didn't know whether their concerns were legitimate or whether they were politely refusing us. Of course, I was upset; it was very discouraging. Yet, I had been warned that these things happen. Paul and I continued on; we placed more ads and took more calls.

I had decided early in the process to quit my engineering job and concentrate on the search. Paul's job as a marketing analyst would allow me to be a full-time mom once the baby arrived. Since the adoption process required so much energy, it made no sense to keep working. It was far better for me to be available to answer the baby phone myself rather than hook it up to an answering machine. What birth mother wants to pour her heart out to a machine?

Certainly not Annie, a sixteen-year-old Iowa girl who was expecting twins. Annie liked our ad, called us, and struck up a friendly rapport with me. A needy young woman, Annie would sometimes call me as often as three times a day. I spent hours and hours on the phone with her. We discussed virtually everything. After several months of dialogue, she verbally committed to placing her babies with us. Naturally, Paul and I were elated! Not one, but two babies! It seemed too good to be true. It was.

The first setback came after Annie talked with our attorney. There was a mix-up with some paperwork, and she said the attorney was so mean and rude to her on the phone that she never wanted to speak to him again!

This was the second time we had heard negative remarks about our attorney. It was the last straw! If you are going to be an adoption attorney, you have to be prepared to do a lot of hand-holding for young girls who are nervous, even hysterical. Our attorney's abrupt "New York" manner was not what these Midwestern girls wanted to hear. We immediately fired him.

Not long afterward, Annie confided that she had severe epilepsy. This did not pose a problem, until she mentioned that she was taking an antiseizure drug on a daily basis. I immediately phoned my pediatrician and discovered that there was a very high chance that the twins would be born with multiple birth defects—spina bifida, a cleft palate, even brain damage.

Could we take this chance? Paul and I were forced to do some serious soul-searching. What would it be like to care for not one but two babies, possibly with very high needs? Could we do it? In the end, we decided we could not take the chance. Birth defects are a terrible thing, and Paul and I decided that we were not willing to adopt two children who could be seriously impaired. Then came the hardest part of all—telling Annie that we had changed our minds. It was one of the most difficult things I've ever had to do. We had developed a very close relationship over the phone, and I knew she was going to be devastated. She was. I tried to be as gentle and as loving as I could. I did not mention the possibility of birth defects. I felt this information should come from her doctor. Instead, I told her we were simply not equipped to care for twins.

We both cried on the phone. Annie sobbed uncontrollably. I tried to reassure her that with hundreds of couples out there looking to adopt, surely she would find someone to provide a loving home for her babies.

As it turned out, Annie went into labor the very next day, six weeks before her due date. She delivered a girl and a boy. Sadly, the boy died a month later. Annie ended up raising the girl herself. Surprisingly, she continued to call me from time to time. We had a strong emotional connection, and she looked to me for support. She ended up going away to college, only to become pregnant again within five months! Since then, I have not heard from her.

After Annie, we had a few calls, but nothing promising. The next few months were totally uneventful. I was feeling discouraged and wondered whether it made sense to continue the ads. I questioned what we could have been doing wrong.

Around this time, we hired a new attorney on the recommendation of the state agency that handles adoptions. The new attorney, Ray Godwin, suggested advertising in a newspaper in an urban area about forty miles from our home. I was skeptical but figured we should give it a try.

Within three days after we ran the ad, a pleasant, articulate woman named Hayley phoned us. Unlike the other callers, Hayley was not a birth mother. She was the best friend of a woman who was due in exactly two days. This young woman wanted very much to place her baby for adoption, yet could not bring herself to make the calls or even talk about the situation. Hayley was very generously acting on her nineteen-year-old friend Diana's behalf.

Well, Hayley and I just hit it off fantastically. Here we were, two strangers talking on the phone, yet it felt as if we were old friends. At the end of our conversation, Hayley said she felt as though we had just gone out together for a long, chatty lunch. More important, she couldn't wait to tell Diana about us!

Later that night Hayley called again and spoke to Paul. Initially, he'd been skeptical, but like me, he started to get excited about the possibility. Things were looking very promising—yet I didn't want to get my hopes up too high. I'd already seen how easily things could fall through.

The next step was to speak to Diana herself. Hayley warned us that Diana was a very shy, very insecure young woman. She was a bank teller who lived at home with her mother and brother, neither of whom had been supportive of her decision. She had a long-term boyfriend who had fathered the child, but they were not ready to marry or raise the child themselves.

Hayley was very much on target—her friend was extremely shy. Our phone conversation was strained. I tried to get as much detailed information from her as

I could the two times that we spoke: Was she right- or left-handed? What were her likes and dislikes? What did she and her family members look like? During our second talk, she agreed to place her baby with us!

We were thrilled! Soon, very soon, we'd be parents. Paul assembled the crib, relatives loaned us a bassinet, and we bought diapers, formula, and bottles. The anticipation, the excitement, and the thrill of it all were just overwhelming. In a matter of days, we'd actually have our baby! Or so we thought.

About a week later (like many first-time moms, Diana was late), Hayley called with some grim news. Another couple had offered Diana $10,000 for her baby. (Although it's illegal to "buy" a baby, many desperate couples are said to do so.)

Paul and I thought long and hard before we came up with a strategy. We got Diana on the phone and asked her outright, "Is your child's life worth money?" "Do you really want to turn your baby over to a couple who would buy him?"

Our tactic worked! A day later Hayley called to say that Diana definitely wanted us as parents. Whether the other couple had ever existed, we'll never know. Needless to say, these ups and downs were emotionally draining. We were exhausted.

A few days later, on a Thursday, Diana delivered a healthy baby boy! We were ecstatic. We had a son! Ray Godwin assured us our baby would be home within a few days.

Once again, however, trouble loomed. Mysteriously, the hospital staff would not allow Ray inside to see the baby. The staff began pressuring Diana to turn the baby over to Catholic Charities and telling her they would not release her unless she carried the baby out herself.

Like most birth mothers, Diana had been under the impression that the adoptive couple would be taking the baby home directly. Neither did she expect to have to feed and change the baby, which the hospital required her to do.

In the meantime, we were at home, pacing, worrying, and praying, waiting for Diana to call. Ray urged us not to panic or lose faith. Diana would call us. We kept hoping in our hearts that he was right. But Saturday came and went with no calls. We called it Black Saturday—it was a horrible day. Late that night, truly alarmed, we slowly began resigning ourselves to the reality that we'd lost another baby.

When Ray called the hospital on Sunday, he found that both Diana and the baby had been discharged. No one answered when he phoned her home. We had no idea where she might have gone. Did she take the baby and flee? Did she accept the $10,000 offer from the other couple? By Sunday afternoon, Ray still hadn't had any contact with Diana. Gently, he told us that we might as well just forget it.

Paul and I couldn't stop crying. We knew in our hearts this was our baby. We had already named him David. How could this be happening? To be so very close and have the baby just slip away was devastating.

Sunday, ironically, was sunny and crisp, an absolutely gorgeous day. We drove to the beach where we walked for miles and miles all afternoon. At times, I would just collapse in a heap and cry. Paul would stop and console me, and I did the same for him.

As the afternoon went on, we decided to take a few weeks off, go away somewhere, grieve a little, and then renew our energies. We'd come back and resume our search.

When we finally got home from the beach that night, I couldn't even bear to walk past the baby's room. I asked Paul to take down the crib and bassinet and put them away in the basement. I didn't want to look at them.

I had started to prepare some dinner when the phone rang. It was Hayley.

"What's the matter?" she asked. "Don't you want the baby?"

I was speechless.

"I've been calling you all afternoon, and no one's been home," Hayley explained. "Diana figured it would be easier for her to just go home, rather than deal with the hospital. She's staying here at my apartment."

This was unbelievable! These two young girls had simply brought the baby home and were playing "Mommy" for a day.

While I kept Hayley on the "baby phone," Paul called Ray Godwin on the other line. Ray, his wife, Laura, and daughter Erika were at a party that afternoon, and we reached him through his beeper. He told us to get to Hayley's apartment immediately. He'd follow with all the paperwork.

I'd been crying all day, and I looked terrible. I needed a complete makeover, but there was hardly enough time to change clothes. Instead, we sped off to Hayley's to pick up our baby. Everything had an edge of unreality to it. Just hours earlier, we'd phoned all our relatives with the bad news.

Paul and I kept each other calm during the thirty-minute drive. I hoped and prayed that nothing would go wrong this time. Ray did warn us about one thing. Diana did not want to meet us face to face. Although she would be there in Hayley's apartment, the thought of meeting us was overwhelming, too much for her to handle. But she did want to see what we looked like.

It would have been wonderful to meet her, to be able to thank her for all she'd done for us. But we understood how she felt.

When we arrived at the apartment complex, Ray, Laura, and their daughter had already gotten there. Diana had completed all the paperwork.

Just as we stepped into the apartment, Hayley slowly walked out of the bedroom, holding a tiny baby swaddled in a blanket. "This is your son," she said and handed David to me.

When I saw the baby's beautiful little face, tears flowed down my cheeks.

It was wonderful; it was all you could imagine. Hayley and I gave each other a huge hug. But there was no time for heavy emotional exchanges. Ray had urged us beforehand not to dilly-dally. He recommended keeping the exchange as brief as possible.

As we bundled the baby into the car, I glanced back up at the window and saw the curtains fluttering. I knew Diana was watching us.

• • •

David, now fourteen years old, is a happy child who has brought much happiness to his parents.

Chapter Six

Who Are Birth Mothers, Fathers, and Grandparents?

Exactly who are birth mothers, and why do they place their babies for adoption? As you begin your search for a birth mother, you'll probably be wondering about what kind of person she might be and why she has chosen to place a child with an adoptive family. You might be anxious about meeting her. But the more you know about the birth mother, the more comfortable you will be when you do meet each other. Even more important is the fact that usually, if the birth mother is comfortable with you, she will be more likely to go through with the adoption.

In most independent adoptions, the prospective adoptive couple will meet with the birth mother and possibly the birth father before the baby's birth. Most encounters that we know of go very smoothly. The personal contact that you have with her is one of the main reasons that a birth mother chooses the independent adoption route. You are not adopting an anonymous woman's baby; you are meeting a person who will give birth to your child. A birth mother deserves much respect. She is not a commodity or merely a person who is a means to an end; a birth mother is a woman who has gone through nine months of pregnancy, labor, and birth, and has probably agonized over her decision.

A HISTORICAL PERSPECTIVE

Adoption has not always been viewed in a positive manner. It was once a solution for "bad" women who got pregnant, for couples who could not "have children of their own," and for "illegitimate" children. In other words, it was considered a second-rate choice for all parties involved. While adoption has certainly become more mainstream, the myths of the birth mother still linger. The following are examples of reasons why birth mothers have been stereotyped. As you read them, keep in mind the impact that such attitudes could have on the adoption process.

1. Birth mothers were told to "forget" their babies. Pregnant women were told to have their babies, surrender them to the agency, go home, forget what happened, and get on with the rest of their lives.

2. Birth mothers were treated as though they were shameful. Some were sent away to a home for unwed mothers so that no one would know about their pregnancy and adoption plans.

3. Birth mothers did not see their babies at birth or ever again. In the delivery room, physicians sometimes instructed nurses to cover the birth mother's eyes so that she would not see the baby.

    Once the baby was relinquished, a woman did not know what sex the child was or what he looked like, much less what happened to him. She also had to bear a secret for many years in her attempt to "forget it all." This level of secrecy led to much anguish.

4. It was believed that a birth mother was a poor judge of what was best for the child. Not only was it assumed that the less a birth mother knew, the better, but it was also assumed that a woman who allowed herself to get pregnant could not possibly be a good judge in selecting adoptive parents. Therefore, agency workers selected the best parents for the child.

5. It was believed birth mothers cared very little about their children. This attitude is probably best expressed by the term "unwanted child," but birth mothers in general do care very much about their children.

Today, we know that many birth mothers are simply women whose birth control method failed. These women believe that their child can be given a better life with other parents than with themselves or their families. Generally, they have chosen placing their child for adoption over abortion or the possibility of raising the child alone without financial support.

PREDICTING THE LIKELIHOOD OF PLACEMENT

Only a few studies have been conducted to determine the likelihood that a birth mother will actually proceed with adoption plans after the baby is born. These studies have examined birth mothers who have used agencies. Yet, for the most part, the same factors that determine if a woman is more likely to place her baby with an agency for adoption can also be applied to an independent adoption.

According to studies conducted in the late 1950s and 1960s, birth mothers who placed their babies for adoption were primarily white, middle to upper-middle class, with white collar or professional employment. They generally lived in a shelter for unwed mothers during their pregnancies, where they received group counseling. A 1971 study analyzed data from 1967 to 1968 and came to similar conclusions—birth mothers with fewer emotional, social, and economic resources were more likely to retain their babies.

In a study published in 1988 by Steven McLaughlin, birth mothers who chose to give their children to adoptive parents were more likely to marry later and less likely to be unemployed. These findings are confirmed by Christine A. Bachrach of the National Center for Health Statistics. She stated that birth mothers who retained their children had fewer educational or career goals, whereas birth mothers who placed their babies for adoption had significant life goals. Bachrach also found that birth mothers who made adoption plans were similar in income and education to birth mothers who married before giving birth or who had abortions. More often, it was middle-class women who were more likely to place a newborn for adoption, contrary to the popular opinion that only lower-class women place babies.

According to a 1993 study done by Medoff, it was found that women who were also religious fundamentalists and had a high school education were more likely to place a child for adoption, whereas women receiving Aid to Families with Dependent Children (welfare) were less likely to place a child for adoption.

In applying these statistics to private adoptions, there are certain "red flags" that can indicate whether or not a birth mother will relinquish her baby. Usually, those women who ultimately decide to keep their child are on public assistance or have unmarried friends who have children and are also on public assistance. On the other hand, women who are likely to place a baby for adoption communicate frequently with the adoptive parents beforehand and have family members who are supportive of the adoption.

Before 1979, about 9 percent of women who had children out of wedlock placed them for adoption. This number has dropped over the years, and in 1995, only about 1 percent of unmarried women placed babies for adoption.

It is believed that African-Americans are less likely to place a child for adoption because of family pressure, and some studies show this. Yet other studies have shown that black women are not more or less likely than white women to place a child for adoption. In our experience, black women are more frequently placing infants for adoption than in the past but usually make adoption plans a couple of months later in their pregnancies than white women do. White birth mothers will often make adoption plans at six or seven months into their pregnancy while black women will often wait until they are eight or nine months pregnant to consider placing their child for adoption.

The women who choose to place their babies for adoption are generally sixteen to twenty-nine years old. The younger birth mothers have life goals to reach for and are motivated to place. Older birth mothers do place their babies in order to focus on life objectives, but more often it is because of financial straits. While most birth mothers do not have children, many have at least one child. She may have one or two children in or out of wedlock, is now single, and just cannot afford or manage another child.

CHOOSING TO PLACE A BABY

In general, birth mothers care very much about their children. It takes a lot of love to make adoption arrangements to ensure that a child goes into a loving, stable home in which emotional and material needs can be met. Birth mothers do not make their decision lightly. Even the woman who knows right away that she cannot have an abortion or rear the child usually spends time soul-searching and agonizing over her decision.

According to Anne Pierson of Loving and Caring, Inc., a Christian organization that provides counseling for birth mothers considering adoption, the advice her clients would give to others in the same situation includes the following:

1. Make a decision that benefits the child as well as you.
2. Look at the future and outline your goals and plans.
3. Think of the consequences of your decision.
4. Pray and seek God's help.
5. Think of the adoptive couple.
6. Never forget your child and always think of him or her.
7. Choosing adoption with the right intentions is positive and rewarding.

In Pierson's 1989 book, *Helping Young Women Through the Adoption Process*, she lists some conditions and attitudes that help birth mothers:

1. Knowing that the child is going to a parent or a couple who would love the child as much as the birth mother would
2. Loving support from friends and relatives
3. Faith in God
4. Counseling
5. Having much information about adoption and the adoptive couple
6. Exchanging letters, gifts, and pictures with the adoptive couple
7. Surrounding herself with understanding people who do not condemn her
8. Being able to see the baby and say good-bye
9. Meeting other birth mothers and adoptive couples
10. Providing for her physical needs (e.g., clothing, medical)

However, Pierson also mentions some experiences that birth mothers say are not helpful:

1. Acquaintances approaching them and confiding in them that they would have adopted the baby
2. Not being treated with the same respect as other mothers in the hospital
3. The awkwardness they encountered with friends and acquaintances when discussing the baby
4. Being told, "You're doing the best thing"
5. Not being given enough time to say good-bye to the baby and being ignored by the adoptive couple once the baby is placed

Qualities Birth Mothers Look for in Adoptive Couples

Because most birth mothers care about their children, they want to be part of the adoption process. A birth mother usually wants to know the couple and wants some contact after placement to assure her the baby is doing well.

Pierson's book lists certain traits birth mothers seek in adoptive couples:

1. Financial security and good jobs
2. Some type of spiritual commitment to provide the child with a religious upbringing and strong family values
3. Emotional stability and readiness for a child
4. A strong marriage of at least four to five years
5. No history of substance abuse
6. Nurturing and loving qualities
7. Being supportive of the birth mother
8. Willingness to send letters and pictures to the birth mother
9. Willingness of the adoptive mother to stay home with the child
10. Infertility
11. A good sense of humor

For more on the kinds of questions birth mothers will ask you, see Chapter 7.

BIRTH FATHERS

A survey completed by the Catholic Charities Adoption Services found that:

1. Most birth fathers (81.8 percent) are more than "casually" involved with the mother.
2. Most (62.5 percent) are committed to the relationship.
3. Most (52.3 percent) dated the birth mother for more than six months.
4. Most (73.9 percent) acknowledge paternity.

Based on our experience, these statistics are not exactly representative of birth fathers' attitudes and intentions at the time the baby is placed with the adoptive couple. They may more or less be descriptive of his feelings and actions months before birth, but at some point prior to birth, the birth father is usually not around. This means, of course, that he is often not part of the adoption decision. Frequently, the birth mother and her family do not want him to be part of the process. Usually, the less romantically involved the birth mother is with the birth father, the more likely she is to place the baby for adoption.

Until 1972, birth fathers had no legal rights. Today birth fathers can gain custody of their child based on their emotional and financial commitment to him or her. (See Chapter 8 and Appendix A for the laws of each state that relate to birth fathers' rights.)

BIRTH GRANDPARENTS

Prospective adoptive parents may find themselves dealing with not only the birth parents, but also with the birth grandparents. If the birth mother is living at home, it is more likely that her parents, particularly her mother, will want to meet with you and discuss the adoption plans. Jeanne Warren Lindsay, in her book *Parents, Pregnant Teens and the Adoption Option*, cites cases that describe the experiences and emotions that birth grandparents often have throughout the process.

1. When parents hear of their daughter's pregnancy, they are usually in shock. Then they often react with anger and bitterness before they move to the next stage of love and acceptance.
2. Many parents of pregnant teenagers never consider adoption. Most parents believe they and their daughter must rear the baby.
3. Birth grandparents feel very alone in what is happening to their family. Some want to talk with friends and family, while others want to be left alone.
4. Of those families that consider adoption, the birth grandparents need to allow the birth mother to feel secure in her own decision. Although it is difficult for birth grandparents not to give advice, the birth mother must ultimately be the decision-maker.
5. No matter what the birth mother's age, by law she has the right to have an abortion, select adoption (in some states if she is under eighteen, a guardian is appointed), or rear the child herself. This can make the birth grandparents feel very powerless, especially when they are still responsible for many of their daughter's other actions.
6. No matter how disturbed the birth grandparents are about the pregnancy, their daughter and the baby's father need much support during this time.

7. When parents say to their teenage daughter, "You can keep the baby, but you cannot live with us," they are, in essence, not giving her a choice.

8. Often the baby is their first grandchild.

9. When adoption is the choice, the birth grandparents need to grieve, just as the birth parents need to grieve, for the loss. Also, as the birth mother goes through other life events, such as marriage, this can be a time when the grandparents grieve again for the child placed for adoption. Just as birth parents can grieve at various points in their lives, so do grandparents.

10. Birth grandparents need to consider the hopes and dreams they have for their daughter as she considers whether to raise the baby or to make adoption arrangements.

11. Often the younger the birth mother, the more difficult it is for the birth grandparents to go through with an adoption plan since they feel more compelled to raise both their daughter and the baby. In fact, most birth mothers that Ray talks with are between nineteen and twenty-four years of age. Other statistics also indicate that most birth mothers are between these ages.

12. Often the birth grandparents are younger than the adoptive parents. This can cause the birth grandparents to feel guilty; if the adoptive parents can rear the child, they ask, "Why can't we?"

13. Some birth grandparents do help their daughters interview prospective adoptive couples. The questions they ask are often more sophisticated than a teenager's would be.

14. It is very important for you, the adoptive parents to know how the birth parents' parents feel about the adoption plans. Their input can have a great impact. Many grandparents have caused a woman's plan to place a child for adoption to be stopped. This is especially difficult when the parents of the birth father intervene and want to rear the child. The birth mother, who may not want them to rear the child, may have little choice, if they have a great deal of control over their son's decision to sign a relinquishment.

15. Recognize that even if the birth parents do not want any updated pictures, the grandparents may desire this. You probably will want to honor their wish and send updated pictures. If you are comfortable, you may want to establish a more open relationship with the grandparents after the baby is placed for adoption. One grandmother, whose daughter placed a baby for adoption about four years ago, expressed how she longs to have a relationship as a grandmother or aunt with the child. The child lives in the same area; so such a relationship could easily be established. Although the adoptive parents regularly send pictures, they choose not to have any other contact. Knowing what a great grandmother this woman is to her other young grandchildren,

this adopted child could have one more person in her life who loves and adores her.

Talking with Birth Grandparents

The ideas listed previously can provide you with some understanding about birth grandparents. By recognizing their situation, you can better communicate with them if the occasion or need arises.

These pointers will help you talk with birth grandparents:

Provide a listening ear. Unfortunately, they may not have many other people who are supportive of their daughter's or son's decision. Often people seek counseling from those who are most understanding of their situation. You may be the most understanding person in their lives.

Let them talk out the option of rearing the child. As they discuss this option and the details involved, they probably will realize that adoption is the best plan. If they do not bring up the subject, you may ask, "Why did your daughter choose adoption instead of deciding to raise the child herself?"

At first this may seem like a question that could cause the family to change their minds, but actually their answers will reinforce their reasons for making adoption plans. The reasons birth grandparents and birth parents give you for making adoption plans will later provide them with rational guidance once the baby is born—a time when everyone's emotions take over.

If they really have no reasons for adoption, then perhaps they may be considering raising the child. It is better to find out during the pregnancy than afterward.

Discuss with them their hopes and plans for their daughter. When birth grandparents begin to discuss their children's college education and other matters, they realize that she would have difficulty achieving her goals while raising a child.

Let them know that you appreciate their involvement and commitment as well as their daughter's. Everyone wants to be appreciated and understood. Also, this is an opportunity to let them see that an unplanned pregnancy can touch other lives in a miraculous way.

By understanding the families' feelings about adoption, you have a better idea of whether the birth parents will go through with the adoption plans once the baby is born. For example, if a birth mother wants to place the baby for adoption but the birth father is ambivalent and the birth father's mother thinks the baby should not be placed for adoption, there could be trouble ahead.

In situations in which an adoption is questionable, counseling could be useful. It could help guide all the parties involved so that they can manage their emotions and understand the facts. Also, counseling will assist all the family members to consider their options and find out who is going to be emotionally and financially responsible for the child if she is not placed for adoption.

It is our belief that a birth mother should not allow family pressure to influence her ultimate decision. The decision to rear a child or to place a child for adoption must be made by the birth parents.

In some states, birth parents' rights are terminated shortly after birth, whereas in others, it could take months. If birth parents can change their minds after the baby is with you, perhaps you may not want to take the baby home unless the birth parents and other family members are secure in their decision. The birth grandparents and other family members can strongly influence a woman who has just had a baby and may convince her to change her mind. Perhaps if the family seems uncertain, ask your attorney about the possibility of foster care placement until the birth parents' rights are terminated.

If you are older than the birth grandparents, do not make an issue of it. Explain your situation. Tell them how you tried for years to conceive a child and how much you long to become parents. If you are wealthier or have a position with more status, do not flaunt this. Let the birth grandparents know that you want to provide the child with the best in life, especially time and love.

Because birth grandparents can ask sophisticated questions, be prepared. Often the birth grandparents are looking for the same traits in adoptive parents that more mature birth parents look for: a stay-at-home mom, financial security, lots of love and warmth, a stable marriage, and, in some cases, a commitment to a religious faith.

Chapter Seven

Meeting the Birth Mother

n most cases, the first contact with a birth mother is by telephone. This is an emotionally fraught moment for everyone. You and she will both have many questions; both of you will want to present yourselves in a favorable light. After all, this could be the beginning of an important relationship.

The birth mother is considering you to be the parents of her child, and she is likely to be curious about your home, other family members, your religion, and your employment. Answer her questions honestly, but do not feel you have to provide more information than is necessary. For example, she may ask if you go to church. If you do, say yes. You do not need to go into detail about your religion and the tenets of your faith.

If you get the feeling that one of your answers is not the "correct" one and you cannot change the situation, then ask her if the issue is a problem. For example, perhaps she asks whether you have any other children, and you say yes. If you sense that this is not the answer she wants to hear, then simply ask her kindly, "Is that a problem?" You cannot change certain factors in your life, such as your religion, your age, or where you live, but depending on how she responds when you ask, "Is that a problem?" you may be able to tell her other things that help her feel more comfortable.

WHAT TO TELL HER, WHAT TO ASK

Early on you will want to let the birth mother know what your level of openness is toward an adoption arrangement. A birth mother usually cares very much about the child's welfare, although she may not know how to express that she is interested in knowing about the baby after it is born. You may want to offer to send photos and letters to her.

Do share a special interest, hobby, or sport. Sometimes one common interest is the reason a birth mother pursues you as parents.

There are several things you will probably want to ask a birth mother in your first conversation with her. For example:

Why she wants to place the baby for adoption. She will probably confide her reasons before you even ask. If she does not, try to determine her reasons and whether they appear to be valid.

Her health history. It is not easy to ask someone outright, "What is your medical background?" You may instead ask, "How is your pregnancy going?" Be cautious in asking direct questions. Your attorney will also be asking her these questions, and you may want to wait for him to do so.

Needless to say, asking someone point-blank about possible drug use is not tactful during a first conversation. Asking about school, work, hobbies, and interests may help you get a sense of how well this birth mother is caring for the unborn child. If she says she spends most of her spare time in pool halls with the guys in a rock band or at bars, you may have cause for concern. On the other hand, if she says she spends her time studying, swimming, and participating in a church youth group, she is probably living a clean life.

Asking someone about her life without prying also demonstrates that you are a caring person. Your concern for this unborn life can indicate that you will care about the baby later.

The birth parents' ethnic backgrounds. If you want a Caucasian infant or any other kind, then it would be appropriate to find out early about the parents' ethnicity. You may simply ask, "What ethnic background are you and the birth father?" Don't make this your first question, but do raise it the first time you talk with her.

Money. Do not bring up the subject of money unless she does. A woman who is just looking for someone to pay her medical and living expenses and has no plans for adoption will probably ask for money in the first conversation. A woman who mentions that she does not have insurance and would like to receive money for medical care, on the other hand, is not necessarily insincere.

When you are ready to end the telephone conversation, you might say something like, "I've really enjoyed talking with you, Jane. Perhaps we can meet each other so that we can talk further, and you can get to know us a little better. Would you like to meet in a diner somewhere between our location and yours or at our attorney's office?"

Here are a few more pointers about telephone contacts with birth mothers:

Don't pose questions as if you are reading from a list. Ask in a conversational manner, and listen to her responses carefully and thoughtfully. It is a good idea to practice this with a friend before you actually talk with a birth mother.

Jot down any questions that occur to you while she is speaking so that you are not tempted to interrupt her. You will probably be nervous (and so will she); however, give her time to complete her statements before you ask another question.

Maintain good records so that you can give any information you have to your attorney.

Do not expect to complete a full interview with every birth mother. Some women call many ads. Some are just thinking about adoption and are still unsure. Other calls will be pranks.

Always ask the birth mother for her phone number. This is a good way to find out whether the person is sincere or just someone making prank phone calls. Most genuine callers will leave a phone number, whereas most prank callers will say they can't or that they are calling from a phone booth.

If a woman gives you a phone number, call her right back after you end your conversation with "just one more" comment or question. This lets you know whether she really is at that number. When you do call back, you may say, "I just wanted you to know my lawyer's number in case you also wanted to talk with him. If you would prefer, I can have him call you at a convenient time." (Of course, if she is very far along in her pregnancy, she must talk to your attorney as soon as possible. Most birth mothers are unsure of the legal process and do want to know what to expect.)

Following is a list of questions you will want to ask in your first few telephone conversations with a birth mother. It is a good idea to copy this list and post it near your baby phone so that you will not have to think about what to ask when you are under pressure. Do not try to ask every question on the list during your first conversation. Concentrate on the ones that seem the most important, and be sure she has a chance to ask all her questions, too.

1. Birth mother's name. (She may choose to give just her first name.)
2. Why do you want to place the baby for adoption?
3. How do you feel?
4. How did you find our number? (Friend, ad, business card? If in a newspaper, which one?)
5. How old are you?
6. Is the birth father involved in your life?
7. How does he feel about your adoption arrangements?
8. Does your family know that you are pregnant?
9. (If yes.) How does your family feel about your adoption arrangements?
10. How many months pregnant are you?
11. Where do you live? (state or general area of a state)
12. Where do you plan to deliver the baby? (hospital and state)
13. What medical care have you received? Did it include an ultrasound?
14. What other results did you get from the obstetrician?
15. Are you taking any medications?
16. How has your pregnancy gone? Are there any complications?

17. Do you live with your family, by yourself, in a dormitory, or with friends?
18. What nationality are you?
19. What ethnic background is the father?
20. May I call you back? (if she is comfortable giving you her phone number)
21. Where can we meet? (if she wants to meet)
22. Other relevant information.

THE FIRST MEETING

Once a birth mother has called and seems sincere, arrange to meet her, if this is what everyone wants. You will probably not agree to meet after the first phone call—more likely after the second or third.

You will need to decide where to meet. If you made contact through a mutual friend, relative, or acquaintance, then you may want to meet at that person's home for the first time. For more confidentiality, meet at a park, library, or restaurant. Make sure you describe yourselves on the phone so you can identify each other easily. If you meet at a restaurant, pick up the tab!

If she selects a place that is familiar to her but not to you, visit the destination (if it is not too far away) so that you know the place really does exist and so you will not get lost when it comes time to meet her.

You could agree to meet at your attorney's office, but this might be a bit intimidating for a first meeting.

Overcoming Your Fears About Meeting

Meeting a birth mother is important for your peace of mind. It will give you at least a sense of the kind of person she is. If she is neat, clean, and dressed in a turtleneck, khaki jumper, and penny loafers, chances are slim that she is taking drugs. If she is disheveled and smells of tobacco and liquor, she is probably not taking care of herself, and she may be taking other substances. Seeing her and speaking to her will go a long way toward allaying your anxieties—or may warn you if something isn't right.

There's no question, however, that meeting a birth mother face to face is difficult for all parties. Everyone is nervous. To relax yourself, think of all the other firsts in your life and how nervous you were: your first day of kindergarten, your first date, your first good-night kiss, and so on. This is just another first—the first time you have ever met a birth mother. For additional reassurance, talk to other people who have met with a birth mother and adopted.

Be yourself. Isn't that what your mother told you as you went on your first date with the guy you were crazy about? But being yourself and knowing what to say are not always easy.

Birth mothers are no different from other people: Some are talkers, and some are quiet and reserved. If the birth mother is shy, making conversation can be difficult. Do not feel that you have to make great conversation. It should be pleasant and polite.

You could start the conversation by asking her how she is feeling. If you begin to feel comfortable with her and you both agree, you can go on to give identifying information such as your place of employment, the town you live in, and your last names. If you've met through a mutual acquaintance, she may already have this information.

Some birth mothers have no idea what to ask. You may have to take the initiative. Explain why you want to have a baby, and ask her why she is making this decision. A teenage mother may be accompanied by one of her parents, who will usually know what to ask, even if the teenager does not. Be aware of the birth mother's behavior if she is young and accompanied by her mother. Sometimes the adoption is her mother's idea, not hers, and she does not want it to happen.

If you have talked on the telephone with a birth mother, you have probably already shared some facts about your lives. As birth parents become more sophisticated about adoption, seeking greater control, some will want to know very specific facts about you. Naturally, you will present your finest points and discuss your interests. Be honest but not controversial. Birth mothers are looking for assurance that you will be a good parent—not that you are a Democrat or a Republican.

Here are the questions about your life that birth mothers usually want answered:

- What is your family like? Your parents, brothers, sisters, etc.?
- How do you spend the holidays? Birth mothers find it reassuring that the child will be in a home in which extended family members share important occasions together and carry on warm traditions.
- What activities do you enjoy? Sharing your interests in sports, music, and community activities indicates that you will probably share these interests with a child.
- What kind of a community do you live in? The kind of community you live in says something about what kind of life a child will have. Talk about any parks, beaches, mountains, or other recreational sites close by. Tell her if there are other children in the neighborhood.
- Will a parent be staying home with the baby? For how long? Some birth mothers feel that if you are going to place the child in a day care center, she might as well raise the child herself and make the same arrangements. No matter how untraditional her life may be, chances are she wants a

traditional home for the baby. A birth mother wants to know that the mother (or father) is going to be home to care for the child for as long as possible. If you know that staying home full-time is not possible, you may want to share your intention to have the child cared for at your home by a motherly figure or a relative of yours. Never lie about your plans. If you are unsure, tell her that you plan to stay home as long as possible. If you tell the birth mother that you plan to stay home full-time to care for the baby when you really plan to go back to work, you will probably feel guilty once you return to work. Going back to work and leaving a baby in someone else's care can be difficult enough. Do not add extra guilt to the situation.

Remember, if you choose not to meet face to face, you will want to keep in contact by telephone or letters. This happens often. Some birth mothers avoid emotional involvement by making all arrangements through a third party—the person who told you about each other or an attorney. You will simply want to do your best to stay aware of how she is feeling about her adoption arrangements and whether she is getting the care and counseling she needs.

TALKING TO BIRTH MOTHERS

When talking to a birth mother, take cues from her about her conversational comfort level. If she is a soft-spoken Midwesterner, do not overpower her with your Northeastern accent. If she is animated and lively, then you will want to be positive as well.

It is appropriate to ask questions and make statements like these:

- What plans do you have for your future?
- Why do you want to place the baby for adoption?
- Have you discussed your plans with anyone else? What do they think?
- Why do you think adoption plans are best?
- Is there anyone in your family who would not want you to place the baby for adoption?
- Is there anyone in your family who has said that they would take care of your baby for you?
- I understand that placing a baby for adoption is a difficult decision; if you need counseling, we will be glad to assist you financially.
- I believe that you want what's best for the baby. As a couple, we want what's best for the baby, too.

- It must be difficult not to have your parents support your decision (if this is the case). Is there anyone else who supports you? (If not, then offer to provide her counseling from a professional, if she so desires.)
- We will be praying for you as you go through this difficult time in your life.
- From what I understand, placing a baby for adoption can be painful and fulfilling at the same time. I know of a group of other women who are facing the same issue. I can give you the phone number of this support group.

Such statements acknowledge that the adoption decision is difficult, while offering her constructive means for making and accepting that decision. Again be sure not to ask question after question; it is not as important to have every question answered as it is to "connect" with her, to have her like you.

SUPPORTING A BIRTH MOTHER EMOTIONALLY

You may well become part of the birth mother's support system, and you do want to be a considerate, thoughtful friend. As with any relationship, however, there are appropriate limits. You may not mind becoming "counselors" for the birth mother—many couples do; but you will not want to provide a twenty-four-hour-a-day counseling service. That can drain you and make you feel negative toward the birth mother. If you begin to dread the ringing telephone for fear that you will have to listen to a birth mother's problems for another two hours, you will need to set limits. Similarly, if you are uncomfortable about the discussions you are having, perhaps you can offer to pay for counseling for the birth mother.

Let her know that you will do what you can to make each part of the adoption process as easy as possible. If you can, help her set up her doctor and counseling appointments. If she needs transportation, make arrangements for this as well. Let her know that you understand her need to get on with her life while demonstrating that you are willing to maintain a certain level of openness within the relationship.

SUPPORTING A BIRTH MOTHER FINANCIALLY

Expenses that an adoptive parent legally can pay for vary according to state law; so you may be limited by more than your own finances. Even if there were no such limits, however, you would not want to be taken advantage of by an insincere woman who has no plans to place a baby for adoption or one who believes that doing so entitles her to a nine-month luxury vacation.

Living Expenses

Paying for a birth mother's living expenses is a very delicate balancing act. Some couples resent paying anything, making the adoption process difficult. Some attorneys offer birth mothers excessive living expenses, making it difficult for couples who cannot afford to pay, for example, $1,000 a month in living expenses for seven months.

Some birth mothers ask, while others expect, to be assisted with rent, phone, utilities, food, gas, car repairs, and so on. All such financial assistance should be handled through your attorney or agency. Your attorney should give the final approval, with funds coming through his trust account. In most states, a judge must approve these expenses, usually at the time of the adoption hearing. You do not want your adoption questioned because living expenses were excessive or inappropriate. Having your lawyer handle the finances also keeps you from having to say no to a birth mother when expenses cannot be paid. Instruct your attorney to contact you before sending out monies that were not prearranged. One attorney sent a birth mother in California $1,500 to have her car fixed without first asking the couple whether it was all right.

Medical Expenses

It is appropriate to support a birth mother by allowing her to see a private physician (if she has no health insurance or does not qualify for Medicaid) or by purchasing vitamins and healthy foods. It shows you care about her and the baby.

Counseling

Paying for counseling also shows that you care about her emotional needs. Sometimes a birth mother has more difficulty after she places the baby than before. Many adoptive parents pay for her counseling fees during this time.

Legally, most expenses can be paid only up to six weeks after birth. Yet counseling may be required for an extended period of time. If your birth mother needs counseling, try to see whether you can get special court approval through your attorney to pay for counseling beyond six weeks if necessary.

Lost Wages

In some states, birth mothers are permitted to be reimbursed for lost wages resulting from pregnancy and postnatal recuperation. This can be very expensive and is sometimes used as a "legal" way to "pay" a birth mother for placing her child with you. If a birth mother earns, for example, $300 a week and is out of work for six weeks before birth, some attorneys will tell her that she can be given $1,800 at birth and another $1,800 after if she is out of work for another six weeks—possibly even on top of whatever she receives in living expenses.

This is an area where paying lost wages can look like baby buying. If you are giving a birth mother this kind of assistance, be sure she is not also receiving disability or paid sick leave.

RELATING TO MORE THAN ONE BIRTH MOTHER

What do you do when you receive calls from more than one birth mother? If you have advertised diligently, especially in the newspapers, you can have more than one birth mother who is interested in placing a baby for adoption. This offers you more options but also means you must make some difficult choices. It is not unethical to be making arrangements with more than one birth mother for a very short time period without disclosing that to both birth mothers; you have the right to change your mind, just as she does. However, it is unfair to string someone along for more than a couple of months. Here are some scenarios that could arise, and some suggestions for handling them:

A birth mother calls you on Tuesday, and another calls you on Wednesday. One has a delivery date in two weeks; the other is due in six months. If both women seem sincere, agree to meet both of them. If both agree to place a baby with you after meeting with you, your choices are as follows:

a. Decide which birth mother you would rather deal with based on her background and interests.

b. Select between the birth mothers based on the earlier delivery date. All other things being equal, if one birth mother's due date is in two weeks and the other's is six months away, it is best to make adoption arrangements with the former while maintaining communication with the latter. If the first birth mother changes her mind, you can then make arrangements with the birth mother whose delivery date is in six months.

c. Agree to make arrangements with both women, and if neither changes her mind, be ready to have two babies—five to six months apart. Good luck!

Two birth mothers call, and each one has a delivery date about five to seven months away. You meet each birth mother and agree that you like both equally.

a. Continue arrangements for a few weeks with each woman until you sense which one you would prefer and which seems most sure of her decision.

b. Make arrangements with both birth mothers, and if both place the babies, be prepared to have two babies a few weeks apart!

Here are some general guidelines for relating to more than one birth mother at a time. Note: Should you become pregnant while pursuing adoption, you may want to use similar strategies, given the uncertain outcome of your pregnancy.

1. While you are still choosing between two birth mothers, never let one know about the other.
2. If you cannot bear to call a birth mother to tell her that you did not choose her, have your attorney do so for you.
3. Have a network of other prospective adoptive parents so that you can give their names to a birth mother if you are not going to commit to her. Alternatively, if your attorney is permitted to act as an intermediary, he can provide another couple.

Chapter Eight

Birth Fathers and Their Rights

To deal with contested adoptions by birth fathers, some states have established putative father registries. A putative father registry allows the biological father (the "presumed" or "reputed" father) to record his interest in the child. The state is then required to notify the birth father of any legal proceedings that relate to the well-being of his child. About thirty-two states have laws related to putative father registries. (See Appendix A to learn if your state or the state from which you may adopt has a registry.)

Here is an instructive story from our own experience of working with adoptions.

The moment Mary and John had long awaited finally arrived when they took home their beautiful baby girl. They had not expected problems since both of the sixteen-year-old birth parents supported the adoption. In fact, both the birth mother, Sally, and her ex-boyfriend, Tom, had responded well to counseling. Then Tom unexpectedly threw a wrench into the works. He decided that the only way to win Sally back as his girlfriend was to insist upon having the baby back. Surprisingly, Tom's mother supported his wish, even agreeing to help raise the baby.

Tom hired a high-profile attorney he had seen on television who argued that the "natural" parents are always best for the baby. Sally knew that Tom's family had many problems and that this was not the ideal household for the baby. Her only choice was to raise the child herself. Naturally, it was not her first choice. Sally had hoped to go to college. Nor were her parents able to help. Her mother worked full-time, and her father was partially disabled.

Ray and I will never forget having to pick up the one-week-old infant from John and Mary's home and take her back to Sally. Of course, Ray could have taken the case to court. But with no guarantee of winning their case, the adoptive parents would have risked losing the baby after she had been in their home for nine months or more, an even worse scenario.

Two weeks later, Sally, the baby, and her family moved to a new city 800 miles away from Tom. Tom received visitation rights that he has yet to exercise. The baby is with the birth mother, and her life goals have been severely limited. If Tom's goal was to punish Sally, he succeeded.

LAWS AND PRECEDENTS

These events took place in New Jersey, where Tom has the same right to change his mind about an adoption as Sally does, provided he has a means of caring for the baby. Birth mothers in New Jersey do not have the right to say they want their child to be placed for adoption instead of being raised by a birth father, even a birth father who has not been supportive of her during the pregnancy.

The story illustrates the impact of various state laws on adoption outcomes. Had Sally agreed to take part in an identified adoption, working with an adoption agency, she and Tom would have been asked to sign a termination of rights seventy-two hours after the baby's birth. If Tom had refused, the baby would never have gone to Mary and John's home, saving them untold heartache.

If Mary and John had lived in South Carolina, the birth parents' rights could have been terminated immediately after birth in either an agency or private adoption. Across the border in North Carolina, on the other hand, where parental rights are terminated seven days from birth whether the adoption is agency or private, getting an agency involved would not have changed the circumstances. There is no national policy on adoption. Every state has its own laws, and invariably there are unintended consequences.

One area in which state adoption statutes have been affected across the board, however, is that of birth fathers' rights. Until 1972, "unwed" or "putative" fathers had relatively few rights. States did not include an unwed father in the definition of "parent," meaning that his consent was not needed for adoption placements.

These laws cut both ways. An out-of-wedlock child could not demand support or inheritance from his birth father; the birth father had no legal status to influence the child's upbringing. Not only was the birth father's consent not needed in many states, but he was also often not even entitled to notice of any adoption hearings or proceedings. Unless he took the extraordinary step of asserting his paternity, an adoptive couple had no need to worry about the birth father. An adoption was routinely initiated and finalized without any regard to him.

Since 1971, however, the Supreme Court has rendered several decisions that provided, under certain circumstances, the same rights to a birth father as are given to a birth mother. All state adoption statutes must provide these rights as long as the birth father meets certain conditions or takes certain steps to establish his paternity. Usually this means taking one or more of the following actions:

1. Establishing paternity by obtaining a court order.
2. In states with a putative father registry, submitting his name to the registry.
3. Having his name placed on the child's birth certificate or similar document.
4. Maintaining a relationship or attempting to maintain a relationship with the

child being adopted—including providing financial and emotional support. New Jersey law, for example, emphasizes maintaining an emotional relationship with the child. Many state laws stipulate that this relationship must be maintained during the six months (or some part thereof) following birth.

5. Supporting the birth mother during her pregnancy, making reasonable payment of medical expenses, appearing at the hospital at the birth, and assisting with postpartum expenses.

Which of these steps are regarded as indispensable varies from state to state, but in most, if the birth father puts his name on a putative father registry or on the birth certificate without attempting to "act like a father," it will probably not be enough to prevent an adoption, and in fact, some states with birth father registries mandate not only his registering, but that he also do those things which characterize the duties and responsibilities of fatherhood.

While the birth father registry is a viable idea in theory, it is not a cure-all in practice. A court will look at whether he has done any of the following: if he lived with the child and birth mother after birth or with the birth mother before birth for a certain period of time; opened a bank account or put money aside for the baby; established a nursery; provided the birth mother diapers, food, furniture, and money to buy necessary items; and whether he has visited or shown a desire to visit with the baby or child.

Similarly, if he tries to establish paternity just prior to or just after the adoption finalization, his rights are limited unless he can show that his inability to assert his parental rights was the result of circumstances beyond his control, such as the birth mother hiding from him and preventing him from seeing the baby or offering support. A birth father who "sits" on his rights as time goes by and fails to show paternal interest weakens his position to contest the adoption. How long must he sit on his rights in order for a court to declare that he has abandoned them depends on the state—thirty days in some to six months in other states.

In 1979, the U.S. Supreme Court stated that an unwed father who has "manifested a significant paternal interest in the child" must be allowed the right to veto his child's adoption. What constitutes "significant paternal interest," of course, is left to the interpretation of the states. Let's consider a 1983 case involving a New York birth father. In *Lehr v. Robertson*, a putative father attempted, after the fact, to contest the final adoption of his daughter by the birth mother's husband. The birth mother consented to the adoption. The case went all the way to the U.S. Supreme Court, which stated that an unwed father who had failed to establish and maintain "any significant custodial, personal, or financial relationship" with his daughter was not entitled to notice of the adoption proceedings.

The birth father had lived with the birth mother before the child's birth and had visited the hospital several times after birth. However, he provided no financial support, nor did he offer to marry the birth mother. Of equal importance, he did not take the steps required under New York law to establish his paternity, which included putting his name on the birth certificate or mailing in a postcard to New York's putative father registry.

Noting further that the birth father did not live with the birth mother and child after birth, the court declared that "the mere existence of a biological link does not merit" constitutional protection when the birth father in essence "sat on his rights." This decision incorporates the principles of all recent U.S. Supreme Court decisions pertaining to the putative father's rights to contest an adoption.

As Justice Stevens noted in the *Lehr* decision, "The rights of the parents are a counterpart of the responsibilities they have assumed." These principles have been incorporated into the laws of every state. In any adoption situation, the adoptive couple and attorney must determine what role the birth father desires to play, if any, and to what extent he will be involved.

A strategy to deal with his involvement should be developed at an early stage to avoid any "surprises" at the time the baby is discharged from the hospital. If the birth mother's honesty can be relied on, then the adoptive couple and attorney must decide when to confront him about the adoption plan. If he has moved on to another relationship and neither he nor his mother have shown any interest in the unborn child by way of support or general contact and comments, then it may be wiser to contact him after birth and placement; this tactic presents the adoption as a "done deal," thus making sure that he does not feel he has new found leverage—not to parent his child (his actions show otherwise) but to either get back at the birth mother or to get her back to resume the prior relationship!

Many birth mothers, of course, do not want the birth father to be involved, particularly if they have parted ways, as it appears to be in the majority of adoption plans. However, if the birth father lived with the birth mother for several months before or after birth, supported her and the child, or has shown some level of interest in being a father, then the tactic of confrontation must be employed as soon as possible. Once a birth mother learns that under these facts the birth father has equal rights and could cause the adoptive couple problems, she will usually agree to provide the necessary contact information and agree he should be confronted as to his interest in the child.

She, a family member, or the adoptive couple's attorney can then approach him, perhaps for the first time, about the adoption plan. Is he really interested in being a father to this child or was he just "saving face" in front of family and friends by providing support or voicing a desire to parent the unborn baby? Once he learns of an adoption plan, he may be relieved, or he may express renewed determination to be a father. In either way, everyone knows prior to birth. The adoptive couple can move on, and the birth mother can adjust her expectations as to her future.

The couple's attorney must be aware of the state statute and case law dealing with the birth father's rights. If the birth father has not assisted with pregnancy-related expenses and has not taken other steps prior to and after birth, then the attorney can consider simply serving the birth father with either notice of the adoption or with the adoption petition or complaint. These legal papers name him as the birth father, tell him the child has been placed for adoption, and inform him that his rights will be terminated.

Very few states today allow a *Lehr* birth father not to receive some type of notice of the adoption proceedings in court. Most state adoption statutes have taken the guesswork out as to whether a birth father has forfeited his right to even be notified under *Lehr*. Most of the recent U.S. Supreme Court decisions have required in general that if a birth father's rights are to be terminated that he must receive notice of the adoption proceedings. This notice is provided by way of the actual adoption petition or complaint or by way of a separate legal document. The notice must provide in clear language that unless the birth father communicates his opposition to the court, his rights will be forfeited forever. It must state how much time he has to act and how he can communicate his opposition, which is usually by writing the court or adoptive couple's attorney or both.

The time period in which to respond is usually ten to forty-five days, depending on the state. If he is opposed to the adoption, he must usually communicate this in writing to the court or appear at the adoption hearing. Appearing at the hearing, however, would probably be too late under most state adoption laws. If he does write the court or engage an attorney who files a formal objection, the adoption is classified as a contested adoption. Most states will appoint an attorney for an indigent birth father or for one who is incarcerated.

WORST-CASE SCENARIOS

Most adoptions go through smoothly. Sometimes, however, questions about the identity or whereabouts of the birth father can lead to serious complications. One—fortunately rare—illustration has to do with the naming of the birth father. A birth mother can name any man as the birth father. As long as he signs the consent or surrender and the true genetic father is not in the picture, there is no problem as to the adoption proceeding.

But if she or the real birth father changes her or his mind, the birth mother who has given an irrevocable surrender (or whose rights have been terminated in court) can ask the "real" birth father to come forward and ask for the child back. In other words, a dishonest birth mother can ask her cousin or some friend to say he is the birth father, use his name on the birth certificate, and ask him to give consent or sign surrender documents. Then if she changes her mind, all she has to do is ask the true birth father to identify himself and say that the birth mother miscalculated her menstrual cycles and that he would like the child back.

The birth parents' surrenders mean nothing if the genetic father is not the person giving the surrender. This situation does not often come up, but it highlights the need to focus on a birth mother's honesty and perhaps the advantages of the adoptive couple developing a rapport with the birth mother. The majority of birth mothers are honest and want a loving home for their child; they feel more comfortable and accepting of an adoption plan when they are comfortable with and approve of the adoptive couple. This emotional connection with the couple means that a birth mother will usually not risk the placement by playing games about the birth father's identity.

Another scenario that can create problems is when there is an unnamed "out of the picture" birth father. This is usually a man who had sexual relations with the birth mother but has had no more contact with her and did not know she was pregnant. If, fourteen months after conception, he suddenly finds out the child was placed for adoption, he may decide that he wants to raise the child himself.

This came up in New York in the case of *Robert O. v. Russell K.* The birth father had learned two years after placement that the birth mother, with whom he had sexual relations, had become pregnant, delivered the baby, and placed the child with an adoptive couple. He took the matter to court, stating that had he known she was pregnant, he would have wanted to parent the child. The court ruled that a birth father's "opportunity to manifest his willingness" to parent a child after his birth must be of short duration because of a societal need for adoptions to be finalized promptly and efficiently.

It further declared that "promptness is measured in terms of the baby's life, not by the onset of the father's awareness" that a child was born to a woman with whom he had sexual relations. In *Robert O.,* the court stated the birth father was too late; he had an obligation to confirm whether the birth mother became pregnant after the relationship and take the appropriate steps to pay pregnancy-related expenses, register with the birth father registry, pay postpartum expenses, and maintain contact with the child. Since he did not, it was in the best interests of the child to remain with the adoptive couple.

In sharp contrast is a 1990 North Carolina case, *Adoption of Clark*, in which the birth father was in a Marine boot camp in another state and did not know of his child's birth and placement. The agency, which knew his identity but not his whereabouts, did not attempt to locate him and notify him of the proposed placement. The court recognized that the birth mother had withheld information from the adoption agency as to the birth father's whereabouts, but ruled that the agency had failed to exercise "due diligence" in seeking out the birth father and notifying him of the adoption proceedings. In other words, the agency hadn't tried hard enough. The horror of this case, as pointed out by one of the justices who disagreed with the decision, is that the litigation had lasted six years, during which time the child lived with his adoptive parents.

The ruling did not consider whether it would be in the child's best interest to remain with the only parents he had ever known. North Carolina is not the only state that fails to consider the child's best interest if the birth father's rights have not been properly terminated under state law, even when it can be shown that a child has bonded with a couple and will suffer psychological and emotional harm by being taken from his home. It seems to defy logic when a child who is flourishing with an adoptive couple for several years is turned over to a birth father she hardly knows, if at all.

The California courts have articulated a standard that a birth father's parental rights cannot be terminated if he is exercising due diligence in pursuing custody of his child, unless it can be shown that he is an unfit parent. In one case, the California Supreme Court stated that it would not presume "either as a policy or factual matter, that adoption is necessarily in a child's best interest," going on to say that a child's best interest is not automatically enhanced because a birth mother places him with an adoptive couple instead of the birth father *(Kelsey S., 1992).*

Having made this judgment, however, the court then went on to say that all factors must be considered in deciding whether a birth father is fit, including a father's actions prior to and after birth. At the time he knows or should have known about the birth, he must present himself as one who can and will assume full custody. If there is any hesitation or lack of ability to parent, this will be held against him. Practically speaking, this covers most cases.

Nevertheless, it is clear that the birth father's rights cannot be ignored and that his status must be resolved as expeditiously as possible. Although his rights are as viable as the birth mother's, they weaken with time if he does not assert them or act upon them either during the pregnancy or after the birth of his child. As the Arizona Supreme Court stated, "an unwed father's parental rights do not attain fundamental constitutional status unless he takes significant steps to create a parental relationship. . . . for, in the child's eyes, a valiant but failed attempt to create a relationship means little" *(Appeal in Pima County Juvenile Severance Action, 1994).*

Chapter Nine

Openness in Adoption

Openness in adoption means communication between you and the birth parents, primarily after the placement of your child in your home and after finalization of the adoption. This can range from sending your attorney pictures and progress notes about the baby for him to forward to the birth mother to having the birth mother visit you and the baby at your home and perhaps even celebrate holidays with you. Openness can consist of contact for a very short period of time—six months—to contact for a period of several years.

In most adoptions openness is minimal, but attitudes are changing. More adoptive couples are becoming comfortable about sharing the details of their child's life with the birth mother. There are, it is true, situations in which openness would not be appropriate, some of which are discussed in Chapter 15: Special Needs Adoption. For many children who are adopted internationally, there is little, if any, possibility of maintaining an open relationship with the birth parents. But in most other cases, open adoption is coming to be seen as a healthy alternative to the anonymity and secrecy of the past.

IS OPEN ADOPTION FOR YOU?

Couples involved in an open adoption will want to attend workshops and read books to learn as much as possible. Although it is important to agree on a plan for openness before the adoption takes place, adoptive parents must be willing to allow the openness to be an evolutionary process and not a specific set of terms. In most cases, the adoptive couple and the birth parents get together more when the children are young; the need for openness usually dissipates over time. You may want to ask yourself how you would feel if the birth mother visited the child the first year and then did not visit after that. To turn the question around, how would you feel if the birth mother wanted to visit more often than originally planned? Would you feel a sense of entitlement to your child? Would you worry that the birth mother might interfere too much?

OPEN ADOPTION: ADVANTAGES

Open adoptions are a relatively new phenomenon, and we lack long-term models for them. Advocates point out that the secrecy associated with closed adoptions has been detrimental to all involved—concluding that if closed adoptions are bad, open adoptions must be good. However, there is more anecdotal information than hard evidence to back this up. Indeed, there is no question that open adoption can sometimes be difficult. The fact that a birth mother chooses you does not guarantee that you and she will have a wonderful, communicative relationship, even if you all initially agree on the level of openness you want.

This is why it is best to allow the relationship to evolve gradually. For example, you may initially agree that you will talk on the phone and send letters and photographs. If you and she find that the relationship is very comfortable, you may want to meet without the baby. From that meeting, you may decide that she can come to your home to meet the baby.

Open adoption offers psychological advantages for everyone concerned: birth parents, adoptive parents, and child. To the birth mother, for instance, it offers the opportunity:

- To resolve many of her feelings as she grieves placing her child for adoption
- To have peace of mind
- To see firsthand the kind of family the child lives in
- To know the status of the baby's health
- To minimize her fears and insecurities
- To be part of the adoption process
- To have an honest and realistic picture of the child, not an idyllic fantasy

It allows the adoptive parents:

- To see the birth parents' traits firsthand, including physical appearance, intellectual abilities, personality, and skills
- To assess the birth parents accurately instead of fantasizing about them
- To have fewer fears and insecurities about the birth mother
- To answer the child's questions about why the birth mother placed the child for adoption and about the birth mother's love for her child

Finally, it allows the adoptee:

- To understand her biological roots
- Not to feel that her life is filled with "secrets"

- To know the circumstances surrounding her placement. This allows her to move beyond the sense of rejection that can occur in a closed adoption.
- To grieve the loss of biological parents. Unlike adoptive parents, who choose to adopt, the child does not choose to have no biological link with her family. It just happens.
- To have a more realistic picture of the birth parents instead of fantasizing about an ideal parent
- To know that she was born and did not just arrive on planet Earth. This may seem simplistic, but it is very important for a child to know that she was born as well as adopted.
- To have a family medical history. As the birth parents' families age, their medical histories can give the adoptee a better picture of her genetic history. The child's birth parents and grandparents will probably be healthy at the time of the child's birth because they are young. But they may later develop genetically linked health problems. This knowledge could help save an adoptee's life later.

OPEN ADOPTION: DISADVANTAGES

Given the emotional factors associated with adoption, it is not surprising to learn that there may be stress in some open adoption relationships. Expectations, for example, can sometimes evolve to an uncomfortable point. You and the birth parents may both agree to one set of expectations at the baby's birth, only to find the birth parents pushing for more openness than you want at a later time. Especially if the birth mother is a teenager, she may have unrealistic expectations about her role in your family, expecting in some way to become a part of your family—to be "adopted" herself. These expectations may be more apparent in girls who have families with profound problems and who view the adoptive couple as the perfect family.

Another problem associated with open adoption is that the birth mother may not properly grieve for the loss because she does not fully experience the adoption as a loss.

Of course, there is always the possibility that the birth mother will not want an open relationship; many do not. If so, you cannot coerce her into one. A birth mother does have the right to place a child for adoption, grieve the loss, and move on with her life. In fact, in a survey of fifty-nine biological mothers (aged sixteen to forty-five years) who placed a child for adoption through an agency, it was found that those who chose an open adoption felt more social isolation and despair and expressed more dependency than those who opted for a confidential adoption. Although it could be that these particular women simply had more difficulties, it could also be that open adoption prevented them from "moving on" in their lives.

Finally there's no denying that some birth mothers are more mature than others. Although we have enjoyed working with nearly all of our birth mothers, not all have been stable people. Having said that, not one who knew the address and phone number has ever yet shown up at the adoptive parents' home. One birth mother, who does have a mental illness, did call the adoptive parents once and harass them, but after that incident, all other limited communication between them was cordial.

In other words, even when there was a history of mental illness or instability, no birth mother has ever caused problems in any of the adoptive couples' lives. Even so, just knowing that a birth mother's mood can swing can cause some people so much consternation that they find themselves living in a state of "what if."

One thing to consider about open adoptions: In most states, a signed agreement between you and the birth parents to maintain an open adoption is not legally binding. Where states have addressed the issue of open adoption rights, only one-third have held that open adoption agreements are valid and that they do not go against public policy as long as the openness is in the child's best interest. The cases in which openness was allowed came as a result of a lawsuit in which birth parents wanted to challenge the adoption. In these cases, visitations were allowed in exchange for dropping the lawsuit.

HOW OPEN IS OPEN?

When you first make contact with a birth mother, all you will know about each other is your first names. As you become more comfortable with each other, you and she may want to share last names, too. Then, if you decide to correspond directly with each other, you will exchange addresses and perhaps telephone numbers. (Note: In a few states, you are legally required to reveal your last names and addresses to the birth parents, in which case anonymity is no longer an issue.)

If you are not comfortable sharing such information or if the birth mother is from another state, you may arrange for all contact to be handled through your agency or attorney's office. Your attorney may include this service as part of the adoption arrangement, or he may charge extra each time his staff handles correspondence and telephone calls. The fee for such services should be reasonable.

Remember, no matter how careful you and the birth parents are about retaining your anonymity, it is all too easy for a professional to slip and reveal your last names. If your attorney's staff is accustomed to addressing you as Mr. and Mrs. Sanders, for example, they will have to change gears to refer to you as Chuck and Doris when speaking to the birth mother. Forgetting to conceal last names on documents is another common slip. Mistakes do get made. We've often known the judge who presides over the court hearing to reveal the last names of the birth parents.

STAYING IN TOUCH

There are various ways to maintain openness in an adoption arrangement. Here are some of the most common.

Correspondence

Many couples exchange letters and photographs with birth mothers. Most birth mothers want to maintain some level of correspondence, at least for the child's first year of life. Letters telling of the baby's progress are usually sent at Christmas and the baby's birthday. You may want to send a note once a month along with a picture, especially during the baby's first year.

Sending Pictures

Nearly all birth mothers want pictures and letters sent to them. Even those who did not make an adoption decision but had the child removed from them want to know that the child is all right, and pictures are the most obvious way—short of seeing the child in person—of knowing that she is alive and well. Videotapes are very easy to produce, and a growing number of adoptive parents and birth parents exchange them.

The birth mother may likewise send you pictures of herself, her family, and the birth father. These can be important keepsakes for your child.

Telephone Calls

Calling the birth mother or having her call you will probably occur more spontaneously than an arrangement to send letters and pictures, but adoptive parents could agree to call the birth mother once a month or so to let her know how they and the baby are doing. The birth mother could also have permission to call the adoptive parents for information about the baby. If this is too personal, she could call your attorney's office for information about the baby; then the attorney's office personnel could call you and get a verbal progress report to pass along.

Sometimes a birth mother just does not want to communicate with the adoptive parents. Perhaps she is living with a boyfriend or husband, someone she does not want to know about her past. In such cases, it is sometimes a relative of the birth mother who stays in touch.

E-mailing Each Other

E-mailing is probably the easiest and least intrusive way to communicate with a birth family. You can easily share information in a quick, spontaneous way. Pictures can also be sent just as readily.

Even if you would be uncomfortable maintaining contact via a direct exchange of letters to each other's homes, e-mail allows a personal touch while maintaining anonymity without having to rely on your agency or attorney to forward letters and pictures to the birth family.

Exchanging Gifts

A birth mother or her family may want to give the baby a special gift, perhaps one with sentimental value. This can be a special keepsake to share with your child to let her know that the birth mother cared very much about her.

After the adoption is finalized, you are permitted to send the birth mother a gift. (It may be illegal to do so before then in your state.) You may want to give her a token to remember you by.

Exchanging Other Mementos

Some birth mothers may request other sentimental tokens from you. Our younger daughter's birth mother asked that we send her a lock of hair when she got her first haircut. Other personal tokens can be the child's artwork or one of the child's favorite dolls or rattles after she has outgrown it. Some people like to send a special book, a Bible, or jewelry.

Sample Letters

Following are samples of the kinds of letters that you or your child's sibling may want to send to the birth mother. Always respond to a letter sent to you from the birth mother.

LETTER FOR THE BIRTH MOTHER
WHEN SHE RELINQUISHES THE CHILD TO YOU

Dear Cindy,

Thank you so much for all that you have done for us. Your love and commitment to David's well-being are magnificent, and the joy that he will add to our lives is immeasurable.

We loved David before we even met him, and we look forward to caring for him and sharing our lives with him. He will truly be a special person, not just for the love that we will provide him, but also for the love that you have expressed in making plans for his life.

Christopher is already so excited about the campsites and ball games that he wants to take David to. I have to remind him that it will be a few years before David will be playing ball and camping.

Cindy, Christopher, and I wish you well in your education. You have been so diligent in all that you have done. I trust that you will find just the right job when you graduate from school next year.

You will certainly always be a part of our lives and in our prayers. We truly love you for all that you have done. Do keep in touch. As we have promised, I will send you lots of pictures of David each month. (I can hardly wait to start photographing our beautiful baby.)

Do take care, Cindy, and I will write to you next month.

All our love,
Sharon, Christopher, and David

LETTER TO A BIRTH MOTHER WHEN THE CHILD IS SIX MONTHS OLD

Dear Jenny,

I can hardly believe that James is six months old. He is now starting to creep and to make the funniest sounds. He is very alert and loves to watch his older sister play. James especially loves music. When Jodi's singing her favorite nursery rhymes, he nearly hums along with her while his body rocks back and forth. Sometimes I play some lively classical music, and again, his body sways to the music. Everyone says James is very good-natured.

Enclosed are pictures from Thanksgiving. We had a wonderful day at my parents' home in the country. All thirteen of James's cousins were there. My favorite picture is Tom holding James next to the turkey. The turkey and James weighed about the same—20 pounds.

We and all the relatives will be back at my parents' house again for Christmas. As soon as we get pictures of James's first Christmas, I will send them to you.

Jenny, I trust you are doing well. I was very pleased to hear about your new adventures. Please continue to keep us updated about your activities and plans.

Thank you so much for the letter and pictures you sent James. We will keep them in a very special place for him. Someday James will know how blessed he is that you loved him enough to make adoption plans for his life.

John and I trust that you will have a warm and special Christmas. We understand that this time of year may be difficult for you. You have made a very difficult but loving decision, and I hope you are especially comforted knowing that James is loved immensely by us and his relatives.

We'll look forward to hearing from you.

Love,
Sandy and John

LETTER FROM THE CHILD'S SIBLING TO THE BIRTH MOTHER

Dear Stephanie's birth mother,

Thank you for giving us a baby sister. She is so cute. We love her, and we love you. Mommy and Daddy said you are a really nice person. We will take good care of her.

Love,
Jason and Brian

SEARCHING FOR BIRTH FAMILIES

Although open adoption has received much attention over the last ten years, the reality is that most adoptions have not been open. Even in cases where letters and pictures are initially exchanged between the birth parents and adoptive family, as the years pass, the contact may diminish or end. Even so, adoptions that have been somewhat open provide at least some identifying information exchanged between birth and adoptive families. As a result, there will be a future generation of adoptees who will be able to find and meet their birth parents if they so choose.

Currently, however, nearly all adult adoptees and those now reaching adulthood were never given detailed information about their birth parents. Sometimes the agency or attorney did not obtain the information. Many times adoptive parents, for whatever reason, did not share what information they had with their children. At other times, adoptive parents did not share birth family information with the adoptee because they considered it superfluous, but this information could be essential to finding a birth parent. In fact, most adult adoptees feel that their parents withheld information surrounding their adoption from them.

Although parents and relatives should be the first place that adoptees go to get information, adoptees often say that if their parents ever knew they were searching for their birth parents that it would "kill" them. The tone that was set in the home may let the adoptee know whether searching for information about their birth history is or is not "open for discussion."

First, a word about terms often used in searching for a birth family—*reunion* and *triangle*. When, for example, a birth daughter and birth mother find each other, this is sometimes called a reunion. Yet others find this term to be inappropriate because a reunion is usually a celebration when family gets together because they share a heritage. Those who search are not necessarily looking to reunite with their birth families; they may just want to have some questions answered or find out some information. They may seek and find the birth relatives, but these encounters may be not positive and could hardly be called reunions. Therefore, the term meeting rather than the word reunion is used when two birth relatives meet. If they continue to see each other, then they have an ongoing relationship.

Another misnomer is the term *triangle*—meaning adoptive parents, adoptee, and birth family; the word *triad* is more appropriate to describe the three parties involved in the adoption.

So Why All of the Interest in Searching?

As one adult adoptee said, "I never thought it was possible until I had seen a television program where a birth mother and daughter met each other." In this day of sensational talk shows, the meeting of birth parents and children is probably not very titillating, but just a few years ago, it was news! Now there are search support groups all over the country, and laws have been passed to help those in the adoption triad find each other. The Internet has also made the logistics of such a search more affordable and likely.

How Many People Search?

The numbers vary greatly, but one Web site, the Adoptee Search Center Registry, which has been in existence since 1996, currently has more than 27,000 people registered who are looking for birth relatives and grows at a rate of 1,000–1,500 persons per month. According to Merry Block Jones, who wrote *Birth Mothers: Women Who Have Relinquished Babies for Adoption Tell Their Stories*, when she interviewed birth parents, she found that nearly all of them continue to wonder how the child they relinquished for adoption is doing. These feelings surface especially when the child reaches the age that he or she would be starting school, graduating, getting married, or having children.

Who Searches?

Anecdotal evidence suggests that mostly female adoptees and birth mothers are searching. It is understandable that more birth mothers than birth fathers would be searching—after all, the woman is the person who gave birth, and the birth father may not even know that he has a biological child. Why more women adoptees search is not so well understood. People who search are from all age ranges, but as may be expected, many are in their early twenties. If adoptees are under eighteen years old when they search, they usually have the support of their adoptive parents

Why Do People Search?

The most prevalent reason given is to obtain medical histories; this is reasonable as most of us know our genetic and medical background. However, for adoptees who were placed as infants, there may be a limited medical background because their biological grandparents may only have been in their early forties, and certain diseases may not have manifested themselves. Also, the birth mothers and their siblings were probably healthy at the time the adoptees were placed for adoption. However, as the birth parents' parents age and the birth parents and their siblings go on to have children, it is very likely that someone is going to have a medical condition that has a genetic component. Even as open adoptions become more prevalent, most adoptees will not have updated, ongoing medical information. Obtaining a medical history is not just about what is happening now. It's about going to a health professional and the adoptee always having to say, "I don't know my family history. I'm adopted." Health information can also provide insight as to what may happen in the future and may mean taking measures to prevent a disease. If this were not so important, then why do medical forms ask about family history?

Although adoptees often identify wanting their medical family history as the primary reason to search—perhaps because it sounds acceptable and is the most tangible reason that can be expressed—the real reason may be curiosity. Although "curiosity" does not sound very meaningful, it is reason enough. Yet others may not understand this concern.

Some people advise that if the adoptee has no compelling health problem and if the search is going to hurt the adoptive parents, then the adoptee shouldn't do it. But this advice can be missing the whole point. The person may really be saying, "I want to know why my hair is red and my eyes are blue." Also, when an adult adoptee considers having children, she may begin to grieve the fact that she does not know the genetic history she is passing on to her child. It's not just the medical background that she is passing on, but hair color, height, and even personality traits.

But beyond wanting to know their medical and genetic history, adoptees say that they want to know why their birth mother placed them for adoption. Likewise, birth mothers search for their birth children so that they can see that they are happy and to tell them why they were placed for adoption.

Because the outcome of the search is not always favorable, being emotionally prepared for who and what you will find is very important. One birth mother who belonged to a support group in which the group discussed all the possible outcomes was not prepared for the fact that her birth son had died a few years previously from a genetic disease that she did not even know she carried.

Two other birth mothers who searched for and found their birth children discovered that each child lived in a home where one parent was an alcoholic and that the adoptive parents had divorced. Even with this information, one birth mother said that adoption was the right choice, but she wished that she had more input into the selection of the family at the time. She even said, "I wish that I could have made them sign a paper that the couple would never divorce." The other birth mother has a warm ongoing relationship with her adult birth daughter. She also wishes that she had more control in the selection of a family at the time.

Of course, not all searches are so heart wrenching. Birth parents often find that the adoptive parents were good parents and that the birth children are doing fine.

HOW ARE SEARCHES CONDUCTED?

The first place to start is a support group. Beyond emotional support, other searchers can give advice as to how to search. Also, their successes probably will encourage you if you have snags in your search. Whether your support group is people that you talk to on the telephone or through e-mail or who you meet at a group meeting, be careful about the information you get and of others' reasons for searching. For example, someone you meet or e-mail may try to convince you that something is wrong with you if you have doubts about searching for your birth parent or child. Perhaps all you want is information and do not necessarily want to meet the other person. When some people join an organization, the "cause" becomes their focus in life, and they may try to convince you that this should be your whole focus as well. Others who are searching are very angry about being adopted and may project their anger onto you. A support group should provide common sense advice and let you know that your feelings are "normal." You do not need to have someone causing you angst about your past.

Next, you may want to contact the adoption agency or attorney who handled the adoption. Larger agencies may even have a registry and someone on staff who assists those who are searching. If they do not have a registry, they may at least give you nonidentifying information about your birth family. Also, ask them if you can sign "a waiver of confidentiality" statement giving your birth child or birth parent permission to contact you should he or she contact the agency.

There are now national and state registries. You can contact the National Adoption Information Clearinghouse to find out if your state or the state you were born in has a registry. Getting your name on a registry can be an active way to find a birth relative. On the other hand, a registry can be for those who are not actively searching but who are willing to be contacted by a birth relative.

The Internet is probably a great place to search if you are not able to contact an agency. The search is done using date of birth, social security number, addresses, and other types of information. At the Adoptee Search Center Web site, the staff and volunteers are also searchers. First priority is given to those who have a demanding medical need. This Web site and others have links for other mailing lists, other registries, prison sites, and telephone databases. If the person you are looking for is not listed, the site's resources may help you find that person.

If your search is getting nowhere, you may consider hiring a private investigator. The fees can be high; start your own search first and see where this leads. Keep good notes. Then if your search is not going anywhere, share what information you do have with the investigator. Be sure to use someone who is experienced and is familiar with looking for birth relatives.

POTENTIAL OUTCOMES OF SEARCHES

What can you expect to find when you do a search? If you were placed for adoption through the foster care system, you can probably expect your parents' lives to be still in turmoil. If you were abused or neglected and you find that one of your parents is working and leading a seemingly "normal" life, you may be angry that you were abused and now their lives are "fine."

Rachel, who is now a teenager, was adopted along with her two older brothers by her foster family when she was a baby. She recently began to search for her birth family. She already knew that her birth mother had used drugs and permitted men to sexually abuse her. However, she also knew that her birth mother was a nurse and could still be employed as one.

Her biological brother, who knew that she was going to search with the support of their adoptive parents, asked that she not share any information with him unless it was part of his medical history. Rachel discovered that the man whom she thought was her biological father was not, but rather the man who had sexually abused her and her brothers. Within a matter of days, Rachel went from searching for a birth mother to finding out that she was not her brother's full biological sibling but had a different biological father than he did. She also found out that she had five other birth siblings who were also placed for adoption with other families.

Because Rachel and her adoptive mother were permitted to read the file that social services maintained and because most of the social workers involved in the case when Rachel was placed for adoption were still working for social services, they were also able to get a full report of the abuse that occurred in her birth family. These reports confirmed what her older brother had said when he was a child. The adoptive mother said that she had always believed her oldest son's reports of what happened in his birth home; however, she felt that because he was only five or six years old when he shared this information that his story was clouded by a six-year-old child's perception and limited ability to relay the facts.

As a result of her search, Rachel did not just learn what her birth mother looked like and what she was doing now in her life. She also learned a lot about her past—all in a very short period of time. Of course, without the right support from her family and social workers, this information could have been overwhelming. With this support, she will continue her search, knowing that more questions will arise as more information is gathered.

Rachel knew that she was most likely never going to connect with her birth parents, and based on the circumstances of her adoption placement, this is understandable. Others who have searched, however, have said they have found "another" family. Not that a birth family is there to replace the adoptive family, but sometimes birth siblings find that they actually can enjoy each other's company and want to see each other a few times a year.

Like other adoption-related stories, the ones with more colorful details are the ones that get media attention and are more memorable. The story of a birth mother and daughter who find each other, visit each other a few times a year, and have a pleasant, cordial relationship is not exactly the plot for a movie. But in reality this is probably what is lived out.

SEARCHES AFTER INTERNATIONAL ADOPTION

When you read about the compelling need for some to find their birth parents or at least information about their backgrounds, you may wonder, "What about children who are adopted internationally? Will they be able to even consider searching?"

The fact is that when adoptions are conducted today, the birth mothers are usually known. In fact, a birth mother often signs a relinquishment. Most adoptive parents are given their child's original birth certificate, and much of the information on that can be used to find a birth mother.

Perhaps the greatest barriers to searching for a birth relative in another country are language and custom. Birth mothers in other countries may not be familiar with the concept of open adoption and may never expect that children they have relinquished for adoption may look for them. Internet searches and registries probably just do not exist in many countries. But for those being adopted now, the chances of finding a birth mother will improve. Countries in Eastern Europe are becoming more "Westernized," English is spoken by young people, and computers and the Internet are also growing.

If you feel that your child will never be able to find his birth family overseas, then you may want to at least encourage your child to visit his country of origin. Those adopted from Korea have formed groups that visit the country. If a group of teenagers and those in their twenties have a shared experience of traveling to Korea, this may also provide a support group of people who share the limited possibility of ever finding their birth parents. The group can be a place where your child can share the losses and the gains that he has experienced.

In some countries, such as Guatemala, there are groups on Listservs who have sibling registries so that families who adopt can see if the child whom they adopted has a sibling also placed for adoption here in the United States.

CONTACTING A BIRTH RELATIVE

Where do you begin to start your search? The first place to start is to contact the adoption agency or attorney who handled the adoption. If the agency is uncooperative, the adoptive family may want to contact the attorney since he can disclose the information in his file to the adoptive parents. If a birth parent is searching, she can contact the attorney who represented her and ask for the information regarding the adoptive parents. If the attorney is not comfortable giving all this information to the adoptive parents or birth family, then he may want to contact the birth family or adoptive family directly based on the information in the file. An attorney can have all parties sign a release at the time of adoption or later so that information can be disclosed.

Others do their own Internet search and join school registries if they have an idea of where the birth parents may have attended high school. Professional services are also available to assist a birth family or adoptee in the search.

How do you handle that initial contact? Making that first phone call to a birth parent or child can be worse than standing before a crowd of a thousand. You will be very nervous. Ideally, it would be great if you can obtain an e-mail address and first e-mail each other. When you call, of course, you will be very nervous. So have a pen and paper ready. If you are calling your birth mother, she may expect you to be angry. She may immediately tell you why she placed you for adoption and sound apologetic. One adoptee who had a wonderful life with her adoptive family made an effort to reassure her birth mother that she grew up in a great home. One adult adoptee said when she got ready to call her birth mother after much time spent searching, she made sure her children were not around; when she made the call, she realized the voice sounded familiar—it sounded like her own voice.

Perhaps the happiest search story we have come across concerns clients who are now adopting themselves. This couple, John and JoAnn, were high school sweethearts, and JoAnn became pregnant when she was about sixteen years old. JoAnn's parents forbade her to ever see John again. JoAnn went on with her life and married. Her daughter, Claire, had never known her biological father but wanted to find him. JoAnn supported Claire's decision to search and gave her as much information as she had about John. After Claire found John, who had also been looking for her, the father and daughter communicated regularly. Then Claire's mother and John remet each other. Both of them had been divorced, and they started dating. They are now married and are in the process of adopting children with special needs. Claire now has both her mother and biological father in her life, and John and JoAnn are finally able to have a family together.

LEGAL ASPECTS OF SEARCHING

Many groups have advocated at the state and national levels for birth and adoption records to be opened. For those advocating, progress is slow. Florence Fisher, founder of the Adoptees Liberty Movement Association (ALMA), is outraged that she cannot have what is afforded to every other American—her birth certificate and records. Most states will not give an adoptee their birth certificate and records without some compelling reason to do so. The reason given for not changing the laws is that women and men who placed children for adoption should be allowed privacy for the rest of their lives. Also, some feel that the adoptive family should not have to be concerned with birth families contacting them.

People have access to medical and other family history without interfering with others' privacy in nearly all states. In some states, only nonidentifying information is permitted. Nonidentifying information is usually a description of the adoptees' birth relatives. The information may include date and place of the adopted adult's birth; birth parents' age and physical description; birth parents' race, ethnicity, religion, and medical history; type of termination; facts and circumstances relating to the adoptive placement; age, sex, and health status of children of the birth parents at the time of the adoption placement; and educational levels, occupations, interests, hobbies, and skills of the birth parents. States usually place more restrictions on the birth mother than on the adoptee.

Some states have mutual consent registries that provide identifying information to the parties in an adoption only if all have agreed that they wish to be found. In some states, the registry is centralized by the state, and in others it operates across the state through the agencies or courts that handle adoption. Some states will not release information to a requesting person if the other party is deceased. Sometimes information will not be released if the adopted adult has not received the permission of the adoptive parents. This, of course, gets ridiculous when a thirty-five-year-old adult cannot get information without his parents' consent. When requesting information about another birth relative, the person usually has to make the request in writing and provide identification, such as a copy of his or her driver's license.

Passive registries, also called *mutual consent* or *volunteer registries*, require both parties to register before information is released and a match is made. Once a match occurs, both parties are notified. Passive registries in the United States currently have a match rate of about 10 percent.

Active registries do not require that both parties register their consent. Once one party is registered, an agency or court representative usually contacts the other party being sought and finds out if it is all right to release information. These registries have a match rate of 50 percent to 90 percent.

Search and Consent authorizes an agency to assist a searching party in locating a triad member and to find out if information can be released or if they want to meet. If, for example, a birth mother agrees that information can be given to a birth child, the court then authorizes this. In many states, counseling is required before information can be received.

Some states have confidential intermediaries who are permitted to get court-sealed information and then contact the parties involved.

In an *affidavit system*—also called a *consent, waiver,* or *authorization*—each party gives written permission to release identifying information. The affidavit system is often used along with the search and consent system.

Veto System. When someone in the adoption triad does not want to be contacted or have her identifying information released, she files a veto document. Tennessee is the only state with contact veto.

Court Orders. In most states in which adoption records are sealed, an adoptee can petition the court to receive identifying information. Usually "good cause," such as a health reason, must be present for the information to be given. Alabama's statute lets parties with a "compelling need" for medical information petition the court for permission to make contact in order to get that information.

In many states, new adoption laws only affect the adoptions finalized after the date the law is passed. This means in one state there can be two set of rules.

Here are some resources on searches:

Adoptee Search Center Registry
P.O. Box 281223
Memphis, TN 38168-1223
www.adopteesearchcenter.org

Internal Revenue Service Disclosure Office
Stop 1020
300 N. Los Angeles St.
Los Angeles, CA 90012-3363

The IRS requires that you provide the name and social security number of the person whom you are seeking. It is unlikely that adoptees know their birth parents' social security numbers, but it is possible. The adoption agency or attorney you used may know the social security number, and you can ask the staff to forward a letter to the IRS.

International Soundex Reunion Registry
P.O. Box 2312
Carson City, NV 89702
Phone: (702) 882-7755

It is best to send them a self-addressed, legal-sized envelope with your written request. This organization does not charge a fee, but it does accept donations.

National Adoption Information Clearinghouse
E-mail: *naic@calib.com*

Chapter Ten

Special Families, Special Considerations

I n the majority of cases, the parents of an adopted child are a married couple. In this chapter, we'll discuss the available options and special concerns of others who may wish to adopt—single parents, gays and lesbians, and unmarried couples. We also talk about another group that, perhaps surprisingly, often has difficulty in adopting children—military families.

SINGLE-PARENT ADOPTION

If you have made the decision to become a single parent through adoption, you can achieve your goal if you have the qualities that make anyone a good candidate for adopting a child. The attitude toward singles adopting has changed dramatically over the last 25 years. It is very well accepted that singles can be good parents—and in some cases more appropriate parents for certain types of children. The number and percentage of singles adopting are climbing. In fact, about one-third of all adoptions through the social services system are by singles.

Being single may require some extra diligence on your part. You may need to prove that you are more "normal" than a married couple seeking to adopt and that you have outside resources for caring for a child. Also, singles, especially those adopting internationally, either overtly or covertly must "prove" that they are heterosexual.

It the past, it was expected that singles would be more willing to take older children and those with special needs. Now, singles can have the same opportunities to adopt healthy babies as couples. There is still prejudice against single men adopting, and there is still an assumption that men will adopt boys—usually older boys.

All areas of adoption are open to singles—especially single women.

According to Shirley Roe, a single mother who adopted from China and the former copresident of RESOLVE of Greater Hartford, Connecticut, adoption is now very possible for single people, even adoption of young babies. Whereas in the past, unmarried individuals may have been restricted to adopting older children, new flexible policies in foreign countries mean that babies are available to single parents. Even domestic agencies are broadening their policies and allowing singles to adopt.

At least one study suggests that being single has little, if any, effect on adoption outcome. Single-parent families were shown to be as nurturing and viable as two-parent families. In fact, without the demands of a marital relationship, a single parent may be better equipped to give the level of involvement and nurturing needed by a child who has had severely damaging experiences. Mature single parents can offer a child many benefits.

It is essential to consider carefully the unique requirements of single parenting before taking this step.

What to Ask Yourself

Jane Mattes, founder of Single Mothers by Choice, recommends that you begin by asking yourself whether you are ready to become a parent and whether you are seeking parenthood for the right reasons. She has drawn up the following questions to help singles explore these issues. Answering them will also help to prepare you for the home study process. Of course, these are questions that are very important for all potential parents to consider, not just singles.

1. Have you accomplished all the personal and career goals that are necessary for you to feel good about yourself? How will you feel if you are not able to achieve some of these goals?
2. How will you feel about some people being critical of your decision to be a single parent?
3. Are you able to support yourself and a child emotionally and financially?
4. Do you have elderly parents who may need your assistance just at the time that you will be devoting yourself to a baby or young child?
5. Do you understand why you are not with a partner and how this will affect your relationship with your child?
6. If you still feel the need to date often, how will you feel about working, dating, and caring for a child? How will a child affect your likelihood of finding a mate? Can you make a distinction between which needs can be fulfilled by a child and which ones can be fulfilled only by a spouse?
7. Do you have a good support system of friends, family, church/synagogue, and work to help you during stressful times? If you do not have family who can help with the child's care, are you prepared for the twenty-four-hour-a-day responsibility of caring for a child with no assistance except from friends and paid child care?

8. Is your job flexible enough so that you can meet your child's needs when he is sick, has a special event, or needs extra attention?

9. How do you handle stress? Will you be able to meet the challenge of caring for a baby while working? Will your coping skills enable you to deal with the stressful situations that having a child will bring, like a baby crying all night, ear infections, etc.?

10. If you are considering adopting an older child, are you prepared to meet the child's special emotional needs and issues? Do you have time to take your child to a therapist in addition to Girl Scouts and other school and community activities?

Options for Single Parents

In the past, adoption professionals have had difficulty justifying the placement of children in single-parent homes. One reason is that statistically the 15.5 million children raised by only one of their biological parents have far more problems than those children who are raised by both of their biological parents. We now have much more information specifically on the outcome of adopted children in single-parent families, and this story is quite different. Adoption by singles has been very successful. As mentioned previously, at least one study has shown that adoption outcome in single-parent families has little, if any, difference from adoption outcome in two-parent families.

While our society's goal may be to promote two-parent families, without evidence that children are harmed by unmarried adopters, states should not discourage single-parent adoption. Today, most adoption professionals are very supportive of singles adopting internationally and adopting children who have been in the foster care system.

However, if you are single, finding a birth mother who will select you can be just as difficult as it was twenty years ago. A birth parent will feel if a single woman can raise the child, then so can she. The argument about whether a child is better off with an adoptive mother than his teenage birth mother has become a class issue, keeping us from focusing on what is better for the child. Many articles have been written to suggest that adopters are in a class tug-of-war with women who cannot afford their children. The practical reality, however, cannot be glossed over by talk of "class tug-of-wars." More often than not, single adoptive mothers do have the maturity, financial wherewithal, and support system to provide a healthier environment for a child than a teenage mother does. From the adoption agency's standpoint, presenting a two-parent family to a birth mother is a way of staying out of this battle.

Of course, even if the single adoptive mother has the necessary maturity, finances, and support system, a birth mother is still likely to be concerned. If she has had lots of boyfriends—no matter how destructive or otherwise unsuccessful the relationships were—she will wonder, "What's wrong with this woman, and why couldn't she find a husband?" Birth mothers are more open to a single adoptive mother if she is divorced, widowed, or presently involved with a man. If the birth mother senses that the adoptive mother will eventually marry, she may be more open to placing her newborn child with her.

However, some birth mothers—especially those who grew up in single-parent homes or who already have one child and are able to maintain a family life—believe that the stability of family life is determined solely by the issue of income. Their experience tells them that a single mother can provide a suitable home for a child if her income level is adequate. In fact, many birth mothers' experiences are positive enough that they would parent the children born to them if they could afford to do so.

An agency or attorney should be honest with prospective adoptive parents who are single and let them know that in this country the reality is that very, very few successful agency and independent adoptions involve single mothers. Although it is not impossible, prospective adoptive single parents need to know that the image of a "June and Ward Cleaver" family strongly dominates the typical birth mother's thinking. Certainly domestic adoption of a newborn is an option, but you should be willing to be patient and, of course, go with an agency or attorney that is supportive of a single-parent adoption.

Single Parents and Special Needs Adoption

It should surprise no one to learn, however, that agencies that place children with special needs are usually very accepting of single adoptive parents, as long as they have an income sufficient to meet the child's needs. Most social services departments will not allow you to adopt, however, if the child's monthly subsidy from the state is going to be your main source of income.

Singles may have fewer resources than a two-parent family, yet special needs children usually require extra resources. Many single people, however, can meet these demands very well, especially with special needs children whose behavior improves because of the one-on-one attention and understanding that single parents can provide. Indeed, children who come from chaotic backgrounds and have been physically and sexually abused often do better in single-parent homes where the family dynamics are simplified.

Single Parents and International Adoption

Nearly all countries permit singles to adopt. For the last few years, China has been very restrictive as to the number of singles who can adopt, but most other countries permit singles—that is, single women—to adopt. Very few countries permit men to adopt, and usually when they do, they are scrutinized more closely. Now countries are becoming stricter that singles who adopt in no way present themselves as homosexuals. For example, it is usually better if you are single to travel with a relative and not with a friend.

If you are a single person about to arrange for a home study, you can expect to be asked to address issues related to marriage, including what plans, if any, you may have for marriage, how marriage would change your relationship with the child, and how being a single parent might change your prospects for marriage. If you answer that you would consider marriage, the caseworker may want to know what kind of a person you would seek to marry. You may be asked about your living arrangements and whether you are gay or lesbian.

During the home study process, it is crucial that you understand as quickly as possible what bias the caseworker may have about you as a single prospective adoptive mother. Tune in to any common theme in the caseworker's questions. General questions about your employment, for example—hours, responsibilities, stress level, etc.—may lead to the all-important issue of child care arrangements, and you may be expected to address arrangements in greater detail than a married couple, even if both of them plan to work. The caseworker will want to know whether you will have any time and energy left over from the workday for your child.

ADOPTION FOR SINGLE MEN

Men have a much more difficult time than single women adopting children.

Regardless of what route a man takes to adopt, his motives are questioned. Simply put, single men seeking to adopt are suspected of being child molesters. (Most known child molesters are men.) Most men do not choose to adopt until they are past thirty years old, and at this age, men are often assumed to be gay.

As U.S. attitudes toward gays and lesbians are changing to become more open, the attitudes of officials in other countries are becoming more strict. This attitude has resulted in such countries as China greatly limiting the number of singles who can adopt and other countries such as Guatemala asking for more paperwork from singles, as well as making the possibility of single men adopting more and more difficult. Most countries outright deny single men the option of adopting.

Although not impossible, it is very unlikely that a single man will find a birth mother to place a child with him. Sometimes an attorney or agency will have a birth mother who allows the professional to select the adoptive family. If a single man knows an attorney, has a wonderful relationship with the attorney, and knows that he will be at the top of the attorney's list, then this could be a possibility for him. However, if you are single and male, it could be years before the "right" situation comes along.

The best adoption route for a single male is through the social services department. Social service professionals will point out that boys who need a strong male role model, firm discipline, and guidance have been proven to do well with single fathers—especially boys with emotional problems.

You must be willing to be proactive, but not so pushy that caseworkers will brush you aside. If you are questioned as to why you are single, you should present yourself as an average guy who just has not found a woman he wants to marry. You may even offer to take a psychological exam to prove you are "normal." This may appear sexist and biased, but the reality is that no one at a social services office is going to say, "I'm sorry, you are a single man, and we are just not comfortable with you." Instead, someone may conduct your home study and approve you, but your approved home study could very likely be put at the bottom of a stack somewhere.

There are stereotypes of the type of children men should seek to adopt. Most social service department staff would permit a white, single female to adopt a biracial boy. However, single black men can expect a cool reception if they seek to adopt any child other than a black male.

Therefore, if you are willing to adopt a male child—especially a boy who is older than five years old or a sibling group—you will improve your changes of adopting. You might also volunteer with a program such as the Guardian ad Litem program (in which volunteers serve as advocates for children who become involved in the court system) or a big brother type program sponsored through your social services department. If you are matched in such a program with a child who is eligible for adoption, you might then pursue the adoption of that specific child.

Also, having an approved home study before inquiring about specific children available through photolistings can enhance your opportunity to adopt. The adoption professionals then know that you are "preapproved" to adopt.

Again, you will have to be persistent yet patient. Making four phone calls to the same social worker in one day will not impress anyone. Conversely, if you wait for a social worker to call you back, you will probably get nowhere. You will need to make regular phone calls to find out the status of a child. If you feel that you are being given the cold shoulder simply because you are single and male, you should be honest with the caseworker and ask in a matter-of-fact way if this is a problem for her or her supervisor or if the issue is that placing a particular child with a single male may simply not be in the best interest of the child. If the caseworker explains that the agency wants the child to go to a two-parent home, ask her the reasons. Sometimes a two-parent home is better for a child, but not always. In fact, sometimes a single-parent home is better.

An organization that provides help and support for single women and men looking to adopt is the National Council for Single Adoptive Parents *(www.adopting.org/ncsap.html)*.

ADOPTION FOR GAYS AND LESBIANS

In most states, gays and lesbians are permitted to adopt; only one state at this time—Florida—has an outright ban on gay adoptions.

Historically, homosexuals have adopted internationally since there have been few restrictions as to singles adopting. The home study that was presented overseas either did not mention that the adoptive parent was living with someone else or did not reveal the kind of relationship the housemates had.

Now, adopting internationally has become much more difficult for gays and lesbians. First, the number of countries permitting a man to adopt has dwindled down to a few, and for the countries that do permit a male to adopt, such as Guatemala, the prospective adoptive father can expect to come under greater scrutiny. He usually must state that he is a heterosexual, and he may even be required to submit a letter from a psychologist indicating he is "normal." For a woman who wants to adopt internationally, there can be no hint in the home study or other documentation that she is a lesbian.

In the last few years, in an effort to stop gays and lesbians from adopting, China has not only greatly reduced the percentage of singles adopting from 40 percent to a quota of 8 percent, they also now only permit females to adopt. For the fortunate few who can get on a waiting list to adopt, they must sign a form indicating that they are heterosexual.

Adopting internationally means that the home study provider must be willing not to reveal prospective adoptive parent's true sexual orientation and probably the person's living arrangements. Gays and lesbians who want to adopt must first find a home study provider who will conduct the home study. Finding such an agency is usually not difficult.

If a homosexual couple wants to adopt domestically, it can be difficult. Most agencies that place infants with adoptive parents give the birth mothers a role in the selection of the adoptive parents, and most birth mothers want a traditional two-parent family for their children. An agency whose policy is to present a few prospective adoptive parents' portfolios to a birth mother will most likely hesitate to offer a portfolio of a gay or lesbian couple, for fear of giving offense. It is a rare birth mother who walks into an agency and says that she wants to place the child with a gay couple.

Attorneys who do direct placements will experience the same kinds of responses from birth mothers. An attorney who has experience with helping gay couples adopt will probably be the best person to facilitate the process and can give advice on where to place ads and all parts of the process.

Gay couples can encounter other obstacles besides finding a birth mother. Once a birth mother is found, the couple must seek an attorney to handle the paperwork, including the relinquishments. They must also count on a judge who will finalize the adoption. In most instances, judges will not object to a gay couple adopting, as long as the couple meets all the criteria that a straight couple would have to meet and as long as the birth mother is fully aware that the couple is gay. In other words, no deception is involved.

ADOPTION FOR UNMARRIED COUPLES

Except in rare cases, unmarried couples are usually not permitted to adopt. Unlike gay and lesbian couples, marriage for heterosexual couples usually is as simple as getting a license and saying "I do." For this reason, even when unmarried couples are permitted to adopt, the question of why they don't get married will be a focal point in the home study process, and their level of commitment to each other will be closely scrutinized. Because the stability of the couple's relationship is essential to approving a home study, an agency caseworker may find it difficult to approve such a home study. A social worker conducting a home study for a private domestic adoption may simply write up the home study without strongly addressing these issues.

Courts are beginning to allow unmarried couples to adopt in certain situations. This is particularly true in states that recognize common-law marriages. (If a couple has been together for a certain number of years, the state recognizes their relationship as a marriage.) The main things that are considered when evaluating whether or not an unmarried couple should be able to adopt are: how long they have been together, how committed they are to each other, whether they are stable people, and whether they are committed to having children. For example, one court judge in South Carolina approved an adoption of a hard-to-place child with an unmarried couple who had lived together for seven years.

What about those who are living together and one person wants to adopt? With no wedding plans in the near future, the woman may want to move on with parenthood, while the decision to marry is "on hold." This scenario is rather complicated; there are many issues to address in how the child and others will view the live-in partner. It must be a serious matter of thought, not only for the adopting parent, but also for the partner who does not want to adopt since it can have serious repercussions for both.

In one case, a woman named Kelly adopted a baby girl, Emily. At the time of the adoption, Kelly was living with her longtime boyfriend, Scott.

A few years later, "Daddy" was reading to Emily, and Scott and Emily fell asleep together in one room as Kelly fell asleep in another.

This situation created a great deal of tension in the relationship between Kelly and Scott because Kelly felt that it was inappropriate for Scott to be sleeping with Emily. Had Scott been the adoptive dad, this scene would probably not cause anyone any concern. After all, lots of children come into bed with their parents in the middle of the night or fall asleep with a parent. One the other hand, had Scott been a boyfriend, he could be accused of sexual misconduct. In this situation, Scott was essentially the child's father, yet an artificial line was established as to what he could and could not do as the father.

Sleeping arrangements are just one issue that a single adoptive parent must deal with. Day-to-day decisions about the child can cause great conflict between two persons—especially when a child is adopted when two people are living together, yet only one person is the parent.

A child being adopted by one person in the household can be compared to a child in a stepparent/stepchild relationship. Nevertheless, unlike a stepparent entering the life of a child through marriage, the relationship between two live-ins is much less secure than two married persons. One partner can leave the relationship at any time, and the nonadoptive parent has no rights.

Kelly and Scott did break up over this issue. Scott has no right to see Emily, even though he coparented her for four years, and this child has lost her "Daddy." In the meantime, Scott has an attorney and is seeking visitation rights with the child.

Singles Who Are Living with a Housemate

If you are living with someone—regardless of the relationship you have with them—that person will have to be a part of the home study process. Whether the person is a relative, friend, or a partner, that person will have to undergo all the same criminal and child abuse screenings that you must go through. Of course, this is true for an adult living in a married couple's home. However, you could expect the social worker to scrutinize the relationship in more detail if you are single.

You cannot eliminate the person from the home study process or deceive the person who is conducting your home study. Before you begin the home study process, be upfront with the social worker about your living arrangements. If you feel that the home study provider is not supportive of your living arrangements, you can hope that the social worker will be upfront with you about this. If you are adopting through a state agency, most likely the caseworker will have little say about your living arrangements. However, private agencies in most states can choose not to conduct a home study for individuals. That is also the right of the agency. In a perfect world, both parties are honest about their circumstances and their beliefs. If you feel that your home study provider is biased against your living arrangements—whether or not they say so—you may need to find a different agency or request a different social worker.

• • •

In summary, adoption is a viable choice for many singles. Before you proceed, though, you have to make sure that you have the resources in place to care for a child. You also want to make sure your child will have access to positive role models of both sexes. In addition, you will have to face all the other issues that adoptive parents face.

As a single, you may have many qualities that in some circumstances make you a better candidate than a couple for the parenting of certain children.

MILITARY FAMILIES

Special considerations need to be given to military families. Traditionally, if military families wanted to adopt a child through the social services department, they experienced difficulty—not necessarily because they were in the military but because they did not live in one place long enough to get through the trainings, home study, and waiting for an assignment of a child.

This barrier has prevented military families from adopting, even though they may be the ideal candidates. What makes them ideal? First, they are often a racially diverse group, and one third are minority families—even more so than the average population. If a family were to adopt transracially, they would most likely find that other military families are very accepting. This could be one of the most ideal settings, especially for a biracial child.

Also, military families usually have ready access to no-cost medical resources, including occupational and physical therapists, speech pathologists, and mental health professionals. The military covers even pre-existing conditions. If treatment is not available at a military medical site, then the patient is referred to a civilian hospital. If a patient receives treatment at a civilian hospital, then his or her health care is covered under CHAMPUS, a health insurance program; however, using this insurance policy requires a copayment.

If a military family pays a copayment, it can easily add up to thousands of dollars. Therefore, it is advised that when a adopting a child in the United States with special needs that the family should apply for their child to receive any special benefits—even if the family does not receive adoption subsidies. It is a wise precaution to take these benefits even if they are never used. Mounting medical bills can be devastating.

If a child has special medical needs, the child will be permitted to stay in an area where medical treatment is available. This dismisses another concern adoption professionals may have—that the military personnel may be transferred to an area where adequate medical services are not even available. Fortunately, the Exceptional Family Member Program states that no member of the military can be transferred to an area where specialized medical care is not available for a family member. Of course, these provisions include adopted children.

As special employees of Uncle Sam, military families can receive adoption benefits of up to $2,000 a year. There is a maximum of $5,000 in a given year, even if both parents are in the military. Reimbursements are made after the adoption is finalized and only if the adoption was done through a state or nonprofit private agency. Fees that can be reimbursed include adoption fees, legal fees and court costs, and medical expenses.

A disabled adopted child also may be eligible for up to $1,000 a month in assistance under the military's Program for Persons with Disabilities. Furthermore, the military's Exceptional Family Member Program is designed to ensure that the adoptive families of children with special needs are assigned to duty stations where the child's needs can be met.

For more information, contact The Adoption Exchange, Inc. at 1-303-755-4756 or contact the National Military Family Association at *www.nmfa.org*.

Although it is not a great deal of money, the benefits are broad and even include medical expenses incurred by a birth mother. Military families, like all other Americans who fall within the income age, are eligible for a $10,000 tax credit.

The Home Study

Military life is not always considered "normal" life, and there are positives and negatives associated with the lifestyle. If you are in the military, you will want to acknowledge to the social worker conducting your home study the realities of being in the military and how this could impact a child. You will also want to address what you do already to compensate for the downside of this life—regular moves, one parent being absent in a time of war, and so forth. For example, you may state the support system you have through other military families, that you make friends easily, and that you get involved in community activities. You will also want to share with the social worker the advantages of a child being reared in a military family. For example, if you are adopting internationally, you may want to discuss how diverse your neighborhood is and how comfortable your family is in traveling.

What If You Are Transferred Overseas?

If you are transferred overseas, there should not be a problem. But you may have to educate your agency about this. Those living on military installations can adopt children from the United States through the Interstate Compact on the Placement of Children because U.S. military bases are considered U.S. territory. You are simply conducting an interstate adoption. A social worker or clergy member on the overseas base can do the home study or postplacement follow-up visits once the child is placed with the family.

Some agencies, such as the Pearl S. Buck Foundation in Perkasie, Pennsylvania, have worked with military families in Asia for years. The Buck Foundation has branches in countries with large U.S. military populations. The agency even employs social workers to work with the military personnel stationed in these countries. If an agency does not have an overseas branch, however, it can use the services of International Social Service, American Branch (ISS/AB). ISS/AB is an international network of professional social work agencies working in more than thirteen countries where U.S. military personnel are often stationed, including Germany and France. ISS/AB can help agencies monitor families who have been transferred before an adoption has been finalized.

Also, see Chapter 12: International Adoption for the section on International Adoption for U.S. Citizens Living Abroad.

You will also want to join the Listserv to communicate with others in the military who have adopted, located at *http://groups.yahoo.com/group/AdoptionSupportGroupForMilitaryFamilies/*.

Chapter Eleven

Relative and Stepparent Adoption

The most common form of adoption in the United States is stepparent adoption. This adoption occurs when the child of the biological parent is adopted by that parent's spouse. A relative, or "intrafamily," adoption is usually defined as one close relative and possibly that person's spouse adopting another relative. This child can be related to the wife or the husband (as with a niece or nephew) or to both (as with a grandchild). The degree of relationship permitted varies from state to state.

Unlike other adoptions, one generally does not plan to become a parent through stepparent or relative adoption; the adoption occurs because of other life circumstances. Neither do people set a goal for themselves of becoming stepparents. Instead, marriage to a particular person is a package that includes children. A stepparent often wants to make an investment in the child's life, and the child and parent believe that it is important to cement that commitment through adoption.

In many states, a home study is not required for a relative or stepparent adoption. If a home study is not required, a child abuse and criminal history clearance are usually required. If such are not required, it is good practice to have an attorney submit these clearances to the court. If a home study is required, it is often conducted in a simplified form and is mainly intended to confirm that the placement was voluntary and that the adoptive family is functional and can provide for the child. The adoption is viewed as a family matter. Having children is a fundamental right that extends to family members who adopt the child, as long as the child is not abused or neglected. However, one very important component of the home study is educating the adoptive couple about adoption-related issues. If a home study provider does not meet with the family, the opportunity to examine adoption issues and educate the family is missed. Learning about the adoption may be all the more important in a relative or intrafamily adoption because the issues may be more complex. Since families involved in stepparent and intrafamily adoptions do not usually seek out adoption information, there may be no other such opportunity.

ADOPTION BY RELATIVES

As a rule, the relatives included in the definition of an intrafamily adoption are the child's grandparents, aunts, uncles, and siblings. Children are placed with relatives at different ages and for different reasons. Often a girl or woman becomes pregnant and wants to place the child for adoption, and another family member who cannot have a biological child adopts him. As with any other infant adoption, in this situation the birth mother (and perhaps the birth father) makes a decision to place a child for adoption because her life circumstances make it difficult to raise a child. Most often relative adoptions occur because a parent has life-dominating problems such as an addiction to drugs or alcohol, and another family member, usually a grandparent, starts to care for the child. At first the arrangement may be more or less informal. Children are expensive to raise, and relatives need legal protection so they can provide for the children. More formal arrangements are often needed.

There are obvious advantages and disadvantages to relative adoption of an infant. One long-term benefit is that the child can grow up with his biological relatives and have a stronger connection to his genetic background—as long as the child is aware that he has been adopted within his biological family. It may also be easier to have contact that is more consistent with the birth mother so that the child can know his birth mother's health history.

A legal advantage to a relative adoption is that the adoption itself is usually less complicated, and in some states, the laws are more lax. In the four states where independent adoption is illegal, it is all right to pursue a relative adoption, although a home study may be required, and if the child is born in one state and you live in another, you will not have to go through the Interstate Compact on the Placement of Children (ICPC). (The adopted child must be a close relative, such as the first generation niece or nephew or grandchild to the adoptive parents, to waive going through ICPC.)

The disadvantages of relative adoption can be more or less pronounced depending on the birth mother's location and situation and how the rest of the family handles the adoption. If she is a close relative and lives very close by, you may be concerned that she will want to share in parenting decisions. If you have a difficult relationship with her, you may worry about her interfering or saying inappropriate things to your child. A woman's reasons for placing a child for adoption can also influence how she feels about setting boundaries. For example, an older sister who is divorced and already has four kids would probably have a very different attitude from the fifteen-year-old cousin who places a baby with you. Your sister, because she is older and a mother already, may feel that she has a right to give input about the raising of your adopted child—her birth child.

If you have such concerns, discuss them up front. Sometimes attitudes can be deduced from comments by the birth mother and other family members and from the way the birth mother has handled other situations. If she is very unstable, you may need to create some distance between her and your immediate family once the child is born. Remember, unlike other birth mothers, she will probably always know where you live.

Other family members may feel the need to give their advice as well. You may find yourself pressured by suggestions and negative comments made by other family members. Although you want your family's support in your adoption decision, all communication should be between you and the birth mother. For example, if your mother tells you that she was talking to your Aunt Edna, and Aunt Edna mentioned that her teenage daughter, your cousin Tracy, is pregnant and wants to make adoption plans, and your mother told Aunt Edna that you may be interested, your Aunt Edna and your mother may feel that they should be privy to all future conversations between you and your cousin. It is nice that your mother took the initial step to "feel out" the situation, but the remaining communication needs to be between you and your cousin. Of course, her parents, your aunt and uncle, may be involved because of the birth mother's age. This no longer is an issue between your mother and aunt, however; it is between you and the birth mother.

If you were adopting a nonrelative, you might share with your parents details of your conversations with a birth mother and how all the plans were going. In an intrafamily adoption, you need to protect your privacy as well as the birth mother's. This means setting up very clear boundaries, if possible without hurting anyone's feelings. Let family members know, very tactfully, that you are glad they are concerned but that you want your cousin Tracy to be able to make her plans as she sees best. You would not want to say anything to anyone that would influence her decision or make her upset. Remind them that it is important to protect Tracy's privacy. If she wants to share information with others, that is her decision.

You will also want to establish some boundaries with the birth mother if she does live close by and if you normally see her for family gatherings and holidays. Having her remain in your life as much as she was before the child was placed with you can be appropriate, but because you will need to feel entitlement to the child, there may need to be limited contact initially.

What if the birth mother changes her mind? A woman named Katie who was in her late thirties wanted to have another child with her second husband, but infertility problems prevented her. When her son's girlfriend became pregnant, everyone involved decided that the child would be placed with Katie and her husband. Toward the end of the pregnancy, however, the birth mother changed her mind. Katie and her husband were very disappointed. It was difficult because they felt they could not express their disappointment to the girlfriend since they wanted to have a relationship with the child as the child's grandparents. They had already prepared a nursery in anticipation of adopting the child. They kept the nursery instead in anticipation of their grandchild. Once the child was born, the grandparents had to be careful that they maintained appropriate boundaries. Otherwise, in time, the child's mother might have come to see the grandparents as full-time babysitters, rationalizing leaving the child with them for extended periods by saying to herself that they were going to adopt the baby anyway.

How to Tell Your Child
Unfortunately, because a relative adoption is so close, some adoptive parents do not share with the child that he is adopted. Perhaps they assume it is not important since the child is already "family" and he already "knows" his birth mother—even though he does not know, for example, that his older sister is also his biological mother. Perhaps they tell the child that he is adopted but leave out the fact that his aunt Jane is also his biological mother. However, this can create problems in the future since the lie conceals the child's genetic background.

When children are adopted, a birth mother has a dual role: one of biological parent and one of relative. According to Sharon Kaplan Roszia, it is best in these cases that a child calls the adoptive parents "Mom" and "Dad" and the birth mother "Aunt" or whatever relation she is to the child based on the child's adoption.

Young and Older Child Placements
Most adoptions among relatives start as informal arrangements. A relative may serve as a guardian for a time, and then eventually adopt the child. Knowing each other and having a blood connection can make intrafamily adoptions both easier and harder. The common heritage, family lifestyle, and traditions are already known to the child, smoothing the transition; however, in most situations in which a young or older child is placed with a relative, it is because of the parent's inability to care for him. The birth parent may be viewed negatively in the family, an attitude that can extend to the child. The relationship can be even more complicated if, for example, the husband has a very negative attitude toward his wife's sister—the biological mother of the child. When a woman adopts her incarcerated sister's baby, for instance, the husband may have ambivalent feelings over the decision, a tension that will be heightened if the wife adopted her sister's child because it was the "right" thing to do—not because she especially wanted to expand her family.

Why Relatives Choose Adoption
Adoption is not always a choice, especially in cases where it will be difficult to terminate the parents' rights. However, if the parents are willing to have their

rights terminated, or if their lives are in such disarray that they would have trouble making a case for their suitability as parents, or if the social services department has declared that the relatives are the permanent foster parents, then adoption may be considered. The great advantage of adoption is permanency. Permanency not only benefits the child, but the relatives are also reassured to know that the parents, whose lives are not together, cannot remove the child from the home on a whim. If a child is removed from his biological parents because of neglect or abuse and the parents have not complied with the requirements for getting him back, adoption can be a message to the child that someone is going to take care of him and love him unconditionally. It also means an end to intervention by the social services department, which will no longer have the power to separate the child from the relative's home or otherwise interfere in the life of the family.

Because adoption is permanent, it usually means a severing of the relationship between the child and his biological parents. Depending on the situation, this step may be too extreme. A kinship adoption can allow some aspects of the birth parent and child relationship to stay intact, if appropriate, by establishing a certain level of openness between the child and biological parents.

KINSHIP ADOPTION

"Kinship adoption" is a term used when a parent can no longer parent a child and a relative takes over that role.

When social services removes children from their homes because of abuse or neglect, for example, and relatives who can adequately care for the child are called upon, the term "kinship adoption" comes into use. Kinship adoption traditionally has been a more informal arrangement between the parent and the relatives; now the arrangement is becoming more formalized as more social service departments are accessing relatives as foster and adoptive parents. Nationally, kin caregivers are usually African-American maternal grandmothers with an average age of forty-five.

A social service agency will often seek out relatives to care for a child instead of placement in a foster home. Often this makes a great deal of sense, especially if the child has had regular contact with the relatives. According to a study by the National Black Child Development Institute in 1986, when an agency asked relatives to care for the children, more than 50 percent said yes. The care of children by relatives helps preserve families, traditionally one of society's most important support systems. "Traditionally grandparents have been viewed as the keepers of the family culture and the thread that ties the family together, by providing the wisdom and emotional support that serve as the forces for continuity." When it comes to adoption, however, it is important to realize that social service staff does not automatically award first preference to family. Although the courts may decide that a family relationship best fulfills the child's interest, the family relationship itself will not be the deciding factor. A judge is to rule on what appears to be best for the child.

According to Ann Sullivan of the Child Welfare League of America, more and more children are living with relatives in general and grandparents in particular. The reasons for this go beyond parental divorce and death to reflect a range of social ills: teenage pregnancy; joblessness; child neglect, abuse, and abandonment; incarceration of the parent; drug addiction; and diseases like AIDS. Many family members believe that to adopt another family member's child would cause great conflict in the family, so they do not take this step. In informal situations, in which the family is being assisted by social workers but the child is not in the custody of the child welfare agency, adoptions are particularly rejected. Most relatives see adoption as unnecessary since the child is already with family.

In some states, social services especially encourage the adoption of children by relatives. For example, a child who has been removed from his home due to abuse or neglect will often first be placed with a relative who is available. These relatives are then the foster family. If the biological parents do not appear to be following a treatment plan to have the child placed back in the parental home, then the relatives must either adopt the child or the child will be placed for adoption. In these situations, the relatives usually receive the same social service benefits, such as monthly subsidies, that nonrelative foster/adoptive parents would receive.

Sometimes an abused and/or neglected child is placed in a nonrelative foster home because the relatives were "afraid" to get involved. Family relations can be complicated, and some people do not want to interfere with a relative's child. If the child then becomes available for adoption because the child will not be returned to the biological parents, the foster family usually has the first right to adopt when the child becomes available for adoption. It is at this time that some relatives then want to adopt the child. This can cause a protracted legal battle for the child between the foster family and the relatives.

If you have been caring for a relative's child because the child was abused or neglected and you decide you would like to adopt her, the public agency that first got involved in the placement can usually handle the adoption. This agency and the court must believe it is in the child's best interest to terminate the parents' rights and for you to adopt the child. Talk with your caseworker about the possibility of the child becoming your full charge instead of the state's responsibility. You may need to hire your own attorney to get the process moving faster and to see that your rights and the child's are fully protected.

If the agency has legal custody of the child and you have been a foster parent and receiving subsidies, you most likely will be eligible for subsidies even after the adoption takes place.

ADOPTION BY GRANDPARENTS

There are 4.5 million children under the age of eighteen living with 2.4 million grandparents (6.3% of all children) and another 1.5 million live with other relatives for a total of 8.4% of children living with relatives. This number has grown 30 percent from 1990 to 2000. In a third of these cases, the grandparent provided care without the assistance of the parents. One study found that 50 percent of the relatives caring for the children were grandmothers.

If a girl has a child at the age of sixteen and her parents are about twenty years older than she is, that means her parents are in their early forties—an age when some couples today are beginning (or continuing) to have children. As lifestyles have changed, many grandparents in their forties and early fifties are able to take on the responsibility of caring for young children. Sometimes grandparents deliberately plan to adopt the child who is about to be born out of wedlock; for others, the decision evolves out of circumstances. If a daughter has a child at sixteen and over time realizes that the task is more than she can handle, her parents may assume more and more responsibility until they are making the major life decisions for their grandchild. At this point, the grandparents may decide that adoption would be in their and the child's best interest. At least it would mean that the child could be covered by their health insurance and could receive benefits such as Social Security. Also, grandparents, who often have lower incomes, may be eligible for food stamps to meet their children's needs.

One set of grandparents, for instance, adopted their fifteen-year-old daughter's infant, initially for legal reasons (the family was traveling internationally), even though both mother and grandparents were sharing in the parenting role. Over time, however, the grandparents took full responsibility for the child because the daughter—the child's biological mother—was doing other things in her life. Now the child is seven years old, and the grandparents are still his primary parents. He knows that he is adopted and that his "sister" is his biological mother. He calls his grandparents "Mom" and "Dad," and his birth mother by her first name.

Nancy, who is in her late thirties, says her grandparents adopted her because her mother was only fourteen years old at the time of her birth. Although her birth certificate was changed to name her maternal grandparents as her parents, her mother maintained a relationship with her, mostly by telephone, and she called her mother "Mommy." As Nancy got older and her mother matured, her mother was able to communicate with her and help Nancy make decisions. Today the two have a close relationship. They live near each other and see each other regularly.

Most grandparent adoptions come out of less planned circumstances. Usually the adoptions result from parents' lives deteriorating and the grandparents becoming more and more involved in their grandchildren's lives and then finally becoming their primary caretakers and then finally their parents. Much information and support are now available for grandparents in such circumstances. The American Association of Retired Persons has a newsletter dedicated to such grandparents.

Other resources include:

American Association of Retired Persons Grandparent Information Center
Phone: (800) 424- 3410
E-mail: *gic@aarp.org*
www.aarp.org/grandparents

Brookdale Foundation Group
Phone: (212) 308-7355
www.brookdalefoundation.org

Generations United National Center on Grandparents and Other
Relatives Raising Children
Phone: (202) 289-3979
www.gu.org

Grand Parent Again
www.grandparentagain.com

National Committee of Grandparents for Children's Rights
Phone: (866) 624-9900
www.grandparentsforchildren.org

The Child Defense Funds has materials about subsidized guardianship programs. Visit *www.childrensdefense.org.*

For more information about medical benefits go to *http://cms.hhs.gov/medicaid/consumer.asp* or call (800) 362-1504 or contact ALL Kids at (800) 441-7607.

To download benefit guides for grandparents and other relatives go to *www.childrensdefense.org* or call (202) 662-3568.

ADOPTION BY STEPPARENTS

As divorce and out-of-wedlock birth rates rise, stepparenting is becoming more common. Remarriages accounted for nearly 46 percent of all marriages in 1990, compared with 31 percent in 1970. Every year more than 1 million children are involved in a divorce, and in several million families, at least one spouse has had an out-of-wedlock child before getting married. As a result, more and more families will be made up primarily of a biological mom and stepdad. Today, nearly 7 million children live in stepfamilies, making up 15 percent of all children living in a two-parent household. In the 2000 Census, stepfamilies were not mentioned, but according to the Stepfamily Foundation, about 50 percent of children thirteen years old and under live with one biological parent and that parent's partner.

Only a fraction of these stepchildren, however, is ever adopted. Why? One reason may be the ways in which general adoption laws are applied to stepparent adoptions. One study, for example, found that stepfathers wanted to adopt but thought it would be impossible because of the biological fathers' involvement in the children's life. As the courts allow more flexibility in stepparent adoption, we may find more stepparent adoptions taking place.

Stepmothers/Stepfathers

Most stepparent adoptions are cases of stepfathers adopting their stepchildren. In 1988, only 11 percent of stepfamilies were made up of the biological father and the stepmother. Custodial stepmothers seldom adopt their stepchildren—even when the father is widowed. Perhaps this is because the children and the stepmother all share the same last name, meaning that the stepfamily does not appear any different from a fully biological family. One study found that children tend to do better in mother/stepfather homes rather than in father/stepmother homes. Also, girls do not appear to be more disturbed than boys. The same study demonstrated that the stepparents' interpersonal relationship with the child played a crucial role in the child's academic achievement.

Why Adopt Stepchildren?

Here are some of the reasons to consider adopting your stepchild or stepchildren:

1. *You will still be the child's parent should the biological parent die, become disabled, or divorce you.*
2. *Should you die or become disabled, the child will be entitled to Social Security benefits.*
3. *You can feel like a real parent.*
4. *The child can have a sense of permanency.* Children's security is often tied to being in a "forever" family. The adoption by a stepparent can provide this "foreverness." Adoption can provide other emotional benefits, too, if your child is from a previous marriage or relationship and you now have another child with your husband. In a situation like this, your older child may feel "second best" because he is not your husband's child. Adoption can help him feel that he belongs permanently to both you and your husband.

5. *The child can take on her parents' last name.* If you are a woman and have taken your husband's last name, your children may still have your last name (if they were born out of wedlock) or their father's last name. Adoption means the whole family can have the same last name. If adoption is not feasible because your ex-spouse objects, you can still consider a name change. Conversely, if the child is older, adoption can happen without a name change. If the biological father has died, the child may see a name change as being disloyal to the deceased parent.

6. *The child's birth certificate changes.* Unlike the simple name change that sometimes occurs in stepfamilies, with adoption the birth certificate changes to indicate the stepparent as the original parent. If the child is older (usually ten years and up), the child's permission is needed to do this.

7. *If the child's parent is deceased and the child receives Social Security benefits, these will not stop if the child is adopted by a stepparent.* If your child is receiving Social Security benefits, it is probably best to get a letter stating that the benefits will continue in the event of an adoption.

Disadvantages of Stepparent Adoption

Here are some concerns to consider before taking the step to adopt:

1. *The stepparent may have to make child support payments in the event of a divorce.* If you are the primary wage earner and you and your spouse divorce, you will probably be responsible for child support payments if the child lives with her mother. If your spouse were to leave you for someone else and take the children, you could still end up being responsible for child support payments.

2. *The child may feel disloyal to her noncustodial parent.* She may feel that if she is adopted she can never have a relationship with her other biological parent and that to proceed with the adoption would be to reject that parent. Such feelings are not easily overcome.

3. *The noncustodial parent could interfere.* Trying to gain the cooperation of the noncustodial parent could turn into litigation if the parent contests the adoption. Your family also runs the risk of counterclaims by your ex-spouse if you mention your adoption plans to him or her.

    A man who has not visited his children nor paid child-support may all of a sudden want to be "father-of-the-year" when he hears that his ex-wife's husband wants to adopt "his" kids. Indeed, most couples who want to proceed with a stepparent adoption are not trying to get the other biological parent out of the picture. Usually the father is already out of the picture and is not paying any child support.

Many stepparents say that they want to adopt but believe that it is impossible because of the previous spouse's interference. Check with a lawyer in your state or where the parent lives to see what his rights are. Bear in mind, however, that no matter what those rights, there is always the possibility of a dragged-out family conflict in which the child will be exposed to the problems of both of his parents.

4. *Any child support being paid by the noncustodial parent would stop.* A parent who is faithfully paying child support usually cares very much about his child and is involved in her life. Many stepparents prefer not to assume full financial and legal responsibility while the noncustodial parent still has this close relationship, especially if the parent and ex-spouse have had a bitter divorce.

Grandparent Issues

You and your children may have a relationship with their grandparents even if they have little contact with their noncustodial parent. This may be especially true if the parent lives in another state while his parents live close to you and your children or if your first spouse has died. In either case, but especially the latter, the grandparents may feel that your husband's adopting the children is removing your late husband's place in the family. It would be wise to discuss the adoption plans with them before you proceed—not to get their permission but to reassure them of the important role that they will continue to have in your children's lives.

Parent-Stepparent Issues

If a stepparent has been married to the biological parent for a year or more (in some states six months) and the other biological parent is essentially not in the child's life, you can consider adoption. If the other biological parent is involved in the child's life, the noncustodial parent must consent before the adoption is finalized.

Children in stepfamilies are likely to have known and to have had an emotional relationship with the parent who is not living with them. In such cases, there is a strong argument for establishing what is called an "open arrangement"—proceeding with adoption, but continuing at least limited contact with the noncustodial parent. This allows children to express their preference for being adopted without breaking allegiance to the biological parent who no longer lives with them. Of course, if the child has not known the biological parent, the biological parent abused or neglected the child, or the biological parent has never paid any child support or provided any emotional connection to the child, then an open arrangement may not serve any purpose.

If parents are pressing for an adoption, the child may feel ambivalent and confused. You will want to discuss both sides with your child, even though you may feel strongly about proceeding with the adoption. A child over the age of eight should have freedom of choice about the adoption and what last name he will use, unless the adoption is sought in an emergency. An example of this is if the mother has a life-threatening illness and wants to solidify the legal relationship between her spouse and her children in the event of her death.

If the biological parent will not consent to the adoption, you may need to wait to find grounds for termination. If several years of not paying child support and lack of contact are grounds for involuntary termination in your state, it would be better to wait out the time period than to initiate an adoption that might only serve to draw the biological parent back into your lives.

The best stepparent adoptions occur when the whole family wishes for the adoption as a legal means of expressing their emotional security. The least successful are those in which the parent coerced the child into the decision. Sometimes when there is friction between the stepparent and child, families may suggest adoption as a way of solidifying the relationship. This is a mistake. Adoption should take place when the relationship between the child and stepparent is positive and always with the agreement of the child.

When a child reaches adolescence, as with any child who is adopted, he may want to reexamine his adoption and ask questions about his origins, identification, and original name. The child may also want to search for his biological parent. During this time, it is important for his parent and adoptive parent to reassure the child of their commitment to him, while allowing the child to explore his identity.

For a child, living in a household with only one biological parent represents a loss. Despite the commonness of divorce and remarriage, children are well aware that the "ideal" family consists of two parents who stay together. The divorce itself is a loss for children. If the original marriage was horrible and the noncustodial spouse was abusive or deserted the family, divorce for the child represents the lost possibility of a good biological parent. Even if the next spouse is "Mr. Wonderful," loves the child, and wants to adopt him, the child may still need to grieve for the "lost" parent, the lost marriage, and possibly the lost "ideal" parent.

You may have very negative feelings toward the parent, and your child may share those feelings. Remember, however, that just as you may have wished your first marriage could have been better, your child will probably wish the same thing. Try to acknowledge his loss. You may say, "I wish that your dad could have been more caring, and I know it hurts you that he was not kinder. One thing that I am glad about is that you are my child and that you have another dad who really does care about you."

If your child has never met her biological parent, then she may have a need to know about him as well as a desire to meet someday. This desire on the part of a child is comparable to that of those conceived through donor insemination. It is not that she wants to change anything; rather, as she matures, she may need a greater understanding of her genetic background. She needs to know "who I am."

If a woman has a child out of wedlock and marries a man who is not the child's biological father when the child is still very young and he adopts the child, then this adoption needs to be explained to the child from the earliest age possible, whether or not the birth father is in the picture. This may not feel comfortable at first. You may begin by saying to a one-and-a-half-year-old, "Mommy and Daddy love you so much, and Daddy adopted you because he loves Mommy and you so much." This may feel contrived and awkward, but the alternative is not saying anything until the child is older, which can be damaging. Finding just the "right" age may be awkward. If you wait until she is old enough to "understand" that she is adopted, she may have already found out through documents or through others' comments.

If your husband has legally adopted your child, you may want to place the paperwork and pictures associated with the occasion in the child's baby book. If you can find other mementos surrounding the adoption that demonstrate your husband's commitment to and love for the child, include these as well.

As with other adoptions, sometimes parents withhold information about the child's birth from her because it causes embarrassment to the parent—especially if the child was born out of wedlock. Some people would also prefer to forget a previous marriage, and in trying to re-create their new family, they never share with the child her relationship to the nonbiological parent. It is very important that parents share with their child that she has been adopted and that the child has a biological parent as well.

As difficult as it may be, share with your child the circumstances that led to her being adopted by your spouse. Of course, the information needs to be age-appropriate, but in general, most information should be shared before the child reaches adolescence.

Most adoption authorities agree that adoption information should be shared with the child, regardless of how much you want to protect your child. In the case of stepparent adoptions, your child will know eventually—first, your wedding date will come after the child's birth. Obviously other people will know that your husband, for example, is not the child's biological parent, and it is very unfair to your child to have others know about her parentage when she does not. Adoptees often feel angry, betrayed, and hurt when information regarding their adoption is withheld from them.

One woman shared with me how upsetting it was for her after her mother died when she found out that her father was not her biological father; the woman seemed more hurt because her mother could not share a part of her life with her daughter. The adoptive father had always wanted to tell the daughter, but the mother was too ashamed to discuss this because she had given birth to her out of wedlock. When her mother died, so did her mother's story.

The woman had wondered about her biological father since she was in her twenties. This woman, now in her forties, went on the Internet and was able to locate her biological father. At first, his name did not come up, and then a few days later she tried again. Her biological father had just been given a Web television, and she found him days after he set it up. When she called him on the telephone, she began by asking him questions to make sure she had identified the right person. In the conversation, he said that he had always wondered what had happened to her and was very concerned about how she was. Since talking with each other, they have met and regularly communicate through e-mail. The woman's adoptive stepfather understands and supports the relationship that this woman has with her birth father.

THE STEPPARENT ADOPTION PROCESS
Here are the basic steps toward a stepparent adoption:

1. Depending upon the state and county in which you live, you may have to have a home study and a criminal and child abuse clearance conducted.

2. The other biological parent's rights must be terminated, or he must sign a consent to an adoption. If the biological parent has been out of the child's life, he may be served legal papers (the adoption complaint or petition) informing him of the adoption hearing. If he objects, he can contact your attorney or show up at court to contest the adoption. If he does not respond by a specified number of days, usually twenty to thirty-five, he is presumed to have waived his right to object to the adoption.

3. A hearing is held, usually two to six months after the filing of the adoption petition. At the hearing, the adopting parent must say why he wants to adopt the child; testify that he contributes to the financial stability of the home or that he and the biological parent together can provide financial support to the child; and state his belief that it is in the child's best interest to be adopted by him. The biological parent must testify that she consents and that she feels it is in the child's best interest to be adopted. If the child is over the age of ten (in some states twelve or fourteen), he is questioned by the judge either in the courtroom or in chambers to confirm that he wants to be adopted. At the hearing, the attorney must present to the court either the signed consent of the noncustodial parent or proof that he was served the legal papers and did not respond.

If the noncustodial parent cannot be found, the attorney must place a legal notice of the adoption proceedings in a newspaper published in the last county in which the parent is known to have lived. If he does not respond, the effect is the same as if he had been served personally.

The Stepfamily Foundation has a Web site with many articles and information related to divorce, remarriage, and stepparenting. They have a 24-hour information line at (212) 799-STEP or you can visit their Web site at *www. stepfamily.org.*

Using a Private Attorney

An agency cannot file papers for you. Most people file the necessary legal documents through their attorney. Because many stepparent and relative adoptions are uncomplicated, nearly any competent attorney can facilitate the adoption. However, if you think that the adoption may be contested, you will want to retain an experienced adoption attorney. These are the steps that must take place before the adoption can be finalized:

1. Depending on what state you live in, you, the adoptive parents, may need to have a home study, a child abuse clearance, a criminal clearance done by your local police department or your state agency, and possibly an FBI clearance, carried out through a fingerprinting check.
2. If you are adopting an infant who will be placed with you upon her release from the hospital, the biological parents must sign consents that terminate their parental rights.
3. If the child is older and you have been caring for her but the birth parent(s) have not signed consents, they must be contacted for their consent or at least notified of an adoption hearing so that they have the right to object to the adoption if they so choose. You may need to employ a process server to serve the papers on the biological parents. They do not have to sign anything; the papers are simply to inform them that their rights are about to be terminated and an adoption is about to take place and that they can contact your attorney or be at court if they want to contest the adoption. Some states require consents unless the child has resided with you for at least six months.
4. Legal papers, including a Judgment of Adoption, are filed with the courthouse in your county. A date is then given to your attorney as to when the adoption will take place.
5. You go to court to adopt the child.

Chapter Twelve

International Adoption

In the early 1990s, many families were moved to adoption and took action when they saw the plight of the children in Romania. Many believed that with enough love and good medical care these children would be all right. Most of the children are doing well, but some have permanent scars. Again, pictures moved us the day after Christmas 2004 with the great tsunami disaster in the Indian Ocean. Many people inquired if these orphans could be adopted. Unlike the babies and children of Romania, these children could not be adopted. Officials in poorer countries usually do not permit candid shots of orphans who live in desperate situations; yet these children do exist. They need homes just as much as the orphans that we have seen in the news.

International adoption may be the right choice for you if you:

- Have the ability and resources to be a good parent and feel compelled to help an orphan
- Want to adopt a baby within about nine months
- Have the resources to pay for an adoption and related expenses that may come to about $30,000, have some time to travel, are interested in other cultures, and understand that there are many unknowns about the child's background
- Have other children and want to add to your family but possibly could have more biological children if you so chose.

With an international adoption, you are not waiting for a birth mother to select you. You can proactively start the adoption process, and you can adopt a child usually well within one year. Although there is paperwork to negotiate, it is manageable.

If you want to adopt a toddler and not an infant, you are much more likely to find such a child internationally than you would either through private or agency adoptions or through public agencies. Here in the United States, birth mothers almost always relinquish only infants, and the majority of children available through the social services departments are school age and older.

If you want to adopt an older child or a child with special needs, you can make a difference in a child's life. Remember, you will not be provided the same public services as someone adopting a child that has been in foster care.

If you are interested in adopting a child from Asia or South America and are Caucasian, then you should be willing to be part of an interracial/ethnic family and be comfortable accepting your differences.

Millions of children around the world need a family, not just for their emotional well-being, but also often for their very survival. Although only a fraction of these children are legally free for adoption, this fraction still translates into tens of thousands of children being available and waiting for adoption. During the 1980s, the number of international adoptions rose from 5,700 in 1982 to nearly 10,000 in 1987. The numbers dropped in the early 1990s, mostly because South Korea reduced the number of children placed for adoption. In 1992, about 6,500 orphans were adopted from other countries. In 1994, the number climbed to 8,200, a 12 percent increase over 1993, and the numbers are continuing to rise, largely because of an increase in adoptions from China, Russia, and Eastern European nations. In 2003, more than 21,000 children from overseas were adopted by Americans. Since 1956, when adoptions first began from Korea, about 250,000 international children have been adopted by Americans.

INTERNATIONAL ADOPTION: ADVANTAGES

The advantages of international adoption are considerable. Here are several:

1. *There are plenty of young children available.* There are significant numbers of healthy babies and young children available, many more than there are in the United States. Countries in which babies can be adopted are by far the most popular countries. In fact, about 50 percent of the children adopted internationally are under twelve months old and 90 percent are under five years old.

2. *Standardized requirements are set by the country—not arbitrarily by the birth mother.* Adopting from another country is sometimes a more viable choice than a domestic adoption, especially for those who are single, have other children, or are older. In domestic adoptions, birth mothers are usually seeking to place their babies with married couples in their late twenties to late thirties who cannot have children because of infertility or who have no more than two to three children. When adopting internationally, the countries set the standards. Therefore, singles are much more likely to adopt, as well as those over forty. China, for example, requires couples to be at least thirty years old. Other countries set very broad age ranges for prospective adoptive parents.

3. *The wait can be shorter.* Because of the abundance of children available, a baby or child can be adopted within months after your paperwork is completed. Usually a family can expect to have a child in their home within one year after beginning the paperwork.

4. *Once you have an approved home study, you are virtually guaranteed a child.* Unlike adopting in the United States, where you can comply with all requirements and still not have a child, when you are adopting internationally, you are almost guaranteed success. You are not counting on a birth mother selecting you; instead, you and a child are matched.

5. *The cost of adoption is well defined.* The cost of an international adoption usually ranges from about $15,000 to $30,000. Although the cost is fairly high, principally because of the traveling and overseas fees, you know what to expect. With a domestic adoption, you can pay for a birth mother's living expenses, and if she changes her mind, those expenses cannot be recouped. With international adoption, expenses may unexpectedly increase, but you are almost certain to adopt a child. True, there are horror stories of those who have gone overseas and been swindled out of large sums of money. But laws have been changed. Now there is less opportunity for exploitation, but always consult with others who have used the agencies or organizations you are considering using before paying any fees.

6. *Healthy children are available.* Some of the medical problems children have are related to living in an impoverished country, and these conditions are usually treatable. Younger children usually have fewer adjustment and emotional problems.

7. *Once your child is home, it is next to impossible for the adoption to be "undone."* When adopting internationally, birth parents only rarely contest the adoption. When this does happen, the adoption process can turn into a lengthy one, or you may even lose a referral of a child. But once the child is adopted by you and is home, neither the child's birth family nor country of origin is coming back to claim him. If they tried, as has happened only once in more than 400 adoptions that we have been involved in, no child has been deported back to his country of origin. In fact, there is no documented record of a child being sent back to his country of origin unless the child is not a U.S. citizen and the child commits a crime.

INTERNATIONAL ADOPTION: DISADVANTAGES

Having considered the advantages of international adoption, let us turn to the disadvantages.

1. *You will probably have to travel to another country.* Couples with busy schedules often consider this a great disadvantage. If they already have children,

staying a week or more in another country can mean making extensive child care arrangements or taking their children along. Traveling by plane and staying in hotels can also be expensive. Fortunately, traveling can be an advantage as well. It is an opportunity to learn about your child's country. While you are there, you can press the orphanage caretakers and medical personnel to give you more information than may be included in the written medical and social reports. Immediate adjustment issues can be handled by finding out little details, such as the temperature your child likes his bottle, sleeping habits, and food likes and dislikes. Also, some orphanages will allow you to feed, dress, and otherwise interact with your child during the time you wait for approval to leave the country. This is a great time to allow your child to transition from being in an orphanage to being with you.

2. *You cannot bring home a newborn infant.* The "infants" that are available are usually between a few months and one year old at the time of placement. Although many children are abandoned at birth, the complications and laws of other countries make it difficult for a child to be placed with adoptive parents right away. Some countries require that a child be on registry for at least six months before he can be adopted.

3. *The child's background is uncertain.* There is usually a gap in the information available about the child and his family background. Even in domestic adoptions, the child's biological parents' full medical backgrounds are often unknown; yet most couples in the United States have at least some medical and social background on the birth mother and could perhaps track down the birth father if necessary. Studies of adopted children do show that it is important for parents and professionals to obtain accurate and detailed information on the child's background whenever possible.

4. *The child is unlikely to ever know her birth parents.* Openness in adoption is considered an advantage to the child, especially when she comes to inquire about her genetic background. In an international adoption, no matter how much you share the child's culture with her, she will probably know little about her biological parents and may never have the opportunity to exchange information with them or to meet them. Even in situations in which the birth mother relinquishes her rights and is known, the attitude of the professionals in these countries can be similar to the attitudes of adoption professionals in the United States thirty to forty years ago: Contact between the birth family and adoptive family is just not important. Although this is beginning to change and some adoptees do go back to their country of origin and find their birth mothers, this is the exception.

Some people choose international adoption because they do not want to "worry" about the birth parents interfering with the adoption. If this is how you feel, you may need to give some more thought to the roles the birth parents will play in your child's life, whether or not they physically cared for your child or could ever contact your child in the future. Birth parents matter to children, and this is true even in the thousands of adoptions in which there is no contact with a birth mother or father. Children need to know why or the possibility of why they were placed for adoption and that their birth parents on some level cared about them. A birth parent cannot simply be emotionally "dismissed" just because she speaks another language and may be nearly impossible to find.

5. *The wait for a child, once he is identified as your child, can be very emotionally taxing.* Waiting for a child is always difficult, and in some countries, it can take months before your identified child can come to the United States. Knowing that your child is in a foster home or in an orphanage with less than optimum care is difficult for you as a parent. Your child is somewhere where you cannot help him. Some adoptive parents go to the country beforehand and care for the child themselves until the paperwork is completed.

   If you must wait for your child while she is in one country and you are in the United States, you can comfort yourself with the knowledge that she is going to get the best possible life once she comes home to you. You did not do anything to cause your child to be in an orphanage, but you are doing something to bring her out of it. If you had never made plans to adopt her and you did not allow yourself to experience the emotional agony of being separated from your child-to-be, then she might never have had the opportunity to live with a family.

6. *The paperwork and repetitive procedures can be difficult.* The hardest requirement in adopting a child from another country may be completing what appears to be endless paperwork and dealing with bureaucracies both at home and abroad.

   Nevertheless, it is doable. One adoptive mother, whose child is now thirty-one years old, says that when she began to inquire about the process twenty-eight years ago, she was told by a legal secretary that the paperwork was so overwhelming that she should not even bother to proceed. This mother thought that if a legal secretary, who deals with paperwork and forms all day long, found the paperwork burdensome, then she was in no position to tackle such a task. Then she met a woman who belonged to an adoption support group, Latin American Parents Association, and this woman was planning to adopt from Colombia. This woman had done her paperwork and was so confident that she would be returning from South America with a child that she was already decorating the nursery. The prospective adoptive mom thought that if this woman could do it, so could she. So can you! (As it happened, both women adopted within months of their meeting each other.)

Fortunately, some countries, such as China and Korea, have made the paperwork process easier. To help minimize your paperwork, ask your agency staff what paperwork will be completed and processed for you. Agencies vary considerably on this matter. Some assist you greatly, while others provide you with an outline and you must manage all the paperwork yourself.

7. *Few support systems and little government funding are available for an internationally adopted child with special needs, especially a child who may have psychological problems.* Although there are many governmental programs for children who have been adopted through state social service departments, many governmental agencies are not offering such programs for internationally adopted children due to budget constraints.

8. *You will most likely be forming a transracial/transcultural family.* While this need not be a disadvantage, certainly you need to consider the impact of how being a "conspicuous" family will impact you, your family, and the child you are adopting.

9. *Older children adopted internationally can have the same problems as older children adopted in the United States.* Families who would not consider adopting older children here in the United States will consider older children from other countries. Yet, these children enter the system for the same reasons that children enter the foster care system here: abuse and neglect. Often the neglect has to be more pervasive for social services in other countries to get involved and remove children from their families. If a parent does place an older child for adoption, chances are the home life was far less than ideal for a parent to make this decision. Poverty alone may not explain why the child is placed. Therefore, the same issues that children have who are in foster care here in the United States are the same issues that children from other countries can carry with them as well.

10. *International adoptions can be the most expensive adoptions because, in addition to the agency's and the in-country fees, there are many expenses associated with traveling to another country, as well as immigration and visa fees.* For example, if a couple is adopting from Russia and must travel twice to the country, the airline tickets to Moscow can cost more than $5,000. Then if the couple travels to a region within Russia, the in-country flights can add up to another $3,000. Then if you add in hotel costs at $200 in Moscow for five nights, there is another $1,000, and hotel costs in a region could easily come to another

$1,000. A home study will usually be about $1,500 and immigration fees including the child's visa are about $1,000. Without even the cost of an adoption, a family could spend $12,500 just to travel and stay in Moscow and for fees related to the home study and citizenship and immigration services.

THE INTERNATIONAL ADOPTION PROCESS: EIGHTEEN STEPS

When adopting internationally, you must meet the requirements of your state of residence, the agency that is conducting your home study, the placing agency (if different from your home study agency), the United States government, and the foreign country. You cannot change the requirements that your state places on you, unless you move to another state, and you have no say in the requirements imposed by the United States. But you do have a choice in the agencies that you select and the country from which you adopt.

To adopt internationally, you will have to go through a number of steps, as shown in the following list and in the sections that follow it, which will explain each step further. It is not essential that you do every step in the order given here, but you should make sure that each one is properly completed.

1. Think carefully about your reasons for choosing an international adoption.
2. Gather information. Talk to others who have adopted internationally. Join a support group, if available, or check out what people are saying on the Internet. (Just don't take everyone's comments seriously—see if there is a consistent pattern.)
3. Decide on a country from which to adopt.
4. Select the type of organization to conduct your adoption.
5. Select a specific agency, organization, or facilitator.
6. Consider the age, sex, and race of the child you want to adopt.
7. Learn what "special needs" means in international adoption.
8. Satisfy your state's requirements for adoption through the home study.
9. Fulfill Citizenship and Immigration Services (CIS) requirements (formerly called INS).
10. Meet the requirements of your child's country of origin: collecting documents for your dossier.
11. Consider the child who is assigned to you or selected by you.
12. Commit to adopting a particular child.
13. Make travel arrangements to your child's country.
14. Meet your child.
15. Get to know your child.
16. Adopt your child in his country.

17. Complete the paperwork after the adoption and before returning home.
18. Bring your child home!

There are further steps you will have to take after bringing your child home. You will have to complete the final legal paperwork by readopting your child in the United States, making sure you have proof of his citizenship, obtaining your child's Social Security card, and sending final documentation to your child's birth country. You will also need to arrange for a medical evaluation.

#1: Think Carefully About Your Reasons

As you contemplate international adoption, you must recognize that if you are Caucasian, adopting a child from another country—unless it is a European country—probably means that the child is not going to look at all like you. If you adopt a child from Asia, for example, your family is entering into a transracial adoption. For a Caucasian couple, adopting an Asian child is certainly a different cultural experience from adopting an African-American/biracial child; yet there are many similarities. You and your spouse need to review some of the issues involved in entering into a transracial adoption before deciding to adopt a child from another country.

#2: Gather Information

First, you should talk to a few people who have adopted internationally. Ask what their experiences have been like. Most agency referrals are made this way. Satisfied clients tell others about their experience adopting a child from another country and the agency that they used. Your first two decisions are which country to adopt from and which agency to use. You may want to decide which countries you want to adopt from before you decide on an agency.

You will probably want to join a support group of parents who have adopted internationally and those looking to adopt. (See Appendix B for a list of support groups.) If no support group is available, you may want to use the Internet to link up with other people who have gone to the country from which you want to adopt. You may stay in touch with others who are using the same agency that you are so that you do not feel alone throughout this process.

Until the last few years, most families' primary means of sharing information with other adoptive families was through local adoption support groups. These groups are still very popular, especially for families once their children are home, since they provide a means for internationally adopted children to get together. If you attend an adoption support group, find out how people in the group adopted their children. Not only can they tell you the best agencies to use, they can also fill you in on all the little things you need to know about the process, the trip to the foreign country, what you need to pack, and what costs can be expected. Local support groups sometimes have speakers come in and discuss various aspects of international adoption. Agency personnel, for example, can offer very practical advice while promoting their services.

In addition to meeting people locally, you can now, through the Internet, join a group specifically related to the country program that you are considering or have selected. There are even Listserv groups for various topics within a country, such as children with special needs from China or groups based on the specific region you are adopting from in Russia.

Once you join a Listserv group, you can then find people in your own area if you want to meet in person with families adopting from a specific country. These are some of the greatest advocates of international adoption. These Listservs can also provide lots of practical advice. If, for example, you ask if you should bring a stroller to China, you will receive many e-mails giving you the pros and cons of strollers and what brands are best. To join such a group, go to Yahoo.com and search for *adoption support groups*. There are scores of groups with new ones being added.

The more information you gather, the better. Contact several agencies and ask them to send you their literature related to their program. Attend a few different agency meetings to find out what kinds of programs they offer and the countries in which they operate.

From the time that you decide to adopt internationally, it is important to have a complete understanding of the adoption procedure. Each country will be somewhat different, but many of the steps and documents required will be the same everywhere. You may be handling much of the paperwork yourself; regardless of what agency is responsible for it, you must keep close track of who has your paperwork, where it is, and where it must go. This means you take responsibility for getting your paperwork done and seeing that whoever is supposed to receive it has actually gotten it. You must be an advocate for yourself and your child.

There are hundreds of agencies and child placement entities in the United States that handle international adoptions, as well as a number of attorneys. You may want to decide which countries you want to adopt from before you decide on an agency. Most agencies or entities work with at least a few countries because one country may suddenly ban adoptions; no one agency can handle adoptions from every possible country. If you decide you want to adopt an Asian boy between the ages of three and five, you may want to work with an agency that has a China program or other Asian countries in which boys are available. If you want a Caucasian child, you will want to work with an agency that conducts adoptions in Russia and Eastern Europe.

#3: Decide on a Country

Because you must meet the requirements of a particular country, you will want to begin by investigating which countries will accept you and what kinds of children are available. In addition, you will want to know what the wait is for a child, travel requirements, and the expenses associated with adopting from that country.

A country's status can change quickly (whether or not it is allowing adoptions and its requirements for adoptive parents); getting up-to-date information is crucial. The agency or attorney working with you should be able to provide the information you need. You can also check the State Department Web site, which lists the laws, requirements, and procedures for adopting from different countries on the Internet. The Web site is *http://travel.state.gov/family/adoption_resources.html.*

The first variable you must consider is a country's policies regarding who can adopt. Agencies may have few requirements, but the country from which you seek to adopt may impose restrictions related to your age; marital status, including number of years you have been married; number of previous divorces; your weight; number of children you have; and your health issues or use of certain medications, such as antidepressants. Some countries require both parents to be U.S. citizens. Find out whether you will be accepted before you set your heart on adopting a child from a particular country.

The ages of the children available may vary widely by country. Some countries, such as Russia, do not allow children to be adopted until they are at least six to eight months old. If you want a very young baby, you will want to choose a country that has a policy of allowing children to be adopted without having to be on a registry or having artificial age requirements before being adopted.

Finding a reputable agency or facilitator to handle the adoption is crucial. If you can't find such a person or entity for a particular country, you will be better off looking elsewhere. Without the help of a professional, you can wait for a long time before a child is assigned to you or until the adoption of your child is completed.

To obtain the most comprehensive information about a country, you will need to make use of several resources. Find out what the country is like, what it is like to travel there, what to expect once you get there, and how easy it is to process the adoption papers once you are in the country. Second, read. Go to Web sites that address adoptions from that country. Borrow a few books and read up on the country's history and culture.

Expenses can be another issue. Most often the agency fee is just a fraction of the high cost of the adoption; the overall high cost arises from the fees of the in-country coordinator, the orphanage donation, traveling expenses, and required length of stay in the country. Agency fees do also vary quite drastically. Make sure you get an itemized list of all fees, including estimated traveling and lodging expenses. Some country programs, such as Guatemala, have a higher fee. But the expenses associated with the adoption are well outlined, and there are few surprises. Whereas if you adopt from a country that requires you to travel twice, the expenses associated with travel can be very high and not always predictable.

The section of this chapter titled "The Most Popular Countries and Regions" discusses the particular climate for adoption in numerous parts of the world.

#4: Select the Type of Organization to Conduct Your Adoption

International adoptions can be conducted by an adoption agency or by an individual facilitator or liaison, who is sometimes an attorney. You can also choose to handle the adoption process yourself. Your choices include:

An adoption agency that conducts international adoptions. Licensed adoption agencies in the United States can help you facilitate an adoption by providing guidance, direction, and contact people overseas. If you are adopting from certain countries, such as China, Kazakhstan, Korea, or Russia, the foreign country may require that only adoption agencies that are licensed (in your state or in another state) can administer the adoptions. They do not accept adoption facilitators. Also, these countries will not accept home studies by independent social workers.

Direct placement agencies are licensed both here in the United States and officially recognized in the foreign country. They maintain a direct relationship with the authorities to place international children directly with American families. These officially recognized agencies often are available to work with other licensed agencies in the United States. For example, there are about 100 licensed adoption agencies in the United States that have a direct agreement with China. If you work through an agency that does not have a direct agreement with China, your agency will process your adoption through one of the officially recognized agencies.

Therefore, if you select an agency that is not directly licensed in China, that agency must be working through an agency that is directly licensed in China. Usually the agency that is licensed in China will "split" its agency fee with the other agency that is not licensed in China. The second agency will be recruiting families and then will handle the clients' paperwork.

An agency's role in an adoption is to manage the paperwork, including the foreign application, assign a child to you, and communicate with those in the child's country. Many aspects of an adoption are out of an agency's control. For example, at different times in the last ten years, families waited for an assignment of a child from China from four months to more than twelve months. Regardless of what agency the families were working with, the wait was essentially the same for an assignment of a healthy baby from China.

Some agencies are only as good as their in-country contacts. If the in-country coordinator can conduct adoptions smoothly, then the agency has a "good" program.

Usually the success of a program is a hybrid between the agency and the in-country source. An agency that moves your paperwork through quickly, maintains good in-country resources, and is sympathetic to your needs is generally a good agency.

On the other hand, if you cannot reach your agency staff, the in-country coordinator is marginal in his ability to complete the work, and the staff does not take your concerns seriously, then you will not be happy with the program.

Regardless of how good the agency staff is and how efficient and knowledgeable the in-country coordinator may be, international adoptions can face bureaucratic delays.

Child placement facilitators, liaisons, and attorneys. Some individual facilitators, individual liaisons, and attorneys have contacts or sources in other countries and know how to proceed with an international adoption. Some of these liaisons are people who have adopted themselves, have learned what must be done, and are now assisting others to take the same route they have taken. They have established and maintained strong contacts in the foreign country and may work with contacts who prefer to work with an individual rather than an agency. Like agencies, these organizations handle the red tape and can help with the language barrier.

In many states, using a facilitator (rather than an agency) to conduct an international adoption is illegal, although it may be legal for you to use a facilitator in another state. For example, in South Carolina a facilitator cannot conduct adoptions nor can that person work for an agency outside the state of South Carolina. Yet, South Carolina residents can use a facilitator of international adoptions who resides in Kansas.

Parent-initiated international adoption. Some people do not use an agency or facilitators but instead coordinate the adoption themselves, which is called a "parent-initiated," "direct," or "independent" adoption. The prospective parents have a home study conducted by an agency or a certified home study provider, then take full responsibility for adopting a child.

A parent-initiated adoption can be less expensive than an agency adoption. Nonetheless, if you make mistakes along the way, the financial and emotional costs can be far greater.

Remember, no matter which method you select, you will have certain expenses: processing fees, a home study, translations, a donation to the orphanage in some cases, foreign attorney fees, airfare, and so on. If you are going to invest that much money, you may want to improve the likelihood that the process will go smoothly and spend the few thousand dollars more to have an agency handle the red tape. If you do decide to conduct an adoption independently, make sure you seek guidance from others who have preceded you. Join a support organization and talk to the people who have completed an adoption from the country where you plan to adopt.

Before you proceed with an independent adoption, you should certainly e-mail the U.S. Embassy of the country where you are thinking of adopting and find out what the requirements are for adopting a child from that country. If you have a particular child in mind, make sure she is legally eligible for adoption.

Here is the process you will probably follow: First, you will deal directly with a foreign child placement source. Your responsibilities will include fulfilling your state's requirements and getting a home study, sending your home study and documentation to the international source, assuming full responsibility for your child, and complying with CIS regulations, which are discussed later in this chapter.

Next, you will adopt your child in the foreign country. You must then also comply with CIS regulations before you can bring the child to the United States. The in-country facilitator should know what documents are required by both the child's country and the U.S. Embassy/Consulate.

#5: Select a Specific Agency, Organization, or Facilitator

To be sure of a given agency's or facilitator's credibility, call the adoption unit of your state and ask about the agency or the organization; if you can, talk to members of an adoption parent support group.

Agencies range in size from small local organizations to large national ones. As a rule, the safest and easiest way to adopt a child from another country is to involve an adoption agency in your state and to adopt the child through that agency. Of course, this is not always possible since some international adoption agencies handle only certain countries. If you want to adopt a child from a certain region of the world and the agencies in your state do not handle them or if the agency is very expensive, you will want to go through another agency. There are many agencies; gather lots of information from several of them before you decide.

When you call an agency, do not expect the staff to have time to cover every last question. Begin with general questions and ask to receive their literature. Once you decide what particular agency or organization you would like to work with, then you can begin to ask more in-depth questions that are not covered in its literature. Watch out for agencies or others who guarantee you something that no other agency can promise. Unrealistic expectations are the cause of much frustration in international adoption, and the agency should not set you up to have false expectations. If an agency says that all the children are healthy or says that the time to bring home a child is much shorter than information that you have heard from any other agency, beware.

Here are some questions to ask:

1. What countries does the agency work with, and what kinds of connections do they have with that country?
2. What criteria must you meet? (List the specific countries you are interested in adopting from.)
3. What services does the agency offer? Get very specific information; some agencies provide workshops, educational materials, and postplacement services.
4. Does the agency provide help with the paperwork, putting together a dossier, finding a translator, and making travel arrangements? What services does it help you obtain in the foreign country? Finding an interpreter and a lawyer?
5. How is the agency aware of the children who are available?
6. What are the adoption laws of the country?
7. Can the agency provide you with the names of families who have adopted there? With the names of professionals who work with the agency?
8. How many adoptions has the agency conducted in that country? (If you are looking to adopt in Korea and you are dealing with a large organization such as Holt, this is an unnecessary question.) Also, some programs are just opening up in certain countries. The key is for the agency or facilitator to be honest with you in stating what she does and does not know.
9. What are the fees and other expenses? Agency quotes can often vary by thousands of dollars. Some of this discrepancy can be explained by what the agency includes in the cost and what it omits. Some families create a grid—listing the "agency" fee, overseas facilitator's fee, and other expenses—in order to fairly compare the total cost of different agencies. Certain country programs such as Guatemala have what appear to be the highest fees. Yet, when you consider the few extra expenses associated with adopting from Guatemala and the fact that you have to be in the country for only a few days if you choose to travel, then the overall cost can be much lower than other programs.
10. How are monies for in-country expenses and fees handled? Foreign country fees should, as a rule, be deposited into a separate escrow account and released by the agency as needed. In most cases, there should be no need to take large sums of cash with you.
11. What can be known about a child's health and background? In most countries, little may be known about the child's family. If this information is not usually available, the agency should say so.
12. Must you and your spouse travel to the country, and if so, for how long? Not only are you losing time from your employment, but also staying in another country—even a "third world" country—can be very expensive.

13. How long can you expect to wait for a child to be assigned to you once you complete your paperwork and receive approval from CIS?

#6: Consider the Sex, Age, and Race of the Child You Want to Adopt

Here are some of the things you will want to consider before adopting:

Boy or girl? Why are more girls adopted than boys? In 1996, 64 percent of the children adopted by Americans were girls. Part of this high percentage is due to the fact that China, which places mostly girls for adoption, was the most popular country from which to adopt.

The availability of more girls from China—which accounted for more than 6,000 of the 21,600 plus adoptions in 2003—explains these percentages, but agencies report that couples request to adopt girls much more often than they request boys. Often families who already have boys will want to adopt girls. This is understandable. But why is there not the same number of families with only girls seeking to adopt boys?

In fact, many families choose international adoption over a domestic adoption because they can definitely know that they can adopt girls. Sometimes people feel that girls are easier to handle and cuter to dress. Yes, couples expecting biological children also express these same reasons for wanting girls, but many express their desire for boys. Perhaps, families want a boy to carry on the family name and value system and do not think of adopting children for those same reasons.

Another reason more girls may be placed is that international adoption is usually a single person's first choice. Because most singles adopting are women, who usually seek to adopt a same-sex child, it is only natural that more girls would be placed with singles.

Except for China, more boys are usually available than girls. If you do not have a strong preference for a female child, then seriously consider adopting a boy. If you cannot consider adopting a boy, perhaps you need to ask yourself why.

If you feel that you can only accept a girl from a particular country because of the child's ethnicity or race, remember that child may someday have sons who will be your grandsons. Certainly you have the right to request whatever sex you desire, and the agency should not judge you. Nonetheless, for your sake and the child's, you may need to examine why you feel that you must adopt a girl.

The child's age. Adopting an older child is invariably more of a challenge but has its own joys as well. When adopting an international older child in particular, you will get to see firsthand your child's delight in many of his "firsts" with you. These may include his first bicycle ride, elevator ride, car travel, pizza, McDonald's, listening to CDs, watching TV, and having a pet. Your family may offer other unique experiences such as going to the lake, trips to the beach, horseback riding, living on a farm, or living in a high-rise apartment.

An older child can help the whole family see their everyday experiences in a new light. Also, the older child can quickly enter into a family's activities. Parents describe how they enjoy having a child to go to ball games with, to the beach, or even to the grocery store. With an older child, your focus can be on enjoying your child's experience, rather than on caring for an infant or toddler's many needs.

Of course, not every older child fits in easily, and there can be significant concerns in adopting older children. The first issue to be addressed can be to determine your child's exact age. Malnutrition and lack of emotional attention can influence growth; tooth eruption and head circumference are sometimes the only measurements available to estimate age. If the child was abandoned, moreover, her history before being placed in an orphanage or with a foster family can be completely unknown.

If she has been raised in an orphanage, she may be very developmentally delayed. Such a child may have a host of emotional and behavioral problems—including a possible attachment disorder. Unlike the adoption of a child with special needs in the United States, where his background is likely to be well documented, in an international adoption, the child's background may be unknown or undisclosed.

Many families select older children from photolisting sites. On the other hand, the agency may assign a child to you. They will provide any known background information and a health report on her. It is expected when you are considering the adoption of an older child that you will want as much detail as possible about the child that you adopt. This can be a similar process to adopting an older child in the United States. You will see a picture of the child and possibly a videotape. Once you select a child, he will be tentatively assigned to you before you travel to the country. At that time, you will be told more about him—his likes and dislikes, temperament, learning ability, and any health problems.

It is highly recommended—although not always practical—that you visit with the child when he is assigned to you and before you make a 100 percent commitment to the adoption and then make a second trip when all the paperwork is completed and it is time to complete the adoption. Some parents do not want to proceed with the adoption of a particular older child once they meet him in person; this usually occurs when the child has more profound medical or emotional problems than the parents had anticipated.

The race/ethnicity of the child. As stated previously, about 75 percent of all international adoptions have historically been of Asian children. Now, at least 50 percent of all children adopted internationally are of Asian or Hispanic origin. If you are adopting such a child, you must recognize that your child will most likely look different from you, and therefore, you and your family will face certain issues that all transracial/transethnic families face. (See Chapter 16 for more on transracial adoption.)

It is very important regardless of where your child is from that he feels that you value his culture. If your child looks very different from you, it is also important that your child be exposed to other children who look like him.

Interestingly, Caucasian families do not necessarily consider the fact when they seek to adopt a child from Latin America or Asia that they are adopting across ethnic/racial lines. Others will contact an international adoption agency and say that they are not concerned about the race of the child; their main goal is to adopt a child. If you are considering adopting internationally and you are comfortable adopting a child of any race, you may first consider an African-American child in the United States. The first place to consider adopting such a child would be through the foster care system. If one considers that more than 100,000 children need a permanent home and almost 60 percent of the children in the foster care system are black or Hispanic, that means more than 60,000 children could be available, and one of these may be your child.

#7: Learn What "Special Needs" Means in International Adoption

Just as there are thousands of special needs children in the United States waiting to be adopted, so it is in countries around the world. Sometimes only children who are considered to have a special need are permitted by the placing country to be eligible for adoption. The officials in charge of an orphanage may classify a child as having a health problem just so he can be released for adoption. If the child is not given one of the handful of diagnoses which will place him on the list of available children for adoption, he will not be considered "special needs."

Unlike in the United States, usually a child's background is not one of the criteria in labeling a child as having a special need. For example, if a child entered an orphanage after being abused and neglected by the birth family, this fact is not part of the "special needs" list. There are three basic criteria that usually will qualify an internationally adopted child as having special needs:

1. *The child is older.* Because finding adoptive homes for older children is more difficult, the agency and in-country facilitator may view an older child as being special needs.
2. *The child is part of a sibling group.* Sometimes children are available only as siblings since an agency, orphanage, or government may be opposed to breaking up the family unit. There are distinct advantages to adopting sibling groups: The children may have an easier time adjusting because they "have each other,"

and you can grow your family faster than if you adopt singly. Adopting more than one child at a time can be far less expensive in the long run, too, especially when you consider traveling expenses.

If you are considering adopting siblings or more than one child at the same time while you are in another country, your home study must qualify you for the exact number of children you wish to adopt. Just because you are qualified to adopt one child does not mean you are qualified to adopt a sibling group of three. A social worker doing the home study will want to know how many other children you already have, what experience you have with children if you do not have any children, your extended support system, how large your home is and how many bedrooms it has, and whether your income can support a larger family.

Some families request the "ideal" situation: a baby under one year old and an older sibling who is about two years old. Such a sibling group, however, is seldom available. To have two children who are available in that situation usually means that a birth mother relinquished a newborn infant and the child's older sibling or that a two-year-old child is in the orphanage after waiting two years for an adoptive family and now his baby sister is in the orphanage.

If you have no children, you may be tempted to adopt two or three siblings. You may have longed for children for some time, and now you feel you are ready to settle down into a large family. Yet, you need to think hard about the impact this decision will have on your life. Adding just one child to a childless home changes life completely. Babies are a lot of work, but they do sleep a lot. It is possible to adjust to their schedule. If you suddenly find yourself with three children under five years old, you will have young children all going through a cultural adjustment while you yourself are going through a major life adjustment. If you plan to be a stay-at-home parent, staying at home and caring for children will be pretty much your life. Lots of people, of course, have three children close in age, but they've had time to "grow" with the job—their children are not making the cultural and emotional adjustments that yours will be.

This is not to discourage you from considering siblings but only to help you think about what it might involve. Actually, the decision to adopt sibling groups can be good for you and certainly for the children. A study shows that international children who are adopted as siblings actually have fewer disruptions and behavior problems than those adopted singly. If you are seriously considering this option, we suggest you offer to have two or three of your nieces and nephews over for a few days or more and see how you cope. If it feels manageable and you have good support systems and the financial resources to meet their needs, ask your social worker to approve you for up to the number of children you want to adopt at the same time. The CIS does not place restrictions on the number of children you can adopt as long as you have sufficient income or assets to meet the needs of the children.

3. *The child has a correctable or noncorrectable medical condition.* Usually special needs are divided into two categories: correctable and noncorrectable. Correctable are usually mild developmental delays or physical problems that can be corrected with surgery, such as club foot or cleft palate. Noncorrectable problems include missing limbs, deafness and blindness, and more profound mental disabilities.

Many families choose to adopt a child with medical problems that are correctable here in the United States. These same conditions can be life-threatening to a child in a third world country—and perhaps worse. If the condition is not life-threatening, the child is destined to be an outcast the rest of his life.

In some areas, a cleft palate can result in a child being very malnourished and therefore underdeveloped and more prone to diseases. If the child is able to get sufficient nourishment without corrective surgery, it could mean that the child can never fully enter into society and be a productive adult. However, if a child has cleft palate in the United States, he can have surgery so the condition is not even recognizable and go on to live a complete and successful life.

In some countries, the stipulations as to who can adopt may be very narrow, and only those adopting a child with a medical condition may have the restrictions broadened. If you want to adopt in a particular country and you do not qualify because of an arbitrary guideline, you may indicate that you are willing to adopt a child with a "minor, correctable disability or health condition."

#8 and #9: Satisfy Your State's Requirements for Adoption and the CIS Requirements

When adopting, you must satisfy the requirements of the home study agency, the placing agency (if different from your home study agency), your state's regulations, the U.S. requirements as established through the Citizenship and Immigration Services, and the foreign country from which you want to adopt. Most home study agencies' requirements are based on the state's requirements. The following must be satisfied in order for you to adopt:

An approved home study. When pursuing an international adoption, you will probably have two home study reports: one that meets the requirements of your state and the CIS and another usually shorter version for the country in which you will be adopting.

The home study needs to include a child abuse clearance through your department of social services, in addition to a criminal clearance through the FBI. The documents that must accompany a home study are determined by the state in which you live. An agency can add additional requirements.

Many of the documents required for your home study are the same or similar to the ones required by the country from which you are adopting. If original documents are kept by your home study agency, be sure to get these documents in multiples if also needed by the country from which you are adopting. The documents usually required to accompany an international home study are generally the same as for a domestic adoption.

The CIS requires that your home study indicate whether or not you have a history of substance abuse, sexual or child abuse, or domestic violence, even if no arrests have been made. If there is a history, you must document how the issues have been resolved. The home study must also include whether or not you have been rejected as a prospective adoptive parent or have had an unfavorable home study in the past. If you have, you must explain why and how you are addressing past problems. If you seek to adopt a child with special needs, your home study must state that fact. Finally, a summary of the preadoption counseling you have received must be included in the home study. It should state that the counseling included a discussion of the international adoption process and its possible expenses, difficulties, and delays.

Begin your home study process as soon as possible; it can sometimes take a few months to complete, especially if there are only a few licensed agencies in your state that can conduct home studies. If your state permits certified individual home study providers to conduct home studies, make sure that the country from which you are adopting and the child placement agency will accept a home study from a nonagency professional. For example, China and Russia only permit licensed adoption agencies and not individual certified social workers to submit home studies.

In selecting an agency or certified home study investigator, check that the person doing the home study is familiar with the requirements of the Citizenship and Immigration Services, the agency you will be working with, and the country from which you will be adopting. The agency hired to conduct your home study will usually not place restrictions on you beyond those imposed by the CIS and your state. If you are fifty years old, for example, and both the country from which you are adopting and the child-placement agency accepts applicants of this age, then the agency conducting your home study most likely will permit you to adopt. If you feel that the home study agency believes those over a certain age should not adopt, then you need to find this out before you start the process with them.

If you are adopting through an agency in your state, then usually that agency will also conduct your home study.

The CIS will accept only a home study that has been completed within the last six months. If you already have a home study, the original agency or investigator may have to be contacted to visit with you in your home and update the study. Although there is a charge to do this, it is not the same cost as a full home study. It is not legal for another agency simply to add information and then "sign off" on another agency or investigator's home study. You must have a home study conducted by an agency or social worker in your state of residence.

The home study that goes to the country from which you are adopting is usually shorter than the one sent to CIS and contains fewer details. If there are any sensitive issues in your home study, be sure to discuss this with your home study agency and ask if they are willing to leave such information out of your dossier home study that is going overseas. Be very careful that you are not in any way implying that you want the home study provider to lie about you. Leaving information out is not lying. Making a false statement is lying. Also, if a country has very specific rules as to who can adopt, such as China, which requires no more than four children at home, then there should be no deception as to how many children you have.

The CIS is very strict about what needs to be included in a home study. Yet, they very seldom reject families based on the information presented. The CIS's intent is to make sure that the family has dealt with issues from the past—not to keep families from adopting. Therefore, the home study agency must include much information in a CIS home study that is often too sensitive to send to other countries' authorities.

For example, if your home study discusses a less than perfect childhood or indicates that one of your siblings has a psychiatric history, leave that information out of the shorter home study going overseas. Also, if you have a health problem that is controlled through medical technology (but would be fatal or incapacitating in a third world country), be sure the home study provider uses very careful wording when addressing this issue.

For instance, if an adoptive parent has a condition such as multiple sclerosis and it is controlled by medication, the home study provider can simply write that the adoptive parent has the condition and that it is controlled by medication. The report should also include the types of activities that the parent engages in, so that it is clear that the parent can properly care for the child.

In addition to asking home study agency staff how they handle sensitive issues, ask them if they will approve you to adopt more than one child, if this is your desire. Some agencies will not permit families to adopt multiple children who are not related to each other. They feel that each child should be allowed to come home and adjust first to his new home environment before a second child arrives. They may also feel that families have a more difficult time adjusting to multiple children. These same agencies, on the other hand, permit siblings to be adopted together.

Many agencies are opposed to families adopting two children who are close in age. Some adoptive families want to adopt two babies at the same time; these babies may be just a few days to a few months apart. Some professionals feel that it will be too much for these children to have to explain why they are sister and brother and not more than nine months apart in age. Some feel this means that throughout their lives they will be explaining that they are adopted.

Although a family should consider the ramifications of adopting more than one child and the added issues associated with the children being very close in age, families must also realize that adopted children who do not look like their parents or their other siblings will probably already be explaining why they look different from other members of their family. Having two children close in age will be just one more element in growing up in a "conspicuous" family.

If you feel strongly that you want to adopt two children who are unrelated, then you must first make sure that the home study agency as well as the placing agency will approve this.

Approval from the placing agency. It is very difficult for a home study agency to give someone an unfavorable home study or to disapprove them outright. For a family to be denied a home study would mean that the family lacked the social, emotional, or financial resources to parent or had a serious or recent criminal history. A home study provider cannot arbitrarily reject a family. The agency is permitted to add further criteria before approving a family, such as counseling, if they suspect that the family has some issues that need to be addressed. It is the home study provider's responsibility to restrict the number, ages, and types of children the family can adopt.

Yet, even when a home study provider is fairly restrictive as to the types and number of children a family can adopt, there are certain children who fall within the approved categories that may not be appropriate for a family to adopt. Then it is up to the placing agency to decide what program or ultimately what child may be best for a family.

For example, a family may be approved to adopt up to three children with minor or correctable health problems or developmental delays. Yet, this family may not have the financial and other resources to parent three children who all have cleft palates that require extensive surgery. When a family is matched with a child who has special needs or is older, the placing agency staff should consult with the home study agency staff as to whether the assignment is a good fit for all parties involved. After all, it is the home study provider who has personally met with the family.

In addition to restricting the type of child (or children) a family is assigned, the placing agency may restrict a family as to the country they adopt from. For instance, a home study approved family who is very cautious and who does not adjust well to change or to germs probably is not best suited for an adoption program in which they will be in a small village overseas in a third-rate hotel for several weeks.

Approval from Citizenship and Immigration Services. Citizenship and Immigration Services (CIS) is the U.S. government agency (under the Department of Homeland Security) that oversees the immigration of any foreigner into the United States, including children adopted abroad. The CIS wants to ensure that you are suitable as a parent, as indicated by your home study, and that you have no serious criminal history or valid child abuse history. One adoptive parent must be a U.S. citizen, and the citizen must be the petitioner. The noncitizen must be a legal immigrant. The CIS requires that all members of the household eighteen years and older obtain FBI clearance. Therefore, you will be fingerprinted at one of your local CIS offices. The fingerprint clearance is good for only fifteen months after your fingerprints are cleared (which is usually a few days after they are taken).

One of the first steps to take in your adoption process is to file the I-600A form "Advance Processing of an Orphan Petition." You will submit this form to the CIS office that has jurisdiction over you. Ask your home study provider which CIS office to mail the I-600A form to. Regardless if you are just starting the process or if you have a specific child whom you are seeking to adopt, you will file the I-600A. Do not file the I-600.

You will need to submit this form with the following documents:

- A check for the one-time filing fee of $525, plus $70 for each adult eighteen and over in the home for fingerprinting fees. The fees go up regularly; check with your agency as to the exact fee.
- Birth certificate of each petitioner (husband and wife). These can be copies, but they must be copies of a certified document.
- Marriage certificate, if married. These can be copies, but they must be copies of a certified document.
- Divorce decree(s), if applicable. These can be copies, but they must be copies of a certified document.
- A certified court disposition of any crime that has been committed, no matter how minor. This includes misdemeanors or any time that you have been fingerprinted in relation to a crime, even if you have been shown not to be involved in any way.
- A signed and notarized letter from you, if you have been involved in any "crime," explaining the circumstances of the crime. If you were found

guilty, you must indicate that you are contrite and how you have been "reformed."

After you file your I-600A, your home study is filed at the same CIS location. You will be fingerprinted at a CIS office as indicated on the permission paper given to you after you file the I-600A.

As of October 1995, CIS requires child abuse clearance on all those adopting, unless your state does not provide this service. Your home study provider will most likely ask you to sign a form, which she will process with the social services department in your state. This is to determine if you have a child abuse or neglect history in your state only. Because there is no national child abuse or neglect registry, your social worker could require you to have a child abuse or neglect clearance in other states in which you have lived.

Once your home study and FBI clearance are received by the CIS adoption unit, you will be approved by CIS. CIS may approve ("adjudicate") your case in a few days or in a few months. The time varies from one office to another, usually based on the number of staff members. The CIS will send your approval, the I-171H (sometimes called the I-797), to you by regular mail. This is very important—this is your approval notice! The letter sometimes is printed on green-shaded card stock or on plain white paper and looks more like a copy than an important document. Therefore, it is very important that you watch carefully for the arrival of this document and immediately make copies of it.

The best way to deal with the CIS is to be sure that you do everything correctly the first time. For example, if you fail to sign a form or if you send the wrong amount of money, your application will be rejected, and your time for approval can be delayed.

If you have any questions or experience delays with your CIS office, you may contact the office by phone or fax. If you cannot reach the CIS, ask your agency staff to contact the office. However, some offices are nearly impossible to reach—even by a professional adoption agency—and you may have to contact your congressman's or senators' immigration liaison staff person to advocate on your behalf.

When completing the I-600A form, either spouse can put his or her name in question #1, as the main petitioner, as long as the spouse is a U.S. citizen. If only one spouse will be traveling, it is better to put this person as the main petitioner. If you check off that you want to adopt more than one child, be sure that your home study also approves you for the same number of children.

FBI clearance. All those adopting internationally must be cleared through the FBI. The FBI will run your fingerprints through their computer databases to see if you have any type of criminal background. The CIS requires that the fingerprints used for FBI clearance be taken only at designated CIS offices, which are usually the offices closest to you. Your fingerprints are sent electronically to the FBI and are "cleared"—usually within twenty-four to forty-eight hours—and then sent back to CIS electronically. Your approval and date of FBI clearance are then cabled to the U.S. Embassy/Consulate that will issue your child's visa in the foreign country.

If you mail your I-600A form to CIS, the CIS will send you a letter permitting you to get fingerprinted at the designated CIS site for your jurisdiction, or in some instances, you may turn in your I-600A form at a local CIS office if you make an appointment online. To visit any CIS office, you must first go to *http://infopass. uscis.gov* to make an appointment online. Once you go the office, the CIS staff will give you a receipt and a letter giving you permission to immediately get fingerprinted at the CIS offices that provides fingerprinting services. Check with your home study provider as to the exact procedure in your state. This can vary greatly from one location to another, even within a state.

You may want to wait until your home study is nearly completed before having your fingerprints taken by CIS since your FBI clearance is valid for only fifteen months. Therefore, your FBI clearance will expire before your CIS approval expires. Some CIS offices will not permit you to have your fingerprints taken until after your home study has been submitted to the CIS office. Some CIS offices only have this rule if you are adopting from China, in which case the wait for an assignment of a child can take from six to twelve months, and therefore, your FBI clearance may expire before you receive your child's visa. The date when your FBI clearance expires is usually typed onto your I-171H. Keep very careful track of such expiration dates.

If you must have your fingerprints taken again, you do not have to resubmit any other supporting documentation such as a court disposition, if you have a "criminal" history. It is wise, however, to submit a copy of your I-171H when you request to have your fingerprints retaken for FBI clearance. There is a fee per person to be fingerprinted again.

Let's look and see when documents will expire. You submit your I-600A on September 5, 2007; you go to your CIS office to be fingerprinted on October 19, 2007; your home study agency submits your home study to CIS on November 29, 2007; and you receive CIS immigration approval December 15, 2007. The FBI clearance, which takes about 48 hours after having fingerprints taken, will expire on January 21, 2009. Your CIS immigration approval is valid until June 14, 2009. Therefore, if your child's visa is not issued before January 21, 2009, then you will need to have your fingerprints taken again and obtain the results. If your child's visa is not issued before your CIS immigration approval expires, you will need to have a new home study with updated supporting documentation and have a new

I-171H issued. Fees must be paid for each step that must be redone. If and when you obtain FBI clearance again, the CIS office does not notify you of the clearance. The overseas U.S. Embassy is notified by your CIS immigration office that the fingerprints have been cleared. Sometimes this information is sent but not "received." You will want to check with the overseas U.S. Embassy/Consulate to make sure that they have your clearance.

Note: You will never receive the results of your FBI check; neither will your adoption agency nor the foreign government. If you have any type of criminal background for which you have been fingerprinted, even if you were not guilty or if it is only a seemingly minor infraction such as nonpayment of a small check that happened when you closed your bank account and joined the Army, you must still obtain a court disposition from the courthouse where the hearing took place. If no hearing took place, there must be a statement indicating this, noting the "crime" for which you were arrested. If the crime was committed several years ago, the crime most likely will not be on record. If there is no record, you must obtain a statement from the court stating that there is no record. If the court disposition is not sent with the I-600A, then the court disposition must be sent to CIS along with your home study. It is best to get two original certified dispositions in case one gets lost at CIS. Sometimes obtaining a court disposition can require more than a simple telephone call from you. Your agency may need to be involved. If the agency staff does not get a response from the court, then your attorney may need to get involved.

Help from your congressional office (if necessary). Many times in adoption, clients need to ask their congressman's immigration liaison person to get involved. Some Immigration offices cannot be reached by just picking up the telephone and calling the adoption unit. If you need to know right away if all the right cables have reached the U.S. Embassy overseas, you may not be able to e-mail the adoption section of the Consular office there. Calling may prove to be more difficult. This is not to say that all Immigration offices and U.S. Embassies and Consulates around the world are not responsive. Some staff write or call right back within a day or so. However, when dealing with some Immigration offices or embassies/consulates, you could wait weeks before you get a response. Therefore, you may need to get your congressional or senatorial office's staff to reach these offices for you. Most congressional and senatorial office staff are very helpful. Some are not. You do have a choice of three offices: your congressman's office and your two senators' offices. It is usually better to call the local offices and not the Washington, DC offices of your representatives.

Explain to the immigration liaison in your representative's office what you need. You may need to get your agency to write an explanation that can be faxed to the representative's office. Your representative's staff, however, is usually not interested in speaking with your adoption agency staff, unless the agency is in your district or state. You are the voting constituent—not the agency.

If you feel that you are not getting good service from one of your representative's staff, move on to another office. Do not contact all three offices at the same time; this can result in triplicate work and most likely will upset all parties involved, especially the government agency (e.g., your CIS office) that is being contacted.

Also, before you ask the immigration liaison in your representative's office to contact your Immigration office on your behalf, be sure that the Immigration office will not take revenge on you. Ask your home study agency about this matter. One Immigration office is known for its nearly draconian policies: If you have your congressional rep contact them, your case is placed at the bottom of the pile. On the other hand, one Immigration office was notorious for not sending out approvals until the adoptive parents' congressional reps were involved.

Your congressional representatives can almost never be involved in any difficulties that you may have with a foreign government's adoption policies. For example, your congressman's staff cannot contact someone in Russia to speed up the process of an adoption.

A form for changing countries (if necessary). If you have been approved by CIS to adopt from a specific country and later decide to adopt from a different country, you will need to file form I-824 to transfer your I-171H approval to another country and to have your Immigration office cable your approval to the appropriate overseas U.S. Embassy/Consulate. The fee for filing this form is currently $195.00. This form can be found at the CIS Web site.

#10: Meet the Requirements of Your Child's Country of Origin

When you adopt, the country from which your child is adopted will require certain documents to be submitted so that they can also "know" who you are. This is called your "dossier." Your dossier is the centerpiece of your adoption. It is a collection of official documents about you and your family. The required documents vary from country to country but generally include birth certificates, marriage license, physicians' letters, and police clearances. The documents sent to the foreign country are reviewed by the government officials, judges, orphanage directors, or others who will ascertain your ability to be a good parent. Having a completed home study and approval from CIS is not enough. Each country wants to see other supporting documents.

Some of the information contained in these documents is straightforward. Your birth certificate is your birth certificate; there is no flexibility in how that is presented. Still, other documents, such as the physician's letter, must be carefully worded.

The dossier may seem like an endless paper chase while you are assembling it but do not underestimate the importance of doing it well. Your adoption will not be finalized until your dossier is complete. Most often, your dossier documents can be completed before you receive your I-171H from CIS. It is a good idea to begin working on it as soon as possible.

Few people really like to complete forms. If you are someone who cannot even stand to complete a credit card application, you will want to select an agency that leads you through the process, reviews your forms, and handles much of the processing for you.

Try to obtain two sets of every document—especially vital records. It will cost a little extra, but there is no more effort involved in getting four birth certificates than in getting one. Keep a set of originals in your possession at all times. If a document gets lost, you always have the extra one, and you won't fall a few weeks behind in the adoption process.

The following documents are likely to be required of you for your dossier or in the adoption process:

The dossier home study. As mentioned earlier, two home study reports will be produced: the home study that is sent to CIS (the CIS home study) and the home study that is sent to your child's country, the "dossier home study." The dossier home study is the key document in your international adoption.

It is essential before you select a home study agency that you have an understanding with them that if there is sensitive information in your background, the home study provider will carefully word or omit in your dossier home study certain facts that must be included in your CIS home study. Not all agencies will do this; you need to ask them about this before you choose the agency that will conduct your home study. For example, CIS requires that any type of "crime" be reported to them—even if it is clear that you were not guilty or if a crime was committed in your youth. These types of incidences, addressed in a dossier home study, may cause a rejection or delays in the adoption proceedings by the authorities in the placing country. After all, the foreign officials, unlike the officials at CIS, do not get to see your FBI report, which indicates not only the charges, but also if the charges have been cleared.

Additionally, certain crimes committed when you were young have little or no bearing on your ability to parent. If you were convicted of a DUI when you were eighteen years old, this fact mentioned in a dossier home study could keep you from adopting in certain countries. Instead of stating such a fact in a dossier, the home study could read that according to the police report, Mr. Smith has no criminal record in Monroe County.

Certain diseases or taking certain medications such as Prozac could keep a country from approving you. Again, the home study could state that according to

Dr. Hall, Mr. Smith is in good physical and mental health and takes medicine to control elevated cholesterol so that his cholesterol levels are well within a normal range.

Although certain facts from your background may not cause you to be rejected, there is no need for a home study provider to include in a dossier home study the fact that you were sexually abused or that one of your parents was an alcoholic. Although these facts need to be included in a CIS home study, these facts do not need to be sent in a home study that may go to the Secretary of State, a country's embassy, and then on to the country itself.

Also, if you belong to a religious sect, such as the Mennonites, you may want to have the home study simply say that you are Christian and not go into detail about your distinctive denomination. It is sometimes difficult to predict how those in other countries are going to perceive others who express their faith more openly or differently from what is considered the "norm."

Vital records. You will need to obtain certified copies of your birth certificate, spouse's birth certificate, marriage license, and any divorce decrees or death certificates of former spouses. "Certified copies" are issued with a seal on them and a signature of the person who is now in charge of vital records for the state in which the document was issued. For birth certificates, this is the state where you were born; for marriage licenses, this is the state where you were married, etc. You can order vital records from *www.vitalchek.org.*

It is best to order at least two copies of each of your vital records. They can usually be ordered quickly online using a credit card. Many people have birth certificates and marriage certificates at home and ask if they can use those for their dossier. In general, the answer is "no" because the foreign country wants to see a certification date on the document that is under one year old. Also, many of these documents are obtained from a local health department and are not certified.

Certified birth certificate. Be sure to order "certified" long forms with a "live" signature. Sometimes your children's birth certificates will be required for the home study.

Certified marriage certificate. When you filled out your marriage certificate, most likely you were required to indicate if this is your first, second, or third marriage and so forth. Therefore, if divorce decrees are required for the dossier, be sure that you have a divorce decree for each of your former marriages!

Divorce decree and certified death certificate. Usually you can order a divorce decree from Vital Records in the state in which it was issued. Sometimes, if the divorce was more recent, the divorce record may not have been sent to Vital Records yet, and it must be ordered from the clerk of court where the decree was issued. Because divorce decrees can contain much sensitive information, you may want to request a divorce certificate that looks like a marriage certificate or birth certificate. You can send this document to the foreign country. If a former spouse has died, order a death certificate from your state's Vital Statistics department.

Medical statements/letter from your physician. Usually the medical statement or letter from your physician indicates that your health is appropriate for parenting and may include the dates of your last physical exams. A home study agency cannot disapprove you because you have had certain diseases including mental illness or because you are HIV positive. They can only disapprove you if your medical condition would keep you from appropriately and safely parenting a child.

On the other hand, a medical report that indicates certain illnesses can keep a country's authorities from approving you. Check with your physician on how he would write a medical report if you feel that certain information should be very carefully phrased in the letter that will be sent to the foreign country. If you have a medical condition that would keep you from adopting in another country, it is best to find this out beforehand.

Some countries, such as China, require a medical form to be completed. On this form, a physician would most likely be required to indicate if you are taking psychotropic drugs, such as medication for depression, anxiety, or a bipolar disorder. It is one thing for a physician to write that you are in good physical and mental health. It is another matter for a physician to write "none" by a statement when asked what medication you are now taking. If the physician indicates you are on such medication, most likely you will be denied from adopting, especially if the medication is being used for depression or anxiety, instead of perhaps to control periodic headaches.

If the physician's medical report is also being used as a document for your dossier, most countries want the medical report to include a statement from your physician that you can expect to have a full life span; are in good mental health; have no communicable diseases; are not infected with the HIV virus (you may have to take an AIDS test); and do not use illicit drugs or abuse alcohol.

If you are just beginning to gather all of your documents and are still exploring from which country you may be adopting and you are in good health, you may want to wait until you have gathered all of your other documents before getting a medical exam. Then at the time that you get the physical exam, ask the physician to complete the letter or specific form as required by the country from which you are adopting. All letters and some forms need to be on the doctor's letterhead, and the document should be signed by a physician and then notarized.

Sometimes clients ask if a nurse, nurse practitioner, or physician's assistant can sign the letter. In order not to create confusion or to have a possible delay in your adoption, it is best to always have letters signed by a physician.

Some countries also require a copy of your physician's medical license.

Police clearance letter. Most likely you will be required to obtain a state police clearance for your home study. This is not the same as being fingerprinted, although some states, such as New Jersey, do require adoptive parents to be fingerprinted as part of the home study process so that the family can receive FBI clearance. Also, the country from which you are adopting will require either local or state criminal clearance confirming that you and your spouse have no criminal records. When you ask an official to sign this letter, ask that it also be notarized. If you are fingerprinted by the police department in your state, you must also be fingerprinted by the CIS office.

Letter to the agency or entity who is finding your child. As part of your dossier, some countries require you to write a brief description of yourselves, any children you may have, and the kind of child you wish to adopt, including their age, sex (if you have a preference), and any medical conditions you are willing to accept. This type of letter is required for the China dossier. Although it is acceptable to mention that you believe in God or that you go to church/temple, your letter should not have strong religious overtones.

Financial statements. When submitting any financial information, such as your IRS 1040 form or statements from your employer and your bank, be sure that your numbers match. In other words, if you tell your home study provider that you earn $70,000 per year, make sure your employment letter(s) also states this as well.

Bank statement. A statement from your bank or other financial institution in which you have deposits, usually providing the following details:

- The date the account was opened
- The total amount deposited during the last year
- Your current balance

It is not expected that you have much money in your checking or savings accounts since interest rates are so low, and it is understood that your funds would be in a mutual fund or 401(k).

Employment letter. A statement from your employer on business stationery that provides the following:

- The date and nature of your employment
- Your salary
- Whether your position is permanent or temporary. Some employers will not put this in writing, but try to get a statement that states your future employment is positive.

If you are self-employed, usually you must provide a letter from a CPA indicating your salary and expected earnings.

I-171H CIS approval. This is your "Notice of Favorable Determination" and is sometimes also referred to as an I-797. Before you can adopt a child from another country, you must get permission from the CIS.

Letters of reference. In most instances, your home study provider will require that you submit at least three letters of reference from those who have known you at least one year. Sometimes letters of reference are required for your dossier as well. Depending upon your state laws or the agency's policies, you will be required either to gather the documents yourself or provide the names and addresses of the references, and the agency staff will contact the references directly so that the reference letter is not necessarily seen by you. If you are asking someone to write a letter to accompany your home study, the letters usually should include how long the person knew you, how they know you, what your positive characteristics are, and why you would be good parents to an adopted child. If you are already parents, the reference should mention what good parents you are now and how well loved another child will be in your home. Ask others never to use the term "children of their own." For example, they should never say, "They will love an adopted child as much as their own children."

If your letters of reference will be sent to another country, mention your religion or faith described in terms of practicing your faith, but you should not go into much detail. Certainly someone saying you teach a Sunday School class at your church is acceptable. Because many countries that place children for adoption have a strong history of communism, Buddhism, or Hinduism, your having a strong faith can lead officials to believe that the child will be losing a strong part of his heritage.

Pictures of applicants. Most dossiers sent overseas include pictures of the applicants in front of their home, as well as individual, close-up photos of each member of your family. You will usually need two family pictures and two of your home for your dossier. In these pictures, it is better not to include pets. Also, you should not be lying down, smoking, or drinking what is obviously an alcoholic beverage. Dress only in modest clothing, and it is better not to wear shorts unless at the beach since in many countries shorts are considered beachwear.

Passports. An adult passport is valid for ten years; you will want to get one while you are completing all the other paperwork. In many countries, your passport number is your identifying number; therefore, both spouses should get a passport, even if only one spouse will be traveling. Some countries require you to submit copies of the first page (photo/data page) of your passport. The exact name on your passport is the name that you should use on nearly all of the other documents and forms that you are submitting.

Statement of residence. This is a form that indicates you live at a certain place and rent or own the home and includes a description of the home. You may be required to get a statement from your city or county clerk's office to fulfill this requirement.

Legalization of documents for your dossier. Most countries require that your dossier documents be notarized by a notary public. A notary public affirms that she has seen the person sign the document on that specific date. Most likely the notary public's signature will need to be verified in some manner. This can require multiple steps or just one step after being notarized, depending upon the state where you live and the country from where you will adopt. Some states, such as Michigan, are very particular as to how the notary public signs the document. It is best if the notary public states, for example:

> Signed and sworn before me, Carl Roosevelt, MD, on this _____ day of June, 2006, in the county of Greenville, in the State of South Carolina. My commission expires on April 23, 2011.
> Signed, John Franklin, Notary Public

Some states require the notary public's signature to be verified at the county clerk's office in the county in which the notary public is commissioned before it can be authenticated at the state level. Therefore, if you have a document from one of these states, you will need to take the notarized document to the county clerk's office in the courthouse to be verified. States that require county authentication are: Alabama, Delaware, Georgia, Kentucky, Maryland, New York, Ohio, Oklahoma, and Tennessee. In all states, except New York, vital records such as your birth certificate and marriage certificate do not need to be county authenticated since they are issued by the State Vital Records Office. Once the documents are authenticated at the county level in these preceding states, the documents can then be sent to the Secretary of State.

The document that is notarized is then sent to the Secretary of State's office, which will authenticate—or apostille—the document. Authentication or apostilling is the next step that confirms the notary public is commissioned properly in the state. For example, if a document originates in Louisiana, the document will be notarized by a notary public who states that she signed the document in what parish (county) and on what date. Then the document will be sent to the Louisiana Secretary of State. If a document is signed in Ohio, the document is first authenticated by the county clerk's office in which the notary public is registered and then is sent to the Ohio Secretary of State.

The document of authentication or apostille is a piece of paper with seals on it that is attached to the notarized document. People may refer to authentication by the Secretary of State as "The Great Seal" or "legalization."

If the country from which you are adopting is part of The Hague Convention of October 5, 1961, called "Abolishing the Requirement of Legalization for Foreign Public Documents," the document does not need to be authenticated at the country's embassy or consulate. Instead, the document is apostilled by the Secretary of State in which the document originated and then sent to the foreign country.

Just because a country is part of The Hague Convention does not mean that it is part of the The Hague Convention on "Private International Convention on Protection of Children and Cooperation in Respect of Intercountry Adoption." For example, Russia is a country in which the documents for the dossier are apostilled, but they have not ratified The Hague Convention regarding international adoptions.

Find out the rules for the country from which you will be working. The authentication process can be expensive, and you do not want to take any unnecessary steps or make any mistakes. Your agency or facilitator should let you know exactly what must be done. In some instances, he or she can help you complete the process.

If the documents have apostilles on them, they are ready to go to the country and be translated. Conversely, if the country where you are adopting your child is not part of The Hague Convention for "Abolishing the Requirement of

Legalization for Foreign Public Documents," then the documents will have to be further authenticated at the foreign country's embassy or consulate here in the United States. Where you or your agency sends your documents depends upon where they originated. For example, if you are adopting from Guatemala, a document that originates in Pennsylvania will be signed and notarized in Pennsylvania and be authenticated by the Secretary of State in Harrisburg, Pennsylvania, and then sent to the Guatemalan Consulate in New York City because Pennsylvania is in the jurisdiction for the Consulate of Guatemala in New York City. If your birth certificate is from Virginia, that document would be authenticated by the Secretary of the Commonwealth of Virginia in Richmond, Virginia, and then sent to the Consulate of Guatemala in Washington, DC, to be authenticated.

The embassy's or consul's seal, stamps, and signature attest to the documents' authenticity and the Secretary of State's legalization.

The "Assistant Stork" operated by Steve and Laura Morrison, adoptive parents, provides excellent courier service in the Washington, DC area. They can also put you in contact with other couriers around the country.

Note: Once your documents have been submitted and have all the proper certifications placed on them, they are usually sent to the country from which you are adopting to be translated. Some country programs do not necessarily do this in this order.

#11: Consider the Child Who Is Assigned to or Selected by You

In general, once your home study is completed, you have received approval from CIS, and your dossier is complete, you will then be assigned a child. Sometimes a child is assigned to you before you receive CIS approval, but, of course, you can never adopt or receive your child until you have such approval, as stated on the I-171H form from Citizenship and Immigration Services.

Depending upon the program or agency you are using and the country from which you are adopting, there are different methods of having a child assigned to you. The countries placing children for adoption want to make sure you want the child you are adopting. That is one reason, for example, that in Russia one of the adoptive parents must visit the child before proceeding with the adoption. As with any adoption, the older the child, the more you will want to know about him in order to be fully aware of his physical and emotional needs.

Years ago prospective adoptive parents would sometimes go into an orphanage and select the child they would like to bring home. This is not the way adoption happens today—not even when there are scores of children in one orphanage. A child is generally assigned to you after all your paperwork is done and you are approved to adopt, but before you actually travel to the country.

Sometimes adoptive parents go to an adoption agency's workshop and see pictures of children available for adoption. They may want to know whether they can adopt a particular child. Usually the child cannot be held for a family while they are completing their paperwork and waiting for approval from the CIS. Sometimes a child—especially an older child or one with special needs—can be held for several months for the adoptive parents to complete their paperwork.

If at a workshop or on the Internet you see a picture of a child who is waiting to be adopted and you have some facts about her, go ahead and get all your paperwork done. The child may still be available; if she is not, there will be others. Some agencies try to get people to go with their program by getting prospective adoptive families attached to specific children. This method of attracting a family can be very emotionally devastating if the child, for whatever reason, is no longer available.

Because there are so many available children now posted on the Internet, some people are finding their children this way—especially older children. Yet, as a rule, babies and toddlers are assigned to families and do not get posted on the Internet. Once the family accepts the referral of a particular child, the parents wait for all the paperwork to be processed before they can adopt their child and bring her home.

The Report on the Child Assigned to You

Usually when a child is referred to you, a report will be given to you that includes details about the child and his background. Some reports are comprehensive, but most have minimum information because little is available. The younger the child, of course, the fewer details about her personality and milestones will be provided. In a country such as China, where most of the children are assigned to you at about nine months old, you will just be given a picture of the child and as much information as possible about her and her medical history. Regardless of all the discussion you may hear in workshops on how important medical records are in assessing your child's health and possibly his future treatment, little information is give by the staff in other countries.

Some of this is due to lack of trained personnel. Some is due to the fact that there are multiple caregivers who do not observe the child everyday. Mostly, it is due to time constraints and attitudes. Even in the United States, a school counselor wanted a foster child's school records from the schools he previously attended. Yet, few records could be obtained. Social service personnel experience the same frustration in trying to get children's medical and educational records. So if here in the United States, where we have many resources, it can be difficult to obtain comprehensive background information, fewer medical and social/educational records can be expected from the staff in poorer countries.

Some countries do have a system in place in which excellent medical background and family history are provided. For example, families adopting from Korea are provided a comprehensive medical report as well as a family social history and medical report. These family background reports are only as good as the birth mother's information.

Lithuania also provides comprehensive medical and family social reports that tend not to minimize or embellish a child's medical issues or social background. Also, in this small country, it is easy to find a well-trained physician to travel to an orphanage to examine the child before you commit to the child.

Although medical and social records are very important, people make their assessment of a child usually on the pictures. Although it is not the most objective way to decide on a child, the reality is that the picture is the most important factor to adoptive families. Although social workers say that it is the medical report that is most important, families know that they have to feel an affinity for a child. Also, regardless of the health report, some children just look as if something may not be quite right. These children used to be called FLKs—Funny Looking Kids. The term is not about their being cute, but that the children had features that caused concern. We now know that sometimes these children had fetal alcohol syndrome or their dysmorphic features meant that other problems were present and part of a syndrome. Knowing that your child looks "normal" can be just as important as the child testing negative to certain diseases.

People often worry about how they will react when they receive an assignment. They think, "Will I like the baby?" "Will she be cute or ugly?" Remember, you do have a choice. Nearly all adoptive parents we have known have been pleased with the child assigned to them and considered him the most wonderful child ever. Still, there are others who did not feel connected to the child in the video. That is all right. Unless a family starts to arbitrarily reject baby after baby shown on a videotape, an agency should accept the fact that the couple did not feel comfortable with a particular child. In some countries, such as Kazakhstan, the children can vary greatly in coloring, and sometimes after seeing videotapes, a family will say they want a child who has lighter or darker skin and hair.

Choosing Not to Adopt an Assigned Child

If an agency refers a child to you who has severe medical problems and this is not the type of child you are prepared to adopt, then clearly state so. One family contacted me after working with an agency that assigned two children to them who had severe neurological and medical problems. The family had given the agency $17,000. Then when the family said that they were not prepared to adopt such children, the agency tried to make them feel guilty and said that they had to take the children or their money would not be returned.

Do not allow an agency to do this. First, never give that much money to an agency without being assigned a child whom you truly feel comfortable adopting. Second, find out what the agency's risk statement includes and ask under what circumstances funds are returned or applied toward another adoption. Third, make it very clear to your agency the type of child you are approved to adopt. That is why the CIS has clearly stated in your home study the age range, sex, and type of child(ren) you are prepared to adopt. You cannot arbitrarily decide to adopt a twelve-year-old child with cerebral palsy when your home study has approved you for a child between six months and thirty-six months who has minor, correctable health problems. Yes, an addendum to your home study can be sent in to CIS, but the home study will have to address more issues than just the fact that you want an older child. This is not like an addendum to a home study where you first state that you want to adopt a female child and then broaden it to a male.

Medical Evaluation of a Child

When you receive the medical information on your child, it is recommended that you present the information to a physician for interpretation. If you give the report to your local pediatrician, she may see any health problem as a reason not to go through with the adoption. Sometimes if the child has a serious health problem, you will not want to proceed with the adoption. Then again, that is not always the reason for an evaluation. Many adoptive parents just want to know what to expect and to be prepared. Therefore, it is best to send a videotape of a child to a specialist who regularly evaluates international children. These physicians see children before and after adoption and know what to look for. They can decipher the medical conditions described by the in-country physician. For example, some of the medical diagnoses of children from Russia sound like the children have gross mental and neurological problems. Yet, a physician who sees these diagnoses knows what they mean and if the child truly has a medical problem. Also, unlike your local pediatrician, the physician will not make a judgment about adopting the child; he will just give you the facts and usually his perception of the child's long-term prognosis.

Although these physicians can view hundreds of videotapes and can make careful assessments, they are only looking at a videotape and a medical report. Therefore, the assessments are usually not definitive but are meant to help you decide if the child is indeed healthy and if there are any serious medical or developmental concerns. Remember, the physician can describe a disease or condition and possible problems associated with a given condition, but do not expect her to make a full evaluation based on the notes presented.

For example, the Evaluation Center at Schneider Children's Hospital states that its goal is to help parents make as informed a decision as possible, based on the child's medical record and videotape.

According to Schneider Children's Hospital, the medical evaluation of the child assesses:

- Past medical conditions
- Child's current weight, height, and head size using age- and sex-appropriate norms to see if these indicate malnourishment, failure to thrive, poor growth, or microencephaly (if photos or a video are available), and the child's facial features, looking for signs of fetal alcohol syndrome or other medical or genetic syndromes
- Medical problems or conditions
- The need for further medical evaluation
- The need for medical treatment
- How medical status will affect future health

Developmental Evaluation of a Child

The developmental evaluation of the child assesses the child's current level of functioning with respect to motor skills, cognitive development, adaptive skills, speech/language development, and personal-social skills. In particular it identifies:

- Any developmental disabilities or delays
- Whether the child's environment has caused developmental delays
- Factors that are likely to have a long-term impact on the child's development

Because most agencies ask that a family make a decision about a child in about ten days, these medical centers are sensitive to adoptive families' time constraints. Usually results are sent by e-mail or fax. When there are questions regarding the child's health status, the adoptive family will want to speak with a physician to clarify any issues. These centers may also suggest that the adoptive parents ask more detailed questions about the child so that staff can recommend further assessments as needed. In addition to verbal feedback, the staff will give parents a typed list of medical and developmental concerns.

The staff at Schneider Children's Hospital will also communicate directly with other physicians and agency personnel about a particular child's medical and developmental status and needs. If a family is overseas, they may also call the hospital if questions arise. This is especially important for families who go to a country and select their child there. At other times, a child's health status may change, and the family may need to have a consultation before taking a child home.

If the child is very young, making an assessment is relatively easy; most problems, if they exist, are medical, not developmental. True, infants in orphanages often do not receive the emotional love and stimulation that they need, which can cause some developmental delay. Fortunately, most catch up quickly. A child under the age of one will probably not have moved from one caretaker to another, nor will he likely have suffered from the emotional problems associated with abuse or gross neglect. The physical examination he will have before leaving the country will tell you whether he has any congenital health problems or other medical conditions. The major risk is unknown genetic factors, which is true with domestic adoptions, too—especially when a birth father is not identified.

Many couples seeking to adopt never "hear" what the social worker is telling them about the child's problems. They see the beautiful child's picture and "fall in love with her face." As difficult as it may be, try to be objective. Listen carefully and understand what problems the child may have. Yes, you can make a difference in a child's life, but a very disturbed child can also make a difference—for the worse—in your life. You must be prepared to handle the potential problems.

For example, even very young children who have grown up in poorly staffed orphanages may have attachment disorders. This condition is not going to be documented, and the only way you may be able to tell whether the child is going to be able to bond with you is by visiting him and seeing what he is like. Such a child will generally not respond to you, and when you look at him, his eyes will appear to be "hollow." Agency staff may gloss over such conditions and state that within a few months of living with you, the child will be very normal. Be diligent in your investigation. Attachment disorders are very difficult to treat, and the course of treatment can be extensive and expensive.

If you were to adopt such a child in the United States through a social services agency, the child would probably be entitled to special services paid for by Medicaid and other funds. This is not so with an international adoption; if your health insurance does not cover extensive mental health counseling, the cost can be very high, although there are limited state funds available.

#12: Commit to Adopting a Particular Child

Once you have decided to adopt a particular child, this can be the beginning of one of the hardest times in the adoption process. Usually at this point, all the paperwork is completed, and all you can do is wait for the adoption to be completed overseas. Also, once you have a picture of your child, it is difficult not to worry about your child.

In some instances, payment for the care of the child in a foster home or orphanage may become your responsibility. In some countries, it can take several months before the child is actually placed with you (depending upon the country's regulations); in the meantime, you want to make sure that your child is as well cared for as possible. Make sure the amount being requested to care for your child is in accord with the country's average wage. If the average family income is $150 per month, you should not be sending $500 per month to a family or orphanage to care for the child. If you are concerned about poor foster care, make sure your facilitator or agency knows how you feel (in writing, not just verbally) and that you want to make sure that the monies you are sending for the care of your child are doing just that.

Depending upon the country from which you are adopting, it is possible to visit your child while you wait for her adoption to be completed overseas. For example, it is very easy to visit your child in Guatemala because adoptions are private and not run by the government. Some parents even choose to take care of the child in the country while they are waiting for the adoption to be finalized—they rent a small apartment and stay for a few months. In other countries, such as Russia, this is not practical. You are not permitted to take your child out of the orphanage until the adoption is finalized. Although you could stay in Russia between trips, most families do not choose to do this.

#13: Make Travel Arrangements to Your Child's Country

Most people who adopt internationally travel to the child's country for the adoption hearing and to obtain the child's U.S. visa and then take him home. Some countries will require you to stay for several weeks. Others may require you to make two trips. In other countries, the adoption takes place before you need to travel there; you simply travel to receive your child and to obtain his U.S. visa. How you pack and the precautions you take will depend on where you are going, the season you are traveling, how long you will be there, and how long it takes to get there.

The main reason many Americans do not want to adopt a child from another country is fear of travel. People will cite the usual disadvantages of traveling—being away from your job, traveling with your children, or making child care arrangements. The real reason may have more to do with fear of the unknown. If you are traveling to another country to get your child, you will want to make sure that you are as prepared as possible. If you can, go during "tourist season." Tourists are particular and want to be comfortable—you will also want to be as comfortable as possible, especially with a new small child.

#14: Meet Your Child

When you get to the child's country, you will probably be meeting your child for the first time and then adopting her in the next few days.

Upon meeting their children, whom they have seen only on videotapes or pictures, most adoptive parents love their babies immediately. Yet, not all children look like the child in the pictures or videos. If the child is several months older and has gone from being a newborn baby to a six-month-old, of course, the child will hardly look the same at all. Even if your child does look the same as you expected, you cannot predict your emotions and how you will feel when you first see her.

You do not have to adopt the child you have agreed to adopt based on a videotape and medical report if the agency or facilitator has not filled you in on other details about the child, or if the child has developed an illness that you were not aware of, or if the child appears to have emotional problems that seem more profound than other children in the orphanage. To change your mind would be very difficult and devastating and perhaps sounds harsh, but if you have selected a child based on his health and you were not told the truth or not given accurate updates when a problem arose, then you have a right to change your mind.

Before you sign up with an agency, find out what its policy is regarding a change of mind. Most of the time, if the child has a serious health condition of which you were not aware, you can adopt again with no extra fees; you will incur only travel expenses again.

This situation very rarely occurs, but it sometimes happens that agencies withhold information from clients. In one case, a family was traveling to receive a child with a serious medical condition. The heart condition was serious but treatable, and the child was thought to possibly have other syndromes that may be associated with mental retardation. The parents were prepared to receive the child in whatever condition he was. The day before the clients were to leave to get their son, the agency called them and said that another medical diagnosis had been made, but the staff would not share the results with the parents. Needless to say, the adoptive parents were angry because information was being withheld. They were very worried but proceeded with their travel plans. Fortunately, when the family met their son, he was in good health, and a serious thyroid condition had been diagnosed and was beginning to be treated. The child is now two years old. He appears to be bright, and his speech development is advanced for his age.

If you must select your child once you get to the country, be sure that a thorough medical exam is done and that a complete health history is given to you. Usually when you see your child, you can tell where he is developmentally compared with other children in the orphanage.

Make sure that the child begins to respond to you. For example, he should smile, and his eyes should shine. When you go to meet your child, depending upon the child's age, you may want to bring a small, soft toy and some sweet crackers or plain sugar cookies. Often children in orphanages are not used to chocolate or other rich desserts, so keep the treats simple.

Because you will be spending a few days with your child, taking her to the U.S. embassy and other offices, have some light snacks and juices available. You may not be able to eat in certain offices, but a child could have a bottle. Also, have some small, entertaining toys to keep her occupied.

#15: Get to Know Your Child

Although many families choose a country from which to adopt based on the fact that they can be in the country for only a few days, this is usually not best for the child. When it is time to receive your child in the foreign country, if at all possible plan to spend time with him in his own environment so that he can make a more gradual transition to being with you. Overall, the older the child, the more important this time of transition is. This time is especially important for preschool children, who are aware of what is happening, but do not have the language skills—even in their own language—to understand what it means to go from an orphanage or foster home to an adoptive family.

For example, if your child is in a foster home, you may want to visit with the child and his foster mother and learn about his routine. Knowing his naptime and bedtime, as well as familiar foods and routines, can be helpful when you take him home. Of course, you don't need to replicate this environment at home, but you can use this information as you organize his new life at home. Orphanage staff often find it disruptive to have parents visit for long periods of time.

Unfortunately in some countries, as important as it is to spend time with your child in his own environment, you may be permitted to visit him in the orphanage for only one or two hours a day until the adoption is finalized. Although it would appear that foster families would be more flexible about your visiting your child for an extended period of time each day, most facilitators in the country would find the logistics of accommodating you too difficult. If you really want to slowly transition your child from his foster home to you, you probably will have to pay someone extra to take care of your traveling from your hotel to the foster home and back.

If you are staying in the country for a few weeks, bring a soft toy to give to your child so that your child can identify the toy with you even when you are not there. Then you can bring that soft toy home. If you can, try to keep a toy that your child had with him; yet, many orphanages will not allow this. Perhaps they will allow you to give him a new toy and clothes in exchange for your child's "old" ones that are familiar to him. Some will not even allow you to keep the child's clothes, but require you to bring your own.

If you are adopting a young baby, keep him on the same formula to keep his tummy happy. If sugar is put in his formula, this is not the time to decide that your child no longer needs added sugar. Once you are home, you can start to mix his formula with the formula from the United States. Also, gradually reduce the sugar, if added to his formula. If he sucks on a pacifier, let him continue to do so. If your child is from an orphanage and was weaned off the bottle at an early age, you may want to reintroduce a bottle to your child to help with the attachment process (holding him while he drinks his bottle), even if your child is a preschooler.

Your child probably had a very bland diet if he was living in an orphanage. Fortunately, this doesn't necessarily mean that he prefers bland foods. He may want to try all sorts of new foods and eat what seems to be enormous quantities. These children are usually undernourished and are catching up. Your child also may need to learn that enough food will be available at each meal and that he doesn't need to eat as much as possible now in case there is not much later. It is best to let the child learn to "listen to his tummy" to tell him when he has had enough to eat, rather than limiting his food intake. You will want to make sure your child has plenty of protein and lots of other nutritional foods. Do not be surprised if your child does not particularly like sweets since he probably seldom had any.

Your child may have been given very mushy foods and may have difficulty in chewing. Also, babies are sometimes given bottles with large holes so that they drink quickly. Therefore, your child may have difficulty with sucking properly on a bottle. Also, these children can have sensory integration problems related to food. Some children cannot tolerate crunchy foods while others cannot tolerate very soft foods. You will have to adjust your child's diet accordingly until he can adapt to a normal diet.

If you adopt a baby, you will most likely want to keep him on formula for an extended period of time to be sure he gets all the protein and nutrients needed while introducing new foods into his diet.

When adopting a child overseas, you will want to know what size clothes to take with you. This decision needs to be based on height and weight of the child—not her age. In general, children are much smaller than their U.S. counterparts; a 3T will most likely fit a four- or five-year-old child, not a two- or three-year-old as here in the United States. Even knowing your child's measurements may not always lead to buying the correct size, as many have experienced after going shopping for children we see every day. For an in-depth look at adopting a toddler child and facing these practical issues, you may want to read the book *Toddler Adoption: The Weaver's Craft* by Mary Hopkins-Best.

#16: Adopt Your Child in His or Her Country

Once you accept a child and your dossier is in the country and the child is free for adoption based on the country's laws, the adoption process in the foreign country usually begins. Usually you will be present for your child's adoption hearing. Like marriage, so much goes into the preparation of the event, but the actual event usually lasts about thirty minutes. In some countries, such as Guatemala, the adoption takes place by proxy, and you are not present for the signing of papers.

In some countries, especially former Eastern bloc countries, there are post-adoption waiting periods. So even after the adoption takes place, you cannot take your child out of the orphanage to be with you until the end of this waiting period. These waits are anywhere from ten to forty days, depending upon the country's laws. In some instances, the waiting period is waived.

#17: Complete the Paperwork

Your facilitator in the country will make sure that proper papers are obtained not just for the in-country adoption, but also to prove that the child is an orphan by U.S. standards. A child must not only meet the orphan status for his own country to be available for adoption, but he must also meet U.S. status as well. If not, a child can be adopted in the country, but the U.S. Embassy/Consulate will not issue the child a visa. This is a situation that occurred several times in Vietnam and is one of the worst possible situations to be in. You have a child that you have legally adopted, but you cannot enter the United States with your child. Your only immediate solution is to live in your child's country with him or take him to another country that will allow you to enter until your child can be shown to meet U.S. orphan status.

A reputable, in-country facilitator will only place children for adoption who meet the orphan status as set by the United States. Sometimes families will identify a child, for example, on a mission trip in another country and then want to adopt that child. Unfortunately, one of the roadblocks they may face is getting the child to meet the orphan definition as defined by the State Department and Department of Homeland Security.

An orphan is a child whose parents have both died or a child whose "sole parent" is placing the child for adoption. Under U.S. law, a "sole parent" is an unmarried person. This single parent can sign a release of parental rights for his or her "illegitimate" child to be placed for adoption. However, the other parent must have severed all ties to the child. If the child has two known parents, her parents must abandon her since two parents cannot sign a relinquishment.

In some countries, steps are taken before the adoption actually takes place in the country to be sure that the child will meet orphan status and that no fraud is involved. A facilitator or lawyer will present the case to the U.S. Embassy to review to make sure that the child meets orphan status—before the adoption is finalized in the country. In Guatemala, for example, a very formal structure is in place to be sure that the child meets all the guidelines of being an orphan. In certain countries such as the Philippines and Sierra Leone, the U.S. Embassy has a special program in place for parents who want to make sure that their child is an orphan by U.S. standards before they proceed with the adoption.

Obtaining Your Child's Visa to Enter the United States

When you receive approval from CIS—that is, your I-171H has been sent to you—the CIS office also faxes or e-mails the approval (called a Cable 37) to the U.S. Embassy/Consulate where you will be receiving your child's visa, which may not be in the country from which you are adopting. For example, if you are adopting from Lithuania, the U.S. Embassy there does not issue orphan visas; therefore, parents must go to the U.S. Embassy in Warsaw, Poland, to obtain their child's visa.

All of the documents submitted to the U.S. Embassy that support the child's status as an orphan must be typed and translated into English. An affidavit affirming that the translator is qualified to translate from the given language to English and that the translated document is accurate, complete, and true must accompany the translation.

Following are the documents and other items necessary to apply for a visa:

Orphan petition. CIS Petition to Classify the Orphan as an Immediate Relative (I-600). If you will be traveling to the child's country, you will take the I-600 form with you so that you can get the child's visa to enter the United States. Leave the child's name blank on the form and complete that information once the child is definitely going to be placed with you. If your spouse is not traveling with you, have him or her sign the document and have it notarized before you leave. Always take two copies with you, with your spouse's signature on each, in case one is lost or the wrong information on the child is entered.

Once you have adopted the child, the petition must be filed immediately. One petition is necessary for each child adopted. Therefore, if you are adopting siblings, the visa fee, which at this time is $380, will be charged for each child. If you are adopting nonrelatives together and have only filed one I-600A form at your CIS office, then you will be charged another filing fee for the second child. (As of this time, it is $525.) Therefore, if you are adopting two unrelated children at the same time, the filing fee will be $525, and total visa and filing fees together will be $1,285.

Alien Registration and Visa Application (DS-230). This form can be quite confusing since all the information on the form is about your child—*now* that he is adopted. You can download the form at *www.state.gov/documents/organization/7988.pdf.*

Pictures of the child for the visa. You need to obtain three identical color photos on a white background. The photo must be one-and-a-half inches square, the head size must be about one inch from chin to hair, and the child should be shown with three-fourths frontal view, with right face and right ear showing. Lightly print the child's name on the back of each photo and sign your name on the front side using pencil or felt pen.

Passport for your child. Your in-country facilitator will need to obtain a passport for your child.

Your child's original birth certificate. If the original birth certificate cannot be obtained, an explanation of circumstances needs to be submitted. The birth certificate should show the date and place of the child's birth. Most countries also issue a new birth certificate to show the child's new name and the names of the adoptive parents.

Statement of release of child for adoption. The statement of release shows that the orphan's only surviving parent cannot provide for the child and has forever and irrevocably released the child for adoption and emigration. The release must state why the mother (or possibly the father) relinquished the child. If the birth father's name is known, it should be listed. Certified copies of this form must be retained to use in adoption proceedings in the United States.

Certificate of abandonment (if the child has not been relinquished). This document is issued by the court after publishing for the child's parents. If the child was in an orphanage, it must show that she has been unconditionally abandoned to the orphanage.

Death certificate of orphan's parents (if applicable).

Adoption decree, permanent guardianship, or custody transfer to adoptive parents. This should confirm the child's legal status as an orphan. A resolution is sometimes given instead of a final decree, which is issued later. The resolution is as acceptable as an adoption decree and will give the adoptive parents custody of the child.

Medical evaluation of the child. The U.S. Embassy/Consulate in your child's country lists the names of U.S. Embassy-approved clinics or physicians who can complete this form. This exam is performed so that parents are fully aware of a child's medical problems or disability and that they will take full responsibility for the child. They also want to ascertain if the child has any serious communicable disease. Once your child is examined, the doctor will give you his or her assessment of your child, and you will receive a medical form enclosed in a sealed envelope. Do not open the envelope; it will be given to the staff at the U.S. Embassy/Consulate when you apply for the child's visa.

You may be required or advised to bring the following documents with you:

Your home study that was submitted to CIS or a new notarized home study reflecting anything significant that has changed in your life such as your address, or if the child you are adopting is not the same sex or the age range that you were originally approved to adopt, or if you are adopting more children than you were originally approved to adopt.

I-171H form.

Your tax forms from last year.

A copy of your spouse's passport data page, if your spouse is not with you.

If your child has not been seen by you and your spouse before or during the adoption, then you must also bring the following documents with you to the U.S. Embassy/Consulate:

Affidavit of Support (I-864). You will need one for each child you are adopting, even if you are adopting twins. Also, the supporting documents must be in duplicate if adopting two children.

Tax forms for the last three years.

Your employment letter (may be required).

Proof that you have met the preadoption requirements of your state. You will need to ask your home study provider about what requirements, if any, other than a home study, are required to meet the preadoption requirements of your state. The U.S. Consulate in China is especially strict about this requirement; whereas, in Guatemala the U.S. Embassy is not.

Receiving Your Child's Visa

Once you have your child's visa in hand, you can travel home! The visa will be on the outside of a large, sealed envelope. *DO NOT OPEN THIS ENVELOPE.* Inside the envelope are all of your child's important adoption documents, which you will hand over to the immigration officer upon arrival in the United States. Because you will not have these important documents with you anymore, it is best if you can make sure that you have certified copies for yourself as well. You will need these documents to readopt your child in the United States. If for some reason you are not given a second set, you can order your child's original set from the CIS office once you are back in the United States by filing a G-884. There is no charge for this, but you could wait several months to nearly a year to receive these documents. This could delay your readopting your child in the United States if you do not have certified copies of adoption paperwork in your possession. If your child has come home on an IR-4 visa and is, therefore, not a U.S. citizen, you will have to wait for this paperwork to readopt him. Also, if you live in certain states, you cannot take the federal tax credit until your child is a U.S. citizen.

#18: Bring Home Your Child!

Adopting a child from another country means the child is going through a huge transition—even children who have been in good foster homes. Unlike children who are adopted in the United States, these children are not only changing caregivers, but they are also losing the sights, sounds, smells, and tastes of their own country. While you are in your child's country, you may notice that your child gravitates toward those who look like him and speak his language.

Initially, one of the most difficult transitions for a child who is already talking is changing languages. You can initially communicate with your child by learning basic words for eating, sleeping, and going potty. Young children will easily catch on to the new language. In fact, many children do not want to speak their original language and want to learn their adopted parents' language. Older children find it more difficult to grasp a new language but will likely adapt quite quickly.

Many families' main concern in adopting international children is how will the children learn a new language. The best predictor that your child will learn English or another language quickly is his proficiency in his first language. Children in institutions often lack language skills since the children often use hand gestures and eye contact to communicate.

The loss of the first language before the new language develops leaves the child without any language, and during this time, the child can appear to regress. For younger children, this is hardly an issue because the child will have a few years before school starts to learn the new language. Even though young school age children lose their native language in less than six months, learning and mastering a new language can take years.

A typical six-year-old in the United States understands more than 20,000 English words. Therefore, an internationally adopted child who is five years old would need to learn fifty-four new words every day to catch up to a six-year-old born in the United States. If the child is given two years to "catch up," he would still need to learn twenty-seven new words each day by seven years old. In the meantime, his friends born here have added 5,000 words to their vocabulary. Therefore, to expect an older internationally adopted child to be proficient in English in a year or two is unrealistic. If a child does not acquire language skills, he can then underachieve in school. If your child is having difficulty with language, it is wise to have the child receive speech therapy lessons. All children under thirty-six months old are eligible at no charge if services are needed, regardless of your income. Most children over thirty-six months old would receive therapy through the school system.

For the older internationally adopted child, learning a new language is more of a challenge. He will go through the same process of having to acquire a new language, but a younger child has more time to "catch up." In addition, the older internationally adopted child is placed into school and social settings in which more language skills are required, for which he may not be equipped.

INTERNATIONAL ADOPTION FOR U.S. CITIZENS LIVING ABROAD

Robert Braun, the former director of the International Family Services Adoption Agency, states there is no reason why U.S. citizens living abroad (expatriates) should not be able to adopt from the same countries as do adoptive families who live stateside. However, in some countries adoption decision-makers reject the applications of Americans living abroad, explaining they are afraid the U.S. expatriates will be immune to postplacement supervision and reporting requirements of the countries in which the expatriates are living, as well to the postplacement supervision and reporting requirements that supposedly exist in the United States. Thus, it is quite difficult for U.S. expatriates to adopt in Russia (unless they are long-term residents).

In certain countries, expatriates who choose to adopt locally may be able to adopt independently. However, the majority of expatriates will have to find an agency to help them find and adopt a child from another country, just as U.S. citizens who reside in the United States typically do. The process of finding a good agency can be a little bit harder when you live abroad. Whereas virtually every U.S.–based adoption agency is willing to take out-of-state clients for their various foreign programs, many of those same agencies are reluctant to take expatriate clients, either because they believe they will not know how to effectively serve them, or they are afraid of the reaction of the foreign governments or the foreign intermediary counterparts with whom they have to work every day, or they are afraid that the expatriates will not comply in providing postplacement reports the agency needs to forward to certain countries to stay in good favor. For instance, one of the biggest U.S. agencies working in the People's Republic of China eliminated its program for U.S. expatriates though other agencies will work with families living overseas.

The CIS overseas requires all home studies to be conducted by a licensed adoption agency, not an independent social worker. Therefore, if you use an independent social worker who needs to pay a stateside licensed adoption agency to "endorse" or "counter-approve" the social worker's report, then you will pay more (depending on travel costs, if any,) than if you contract with a stateside adoption agency that uses its own staff to conduct the home study from beginning to end. If the social worker or the licensed adoption agency you choose charges for its travel to your overseas home, then what you end up paying might well stretch thin your budget! Be specific in your questioning of the credentials of the home study provider, how much the agency charges, and how long the process will take.

As with all home studies, the preparer should work closely with the adoption facilitator or placing agency to make sure that all topics the target country wants in the home study are covered in the report and that the process of gathering supporting paperwork will not be overly burdensome for the family.

You must file your I-600A and your home study at the overseas U.S. CIS office that has jurisdiction over your place of residence; to find that office, you can go to *http://uscis.gov/graphics/shared/fieldoffices/worldmap.htm.*

The overseas U.S. CIS will normally accept a police clearance from the country in which you are living (even a military police clearance from the U.S. authorities) instead of a police clearance from the state to which you would be returning; if you choose the former approach, the overseas U.S. CIS will normally not require a child abuse clearance from the foreign country. But if you submit a stateside police clearance, then you will probably have to submit a child abuse clearance from the same state.

If anyone in the household has any history of minor legal infractions, fully disclose this to the home study preparer and be ready to provide full documentation (with copies certified by the court) to the overseas U.S. CIS as to how the matter was resolved.

Everyone over the age of eighteen in your household needs to be fingerprinted as part of the I-600A application, and you should inquire at the closest U.S. Embassy (Regional Security Officer or American Citizens' Services Section of the Consulate) about getting this fingerprinting done. But you probably should not have to pay for the fingerprinting: U.S. expatriates get this free!

Some U.S. expatriates would like to adopt from their home state or from another state in the United States. Although finding the right child might be a challenge, the legal proceedings usually are not, as long as the court is satisfied concerning how the preadoption home study was carried out. The federal government itself has to accept a home study for expatriates if it has been prepared by an agency licensed in any of the fifty states.

Adopting your child for whom you are a guardian when you return to the United States.

If you are a U.S. citizen living overseas and have had legal custody of a child from the country in which you have been residing for at least two years, then you can enter the United States with the child and adopt the child in the United States. Before you leave the country to go to the United States, you must file an I-130 Petition for Alien Relative with the U.S. Embassy/Consulate that has jurisdiction over the country in which you are residing so that the child can obtain a visa to enter the United States. The child can enter the United States with you only if she was under the age of sixteen at the time she came to live with you. The child can come to the United States to be adopted and then be issued a U.S. passport and a Certificate of Citizenship.

Americans who are working overseas, including missionaries, often adopt children under these circumstances when they come in contact with a child who needs a family and then later obtain legal custody of the child. If you are in an unstable area of the world and believe you may have to leave the country on short notice, you will want to make all attempts to legally adopt the child in the country and obtain a visa for the child to enter the United States when the need arises.

Establishing an adopted child's citizenship if you do not return to United States after adopting

If you and your spouse are expatriates and you adopt a child in a country, such as China, and then take the child directly to your resident country, such as England, your child will *not* be a U.S. citizen, even if your child was issued an IR-3 visa. When you arrive in your resident country, you must file an I-130 Petition for Alien Relative with the immigration office that has jurisdiction over your country. (This should be the same office where you originally filed your home study and I-600A.) You must also file an I-485 Application to Register Permanent Residence so that your child is a permanent resident of the United States and, therefore, can enter the United States.

For more information on U.S. citizens living abroad, contact:

International Families Licensed Adoption Agency
www.4adoption.com
E-mail: *intlfam@earthlink.net*
Phone: (215) 735-7171, Fax: (215) 545-3563

Non-U.S. Citizens Living in the United States

If one spouse is a U.S. citizen and one is not, the couple can still adopt internationally as long as the foreign country permits them to adopt and as long as the non-U.S. citizen is a legal immigrant.

If both spouses are non-U.S. citizens, the couple cannot adopt a child outside of the United States and bring the child back into the United States immediately after the adoption, unless they have diplomatic status. The family must wait with their child in the child's birth country until the child is issued a permanent resident card, which can take an extended period of time. Likewise, if a non-U.S. citizen couple returns to their country and gives birth while there, the child must wait for a permanent resident card before entering the United States, even though his parents have resident cards.

On the other hand, non-U.S. citizen couples living in the United States can adopt children born in the United States.

INTERNATIONAL TRAVEL WHEN ADOPTING: HEALTH AND SAFETY CONCERNS

When traveling internationally to adopt a child, it is certainly essential to get whatever immunizations are recommended for the country to which you will be traveling. Start by making sure your childhood immunizations are all up-to-date. In addition, we recommend the following:

Diphtheria/tetanus If you have not had a *diphtheria/tetanus* booster in the last ten years, get one. Diphtheria is a major health problem in all of the former Soviet Union.

Cholera has been an ongoing epidemic in parts of Latin America and much of Africa, as well as in certain parts of Russia. Because a cholera vaccine is not very effective and has side effects, it is not recommended if you are traveling for a short time.

Typhoid has been reported in parts of the former Soviet Union. New typhoid vaccines—both injectable and oral—are available, have few side effects, and are effective in preventing 50 percent to 75 percent of cases.

Hepatitis A: Nearly everyone in the developing world has had it, and about 50 percent of American adults have been infected. If you have been infected, you have antibodies that can prevent your getting the disease if you eat food infected with it.

Hepatitis B: Today all children in the United States are immunized against hepatitis B, which is spread by the exchange of saliva, urine, and other bodily fluids. If you have not been vaccinated, you should do so. The vaccine is given in three doses; even one dose provides some protection if you do not have time to complete the series before traveling.

Influenza. The "flu" can be prevented by taking amantadine during the whole trip. If you are at risk for other diseases associated with the flu, get immunized instead.

Cytomegalovirus (CMV) is a common virus found throughout the world. Infants usually get it through the birthing process but also receive antibodies to the virus from their birth mothers. Yet, for several months after birth, the child can still infect others. The disease is then spread from person to person through bodily fluids.

The disease usually causes no illness, but if a pregnant woman is exposed to it for the first time in her life, she can pass the disease to her unborn baby, possibly causing birth defects in the child. In the United States, about 40 percent to 50 percent of all middle-class women have had the infection and, therefore, have antibodies against the virus. The problem is if you never were exposed to the virus and then become exposed through your adopted child's urine, saliva, or other bodily fluids.

There is no vaccine for CMV. It is advised that you have a simple blood test to determine if you have antibodies to the disease. If not, you may need to take extra precautions against exposure if you may be pregnant while traveling to your child's country or if your adopted child has it. Being in the same home environment as a child with the virus increases your risk of exposure greatly, especially if your infant is still secreting the virus.

Malaria is a significant problem in many areas. If you are going to an area that has a high incidence of malaria, especially in the rainy season, you may need to take an antimalaria drug, starting one week before you leave and continuing for six weeks after you return home. Depending upon where you are going and what kinds of malaria strains are present, you may have to take more than one drug. All can cause severe reactions; you will want to discuss with an expert whether they are necessary.

YOUR TRIP ABROAD

When preparing for your trip, remember to pack lightly. The United States is the only country where you are expected to wear a different outfit every day! Remember, when you get to the country, you will have a child to carry as well as his belongings.

What to pack and bring for a baby or child:

- Baby carrier (cloth and lightweight)
- Baby bottles and nipples, preferably disposable
- Disposable diapers and baby wipes

- Tylenol
- Thermometer
- Pedialyte (or you can make it with bottled water and sugar and a dash of salt)
- Diaper rash ointment such as A&D ointment
- Hygiene products
- Benadryl

Many parents do not know what size clothes to take for their child; try to estimate or take a few different sizes. The sizes that do not fit can be left for other children in the orphanage. In many countries, you can purchase some outfits once you are in the country. The children generally do not leave the orphanage in their clothes; you must bring some for your child.

Carrying Money

Usually you will have to carry some money on your person so that you can pay the in-country facilitator. Most countries have a cash economy; you will need to carry clean, crisp money with you, usually $100 bills. Even the U.S. embassies usually require you to pay them in cash using clean, unmarred $100 bills.

If you must carry a few thousand dollars with you, divide it between you and companion. Keep your money for the embassy very clean and try not to fold it.

To safeguard your money, place it in your passport holder and wear it on your body at all times. Stores sell special passport/money pouches on a string that you can tuck under your clothes.

Sometimes you can wire money to the facilitator so that you do not have to carry so much money with you. However, you may still be required to pay in cash at the U.S. Embassy for the child's visa and for the purchase of other items. Unless you are staying in a Western-style hotel or eating at such a restaurant, credit cards are not accepted. Do not even consider taking travelers checks; they are very rarely accepted.

Travel Documents

A current passport. If you are even thinking about adopting an international child, get a passport now. It is valid for ten years, is not expensive, and is one less piece of paperwork to obtain when you do adopt. If you travel with someone, have a copy of each other's passport data page as a precaution in case one of you loses a passport. If you are traveling alone, put a copy of your passport data page somewhere else in your luggage, in case your passport gets stolen or lost. Also, carry a copy of your spouse's passport's vital pages as identification.

A tourist visa. Some countries require adoptive parents to have tourist or adoption visas. You may want to call a travel agency or airline or contact the consulate of the country you will be adopting from to find out the fees for the visa. Most visa application forms can be downloaded off the Internet, and the embassy's or consulate's Web site will indicate what documents, if any, must be submitted to obtain the visa as well as the amount of the money order. Visas are usually attached to or stamped in your passport; therefore, you will need to send an application, your passport, one or two passport-size photos, and a money order to the foreign country's consulate in the United States. Always send such important documents by an overnight delivery service, such as UPS or FedEx. Visas are only good for a certain period of time; therefore, you will not want to obtain one too early in the process.

Power of attorney. If you are not traveling with your spouse, you will need a document giving you power of attorney on behalf of your spouse, which is signed by your spouse and notarized. Usually your adoption agency can prepare this document for you. Even if both of you are traveling, it is wise to have a power of attorney for each spouse in the event of an emergency and one of you must leave the child's country earlier than planned. For example, if you are in a country and the adoption is completed and there are delays in obtaining your child's new birth certificate, one parent may have to go back home to take care of family matters or return to work. You will need a power of attorney from your spouse to obtain your child's visa at the U.S. Embassy/Consulate if your spouse is not with you.

For more information on international travel, go to *www.cdc.gov/travel.*

Having Someone Escort Your Child Home

Some families select a country from which to adopt based on the fact that the children can be escorted home by someone other than themselves. Some adoptive parents have a severe fear of flying. Others have small children at home and do not want to leave them, even for short periods of time. Others, such as the Amish, may not be permitted to travel by plane. If you do choose to have your child escorted home, the paperwork process gets a bit more complicated and will most likely mean that your child's arrival home will be delayed by a couple of weeks.

Some families go into the process with the idea that their children will be escorted home. Initially, the thought of going overseas to a third world country is just too overwhelming for them. In spite of this, the parents often decide that they can hardly wait the extra time usually required to complete the paperwork for someone else to escort the child home.

If you do decide to have your child escorted home, you will need to file the I-600A form at your CIS office along with the translated adoption paperwork from your child's country. This paperwork is usually mailed from overseas to you, the adoptive family, and you must submit it to the CIS office in which you filed your original I-600A form. Also, the paperwork may first come through your adoption agency, and the staff will overnight it to you. If you, the parents, have not seen the child before the adoption—and most people who have their children escorted home have not—then you must also submit to CIS any paperwork to prove that you have met the preadoption requirements, if any, of your state. Then the CIS adoption unit reviews the paperwork.

Upon approval by CIS, you are then issued an I-171 Notice of Approval of Relative Immigrant Visa Petition. The CIS also sends to the U.S. Embassy/Consulate a Cable 39 indicating that the paperwork is approved and that the child's visa can be issued. Getting approval from your CIS should take just a matter of days. But there have been instances of it taking weeks to be issued. Also, it is important to confirm with the U.S. Embassy/Consulate overseas that they have received the Cable 39 so that your escort can get your child's visa from the U.S. Embassy and bring home your child. You will need to stay in close contact with your immigration office. If you cannot reach them or if you cannot reach the U.S. Embassy/Consulate overseas, you should get your congressional representative involved as you will be very eager to get your child home.

The escort must have a power of attorney given to him by you, the adoptive parents. The power of attorney is a simple document that is signed by you and notarized. This is not prepared by a lawyer. Your adoption agency will provide the format for this document. Then the escort goes to the U.S. Embassy/Consulate where your child's visa is issued and then brings the child to the United States. Most families meet their children at the airport.

If you are torn between receiving your child yourself or having your child escorted, it is recommended that you go to your child's country. You will have an opportunity to see your child's country and gain an understanding of the culture and take pictures for your child. You will get to attach with your child, most likely meet his caregiver or foster mother, and learn about his habits. Your child will also not be taken from his caregiver, be placed with someone else to travel by plane to the United States, and then be handed over to you in the airport. That can be an overwhelming experience for a child who has lost everything he has ever known.

THE MOST POPULAR COUNTRIES AND REGIONS FOR ADOPTION

Following is a list of some of the most popular countries and areas that permit people from abroad to adopt their orphans. Bear in mind that adoption laws in a particular country can change quickly. Countries are often criticized for "not taking care of their own," prompting them to close or slow down their adoption programs. This happened in Korea, whose adoption program drew much attention. After receiving a great deal of criticism from other Asian countries, Korea sharply cut back on the number of children adopted.

Latin America

Most Latin American countries have such restrictive adoption laws that few adoptions take place from this continent except for from Colombia and Guatemala.

Colombia has been a placement country for more than thirty years. Although the number of children placed each year has dwindled, it is still a viable option for those seeking to adopt.

Guatemala, with a population of fewer than 13 million, places nearly 4,000 children for adoption each year. It has the highest rate of adoption of any country. Although Russia and China have the greatest number of children placed for adoption, these countries also have populations far greater than Guatemala.

Guatemala has such a high rate of adoption because of poverty. Most adoptions in Guatemala are through relinquishments; that is, the birth mother makes a decision to place her child for adoption, and her child is most likely placed in a small group home or into foster care until the adoption is completed. Usually the care that the infants and children receive while awaiting their adoptive families is very good.

Unlike other countries with high rates of poverty, Guatemala has favorable adoption laws not only for the adoptive families, but also for the birth family and adopted children. For example, the birth mothers relinquish their babies and know that they are being placed for adoption; this avoids the uncertainty surrounding adoptions in which children are placed in an orphanage.

There are no age limits as to who can adopt from Guatemala. Adoptions take place by proxy. Adoptive parents can have their children escorted home or can go to the country for just a few days to receive their children. In addition, the flight to Guatemala is just a few hours away from Houston or Atlanta.

Asia

Historically, Asian children had accounted for 75 percent of all international adoptions in the United States. Many families select Asian countries because, in general, the overall fees for adoptions are lower than in other countries. Also, there is a much lower incidence of fetal alcohol syndrome in these countries than in Eastern Europe.

Although other countries in Asia may have rules and regulations that change frequently, China and Korea have programs that have remained fairly consistent through the last decade. Changes include China allowing a broader range of families to adopt, such as those with multiple children and those thirty to fifty years old. While the requirements for couples have loosened, China has established tight quotas on the number of singles who can adopt, creating waiting lists at the U.S. agency level.

China

A new adoption law in China went into effect in April 1992, and in October 1992, the China Centre of Adoption Affairs (CCAA) was created in Beijing. Since that time, more than 50,000 children from China have been adopted by U.S. citizens. The numbers of adoptions continues to rise. From 2002 to 2003, there was a 36 percent increase from 5,053 to 6,859 adoptions from China by Americans and in 2004 just over 7,000 children from China were adopted (National Council for Adoption 2003 report). This increase is a result of elimination of quotas and an increase in CCAA staff.

Overall, the Chinese government has been very cooperative about adoptions, and the paperwork required is relatively easy to understand and follow. For the most part, the children are healthy: Chinese women usually do not smoke, and AIDS and other sexually transmitted diseases have not been a major concern so far. Because the children live in poor conditions in orphanages, they may be malnourished.

Adoptions are finalized directly in China, and at least one parent must travel to receive the child and finalize the adoption. The stay is about two weeks. Your agency will arrange for a facilitator in the country to guide you through the process.

If you adopt from China, your dossier will be submitted by the licensed agency at the CCAA. The translations of the dossier must be done in Beijing by the China Translation and Publishing Corporation. The date of the dossier's arrival is very important (Date to China—called DTC). Families track the time of dossier date of arrival to referral of a child. The CCAA selects the region where you and the others from your agency who submitted paperwork at the same time will be adopting your children.

You and this group of families will wait for an assignment of children from one specific region and most likely one specific orphanage. Because everyone in "your group" will have a child assigned to them at the same time you do, this group will then become your travel group. Although it is not an exact science, the guidelines are fairly straightforward.

The time you wait for an assignment of a child has virtually nothing to do with your agency. The CCAA determines who gets assignments based on the date your dossier arrived. If the time frame for waiting for a child is six to eight months, then you must wait that long for a referral of a child. The time frame over the years has varied from about four to twelve months.

You will most likely receive just one picture of your child, although you could receive a few pictures of your child before you receive her, as well as a medical report. Once you decide to adopt the child assigned to you, a form is completed indicating that you are willing to accept this child. Unlike other countries, you do not have a choice in the child assigned to you, unless the child has a health problem.

Although most of the children assigned are infant girls, boys are also available. The wait for a boy can be a little bit longer than for a girl—but not necessarily. Also, if a family indicates that they are interested in adopting a male child with special needs—even very minor correctable medical conditions—this could further reduce the wait for a child.

China has an excellent program of placing children with special needs. The structure provides a balance of allowing families to preselect their children without having children photolisted on public Internet Web sites. You must contact a specific agency before seeing a child who is available for adoption.

Some agencies reduce the fee for such children with special needs; yet, most do not since fees for China adoptions are lower than most country programs, and there are few ways to reduce the fees. For example, the orphanage donation fee is not reduced. The advantage of adopting a child with special needs is that in nearly all cases the time it takes to travel to adopt your child is reduced. Many children are available to various agencies, and you can select a child before you proceed with the adoption paperwork. Also, you can complete the paperwork for a China adoption and then select a child from various agency profiles, or you can submit the paperwork for a child with special needs and let the CCAA assign a child to you.

If you want to have the shortest wait for a child once he or she is assigned to you yet be able to select a child, it is best to complete your paperwork first and then visit agencies' private Web sites of children available. Children are not photolisted on public Web sites, but rather on an agency's Web site using a special code to view the children. If you want to have your paperwork ready and then look for a child with special needs among agencies, you can work with an agency that will assist you in completing your paperwork for a China dossier. You need to let the agency know that you may select a child through another agency since each agency only has a limited number of children with special needs assigned to them every few months. Completing the paperwork for an adoption from China is transparent since standard documents are required. Before you select a child, the agency's role would be to check over your paperwork to be sure that the writing is in accordance with the latest standards of the CCAA.

So if you have completed paperwork through one agency, and you want a deaf child, and your agency does not have a deaf child assigned to the agency, then you can work with another agency.

Some children's health issues are more complicated, and it can take longer to find a family for such a child. These are often the children in which the adoptive parent identifies the child first and then starts the paperwork. This, of course, delays the process and means a child waits while a family prepares the paperwork.

Korea

There have been more than 100,000 adoptions from Korea since U.S. citizens started adopting after the Korean War. Korea has rather stringent requirements as to who can adopt. Only married couples can adopt, and they cannot have more than four other children.

Korea works only with adoption agencies that have child-placement contracts with Korean agencies, and only those U.S.–based agencies in each state can place children in that state. Unlike most other international adoption agencies that assist couples all over the United States, the agency can place children only with families in the state where it is licensed or a state where it has a contract with a home study agency. If you are seriously considering adopting from Korea, your home study should be conducted by the Korean agency that you are adopting through or a home study agency that has a contract with a Korean agency.

Korea remains a popular country because the fees are usually reasonable, the process of adopting from Korea is uncomplicated, and the babies are well cared for in foster homes.

Russia and Eastern Europe

Russia has competed with China as the number one country placing children with U.S. citizens. Unlike China, a couple adopting from Russia does not have to be thirty years old or younger. No artificial limits are placed on the family as to how many children they can have in their home, and there are no quotas as to the number of single women adopting. Therefore, most everyone qualifies to adopt. In general, couples should not be more than forty-five years older than the child unless the child has special needs.

The process for adopting a child from Russia is usually straightforward and the time frame can be quite short. The rules vary from region to region; guidance must be provided by your placing agency as to what these rules are.

Adopting from Russia can be very expensive—even when agency fees are modest. Most families must make two trips to Russia, and each trip requires a visa. The total for two visas to enter the country twice can be close to $1,000. Also, staying in Russia can be pricey. Even if the region where your child is located has fairly inexpensive hotels, you will also have to stay in Moscow to obtain your child's U.S. visa. Moscow is one of the most expensive cities in the world. Therefore, a family can plan to spend about $10,000 in travel-related expenses, including airline tickets, if they adopt from Russia; whereas, families adopting from China can plan to spend closer to $5,000.

Russia has had fairly stable adoption laws; in spite of this, other former Soviet Union and Eastern bloc countries' laws have fluctuated greatly. Certain countries, such as Romania, have essentially shut down their adoption program. Others have restricted adoptions through laws that make the adoption process extremely difficult.

INTERNATIONAL ADOPTION: ONE COUPLE'S STORY
One family tells their story of adopting a preschool girl from Romania.

• • •

On Thanksgiving 2001, we had a picture and a video of a little girl; we had requested a girl between two and five years old. We decided to proceed after showing the video to our family members. On December 19, we arrived in Romania. As the actual adoption process was only three weeks, we stayed through Christmas and returned home before the first of the year. We then went back a few weeks later to get our daughter after the remaining paperwork was completed.

Our daughter Cristina took to us right away. To help with the transition, we sent an album of pictures, and workers at the home told Cristina about us. When we arrived in Romania, she came flying down the orphanage steps into our arms. In fact, she was very protective of us and possessive. She didn't want any other children around us.

The orphanage was operated by a Baptist pastor and had begun only eleven months earlier. The pastor and his people told us that Cristina and others had real emotional problems. The pastor is a good man and ran a home that was like a large family. Also, the members of the church often took the children home over the weekend. Overall, the children appeared to be well adjusted when we visited. When we came in January to pick her up, Cristina was very excited, and about seventeen children and workers from the orphanage came to say goodbye. Cristina said, "Goodbye," and "When I come back, I'll bring gifts." She didn't show any homesickness and didn't look back. She has referred to the family that she stayed with on weekends as her cousins, grandfathers, etc.

Her biggest adjustment was frustration with the language barrier. Cristina seemed to understand us but couldn't speak. At the time, we had four small dogs, one an old beagle, and when we got home, she was terrified of the dogs: "no manka." We said "good manka"; "Manka"—she was saying "Don't eat me." In a few weeks, she played with the dogs.

Before we adopted, we read books about anxieties and habits of children from orphanages and didn't feel there was an attachment disorder. However, looking back, there was a period of biting, scratching, and spitting. We dealt with each situation one by one instead of all at once. We realized that if we tried to correct everything, we would always be fighting with her. Patience is critical. Also, we had to prioritize. She was angry and would have half-hour meltdowns and temper tantrums. There was nothing that was prompting her to be angry. At other times, she would go into the corner sobbing and crying. Each day the tantrums were fewer and further apart; finally she learned to control herself and get a hold of her feelings. For me, it was easy to get angry and think, "Kid, would you just snap out of this?" Family members said all kids do this, but they didn't realize what was happening.

This difficult time lasted a few months. Then Cristina was just more or less a normal, strong-willed child. It didn't take her long to master the language. She came home in January, and by April, she mixed English phrases with Romanian. Before she entered preschool in the early fall, I worked with Cristina to help her improve her English. I also got her together with other children so that she could be exposed to the language. She progressed well in K-4 and continues to do remarkably well; now she is a talker and loves people. She's a real people person.

• • •

The family says that they knew from the moment that they saw the video of Cristina that she was the child for them. "When she was in the orphanage, she would ask for a mommy and daddy. Her first grade teacher said Cristina always talks about her family; we never want her to forget Romania. She should see Romania as a good thing, a place where God was preparing her to be part of this family."

TRANSITION ISSUES

One significant transition for your adopted child can be his or her sleeping habits. Oftentimes, the foster mother or foster parents will sleep with the child. There are many opinions on this topic, but remember this is common in most of the world. Even if your child is in an orphanage, he or she will be used to sleeping in the same room with other children and probably will not want to sleep alone at night.

Therefore, your child will likely want to sleep in the same room with you, if not in the same bed. Your child may not want to sleep in a bed at all, but rather on a mat on the floor.

One mother describes the transition for her son who was adopted as a baby from the Ukraine.

• • •

He had difficulty sleeping through the night since he was used to a roomful of people. It helped to play music. The first month, I rocked him to sleep, even for naps. Also, I put him back on the bottle for bonding—whenever he went down for bed or a nap. Feeding him his bottle definitely helped with bonding.

Also, I used the orphanage's schedule for the first six months that he was home. He liked to keep his sleep schedule even though he was active during the day.

Although my husband instantly bonded with our baby son, it was not so instant for me. I was worried and stressed after having read about attachment disorders and was afraid he wouldn't love me.

Now Alek is like his dad, outgoing and happy. He is all boy!

• • •

Many foster mothers not only sleep with their children, but also carry them and hold them often. Your child may be used to this and not want to be put down. On the other hand, if your child has been in an orphanage and is not used to being held, he may find your holding him and looking him straight in the eyes while giving him a bottle to be too much stimulation. Most likely his bottles were propped up in his crib. Although feeding your child can be an important bonding time, you may need to gradually increase the intensity of your physical and eye contact. Depending on the child, you may need to begin gradually, such as sitting next to him and holding his hand while he drinks his bottle.

If your child is preschool age or older, she probably will know how to dress herself, make her own bed, and do chores. One mother describes how her three-year-old daughter was not interested in playing with toys, but more interested in helping fold the towels. Although it is commendable that the child wanted to interact with her mother, she had no idea how to play. These children need to have their needs provided for them and be allowed to be children once again. Also, these children have essentially had no choices: They were told when to eat—usually with no choice of what to eat, when to go potty, and when to sleep. Therefore, when your child first arrives, be aware that offering him choices can be overwhelming to him. Gradually, begin to offer him simple choices such as between juice or milk or between the red socks or the blue socks.

All children coming from other countries should be protected from too much stimulation when first arriving home. The environment should be calm and tranquil. A minimum of toys, games, entertainment, and outings should be available. Chuck E. Cheese is not the place to take your child in the first few months at home! You may want to bring him home to a colorful room full of toys, but this is not what he needs. A simply decorated room with a few things to do is more than enough. Amazingly, he does not need all of this to entertain himself! Gradually, the typical American lifestyle can be introduced to the child.

The most important goal is that your child bond with you. Dr. Gregory Keck states that it is important for a child to bond with one or two caregivers. He also says that children who have come from orphanages should not be placed in day care environments since this does not promote bonding with a primary caretaker. In addition, a day care is a noisy, overstimulating environment for this kind of child. At least one parent needs to stay home for several months until the child is fully bonded. If this is not possible, then your child should be cared for in his own home environment or by a close relative.

Even as important as early intervention is for your child to overcome early deprivation, exposing your child to too many professionals may limit his ability to bond with you. For example, if your child needs occupational therapy or speech therapy, you may want to delay this for a while. If he is spending a lot of time with the speech therapist, for example, this could be confusing to him.

CITIZENSHIP FOR YOUR CHILD

The Citizenship Act of 2000 allows all children adopted internationally who have come home on what are called IR-3 (IR stands for immediate relative) visas to become U.S. citizens without any formalities. How does a child come home on an IR-3 visa? If your child has been seen by you and your spouse before or during the adoption proceedings, then your child will come home on an IR-3 visa. Some countries, such as Russia, require both parents to be at the adoption hearing; virtually all children adopted from Russia would come home on an IR-3 visa. Other countries, such as China, allow only one parent to be present; if only one parent goes to China, then the child comes home on an IR-4 visa and the child is <u>not</u> a U.S. citizen.

Then there are adoptions that take place in the country—such as Guatemala—without the parents present. If parents simply travel to get their child and receive his visa, then the child will come home on an IR-4 visa. Some parents visit the child before the adoption in Guatemala, and then the child comes home on an IR-3 visa.

If you are adopting from a country in which your child may come home on either an IR-3 or IR-4 visa, you may consider taking the steps to visit your child beforehand or have both parents travel since there are some advantages to seeing your child before the adoption, as follows:

1. Your child is automatically a U.S. citizen when he touches U.S. soil and will be issued a Certificate of Citizenship in the mail—usually a few months after being home.
2. You do have to meet the preadoption requirements of your state (if any) before going to the U.S. Embassy to receive your child in the other country. For example, if only one spouse is traveling to China, the child will not be issued an IR-3 visa, and the parents must then meet the preadoption requirements of their state. This is usually proven by the fact that a home study is issued, but some states such as Wisconsin have more stringent guidelines. It is critical that you check with your home study provider as to your state's requirements.
3. If your child came home on an IR-4 visa, you will need to apply for a Certificate of Citizenship by filing CIS form N-600, Application for Certificate on Behalf of an Adopted Child. The CIS does not require original documents; send only photocopies. Attach a letter and state that they are true copies of the originals and have your signature notarized.

Copies of documents that must accompany the N-600 include:

- Child's new birth certificate from overseas and from the United States.
- Final adoption decree overseas and in the United States.
- If the child's name has been changed since coming to the United States, submit evidence of legal name change if not in the adoption decree.
- Evidence that one of the adoptive parents is a U.S. citizen. If you are born in the United States, your birth certificate will suffice.
- Marriage certificate of adoptive parents.
- Divorce decree or death certificate (if applicable). If either parent has been widowed or divorced, evidence of termination of these marriages must be given.
- Photographs. You will need to submit three identical passport photos of your child; these photos must be no more than thirty days old.
- Green card.

If you need more proof of your child's citizenship quickly, you can obtain a U.S. passport for your child while you are waiting for the Certificate of Citizenship.

If your child is a U.S. citizen, there is no question whether or not you are eligible for the federal tax credit when you file your taxes. In some states, you must readopt your child, making your a child a citizen, before you are eligible for the tax credit. This can delay your getting a tax credit by one year.

Although you may be tempted to forego getting your child a Certificate of Citizenship, once you adopt your child—after all he is a U.S. citizen with or without the Certificate—you should proceed with obtaining the Certificate. It is a bit expensive and does take some time to complete the N-600 form, but it is better to do this now while you know just where your child's important paperwork is located instead of waiting until he is going off to college. A birth certificate is not proof that your child is a citizen. Passports expire; the Certificate of Citizenship does not. Your child, especially if he is not "Anglo" in appearance, may be required more often than other Americans to "prove" that he is a U.S. citizen. Having the Certificate of Citizenship can save your child the hassle of having to get other documentation to prove that he is truly a citizen. Reportedly, some institutions of higher learning and the Armed Services may require a Certificate of Citizenship for those of foreign birth and will not accept a U.S. passport as proof of citizenship.

The N-600 is not necessarily filed in the same CIS where your I-600A was filed. To find out the exact location of where this should be filed, contact your home study agency. If the staff is not sure, then ask your immigration liaison at your congressman's or senators' local office.

OBTAINING YOUR CHILD'S ORIGINAL ADOPTION PAPERWORK

As stated earlier, to obtain this paperwork that is handed over to the CIS at the first port of entry when you enter the United States (found in a brown sealed envelope), you must file a G-884. This form cannot be downloaded from the CIS Web site. You can order the form to be mailed to you at *http://uscis.gov/graphics/exec/forms/index.asp* or by calling (800) 870-3676.

Most families who adopted from Guatemala report that when they order these original forms, they received color photographs of their children and birth mothers (hardly ever birth fathers) as was required for the DNA testing.

READOPTING YOUR CHILD IN THE UNITED STATES

Once your child is in the United States, it is highly advised from a legal standpoint that you readopt her officially in your state of residence. There are a number of reasons for readopting your child in the United States, whether or not you need to do so to obtain your child's U.S. citizenship:

Your child will have a state-issued birth certificate instead of having to present her birth certificate from another country or having to order her birth certificate from another country, such as China, when she signs up for soccer.

Your child's new birth certificate means he will seldom have to prove that he is also a U.S. citizen.

The child's name can be changed if the country issues the adoption decree in the child's original first name and the adoptive family's last name, such as is done in Guatemala.

The adoption is recognized by the state, and therefore, the child has all the same legal standing as a biologically born child.

Your child's new adoption decree and newly issued birth certificate are recognized by all states in the United States.

The foreign country, which may maintain the child's citizenship until he is eighteen years old, can never have claim to the child.

If your child is not a U.S. citizen (and came home on an IR-4 visa), he can be deported to his country of origin if he commits a felony. The Joint Council on International Children's Services cites instances in which adoptees who have committed crimes and who never received U.S. citizenship have been deported to their country of origin. Of course, you do not think of your child ever becoming a criminal. But what if he got into trouble while in college and was deported to a country where he knows no one and cannot even speak the language?

If the child's age needs to be changed in accordance with dental/bone and growth records, he can be reissued a new birth date. Sometimes a child's birth date may have been lowered to make him more adoptable, and therefore, the child is really older. At other times, a child may be made to be older so that he is adoptable by the country's standard. Usually if you are going to change a child's birth date, the judge will require you to submit a letter from a pediatrician explaining the reasons.

If you do readopt, this is the procedure you will probably follow:

1. Have a postplacement home study report conducted (almost always required).
2. Contact a knowledgeable attorney to file papers for adoption. The cost of this adoption is a fraction of an independent adoption. The attorney is simply filing the appropriate papers. Some couples do this work themselves, but getting a birth certificate can be difficult unless all the papers that should be submitted are exactly the way they should be. Be prepared to provide the attorney with a copy of your home study, child's birth certificates, documents indicating parental abandonment or relinquishment, and adoption decree from the foreign country.

3. Go to court for the child's final adoption.
4. Your attorney or the court will submit a Judgment of Adoption to your state's department of vital statistics to obtain a birth certificate. Make sure the Judgment of Adoption lists your child's date and place of birth. Vital statistics offices do not like to have to look at any other paperwork.
5. Obtain a copy of the child's new birth certificate. The new birth certificate will include the child's new adoptive name, you as his parents, and his date and place of birth. In some states, such as New Jersey, when a child is adopted internationally as opposed to domestically, the birth certificate says "Adopted" on it.

GETTING A SOCIAL SECURITY CARD AND PASSPORT FOR YOUR CHILD

Whether your child has come home on an IR-3 or an IR-4 visa, he can still get a Social Security card. Although you can obtain one by mail, it is much better if you go directly in person to the Social Security office. Your child does not need to go with you to the office.

If your child has come home on an IR-3 visa, you can go to the Social Security office and obtain his Social Security card when he receives his Certificate of Citizenship in the mail. If your child was issued an IR-4 visa, you must wait for his "green card" to be mailed to you, which indicates that he is a permanent resident before you can obtain the Social Security card. Sometimes the person at the Social Security office may not know that an "alien" is eligible to get a card; however, because your child is a permanent resident, he should qualify. Your child does not need to be a U.S. citizen to obtain a Social Security card.

If your child is not a citizen or if your child is going to have a name change after the adoption in the United States, you may want to wait until after the adoption to obtain the card so that you do not need to make two trips to your Social Security office to either change his name or to update his citizenship status.

Many families are willing to make two trips since they want the Social Security card right away for tax purposes. If you do not obtain a Social Security card for your child, you can get an Individual Taxpayer Identification Number. Yet, you cannot get an Adoption Taxpayer Identification Number for a child adopted internationally.

Note: If you are having any problems with completing immigration forms or obtaining a Social Security card, your agency may provide postplacement information support, or you may contact the immigration liaison at your local congressional or senatorial office.

Applying for a Passport for Your Child

Your child must be a U.S. citizen upon entry into the United States or must be readopted (and therefore a U.S. citizen) before he can be issued a passport. You do not need a Certificate of Citizenship for your child to receive a passport.

To apply for a passport, both parents and your child if he is under fourteen years old must appear in person at the post office or court house, and you must submit the following documents:

- DSP-11 Application for a Passport (both parents must submit)
- Two identical photographs (2 x 2 inches)
- Parents' valid identification (birth certificate or passport)
- Certified adoption decree, with English translation if necessary, or certified U.S. birth certificate; or Report of Birth Abroad (FS-240); or Certification of Birth Abroad (DS-1350); or Certificate of Citizenship; or Naturalization from CIS
- Child's foreign passport with CIS stamp I-551 or resident alien card
- $70 for children under fourteen years old
- You do *not* need a Social Security number to get your child's passport

All documents submitted must be originals, and these will be returned to you. It is best to have a prepaid self-addressed express envelope so that these precious documents can be tracked when they are returned to you.

FOLLOW-UP DOCUMENTATION FOR THE FOREIGN COUNTRY

Many countries require that follow-up documentation be sent to the foreign country to monitor the child's progress. These reports and documents and especially photos (send photos even if not asked) allow the placing organizations to prove to the courts and authorities that this child is in a good environment and is not being exploited. Sending this documentation can mean the difference between a country's keeping its adoption policy open or closing the doors. Even if the courts do not mandate that you send documentation, send letters, small gifts, a few dollars, and photographs to your child's caregiver or orphanage. In some countries, you should not send large packages since corrupt mail carriers and others will open packages that appear to have valuables in them. Keep your child's orphanage address on your Christmas list and send photos and a letter at least once a year.

ARRANGE FOR A FINAL MEDICAL EVALUATION

About two to three weeks after your child arrives home, you will want to take her for an evaluation. It is preferable that you take your child to a clinic that specializes in international adoption. This is not always possible, so try to select a pediatrician who is sensitive and knowledgeable about international children's needs.

When your child arrives home, you should consider having your child complete the following tests:

- Anemia testing
- Each child should have a complete blood count to screen for anemia and hemoglobinopathies. In addition, your child should be screened for sickle cell hemoglobinopathies if he is adopted from India or Central or South America. Hemoglobin E can be found in children from Southeast Asia, and B-thalassemia occurs in children from India and Southeast Asia. If the child has anemia, the health care provider may then want to investigate a dietary deficiency, intestinal parasite, or other infection or health problem.
- Thyroid function test
- Lead status. In about 14 percent of children adopted from China, there are elevated levels of lead; fortunately, a child rarely needs special therapy for the problem.
- Screening for hepatitis B and C
- Testing for HIV status
- Newborn screening. If a child is under twelve months old, he should receive a newborn screening.
- Audiology. Because so many children who live in orphanages have chronic, untreated ear infections, it is best to see if the child has experienced any hearing loss as a result.
- Dental screening. Many children living in other countries have many cavities; therefore, your child should visit a dentist.

Immunizations

The U.S. Embassy will require you to have your child immunized before you leave the country, or you will be asked to sign an affidavit stating that you will have your child immunized when the child is in the United States. Unless your child has good immunization records, the child should be immunized in the United States.

According to Jerri Jenista, M.D., if the record is written in different handwriting and at different monthly dates, then the record is probably accurate. Conversely, if your child has "perfect" immunization records, this is usually an indication that the records have been falsified.

Although some vaccines may have reduced potency and therefore are not as adequate, most vaccines, even those in developing countries, are reliable. The vaccines for measles, mumps, and rubella are heat sensitive, and an American pediatrician likely will reimmunize your child in the event that the vaccines were of a poor quality or not properly refrigerated.

If a child is under one year old, it is recommended that the child receive his immunizations again, even if he reportedly received them before coming to the United States. If a child is older, the physician may do testing to see whether the child has antibodies for the disease. However, these tests can be expensive—much more so than the vaccine—so many physicians opt to give the vaccine.

ISSUES RELATED TO ADOPTING INTERNATIONAL CHILDREN

Because children adopted internationally often look different from their parents, you may be asked questions such as: "Where did he come from?" "When did you get her?" "How old was he when you got him?" When answering such questions, do so in a way that feels comfortable to your child, helps your child feel like part of the family, and gives examples to your child of setting appropriate boundaries. While at times you may want to give a sarcastic answer, this will only make your child and others uncomfortable about adoption.

Establishing the simple understanding in your family that "not everyone understands adoption" can go a long way in how you deal with other people's reactions and comments. It may be more effective to reassure your child indirectly about his worth. For example, you could say, "It's hard to believe that some people just don't understand adoption." Don't let your hurt and perhaps your own fears about your child being "different" cause you to be overly "gushy" with your child about how wonderful he is. This can communicate as much about your insecurity as about your love.

You will want your child to have a sense of his heritage. If at all possible, try to connect with others in your area who have adopted children internationally and, if possible, from the same country. Although most children will want to be "Americanized," it's also important for them to know about their beginnings, where they came from, why they were placed for adoption, and that you believe their culture is worth keeping.

Special Programs for Paying for an International Adoption

Some grant programs are available for those adopting internationally, and sometimes individuals donate funds toward the adoption fees for a specific child's adoption, increasing the likelihood that the child will be adopted.

It is always best before looking for a child who has funding available to be completely home study ready and immigration approved. Even if you find a child from another country other than where you have been approved, CIS does allow families to change the country from which they are approved to adopt for a fee. Sometimes the home study must be amended as well.

God's Grace Adoption Ministry at *www.ggam.org* helps orphaned children of the world find families by reducing the financial burden to families.

The LOOC Foundation provides financing for the adoption of girls from China to qualified families. Go to *www.looc.org* or e-mail them at *info@looc.org*.

SPECIAL HEALTH CONSIDERATIONS IN THE INTERNATIONALLY ADOPTED CHILD

Children who are adopted internationally come from a wide variety of situations, programs, and cultures; for this reason, there are several health issues that should receive special attention.

Growth Delay

The most common medical problem among children adopted internationally is growth delay. For every three to four months a child spends in an orphanage, there is usually a one-month delay. Therefore, you would expect a child who is twelve months old to be developmentally at the same level as a child who is about eight months old.

A premature infant will be developmentally delayed, yet this is "normal." The growth delay can be due to lack of nutrient intake, including iron deficiency, iodine deficiency, lack of calcium, and overall lack of protein and calories. For example, if a child who was to be born in the middle of April is born in the beginning of March, then on July 1st, you would expect him to function as a two-and-one-half month old baby—not a four month old baby.

When adopting a child from another country, there are special considerations of health issues that are less likely to be a health problem here or may be more easily identified or documented if the child were adopted domestically.

Fetal Alcohol Syndrome

Regardless of what method of adoption a family chooses, infant domestic, special needs through the foster care system, or a child through international adoption, there is a risk that the child can have fetal alcohol syndrome (FAS/FAE).

Unlike adopting an infant in the United States, chances are you will receive little or no birth mother background information, and if you do, there is no guarantee that it is true. Also, unlike a domestic adoption of a child through the social services system, in which you can meet the child and obtain medical, social, and educational reports, there will be limited information in the child's file in an international adoption.

Certain countries have a much lower incidence of children born with FAS/FAE such as China and Korea. Other countries, such as Russia, have a much higher rate. Of course, considering the statistics in a country is only one way to reduce the likelihood of adopting a child with FAS/FAE.

Therefore, to determine if a child has or is at risk for FAS/FAE, you will need to look at the facts presented in the child's medical report and the picture/video of the child. Although few children from Asian countries have FAS/FAE, it is never safe to lull yourself into thinking that a child has not been prenatally exposed to excessive alcohol.

You will want to have the child's medical report and picture evaluated by a specialist in international adoption. Sometimes this is not practical, such as when you are presented with a picture of a newborn infant with only basic newborn information. In countries such as Guatemala where infants are often assigned to families and the initial medical report includes basic information such as height, weight, and head circumference and results from hepatitis B and HIV testing, there is little information provided to determine if the child is at risk for FAS/FAE.

Although such incidences are rare that a child will have FAS/FAE, it is possible. You still may want to have the child evaluated by a specialist when you receive updated measurements and pictures.

Tuberculosis

In most countries where children are adopted, tuberculosis (TB) is prevalent. The orphanage workers are infected and spread it to other children through coughing and sneezing. Most adults are not treated, and thus, the babies and children, who are more susceptible to the disease because of a weaker immune system and may already be nutritionally compromised, become easily infected.

Therefore, to decrease the likelihood of children getting TB or the problems associated with it, children are often given a vaccine against tuberculosis called the BCG. The vaccine is usually given in the upper arm shortly after birth. The scar from the BCG vaccine looks like a smallpox vaccine scar.

Although the vaccine does not protect completely against TB in the lungs, it does protect children from the complications associated with TB, such as the bacteria going to the kidneys or spinal fluid. In fact, TB bacteria can go anywhere in the body, but it most likely goes to the lungs.

When your child arrives home, he must be given a TB test called the PPD (purified protein derivative) to test for exposure to TB. The test is done by injecting a minute amount of TB under the skin and seeing if there is swelling or firmness on the skin. If the site of injection has a reaction that measures more than 10 millimeters, forty-six to seventy-two hours later, chances are very likely that your child has been exposed to TB. This reaction may be due to the BCG vaccine itself or to a latent TB infection. A positive reaction probably means that the child has a latent TB infection in which the disease is in an inactive form and is not contagious. Unfortunately, the child can later develop TB. Also, latent TB will not show up on a chest x-ray.

If your child is malnourished, there is a possibility that he could have a false negative test—that is, he will test negative, even though he has been exposed to TB. Therefore, children should be retested six to nine months later after they have been well nourished.

The child then will have a chest x-ray to determine if he has TB in his lungs. If there is no evidence that your child has an active case of TB, he will be given Isoniazid for nine months. This medication prevents the TB from becoming active and your child getting TB. Like all antibiotics, it is essential for your child to take the medication for the full nine months or more so that TB that may be resistant to the antibiotic does not thrive. If your child does not have an active case of TB, he is not contagious to other children.

Many children, who have been given the BCG vaccine will test positive for the PPD due to the vaccine itself and not to any real exposure to TB. It appears that the measurement of the skin reaction when the PPD is given indicates whether the reaction is from the vaccine or from a true exposure to TB.

When your child should be tested for TB if he has had a BCG is debatable. The test can be done on infants as young as six months old, especially if it is known that the child was exposed to TB. Yet, if the child still has a scar from the vaccine that is still healing, then the test should be delayed for about one year. If the child has an active scar and is therefore not tested, then the child should have a chest x-ray.

Hepatitis B

Hepatitis B is the most prevalent chronic viral disease in the world and is most prevalent in Asia, the Pacific Rim, the Amazon, and southern parts of Eastern and Central Europe, as well as sub-Saharan Africa. It is estimated to be in 10 percent to 30 percent of the population. It is highly contagious, spread through body fluids, and fifty to 100 times more infectious than the HIV virus. It can also live on a surface for a few days. About 5 percent of all children adopted internationally have the infection. Most of the children from China, who have hepatitis B, will have gotten the disease when it was passed from mother to baby at the time of birth or during the first year of life from exposure while living in the orphanage. About 70 percent of children whose mother is positive for hepatitis B when giving birth will acquire the disease at that time. The disease can be prevented if an infant is given immunoglobulin within twelve to twenty-four hours after birth. Unfortunately, this is rarely done in developing countries.

Ninety percent of these early infections become "chronic," which means the infections last longer than six months, and usually they last for life. Fortunately, for most of these children, the liver does not respond to the infection because the virus is seen as part of the body's cells and not as a "germ." If your child tests positive for hepatitis B, when he reaches his teens, he should be further tested by an infectious disease specialist to make sure he does not have the early signs of liver cancer, which is treatable.

There appears to be about a 25 percent chance that a child will later have some complications related to having hepatitis B.

Many children in orphanages do not get tested for hepatitis B because it is impractical to take a specimen and then take it to a reliable lab. A negative hepatitis B outcome can give a false sense of assurance as well. Once in the United States, children should still be tested again for hepatitis B because it can take up to six months after exposure for a child to test positive.

If your child has been immunized against hepatitis B, he will test positive for the antibody but will test negative for the antigen.

Strabismus

It appears that in adopting internationally, there is a higher incidence of strabismus (what people refer to as being cross-eyed) than in the United States. About 30 percent of all infants will have a strabismus at birth, usually exotropic (outward turning), and it will resolve within the first three months as coordination of the eyes develops. The true infantile or congenital esotropia is a large turn, which is easily noticed. A child will never grow out of a true strabismus. Sometimes children look like they have a strabismus because the bridge of the nose has not developed. When the bridge of the nose forms, the appearance of a strabismus disappears. Thus, these children never had a strabismus.

Your child should have a thorough eye exam by a pediatric ophthalmologist to determine if he has any vision problems, as the sooner these are corrected, the better.

Scabies

Scabies is an infestation of the skin with a microscopic mite. Scabies spreads rapidly under crowded conditions where there is frequent skin-to-skin contact between people, such as in orphanages.

Scabies looks like small pimples and the rash occurs on the skin, especially the webbing between the fingers; the skin folds on the wrist, elbow, or knee; the penis; the breast; or shoulder blades. The itching is very intense, especially at night because that is the time when the mites feed.

If the mites are away from the body, such as on sheets, they will not survive more than forty-eight to seventy-two hours. When on a person, the mite can live up to ninety days. If you are exposed to mites overseas and you never had them before, the symptoms may take four to six weeks to show up. You could be home with your child for a month before you notice the itching. If you had scabies before, the symptoms can appear within several days.

Pets cannot spread mites, only humans. The mite living on animals is called mange and can cause you to itch, but the mite will die in a couple of days.

Typically, there are fewer than ten mites on the entire body of an infested person; this makes it easy for an infestation to be missed.

Several lotions are available to treat scabies. Always follow the directions provided by your physician or the directions on the package insert. No new burrows or rashes should appear twenty-four to forty-eight hours after effective treatment. All clothes, bedding, and towels used by the infested person before treatment should be washed in hot water and dried in a hot dryer. A second treatment of the body with the same lotion may be necessary seven to ten days later. Pregnant women and children are often treated with milder scabies medications.

All persons who have close, prolonged contact with the infested person should also be treated. If your health care provider has instructed family members to be treated, everyone should receive treatment at the same time to prevent reinfestation.

Itching may continue for two to three weeks and does not mean that you are still infested. You and your child may need medication to relieve itching if it is severe.

Your health care provider can prescribe medication to destroy the mite and to relieve itching. Permethrin (Elimite) Creme is most commonly used. Another medication, Eurax, is available for use with pregnant women and children under age three. An older medication, Kwell (Lindane), is not currently recommended, especially for young children.

Parasites

An examination for ova (eggs) and parasites, giardia antigen, and bacterial infections is recommended for all international adoptees. Families need to contact the laboratory that processes the stool specimen to see if special handling instructions are necessary with collecting this specimen. Children living in impoverished orphanages are at a higher risk, as are children who are significantly malnourished. It is not necessary for children to have diarrhea for them to have illnesses diagnosed by these tests. Most doctors will obtain three specimens, collected forty-eight hours apart, to make completely sure that the children have no infection, particularly if they are symptomatic.

Children living in an orphanage setting may pass several parasites at one time. If a parasite is found, it is recommended that the stool examination be repeated after treatment. Some asymptomatic parasite infections found in international adoptees will resolve without any treatment. There are also numerous cases of children adopted internationally who have tested negative for parasite infections just after being adopted but have passed large worms months to years later.

For a list of physicians who can evaluate your child before adoption, visit *www.ComeUnity.com/adoption/health/clinics.html.*

Other resources regarding health issues and international adoption include:

www.adoptionsinternational.com
www.adoptionpros.com/doctors.htm
www.globalpediatrics.com

RESOURCES ONLINE

www.karensadoptionlinks.com
Karen provides multiple links and other information related to international adoption.

Our Chinese Daughters Foundation, Inc.
www.ocdf.org
This site provides resources, travel information, and cultural events.

www.eeadopt.org
Eastern European information

www.Frua.org
Information and support for families adopting from Russia, the Ukraine, and other former Soviet Union countries

Korean-American Adoptee Adoptive Family Network
www.kaanet.com
Asian and Korean adoption support and information

Korean Focus for Adoptive Families
www.koreanfocus.org
This site provides adoptive families with support and education on Korean culture.

Latin American Parents Association (LAPA)
www.lapa.com

INTERNATIONAL ADOPTION: ONE COUPLE'S STORY

• • •

For seven long years, my husband and I tried thermometers, surgery, syringes, and just about everything short of swinging chickens over our heads. Still, we had no children. Our doctors had no idea why I couldn't get pregnant. They still don't, but now we have children. They came a year ago from Korea—according to our youngest son, "born on the Christmas airplane when I was three and my brother was five."

How did we come to be at the airport that night? It started four months earlier in August with the blinding realization that what we wanted was not to get pregnant, but to be a family. Our first thought was to adopt an American infant with high Apgar scores. After all, one agency was ready to give us just such a child as long as we paid them $16,000 and didn't ask any questions. But in the end we did something very different. We applied to Catholic Charities' international program on August 21, requesting an infant girl.

In September, two days before completing our home study, we called our caseworker and said we'd done some thinking about diapers and drool and would consider an older child—a girl about two years old. After all, we'd waited long enough for a family and didn't really see the point of waiting still longer for a child to gurgle, "Ma-ma, Da-da." That was when the caseworker showed us the picture—two little brothers, three and five, looking impossibly dirty and infinitely sad. Days later we were petitioning the CIS for visas for these two little boys, whom we were about to adopt from 12,000 miles around the world.

Our families were enthusiastic—my mother pointing out that adoption was infinitely better than pregnancy because you got pictures. We were euphoric—finally able to prowl the children's department at Garfinkel's and Lowen's in preparation for their arrival. We never regretted the decision, but we did get chills.

After all, these were older children. They were probably a little hardened. Bonding certainly wasn't going to be an issue; what we were worried about was, "Why can't we have more treats?" They'd probably test us and be suspicious.

By December, we'd reached such a state that we fully expected them to arrive with beards, smoking cigarettes, and cursing. When the caseworker called my husband at work to say they were to arrive in just five days, he said, "How nice" and threw up in his wastebasket.

So there we were at the airport, ready to face two sullen boys who by that time we imagined as six feet tall and ready to form an alliance against us. Instead, two tiny, terrified children walked haltingly down the ramp and reached out their hands. What we never anticipated is that our sons wanted a family as much as we did. Their need, like ours, was to love and be loved and to build a future. From the moment they put their small hands in ours, that's what we've been doing.

There were never any of the struggles we'd expected. We found ourselves the parents of children who were inexpressibly joyful to have a mama and a papa. They were untiring in their desire to please, expansive in their appreciation of our attempts to please them.

After our son's birthday party in September, we were tucking the boys in, and my husband said, "I'm sorry we weren't together for your first three!" Our older son touched his arm and said, "It's okay, Papa, we're together now." It is okay. We've learned to carpool, bake brownies, make valentines, and clean mud off tiny soccer shoes. I've also learned that the most wonderful part of the whole day can happen unexpectedly—anytime a small pair of arms reaches up to give a hug or a small voice says, "Mama."

Hardened? Our six-year-old got into a fight at school because a boy was teasing a little girl. He explained that the girl didn't know it was just teasing and that she felt scared. He knew how that felt he said and wanted to help her. Hardly dog-eat-dog.

Are they like us? I don't know anymore. I know we fit together tightly, but I'm not sure who changed or whether we were alike from the start. They're teaching us to see our entire world with new, gentle, and eager eyes. Labeled as "hard-to-adopt" because of their "advanced ages," these two children are teaching us to find blessings wherever we look and to know that even when sneakers have "accidentally" been glued to the refrigerator we're happier than any of us would have dreamed before that night when the "Christmas airplane" landed.

Chapter Thirteen

Adopting in Canada

I f there is one generally true statement that can be made about adoption in Canada, it is that no such comprehensive statement really exists! Adoption rules and regulations vary tremendously from province to province. Not only are the diverse provincial laws varied in their content and applications, but they are also in a constant, almost day-to-day state of flux. According to Judy Grove, retired director of the Adoption Council of Canada, "It is a full time job, just keeping up with all of the changes." Because of the fluid nature of Canadian adoption regulations, this chapter does not attempt to be a definitive guide for the Canadian adoptive parent. The goal here, instead, is to provide a brief but accurate overview of Canadian adoption. Adoptive parents are advised to take advantage of the list of resources at the end of the chapter to find people and organizations that can provide them with complete, up-to-the-minute information.

AN OVERVIEW OF ADOPTION IN CANADA

As more mothers consider single parenthood to be a viable option and as birth control and abortion are more accepted, the number of babies available for adoption has decreased dramatically. It is estimated that there are only about 1,400 babies available for adoption in Canada each year, but approximately 15,000 couples wanting to adopt. This is one reason that international adoption has become a popular option. Intercountry adoptions now outnumber domestic adoptions by a ratio of three to two, according to adoption expert Michael Sobol. This is unlike in the United States, where there are at least as many, if not more, private agency/ independent infant adoption placements than international child placements.

According to statistics provided in a phone interview with the Adoption Council of Ontario, 908 children were placed domestically for private adoption throughout Canada in 2002; and in 2003, 2,181 children were adopted by Canadians from foreign countries.

Despite the changes in Canada's cultural climate, married couples still have the easiest time completing both domestic and international adoptions, even though as of August 2004, British Columbia, Alberta, Newfoundland, Nova Scotia, Ontario, and Quebec allow adoptions by same-sex couples.

According to the Adoption Council of Canada, singles may find adopting more difficult. Some foreign countries do not accept single applicants, while others place restrictions on the age of a child to be adopted by a single parent. Canadians living abroad are frequently denied access to Canadian resources for adoption.

PRIVATE DOMESTIC ADOPTIONS
There are essentially three different kinds of private domestic adoptions in Canada: independent, licensee, and direct placement (formerly known as identified adoption). The cost for a private domestic adoption is usually between $10,000 and $15,000.

Independent Adoption
In an independent or self-directed adoption, the adoptive parents contact a birth mother who chooses to place her child directly with them without the assistance of an agency. The adoptive parents usually have to find the birth mother themselves. Independent adoptions are not allowed in some provinces; check with your provincial government before undertaking such a procedure. As of this writing, independent adoptions are becoming less and less prevalent.

Licensee Adoption
According to Judy Grove of the Adoption Council of Canada, Ontario is the only province that uses the term "licensee adoption," but many provinces have licensed agencies. In a licensee adoption, the services of a "licensee," or adoption professional, are engaged. This licensee may be either an agency or a person. Licensed agencies employ social workers to coordinate adoptions and a lawyer to conduct the legal work. In cases where a licensed individual is used, the licensee is usually a lawyer, social worker, or physician.

Direct Placement
In direct placement adoptions, a birth mother chooses you, but a licensee conducts the adoption. The licensee may be associated with an agency or may be an approved individual. Direct placements can be quicker than independent adoptions because the agency you are working with may find a child for you while you simultaneously conduct your own search for a birth mother.

Note: It should be emphasized that in many provinces in Canada it is illegal for adoptive parents to pay a birth mother's expenses during pregnancy.

PROVINCIAL RULES AND REGULATIONS

Those interested in domestic adoption must acquaint themselves with their provincial laws. Private agencies are allowed for domestic adoptions in some provinces but not all.

A summary of each province's laws:

Alberta: Agency required, except in direct placement

British Columbia: Agency required

Manitoba: Agency required

New Brunswick: Government-run agency and lawyer required

Newfoundland: Direct placement allowed; no private agencies; use a lawyer

Northwest Territories: Private placement allowed; use personal lawyer

Nova Scotia: Direct placement allowed; some private agencies; may also adopt
    directly using a lawyer

Ontario and Prince Edward Island: No direct placement

Quebec: No private agencies; no direct placement

Saskatchewan: Direct placement allowed; only one private agency; use a lawyer

Yukon Territory: No direct placement

Provincial laws on domestic adoption are subject to constant fluctuation. To receive the most current information about your province, contact your local government, the provincial authorities found at the end of this chapter, or call the Adoption Council of Canada at (613) 235-0344. The Adoption Council of Canada is a private organization, not a government agency, but it is mandated to keep up with changes in adoption legislation, both domestic and international.

FOSTER CARE ADOPTION

About 2,000 children were adopted through the social service system, although there are 66,000 in foster care and 20,000 are permanent Crown wards.

The *Ottawa Citizen* reported in April 2004 that the Ontario government is planning to change its adoption laws to find families for the nearly 9,000 children in foster care and plans are to increase adoptions by 15 percent. A major obstacle to adoption is terminating parents' rights. About 75 percent of the province's Crown wards have parents who have access and, therefore, are not eligible for adoption. Yet, many of these parents exercise these "access orders" only every few years. It costs the government $40,000 per year to keep a child in foster care; therefore, measures as mandated by law that are taken will save the taxpayers much.

The North American Council on Adoptable Children has an excellent Web site and contact information for Canadians adopting children through the social service system.

INTERNATIONAL ADOPTION

In Canada, most international adoptions are conducted through private agencies. These agencies engage the help of provincial and national government ministries to complete the legalities of the adoption. In 2003, Canadians adopted 1,108 children from China, making it by far the most popular country from which to adopt. The next most popular country was Haiti, from which Canadians adopted 138 children. Chinese adoptions make up about 51 percent of all international adoptions; whereas adoptions from Haiti account for only 7 percent. The number of children from the United States and Russia followed closely behind Haiti.

Overall, the number of international adoptions has remained fairly constant over the past nine years.

The Canadian government, unlike that of the United States, does not place a restrictive terminology on the word "orphan." Often, in fact, when a child is not able to come into the United States because she is not an "orphan" as strictly defined by the U.S. Citizen and Immigration Services, an immediate search will begin for a Canadian couple instead.

The Hague Convention on Intercountry Adoption was ratified in 1994 and is an important aspect of international adoption in Canada. If the country from which you wish to adopt is a country that has subscribed to the standards set forth by The Hague, your paperwork must meet these standards in order to be approved. For a current list of Hague and non-Hague countries, contact the Adoption Council of Canada.

If a family does adopt from another Hague country, all Hague documents have to pass through Canada's central authority: Child, Family and Community (CFC) Division. CFC is in the same location as the former National Adoption Desk:

Child, Family and Community Division
5th Floor, Phase IV
Place du Portage
140 Promenade du Portage
Hull, Que. K1A 0J9
Phone: (819) 994-3831, Fax: (819) 953-1115
www.hrdc-drhc.gc.ca/sdd-dds/cfc/content/interAdopt.shtml

For the Intercountry Adoption Services Unit, contact Manager Patricia Paul-Carson, (819) 953-6610, Fax (819) 953-1115, *patricia.paulcarson@hrdc.drhc.gc.ca*.

The Intercountry Adoption Services Unit shares adoption information with provinces and the community. CFC also represents the provinces and territories in other countries, except for Quebec. Quebec's equivalent of the CFC is Secrétariat à l'Adoption Internationale.

If you are considering an international adoption, it is best to contact your provincial adoption coordinator rather than CFC.

For more on CFC, see News at the Family Helper Web site, *www.familyhelper.net*.

Canadians considering international adoption will want to consult the *Canadian Guide to Intercountry Adoption*, 2004 edition. This book is an indispensable tool that helps parents choose the country that is best for them and assists in the process of choosing an agency. You may order the guide by sending a check for $12.00 (Canadian or U.S. dollars), made out to Robin Hilborn, Box 1353, Southampton, Ontario, NOH 2LO. Robin Hilborn also publishes a quarterly magazine, *Adoption Helper*, which can be obtained by writing to the same address. A subscription for one year (four editions) is $36.00 (Canadian dollars).

An excellent Web site that outlines each province's regulations regarding international adoption is *www.interlog.com/~ladybug/canagen.htm*.

ADOPTING A CHILD FROM THE UNITED STATES

In 2003, seventy-four U.S. babies were adopted by Canadians, according to the Adoption Council of Canada. Adopting from the United States is like any other international adoption in most ways. In a phone interview, Joanne Conlin, a licensee in Ontario, outlined the steps of the process. Bear in mind that some of these steps may be unique to Ontario, but overall, the process is fairly similar from province to province:

1. An agency in Canada is chosen, and the home study package is submitted, with medical reports, references, and police clearance.
2. The local Ministry of Community and Social Services issues a letter of recommendation.
3. Adoptive parents fill out a sponsorship application and get approval from the government.
4. A child is selected.
5. Social and medical history of the birth parents and child are obtained and given to the Canadian government.
6. The government issues a Letter of No Objection and an approval of the placement of this particular child with this particular family.
7. The Letter of No Objection is given to the Canadian Embassy in Buffalo, New York, along with copies of the adoptive parents' passports, approval for placement,

and immigration medical report on the child. This medical report must be performed by a physician in the United States who is approved by the Canadian government to do adoption immigration physicals. The provincial social service department gives this to the Canadian Embassy in Buffalo.

8. An application for permanent residence is filled out.

9. A visa is issued for the child. The usual lapse of time between the child's birth (or selection) and the issuance of the visa is three to four weeks.

10. After the child enters Canada, the adoptive couple is on probation for six months. Reports on the progress of the child are sent to the agency in the United States.

11. The family goes to court to get an adoption finalization order and a new birth certificate for the child.

ADOPTION IN QUEBEC

The province of Quebec is distinct from the rest of Canada in many matters involving culture and law. Adoption is no exception to this separateness, both at the domestic and international levels. Quebec is a very adoption-minded province with almost 1,000 international adoptions per year among a population of just 7.5 million. Proportionately, many more Quebecois adopt than do U.S. citizens. Each year, there are nearly as many adoptions in Quebec alone as in all the rest of Canada put together.

International adoptions are more popular in Quebec than domestic for several reasons. Quebecois are not allowed to publish advertisements seeking a birth mother in their own province. They must advertise outside of Quebec, and adoptions from another province are technically considered "international." Also, there are no private agencies in this province; domestic adoption is a provincial governmental matter. Adopting through the public social services organization, Association des Centres Jeunesse du Quebec, tends to be difficult; the wait for a newborn can be as long as eight years. This is a powerful incentive for Quebecois to adopt their children from other countries.

According to Claire-Marie Gagnon, a Quebec adoption specialist and former president of the Federation des Parents Adoptants du Quebec, those who do decide to adopt within the province have three classes of adoptions from which to choose: open, closed, and Banque Mixte. Open and closed adoptions function similarly in Quebec to how they would in the United States. Banque Mixte, the third route, is a somewhat risky method of adopting a child in that 20 percent of placements are never finalized. In this procedure, a child who may become available for adoption through parental abuse or neglect is placed by the department of social services in a home with parents who wish to adopt her. In 80 percent of cases, parental rights are terminated, and the adoption goes forward. However, in some instances, reunification takes place between the child and her birth parents. This sometimes happens after the child has been in the hopeful adoptive parents' home for years. The tension and uncertainty involved in a Banque Mixte adoption make it a potentially difficult experience, both for the adoptive parents and the child.

International adoption in Quebec is a function of the province, as is domestic, but is perceived by many as being less risky. The Quebecois ministry that has overseen foreign adoptions since 1982 is called the Secretariat a l'Adoption Internationale. Any organization that handles international adoptions must be officially recognized by the Secretariat. There are sixteen such organizations, called *organismes*. While the organismes function somewhat like private agencies, they are, in fact, licensed, nonprofit organizations recognized by the government.

The sixteen organismes presently have working relationships with twenty-one countries. China is the country from which children are most frequently adopted, with over 450 children placed in 2003, followed by Haiti, Belarus, South Korea, and Colombia.

To contact someone in your province, use the following resources:

GENERAL
Adoption Council of Canada
211 Bronson Avenue
Suite 210
Ottawa, Ontario KIR 6H5
Attention: Eugenie Dore
Phone: (613) 235-0344

Parent Finders
Phone: (613) 730-8305
www.canadaadopts.com

ALBERTA
Adoption Services
11th Floor, Sterling Place
9940 106 Street
Edmonton, Alberta T5K 2N2
Phone: (780) 422-0178

BRITISH COLUMBIA
Adoptive Families Association of BC
#200-7342 Winston Street
Burnaby, British Columbia V5A 2G1
Phone: (604) 320-7330

Adoption Coordinator
Ken Bonner, Manager, Adoption Branch (XNG)
Ministry of Children and Family Development
Box 9705
Stn Prov. Govt., Victoria V8V 1X4
Phone: (250) 387-2281, Fax: (250) 356-1864

Adoption Legislation Hotline
Phone: (888) 236-7888

MANITOBA
Adoption Services
6-677 Stafford Street
Winnipeg, Manitoba R3M 2X7
Phone: (204) 944-4360

Margaret Curtis
Adoption and Perinatal, Child and Family Support, Child and Family Services
#201, 114 Garry Street
Winnipeg, Manitoba R3C 4V5
Phone: (204) 945-6962, Fax: (204) 945-6717

International Adoption Specialist: *Juliette Charlebois*
Phone: (204) 945-6958

NEW BRUNSWICK
New Brunswick Dept. of Health and Wellness
P.O. Box 5100
Fredericton, New Brunswick E3B 5G8
Phone: (506) 453-2536

Joan Mix
Adoption Service, Department of Health and Community Services
Box 5100
Fredericton, New Brunswick E3B 5G8
Phone: (506) 444-5970

NEWFOUNDLAND/LABRADOR
Ethel Dempsey
Child Welfare Services, Department of Social Services
Box 8700
St. John's, Newfoundland A1B 4J6
Phone: (709) 729-2668

Post Adoption Services
Health and Community Services
Box 13122
St. John's, Newfoundland A1B 3A4
Phone: (709) 570-8406

Note: Newfoundland and Labrador are not signatories to the Hague Convention on Intercountry Adoption and, therefore, do not have the same policies on international adoptions as other provinces (*Adoption Canada* newsletter, August 2003).

NORTHWEST TERRITORIES
Protective Services
Department of Health and Social Services
Box 1320
Government of Northwest Territories
Yellowknife, Northwest Territories X1A 2L9
Phone: (867) 873-7943

NOVA SCOTIA
Nova Scotia Dept. of Community Services
Family and Children's Services
P.O. Box 696
Halifax, Nova Scotia B3J 2T7
Phone: (902) 424-4279

ONTARIO
Children and Youth Services
7th Floor
Hepburn Block
80 Grosvenor Street
Toronto, Ontario M7A 1E9
Phone: (416) 327-4742, Fax: (416) 212-6799
adoption.unit@css.gov.on.ca

Adoption Council of Ontario
Phone: (416) 482-0021; Fax: (416) 482-1586
Provides workshops for adoptive parents.

Vanier Institute of the Family
94 Centrepointe Drive
Ottawa, Ontario K2G 6B1
Phone: (613) 228-8500; Fax: (613) 228-8007
This group publishes a French/English newsletter covering many family issues, including adoption.

PRINCE EDWARD ISLAND
Provincial Adoption Services
Department of Health and Social Services
16 Garfield Street, Box 2000
Charlottetown, PEI C1A 7N8
Phone: (902) 368-6511

QUEBEC
Centre de Protection de l'Enfance et de la Jeunesse
Service de l'Adoption
4515 St. Catherine Street W
Westmount, Quebec H3Z 1R9
Phone: (514) 935-6196

Luce De Bellefeuille, Directeur, Secrétariat à l'Adoption Internationale,
201 Boul. Crémazie est - RC 01
Montréal, Québec H2M 1L2
Phone: (514) 873-5226, Fax: (514) 873-1709, 1-800-561-0246
www.msss.gouv.qc.ca/adoption

SASKATCHEWAN

Janice Krumenacker, Senior Program Consultant

Adoption Program, Family and Youth Services Division,
Department of Community Resources and Employment

12th Floor, 1920 Broad Street

Regina, Saskatchewan S4P 3V6

Phone: (306) 787-5698, Fax: (306) 787-3648

Postadoption Registry

Department of Community Resources and Employment

1920 Broad Street

Regina, Saskatchewan S4P 3V6

Phone: (306) 787-3654

YUKON TERRITORY

Child Placement Services

Department of Health and Social Services

Government of Yukon

Box 2703 (H-10)

Whitehorse, YT Y1A 2C6

Phone: (867) 667-3476

Chapter Fourteen

Toddler Adoption

You may feel that you do not want to adopt an infant. Perhaps you do not want to go through the infant stage—nightly feedings and diapers for the next two to three years and accumulated paraphernalia that is "required" to care for an infant. You may be older and believe that you either do not have the energy for an infant or that you want the child to be a couple of years old so that there are fewer years difference between you and the child. Instead of adopting a school-age child who may have been institutionalized or has suffered because of years of abuse or neglect and possibly being shuffled around in the foster care system, you may want a child who is young and less likely to be adversely affected by her history. You may also feel that a toddler adopted today would be in school full-time in just a couple of years.

If you are looking to adopt a toddler—that is, a child who is more than one year old to early preschool age—you join the majority of families who adopt internationally. You can adopt a child from a private agency or attorney, or you could adopt through the social services system. Adopting a toddler from the United States can prove more difficult since most birth mothers place infants for adoption and most children placed through social services are school age. However, if you are diligent and flexible, you can adopt a toddler. No matter what route you take, you may want to start with your social services department and take classes through them. If you feel that you may wait forever to adopt a toddler through social services, you may want to get your home study sent to many agencies and attorneys. Most families are looking to adopt infants; therefore, you can present yourselves as wanting to adopt the child who is a little bit older. Although such children are the minority of placements, these children do come along, and if you are diligent, you could have a placement of a toddler.

Usually the fastest route to adopt a toddler is through international adoption, especially if you are seeking to adopt a Caucasian, Hispanic, or Asian child. If you are seeking to adopt an African-American toddler, then the fastest route may be your social services department. You can also submit your home study to multiple agencies and attorneys in the event that an African-American toddler becomes available.

Although it is true that the younger the child, the less likely they are to have emotional and behavioral problems, there are still issues to consider. You should never lull yourself into a false sense of security because a child is less than two years old and therefore will have no "issues."

WHY TODDLERS ARE AVAILABLE

It is well documented that babies and toddlers who are in institutions or who go from one foster home to another before being adopted do not fare as well as children who are placed into adoptive homes at birth. Yet, in spite of this, most children are not placed as infants but as toddlers or older. Essentially, the only way to adopt a newborn infant is through a domestic adoption conducted by a private agency or attorney. If you adopt a child through social services or internationally, it is nearly impossible to adopt a newborn baby. Infants placed into the care of social services usually go to a foster home first before an adoption plan is made. Only 34 percent of children available through the social services department are five years old or younger.

Primarily, toddlers are available through international adoption because laws in many countries require the children to be on registries for a certain period of time before they can leave the country. Even if you are assigned a very young child, bureaucracy can delay the placement, and the very young baby that you saw and was assigned to you can be ten months old when you receive him.

There are obvious challenges when adopting an older child. Usually the child is placed after difficult life circumstances at best and after being abused or neglected at worst. Even if the child grew up in an orphanage and received adequate care and food, the child may very likely suffer emotionally from growing up in an institution. A child's physical and psychological development has much to do with how well the infant had his needs met in the first year of life. It is believed that adopting a child over two years old greatly increases the likelihood that the child will have serious emotional problems. But what about the child who is adopted under thirty-six months old, but not as a newborn baby? What issues can the adoptive parents expect to face? This is the question that everyone who is adopting internationally needs to ask.

If you are adopting a child who is not a newborn infant, you will want to read *Toddler Adoption: The Weaver's Craft* by Dr. Mary Hopkins-Best, an educational specialist. This book is realistic yet optimistic.

So many clients enter into the adoption of an older baby—even though they are often referred to as infants—thinking that as parents all they have missed out on in the first few months of life. However, not only have the parents missed out, but the child probably has also missed out on some very important needs being met during this critical stage of life. Some experts believe that a child learns 50 percent of everything he knows in the first year of life and 75 percent by the end of his second year. This learning includes how he relates to the world and to people and his ability to control his world. How the child's mother or other primary caretaker meets the child's needs through touch, eye contact, smiles, sound, and food can affect a child's overall attitudes. If his needs were not met, he may feel anger, hopelessness, and distrust because the world is not a safe place.

Also, if a child's needs are not met, she can develop insecure attachments, which makes it difficult for her to attach to you. Those who are adopting even very young babies or toddlers will want to know whether or not a child can attach.

Signs of Attachment Difficulties (Birth–1 Year)

- Does not respond with recognition to face of primary caretaker in first six months
- Hardly coos, babbles, or cries
- Delayed creeping, crawling, sitting
- Does not like to be cuddled and will become rigid when held
- Excessive fussiness and irritability
- Passive or withdrawn
- Poor muscle tone, limp

Signs of Attachment Difficulties (Ages 1–5)

- Excessively clingy and whiny
- Persistent, frequent tantrums
- High threshold of pain—does not seem to notice if too cold or too warm; does not feel injury on body
- Unable to occupy self in a positive way without involving others
- Resistant to being held
- Demands affection in a controlling way
- Intolerant of separation from primary caretakers, except on the child's terms
- Indiscriminate display of affection, sometimes to strangers
- Problems with speech development, problems with motor coordination—considered accident-prone
- Hyperactivity
- Feeding problems
- By five, may be manipulative, devious, destructive, hurtful to pets, lies frequently

Of course, some children will display some of these signs and not necessarily have an attachment problem. Also, attachment problems can be on a continuum; it does not mean that a child will have all of the signs. However, if the child you adopt does not want to be held and snuggled softly but is whiny and clingy and will not let you out of her sight and seems very demanding, this can be indicative of an attachment problem. Also, it is the degree of the problem that may indicate an attachment problem. All two-year-olds can be whiny and clingy, have temper tantrums, be hyperactive, and be picky eaters. The problem is not when the child has these characteristics some of the time. It is when these characteristics tend to dominate the child's personality that there is a problem.

Because of the lack of stimulation in an orphanage setting, even young babies in orphanages are not as developmentally advanced as other infants, and usually they are sicker. An American family who lives in Romania adopted two unrelated babies who were three months old at placement. While the children were still in the orphanage, one week before the children's placement, the adoptive parents videotaped their children. A few months later, in viewing the video, the parents had forgotten how different their children looked. They said the babies looked very sickly in the video. At six months old, these babies were alert, healthy, and chubby.

Many families report the great strides babies make while the parents are in the country visiting their children daily while their children are still in the orphanage. More than a few times have babies started to walk while the parents were still in the child's country. The regular attention appears to help the child reach new developmental milestones in a short period of time.

Reparenting is the key to helping a toddler or older child. Many of the child's behaviors have to be unlearned, and new behaviors and patterns have to be established. According to Gail Trenberth in *Promoting Attachment*, some of the best ways to encourage attachment with a toddler is rocking while she is wrapped in a baby blanket, singing in a low, loving, nurturing voice, running fingers through her hair, stroking her face, and maintaining good eye contact.

Even when the child does not want to experience such closeness, if you engage in such activity, the child will usually be calmer and happier. You need to place much emphasis on getting the child to love and bond with you. Yet, some parents do not automatically feel a strong love and attachment to their newly adopted child, especially if he is difficult. Yet, usually if parents begin to demonstrate nurturing behavior toward the child, this creates those fuzzy, warm feelings toward the child.

For additional techniques that promote bonding, contact:

Nancy Thomas
Families by Design
8617 Country Road 245
New Castle, CO 81647
www.nancythomasparenting.com

www.olderchildadoption.com

TODDLERS THROUGH PRIVATE ADOPTION

When toddlers are adopted through private channels, usually a birth mother or more often a grandparent contacts an attorney or private agency and states that she has a child who needs to be adopted. Grandparents who may be aging sometimes realize that a child needs more attention, and they just do not have the health and energy to raise a toddler to adulthood.

If the child was well cared for by the grandparents, the adjustment goes fairly smoothly. It is best if the child can make the transition gradually from the grandparents to the adoptive family. The adoptive family, if appropriate, should allow the grandparents to be in the child's life and be what they were meant to be—grandparents, not caretakers.

Even though the child may not have been abused or neglected, the adjustment to a toddler coming from another home can sometimes be difficult. You do not have the opportunity to "grow" into the job. Toddlers are full of energy and take much time and sometimes too few naps. From our experience, the only situation in which we've had clients change their minds was when fourteen-month-old twins were placed directly from a birth mother to a couple who had no other children. The adoptive mother called a few days after the children were with her and said that caring for the children was beyond her ability. Multiple toddlers who are running in two different directions can be overwhelming to someone who has previously never parented.

Another family adopted their third child when he was sixteen months old, while the two older children were adopted at birth. At the time the third child was placed with the family, the second child was also about sixteen months old. The mother said she looks back and wonders how she did it. She said that she was never educated about the reality of adopting a child whose birth mother most likely had given the child inconsistent attention at best. When the sixteen-month-old arrived in the family, the natural inclination was to view the two toddlers as being like twins. But the reality is that they were very different emotionally and developmentally, and these differences went beyond their being two different children. The differences were clearly a result of being in two contrasting environments for the first several months of their lives.

Now the son is doing well and is very sweet. He has attention deficit disorder, which is well controlled with medication. His parents set clear guidelines for him and provide consistent discipline, and although he sometimes has difficulty following through on directions, he is a happy and delightful child. Most likely, he is very different from the child he would have been if his environment had stayed the same.

ADOPTING A TODDLER INTERNATIONALLY

Adoptive parents who choose to adopt internationally must accept the fact that they cannot receive a newborn unless they go to their child's country and parent the child until the adoption is completed. Accepting does not mean resigning yourself to adopting a toddler, nor does it mean entering into the situation and thinking, "I've only lost a few months with her." You have lost something and so has she. She may have lost being held, being sung to, and being fed on time. You have also lost the opportunity to meet your child's needs during those first few months. Before you adopt a toddler, you may find that you need to grieve not having an infant from birth. Once you get your child and are thoroughly delighted with her, you may need to grieve that you were not there to care and nurture her during those first months of life.

If you are adopting a child from another country, the child may have what is called post institutionalized (PI) issues. According to Susan Ward, who writes extensively on older child adoption issues, PI behaviors are caused by lack of stimulation and affection, having very structured schedules, lack of movement and choices, and not having proper emotional outlets. Ward lists some of the behaviors of a PI child. These problems can be overcome by time and good parenting. Some may require professional intervention. These problems include:

- *Repetitive rocking.* The child usually does this when upset or tired.
- *Head banging.* The child will bang his head when he is frustrated or angry.
- *Inability to change from one activity to another.*
- *Independence and not asking for help.* This can be seen in children who have had to dress themselves and take care of other children. Often it is difficult to convince an older child that he does not need to take care of his younger siblings.
- *Difficulty going to sleep and staying asleep.*
- *Overly cute and seeks attention from adults and other children.*
- *Overly affectionate and will ask for hugs, kisses, food.*

- *Sensory integration disorder.*
- *Little or no sensation to pain.* Some children who have not been fed when hungry or comforted when upset or hurt, as often is the case in an understaffed orphanage, will show no indication of pain or tears when they get hurt.

Families most often prefer programs in which they fly to a country, are there a few days, and take the child home. However, when adopting a toddler or an older child, it is best to transition the child slowly if at all possible. In countries such as Kazakhstan or the Ukraine in which the parents must be there for a couple of weeks, they visit the child each day at the orphanage. The child gets to know the parents, and parents report that they can see a drastic change in their child because he is getting individual attention.

If you cannot stay in the country for extended periods of time and are adopting a toddler or older child, you may want to visit the child intermittently until the adoption is completed. If your child is in foster care, you may want to visit the child at his foster home, take the child and his foster mother to your hotel, and perhaps do some activities together. Short visits in which the child becomes familiar with you are better. This is not always practical due to financial constraints.

If a child is old enough to communicate, your being in the country allows the child to learn who the adoptive parents are and to get familiar with his being adopted. Put together a small picture book of your home and family and leave this with the child's caretakers so your child can look at the pictures after you are gone and before you come back to receive him.

ADOPTING A TODDLER THROUGH SOCIAL SERVICES

Some toddlers may have been abused or neglected and have come from the birth family to your home. Others may have been in a foster home before coming to you. A baby who was with his birth family may have multiple caretakers in that setting or, worse, may have been left alone. If he then was placed into foster care, this can mean he has had at least two caregivers before coming to you. The more caregivers and the less ideal his early life, the more likely a child can have difficulty trusting and attaching.

PREPARING FOR A TODDLER

Susan Ward makes these suggestions when adopting an older child:

Learn as much as you can. No matter how much you have read before your child arrives home, there will be gaps in your knowledge. You can never predict what needs your child will have; you will need to read and learn more in-depth information that pertains to your child. You as the parent will become the expert on your child.

Have a sense of humor. If you can laugh and be silly even in some more difficult times, it will help you stay sane as well as promote attachment between you and your child.

Be flexible. Your schedule and plans can be thrown out. Your child will upset every one of them. You will need to adapt to a new way of coping, even as your child's needs change.

Have a strong inner core and convictions, even when others do not support you. Susan Ward says, "Whatever issues you face with your adopted child, you will need a conviction that it will work out. That the issue WILL be resolved. That you WILL find the support you need. That your child WILL heal. Anything less than complete conviction will lessen your dedication and drain your energy. Your child needs to feel and see this conviction in order to grow and heal."

Know What to Expect

Being well prepared means knowing what to expect when adopting a toddler who has been in less than an ideal setting. You absolutely cannot compare an eighteen-month-old who has recently arrived in your home with your friend's toddler. For those who already have had birth children, the comparison can be quite pronounced. Your expectations must be realistic. One mother, who had three birth children and then adopted two-year-old twins from an orphanage, said one of the children had difficulty attaching, was not affectionate, and showed little or no preference for her parents. The child saw tenderness and kindness as a weakness. The child also did not want her sister to be content and would try to antagonize her.

Because this mother thought that she and her daughters were going to experience the usual day-to-day toddler fun, the mother had to go through a grieving period when she realized that her toddlers could not be like her three biological children were as toddlers. She had expected her newly adopted children to integrate into the family nearly immediately, but once she realized that it would take time, she accepted the fact that there would be a transition period. At nearly four years old, the twins were very well integrated into the family, and family life with them is enjoyable and pleasant.

Fortunately for this mother, she had been a special education teacher, and she quickly realized that the usual way of parenting had to be altered. She knew what normal development was as an educator and as a parent. She also knew what was out of the normal developmental range.

Like this mother, you will want to be able to distinguish normal behavior from that which is not typical. For example, if your child has a temper tantrum, you will want to know if this is "normal." A thirty-month-old kicking and screaming for two minutes is normal; doing this for four hours is not.

Dr. Mary Hopkins-Best encourages parents also to be familiar with developmental milestones. For example, the age at which children begin to speak and walk falls within predicable ranges. If your child's development falls far outside these ranges, this can indicate serious physical, cognitive, or emotional problems.

Children do not have to be scarred for the rest of their lives because they lived in orphanages, had multiple moves early on, or had birth mothers who were neglectful. It's just that these children may need extra time and understanding. Also, parents need to be understanding of themselves and to understand that it would be abnormal for a child coming from a very different environment to suddenly fit into everyday life with a family. Hopkins-Best states that if the child is to develop a healthy autonomy that he must first attach to his primary caretaker.

On the other hand, there can be problems if the child is beyond other children his age raised in the United States. For example, a child reared in an orphanage may know how to dress himself and make his bed at two years old. A fourteen-month-old may already be potty-trained. Actually, the orphanage staff is trained to sit the children on little potties at prescribed times until each child goes to the bathroom.

If your child is fourteen months old and is "potty-trained," it probably is best to allow the child to start using diapers again. The same goes for using a bottle. Allow the child to be a baby again since his babyhood was probably cut short. He needs to experience being held and fed by you. Your pediatrician may not see the importance of this need. In fact, clients have been told by pediatricians that their babies needed to be off bottles as soon as possible. Why, as long as a child does not go to bed with a bottle? These pediatricians did not take into consideration that these children just went from being in a foster home or orphanage in another country, made a long airplane flight, and are now adjusting to new environments. Why must these babies give up their security?

You will, of course, want to hold and rock your toddler. But some toddlers may be seemingly self-sufficient and not want to be cuddled and held, although this is not typical—most really enjoy being held. If this is an issue, you will want to read Dr. Martha Welch's book *Holding Time*; this is an excellent guide to getting a child to be held, even though the child may initially resist. Dr. Welch's method encourages the parent to hold the child, even if he strongly resists, until he finally relaxes and begins to accept and eventually enjoy being held.

Because living in an institution is not the best environment for a child and can cause emotional and developmental problems, some countries place the child in a foster home. Usually in this situation, the child is designated to be adopted, and the child stays in just one home, sometimes straight from the hospital. If the child cannot come home with you immediately after birth, then being in a loving foster home is the next best place for him to be placed at birth. Yet, some adoptive parents actually fear that their baby will bond too much with the foster parents. When they go to receive their child, the parents are sometimes dismayed that the child cries for the foster parents and is not initially smitten with his new adoptive parents. Actually, this is how you want your toddler to respond. If he was receiving love and nurturing from his foster family and you are strangers, for him to want his foster parents is very normal and healthy. Because he has bonded with one set of parents, he will more easily bond with you. On the other hand, if the child has been in multiple homes, he may have difficulty attaching to you because, like his other placements, he thinks you may be temporary.

If the child was in an orphanage, he most likely will be receptive to you. After all, you are probably giving him more and tastier food than he is used to, and you are warm and snugly. In the Ukraine, clients do not know who their child is until they arrive at the orphanage, where they are permitted to select a child. Once a child is presented to them and they agree to that child, the child usually warms up to them in a matter of hours. Previously, no one person has showered the child with so much individual attention, and the child is usually very pleased to have someone doting on him. As the parents visit the child each day until the court hearing, the child becomes more attached to them and then may start to fuss if other children from the orphanage are vying for the adoptive parents' attention. The child's response is appropriate given the circumstances from which he came; however, the appropriate response for a child who is attached to his caregivers is to want them over his new adoptive parents. A child most likely will not be well attached to anyone at an orphanage, but he should be attached to his foster parents.

There are challenges in adopting a toddler because his past, even if he cannot remember it, may have been painful. He has first lost his caretakers, and he must make an adjustment to living with you in your home. This does not mean that the child is necessarily scarred for life. But the parents need to be aware of what the child lost during the first months of life, how the baby or toddler may be different from a birth child or a child adopted as newborn, and what steps can be taken so that the child can reach his full emotional and developmental potential.

If your child has come from an orphanage setting, I highly recommend that one parent care for the child for as long as possible. If one parent cannot stay home, make arrangements for one person to care for the child. It does not make sense to place a child who has been in an institution back into a group setting. Being with other children can be delightful for short periods of time. One mother said her son enjoyed being in a nursery school one or two mornings a week. Another mother said that her twins adjusted to the nursery at church very well. However, these are all children whose mothers stay home nearly full-time with them.

Language Development

There can be a delay in the speech development of a toddler because of environmental influences before he was placed for adoption. If a child came from an orphanage or was in a neglectful home, when he first made sounds at a few months old, chances are that these sounds were not repeated back to him. Also, no one may have spent time talking with him one-on-one. Reading a book and asking a child to point to the man, the ball, and so forth in the pictures is usually not done either. Even a baby who is in a good orphanage or a foster home in another country will most likely not be as stimulated through books, educational toys, and conversation as your child would be in your home.

In addition to your child's language development being delayed, when your child is with you, he will be learning a whole new language. Knowing some simple phrases in your child's native tongue is very helpful, especially those that revolve around food and using the potty. However, children who come to the United States often do not want you to speak in their native tongue. Although they may not be able to speak to you in English (expressive speech), most likely your child will understand you (receptive speech). Also, children love to mimic and may enjoy your pointing to objects, saying the word in English, and then repeating what you have said.

Once your child is home, you will want quality one-on-one time with him. Talk slowly and tenderly to your child. Reading simple picture books can also help a child master new language skills. The repeating of the phrases each time you look at the book reinforces the words and allows the child to develop his expressive speech skills.

If a child is having difficulty learning English and appears to be delayed in his speech development, you may want to consider the program Fast ForWord. The program is pricey. A professional administers the program, but it is reported to be very effective. (See resources at the end of this chapter.)

Older Siblings and Toddlers

In *Toddler Adoption,* Dr. Mary Hopkins-Best discusses the effect of older siblings on adopted toddlers. As may be expected, the more input that the older sibling has into the adoption, the more comfortable the older child will be with the new arrival. Hopkins-Best further states that children over six years old adjust better than younger siblings. If at all possible, I encourage clients to take their children with them to another country when adopting a child. The logistics and finances do not always make this possible; if you cannot take your other children, try to make them as much a part of the process as possible.

Pets and Toddlers

Toddlers coming from another country may never have been exposed to cats, dogs, and other animals. In Eastern European countries, dogs run wild; it may be difficult to assess whether your child's encounter with a dog was positive or negative. In one orphanage, the dogs that stayed around seemed gentle. The children did not seem to especially like them nor did they seem afraid of them.

If you have a dog, especially a big one, this animal is probably the size of your child, if not bigger. Unlike an infant who grows up with the animal, the toddler may be terrified of the creature. If the animal is not used to small children, especially a child who may touch its eyes or pull its tail, the pet may, of course, bite the child. For the safety of your child—and your pet—the two may have to be separated unless they are very closely supervised.

If you have more than one animal inside your home, this may be too much for your child. Just as too many people around can feel overwhelming to a toddler who has just entered the family, so can a few pets—especially pets that meet the child at eye level.

Few adoptive parents give their pets away when a child arrives, but a compromise should be taken. If you have animals, try to find one place where they can go so that the child cannot get to them and the animal cannot get to the child. The child should not feel that an animal is going to come into her space. A child may never have had anything of her own while in foster care or an orphanage, and then to have the dog take her ball or small doll can feel like a great invasion.

ADOPTING MORE THAN ONE TODDLER

What about adopting more than one toddler at a time? Some countries and agencies have a policy that siblings must be adopted together. If you are considering siblings, carefully consider your decision. You must want to adopt more than one child. Making the decision to adopt siblings should not be based on your wanting a young child, but being willing to accept his three-year-old sister because they are a package. Each child should be wanted. If the sibling group is made up of three or more children, plan carefully. Adopting more than two children at one time is very difficult unless you have many resources. One family who adopted three siblings said it took them six to nine months to adjust. Although the family is doing very well, caring for three toddlers is an exhausting task.

It is not uncommon for someone to adopt two unrelated toddlers at the same time. Some believe that it is better to have each child enter the home at separate times, and in fact, some agencies do not permit families to adopt two unrelated children at a time. However, adopting at separate times can mean double the expenses and another trip to the country. Because of financial constraints, some families realize that what is best for them is to adopt another child at the same time. Also, some families say that two children entering the home together help in the transition. Just because children are siblings does not mean that they know each other well. Both in the United States and in other countries, siblings are not necessarily in the same home or orphanage group. In one case, twin toddlers were in two different orphanage groups and did not know each other until they were with their adoptive families. Of course, they should have been placed together, but their placement was essentially the same as two unrelated toddlers being placed in the same home.

CHOOSING TO ADOPT A TODDLER

Although most families, if given the choice, want to adopt a newborn infant, some families deliberately choose to adopt a toddler because the child will fit into their lifestyle more easily. These families may find that the downside of adopting a child who has been in an institution far outweighs the inconveniences of caring for an infant.

Dr. Mary Hopkins-Best, author of *Toddler Adoption*, states that those who deliberately choose to adopt a toddler, after carefully considering such factors as their own ages and the availability of more toddlers than infants, have the most successful experience. These are the people who understand both the positives and negatives of adopting a toddler and are well prepared. The good news is that adopting a toddler is a very viable option because so many are available, and if you are well prepared and realistic, the transitioning of your child into your home will go much more smoothly.

Note: All children up to thirty-six months old who have some special needs are permitted to receive early intervention services at no charge through Child Find. It is called by different names in different states. The organization in your community will provide an evaluation for your child at no charge to you. If your child qualifies, there is no charge to you regardless of your income. Go to the Web site *www.nectac.org* to find the name and phone number of the organization in your state or community.

Chapter Fifteen

Special Needs Adoption

The most drastic change in number of adoptions has been the number of children adopted through child welfare agencies. Each year, more than 50,000 of the children in foster care are adopted. In 2001, these adoptions accounted for about 40 percent of all adoptions. In 1992, the 28,000 children were placed through social services agencies, accounting for only 18 percent of all adoptions (as stated by the National Adoption Information Clearinghouse, 2004). Two factors account for the increased number of children available: parental rights being terminated earlier and therefore children being available for adoption and more funds available to provide parents and children with the needed resources to make adoption feasible. If you want to adopt a child and are flexible about the age and race of the child, you can adopt very quickly if a child has been in the foster care system. If you are looking to adopt a Caucasian or Hispanic child, the wait could be longer, but there are children available. If you are seeking to adopt a young child, again, the wait could be longer, but you could adopt. In general, there are no fees to adopt these children, and often there are monthly subsidies and other resources available to offset the expenses involved in meeting the needs of these children. Because these children come from backgrounds that include abuse and neglect, you will need to educate yourselves about the issues these children face and the resources needed to help these children have the best outcome possible.

Currently in the United States, there are more than 523,000 children in foster care, and more than 118,000 of these children are awaiting adoptive parents. Twice the number of children wait to be adopted as have been adopted. Most of these children will be placed through state operated social service agencies. Others will be placed by private adoption agencies that have been given grants or contracts to assist in the placement of children in foster care for adoption (National Adoption Information Clearinghouse, 2004).

These children in the "system" are called "special needs," not necessarily because of a medical condition or physical or mental handicap but because they have often suffered much.

Many are adopted by their foster parents, many by their relatives, and others by adoptive parents who were selected to be their parents. From 1999-2003 an average of 50,000 children have been adopted each year. The increase in adoptions is due to a change in attitude from professionals who have created the barriers. The ad campaign "You do not have to be perfect to be a perfect parent" demonstrates this change in attitude. Social services agencies have removed many of the restrictions that in the past have kept families from adopting. Research has shown that those who are single, older, and with a lower income can be positive parents. If you do not meet the criteria for adopting an infant or cannot afford to adopt internationally, chances are good that you can adopt a child through the social services system. Also more children are being placed for adoption because financial incentives and support systems are in place so that the adoptive parents and children get the help they need to help make these adoptions successful.

Many of the children who go into the foster care system because of abuse or neglect cannot be returned to their parents. Sometimes the parents are not capable of parenting due to overwhelming life-dominating problems such as drug use and alcohol abuse or inability to hold a job, make proper child care arrangements, or keep their children safe from others. Most of these parents say they want their children to return to them but are not willing or able to take the necessary steps to change their lives so that their children can be returned to them. Not all the parents are overt abusers; in fact, most children in the foster care system are there due to neglect. When it appears that these parents cannot or will not change, the next step is for the children to be placed in loving, permanent homes.

Few of life's rewards equal that of adopting a child who desperately needs a home. Not only will you change the life of a child, but your life can also change for the better as well. If you are up to the challenge of adopting a child who may otherwise be without a home, one of the first places you may want to begin is your local social services department's adoption unit. These children, many with siblings, need loving families to adopt them. More than half are over eight years of age, and many (65 percent) have been in foster care more than two years. Because of their background of abuse and neglect—not a physical disability or illness—most of these children are labeled as "special needs."

Adopting through social services provides a means to adopt a child in a relatively short period of time, with little financial risk, and sometimes minimal legal risk.

WHY ADOPT FROM THE SOCIAL SERVICES SYSTEM?

The advantages of adopting through the social services system include the following:

Expenses can be minimal. If you adopt a child with special needs through your state's social services, not only will there be little to no cost for the adoption, but the child may also be eligible for monthly tax-free subsidies. These subsidies help to defray the costs of raising a child who requires extra parental care and possibly such specialized services as physical therapy or psychological counseling. Even if your adoption expenses are minimal, you still receive the $10,000 tax credit.

Special needs adoption subsidies. Years ago children remained foster children because foster parents who were receiving monthly payments could not afford to lose those benefits if they adopted the children. Other parents interested in adopting a child with complex medical needs or a sibling group could not afford to do so. Now, thanks to the Adoption Assistance and Child Welfare Act of 1980, a whole new pool of parents can consider special needs adoption. This act mandated that all states establish a Title IV-E adoption subsidy program for children previously eligible for funding while in foster care. Title IV-E monies come from both federal and state dollars. Each state also administers other subsidies that come solely from state dollars. Unfortunately, many adoptive parents are not even aware of the subsidies because sometimes social workers neglect to make them aware. In some states, adoptive parents may have to go to court to make sure that their state provides them with the funds that are due them.

Children are available. About 80 percent of these 119,000 available children will be adopted by their foster parents, but about half of them will not.

The wait for a child can be much less than other adoptions. If you are diligent about getting a home study, you could have a child in the time it takes to complete a home study and be approved. Sometimes the wait for a child will be directly related to how long it takes you to complete a series of workshops on adoption and for the social services department to come to your home to conduct a home study, complete the paperwork, and file all the correct papers.

You can know about the child you are going to adopt. Unlike most other domestic or international adoptions, you get to meet the child a few times before she is placed in your home. For some people, the certainty of meeting a child before making the decision to adopt is paramount.

You will have specialized training and workshops. Sometimes the requirements may seem arbitrary or invasive, but most people can benefit from the opportunity to learn more about parenting.

Pre- and postadoption support from the agency. Once the child is in your home, both before and after the adoption is made legal, your social services agency may provide extensive services to help you meet your child's needs. The value of postadoption support cannot be underestimated. Families who adopt internationally may not receive any support from their local child welfare agency once the child is home—

even though their child is a U.S. citizen. If you adopt through social services, your child will probably be eligible for Medicaid and for other benefits that most other adopted children cannot receive. Also, a child could be eligible for counseling and other psychological services paid for by Medicaid. The goal of the child welfare program is to create permanency and to help families be successful. Agencies do not want children placed for adoption to reenter the foster care system; therefore, extra support—which ordinarily can be very expensive—is usually available for those who need it.

You do not need a good income or to be married to adopt. Studies show that those who are not as well educated and have lower incomes actually do better in rearing these children, perhaps because their expectations for the child are more realistic.

You have an opportunity to make a difference in the life of the child. About 40 percent of adults have considered adopting a child. If just one in 500 actually followed through on this consideration, then all the children in the foster care system awaiting adoption would have a home. Many people who have biological children also choose to adopt children with special needs because they want to expand their families and make a contribution to the lives of children. Few other achievements can have such an impact on an individual life and offer you such a reward.

• • •

Concerning the disadvantages of using a public agency, several important—but not insurmountable—challenges must be highlighted.

1. *Working with the system.* There's no denying that working with the bureaucracy can be difficult. You may agree to take a child who is considered a moderate-to-low legal risk and find that because of state laws it takes a year or more to terminate a missing parent's rights.
2. *Demands on your schedule before you adopt.* The agency may expect you to attend twenty-five hours or more of preadoption educational training. Providing preadoption education to prospective adoptive parents is essential to the overall outcome of adoptions. However, some adoption training can be offered at times that are not convenient for both parents to attend; this is especially true for two working parents who have children in the home. More training workshops are being offered at convenient times—not just a few times a year. Also, couples do not have to attend at the same time.
3. *The public agency's home study process may be more demanding than a home study done for a private placement.* Because you are requesting a child with

special needs or of a different ethnic background from your own, the agency may ask you numerous personal questions about your upbringing and your attitudes on many issues. These questions may be necessary, but they can also feel invasive. Because the agency is required to screen out parents who could not handle the challenge of a child with emotional problems, more personal questions are asked. A good caseworker will explain to you why such questions are asked. Public agencies and private agencies that place children with special needs are probably flexible about the size of your home, but they are likely to question you extensively about your attitudes toward marriage, child-rearing, adoption, adjustment to stress, and counseling for your children. After all, the caseworker wants to know how you will be able to handle a child with special needs. She may expect you to understand issues related to the separation and loss the child has probably experienced. The home study is not just to see whether your lives are stable but whether you can adjust to having a child who may be very disruptive.

4. *Mostly older children are available.* The child who you are adopting will most likely not be a newborn, and the quality of care he or she received before being placed in your home may be relatively unknown.

5. *You need to become well-informed.* You will need to become educated about the kinds of emotional problems the child may suffer as a result of his past experiences and be prepared to deal with such issues.

6. *Children can have serious, unpredictable problems.* The child's outcome is less certain than a child who is adopted as an infant under more favorable circumstances.

GETTING STARTED

You may be intimidated about starting the process and with good reason. For many people, the main challenge of adopting through a social services agency is working with the system. Working with a government bureaucracy can be frustrating. Studies show that 90 percent of prospective adoptive parents who contact a social services agency to inquire about adoption drop out of the process before the home study is begun. These dismal statistics demonstrate the need for caseworkers to welcome prospective adoptive parents when they inquire about adoption in general or about a specific child, instead of merely giving them reams of paperwork and a list of "to dos." The broadening of attitudes has included the position that "no child is unadoptable." If no child is unadoptable, then most adults who are willing to be parents should be permitted to adopt.

Because many more children are awaiting homes and more financial efforts are being made to find homes and encourage those who are interested in adoption, you can adopt quickly—usually in six to twelve months—if you want to adopt a minority or school-age child. Another important advantage of using a public agency is cost. Adoption expenses are usually minimal, and often state and federal subsidies are available. Support services after the adoption are also frequently available, and public agencies typically network with other government agencies to provide counseling services to children and adoptive parents.

If you are relatively young and want to adopt a baby or toddler and are flexible about the race of your child, then chances are good that you can adopt a baby. If you are older and are flexible about the age of the child, then chances are good that you will be matched with a child. If you have a lower income but can provide a solid home life, chances are good that you can adopt.

WHO ARE THE CHILDREN IN THE SOCIAL WELFARE SYSTEM?

According to the Department of Health and Human Services, two out of three waiting children have medical, developmental, behavioral, or psychological special needs, and most have more than one condition. About 41 percent of the children are part of a sibling group, making them particularly hard to place.

About one-third of the children who are in the foster care system and then become eligible for adoption are victims of overt abuse. The other two-thirds enter the system due to neglect. Neglect is harder to prove and must be pervasive before children are removed from their home. All neglected and abused children are also emotionally abused.

Virtually all children who are removed from their homes must be placed in foster care before their biological parents' rights are terminated. The trauma of being abused and then going to one or more foster homes can have a profound emotional impact on the child. Unlike high-profile adoption cases, there are no cameras or six o'clock news coverage for these children. Yet, they hurt deeply because they are caught up in the bureaucracy and have no permanent home.

In addition, some children, especially those placed in group homes, become the victims of sexual abuse. The perpetrators are usually older children who themselves were victims of sexual abuse. The child who has gone through one caretaker after another may have deep-seated psychological problems, often expressed in attention deficit disorder (ADD), hyperactivity, daytime wetting and soiling, sexual acting out, detachment, and a host of other behavior problems.

Often these children have a complex relationship with birth parents because of the history of parental abuse or neglect. Usually, the birth parents' rights are terminated only after considerable disruption and pain in the children's lives. Even after the biological parents are physically out of the children's lives, their emotional influence on the children can still be very intense. The children often remember living with their biological parents as well as with previous foster parents, and of course, they remember being placed for adoption. Often, indeed, what makes a special needs child "special" is the fact that he has suffered so much.

Because it is now well documented that changing homes is not good for children, they are becoming available for adoption at a younger age. The average age of the available child is seven to eight years old. However, as parents' rights are more readily terminated, younger children should become more available. Drug-addicted, abusive, neglectful parents are no longer given third and fourth chances. To make adoption a more likely outcome for children, the Adoption and Safe Families Act requires that the birth parents' rights be terminated if the child has been in foster care for more than twenty-two months or if the parents killed or seriously injured another child.

Although younger children are available for adoption, it can appear from looking at photolisting Web sites that only older children are available. More recruiting efforts are made for older children, and more funding is available to place them for adoption because they are more difficult to find permanent homes for. Only 34 percent of children available are five years old or younger; yet 45 percent of children who are adopted fall in the younger age category.

SPECIAL NEEDS CLASSIFICATION

The following listings are explained in more detail at the end of the chapter. What is listed here is just an overview to help you think about whether you could consider a child with special needs. If you are seriously considering adopting a child with special needs, many books and Internet articles discuss the topic of adopting older children. It is very important that you research the issues associated with a child with special needs.

- Physical and Medical Problems—If a child has a physical or medical problem, usually the diagnosis is clearly defined, and the outcome is somewhat predictable.
- Learning Disabilities—Many children have learning disabilities due to in utero exposure to drugs and alcohol as well as lack of stimulation and education. Children often change schools frequently before being adopted.
- Emotional and Behavioral Problems—These problems are less predictable and include ADD, ADHD, depression, and other disorders.
- Attachment Disorders—Serious problems in attaching are perhaps the most difficult of all the problems because an unattached child can make you feel as if you are not parenting and you get little in return. Attachment problems are on a continuum. Most children will have some attachment

problems just due to their life circumstances, but these problems diminish over time with love and attention. The serious disorders almost always require professional intervention.

- History of Sexual Abuse—Many children who are removed from their parents have been sexually abused in their homes or in foster care by other foster children.

- Sibling Groups—For a sibling group to be considered "special needs," usually it must be three or more children who all need to be placed in the same family.

- African-American and Racially Mixed Children—About 60 percent of children available in the foster care system are African-American or Latino. Because a child's racial or ethnic background makes it more difficult to find her a home, she may be classified as "special needs."

- Older Children—Usually an older child is classified as a school-age child. Unlike other classifications of "special needs," a child's age is the best predictor of how the child will adjust.

- Fetal Alcohol Syndrome—Fetal alcohol syndrome (FAS) is perhaps the problem that prospective adoptive parents fear the most.

WORKING WITH A STATE OR PRIVATE AGENCY

Every state has at least one agency that handles adoptions, usually an extension of the state's social services department. There are more than 2,000 such agencies in the United States. In some states, there is one agency; in others, there is one in every county. Consult your state directory for the name of your state's adoption specialist; this office can direct you to the agency in your county or district. Check the directory of the National Adoption Information Clearinghouse, which is regularly updated at *http://naic.acf.hhs.gov.*

Contact your state agency to see how to apply. They may send you a preliminary questionnaire/application and ask that you attend a series of training workshops. Public agencies conduct workshops not only to educate prospective adoptive parents about issues involved in adopting a child with special needs, but also to screen out prospective adoptive parents who are not ready to deal with the emotional and behavioral problems of children in the system.

Some private agencies operate much like public adoption agencies, receiving government monies, networking with their state's social services department, and placing children who have been removed from their parents. Such agencies usually accept children for adoption and assume legal responsibility for them. Often they will function to fill a need not covered by the public agencies. For example, a specialized agency may place older African-American children, whereas a social services department might not have the resources to reach out aggressively to the African-American community for potential adoptive parents. Such agencies do not usually charge a fee because they are serving waiting children; but if they do charge one, it is made considerably lower by the provision of government grants.

In addition, private agencies can negotiate monthly subsidies for families. June Bond, the executive director of Adoption Advocacy, a private agency that assists families seeking to adopt children who have been part of the social services system, states that once a family is matched with a child that the agency can negotiate with the social services agency to help get the family subsidies. Bond states, "With the advent of the 1997 Safe Families and Adoption Act, the face of special needs adoption changed forever." Special needs adoptions were previously the exclusive domain of public agencies. Now, public agencies are welcoming private and faith-based agencies to help place the more than 500,000 children who are currently residing in the public foster care system. Consequently, private agencies are helping families to cross both racial and geographic barriers to look for children in all fifty states of the union. Private agencies assist in the home study and preparation process, with the help of private pay, public and private grants, and purchase-of-service agreements from the sending state. Once the family is considered "home study ready," the family can register, usually free of charge, with national matching agencies such as Adopt: US Kids and Adopt America. These matching services assist families and private agencies with locating a special needs child or sibling group that is available for adoption. The private agency can then advocate for their family in various staffing sessions. Once a match has been made, the private agency can negotiate on two fronts: (1) Helping the family get available subsidies for the children once the children are placed and (2) Helping negotiate a purchase-of-service agreement between the sending state and the private agency for supervision and placement of the child with the family until finalization of the adoption is complete.

Negotiation of a monthly subsidy for the family is a common practice for public agencies and is not that different a process with a private agency. The agency advocates on behalf of the family to meet the child or children's needs. Monthly subsidies can vary from around $300 per child to as much as $1,000 per child, depending on the sending state's formula and the child's needs. The subsidy is usually in place until the child is eighteen years old. Private agencies should be aware that some states have very little money for subsidies and will try to alleviate their financial commitment to the child once he drops off their geographic radar screen. The private agency must remain in touch with emerging trends, helping a family to find the best match with the best available resources that will follow the child into adulthood. It is vital to remember that subsidy agreements can be renegotiated, as the emerging needs surface. These agreements are not tablets of stone, handed down from the "mountain top." Ongoing negotiation is not uncommon as a child enters into puberty or a new phase of life or education. Likewise, special needs children should not be denied services if they are being adopted by a family that has private resources. Often private resources do not cover the breadth of services covered by Medicaid. Likewise, job loss or changes and tightening private insurance may exclude pre-existing conditions that a special needs child may have. The private agency should also be aware that the nonrecurring costs that cover travel for the child and legal fees vary from state to state, with a low of $250 to a high of $2,000 per child. Being aware of different state subsidy plans can help a family to focus on states that are more adoption-friendly. At this moment, some of the most adoption-friendly states for special needs children include Louisiana, Texas, Ohio, and Connecticut. However, these trends may change.

Classes and Support Groups

The extensive preparenting classes that are required to adopt a child through the child welfare system may not be required by a private agency or if you are adopting a child from another state's social services department. Nevertheless, be sure to take some classes to prepare yourself for adopting a child with special needs. Even if you are not adopting a child directly from your county or state social services system, the department will probably let you take their classes—usually free of charge.

You may want to join an adoption support group in which a good number of members have adopted children with special needs. Those who have adopted through the department of social services or through a public agency will know what works with the system and what does not. Call your local public adoption agency and ask if they have upcoming workshops for those who are interested in adopting a child with special needs. These multisession workshops usually cover the legal issues, kinds of children available and their special needs, and relationships these children typically have with their birth families and foster care parents. Your attitudes about adoption, kind of child you can accept, emotional problems, and similar issues will also be addressed. Many people "screen" themselves out of the process after going to these workshops.

Prepare Yourself

The next step is to investigate the special services that are available in your area. If you want to adopt a certain kind of special needs child, find out what services you will have access to, what expenses are involved, and whether Medicaid covers those expenses. Remember, be realistic about what kinds of children are available and about how much impact you can have on a given child. If you want an essentially healthy but older child, for example, you must recognize that any child who has been removed from his home because of abuse or neglect is likely to have some emotional, developmental, or learning problems. If you have successfully raised children through the teenage years, you may feel that you would like an older child. However, the way you measured "success" in raising your children, who came to you at birth or at a very young age, will probably not be the standard for success in raising a child from a troubled background. You need to explore how you feel about dealing with a child's emotional problems, the behaviors that may accompany the problems, and going with your child to a counselor.

Sit down with your spouse and discuss what you can and cannot accept. Your spouse may be unwilling to care for a child who is mentally disabled but feel very different about adopting a bright child with fairly serious learning disabilities—in other words, one whose problems appear more "correctable." Again, be sure that your expectations are realistic.

Beware of social workers pushing you to accept more than you can handle. On the other hand, if you say that you want a girl up to four years old and the social worker tells you of a girl who is five years old, who overall is doing well, do not be offended. Most caseworkers want families to be fully informed, not only about the child's positive and negative attributes, but also about what may be anticipated down the road. Having realistic expectations is the best insurance against an adoption disruption.

Be especially careful about "broadening" your level of acceptance because you find a child so attractive. Sometimes a prospective adoptive family will see a child or a picture of the child and "fall in love" with his cute face and charming personality. At this time, the couple may not "hear" what the caseworker is telling them about the emotional, physical, and/or behavioral problems the child has or is at a high risk of having. They see only the adorable four-year-old who, with enough love, will overcome all his problems. One caseworker says that when families change their minds and "broaden" their level of acceptance, they usually have problems with their adopted child in the specific area they stated on their initial application they would not be able to accept. This broadening of acceptance can be especially true when adopting a child who also has a sibling. You may be seeking a four-year-old child who appears to be just the child that you desire, yet she has a three-year-old brother who has serious developmental delays. You may be prepared for the four-year-old, but you should not just "accept" the younger brother. Each child should be desired for himself.

Although the overall tone of special needs adoption seems to focus more on what is wrong with the child than what is right, this is done to increase realistic expectations. However, once parents adopt these children, like all parents, they also focus in on the children's positive traits and accomplishments. These parents, like most adoptive and biological parents, find the experience rewarding and have felt the same pride in their children.

The Home Study

The next step is to complete your home study. If your state agency conducts home studies, this is a good place to start because they will usually not charge you if you are interested in public agency adoption. The home study they conduct can also be used to adopt a child through a photolisting service. You may want to contact a private agency to conduct your home study if you want to search through photolistings of children from other states. Although you most likely will have to pay for the services, private home studies usually are completed in less time.

Remember, a home study conducted by a public agency may be more stringent than a standard study because the social worker is looking for more than good health, a reasonably clean criminal record, and financial stability. She wants to find out how you cope with setbacks and how you deal with frustration and anger because these relate to the kind of special needs child you want to adopt. The caseworker will also want to see how flexible you are. If you love everything in order and want to adopt a young sibling group, are you willing to let things go a bit? Alternatively, if you are single or if both spouses plan to continue to work, how will you manage your days so that the child's needs are met?

Also, special needs children often require special services. You need to live in an area where such services are available. If you live on a large ranch in Wyoming and the closest large city is three hours away, regularly getting your child to a psychologist or an occupational therapist may be very difficult. Even if you live in a metropolitan area, you must be able and willing to see that your child gets the services he needs.

In addition to the basic documents required for a home study, a state agency may ask for certain kinds of information. For example, if you have had any kind of counseling, even for infertility, the agency may ask for a letter from your counselor or therapist. They will also have forms for your physician and your references to complete, whereas a private agency most likely would simply request letters.

The home study for a special needs adoption will essentially be like any other, except that the caseworker may ask you more in-depth questions, especially regarding certain issues that relate to the kind of special needs child you hope to adopt. The questions will have to do with family values, what you learned from your parents that you want to pass on to your children, how you cope, how you and your spouse deal with disagreements, how accepting of the particular child your family and community would be, what support systems you have to care for a child, your attitudes toward the birth parents, how siblings are going to react, and your attitudes toward counseling. Unlike a standard home study, the caseworker may want you to discuss your attitudes toward sex, what you consider sexually age-appropriate behavior in a child, and how you feel about caring for a child and not receiving much appreciation and affection in return. If both of you work, the caseworker will probably go into depth about your child care arrangements. If the child will need special services, the caseworker will also want to know about the availability of these services in your area. One question the social worker most likely will ask is who would care for your child in the event of your death. If you have other children without special needs and you have appointed legal guardians for them in the event of your death, remember that these same people may not be open to adopting a child with special needs.

Be prepared to explain just what kind of child you want, how much openness with the birth family you are willing to accept, and what legal risk you feel you can handle if the parents' rights have not been terminated. The agency will most likely ask you to complete a list so that you can check off what factors you can accept in a child or in her family background and to what degree you can accept these characteristics. Before answering this section, you may want to do some basic homework to determine what is meant by such terms as "deformity," "physical disability," or "learning disability." These are broad terms, and you may want to attach a sheet of paper explaining exactly what you can accept. The social worker who comes into your home will also want to explore this with you. For example, if you answer that you can accept no history of sexual abuse, the staff may ask you how you will feel if you find out later that the child was sexually abused. Sexual abuse is a very sensitive topic, and the caseworker may want to find out whether there are any underlying reasons that you would not accept this kind of child.

In some instances, you may also be required to get counseling so that issues you have within your own family systems can be clarified and dealt with before you adopt. Couples who have not had to face family-of-origin issues because they have experienced no real crises may suddenly have to face these issues once a difficult child enters their lives. Adding a child to a family always changes its dynamics; adding a child with psychological scars can change the dynamics in the family dramatically. Being prepared to parent an emotionally abused child and having realistic expectations of yourself and the child are necessary. Unlike medical conditions, which tend to fit more or less into textbook models, the emotional problems that these children have can be varied, and the outcome is far less predictable.

THE ADOPTION PROCESS

When you have finally attended all the workshops and completed the home study, the agency has a matching system based on the type of child you want. As children become available, the staff may select you to adopt a particular one. You will be presented a child or sibling group that the agency thinks matches the kind of child you are willing to accept. You do not have to accept the child. If you feel that the child is not one that you are prepared to parent, tell the agency. You may need to work with them to clarify what kind of child you want. In some cases, parents will say they are willing to accept a child with certain characteristics, but then when they are presented a child who has these characteristics, they are disappointed. It is clear they were secretly hoping to adopt a healthy child with few problems. They should have been honest at the outset.

Assuming you approve the child, however, the next thing that will happen is that she will be placed with you or she may gradually be transitioned into your family over a course of a few weeks. At this point, she may or may not be legally free for adoption. If she is not legally free and the birth parents are not making any progress, then you must wait until their rights are terminated. (In some cases, the parents' rights are terminated at the adoption hearing.) Legal adoption can take between several months and several years to accomplish, although there is now a big drive under way to move adoptions through faster.

Most social workers within the system are truly concerned about the children and want to see children in good adoptive homes. The Adoption and Safe Families Act (ASFA) has mandated that children move more quickly from foster care to permanent families since those in the system have seen the harm caused to children who stay in the foster care system. However, a judge who wants to give the biological parents "one more chance" can thwart their best efforts. If you are fostering a child who is to be available for adoption, this could prove to be one of the most difficult situations in which to find yourself. The child whom you are to love, nurture, and protect is then placed back with his biological parent. Children are traumatized by being sent back to abusive homes and then taken out and then finally becoming available for adoption.

Not only must you be an advocate in the adoption process before you have an assignment of a child, but you must also continually be an advocate for your child in the educational system and for other resources that your child may need.

Selecting the Child Based on the Type of Legal Risk Category

Before you begin to be assigned a child or select a child, you will first want to explore how much legal risk you can accept. In most instances, the more legal risk you are willing to take, the more likely you are to have a younger child placed with you who has not been in foster care for a long period of time.

What is a legal risk? Nearly all adoptions are "legal risks," but ones which concern an involuntary termination of parental right or ones in which the birth mother may have given false information about the birth father are considered especially "risky." Although the media has created much of a sensation regarding this matter, the reality is that a child who has been abused or neglected and cannot go back to his original family is not a high legal risk, even if no one can find the child's birth father.

Let's look at three categories of risk: low risk, moderate risk, and high risk.

Low risk. A low-risk adoption means that the consents of the birth mother, birth father, and any alleged fathers have been given or their parental rights have been terminated. If there is no consent from the birth father because he cannot be found, there is documentation to support that efforts were made to find him and tell him of his rights. If the agency says that a child is a low legal risk, ask whether documentation shows that both parents' rights have been terminated or that efforts were made to contact the birth father so that he could not contest the adoption if he chose.

Moderate risk. An example of moderate risk would be a situation in which the birth mother's rights have been terminated, but the birth father cannot be found and only sketchy documentation exists regarding the state's effort to find him.

High risk. High-risk adoption is not adoption—it is foster care, called foster-adoptive placements. It means the birth mother's and probably the birth father's rights have not been terminated. Do not necessarily rule out taking a high-risk child initially as a foster-adoptive child; it may be that the birth mom and dad are never going to get their lives together, but without a doubt not enough of a paper trail was left to prove that efforts were made to find them and explain their rights. Babies are often high legal risks simply because not enough time has passed to allow their birth parents to do a turnaround. If you find out that no other family member is available to care for the child and the birth parents are not making any effort to follow their court-ordered plan, you may want to consider this situation.

Foster-adopt does not mean becoming foster parents as a way of caring for children who "might" become available for adoption. It means taking a child into your home who will probably become available for adoption. Although 50 percent to 70 percent of the children in foster care return to their biological families, others will never go back to their biological families and are not being adopted quickly enough. Many could be eligible for adoption, but the legal steps have not been taken to terminate the parents' rights (TPR), or a certain time has not lapsed until the parents' rights can be terminated, and so the children are technically not available for adoption. While these children are waiting for a TPR, it is best if their foster home is also their potential adoptive family.

About half of these children are already in foster homes in which the foster parents want to adopt them. The others need to be. However, the time from placement in the adoptive home to adoption can be lengthy and the paperwork extensive. When social workers have limited time and resources and have many emergencies to deal with, pushing through the adoption of a child who is in a loving and stable foster-adoptive home is not a priority. The actual adoption is important for the child and parents, however. They need to know that this is forever.

To become a foster-adopt parent, you must meet requirements both for becoming a foster parent and for becoming an adoptive parent. This process can take a longer time, which can be frustrating if you have a particular child in mind. Depending on the requirements of your state for becoming a foster parent, the authorities may place more emphasis on the safety of your home than they would if you were applying to be an adoptive parent. Before a child is placed in your home, you will probably need a safety and fire prevention inspection, and any lead paint in your home (common in older homes) may have to be covered or removed.

SOCIAL SERVICES ADOPTION: ONE COUPLE'S STORY
In the following, a woman named Carrie tells of the experience she and her husband had with social service adoption.

• • •

In the state of Washington, foster/adopt is called fast track. Our two youngest children (now 14 and 26 months old) both came through the fast-track/foster-adopt program. When we adopted our son, David, it was very frightening since we did not even have our foster care license. So when the agency called us and told us about him, they pushed the license through in two days so we could bring him home at three weeks old.

The birth mother had other children, and her rights to all those children had been terminated. We were 90 percent sure that our David would be with us permanently. A year later, David's sister was placed with us. Although we were more familiar with the system and how fast track worked, we were still nervous because a more in-depth search had to be done to find the birth father.

I learned not only the system, but also what not to believe from the birth family. Nearly everything we heard from them went contrary to what the staff was telling us. The birth family would also say, "He is coming home with me" and "You will never get him." At the time, I didn't really know the birth mother's history, didn't really understand the system, and was worried because what she was saying went against everything we were told about this baby.

We didn't do foster care just to do foster care. We went the foster care route to build our family through adoption. One of the greatest fears I had was with our nineteen-month-old baby, Andrew, at the time of David's placement. Andrew immediately bonded with David, and the thought of having to deal with Andrew's grief if David was to go back to his birth family was not something for which we were prepared. This is why we went with the "90 percent guarantee" route. I believe that if we did not have Andrew, I would have been more open to foster care so that we could care for a child who temporarily needed a loving home. We are very pleased we chose this route of adoption since we now have three beautiful babies. In a few years, I hope to grow our family again through the foster-adopt route.

• • •

THE ASSIGNING OF A CHILD

If you are not a foster parent or a relative of a child available for adoption, there are two essential ways that you will be matched with a child: a child will be assigned to you or you will find a child through a photolisting Web site. Of course, there may be other ways that you find out if a child is available for adoption. For example, you could have a friend who is a foster parent who is not in a position to adopt the child, but you would like to adopt the child. So you proceed with the hope that you could adopt the child and keep the child in close contact with your friends, the foster parents.

If the staff assigns a child to you, it is because your request for a certain type of child matches the type of child who is available. Once you are assigned a child or see a child on a photolisting Web site who you are serious about adopting, you will want to get a child's full social, medical, and psychological history. Of course, it is not always possible to know everything. Ask the caseworker what her "sense" is if the record is not complete. In particular, be sure to ask the following, if you feel that the whole background is not presented to you.

- In what kind of foster homes was the child?
- What kinds of emotional, social, or behavioral problems can you expect based on the child's history?
- What kind of counseling and other medical or special services will the child require, and will they be available to her?
- Is the agency willing to provide full disclosure of all records prior to adoption finalization?
- What were the circumstances that placed this child in foster care and for adoption?
- What is the history of this child?
- What kind of abuse (physical, emotional, and/or sexual) has this child endured?
- How long has this child been in foster care and what kinds?
- How many times has this child been moved since birth?
- What are the existing or potential problems for this child?
- What postadoption intervention resources are available should problems arise?

To get more ideas about what adoptive parents need to know before adopting a special needs child, read Keck and Kupecky's book *Adopting the Hurt Child*, especially Chapter 6, "Dreams and Realities."

QUESTIONS TO ASK YOURSELF

When considering a social services adoption, here are some questions to consider:

- Do we thoroughly understand the process of attachment or parent-child bonding and the consequences of children experiencing insecure attachment or broken attachments?
- Do we have the necessary commitment to make an investment in parenthood that raising a child requires?
- Do we know what kind of child we would consider bringing into our home?
- Do we have sufficient knowledge to ask the right questions about a child?
- Do we know how to establish resources before we adopt that we may need after the adoption?
- Do we have the patience to participate in pre- and postadoption placement counseling to be prepared for the problems that will arise?
- Do we have the financial resources, including adoption subsidies, to raise this child?

ADOPTION NETWORKS OR EXCHANGES

Adoption networks are photolisting services that present children who have not been able to be placed by their own social services department. Such children are usually more difficult to place and therefore need a broader exposure to potential adoptive parents. An adoption exchange is not an agency but a networking system where public and sometimes private agencies can register children who need homes. The exchanges do not have custody of the children; they are merely facilitators in bringing children who are in the custody of an agency or foster care system together with prospective adoptive parents. Exchanges often will try, using a computer, to match prospective adoptive parents with children.

You may be very excited about the number of children available in a photo-listing, but remember that many other prospective adoptive parents may be inquiring about the same children and that the children may be in the process of being adopted even as you are beginning plans to find out more about them. As you pore over these books, try not to raise your hopes too high. Prospective adoptive parents have often reported much disappointment.

Exchange Lists

It is best to place yourself on a few adoption exchange lists to increase your opportunities for adopting a child. Different lists cover different geographical territory. Some cover a single state, some a region, and some the entire country.

State—It is probably best to begin your search for a child in your own state. First, you are more likely to be selected than an out-of-state parent because some social workers are opposed to sending a child a long distance away, especially if the child needs a more gradual transition from his foster home to his adoptive home. Second, the adoption process can usually go more smoothly because the Interstate Compact is not involved. Third, it is easier to visit the child before the adoption takes place if you live within a few hours' driving distance.

National—A national exchange certainly allows you to select from a greater number of children. Remember, anytime you adopt a child from a distance, you must consider the cost of transportation. You will probably be expected to visit the child a few times before making a permanent adoption plan. Traveling can be expensive and time-consuming. The most comprehensive list is *www. adoptuskids.com.*

WHEN THE ADOPTION IS COMPLETED

There are a number of things you should do to make sure a social services adoption is successful. First, be sure to share with your close relatives what the child is like and what may be expected. If they live nearby, their assistance could be very important, especially if you have other children in the home.

Finding Professional Assistance

You should begin by asking a pediatrician who is very competent in treating children with special needs to review the records. You may also want to ask other appropriate professionals, such as a child psychologist and an educational psychologist, to review them. Make it very clear that the review is not to determine whether you want to proceed with the adoption but to get a complete picture of the situation you and the child will be entering. Once you feel you have a clear picture, you can begin to arrange for physicians and other professionals who accept your insurance or Medicaid coverage.

The Child's Arrival at Your Home

Depending on the child's age, she will very likely visit with you a few times and spend a weekend before coming to live with you. It is best if you visit her at least once or twice in her foster home first. You and your spouse may want to go visit the first time; then the second time, you may want to take your other children with you, if you have any, and perhaps plan a fun outing all together. The third time you all meet, the child will come to your home, and the fourth visit will probably be a weekend overnight. Again, depending on the child's age, this process should take about two to three weeks.

Before the child arrives at your home, she will have to leave at least one, possibly two, families behind: her immediate foster family and her biological family. Even if she has not lived with her biological family for years, she may still need to "leave" the dream of living with her biological parents. This transition can be very difficult for a child, especially if she has feelings of mixed allegiance to her foster and birth families. If she is older, you or the caseworker may want to arrange a special ceremony in which the birth parents say good-bye to the child. If this is not possible or appropriate, a birth parent will sometimes write a letter wishing the child well in her new home. The child needs to feel that it is all right with her birth parents for her to move on to another home; she may need their "permission." If birth parents are not available, you can arrange a different kind of special ceremony. Buy some helium-filled balloons, one representing the child, one for each of her birth parents, one for each of her foster parents, and one for each of you. You can write each person's name on a balloon and then have the "persons" talk to each other. In the end, the child can hold on to the balloons representing herself and her adoptive parents; you and the child can release the birth and foster parents balloons into the air.

Learning the Child's Routine

The small things in life can go a long way toward making a child's placement successful. If a child needs a lot of structure and routine, that needs to be established when he arrives. If he is very controlling, you will need to decide what is important and what you need to overlook so that not everything becomes a power struggle. Often adoptive parents get upset over minor irritants—how much toothpaste is used, food "stealing," eating habits, and so on. A parent who can handle the child's learning disability may get quite upset if the child is clumsy. Issues such as space, sharing, meals, favorite foods, television time, and how to get along should be thought through as much as possible beforehand and the child's day-to-day activities, preferences, and interests learned. Your caseworker should be able to give you practical tips in dealing with the child.

Depending on the child's nature and background, you may want to keep things predictable and calm the first few days after the child's arrival. It is probably best not to have many visitors to your home during this time so that the child does not feel like a "specimen" that is being examined.

Making It Work

Once a child is in your home, the experience can be wonderful. However, after the newness has worn off—usually about three to six months later and often even sooner—the relationship with the child may begin to deteriorate. Caseworkers see this as the end of the "honeymoon" period, when the reality of the child's problems begins to hit. Before the child comes to live with the adoptive parents, they may not have been able to hear fully what the caseworker was saying to them about their child's needs and problems.

Although most parents of children with special needs experience a great deal of joy and personal satisfaction despite the extraordinary demands, some adoptions do disrupt. Planning and having realistic expectations can help reduce the likelihood of an adoption not working. Here are some suggestions for making the experience as positive as it can be:

Join a support group of parents with special needs kids. If you did not do this before you adopted, do it now. The more information you can gather from others, the more prepared you will be for whatever postadoption issues you will have to face.

Research the special characteristics of your child. Read, read, and read. Once you decide on a particular special need you would be comfortable handling, do as much research as possible on the subject. Get to know other parents who have a child with that particular medical, psychological, or disability problem. Visit them at their home, if possible. See how day-to-day family life goes with such a child.

Get a support system in place. No parent can on his or her own care for a child twenty-four hours a day, seven days a week, especially a child who has many needs that can be emotionally and physically draining. Get someone to help you and give you a break. If you are reluctant to leave your child with yet another person after all the caretakers he has experienced, hire someone to come into the home while you are there so you can make yourself a cup of tea and go through the mail or read a book.

Studies show that in families in which the father plays a significant role the parents were able to stay far more committed. Make sure that you have support from friends and family. If your family is functioning well now, that is a good predictor that you will perform well with an additional child.

Selecting a Therapist

When selecting a therapist, one of the first criteria should be the therapist's knowledge of adoption issues, especially issues related to attachment and to the loss involved in the adoption process. If your child has experienced abuse and neglect, the therapist should have the skills to handle such issues. Many therapists know about these issues in adults but have little experience with children. The therapist must also be competent in working with family dynamics.

The therapist must see you, the parent, as an integral part of the team and should communicate regularly with you about your child's progress. Both of you should have goals for the child.

Your local social services department most likely will have the names of such therapists. In addition, these therapists usually accept Medicaid reimbursement. If your child is not adopted through the social services department or a private agency that has contracted with the social services department, then your child most likely is not eligible for Medicaid. Many insurance companies offer only partial reimbursement for a therapist, and you are responsible for the remainder of the payment. You may have to negotiate with your insurance carrier to select the right therapist for your child. For example, you may need to ask them to allow (and pay for) your child to see a therapist who is not on their "list" of providers.

Many families who will spend a great deal for an adoption are reluctant to spend funds for a therapist. Yet to make an adoption successful, therapy is often required when problems arise.

Be sure that you are comfortable with the therapist. If are you not, select someone else; otherwise, you will either be second-guessing the therapist or yourself.

Some children will need intensive therapy, and there are organizations especially for such children.

It is also very important for a child to feel that he is in his permanent family and not in legal limbo. If your child's adoption finalization is taking longer than is reasonable, you may need the help of your own adoption attorney. An attorney can review all legal documents and adoption subsidy agreements and can expedite the adoption process, especially if one or both of the birth parents' rights have not been terminated.

In addition, you may need to hire an attorney if you feel that the right subsidies and benefits are not in place for your child.

DISRUPTIONS

Not all adoptions work out: the older the child, the more likely it is that there will be a disruption.

An extensive study by the Evan B. Donaldson Adoption Institute demonstrates that most adoption placements are stable and disruptions are not occurring at previous rates. In a November 2004 report, the Institute reports that they have found that disruptions seldom occur. Families headed by single, lower income, less educated parents do better than married affluent, well educated family heads, and postadoption services are essential to reducing the rate of disruptions.

The Institute states that disruptions are lessened when there is improved matching, preparation, and education. Parents who were the most informed about the child, had prepared for the child, and had adoption subsidies were the most likely not to disrupt. Those parents who felt that something was "wrong" or it just did not "feel right" are more likely to disrupt. Those at *www.adoptiondisruption.com* say listen to your intuition. It is better for you and the child if the disruption takes place sooner than later.

If staff provide parents with more information, parents are less likely to have unrealistic expectations. Parents need to know not only what problems the child has demonstrated and to what extent, but also what problems they could face in the future. For example, the behaviors associated with disruption included cruelty, fighting, and vandalism. Being fully prepared may be the most important factor to making the adoption successful.

What Kinds of Adoptions Disrupt?

Overall, the older the child, the higher the rate of disruption. For example, less than 1 percent of infant placements disrupt. We have yet to see any parents disrupt a newborn infant placement. However, in some instances it appears that one of the highest rates of disruption is in preschool children. This may be explained by observing that families fall in love with these children's sweet faces and do not see the problems they have or believe that they can help the children overcome these problems.

When It Is Not Working

Parents need to be very careful about how they handle a disruption. Some social services agencies are not supportive and may feel that the parents are abandoning the child and may then want to put them on the state registry for child abuse/neglect. Parents who are considering a disruption should first seek the advice of an adoption attorney before they contact their social services agency.

Adoption disruption can exhibit these stages:

1. *Diminishing pleasure.* The joy of taking care of the child becomes outweighed by the burden.
2. *The child is perceived as a major problem.* The parents can't cope with the child. They want change, but the child does not change.
3. *The parents complain to others about the child.* They are urged by friends and family members to vacate the adoption.
4. *The turning point.* A specific event leads the parents to believe they can no longer tolerate the child's behavior. The parents imagine and look forward to life without the child and no longer try to assimilate him into their family.
5. *Deadline.* Either the child is given a "shape-up or ship out" message or the parents decide that if the behavior occurs once more, they will vacate the adoption.
6. *Giving up.* The parents give up and return the child to the agency.

TALKING TO YOUR CHILD ABOUT ADOPTION AND HIS OR HER PAST

When you adopt a child with special needs, you are likely to be dealing not just with adoption issues but with issues of why the child's parents could not care for him and perhaps why they abused or neglected him. This kind of abandonment is different from the "abandonment" that occurs in other countries, in which a child is left in an orphanage. "Abandonment" in the United States usually involves overt neglect. Similarly, if the child was abused, he will not understand why his parents would do this to him.

Although hearing about the neglect and abuse and why he was placed for adoption is very painful for the child, at some point he will need to know the details surrounding his placement. Children have a right to know their past—it helps them understand why they feel what they feel. Without this information, the child may feel like a partly blank slate.

Of course, children do not need to know all this information at an early age or all at the same time. Telling your child the truth is a process that may parallel the discussions you have with him about adoption. Just as you do not explain adoption all at once when the child is four years old, never to bring up the subject again, you would not think of sharing the child's past with him all at the same time. Sharing the past is a process in which information is gradually revealed in ways that the child can understand.

Many adoptive parents feel that they want to protect the child by withholding some of the more grim details of her abuse or neglect. This is understandable, but they should know that the child might find out elsewhere. It is better if the information comes from you.

As your child asks questions, try to answer her honestly, providing only as much information as she is seeking and as is appropriate for her age. When she asks about her birth parents, try to tell the facts without making a judgment. Do not be overtly condemning of her birth parents. The child may feel she needs to "defend" her biological heritage, and she may become uncomfortable about sharing her feelings or memories if you use those occasions to bad-mouth her biological parents. Be careful of the way you talk about her biological parents in front of others. Your attitude will come through.

Although it is best, in discussing the child's past, to state the facts without adding a negative interpretation to it, at times you will need to let the child know that what was done was wrong. To say, "Your mother was a wonderful woman who drank too much alcohol, and that is why she couldn't keep you" may confuse the child. The child may think, "Why do you think she was so wonderful when I remember going hungry when she was drunk?" or "If she was so wonderful, why didn't she just stop drinking so that I could live with her?" It might be better to say, "Your first mother loved you, but she drank too much alcohol, which made her do bad things like not feed you often enough." The child will understand that he was not necessarily rejected, but that his mother chose not to get help for her alcoholism and therefore was not able to provide for him. This captures some of the intense complexity of the situation, that his mother loved him but also did things that had a terrible effect on him. If you can and if the situation warrants, talk in terms of the parents' actions and choices that were bad, not a mother and father that are bad. If the parent was an addict, it may help to explain how drugs and alcohol can "lasso" a person and trap them so that they find it very hard to get away. The parents made some bad choices, and then their choices trapped them. It was alcohol or drugs that took his mother from him. In no way do you want to excuse the birth parents' lifestyles and diminish the reality of what the child went through. On the other hand, you do not want to dehumanize the birth parents by painting them as all bad and giving the child that kind of lifelong image of them.

LIFE BOOKS

A life book is a pictorial and descriptive history of a child's life. Like any scrapbook, it can be put together at one time, but it is better if it is made over time. Usually a caseworker assists a child in completing the pages, but a dedicated foster parent may also put in entries.

The older the child, the more important the life book. A child in the foster care system often has had a fragmented life and may have difficulty knowing where he was and what he was doing at various times. The life book can help put the pieces together. Unlike a regular photo album, the life book provides more than pictures of the child's past; the book can also fill in gaps that even his current social workers may not be able to tell him. Also, the life book can help a child express his feelings about different points in his life.

Ideally, a child or his caseworker has a regularly updated life book from the time he enters foster care until the time he is adopted. However, this probably will not be the case. First, many children enter foster care with no pictures of themselves, and second, foster parents often do not take pictures. In addition, social workers may have limited opportunities to take meaningful pictures of the child; the pictures may be only of the child's foster home, his church, and his school.

If your child comes with a life book, do treat it as a special object. Go through it with your child so that he can share his past with you. Do this more than once. The child may tell you more and more each time. You will want to add pictures of your child with your family. The life book is the child's personal history; don't put the book on the coffee table—or in the attic, as one adoptive family did, sending a message to the child that his past was not significant.

A list follows of what goes into a life book, but your child's life book may not contain all of these items. You may want to add some of these entries yourself.

- Information about the child's biological family, along with pictures and letters from or about family members
- The child's birth certificate and Social Security card
- A family tree
- A page about the child's nationality

- A list of relatives, including parents, grandparents, and siblings
- Birth and death dates
- Pictures of your child's family of origin, the homes they lived in, and the pets they had
- The child's health records
- Any family history of diseases
- The child's immunization records
- A record of childhood illnesses and health problems, including injuries
- An education page, including a list of schools the child has attended, photos of teachers, and a list of things the child enjoys
- Pictures of special foster family members and any notes from them you might have
- Illustrated stories by you about funny experiences related to the child
- A letter about why you like and love the child
- A "Heart" page where the child describes with words, magazine pictures, etc., how he likes to show feelings and affection and what makes him feel loved
- A "Bug" page where you or the child draws or writes down all the things that "bug" him (Put a picture of a big bug on this page.)
- A page about church/temple and Sunday School experiences, including pictures of a favorite teacher
- Information gleaned from social workers or the child's previous foster family about his day-to-day routine; foods he likes; sleeping habits; favorite toys, books, blankets; and the kinds of clothes he likes.

OPEN ADOPTION

Openness in a special needs adoption can be very similar to openness in a standard infant adoption, with letters and pictures being exchanged with the birth mother or other family members every six months or so, or it can be quite different. Children who are in the foster care system are often old enough to remember their parents or relatives, and therefore, more openness may be advised. On the other hand, children removed from their birth families have parents or other family members who may pose a danger to the child and should not have contact with the child. Privacy is usually maintained by the exchanging of letters and pictures through the adoption agency.

Initially, the contact may be one-way: the adoptive family sending letters and pictures to the birth family. Whether or not you share the fact that you are sending pictures with your child can depend upon the circumstances of placement. What you do may be less important than how it is perceived by your child. Relationships are complex; it is wise to make sure your child feels free to bring up discussions about his birth family and the level of "contact" that he may want.

Where possible, a certain level of openness is now commonly viewed as beneficial to the birth parents, adoptive parents, and most of all the child. Although the birth parents and the child probably gain the most advantage from openness, adoptive parents and the agency usually have the most control over the matter. Because you will ultimately set the tone for the level of openness that will take place in an adoption, the caseworker will want to know your comfort level and under what circumstances you may or may not be comfortable with openness. Whether or not contact in person or through letters with the biological parents is advised, the caseworker will probably expect that you remain in contact with the child's previous foster parents for at least a few months to make the child's transition easier.

Here are some of the different levels of openness and the times when each kind may be appropriate:

Personal visits with birth parents, extended family members, or foster family members. No one wants to see a child abruptly removed from his home and placed with a new set of parents, never to see his biological parents or caregivers again. We have all heard about children being taken from the only home they have ever known and sent to live with their biological parents. No matter what we believed was the right legal decision, our hearts ached for the children. Yet every day, 2,000 children in the United States and Canada are separated from their parents and placed in another home. Often they are placed with foster parents with whom they become attached before they move on to be with their adoptive parents. The trauma of separation from parent(s) and other relatives is added to the trauma of the neglect and abuse. That is why social services agencies work so hard to reunite children with their parents or to have a relative care for the child if the parent cannot.

Not all children's parents who have neglected them are malicious. Cocaine and crack have disrupted the lives of many parents who come from seemingly stable family backgrounds. A child of such parents may have aunts and uncles and grandparents who lead normal lives. These extended family members may love the child very much and, although they lack the resources to care for her, may desire to see her at least a few times a year. Since they did not neglect or abuse the child, they may be the ideal people to provide her with the link to her birth family and allow her to feel connected to her original family in a positive way.

Other children have parents who have a mental illness or a level of retardation that makes caring for the children very difficult, causing the parents' rights to be terminated. A child may have parents who truly care about him and wish him no harm, but just cannot provide the day-to-day structure needed. He may well benefit from having contact with his parent(s), especially if he has strong memories of them and knows that they care about him. Having contact with the birth parents can give him a sense of continuity and connectedness to his biological roots.

Of course, if you adopt an older child—one who can remember phone numbers and make phone calls—openness may not be an option—it may just be a fact. Children can and will make phone calls to relatives.

The child's response to seeing his biological parents or other relatives when they visited him while in foster care should be taken into consideration when deciding whether such visits are appropriate. Depending on the situation, it is best for such meetings to take place in a public area, such as a restaurant. You probably do not want the family to know exactly where you live.

Letters and pictures. Sometimes children are placed with adoptive families who live so far away from their birth parents and relatives that personal contact with the birth family is nearly impossible, even if it is appropriate. Sometimes parents' lives are too chaotic, or the abuse they inflicted on the child was too severe for visits to take place. In such situations, cards, letters, and pictures may be appropriate. Again, the child's age and history should be taken into consideration. If the child is very young, contact with the birth family is for the birth family's benefit. As the child matures, the contact can be for his benefit.

If the child's parents' rights were involuntarily terminated, you will probably not want the parents to know your address. All correspondence should go through the agency.

No contact. Children who were grossly neglected or abused may be traumatized by any contact. The parents can continue to abuse the child psychologically in letters, even if the content of the letters is not overtly abusive. Parents who used code words when they abused the children could still continue to use those terms in a letter. A letter may remind a child of past trauma in a way he is not ready or capable of dealing with; it may even cause flashbacks that may retraumatize the child.

Even if minimal contact with the parent is not appropriate now, some level of contact may be appropriate in the future. If the child is in therapy and needs to confront his abusers on some level, making contact with his parents may be part of his healing process. He may also have to make contact with his biological relatives to understand his genetic background, especially as it evolves over time.

Contact with foster parents. Children often desire and need to continue contact with the foster parents. Sometimes, however, it is not appropriate for children to have contact with the foster parents if they are trying to sabotage the adoption or are causing the child to have conflicting loyalties.

Accidental encounters. Then there is the bump-in at a store. If you live in a relatively small town, you may not want to risk running into a birth mother or other family member at the grocery store. Therefore, social workers will take measures to place a child in another town so that this is less likely to happen. Sometimes a teacher or someone who knows the child seeks to adopt the child, and the possibility of seeing the birth family can remain. You may want to prepare how you will handle such an encounter. You may want to discuss this with your child, as well as to how he may feel if he sees his birth mother in a public setting.

GETTING TO KNOW MORE ABOUT SPECIAL NEEDS
The following list is just an overview to help you think about whether you could consider a child with special needs. For example, if you are seriously considering adopting a child with special needs, many books and Internet articles discuss the topic of adopting older children.

Physical and Medical Problems
Physical disabilities can include in utero exposure to drugs and alcohol, sensory disabilities such as blindness and deafness, and diseases such as epilepsy. Although the outcome for certain conditions—especially those related to exposure to drugs and alcohol—is uncertain, most conditions have a predictable course. You may believe you have the background and skills to help a child with a particular kind of physical problem. If you are considering an older child with a medical condition, you must also recognize that any child who is older will most likely also have some emotional problems. But studies show that those who do adopt such children have a high degree of satisfaction; placements with the best outcomes were ones in which adoptive mothers were not depressed, had few reservations, had experience with disabling conditions, and had strong religious beliefs.

Learning Disabilities
Adopted children, even those adopted at birth, have a much higher-than-average incidence of attention deficit disorder (ADD), attention deficit hyperactivity disorder (ADHD), and other learning disabilities. Poor parenting, abuse, and neglect can interfere with the child's ability to attach and to learn. Prenatal exposure to drugs and alcohol also increases the likelihood of a child's developing a learning disability.

ADD and ADHD can resemble other mental, personality, and behavioral disorders. Children who have been abused, neglected, or institutionalized can be diagnosed with ADD and ADHD when, in fact, they have other disorders. Nevertheless, ADD/ADHD may often be the correct diagnosis.

Diagnosing the disorder is not always easy, especially when a child is bright or when a child is more passive.

One mother tells the story of her two children, each adopted at birth. Her daughter, Gracie, is eight years old and was finally diagnosed with ADHD at age seven. The mother noticed that her daughter was hyperactive, defiant at times, struggled in math, yet flourished in reading and vocabulary—the mother did not quite know what it all meant. After the mother heard a lecture by a physician who is very cautious in diagnosing children with ADD or ADHD, she realized that Gracie most likely had ADHD.

The mother then went to Gracie's teachers, who were very reluctant to accept the ADHD diagnosis. So the mother went to a physician who had Mom, Dad, and Gracie's teachers complete a questionnaire. With this exercise, each soon realized that Gracie did indeed meet the criteria for a diagnosis of ADHD, and so she was treated with medication. The evening of the day she began taking the medication, her parents were shocked in her change in behavior. Gracie now excels in school, is appropriately compliant, and is eager to please.

Unlike Gracie, Thomas, her brother through adoption, was not hyperactive. In fact, his symptoms were somewhat opposite of Gracie's. Being a boy, teachers were reluctant to diagnose him with an attention deficit disorder because he was not "hyper." Instead, the teachers said he had a mild learning disability. He was very disorganized, often lost things, excelled in math, yet struggled in reading. He underwent the same battery of tests as his sister and was diagnosed with borderline ADD. He takes a smaller dosage of medicine than his sister, and now instead of failing his classes, he is an honor student.

According to psychologist Dr. Anna Kieken, not all children with ADD or ADHD have such a dramatic turnaround. Perhaps the most important thing is a careful diagnosis, which usually includes behavior checklists of the childhood and adult behavior of the biological parents (if available), as well as questionnaires filled out by the child's parents and teachers. It is very common for children and adults with ADD or ADHD to also have mild or moderate depression. Depression can affect every area of the child's life, including bonding with his parents and being motivated in school, and it is important to treat the depression as well.

Dr. Kieken states that medications can be a powerful tool in treating the brain imbalance that causes the symptoms of ADD, ADHD, and depression. New medications have been developed in the past few years, giving parents and doctors more than one medication option. A reasonably structured schedule and home environment, as well as teaching the child organizational skills, such as laying out his clothes at night for the next day and making his bed in the morning, can also go a long way in dealing with these behavior issues. See *www.add.org* for more information on diagnosis, treatment, and management of ADD/ADHD at home and in the classroom.

For a wealth of information regarding children with special needs and their educational needs go to *www.specialchildren.about.com.*

Emotional and Behavioral Problems

Many children who are removed from their parents as a result of abuse or neglect will display a variety of emotional and behavioral problems as a direct result of their traumatic backgrounds. These problems can be further exacerbated by the loss of their biological parents and possibly of their foster parents. Children who are in overseas orphanages also can display the same type of problems as children from the United States who are placed because of abuse or neglect. In other countries, it is poverty that is often the reason for the placement of a child into an orphanage setting. Nevertheless, the environment that the child came from before being placed into an orphanage can be one of neglect by U.S. standards. Orphanages overseas often have very few staff to care for the children and lack other resources for the children as well.

This means that nearly all adopted children, except those adopted at birth and not prenatally exposed to drugs or alcohol, are at risk for emotional problems, although many will not have such problems. Unlike physical conditions, emotional problems are not easily diagnosed and can have uncertain outcomes. Typical emotional problems for these children include fear, anger, low self-esteem, anxiety, depression, lack of trust, and developmental regression. The problems a child has may be known at the time you plan to adopt her and may subside because of her being in your loving and nurturing home environment. On the other hand, a younger preschool child may not have any notable emotional or behavioral problems but may develop problems later on.

Helping a child overcome her emotional problems and the behaviors that accompany them can be very rewarding. It requires a great deal of patience and understanding, as well as realistic expectations.

One family, who is in the process of adopting siblings who were placed into foster care at two and three years old and then placed in their home at ages five and six, says that although the transition has been smooth, the children still express many insecurities. Both children are afraid that the parents "will get tired of them" and give them away and that they will have a new mommy and daddy. The children's fears are understandable because of their history of going from their birth family to a foster home to an adoptive home. Moreover, these children have only been in three different homes! Many children are in far more homes by the time they reach school age. The parents say the most trying aspects of parenting these children are convincing them that this is a permanent home.

Parents report their foster-adopted child saying such things as, "Oh Daddy, you came home again" or "Are you going to leave us?" One preteen asked his foster parents, "What is this," in reference to their living together in marriage. This child had never seen a mother and father living together for any length of time and did not understand the concept of marriage.

Knowing which problems you can and cannot accept is very important. One behavioral problem, even if minor, that one parent can overlook can cause havoc in another family. In addition, the child's age can play a role in the parent's attitude. For example, most parents adopting a five-year-old would accept the fact that she wets the bed; however, some parents cannot cope with bed-wetting in a twelve-year-old. The same is true for lying. A four-year-old who lies may seem cute; a twelve-year-old with the same behavior is often viewed as cunning and manipulative. As will be discussed later in the chapter, you must know what you can handle and what you cannot. Also, even though you may be able to accept a wide variety of behavioral problems, this does not necessarily mean that you are willing to accept a child with many behavioral problems.

The following description includes the behavioral characteristics often associated with children who have been abused, neglected, or have moved from one caretaker to another:

- *Delayed development.*
- *Aggression and hyperactivity.*
- *Indiscriminate affection.* These children have not attached to one particular person. Although overly friendly even with strangers when they are small, as they grow older they may be cold, aloof, demanding, and manipulative.
- *Lack of self-awareness.* The child is not aware of his own needs, including the need to eat or use the bathroom.
- *Control issues.* The child who has had no normal boundaries set for him may try to set his own boundaries to make himself feel secure.
- *Wetting and soiling.* A child who needs to control his environment does so by not going to the bathroom and then becomes constipated or soils or wets his pants during the day.
- *Food hoarding.* A child who has not been able to depend on adults to meet his needs may hide food in his bedroom because he has learned to be self-sufficient.
- *Lying.* The child lies indiscriminately, that is, she lies as a habit, not just to get out of trouble. She will lie even when the lie is obvious or when telling

the truth would not normally lead to punishment.

- *Profound emotional problems, including attachment disorders.* Children with emotional problems are probably the most common special needs children. Some children do not have a specific diagnosis but are at risk for having emotional or behavior problems. Being at risk for a having an emotional problem or a mental illness can also classify a child as special needs. For example, if you adopt a three-year-old child who has been in several placements before being adopted by you, the child's problems may not become apparent until the child reaches school age or puberty. If you adopt a child who has a limited family history but you are told that alcoholism and perhaps some depression may be in his background, your child could be at risk for fetal alcohol effects, or the child may later develop depression.

- *Depression.* About 5 percent of children and teenagers in the overall population suffer from depression, and children who have suffered abuse, neglect, and multiple caregivers have a higher incidence. Children who are under stress, have ADD, are anxious, or experience loss also have an increased risk.

ATTACHMENT DISORDERS

Attachment disorders are different from the usual emotional and behavioral problems a child may have. They are a group of serious, hard-to-treat, and often misdiagnosed conditions. Because they are so difficult to treat, knowing whether a child has an attachment disorder is crucial in making the decision to adopt. Moreover, if you do decide to adopt, you need to know how to get help for the child.

Some children who have been grossly neglected or have gone from one caretaker to another without "bonding" with anyone will probably never bond without intensive treatment. Such children do not respond to standard therapy because they cannot "connect" to the therapist. As a rule, the earlier the abuse and neglect, the more likely the child will have an attachment disorder. Usually the factors that cause attachment problems occur before the child's third birthday. This is one of the most difficult emotional disorders to handle because the child may never respond to your love and affection.

Fortunately, most children who have the risk factors for an attachment disorder—primarily abuse and neglect—will not have one. The greater the degree of abuse and neglect, the greater the chance that the child will have an attachment disorder. Yet, some children who have more risk factors will have a greater ability to overcome their backgrounds, while other children who were not as severely abused or neglected may display gross behavioral and emotional problems. The reasons why some children appear to be more resilient than others are not well understood. A child's response to abuse and neglect appears to be part of what determines whether she will have an attachment disorder. It seems that children who can learn to gratify themselves when their caretakers have not met their needs will usually have fewer symptoms and are more likely to bond with their adoptive parents.

For a diagnosis of attachment and bonding disorders, one or more of the following must have been present:

- *Prenatal exposure to significant amounts of drugs or alcohol.* This causes the most permanent damage.
- *Lack of early bonding with a caretaker and lack of love and nurturing.* The child cries for food or for a diaper change, and when he is not fed or changed, he rages. After a cycle of crying and then raging and learning that no one responds to his needs when he cries for help, he learns to trust only himself.
- *Multiple foster care placements.* When a child has multiple caretakers, he learns not to "bond" with anyone, knowing that if he does, it will be more painful when he leaves that person's home.
- *Other interruptions such as hospitalizations or going from one relative to another.*
- *Abuse and neglect.* A history of mistreatment, including physical or sexual abuse before adoptive placement, affects the child's level of attachment. The younger the child when the trauma occurs, the more impact it has on him.
- *Painful medical conditions.* A child who has pain that the parent cannot alleviate may detach.
- *Chaotic family life.* For example, a mother who is on drugs or who suffers from mental illness.

It is important to be aware of the symptoms associated with attachment disorder, not only so that you can know if the child has the problem, but also so that you can decide whether this is the kind of child you want to adopt. If you are adopting a child from another country, you may be given a very sketchy background on her, making it difficult to know whether she has been grossly neglected or abused. It is important to know the signs associated with an attachment disorder and to look for them in a child that you may adopt. If she does display the signs, finding resources to help may be very difficult, especially if you have adopted internationally.

Here are some of the symptoms of an attachment disorder:

- *Can be delightful initially.* These children have moved from one household to another and learned to "adjust" to many different people and situations.

- *Poor eye contact.* The child may be aloof, make little or no eye contact, and appear to have no conscience. Some people describe such a child's eyes as "hollow." For those who are adopting internationally, this may be the only symptom that can be observed. If the child cannot look you in the eye, he may very well have an attachment disorder.
- *Emotional withdrawal.* The child does not respond to affection and will not snuggle with you if you touch her.
- *Indiscriminate affection.* The child does not seem to "discriminate" between who should be given affection—people she knows and who are loving to her—and those to whom she should not be giving affection. It is not uncommon for such a child to run up to a total stranger to hug her and say, "I love you." It is very difficult for parents to feel close to a child who is acting close to everyone.
- *Overcompetency.* The child may not allow anyone to help him, for example, refusing any help with getting dressed or any other activity. This is a very serious problem that indicates the child has decided that no one but himself can be counted on for help. He doesn't need you or anyone else, and it is very possible that he will not attach to you. This overcompetency is often mistakenly viewed as independence.
- *Aggressive behavior.* A child who is defiant and hyperactive is usually diagnosed with attention deficit disorder. If he improves while taking Ritalin, then the diagnosis is considered to be attention deficit disorder and probably not an attachment disorder.
- *Frequent accidents.* An accident-prone child who is always dropping and breaking things and bumping into things.
- *Cruelty to animals, fire-setting, or bed-wetting or soiling during the day.* When a child shows all three of these behaviors, it is a "triad" that is extremely serious. This is a crystal clear sign of a child who may never "get better," no matter how much you love him and no matter how good a parent you are. It is particularly unwise to adopt such a child without consultation with a child psychologist or psychiatrist and having a clear understanding of what raising this child may involve.
- *Lying.* Crazy lying for no apparent reason; stealing to get caught.
- *Idiosyncratic speech patterns.*
- *Delayed learning; wanting to act "dumb."*
- *Lack of cause-and-effect thinking.*
- *Lack of conscience.*

When deciding to adopt such a child, you must do all that you can to get a comprehensive background of the child. If the child has been in foster care, some of this information about the child's behavior may be gathered from the foster parents, even if a caseworker does not say explicitly that the child has an attachment disorder. If you are selecting a child from another country, especially if the child is in an orphanage, making such an assessment may be far more difficult.

If you think a child may have an attachment disorder or be at a high risk for such a disorder and you want to proceed with an adoption, you must first seriously consider your own family situation. Those who are most successful in parenting such children usually have some experience parenting but do not have small children in the home and have time and energy to give the child the individual time and attention needed.

Families who are "flexible" yet structured tend to do best with such children. They also have realistic expectations and know that progress can be slow.

If a child must be treated for an attachment disorder, the treatment must usually be intense. Generally, the therapy is to help the child rework her negative life experiences and help her reduce anger, resentment, fear, and rage. As she lets go of these negative feelings, the child learns to experience trust and closeness so that she can bond with others. Some children and their adoptive families may be helped through weekly therapy, whereas other children may require an intensive inpatient therapy. Parent participation is crucial to the child's success, so much so that confidentiality between the child and therapist is secondary to having the parents' full understanding and input.

For more information and many excellent resources on attachment problems, see *www.instituteforattachment.org/whatisit.htm*.

HISTORY OF SEXUAL ABUSE

Many children who are removed from their parents have been sexually abused. In fact, it is estimated that a large majority have been sexually abused on some level. The factors that led to their removal from their families are the same factors that increase the risk of sexual abuse. For example, lack of parental protection, parental drug use, and parents socializing with other drug users all increase the likelihood of sexual abuse. Also, children who are neglected or abused are often more passive and emotionally vulnerable, making them easier targets for perpetrators.

Adults are not the only perpetrators. Children also abuse other children. This is particularly true in foster or group homes in which younger children are in contact with older children. Some older children (who are usually themselves victims of sexual abuse) abuse younger children. Ironically, a child who has never been sexually abused may be the victim of such abuse once he is removed from his birth family and placed in a foster care setting. The emotional scars from sexual abuse from a child's peers can be just as damaging as those caused by sexual abuse from an adult.

Contrary to popular opinion, sexual abuse is not restricted to males exploiting girls and boys. Women and older girls also abuse children. However, when women are the perpetrators, determining sexual abuse is even more difficult to diagnose because of the nature of the abuse and because boys, especially older boys, may not view the exploitation as offensive.

Diagnosing sexual abuse is difficult because the abuse can be subtle and may never involve actual physical contact with the child. For example, the child may have viewed actual sexual acts or X-rated films and may have been the target of inappropriate gestures and comments. Second, if the child was abused, he may not view it as abuse but as a display of affection and a way of gaining approval. Children often try to "normalize" such behavior—convince themselves that this type of sexual relationship is normal—if the behavior is done by a parental figure. If the child does view the abuse as wrong, he may have so much shame that he will not discuss it. Also, children often do not discuss the abuse because their two main fears are that they will not be believed and that nothing will be done. These fears are reinforced if therapy and other interventions do not take place.

Even if no one knows that a child has been sexually abused, the child's behavior may be an indication. Children, even young children, who have been sexually abused are generally more sexually knowledgeable, may act out sexually, and may be sexually provocative around adults as a way of getting attention. Many victims also struggle with such emotional problems as guilt, depression, anger, fear, and inability to trust. Depression in particular appears to be present in nearly all victims.

You may feel that you cannot handle the issues associated with raising a child who has been sexually abused. This is understandable. However, do be aware that any child who has been removed from his home may have a history of being sexually abused; it may be a single incident or many incidents. Usually the problem behaviors will diminish once the child is in a stable environment in which proper guidelines and trust are established. As with any child who has been abused, the child will require some therapy to deal with her past. Also, adoptive parents who have themselves been the victims of sexual abuse should enter therapy either for the first time or possibly return to therapy to resolve their own issues that will doubtless come to the surface again because of their adoptive child's sexual abuse.

The most sensible approach to adopting a child who may sexually act out is to adopt only a very young child or one who is significantly younger than any children already in your family. You certainly would not want an eight-year-old who may sexually act out if you already have a five-year-old. This is not to say that every child who has been sexually abused is going to be a perpetrator, but taking such precautions can help the placement of a child in your home go more smoothly.

If you do adopt a child with a history of sexual abuse, remember: A victim may say or do things that others view as perverted. Do not regard the child as a deviant, but rather as one whose actions are a result of his background. Calmly tell the child that his words or behavior is not appropriate; for example, he may not touch others in private places or talk about doing it. Instead tell him how he can show affection appropriately. Similarly, tell him that you imagine he may be quite angry, but that he may not hit or hurt others, or hit or kick or throw things. Work with him to figure out ways that do help him express his anger and hurt, such as kicking a ball against a wall, playing basketball, writing in a journal, drawing cartoons, and eventually talking with you or someone else about it. These things can help him to heal.

Sexual abuse is not a black mark against a child that can never be erased. These scars can heal, and these children can learn to love and be loved. When they begin dating, it will be helpful if they return to therapy at least for a brief period, in order to resolve any issues that come to the surface again. It is also helpful if they return to therapy at least for a few sessions before they get married.

SIBLING GROUPS

For a sibling group to be classified as "special needs," usually there must be three or more children who all need to be placed in the same family. If such children are available for adoption, it is usually because they have been removed from their home because of neglect or abuse, and they are likely to have emotional problems due to their backgrounds.

When abuse or neglect occurs to even one of the children, usually all of the children in the home are removed. These brothers and sisters are often very bonded to each other and may have learned to meet their needs through each other.

Therefore, when adoption is the plan, agencies try to find a family who can adopt all of the children. However, while the children are in foster care, they are often separated because it is difficult to find a foster home that can accommodate three or more children. Sometimes one child becomes very attached to his foster parents, who may want to adopt him but not his siblings. Such a scenario further complicates the emotional issues these children face as a result of being separated from each other during foster care, being removed from their foster family, and then being reunited in an adoptive home.

Finding an adoptive home can be difficult for sibling groups if one of the children has a more serious medical condition or behavioral problem. This may mean, for example, that an adoptable four-year-old may wait a long time for a family because she must be placed together with her eight-year-old brother, who has serious emotional problems. It can be very difficult for social workers to decide when siblings should be separated so that an adoption for at least one of the children is feasible.

The "biological bond" is given more weight than bonds with foster brothers and sisters. For example, if a foster family has been raising one eighteen-month-old child from a five-child sibling group because social services could not find a foster home for all the siblings, the plan may be for an adoptive family to adopt all five children. Yet, the eighteen-month-old could be very attached to the other children in the foster home and not to his biological siblings, whom he may not have ever known. To take a child away from his foster parents who want to adopt him because the foster family is not in a position to adopt the other four siblings can be unfair for all involved.

The decision to separate siblings is not made easily. Many factors are taken into consideration, and the overriding issue should be the bond that the children have together (if they have even been together) and the best interest of each child.

If you do decide to adopt a sibling group, the dynamics among the siblings need to be understood before adopting. Often the older child has been the caretaker of the younger children. The older child may have been playing this role for so long that she may find it difficult to relinquish it even after she and her siblings are placed for adoption. If you adopt such children, you will need to help each child learn new family roles. The oldest child will have to learn that you will meet her and the other children's needs and that she can be a child again. Although the children must learn new roles, the children's transition to a new home can be eased by the fact that they have a connection with each other.

Initially, the concept of having an instant family of more than one child can seem very attractive. However, be aware that meeting the needs of multiple children requires a great deal of time and commitment. If you already have one or two children, you probably have a more realistic understanding of the responsibility involved in caring for two or more additional children.

In some states, if the number of children in your home is greater than six, then you will need to be licensed as a group home. Once your home is licensed, you will be required to maintain a certain level of fire and safety precautions.

Funds are available for those adopting sibling groups. Generally, these children already qualify for subsidies because they are at risk for emotional problems.

AFRICAN-AMERICAN AND RACIALLY MIXED CHILDREN

About 60 percent of children available in the foster care system are African-American or Latino. Because a child's racial or ethnic background makes it more difficult to find her a home, she may be classified as "special needs." A child of mixed racial background is usually African-American and Caucasian. Although "Hispanic" is not a race, a child who is both Hispanic and Caucasian may be classified as racially mixed. A child who is two years old, healthy, and seems to be developmentally and emotionally on target may still be considered "special needs" because of her racial background.

Children who are "mixed race" Hispanics are often easier to place for adoption than a child who is considered to be biracial or African-American. Although a child is labeled "mixed race," finding an adoptive home for the child for adoption may not be difficult.

If you want to adopt a child from a certain ethnicity, you may want to consider the states in which the largest percentage of adoptable children is in that group. For example, if you want to adopt a child who is Hispanic and you live in South Carolina, in which 2 percent of the children placed for adoption are Hispanic, you may want to apply with other states such as Texas, in which 37 percent of the 2,295 children placed for adoption were Hispanic. Some states with a higher percentage than average of Hispanic children may primarily place with the foster parents rather than making them available for adoption, and the actual number of children who are available for adoption may be relatively small. It is important to find out how many of these children are actually available for adoption, not just in the social services system.

OLDER CHILDREN

Age as a "special need" is unlike a medical condition, which can have various but defined outcomes or even a child's race, which may make it harder for him to find a home. The success in adopting an older child has much to do with the child, his background, his age, and the adoptive parents' expectations. Defining "older" children is difficult. Some agencies call any child over one-year-old an "older child." One thing is certain: The older the child, the more emotional problems he is likely to have and the more difficulty he may have in attaching. However, in the context of social services, generally a child who is school age is "older." Fifty-five percent of all children adopted through the social services system are over five years old; yet a higher percentage of older children await adoption because these are the hardest children to place. This is because they usually have backgrounds that make them more difficult to parent and because the adopting parents will lose the opportunity to parent a young child. Everyone loves a baby, but not everyone loves a teenager.

Those adopting older children with special needs have the highest rate of adoptions not working out, or "disrupting."

If you are considering adopting an older child, you will want to read as much as possible about the subject. Most knowledge about the adoption of older children comes from the experiences of those who have actually adopted these children.

Unlike other classifications of "special needs," a child's being older is only one variable in how the child will adjust. An older child has had many more experiences, which can make the adjustment more difficult and less predictable. Susan Ward emphasizes in her "Older Child Adoption" article that you should know everything you can about the child ahead of time.

Fortunately, as more and more "older" Americans consider adoption, more opportunities are available for these children to find families. As Ward writes, the profile of adopting parents is changing: They are older, single, empty-nesters, and those who want to add more children to their existing families. They are often in their forties and fifties. They are healthier and "younger" than before. For those who have raised a family and are now in their mid-forties, adopting a child who is about seven years old could be a reasonable consideration. The child would be in school, and when the child turns eighteen years old, the parents may be only in their mid- to late fifties. Chances are they would not even be one of the oldest parents in their child's class.

An older child may integrate into your life and activities more easily. You may enjoy fishing, playing games, bicycle riding, or going to the beach.

Although most children classified as "special needs" because of their age are five or older, any child over the age of two who has suffered abuse or neglect and often younger children, too, are going to bear the scars of that trauma in their early lives. If you are considering adopting an older child, you are considering adopting a child who has lost at least one caretaker. The process of going from one caretaker to another can have a great psychological impact on the child. If you are adopting an older child, you must be prepared to face special emotional problems that may also cause behavioral problems.

In a study of adoptions that were and were not successful, the child's age was the single best predictor of disruption. Older, more troubled children not only entered the foster care system at a later age, but also remained in foster care longer and waited longer to be freed for adoption and to be placed.

The likelihood that a placement of a child will "work" is increased when you believe that adopting the child is right for you and the child and you have a strong conviction that things will work out, the issues will be resolved, and your child will heal. Anything less than a true conviction will lessen your dedication and drain you. Your child needs to know and feel your conviction as part of his healing process. The most critical of all components for success is commitment: a commitment to helping your child, a commitment to finding solutions. This is the advice of Ward, who not only encourages parents to do their homework and find information and advice, but also to remember that they are the parent and they are the one who knows their child the best.

The older the child, the more likely the child will have some attachment issues. This is not saying the child will have reactive attachment disorder. Most children have not learned to trust another person because they did not have loving caretakers. Read all you can on what you can do to make the attachment of a child easier and the transition smoother. These children cannot just leave the past behind and move on. The past needs to be integrated into their present. Once they learn to trust you, they will have lots of questions.

If your child came to you through the foster care system, chances are she moved from home to home with a plastic garbage bag full of her belongings. Your home may be one more in a series of homes. It may take time to adjust to her new surroundings and your habits, routine, and diet.

Chapter Sixteen

Transracial Adoption

I n adopting a child, we may seek certain characteristics, but humans are complex creatures. We cannot select a child's characteristics based on his or her ethnic background. Every child has her own unique characteristics that need to be valued and cultivated. Children will be who they will be, a fact of life that is as true when adopting as when you have a biological child.

A child's race or ethnic background does not predict the child's characteristics, but it may well predict the reactions of others. That is why the first question that comes to mind when you consider adopting a child outside your racial background (a transracial adoption) is often, "What will my family think?" Perhaps you do need to consider the responses of family and friends, especially if you think your family would have difficulty accepting such a child. Often the lack of acceptance, however, has more to do with what your mother's Aunt Edna may think rather than what your immediate family will think. Sometimes people use nonacceptance by family as a way to cover up the fact that they would find it difficult to raise a child who does not look like them or who belongs to a certain race or ethnic group.

If you are truly comfortable with a transracial or international adoption, expecting acceptance from every last relative, including those you see once a year, is unrealistic. If you are concerned that closer family and friends may have difficulty, you may want to discuss some of their concerns with them and let them know that you want to consider their feelings. Your parents may have to go through the stages of grief related to the loss of having biological grandchildren, and from there they may need to come to terms with having grandchildren who do not look like them. It may have taken you months or years to process the decision to adopt transracially; expect your family members to need some time to process their feelings as well.

Remember, grandparents and other close relatives who say they cannot accept a baby of a certain racial or ethnic background will probably be enthralled with him once he arrives. If they can't accept the child, you may ask yourself, in the words of one adoption attorney, "Do you really want to be around someone who cannot accept a sweet innocent baby because of the color of her skin?"

WHAT TO CONSIDER

If you are Caucasian, for example, and are considering adopting an African-American, biracial, or international child who will look very different from you, here are some questions you may need to ask yourself:

1. How do I feel about raising a child and providing him with a sense of his heritage?
2. How would I handle the comments from others about how my child looks different from me?
3. How would I feel about my child marrying someone of the same racial or ethnic background and having grandchildren of that heritage?
4. How would I feel about my child marrying someone of a different race?
5. Do I have friends or relatives outside of my race or culture?
6. How will I feel if people tell me how lucky my child is to be adopted by an American family?
7. Will my expectations for the child be based on his race or culture?
8. Do I feel differently about adopting a black or Asian girl versus a black or Asian boy?

If you did not answer the questions "correctly," relax. These questions are not designed to trap you; they are there to help you explore your feelings and what biases you may need to overcome.

Some of our biases are sexist as well as racial. For example, there is such a disproportionate number of couples who want to adopt Korean girls that at least one agency will not allow couples to request a girl unless they already have a son. Why the desire for a girl and not a boy? Perhaps it is because we perceive Asian girls and women, who generally are petite, as fitting into our American stereotype of what is feminine, or maybe it is because we have difficulty thinking about having sons—who are supposed to pass on the family name and traits—but who do not look like us.

Even if you have worked through any sexist or racial biases you may have, you may believe that because you live in an all-white neighborhood and did not sign up to lead the diversity weekend retreat at work that no agency is going to accept you for a transracial adoption. One Caucasian couple said they considered adopting a biracial or black child but decided against it after an agency sent them a list of questions regarding the racial makeup of their neighborhood, friends, church, employers, and so on. You should not be intimidated by such questionnaires. If you are open-minded, you can change your lifestyle so that an international child of another race or a black child can feel comfortable with your family and friends while retaining a sense of his heritage and culture.

BROADENING YOUR OPTIONS

Just as people dream of the ideal biological child, you may dream about the ideal adopted child. At first this fantasy may be to adopt a child who looks like you and your spouse. Expecting a child to look like you, however, even if you were to find biological parents who resembled you, is unrealistic. Even to expect biological children to look like you is unrealistic. Accept the likelihood that a child will probably not look like you—although we've seen lots of children who look like their adoptive parents, even those of a different race or ethnic background. Once you arrive at this realization, you may find yourself expanding your ideas about what kind of a child you would be able to accept.

This is not to say that someone who is uncomfortable with adopting a child from outside his or her race is nonaccepting. There are many things to consider when adopting a child, including the child's age, health background, and prenatal exposure to drugs and alcohol. Sometimes, looking at what you can accept emotionally, culturally, and financially allows you to move beyond preconceived ideas about what your child will be like and challenges you to consider adopting a child who does not fit into your original, often unrealistic, fantasy.

Regardless of background, every child needs to be loved and accepted for his unique qualities. We do not adopt children to make a social statement, out of pity, or because we feel some kind of social guilt. We adopt because we want children and because children need a loving and supportive home. The positive environment you provide may not compensate for every challenge your child may face, whether she is biological or adopted, but we know that, regardless of their backgrounds, children do better in stable, loving homes.

WHAT IS TRANSRACIAL ADOPTION?

Transracial adoption is adopting any child outside of your racial background. Many international adoptions are transracial adoptions because most of the world's children who are available for adoption are from China. Indeed, most transracial adoptions involving Asian children are international. Since only 15 percent of Asian births in this country take place out of wedlock, this chapter is primarily about Caucasian parents adopting biracial or African-American children born in the United States or Asian children born in another country. Many of the studies cited and issues discussed about white parents adopting black children could also apply to those adopting Asian and other international children. However, in the United States the experience of being an Asian raised by white parents can be very different from being black and having white parents. Historically, overall race relations between Asians and Caucasians have been more positive than those between blacks and whites. Asians and whites also tend not to segregate socially as much as whites and blacks. For example, Asians are less likely to live in racially distinct neighborhoods, except in very large cities.

Also, the adoptive couple's extended family members may initially be more accepting of an Asian child than a black child. Perhaps this is because interracial marriages between Asians and Caucasians have been historically more acceptable. In addition, many may feel that only African-Americans should adopt black children, a view regrettably shared by some social workers.

BIRACIAL CHILD PLACEMENT

For those who are Caucasian and are considering adopting a biracial child of white and black heritage, there are some considerations that need to be explored.

According to Beth Hall of Pact, An Adoption Alliance, Inc., which places children of African, Asian, and Latino heritage, children are identified by the racial background that they most resemble. Most biracial children appear to be black and will therefore be identified by others as black. In our culture, which is very race conscious, to be identified as black is a very different experience from being identified as white.

Hall asks prospective adoptive parents to explore their reasons for wanting to adopt a biracial child, as opposed to one who is fully black. She says perhaps it is because a white couple has difficulty accepting the "blackness" of that child. If a family has difficulty with the "black" part of the child, that message is going to be sent to the child in some form.

Hall's organization does not permit couples to select a birth mother who will deliver a biracial child instead of a black child. She believes that to accept a biracial child is to accept his black and white background equally, meaning that parents should feel comfortable adopting either racial background. Some biracial children, after all, look fully black. A white couple needs to be willing to accept the biracial child regardless of what she looks like.

When adopting a biracial child, some adoptive parents plan to wait until after the child is born to determine how dark she is before they proceed with the adoption. Such parents have clearly not accepted the child's black heritage. Yes, some biracial children will look nearly entirely African-American. Biracial siblings with the same two biological parents can, like other siblings, look very different.

Hall is right that prospective adoptive parents need to think through why they want to adopt a biracial child and not a black child. However, it is not necessarily right to say that parents need to be willing to adopt a black child if they plan to adopt a biracial child. Parents have different reasons for wanting to adopt a biracial child. Biracial children are both black and white, and some white parents want the child to match part of their heritage. Other parents are attracted to the "distinct" look that can characterize a biracial child. What about couples who are multiracial themselves? They may want to adopt a child who shares both of their heritages. One African-American couple who describe themselves as being "light-skinned" said that they would prefer to adopt a biracial child so that the child would resemble them.

We believe that to say biracial children are black because they are perceived as black by society detracts from who the child is. Is a child more what he is perceived to be or what he identifies himself to be? Indeed, because biracial children are neither fully black nor fully white, some do have difficulty in how they identify themselves. Biracial children who do not try to be either black or white, but both, tend to have the strongest sense of identity.

THE ADOPTION PROCESS
When you adopt an African-American or biracial child, the same laws and methods apply as with any other adoption. The only difference is the time frame for finding a child—about three to six months.

If you want to adopt an infant, it is best to contact several agencies and private attorneys who are permitted to do direct placements. If you have your heart set on a newborn baby, you should plan to wait three to six months, although most couples who are serious about adopting don't wait that long. If you are an African-American or interracial couple, you may not wait long at all before the attorney or agency calls to tell you that a child is ready to be placed.

Private Adoption
If you live in a state where it is legal for an attorney to place a child directly with a couple, the first thing you may wish to do is find a reliable attorney and get yourselves on her waiting list. Some attorneys may waive or lower the retainer fee for placing your name and home study with their office if you are seeking to adopt a black or biracial child. Like many agencies, attorneys like to have couples on hand who are ready to adopt a black or biracial child because many attorneys have too few prospective adoptive parents to present to a birth mother.

What happens next, as with any independent adoption, is that a birth mother either contacts the attorney directly or calls the office after being referred by adoption clients. These are clients who have placed adoption ads and are seeking to adopt a white child. When a birth mother expecting a biracial child answers an ad, the clients refer her to the attorney's office to find another couple.

In our own experience, we have recently seen more African-American women place their babies for adoption. In the past, the pressure to rear the child or to have a family member rear the child is great, not only from her own family, but also from the birth father's family. Private adoption expenses are the same regardless of the child's racial background. Sometimes an attorney will reduce her fee when placing an African-American or biracial child, sometimes not. This is not always possible, especially if the adoption is a complicated one.

The cost of an adoption for a black child is a sensitive issue. The reality is that most families who are seeking to adopt an African-American infant expect a discount since there are fewer families seeking a black infant than those seeking a white infant. Many times, agencies and attorneys do reduce their fees to accommodate these parents so that the child can be placed. Recently an agency from another state said that they had an African-American infant available for adoption and that the fee was $18,000, not including legal fees. We had no families who could afford to pay this much for an adoption. On the other hand, if the same agency had called and said they had a white infant available and the fee was $18,000, there are couples who could and would pay the agency's fee.

Another sensitive area is the birth mother's living expenses. As more families are seeking to adopt biracial and African-American children, the birth mothers are also expecting and receiving reasonable living expenses from the adoptive parents. Although no attorney or agency would have a policy of not paying for a black birth mother's living expenses, the reality is that it may have been difficult to find a couple to pay these expenses since many of these families sought to have a lower cost adoption and would select a birth mother who did not need to receive assistance.

Also, in the past many African-American birth mothers and those expecting biracial babies made more "eleventh hour" decisions to place their children for adoption. Now, this is changing, and these birth mothers are making plans more in advance.

A few times per month a posting will be made of African-American or biracial children available for adoption on Listservs. (Two that you might try are at *http://groups.yahoo.com/group/2adopt/* and at *http://groups.yahoo.com/group/Transracial_Adoption_or_Placement/*.) Usually the fees for these adoptions are higher than if you are working with a local attorney.

Advertising

Most advertising is done by Caucasian parents looking to adopt Caucasian children. In fact, years ago a typical ad would read, "Couple looking for healthy white newborn." Most ads today are not so candid, and many couples get calls from birth mothers expecting African-American and biracial children. If you know of someone advertising who wants only a Caucasian child, let that person know you are interested in phone calls from other birth mothers.

Even if your attorney cannot legally serve as an intermediary, he can tell his clients who are advertising to call you if they receive a call from a birth mother expecting an African-American or biracial child. Joining a local adoption support group or a RESOLVE group can also help you hook up with couples who are advertising.

PRIVATE AGENCY ADOPTION

An agency adoption of an African-American or biracial child will be handled much the same way all other adoptions are handled. However, the agency policy may require you to attend classes so that you can understand some of the issues related to adopting transracially. Also, many agencies have different standards about matters such as age or length of marriage for those adopting transracially.

Private agencies want to place the babies born to birth mothers who come to them. They do not want to send a birth mother away and are usually more than willing to place transracially.

Most private agencies, like all attorneys, permit the birth mother to select the couple. One agency reports that most of their birth mothers expecting biracial children want to place the infant with an interracial couple. Many other birth mothers do not care about the parents' ethnic background. Sometimes a birth mother will specify that she wants to place the child only with an African-American or Caucasian couple. In these agency adoptions, the birth mother's wishes are respected. Sometimes it is difficult, however, to find the match that she desires since there is often not a large pool of prospective adoptive parents.

Some agencies have a different fee scale for those adopting African-American and biracial children, especially agencies of a religious affiliation that raise support. A private adoption agency without outside support will generally charge you its standard fee plus birth mother living expenses, though it may reduce the application fee to increase the pool of applicants.

There are not as many African-American and biracial newborns available as there are Caucasian newborns, but there are also far fewer couples seeking to adopt these newborns—although the number is growing very quickly. The best way to adopt quickly is to make as many contacts as possible. Join an adoption support group and let people who are in adoption circles know of your desire. It often happens that a couple is sought out suddenly to adopt a new baby, and you could be that couple.

PUBLIC AGENCY ADOPTION

Adopting through your social services department essentially means adopting children in the foster care system. If you are flexible and are willing to adopt a toddler-age child or older, you can have a child fairly quickly. Although dealing with the bureaucracy can sometimes be very frustrating, the fees for the adoption service are minimal, and in some cases the state may provide monthly subsidies if the child is considered to have special needs. In some states, coming from a minority ethnic background is considered in itself to be a special need.

Although no social services department or agency that accepts federal funds can discriminate against you because of your ethnic background if you are seeking to adopt a biracial or black child, many of the public agencies have had policies against transracial adoptions in the past, and because of this, their staffs may make the process more difficult for you. You may be asked numerous questions about your neighborhood and your ability to provide the child with a sense of his culture, as well as the acceptance level by your friends and family. Although yours and other people's attitudes are important to explore, you do not want to be excluded just because you live in an all-white neighborhood. People's acceptance level has more to do with their attitudes than with where they live. Nor does every last relative have to favor your decision. If you live close to parents who will be involved in the child's life, you will certainly want your child to feel as loved and accepted as any other grandchild, and if this seems to be a serious issue, it makes sense to think carefully before insisting on more flexibility than your family is ready for. But if their hesitation is a normal one of getting used to a new idea, this should not be a serious obstacle.

It is generally difficult to adopt a newborn child through social services, but get your name on their list just in case. This will mean attending a series of classes and having a home study conducted and approved by your social services department.

THE CONTROVERSY OVER TRANSRACIAL ADOPTION

Why was transracial adoption prohibited in the past? During the 1950s and 1960s, transracial adoption increased sharply as a result of the rise in the number of children in the social services system and the lack of minority homes in which to place minority children. In 1972, however, the National Association of Black Social Workers (NABSW) came out strongly against transracial adoption. Within a year, the number of transracial adoptions was cut in half to 1,569, and by 1975, the number was down to 800.

The NABSW policy was and still is that a black child needs to be raised by black parents in order to develop a positive racial identity and only black parents can help the child develop skills for coping in a racist society. This view, seconded by many others, has had an unintended side effect: children languishing in foster care because no family of like ethnic background can be found. Until recently, many state agencies simply would not place African-American or biracial children with Caucasian parents.

Waiting Children

Despite this, the NABSW continues to argue that placing black children in white homes is black cultural genocide. But does this really make sense? Are there really enough transracial adoptions to wipe out black culture? Even supposing there were, shouldn't the child's best interest prevail over a culture's interest? As Peter Hayes observes, "To compromise a child's welfare in the name of culture, especially when the cultural benefit is slight or nonexistent, is inimical to the purpose of child placement and violates the best-interests standard mandated by law."

Consider these statistics. African-Americans and people of color make up 12.3 percent and 17 percent of the total population, respectively; yet African-American children and children of color make up 34 percent and 47 percent of the children waiting for homes. According to research by Elizabeth Bartholet, nearly half of the children in the United States waiting for homes are children of color. In Massachusetts, for example, about 5 percent of the population is African-American; yet nearly half of the children in need of foster or adoptive homes are African-American.

The number of children in foster care went from 276,000 in 1986 to more than 500,000 in 2000, and these statistics hit minority children the hardest.

Bartholet's research into the practices of adoption agencies responsible for placing African-American children shows that agencies do typically practice racial matching, leading to delays in permanent placement. The costs to the children are great—too great. Six months may be a short time in the life of a bureaucracy, but for a small child, it can have significant impact. Racial preferences can also mean that a two-year-old child can be torn from the foster parents who want to adopt him so that he can be placed with parents of the same ethnic background. There are many cases where foster parents have gone to court to contest such disruptions.

It is useful to remember that racial discrimination is against the law. Since the Multiethnic Placement Act, effective as of October 1995, ethnic background can be a consideration for placing a child with a family, but it cannot be the only consideration. Some felt that allowing ethnic background to be a consideration slowed the process of placing African-American and biracial children into families; so this law has been further strengthened. As of January 1, 1997, a child's or adoptive parents' race or ethnicity cannot be a consideration if it delays the placement of that child. The new law is so strict that it appears that transracial adoptions must take place. However, a child's cultural needs will still be considered as a factor in deciding what is in his or her best interest.

In short, the harmful consequences of transracial adoptions remain merely speculative, while the social and economic costs of keeping children in the foster care system are obvious and monumental.

TRANSRACIAL FAMILIES

What can be said in answer to the argument that only same-race placements give a child a positive racial identity? Our response is that it is not necessary for a child to identify with his entire cultural system whether he is black, Asian, Latino, or white. Many white adoptive parents successfully teach their children about their ethnic/racial culture and help foster in them a sense of ethnic pride.

How well white parents do in raising children transracially has been researched for more than twenty-five years. According to Elizabeth Bartholet, however, few of these studies were designed to look at the positive aspects of transracial adoption, and virtually none were set up to assess the negatives associated with same-race placements only. No studies have been done to compare the experience of children placed immediately with white families to those of children held in foster or institutional care while they waited for a same-race home.

In a long research study on transracial adoptions that focused on African-American, international, and Native American children who were placed transracially, adoptees have been found after twenty years to be stable, emotionally healthy, and comfortable with their racial identity and to have positive relationships with their parents. Most of the children in the study were adopted before the age of one.

According to Bartholet, there are no data to demonstrate that transracial adoptions have a harmful effect on children. On the contrary, the evidence is that those who were adopted as babies into transracial homes do as well as those adopted in same-race homes. In an extensive twenty-year study, 90 percent to 98 percent of transracial adoptees were found to enjoy family life, were well adjusted, and had a strong sense of racial pride.

Another longitudinal study also showed positive results. In 1970, the Chicago Child Care Society began a study of the family lives of African-American and biracial children adopted by Caucasian families and African-American and biracial children adopted by African-American families. The following conclusions are drawn from thirty-five transracial adoptees, twenty interracial adoptees, and their parents when these adoptees were seventeen years old. It was found that: (1) the children's developmental problems were similar to those found in the general population; (2) most of the adoptees had good self-esteem; and (3) 83 percent of those adopted interracially said they were black, 33 percent of those adopted by white parents said they were black, and 55 percent said they were of mixed ethnic background.

Some other interesting facts emerged. Among those with white parents, 73 percent lived in primarily white neighborhoods, while 55 percent of those with black parents lived in primarily black neighborhoods. Those with white parents had primarily white friends, while those with black parents had primarily black friends. Of the adolescents with Caucasian parents, the girls were more likely than the boys to date African-Americans. All those adopted transracially knew of their adoption before they were four years old, while 80 percent of those adopted interracially did not learn about their adoption until after they were four. Finally, 83 percent of those adopted transracially and 53 percent of those adopted interracially had interest in meeting their biological parents.

PROVIDING YOUR CHILD WITH A POSITIVE ETHNIC IDENTITY

One of the arguments against transracial adoption is that black children need a cultural identity. It is logical that a black child should have a positive racial identity; however, it is not necessarily true that black culture is the only route to that positive identity. Several studies have indicated that Caucasian parents of African-American or biracial children usually offer those children a healthy sense of racial identity. Studies conducted by both black and white researchers, proponents and opponents of transracial adoption, show much evidence that adoptees have a strong sense of racial identity while being fully integrated into their families and communities. The studies' positive outcomes also apply to those adopting internationally.

Caucasian parents can support African-American culture and ethnic pride in their children by providing books and music about black culture, encouraging friendships with other African-American children, and participating in African-American cultural events. These activities appear to be associated with being middle class, whether African-American or Caucasian. It is questionable whether a black single parent living in poverty can provide a child with the same positive black cultural background as a white family, though a black middle-class family could probably provide more cultural opportunities and more of the subtle day-to-day experiences distinct to black communities.

What of the argument that only black parents can teach the survival skills needed in a racist society? It is believed that a child's racial identity can affect his ability to cope with the world, and it is true that transracial adoptees are generally less comfortable with African-American children than are intraracial adoptees. However, transracial adoptees associate more comfortably with Caucasian children and do as well as same-race adoptees in interpersonal relationships. African-American children who identify with the dominant cultural values also have higher levels of academic achievement, and transracial adoptees are statistically more likely to get better grades in school than intraracial adoptees.

Children can learn to cope with racism. Caucasian parents who adopt transracial children are in general less race conscious than those who adopt intraracially and so are at an advantage to teach children to be less race conscious. The message from the Caucasian parents that all ethnic backgrounds are equal can carry more weight than the same message coming from an African-American parent, who may seem to have more personal interest in protecting her status as a black person.

Professor Joan Mahoney, who has adopted transracially, reports that she and her daughter have African-American friends, she sends her daughter to integrated schools, and she provides the child with books and toys that will help her relate to her culture. Mahoney recommends investigating your neighborhood for black role models, churches and other cultural institutions, and postadoption counseling.

ASIAN ADOPTEES

The raising of Asians by Caucasians has been less controversial since nearly all Asian adoptees come from other countries, and there are no vocal groups in the United States questioning the practice. It is mostly because of poverty as well as culture that Asians do not adopt. Today, the number one country from which U.S. citizens and Canadians are adopting is China. Guatemala and South Korea are also countries that place a great number of children in the United States, and most of these children will become part of multiracial/ethnic families.

What we have learned about racism as it relates to Asian adoptees is primarily from adult adoptees from Korea. The adult adoptees from Korea have provided a wealth of information on what it is like to grow up in a Caucasian home. The first generation of these Korean adoptees are now approaching fifty, since Korean adoptions to the United States began in 1956. Asian children tended to view themselves as Caucasian while growing up, and then as adults tend to view themselves as Korean-Americans or Vietnamese-Americans, depending on their country of origin.

The adult adoptees expressed that they wished their parents understood more of what it was like to experience discrimination, and they wished that they could have had more exposure to their culture. In addition, these adults wished their parents interacted with the culture so that all members saw themselves as a multiracial family. Looking back, these adult adoptees wanted their parents and other siblings to be part of this racial integration—not just the Asian child being exposed to white and Asian culture.

The attitudes of the 1950s, '60s, and '70s may have changed, but children still experience isolation if they are the only Asian child in their community and still face teasing and discrimination.

ADOPTION POLICIES AND PRACTICES

The North American Council on Adoptable Children believes that a child should be ethnically matched when possible but that children should not have to wait for long periods of time to find a same-race family. How long is too long is not an exact science. The detriments associated with being in foster care while waiting for a family must be weighed against the advantages of ethnic matching.

Some assert that if immediate placement is given automatic priority over ethnic matching, not enough effort will go into recruiting African-American families to adopt. Others believe that agency standards for adoptive parents are biased in favor of Caucasian parents. If more single parents and those with lower incomes could adopt, they say more African-American parents would do so. This may be true, but a child or a sibling group may need the energy of two parents, not just one. Humans are finite, and sibling groups probably need the financial security and time that only two parents can provide.

Still, greater efforts need to be made to recruit African-American families and to build trust in the African-American community so that more African-American families will adopt. Agencies need to provide more thorough training and literature to educate prospective adoptive parents about adopting transracially. In the meantime, Caucasian children are primarily going to Caucasian families, and biracial and African-American children are going to both Caucasian and African-American families. Children are adopted because they need love, and parents adopt because they want to extend their love to the next generation. No child should have to wait for a home because of the color of his or her skin.

Chapter Seventeen

The Home Study

Although each state has its own laws regulating adoption, all require adoptive parents to complete a home study. In a home study, a case worker gathers information about you and your spouse and your backgrounds by asking you direct questions about your family, your marriage, and your attitudes about parenting and adoption. This is a meeting between you and a case worker to discuss the attributes that will make you a good parent.

Historically, a home study was a written investigation conducted by a state's department of social services to ensure that adopting couples were suitable to be parents. Today, most states have delegated this responsibility to licensed adoption agencies or to specially authorized social workers. Some agencies perform only this service and do not place children for adoption. Agencies that do place children do not necessarily impose the same restrictions when conducting a home study for an independent adoption, even if the agency itself restricts applications according to age, marital history, etc., of prospective parents who apply for direct placement.

Most states require that a home study be conducted before the baby is placed in your home. If you are adopting a baby from another state, you must have the home study conducted beforehand to comply with the Interstate Compact Act. In other states, however, the home study is not required until the baby is placed in your home. This is permitted only in independent adoptions, and only when the baby is born in the same state as the adoptive parents.

All states require postplacement supervisory visits—brief visits with a social worker whose job is to note the child's progress and your family's adjustment. The caseworker will visit with you and your baby at least once, if not more often, until the adoption is finalized. These visits usually take place at your home and are usually conducted by the same agency that handled your home study.

The home study is designed to protect children from going into the homes of unfit parents, to assess your ability to raise an adopted child and deal with adoption issues, and to introduce you to the caseworker—your advocate and an invaluable adoption resource. A caseworker is there to help you as a couple develop a philosophy of child-rearing and to provide you with information so that you can learn more about the issues related to raising an adopted child. Some agencies require that you attend adoption seminars or workshops, some of which may be especially designed for those in the home study process, while others address general adoption issues.

Another of the caseworker's tasks is to obtain information about your adoption process. If you have already found birth parents, for example, or if the child has already been placed with you, the caseworker will ask how you met the birth parents and what expenses you paid for. Usually there are two or three interviews. At least one will take place at your home, and the other may be at the agency's office.

WHEN TO HAVE A HOME STUDY

As a rule, it is best to have the home study done just before you begin seeking a birth mother. If an FBI clearance is required, you will need to be fingerprinted; this can take up to a few months to get processed, so start the process as soon as possible. On the other hand, you do not want to have a home study done too soon because it is usually valid for only twelve months, after which a small fee is charged for updating it.

Various states have different regulations concerning who needs to undergo a home study and when. Find out which of these apply to your state:

- In most states, a home study is required before a baby is ever placed in your home. If a situation comes along quickly, usually a police clearance and child abuse clearance must be completed, and an "emergency" home study is done.
- In some states, you must have a home study conducted before you can advertise in that state.

Remember, if you are adopting a baby from another state, you must have a home study done before you can take the baby across state lines.

One reason to start the home study process as soon as you begin looking for a birth mother is that it will help prepare you for meeting one. Many of the questions posed in a home study are the ones you can expect a birth mother to ask. Birth mothers tend to be interested in the same character traits a social worker is looking for in a couple: stability, a good marital relationship, love of children, and strong family values. A birth mother will also be reassured to know that you have met certain state requirements by completing your home study.

Remember, even if you advertise only in your own state, a birth mother from another state may contact you. It is wise to have your home study finished and out of the way in case of the unexpected. Think of it as one less hurdle to jump! With your home study complete, you can focus your attention on pursuing an international adoption or on finding a committed birth mother and getting to know her. Otherwise, you might find a birth mother and then also have to think about gathering the documents for the home study, instead of focusing on the birth mother and the baby.

If you are considering adopting a child with special needs, a child outside your race, an international child, or a sibling group, be sure that your home study addresses the issues surrounding such an adoption. For example, your home study may approve you for only one child, but you may then have an opportunity to adopt a sibling group of three. You cannot adopt more than one child until you are approved for more. In one situation, a Caucasian couple wanted to adopt a black or biracial child or a sibling group. However, their home study did not address the couple's attitudes about a transracial adoption, and when a sibling group became available through an agency, their home study could not be updated quickly enough to include this information. Another couple ended up adopting the children.

If your home study will be sent out to other agencies, remember that an agency that did not conduct your home study can assign only based on the type of child you are recommended to adopt and how ready you are to face the issues associated with the adoption.

WHO QUALIFIES TO ADOPT?

Nearly everyone who seeks to adopt is qualified. Not one of our private adoption clients has ever been rejected after being interviewed. Some families are disqualified through an initial telephone interview usually because they have a recent criminal history. Yet, many couples worry about supposed skeletons in the closet. When a social worker conducts your home study, she is not looking to disqualify you; she simply wants to know that you are capable of providing a child with a loving and secure environment. Most couples who seek to adopt privately are in their late thirties to early forties and often have accomplished other life goals that lead to being good parents, such as emotional and financial stability. When an agency caseworker writes your home study, she is usually acting as your advocate. As honestly as possible, the caseworker is there to present you in the best light.

If you think something in your past may present a problem, talk with your attorney about the matter and get his advice. Some people worry needlessly about arrests made when they were much younger, such as for shoplifting. Other problems are more serious, such as repeated divorces, a recent recovery from alcoholism, or a criminal history. Your attorney may call an agency, explain your situation, and see how the staff would handle it. For example, if you were treated for alcoholism, an agency may simply require that you have a letter from a counselor explaining your situation and stating that you have not had a drink since your treatment five years ago. If a caseworker believes that a couple may have some emotional or psychological problems, she will usually recommend counseling.

Sometimes couples will ask what they should and should not discuss with a social worker. We suggest that there is no need to bring up issues that serve no purpose. If you had a difficult relationship with your parents during your teen years and, as a result, spent most of your summers with your grandparents, then you can state these facts in positive terms. For example, you might say, "I had wonderful summers at my grandparents' farm milking the cows and tending a large garden. I learned to be very resourceful during these years."

Even a very difficult situation need not be discussed. If a teacher or scout leader sexually abused you when you were young and you have received therapy for this or have dealt with it through counseling or self-help books, telling the caseworker may not serve any purpose. Some caseworkers may ask you directly, however, if you have ever been emotionally, verbally, physically, or sexually abused. This is a question when adopting internationally and often for a home study through a public agency adoption. If you must answer in the positive, explain how you have overcome this abuse. You are not disqualified for having experienced it, but you should be able to demonstrate how it may have affected you and how you have dealt with it. The purpose of this question is to make sure that you are emotionally stable in spite of being abused, that you are not going to abuse a child in the same manner, and that a child from a difficult background is not going to "push your buttons" and perhaps trigger problems in your life that you have not sufficiently resolved.

The following "problems" will not disqualify you as adoptive parents:

- *You have been married only a short time.* As long as you are married, you have every right to pursue an independent adoption. Some states can have laws regarding this, and some agencies may require you to have been married a minimum period of time.
- *You are not married.*
- *You are divorced.* If you have been divorced (even more than once), you are still permitted to adopt. A caseworker will ask you about your previous marriage(s), but the agency's main concern is the stability of your current marriage. If someone has gone through multiple marriages because he is unstable, this instability will probably manifest itself in other areas of the person's life as well.
- *You are in therapy.* If one of you has been in therapy individually or if you have had therapy as a couple, your chances of being approved may not

be lessened. In fact, most agency personnel view counseling as a sign of strength. The reasons you give for your counseling are what matter. For example, counseling to deal with issues related to infertility, communication, or family of origin is considered very normal.

Some agencies may require a letter from your therapist stating why you are in therapy and that you are stable and capable of caring for a child. Some agencies may even require a copy of the therapist's case notes. If they do, you will have to sign a letter of release before the notes can be sent to the agency. You should review all notes before allowing them to be sent to another party.

Do some research first to find out what the agency's policy is on such matters. A policy of requiring people to submit their case notes can encourage people to be dishonest about their counseling histories. Suppose you have suffered from depression. Instead of revealing that information to the caseworker and letting her know that, thanks to medication and counseling, you are doing well, you may be tempted just to skip the issue and say that you have never sought counseling. You should not have to face this moral dilemma; finding out the agency's policy will prevent you from being placed in this position.

- *You have a history of drug or alcohol abuse.* If you used illicit drugs in the past, do not have a record, and no longer use them, you most likely do not need to reveal this to a social worker. If you have been treated for abusing drugs or alcohol, however, you will need to tell the social worker. Usually, this information will not disqualify you, but the agency will want evidence from a treatment counselor that you have resolved this problem and that the risk that you will become a substance abuser again is minimal. Most agencies will require a letter stating that you are no longer addicted to drugs and alcohol and that you are doing well. Some agencies may want more information—why you entered treatment, what the course of treatment was, and whether you followed the treatment plan.

- *You have a history of psychological problems.* If you have been treated for a psychological disorder such as depression or anorexia and it has not been a life-dominating problem, then you do not need to mention it. If you are still in treatment, however, and the problem interferes with your life (you are not able to work), then you will probably have difficulty being approved by an agency immediately.

- *You have a chronic health condition.* People with physical disabilities should not be disqualified from adopting as long as they can care for a child.

Neither should a chronic disease like diabetes disqualify someone, provided it is controlled. Even a history of cancer will not disqualify you from adopting as long as you have close to a normal life expectancy. The purpose of the medical report for the home study is to determine that the parent is expected to have a normal life span and be able to care for a child.

- *You come from a dysfunctional family.* If you have come from a grossly dysfunctional family, have dealt with the issues appropriately, and other facets of your life are in order, then a social worker will minimize your family's past and focus on your life now. If you were physically or emotionally abused as a child and recognize that such behavior is inappropriate and you can state reasonable measures for disciplining a child, then a caseworker will simply say so in your report.

The ADA applies to all adoption agencies. Those protected under the ADA are those who have or have had a record of a physical or mental impairment that limits major life activities. Protected impairments include orthopedic, visual, hearing, heart disease, cancer, diabetes, HIV—even if symptomatic—drug and alcohol addictions. The protected mental impairments include mental retardation, emotional and mental illness, and learning disabilities. Mental impairments that are excluded are sexual behavior disorders, compulsive gambling, kleptomania, and pyromania. The ADA also does not apply to those who are currently using illegal drugs. Yet, if someone used illegal drugs at another point or is using drugs but is in rehabilitation, then they are covered by the ADA. Ms. Freundlich states that an adoption agency can use "safety" and "direct threat" issues to screen out an adoptive parent. The decision must be based on actual risk and not just speculation. Therefore, if a prospective adoptive parent is seen as a potential threat to the safety or health of the child, then the agency staff must make a judgment based on objective evidence.

If you have a recent criminal history, are grossly dysfunctional, or display other attitudes or behaviors that would make you unfit as a parent, a caseworker cannot recommend you as an adoptive parent. Following are some examples, usually based on law, of factors that can disqualify you. If any pertain to your situation, talk it over with an attorney. He will not reveal what you tell him to an agency because he is required by law to maintain client confidentiality.

- *You or someone who lives in your home has committed a felony.* If you have been arrested for a crime, even if you were found not guilty, this information may be part of the police department's records. Find out before you begin a home study. Any adult living in your home (including children eighteen years or older) must undergo the same police and FBI screening you do. If your parents live with you and one of them has a criminal history (at least one conviction, not just an arrest), you may be disqualified because that person is living in the home. Convictions for certain felonies (burglary, forgery, etc.) that occurred more than ten years ago are often noted but disregarded if there are no other legal violations.

- *You have been convicted of child abuse.* Even an unfounded investigation for child abuse with no conviction may remain in your record. If you think there may be such a problem, have your attorney contact the government agency from which you may need clearance to see whether there is any record. Any unfounded investigation should be discussed with a caseworker. Again, anyone living in your home will have to undergo the same child abuse clearance you do. If that person has a history of documented child abuse or neglect (not just allegations), that person will have to move out, or you may be disqualified to adopt.

- *You are still in treatment for substance abuse.* Although this appears to be protected under the Americans With Disabilities Act, the home study provider would probably use such issues as DUIs or other factors to say that this situation could pose a direct threat to a child.

- *You are financially unable to support a child or are financially unstable.* This does NOT mean you have not balanced your checkbook, nor are you disqualified if you have filed for bankruptcy. However, if your income is so low that you could not meet the poverty guidelines, you may not qualify to adopt. If you have a very unstable work history, this could also mean that you may not be able to support a child if you were to lose your job. Also, if you earn sufficient income but demonstrate an inability to make wise financial choices, this could also disqualify you. Such an example may be having excessive credit card debt.

- *Your home is unsafe or unsanitary.* Some homes have lead paint in them, and the law in your state may not permit you to adopt. Also, some states require that no firearms be in the home. Smoke detectors should be in all key areas, and the batteries should be current. If your home has a problem such as a broken staircase that could endanger a child, this should be explained to the caseworker, and she may have to revisit to make sure it is properly fixed. A home that is very unclean and disorganized can indicate other problems. You will be rejected if the roaches are carrying off the food and your laundry has not been done in weeks.

- *You have a serious mental illness.* Although you cannot be outright rejected as a prospective adoptive parent for having a mental illness, you will be required to prove that you are capable of caring for a child and pose no threat to the child. Also, the agency will want to discuss if a child added to your family will exacerbate your condition. If someone has a serious mental illness or personality disorder, often other areas of their life will be affected, which would disqualify them from adopting.

SELECTING AN AGENCY OR INDEPENDENT INVESTIGATOR

Agencies are required by state law to obtain specific information from couples seeking to adopt. Some agencies, however, require more extensive information than others. Agencies can also vary widely in their fee structures.

Call several agencies before making a decision. Ask specifically about their fees and requirements. Most agencies have forms that you must complete before a caseworker meets with you. Your attorney should advise you about an agency's minimum legal requirements. Some agencies may require more frequent meetings between the couple and the caseworker or psychological evaluations or participation in parenting classes. Although a more extensive home study may have its merits, the more services an agency provides or requires, the more costly the home study.

Before you select an agency or social worker, you should also ask whether you are permitted to have a copy of your home study and what the agency's or person's attitude is toward issues such as divorce, limited income, or minor criminal history—whatever your concerns. Try to get a sense of the social worker's background. If she is an adoptive parent, chances are she is more understanding of how you feel than an unmarried twenty-five-year-old who may have little experience with children.

THE HOME STUDY PROCESS

Relax. The caseworker is not coming in with white gloves, armed for a psychological examination. If possible, talk with her on the telephone before you meet in person to help you feel more comfortable when you do meet.

Prepare for the home visit by making the mood as comfortable as possible. Have some light refreshments such as tea and cookies ready. If you have no children, have your home comfortably clean and tidy. You will be more relaxed. Do not apologize about anything related to your home. If you are in the middle of a move, just say, "We moved here two weeks ago, and the boxes in the dining room are waiting to be unpacked."

Turn off all distractions like the TV or radio—perhaps even the telephone. Do not set your appointment so that you are squeezed for time. Put pets outside, or confine them elsewhere. For some caseworkers, there is nothing worse than a dog jumping on them or cats crawling around their legs.

If you have children, arrange for them to be there so that the social worker can interview them. If you need to discuss sensitive information, you should also arrange for them to be occupied during that time.

Remember, the caseworker serves as your advocate. Caseworkers have different personalities and styles; you may or may not feel comfortable with someone. Regardless of how well you connect with the caseworker, however, she has specific guidelines to follow and cannot subjectively reject a couple based on personality differences.

A progressive adoption agency will have clear objectives and will focus its questions on your attitudes toward each other and on your parenting style, especially as it relates to an adopted child. The agency will be concerned about adoptive parenting issues and will want to provide you with resources: book titles, the names of adoption support groups, and the names of contact people for play groups once the child arrives.

Preliminaries

Before you have a home study done, the agency may send you an application with questions like the ones the caseworker will pose. Don't be intimidated. Some of the questions may seem invasive or difficult to answer, and you may feel resentful having to answer questions that other parents never have to consider. Such feelings are normal.

When you receive the application, you will also be asked to produce the following documents. It is best (even if not required) to have these ready before you meet the caseworker.

1. *Birth certificates for all members of the household.*
2. *Marriage certificate.*
3. *Divorce decree (if applicable).*
4. *Death certificate (if former spouse died).*
5. *Military discharge (if applicable).*
6. *Photographs of you as a couple or family (if you have children) and pictures of your home.*
7. *Income verification (W-2 or income tax statement).*
8. *Health status statement from physicians.* Some agencies may require a complete physical that is no older than one year.
9. *Personal references from friends.* Usually three to five references are required. Good references are important in establishing your character. Their purpose is to tell how these people feel about you as potential parents and your readiness to have a child. Of course, every reference is going to be good, because you will

select only people who like you. But they will attest that you have the ability to establish solid relationships.

10. *FBI, police, and child abuse clearances.* These requirements vary from state to state. In some you must receive a report from your local police department or from the state police. The FBI clearance is done through fingerprints and can hold up the process by up to three months. If you must get FBI clearance, begin this process before or as soon as you start your home study. Once the clearance comes back, have the caseworker finish and date the home study using the date on which the fingerprints were issued, if possible, so that the home study stays current as long as possible.

11. *Statement from each of you declaring that you are not addicted to drugs or alcohol and that you have never been treated for a drug or alcohol addiction.*

As part of the study, you will be asked to provide identifying information such as your name, address, telephone number, and citizenship. You will also be required to answer questions about your history, lifestyle, and attitudes.

Interviews

The home study provider must interview all persons living in the home and record the number of times she interviewed each and what type of visits and contacts took place. Usually, the social worker will also interview the husband and wife separately.

Autobiographical Information

Autobiographical information includes a physical description and information about where and how you were raised. Did your parents teach consistent values? Did they emphasize education or sports? Were they very involved in your life? Did they encourage independence? Were they domineering? Did they abuse alcohol, or were they violent or undisciplined in their lifestyle? How was love demonstrated, and what was the method of discipline? You will be asked to provide background information on your parents, including their names, ages, professions, and work histories, and to say something about your relationship with and attitude toward them, both when you were a child and now.

The names, professions, and ages of any siblings will be requested, along with a description of your relationship with them. Other questions will cover your schooling and education level, social life as a child and teenager, interests and hobbies, profession and work history, personal strengths and weaknesses, and any history of psychological counseling.

Your Marriage

Considerable attention will be devoted to your marriage. You will be asked about your premarital relationship (how you met, when you were engaged), how you resolve differences, how your relationship has grown and changed over the years, and your spouse's assets and liabilities, including his or her overall emotional stability and maturity as a person and a marriage partner. The caseworker may ask if you and your spouse have had any counseling and what were the issues and how they were resolved. She may also ask if there have been any separations and for what reasons. Also, how chores and finances are decided and handled between the two of you will be discussed. It is not appropriate for a caseworker to question you about your sex life.

Interestingly, as detrimental as divorce may be to spouse and children, most caseworkers place much more emphasis on the issues of the current marriage than they do on previous marriages. If someone has been divorced a couple of times and never sought counseling during or after the divorces, this may never be questioned. Yet, if a couple has sought marriage counseling to strengthen their marriage, they may be required to supply the counselor's notes as well as a statement from the counselor.

If you have been divorced, the caseworker will ask why the marriage ended. If there are children from a previous marriage, the caseworker will also want to know about your relationship with noncustodial children and what visitation rights the other parent has with children living in your home. Although a person cannot be outright rejected for having multiple divorces, a caseworker will usually want to investigate further why someone has had multiple marriages. The caseworker may require a psychological evaluation if she feels that the number of divorces is an indication of other life-dominating problems.

If you are single, you will be asked about your social life, how a child will fit into your life, and if you have any plans for marriage. If you plan to marry in the near future, your fiancé may also be required to be interviewed and have law enforcement and child abuse clearances as well.

If you are separated but not divorced, this can cause some problems in getting approved to adopt since your spouse is to be included in the home study process, and of course, this is not possible. Some people because of religious or cultural reasons are separated from their spouse for years but never officially have a legal separation or divorce. In this situation, you may need to either get a statement from your religious leader, such as a pastor, as to why you are not divorced. If you have not divorced because you just never got around to making your separation into a legal divorce, this should be taken care of as soon as possible. You may be required to make efforts to locate your estranged spouse if his whereabouts are unknown to notify him of your adoption plans since he is still legally married to you.

Others in the Home

Any other adults in the home will need to be interviewed, and they are also required to be asked all questions related to drug/alcohol abuse and criminal history. They will also need criminal and child abuse clearances as well.

Sometimes this gets more complicated than it appears. Families sometimes have exchange students who come and go. The reality is that an exchange student over eighteen years old is not going to have a listed state criminal record and only a criminal record that has been submitted to Interpol (an international database of reported crimes) will show up on an FBI criminal report. Also, sometimes a family may have a visitor in their home who is meant to be there temporarily but ends up remaining there for a longer period of time. If someone may be in your home at the time of the home study or at the time of placement of the child, then this person needs to be part of the home study. If someone enters your home after the home study is completed but before a child is placed there, it is essential that you notify your home study provider. This is particularly true if you are adopting internationally.

Your Religious Background and Values

Another part of the study will look at your values and religion. You may be asked about your religious tradition, church, temple, or synagogue attendance, religious faith as a child, and current religious beliefs and what impact they have on your life. If you and your spouse practice different faiths, the caseworker will want to know whether this will create a conflict in raising a child. If you do not participate in an organized religion, highlight your strong family values and whatever beliefs provide inner strength and comfort.

Some of the questions in the home study will have to do with character. For example, you may be asked about your goals and how you set and reach them. Discussing your values and their origins is another important aspect of the home study investigation.

Parenting Issues

Be prepared to talk at length about parenting issues. Why do you want to be a parent? Why do you want to adopt? What do you see as an appropriate method of discipline? (Some states require a declaration that you will not use corporal punishment.) Some people feel pressured to say that they will not spank their child, even though they know in their hearts that occasions may arise when they will do so. Nearly every adoptive couple we have talked with believes that at some point a spanking may be appropriate, and most social workers will agree. However, there is no point in discussing with the social worker why you think that a spanking should be given at certain times. If you think it would be false to say that you will never spank your child, tell the caseworker that you will focus on passive forms of discipline and not on corporal punishment. Instead, you would remove the child from the dangerous situation. If the child is unruly, you would remove him, take away a favorite toy, or place him in a "time-out" chair.

Other parenting questions will concern the parenting styles of each partner and how your own styles will be the same or different from those of your parents. What attitudes and values do you hope to pass on to your child(ren)? What parenting and child care skills do you already possess, and what is your willingness to acquire new skills? Will one parent be home to care for the child? If not, who will care for the child? How much experience have you had with children? Are you able to give and receive affection? If you have children already, what is their attitude toward the idea of a new sibling?

If both parents plan to work after the child is arrives, then child care arrangements need to be addressed. If you are single, the extended support system that you have will also be discussed.

Infertility/Adoption Issues

Another area the home study will certainly explore will be your attitudes toward infertility and adoption. You will be questioned about the following:

- Your infertility status, if applicable. You will not be required to provide full details—just the fact that you are not able to conceive or carry a child to term.
- Your infertility resolution, if applicable.
- The impact of infertility on your marriage, if applicable.
- How you came to choose adoption and what resources you used to come to that decision.
- What parenting an adopted child means to you. (How will this differ from parenting a biological child?)
- What kind of child you seek to adopt (Caucasian newborn, etc.).
- What your attitudes toward birth parents are.
- How you feel about the idea of your child seeking his birth parents.
- What adoption resources you have access to, including others you know who have adopted.

If you are adopting internationally, the caseworker will address that you are aware of the process involved in an international adoption, including the expenses, financial risks, and possible difficulties and delays.

Type of Children to Adopt

A description of the type of children, ages, and special issues can be addressed. If you are adopting a child from another country or if you are adopting a child of another ethnicity or race, you will need to address how you will preserve the child's heritage and culture. If the child you seek to adopt has any special needs, these need to be addressed. For example, if you are adopting through social services or internationally, the potential problems that a child may face must also be addressed. You must demonstrate an understanding of the issues and a willingness and ability to properly care for such a child.

Background Clearance

You will be required to have a criminal and child abuse clearance completed. Some states require everyone over the age of fourteen to have a criminal clearance. If you are adopting internationally, everyone over eighteen years old in your home will need to be fingerprinted. This can get a bit complicated if you have an elderly parent or other relative living in your home who is incapacitated. Usually, exceptions can be made for this person.

If you are adopting internationally, you and every person eighteen years old and over will be asked about the following.

Your Home

The caseworker may ask what you paid for your home and its current value and what kinds of neighborhood and community resources you have access to—parks, schools, libraries, museums, etc.

Don't go crazy trying to get your home in order. If anything is clearly a potential danger (no cover over the fireplace, frayed wires, clutter that is a fire hazard), take care of it before you have a home study. Have a fire extinguisher and other safety features present in your home. But don't act as if your house is about to be photographed for *Better Homes and Gardens*. The social worker is primarily interested that the home can accommodate a baby or older child. In her report, she will comment on the bedroom or area of the home where the child will sleep.

Don't worry, especially if you already have a child, if your home is not spotlessly clean. Social workers are not looking to see whether Mr. and Mrs. Clean live at your home; they just want to make sure that your home is a safe and healthy environment. If life is getting a little crazy, you could always treat yourself to a housekeeping service before your home study appointment. You will be much more at ease knowing that the cobwebs have been dusted away.

The home study will give a detailed description of the home and the child's room as well as the suitability of the home and if the home meets the state's requirements, if any. If, you, the adoptive family, plans to move, this needs to be addressed.

Your Finances

You will be expected to disclose your salaries, savings, and other resources, as well as your debts, health insurance, and life insurance. Your financial status should indicate that you have enough discretionary income each month to meet the needs of a child. However, a large savings account and a substantial stock portfolio are not necessary for you to pass a home study. A social worker will instead look for savings of perhaps two or three months' salary set aside for emergencies and a general sense that you and your spouse manage your money sensibly. Most likely you will be required to show some proof of your salary such as last year's 1040 IRS tax form or a W-2 form.

You should mention that your health insurance will cover your child's medical needs including pre-existing conditions.

References

Usually, you will be asked to gather your own reference letters and then give them to the caseworker. However, some agencies prefer or require that references be confidential and that they send out forms that go directly to your reference, which are then sent directly back to the agency. Some agencies may also call some of your references since sometimes people will be more explicit on the telephone than they are on paper. It is expected that all references will be very positive. If there is a negative reference that is first given to you, of course, you will not use it. Most people will tell you first if they are not comfortable in providing a reference for you.

If your references submit letters confidentially to your caseworker and one is negative and far different from all others, the caseworker will most likely call the reference and investigate why they provided a negative response. It is very rare to ever receive a negative reference. Sometimes people will call an agency to say they have concerns about the person. Also, people will be more forthcoming in a telephone interview about apprehensions that they may have about your adopting. Adoptive families are not going to ask their next-door neighbor who sued them for cutting down the oak tree to be a reference for them.

Some agencies have forms with a question and answer format for your references to complete. Usually, the questions on the forms include how the person knows you, for how long, and what assets you have that would make you good parents. They may also ask how often the person sees you and if the person has seen you around children. Also, questions about your health, emotional well-being, and if you have been known to have any problems with drugs or alcohol may also be addressed.

A reference letter should have an overall tone of being warm and personable and make the caseworker feel that the person knows you well and believes that you have assets that will make you a good parent. The reference letter should list the specific traits that indicate you will be a good parent. If you have no children, your references may want to share how you take care of their children, teach Sunday School, and are fun-loving, warm, affectionate, financially stable, caring, and devoted to each other.

If someone is writing a letter for you, they should state everything in the positive, unless the agency specifically asks them to address certain issues. Otherwise, there is no need for someone to write in a reference letter, "Jerry and Suzie have not demonstrated any problem with drugs or alcohol, nor do they demonstrate any emotional problems."

References are meant to be glowingly positive statements about you. A caseworker is not so much looking to see how positively the person is writing about you, but rather, that indeed you have personal relationships with people who know you well and support your decision to adopt. If someone does not have enough social contacts to provide at least three references, then that could be an indication that the person has no contact with neighbors, support systems, is not involved in community activities, nor does the person have any friends through her employment.

Recommendations

In the recommendation section, the caseworker will say what emotional, spiritual, financial, and other assets the family has that qualifies them to adopt. The recommendation should include the specific number of children you are approved to adopt, any restrictions related to health, age, sex, and number of children, and, if adopting internationally, what country the family is approved to adopt from.

A SAMPLE HOME STUDY

Following is a mock home study to use as a guide. Although it may seem overly perfect, remember: Most home studies are written to show your best assets. This one is very similar to ones used in actual adoptions.

• • •

Social History

John Smith is a Caucasian American male, born July 4, 1965, in Cape May, New Jersey (verified). Mr. Smith is six feet one inch tall, weighs 190 pounds, and has brown hair and eyes.

John is warm, sincere, and genuine. He openly expresses his desire to adopt a child and raise a family.

John was born and raised in Cape May, New Jersey. In 1983, he graduated from Cape May High School and attended Rutgers University in New Brunswick, New Jersey, where he received a degree in accounting in 1987.

John states that his family was very traditional. His father is vice president of a bank in Cape May, New Jersey, and his mother is an innkeeper, also in Cape May. Although his father worked hard, he still managed to spend time with John and took him to the shore and on skiing trips. He describes his mother also as hardworking. He vividly describes the fun he and his cousins had living at the shore. Both of his parents are described as people who emphasized values and were fair and consistent.

John and his three siblings hardly presented any discipline problems to their parents. When John had to be disciplined, both of his parents were fair and consistent. Very infrequently did they spank him, but rather talked to him about what he had done wrong.

John has two older sisters and one younger brother. All of his siblings live within the Cape May area. He maintains a warm, close relationship with all three.

Upon graduation from college, John took a job with a large real estate firm where he worked as an accountant for two years. He took time away from this job to travel through the United States. He states that he was feeling restless and did not want to spend his youth behind a desk working with numbers. He feels that the two and a half years he spent traveling have now helped him to feel more settled. If he had not taken this adventure, he would never have met his wife, Carol.

After traveling, John came back to Cape May and joined an accounting firm in 1992. In 1998, he was named a partner. He says he enjoys his job, but sometimes finds the work tedious and exhausting. He jogs and plays tennis to release his stress.

John and his family are still very close and enjoy activities together. His father has assisted him in business. They still enjoy playing golf together as well as working on home projects. It is clear that his desire to have children is based on his happy childhood as well as his love for his nieces and nephews.

Social History

Carol Jones-Smith is a Caucasian American of Irish background who was born on January 16, 1966, in Philadelphia, Pennsylvania (verified). She is five feet five inches tall and weighs 125 pounds. She was reared in the suburbs of Philadelphia, Pennsylvania. Carol's mother stayed at home to rear her children while her father worked as a plumber. Carol's parents and one of her two sisters reside in Pennsylvania. Her other sister lives in California.

Carol is very sociable, warm, and easygoing. Carol desires to be a full-time homemaker and stay-at-home mom until the child is at least two years old.

Carol states that her family is loving. She is close to both parents and believes that they taught her values such as respect and honesty. Although she was never a difficult child, she states that at times she was mischievous. She believes her parents raised her well and disciplined her fairly. Her parents usually took away privileges as a means of discipline.

Carol was very sociable growing up and was involved in Girl Scouts and church activities. She believes that her association with her church instilled many positive character qualities. She enjoyed the many church-related activities as well as camping with the Girl Scouts. Her mother volunteered for the Girl Scouts as well as for the PTA and school library. After high school, she went to Pennsylvania State University where she graduated with a degree in elementary education in 1989.

For two years after graduating from college, she substitute-taught because no full-time teaching positions were available. She and John maintained a long-distance relationship until she could find a job in Cape May.

In the fall of 1991, she took a position as a second-grade teacher. She enjoys teaching and says that second-grade children are old enough to learn, yet young enough not to be a discipline problem.

Carol's hobbies include reading, golf, music, and home projects. She and John enjoy day trips, long walks, and bicycle rides. For special occasions, such as Christmas and baby showers, she enjoys making gifts. She loves having the summers free to focus on such activities.

Marital Relationship

John and Carol were married on June 10, 1992, in Philadelphia, Pennsylvania (verified). They met in the summer of 1990, while she was visiting her sister in California. He was attracted to her right from the beginning. She was a little bit unsure of a man who was taking such an extended "vacation." After talking to and then maintaining a long-distance relationship with him, she began to understand his commitment to a secure lifestyle, while still having a spirit of adventure. In 1990, they became engaged. In the fall of 1991, she took a position as an elementary school teacher in Cape May.

In the initial stages of their relationship, Carol's parents were concerned about his job situation. But after he went back to work for a large accounting firm and seemed settled, they soon began to like and trust John. Today, they have a comfortable relationship with all four of their parents. John and Carol enjoy spending the holidays with family members. In fact, they say that the more extended-family members present for celebrations, the better. Birthday parties for family members are celebrated by parents and siblings.

The Smiths' good relationships with family are also expressed in their marriage. John and Carol state that they communicate well and often have deep discussions while taking long walks on the beach. They seldom argue, and when they do, they usually compromise until the difference is resolved. They state that their marriage is excellent.

Carol and John appear to be thoughtful of each other's needs. For example, John did not want Carol to continue infertility treatment that would cause her emotional or physical discomfort or to take medications that could have adverse side effects.

Carol and John share in the household responsibilities equally, although they admit they tend to divide chores along gender lines. Carol does more of the traditional female tasks since she loves to cook, while John enjoys yard work. They both discuss finances and have a budget; Carol pays most of the bills, and John balances the checkbook.

Values and Religion

Both John and Carol attended church as children and believe it is important for children to receive a solid religious upbringing. Carol said that her family placed a great emphasis on honesty, integrity, and "doing what is right." Her family's values were also part of her spiritual training as well. As children, John attended a Presbyterian church, and Carol attended an Episcopalian church. John and Carol are currently visiting churches and believe they will select a conservative Presbyterian church in Cape May that is very family oriented and provides special programs for children.

The Smiths both value family life, marriage, and hard work and commitment. They say that they obtained these values from their family and from their friends. John and Carol also have seen the problems in children's lives when parents are not fully committed to the responsibility of parenting or to the marriage.

The Smiths have set several goals that they have reached, including purchasing a home, planting a vegetable garden, and establishing a savings account for a child. Each year they sit down on January 1 or the weekend of the holiday and set individual goals and goals as a couple. This year they decided that they will each read a good book a month. They also want to finish the basement and have already made arrangements with a contractor. Their primary goal is to adopt a child, and they have set aside money to begin the process.

Parenting Attitudes/Child Care

John and Carol believe they will raise their children according to the positive set of values that helped to shape them. They love children and often care for their siblings' children. This love for family makes them long even more for a child of their own.

In disciplining their children for wrong behavior, they plan to use "time-out" or take away a favorite activity or toy. Once a child is placed with the Smiths, Carol plans to stay home full-time. She may continue in her teaching position until the end of the school year, depending upon when a child is placed with them. If a child is placed toward the end of the school year, then John will take up to twelve weeks off as permitted by the Family Leave Act.

There is an opportunity for Carol to have a part-time position in the school district. If she decides to go back to work, her sister will care for the baby, and John will also work from home so that the child will always be with family.

Attitude Toward Adoption

John and Carol have undergone about four years of unsuccessful infertility treatment. Carol has endometriosis, and John has a low sperm count. Carol has had surgery and has taken infertility drugs while having intrauterine inseminations done. They decided that more advanced treatment would be too financially and emotionally draining for them. Carol and John both state that the hormonal therapy has not caused any adverse physical or emotional reactions.

They have chosen to end infertility treatment since successful pregnancy is very unlikely. Also, they decided that they were not seeking a pregnancy but wanted a child and that adoption would provide them with this opportunity. Both John and Carol feel adoption is a very positive alternative to biological children.

The Smiths have read a number of books about the adoption process as well as the raising of an adopted child. They appear to have a good understanding of adoption. For example, they both agree that openly sharing information with a child about her adoption is important. Yet, they state that they do not want to overemphasize the difference and perhaps make the child feel out of place. John and Carol are comfortable in communicating with a child's birth parents (i.e., sending photos and letters). Also, they recognize that their child may someday seek her birth parents and understand that this would not be a negative reflection on their relationship with their child.

Carol said that once she adopted, she would want to communicate with other adoptive moms. The Smiths are members of RESOLVE. If they have a child, Carol plans to join a play group in which many of the children are adopted.

Finance and the Home

John and Carol live in a lovely, well-maintained Victorian house that is within walking distance of the beach. The home has a large eat-in kitchen that John completely renovated. John also renovated a playroom/den. The child's bedroom is spacious and comfortable. In this room, there is already a child's toy cradle filled with stuffed animals.

The home is valued at about $360,000, and as John continues to make further improvements, the home may increase in value.

John earns about $98,000 per year, and Carol earns $52,000 per year (verified). The Smiths have no debts except their mortgage payment of nearly $1,700 per month and property taxes of $600 per month. He has a life insurance policy worth about $250,000, and she, through work, has one valued at $104,000.

Type of Child Requested and from Whom

The Smiths are interested in adopting a healthy Caucasian infant. They have sent letters to friends expressing their desire to adopt. Many people have responded, wishing them well. Next week, an advertisement will be placed in a small newspaper in Central New Jersey. An attorney, John Johnson, has been retained by the Smiths.

References

Each reference (verified) cites the Smiths as a couple who would provide a loving, moral, stable home for a child. Those who know them say that they are respected by friends and family, are committed to each other, and are energetic, fun-loving people who would provide much happiness to a child.

Health Status

Both Carol and John are in good health, according to Dr. Laura Jones, are able to care for a child, and are expected to live a normal life span (verified). Neither person is a smoker. The Smiths present themselves as emotionally stable and healthy persons.

Recommendation

John and Carol Smith appear to be open, expressive, and caring individuals who have strong family relationships. It is clear from the love that they express for each other and for their family members that they would offer a truly loving home to a child. They have the emotional, spiritual, family, and financial resources to be excellent adoptive parents. They are recommended as adoptive parents.

• • •

POSTPLACEMENT SUPERVISORY VISITS

Postplacement supervisory visits are a series of visits made to your home by a caseworker or social worker to ensure that the family is adjusting well to the child and that the child herself is doing well. In infant adoptions, supervisory visits are simply a time for you and the caseworker to share how the baby is developing. For children who are older, adjustment issues will need to be addressed.

Information gathered at a postplacement supervisory visit will begin with the child's medical progress. You should keep a record of his doctor's appointments, illnesses, and routine vaccines. Most people will simply tell the caseworker when the child had his last well-baby checkup and whether he had any reaction to the vaccines.

The caseworker will ask about the child's eating and sleeping patterns, which will change as the child progresses. If the caseworker visits you when the child is two months old, you may share, for example, that he is taking about six four-ounce bottles per day of Similac with iron and that he generally sleeps from eight P.M. to six A.M., wakes up once in the middle of the night, and during the day has a morning nap, an afternoon nap, and a later afternoon nap. When the caseworker visits you again in two months, you will tell her that the baby is now having applesauce and rice cereal twice a day, goes to bed around eight P.M. and gets up at six A.M., seldom wakes up in the middle of the night, and generally sleeps for two hours in the morning and an hour and a half in the afternoon.

At each visit, you will share with the caseworker the progress your child is making. For example, if the caseworker visits you when the child is two months old, you will probably say that the child smiles and responds to facial expressions. At four months old, you will say he can play with his feet and hold an object in his hands. At six months old, he may be crawling, sitting up, and cooing.

Some agencies focus on you and your child's appearance as well as the appearance and cleanliness of the home. If you are feeling overwhelmed, hire someone to clean your home before each visit. The investment is well worth the expense simply because you will feel so much more comfortable during the caseworker's visit.

Finally, the caseworker will want to know how your family is adjusting to the child's arrival. Both of you will be required to be present for at least some of the visits. Sometimes husbands, either because of nervousness or because they do not want to steal the limelight from their wives, do not interact with the child during a caseworker's visits. However, it is very important that the social worker see both parents holding and feeding a baby or attending to the needs of an older child.

The question of how much time the adoptive parents spend with the child will probably come up. The only wrong answer is "none." Social workers are aware that one spouse may work ten- or twelve-hour days and that both parents may work outside the home. Again, a commonsense approach is all that is required.

Chapter Eighteen

Adoption Expenses

A n 2003, the Dave Thomas Foundation for Adoption reported that the average cost of an adoption is $15,000, but this amount can vary greatly. Adoptions through social services are usually provided at no cost, and usually subsidies are available to help you care for the child's extra needs. On the other hand, agency adoptions of newborn infants including all expenses can come close to $30,000. Likewise, an international adoption can easily cost this much when all expenses are included.

Money can be an emotional issue, and the way you feel about it can affect the way you approach adoption. Some people can have a sense that it is not "fair" that other people do not have to pay money to have a child. Many people also feel that if children so desperately need a home, then why is adoption so expensive. After all, the goal is to get children into good homes, not for people to profit by other's unfortunate circumstances.

Although adoptions can be costly, there are programs and services available to help defray the cost. There are tax credits and possible deductions. Many employers now offer adoption benefits, much like health benefits.

Also, many families find that others are willing to assist them financially in their endeavor to make a difference in the life of a child. Not everyone can adopt a child, but nearly everyone can contribute a little bit to helping someone else adopt a child.

DOMESTIC INFANT ADOPTION
Many people become involved with adoption after spending a number of years and thousands of dollars on infertility workups and unsuccessful treatments. Often there is a sense of anger about spending even more money on another procedure—adoption—that, like infertility treatment, has no guarantee of success.

If you are planning on adopting a newborn baby and are engaged with a birth mother, paying out thousands of dollars in living expenses and other fees with no tangible return can make you feel victimized and out of control. Feelings of "Why me?" are natural and common, as are feelings of anger and a sense of futility. The question is, "How do we cope with these feelings?" Some people cope by developing an unhealthy defensiveness and extreme skepticism toward the idea of adoption. You should try to deal with these attitudes before you start the process. If you don't, your negative feelings will be communicated to the birth mother; you will not be comfortable meeting her, and she will know it.

Adoptive couples can indirectly project their own feelings onto the birth mother. She will not understand the uneasiness she feels about you; all she will know is that she has "bad vibes" about you. Understandably, a birth mother does not want to choose this kind of person as an adoptive parent.

Even more self-defeating than projecting feelings onto the birth mother is discussing with her their own feelings of victimization in your past attempts to become parents and how this makes them afraid to lose again, whether financially or emotionally. This will most likely make the birth mother feel that you doubt her honesty and her motives. One birth mother let a prospective couple know that she did not want to hear about their disappointments with unsuccessful infertility treatments and other previous adoption plans. She felt that she had enough of her own problems and did not need to hear the adoptive mother pour her heart out about the lost money and failed attempts.

Later in the relationship with the birth mother, it may be appropriate for you to share your feelings about your emotional and financial investment. However, several birth mothers have experienced this sharing as attempts by adoptive couples to "lay a guilt trip" on them. Remember, a birth mother usually assumes you are middle class or upper middle class and that your life is structured and in control. It is her life that is out of control, and placing her child for adoption is a way of regaining control. The last thing she wants and needs is to feel that you have reservations about her honesty or her intentions. Adoption author Patricia Johnston writes that finances can be a most uncomfortable issue for everyone involved in the adoption process. Prospective adoptive parents do not like to think about the costs because it reminds them further of how they are different from those who can give birth to a child. Professionals who have to ask clients directly for fees are sometimes uncomfortable charging them, although they rely upon these fees for their livelihood and the functioning of the agency or office. Nor does the issue of fees end when you receive your child. Feeling like a victim during the adoption process, including paying a great deal of money for something that most people get "for free," can color our attitudes for a long time.

It is important to recognize the fact that you may be feeling out of control about having a child. For example, your having a child depends on a birth mother who has to "choose" you and who even then may change her mind. It is important to begin to be aware of the fact that you may be feeling like a victim. For example, you are paying large amounts of money for unsuccessful infertility treatments, when many women conceive effortlessly and thoughtlessly. When you can recognize and confront these feelings of being out of control, this can help to minimize your anger and bitterness. If you do not deal with these feelings, there is a good chance that your feelings about past experiences will contaminate your future experiences: with the birth mother and with adoption professionals whom you may be paying a great deal of money. To some extent, you can avoid feeling victimized again by making sure that you and the agency or attorney with whom you are working are very clear about what their fees are and what you can expect to pay. To maintain a good attitude throughout the adoption process, make sure not to let misunderstandings get in the way or questions go too long unanswered.

If you are pursuing a public agency adoption of a child with special needs, plan to spend up to $2,000; for an independent adoption, $5,000 to $25,000; for a domestic agency adoption, $7,000 to $30,000; and for an international adoption, $15,000 to $30,000. Fortunately, there are now adoption tax credits available, and your employer may offer adoption benefits.

Be aware that some attorneys and agencies do overcharge. As Christine Adamec writes in *There ARE Babies to Adopt*, a higher fee does not mean a "better" baby or a better quality of service.

The expenses you can expect to incur for different types of adoptions follow.

INDEPENDENT ADOPTION

An independent adoption is usually less expensive than an agency adoption but still can total more than $25,000. In this type of adoption, you most likely will be paying for at least some of the birth mother's expenses. When a birth mother begins interacting with an adoptive couple, she often has no desire or need to accept monies for living expenses. As her pregnancy progresses, however, her circumstances may change, causing her to need assistance. When a birth mother requests help at that point, couples are often quick to feel taken advantage of. They should know that most birth mothers are quite reluctant to ask for and accept money and do so only in time of great need. If that need arises shortly after a couple begins working with a birth mother, the couple must be careful not to overreact. Any rapport that exists between the birth mother and the couple could be ruined if the couple suddenly becomes defensive about money.

Then there is the birth mother who asks for money up front, sometimes in large amounts. One birth mother told an adoptive couple that she wanted $12,000 as soon as the baby was born. The couple was speechless. Fortunately, they realized this was a situation in which their own emotions would get in the way, and they asked her to talk to their attorney. When the attorney asked why she chose $12,000, the birth mother replied that she knew that was the amount adoption agencies were paid, and she assumed she would be paid the same thing since an agency was not involved. Once the attorney explained that such an amount was not legal to pay and that only reasonable living expenses were allowed, things were fine. She did place her baby with the couple, and she received reasonable living expenses as allowed by law. Later in this chapter, we will say more about how to handle this kind of situation.

An independent adoption is usually less expensive than an agency adoption. Expenses you are likely to incur include the following (amounts are approximate):

Attorney's fee: $2,500–$8,000: In some situations, an attorney's fee is lower than others, especially in the placement of children with special needs or when placing an African-American child. Also, if an agency is involved in the adoption and the attorney is simply going to court, then her fees may be lower. If you have found a birth mother, she is far along in her pregnancy, and she lives in the same state as you do, then the attorney's fees will most likely be lower.

On the other hand, if two attorneys are involved, such as when one attorney takes the birth mother's relinquishment in the state where the baby is born but the adoption is finalized in your state and your attorney is handling all the paperwork, then the attorney taking the relinquishment should charge much less. However, in some states, only an attorney who belongs to the American Academy of Adoption Attorneys can take the relinquishment, so her fees can be much higher because there may be just a few attorneys who can handle this process.

Advertising costs: $250–$450 per month: The low figure is the approximate cost of placing an ad in a daily newspaper (usually for a small- or average-size town) twice a week. The high figure is the approximate cost of placing an ad in two big-city newspapers twice a week. Sometimes you must hire two attorneys—one in each state or two in the same state—so that there is no conflict of interest. Usually, the fee is not double.

Counseling for birth mother: $50–$100 per hour: Many birth mothers do not ask couples to pay for counseling, but the professional involved should mention this option to a birth mother. The birth parents often receive counseling if the adoptive couple wants to pursue an identified agency adoption.

Birth mother's obstetrical and delivery bill: $2,000–$3,700: Most birth mothers receive insurance or Medicaid benefits, and you will seldom have to pay this cost. You may need to help her pay her insurance premiums, however.

Birth mother's hospital bill: $3,500–$7,500: This is for a simple delivery, without complications. Again, most birth mothers have medical care coverage, and few adoptive parents ever pay this bill.

Infant's hospital nursery bill: $1,000: Many hospitals will not process the infant's bill under the birth mother's coverage (private or Medicaid) once it is disclosed that the baby will be placed for adoption. Your own insurance should pay for this bill. The key language in your medical insurance benefits booklet is the definition of "dependent," which should include the child to be adopted, over whom you have "dominion and control" (meaning coverage should be automatic). Some booklets still specify that coverage begins upon the finalization of the adoption. This simply reflects the drafter's ignorance of the adoption process since finalization can occur up to one year after placement. Your attorney should provide an explanation to your benefits office or to the insurance company.

Infant's medication, pediatric exam, and circumcision: Again, your insurance should cover these items.

Living expenses: Depending upon the state in which the birth mother lives, you can pay for certain living expenses. The total can range from $0 to more than $1,000 per month from the time that she contacts you until about six weeks after she delivers the baby.

Keep close track of all your expenses. You may be eligible for a tax credit (see page 339).

AGENCY ADOPTION

If an agency places a healthy infant directly with you—that is, if you did not find your own birth mother—its fee may range anywhere from about $7,000 to $35,000. The agency may have a standard fee regardless of the birth mother's needs. It may charge you a fee of $12,000 to $15,000 and then add on to that the birth mother's medical, living, and counseling expenses, as well as attorney fees. It is crucial that you understand whether the fees quoted to you by the agency include the birth mother's medical, living, and counseling fees. It would be easy to misconstrue the agency's quoted fee of $12,000, for example, as being your total cost. More than one couple has been stunned when presented with doctor and hospital bills after having already paid the agency fees. If you hire your own attorney to represent you, that will be an additional fee.

In states in which only agencies can legally conduct an adoption, it is not uncommon for agencies to charge an outrageous amount.

Identified and Facilitated Adoption

Some agencies specialize in identified adoptions, in which you find the birth mother, but instead of seeking the services of an attorney only, the adoption is processed through an adoption agency. In this kind of adoption, the agency will generally charge a standard identified adoption fee of $4,000 to $12,000, in addition to legal fees and birth mother expenses, usually making an identified adoption more expensive than an independent adoption.

HOW TO KEEP YOUR EXPENSES TO A REASONABLE LEVEL

Like any other legal process, adoption requires professional assistance, and adoption specialists deserve to be paid a reasonable fee for their services. Some professionals, however, prey on the emotions of desperate couples, claiming that if they do not pay a certain amount of money immediately, they will lose this once-in-a-lifetime opportunity to have a baby. Sometimes you need to rely on your instincts to tell you whether an attorney or an adoption agency social worker is pushing too hard or seems overly concerned with money. Here are some guidelines you may find helpful:

1. *View with caution any agency or attorney who asks for more than $1,500 up front without any service being rendered.* Having said that, you should know that there are several reputable agencies that are charging up to $4,000 to initiate your application. These agencies have written refund policies stating that the bulk of the monies will be refunded to you in a year or so if no placement occurs. Have your attorney check the agency's references, and telephone other couples who have obtained placements from the agency to find out whether they were satisfied with their experience.

2. *Make sure that any agency or attorney who charges you gives you an itemized bill.* An attorney may say that her fee is $3,000 for all services. This is fine. But if the bill keeps getting higher as the attorney does more work or because new expenses keep popping up, make sure you receive an itemized bill.

3. *Find out whether there will be any additional charges for birth father issues.* This is one aspect of the adoption procedure that many attorneys and agencies do not make clear. For example, find out whether there will be an additional fee if a birth father's rights must be terminated in court by a separate proceeding. Many agencies state that the adoptive couple's attorney must take care of the termination of the putative (usually the birth mother's husband) and alleged birth fathers' rights if the stated birth father(s) each do not sign an agency surrender. Again, ask for a written schedule of fees and what it covers.

PAYING FOR A BIRTH MOTHER'S LIVING EXPENSES

Most states permit an adoptive couple to pay for the birth mother's living expenses. The amount paid may have to be preapproved by a judge, however, to ensure that there is no appearance of "baby buying." Some judges are very particular about this matter. Your attorney should guide you so that you do not pay too much. Document all payments. It is best if all monies go through your attorney's escrow account to avoid any appearance of wrongdoing.

Legal living expenses usually include a few months of average rent (about $400 per month), food ($50 per week), and transportation to the doctor's office. However, what is deemed reasonable depends on the state and even the region of the state. The cost of living in a given place is what determines the appropriateness of expenses. It would be difficult to obtain a decent apartment in large metropolitan areas for $400 per month; the law would most likely permit you to pay a higher rent if the birth mother lived in such an area. The standard of reasonableness will also change if the birth mother has to care for one or more children.

Birth mothers do have crises—emergency car repairs and other unforeseen expenses. You should have your attorney or agency deal with these on a case-by-case basis. Always have your attorney get your permission before advancing money that you did not discuss beforehand.

Sometimes a birth mother will request money for placing a baby. Perhaps a friend or relative told her that this was a common practice, or perhaps she saw a television program or a magazine article about attorneys and agencies charging $25,000 to $50,000 for an adoption and asked herself, "If the attorney gets that much money, why can't I?" After all, she is the one going through pregnancy, labor, and delivery.

If a birth mother asks you for "placement money" or tells you of another couple who has offered her $10,000 for the baby, tell her that you do not want to jeopardize the baby's welfare. Tell her you would hate to see the baby removed from your home because the authorities discovered that you had paid her monies that are not allowed by law. Emphasize that you are willing to pay what is legal and that you would want to help in her time of need (assuming this is true), but your attorney must approve everything involving money. You should ask the birth mother to contact your attorney to discuss the money issue further. One couple asked a birth mother, who said she had an offer for $10,000 from another couple, "Would you really want your baby to go to a couple who is willing to pay you $10,000 illegally?" The birth mother placed the child with the honest couple.

Some people can afford to take risks and others cannot. If a birth mother is asking for $1,000 a month in living expenses for herself and her three children and you make contact with her when she is three months pregnant, these expenses alone will be $6,000—money that you could lose if she changes her mind. Some people can afford to lose this kind of money and move on to another adoption. If you are not among them, you may need to forego that situation and look for a birth mother who is further along in her pregnancy or has fewer living expenses.

This kind of risk is one of the things that can make international adoption so attractive. You are not dependent upon a particular birth mother. Unless a country suddenly closes its doors to adoption, if you work with a reputable agency, you are virtually guaranteed that your money will result in a finalized adoption. If you have access to $17,000, for example, that would cover nearly all fees and expenses for an adoption from China, and you could be fairly certain that in a matter of eight to twelve months you will have a baby.

INTERNATIONAL ADOPTION

If you are dealing with an agency, the costs are generally well defined, and payments are expected at regular intervals. The fee will vary depending upon the country from which you are adopting, but you can expect to spend between $15,000 and $30,000. Out of this amount, the fee that the agency receives is usually between $3,000 and $5,000. The remaining fees are for the facilitator overseas, in addition to expenses such as transportation, lodging, meals, and having documents authenticated.

To keep costs down, check around. Agency fees vary widely. A more expensive program does not necessarily equate with better service or a faster adoption. For example, if you are adopting from China, the process is virtually the same regardless of what agency you use. Some agencies can offer you more services and more information, but the wait for a child will be identical.

No matter which program you select, there will be travel expenses—even if your child is escorted here rather than your traveling to another country to bring your child home. Airline rates can vary significantly depending upon when you travel. Usually rates are highest during the summer. Even the specific date you travel on can affect the price of the ticket. For example, leaving on Thanksgiving Day instead of the day before or after can save you several hundred dollars.

When planning your stay in the country, find out if there is a host family with whom you can stay instead of at a hotel. The cost to stay in a home will probably be very reasonable, whereas the charge for staying at a Western-style hotel can be $100 to $300 per night.

If you plan to take gifts with you, start to look for gift items as they go on sale instead of shopping at the last minute. Ask your agency or do your own homework to find out what gifts are appreciated in the country where you are going, to whom you should give gifts, and the appropriate dollar value of the gifts.

PUBLIC AGENCY ADOPTIONS

If your funds are very limited, you may want to consider adopting through a public agency. Not only do you pay little to nothing for these adoptions, but you may actually receive subsidies each month to help you support the child. Also, you can receive a one-time $10,160 tax credit, regardless of the total expenses of your adoption.

The fact that you cannot afford another route is not enough of a reason for selecting a public agency. Children available through public agencies are those who are less "adoptable," and you must be prepared for this and have a strong support system to handle the special needs that a child adopted through this avenue may have.

If you want to adopt a child from a minority ethnic background, adopting through a public agency will probably be your least expensive route. However, there is no guarantee that you will be chosen when a committee meets to select a family for the child. You may end up waiting a long time.

PAYING FOR YOUR ADOPTION

You may not have $20,000 in the bank to adopt privately or internationally. Indeed, even a relatively inexpensive adoption will stretch most couples' resources. In her book *There ARE Babies to Adopt*, Christine Adamec discusses various techniques for meeting these expenses, from asking relatives for help to taking out a second mortgage. There is nothing shameful about taking out a loan to adopt a baby, but the bank may not approve you because there is no "collateral" except the world's most valuable possession—your baby. You may find yourself thinking along the same lines as your bank at first—a baby is not a financial investment. But if you consider that an adoption costs less than most new cars, you may gain a different perspective. Why not keep your car another year or so instead of buying a new one? Then you can take the payments that you would have used for a car and pay back your "baby loan," while you are in the process of adopting your child. When the adoption is complete, you can pay off the entire loan when you receive your tax credit and possible other adoption benefits.

Compare adoption expenses with the costs of infertility treatment. Some infertility treatment is covered by a third party—your insurance company. When another party is paying the bill, the costs do not seem so bad. However, many insurance companies do not pay for certain treatments, especially high-tech reproductive procedures such as in vitro fertilization. These kinds of procedures can cost $10,000 to $15,000 per cycle. Moreover, only a certain percentage of couples will achieve a successful pregnancy. Certainly, economics is not the only reason for choosing adoption over continued infertility treatment since some couples feel that they must pursue infertility before starting the adoption process. Nevertheless, you need to weigh whether the pursuit of having a biological child is really worth the financial investment if it eats away at your resources and limits your opportunity to adopt. For example, if you were to take the money for two in vitro fertilization cycles, you could easily adopt a child and, in most instances, in less time than it would take you to conceive and carry a child to term.

The truth is people often decide they cannot afford adoption before they have really explored their options. Even if you have only a few thousand dollars in the bank, you can proceed with an adoption. Most attorneys and agencies do not ask for all the adoption fees and expenses up front—and if they do, you should probably not be dealing with them. As you look over the expenses associated with an independent adoption, you will see that you are not required to pay a lot of money up front. You start by advertising and then you may begin helping a birth mother with living expenses—which can be paid monthly—and along the way, you may be paying the attorney or agency its fees. If your budget does not allow you to pay an agency or attorney $5,000 to $10,000 up front, then don't. Most agencies charge $1,000 to $4,000 to begin processing your application and then ask for the next installment when a birth mother is matched with you. Even international adoption programs have a fee schedule, and monies are paid over time. Adoptions usually take place in stages, giving a couple time to save money as they go along. Some agencies will even work with you and wait to receive some of the funds after you have received state subsidies or employment benefits.

ADOPTION ASSISTANCE AS AN EMPLOYEE BENEFIT

Some companies are beginning to see the goodwill and financial value in providing adoption coverage to their employees. According to the National Adoption Attitudes Survey, 95 percent of Americans think adoptive parents should get the same benefits from their employer as biological parents. For companies that are self-insured (meaning that the company and not a medical insurance company covers its employees' and their families' medical bills), the decision to provide adoption assistance can be even more of a financial incentive. The average birth costs about $9,000. If a self-insured company pays all or part of the costs associated with infertility treatment, as well as the medical costs associated with pregnancy, delivery, and care of a newborn—about $7,000 to $50,000 and up if there are complications—the company may view adoption assistance as very cost effective. Instead of paying up to $20,000 in infertility and birth-related expenses, the company can have a policy of paying, for example, up to $5,000 toward an adoption. In South Carolina, as of this writing, state employees can be reimbursed $5,000 in adoption expenses for a healthy child and $10,000 for a child with special needs. As politicians begin to see the value of adoption, perhaps more states will begin offering their employees such benefits.

If your employer provides employee benefits, up to $10,160 of the benefits is not taxed. In addition, you can take the adoption tax credit.

For more information about companies that provide adoption assistance, contact the Dave Thomas Foundation (their Web site is *www.davethomasfoundationfo-radoption.org*). Another source for information on employee adoption benefits can be found at *www.adoptionfriendlyworkplace.org*. If your company does not offer adoption assistance, you may want to advocate for such a policy. If you talk with them about ways in which the company itself can benefit, the decision-makers will be more likely to be open to this kind of change.

THE ADOPTION TAX CREDIT

The adoption tax credit is perhaps the greatest financial incentive for adoptive families. You can now earn up to $10,160 in tax credit on your federal taxes for each child who you adopt. A tax credit is not the same as a tax deduction; a credit is far more generous.

Qualified expenses include adoption fees, court costs, attorney's fees, and other adoption-related expenses such as travel. For example, if you paid $15,000 in adoption expenses in 2005, the adoption was finalized that year, and you paid $5,000 in federal income tax for 2005, then when you file your 2005 taxes, you will receive a $5,000 refund. The following year, you can receive a refund up to the total amount you paid in taxes until you reach the tax credit total of $10,160. If you adopt two children in one year, then you are eligible for a $20,320 tax credit.

If your modified average gross income is more than $152,390, then your credit will be reduced, and the credit is eliminated if you earn more than $192,390. Therefore, if you have a tax credit of $20,320, you will almost certainly receive a refund of all of the federal taxes you paid that year. This credit can be carried over for five years so that each year you can receive a portion of the $20,320.

You cannot take the credit until the adoption is finalized—whether domestic or international. If your child is placed with you in 2006, but the adoption is not finalized until the following year, you must wait until you file your 2007 taxes to receive the tax credit. Your internationally adopted child might not be a U.S. citizen if he came home on an IR-4 visa. According to the IRS publication "Tax Benefits for Adoption," your child must be a U.S. citizen before you can take the tax credit, which means you must readopt the child in the United States. However, in some states in which the foreign decree is recognized, you may still be able to take the tax credit.

The tax credit can include expenses incurred from an unsuccessful adoption.

If you incurred $2,000 in adoption expenses in 2005 from a failed adoption and you adopted a child in 2006 and incurred $8,000 in adoption expenses, then you can take a $10,000 tax credit. Although it sounds generous to get a tax credit for a failed adoption, the truth is that by the time you pay for another adoption you most likely will have exceeded the $10,160 cap. This credit does not permit you to count each adoption attempt as an adoption.

If in either a domestic or international adoption you make payments after the adoption is finalized (which is seldom done), then you use the tax credit the year of payment.

Adopting a child who is related to you, except for stepparent adoptions, appears to be covered by this legislation.

Remember that you are dealing with the IRS. They have improved their public image considerably, but they are not a social services agency. The IRS states that fees paid must be reasonable and necessary; keep a receipt of everything to prove what you spent. Also, keep track of the little things: mileage to your adoption agency, medical expenses incurred before you even adopted, and every meal eaten out that was related to the adoption.

How to Take a Credit or Employer Benefit Exclusion

You must file form 8839 with your federal income tax return (1040 or 1040A) in order to receive the credit or exclusion. If you are married, you must file a joint return. (There are exceptions for those divorced or separated.) Also, you must provide the child's identifying number on form 8839. If your child does not have a Social Security number and is not eligible for one, apply for an individual taxpayer identification number on form W-7A. You can also apply, using form W-7A, for an adoption taxpayer identification number for U.S.-born children who are in the process of being adopted.

If your employer pays for an adoption in 2005 (up to $10,160) and the adoption is not finalized until 2006, you still do not have to pay taxes on the funds given. The exception is if your child is not a U.S. citizen. Most employers do not pay for an adoption until after the adoption is finalized. If you are adopting internationally, your employer is assisting you in the payment of your adoption, and your child will be coming home on an IR-4 visa and, therefore, will not be a citizen, you can then be taxed on these benefits.

Getting a Social Security Number for Your Child

One important thing to note: you should get a Social Security number (SSN) for your child as soon as possible. If a child receives an SSN under one of the birth parents' last names instead of yours, you will have to reapply. Most people find getting an SSN to be very simple. Usually, you must go to the Social Security office and apply in person with your child's birth certificate and adoption decree.

STATE SUBSIDIES FOR "NONRECURRING COSTS"

States provide what are called "nonrecurring costs" for the adoption of a child with special needs. This is a one-time subsidy that must be requested before the child is adopted. Some states are very strict about who can qualify for this subsidy and require that the child could not have been placed without subsidies and that no other home could be found for the child. Some states are more flexible and allow children who are adopted internationally and independently to be eligible as well.

Most states provide between $500 and $2,000 for this subsidy. In South Carolina, for example, families adopting internationally receive $1,500 per adoption, and nearly all children adopted from another country are considered special needs because they have very limited family history and medical background reports—or none at all—and usually have been in an orphanage. If your state provides this subsidy and you are adopting from a country such as Ukraine, where you do not know who your child will be until you get to the country, you still must apply for the subsidy before the adoption is finalized (while you are still in the country where you are adopting). You or someone else must send to the subsidy specialist in your home state the name and birth date of your child. The specialist will then fax the agreement to you; then you sign the agreement and fax it back. Remember that this is something that must be done before you adopt your child. There is no maximum income to be eligible for this subsidy, but the document given to you does ask, "Do you need this subsidy to complete the adoption?" This seems like a trick question since the government does not give you the subsidy monies until after the child's adoption is finalized and you have usually paid all of the expenses. If you could not afford the adoption, you would not be doing it. Some clients answer this question, "Yes, it would help."

One adoptive mother, who is a pediatrician, and her husband, a general practitioner, were about to adopt a child who was born with nerve damage to the inner ear. Because of the child's special needs, they applied for the nonrecurring expenses subsidy. The ear problem miraculously corrected without medical intervention. The parents had already received the subsidy; the mother contacted the state and tried to return the money. The state does not take money back! Their other adopted child had profound learning delays, even though she had excellent prenatal care. The parents never even considered applying for subsidies for her since there was no indication at all that she would have special needs. The mother decided, "Well, the subsidy money that we received can go toward the expenses of the child who truly has special needs."

STATE AND FEDERAL SUPPORT FOR CHILDREN WITH SPECIAL NEEDS

As with many government programs, the language and terms can be complicated. Do not let this intimidate you. You can get subsidies for your child if she has special needs and was adopted through the social services system. Your child may even be eligible if she was adopted through a private agency. Do your research, get outside help if you must, and be persistent. Receiving monthly subsidies for your child can mean the difference of your child receiving hundreds of dollars per month that can be used to give him the "extras' in help that he may need—even if not now, but down the road.

Title IV-E

In general, for a child to receive federal monthly adoption subsidies from Title IV-E, he must have sufficient medical, developmental, or psychological problems or disabilities or be at risk for these problems because of unknown parental background. For a child to be eligible, he must meet the state's criteria for having special needs, and he must come from a birth family or relative's home that was receiving or was eligible to receive Aid for Families with Dependent Children (AFDC). (This program no longer exists at the federal level and was replaced with TANF—Temporary Aid to Needy Families.) However, the rules for AFDC as of June 1996 are used to qualify a child for the Title IV-E Adoption Assistance Program. If a child has a birth family who is low income and was not receiving support from the other parent, then the child is most likely AFDC eligible.

If the child has special needs but does not meet the other criteria, he may be eligible for an equal state subsidy instead of a federal subsidy.

Children who are receiving Title IV-E federal foster care maintenance payments are eligible for federal adoption assistance benefits. Many foster children are receiving state and not federal funds, however, so the child may or may not be eligible for federal funding once adopted.

Children who are eligible for Supplemental Security Income (SSI) automatically are eligible for Title IV-E adoption subsides. Children who are receiving SSI benefits at the time of adoption are financially and categorically eligible for adoption assistance; in fact, even if they have been not receiving SSI benefits, if they meet SSI criteria at the time of adoption, they are eligible for adoption subsidies. With SSI benefits, only the child's income is taken into consideration at the time the adoption petition is filed. This means that most children who meet the disability criteria for SSI are eligible for SSI based on income because few children have any earnings. The disability determination is the only requirement for the child's receiving SSI. If a child meets the eligibility standards for SSI, then it does not matter if the child was in the state's care or not.

Remember, prospective adoptive parents cannot receive the maximum amount of federal support from both SSI and the adoption assistance program, even if the child is eligible for both programs.

Following are the general categories of SSI eligibility. This is not a comprehensive list; be sure to contact your local Social Security office at 800-772-1213 for more complete information on eligibility criteria and application forms.

- Growth impairment of the musculoskeletal system (e.g., arthritis, disorders of the spine)
- Blindness or hearing impairment
- Respiratory problems (e.g., asthma or cystic fibrosis)
- Cardiovascular problems
- Digestive system disorders
- Malnutrition
- Endocrine system (e.g., thyroid) disorders
- Diabetes
- Blood and lymph disease (e.g., sickle cell disease)
- Cancer
- Multiple body defects
- Down syndrome
- Immune deficiency
- Neurological problems (e.g., cerebral palsy)
- Mental and emotional problems
- Attention deficit hyperactivity disorder
- Developmental and emotional disorders of newborns and infants
- Genitourinary problems

If a child is not receiving federal foster care maintenance payments or is not eligible for SSI, two categories must be met in order for her to be eligible for the federal adoption assistance program. The state must determine that the child has special needs, and the child must meet the financial and categorical criteria of Aid to Families with Dependent Children, both at the time she was removed from her parents' custody and at the time of adoption.

Each state establishes specific guidelines as to what defines a "special needs" child. In one state, a child may have to be six years old to be considered special needs; while in another, she must be ten years old. A child who is African-American or of mixed ethnic background will have a lower age requirement than a Caucasian child in order to be considered special needs.

A child is considered to have special needs when she has met these three factors:

1. She cannot or should not be returned to her biological parents. This includes children whose parents have voluntarily released them for adoption.
2. The child has a specific condition, including minority ethnic background, age, being part of a sibling group, or having a medical, mental, or emotional disability or being at risk for one that would make adoption difficult without a financial incentive.
3. Except where it would be against the best interest of the child to place him, efforts to place the child without offering medical or adoption assistance have been unsuccessful. Federal officials have finally recognized that a focus on "shopping" a child until adoptive parents who do not need the subsidy can be found is contrary not only to sound adoption practice, but also to the intent of the adoption assistance program. If parents cannot or will not adopt without the subsidy, then the requirement is met. Asking parents whether they are willing to adopt without subsidies does not put the placement at risk for them. As a practical matter, however, children with special needs who are easily adoptable, such as a cocaine-exposed Caucasian six-month-old, can easily be placed without subsidies. A few couples will usually be considered for the child, and the one willing to adopt without subsidies will be selected.

Foster parents who have had a child in their home for a significant time do not need to consider whether they are willing to take the child without a subsidy. Because of the emotional ties involved, this requirement is waived.

Aid for Families with Dependent Children

There are two classifications of AFDC requirements: need and deprivation. Deprivation requirements are met if a parent is absent or if parents' rights have been terminated. To qualify for the need category, a child must have been eligible, even if an application was not made for AFDC, at the following times:

- In the month that a petition was filed with the court for the removal of the child from his home, or six months before
- In the month before the child's parent voluntarily signed an agreement for the child to be placed outside the home, or six months before

In other words, even if the child was not receiving AFDC at the time he was removed from his home, if his biological family qualified for it, he still will meet the AFDC criteria. He must also be eligible when the adoption is petitioned. Children who meet the AFDC requirements at the time they are removed from their parents' custody may or may not meet the criteria when the adoption proceedings are initiated.

Requiring children to be AFDC eligible seems arbitrary, and as of this writing, federal lawmakers are reconsidering the requirement. Meeting the AFDC requirement is not as simple as it may look. More and more children entering foster care who then become eligible for adoption are not coming from welfare homes but from working families. Moreover, even if the child's biological family was AFDC eligible at the time he was removed from his home, his family's work status may change from the time he was removed from the home to the time the adoption petition was put into place. Often the employment status of one of the biological parents does change between the time the child is removed from the home and the time the adoption petition is filed. The biological mother may have gotten a job, making the child ineligible for AFDC status.

Note: A child who is receiving Title IV-E foster care payments at the time the adoption petition is filed meets the AFDC relatedness test.

STATE ADOPTION SUBSIDY PROGRAMS

Most states have an adoption subsidy program for children with special needs who do not qualify for federal adoption assistance under Title IV-E—usually because they do not meet the SSI/AFDC requirements. In many states, Title IV-E adoption assistance and state payment subsidies are administered as the same program, with the same payment rates for families. If a child meets the criteria for special needs but not for the SSI/AFDC requirements, the payments come from state instead of federal funds. Most states have fairly broad standards for defining "special needs." Some even say that if a child has been in your home for eighteen months as a foster child, she qualifies as special needs because of the emotional trauma that would be caused if she was removed from your home. Be aware that as federal and state dollars become tighter, fewer benefits may be offered.

Depending on your state and your particular situation, available programs may include:

Monthly benefits. Once a child is considered to have special needs, she is eligible for monthly assistance, usually in the amount you would receive if you were foster parents. Each state sets up its own fee schedule. As a rule, the higher the cost of living and the older the child, the higher the payments. Some states provide a higher foster care rate for children who require special care. This is called specialized or accelerated care rates. If the adopted child was eligible for specialized care rates when she was in the foster care system, the rates would stay higher after the adoption.

Medical assistance. Children in the federal adoption assistance program are automatically eligible for Medicaid benefits. Many states also choose to provide Medicaid coverage for children who are receiving benefits from state or local (non-federal) adoption assistance programs. Although states have broader standards in defining who is a special needs child, the definition for special needs is directly related to having a special medical or psychological need, as opposed to being in a certain age or ethnic background category. A healthy two-year-old African-American child would not necessarily qualify.

Minimum Medicaid benefits for children include inpatient hospital services (except for tuberculosis or mental disease), outpatient hospital services, laboratory and x-ray services, screening and diagnosis, and medical and dental services provided under state law. Children are also entitled to optional services to correct or lessen the effects of physical or mental illnesses or conditions discovered during a health care screening under the Early and Periodic Screening, Diagnosis and Treatment Program (EPSDT). These services include home health, private duty nursing, clinic services, dental services, physical therapy, prescription drugs, dentures, prosthetic devices, eyeglasses, inpatient psychiatric services, respiratory services, and other medical care.

Even if you have comprehensive health care insurance, you may want the extra security of Medicaid in case your situation changes.

If your child has special mental or physical needs and is to receive Medicaid, try to negotiate as much other assistance as possible. Many physicians will not accept Medicaid, which can be difficult, especially if you have other children who are already going to a particular physician.

Medicaid is especially useful when you are using specialists and not general practitioners and for getting specialized hospital care. You can also request that the state pay for psychological counseling and for one-time medical needs and equipment, such as a wheelchair ramp.

Social Security Block Grants (SSBG; formerly called Title XX) govern the social services grant, which gives federal money to states to use for helping families maintain self-support, remedying neglect and abuse, and preventing or reducing the need for institutional care by providing these supportive services to adoptive families.

These funds have not been actively promoted by child welfare workers, and the individual states have much latitude in designing the programs. Each state has an outline for services and established activities to be supported and who will be served. Types of services vary from state to state. Potential services include day care, respite services, in-home support services such as housekeeping and personal care, and counseling.

Unlike the Medicaid program, SSBG is not given automatically to dependent children or children eligible for AFDC. However, the program is designed to make sure that children in the adoption assistance program will not be excluded from services that the state provides children who do receive AFDC. For example, if the state operates a day care program funded by these block grants and gives preference to AFDC children, then a child in the adoption assistance program will have the same preference regardless of the adoptive parents' income.

Early Intervention Programs

If your child has health problems and needs intervention, each state provides intervention through the Early Childhood Intervention Program for children from birth to three years old. The services provided are not income-based. Regardless of how much money you earn, if your child has some special needs such as speech impairment or has physical delays, he may be eligible at no cost to you. The usual services include physical, occupational, and speech therapies. To find the program in your state go to *www.nectac.org/search/mapfinder.asp*.

Other Services and Assistance

The federal law also requires that the adoption assistance agreement include any additional services that are needed for the family or child. Prospective adoptive parents should closely monitor their child's needs and anticipate any future needs. For example, a family may have to change their home to accommodate the physically challenged child now or in the future. If you are considering the adoption of a child, be sure to ask if the child needs special education, has medical problems, or needs any counseling.

Service subsidies. Many states provide medical, mental health, and other postplacement services that are not covered by the adoptive family's health insurance or by Medicaid. Service subsidies should be established before the adoption is finalized. Some states do provide service subsidies to adoptive families after finalization.

Education. This may include speech and physical therapies.

Reimbursement for nonrecurring adoption expenses. Since 1987, the federal adoption assistance law has required states to pay nonrecurring adoption expenses in the adoption of children with special needs through a state or nonprofit private agency. The cap is usually $2,000 per child. A child need only meet the federal Title IV-E definition of a special needs child to qualify for this one-time subsidy; he does not have to meet SSI or AFDC eligibility. Even if a child is at risk for a certain problem because little or no birth father family history is available, this will make a child eligible for nonrecurring adoption expenses. Therefore, nearly all children will meet the definition of being special needs, even if they do not qualify by other state standards.

You must apply for reimbursement of these expenses in the state where the adoption assistance agreement is signed. If you are not receiving adoption assistance, you must apply in the state where the adoption will be finalized. The subsidy covers:

- Adoptive parents' home study, medical exams, and postplacement supervisions
- Legal and court costs
- Transportation, meals, and lodging
- Adoption fees

To obtain the latest information, contact North American Council on Adoptable Children (NACAC). Although the Web site is kept up-to-date, you may want to talk to someone to determine what your state provides and if you think that you and your child may be shortchanged. The staff at NACAC can advise you accordingly. Their number is 800-470-6665, and their e-mail address is *adoption. assistance@nacac.org.*

If you adopt through a private agency, your child still may be eligible for benefits. *The Child Welfare Manual* indicates that the state or legal agency is responsible for letting you know this. However, they may be totally unaware of your adoption. Therefore, the adoptive family must take this initiative. If you are adopting through a state agency, the staff are familiar with subsidies, and even if you had to negotiate the amount you wanted, you most likely would obtain some monthly benefits for your child. However, if you are adopting through a private agency, chances are good that the state is not going to provide you monthly benefits without you first asking for them and perhaps getting an attorney involved.

If you are adopting a child through a private attorney and your child has special needs but his disabilities are not so profound that he qualifies for Supplemental Security Income, it may be better to turn your adoption into an agency adoption if this will mean that your child qualifies for monthly subsidies.

TAX BENEFITS

Many people are aware that adoptive families are eligible to receive a $10,000 tax credit. (Actually, for the 2004 tax year, this limit was set at $10,390.) This credit is based on income and the amount of funds paid for the adoption. In most instances, a family can easily spend $10,000 for an adoption of a child adopted through a private agency or internationally. However, when adopting a child through the social services system, there are few fees except legal fees to finalize the adoption and some expenses. A family can expect to spend less than $3,500 in adopting a child with special needs. Yes, if you adopt a child who qualifies as special needs, even if you spend little or no money, most likely you can qualify for the $10,000 tax credit.

Be sure to keep evidence that your child is considered special needs. Then you can take the $10,000-plus tax credit. Let's look at a likely scenario that could benefit you, even if your income is moderate. You adopt a child who is determined to have special needs, and you will be receiving monthly subsidies or perhaps zero-based subsidies in the event that your child later needs assistance. Your out-of-pocket expenses total $2,000, which are covered by the nonrecurring cost that your state allows. Therefore, you have no net adoption expenses. Your income is $35,000 per year, and you pay $2,500 in federal income tax. In the year that the adoption becomes final, 2005, you can take the tax credit. When you file your taxes with the IRS in 2006, you can take a credit up to $2,500. Therefore, the IRS will reimburse (or credit you, if you owe taxes) $2,500 in 2006. You can continue taking the credit each year for five years until you reach the $10,000-plus credit.

State Income Tax Deductions

In some states, if you adopt a child with special needs, you may be eligible to also take a tax deduction on your state income tax.

If adopting a child with special needs, you could potentially be receiving monthly state subsidies, have your complete adoption paid for through nonrecurring subsidies, receive a tax credit of $10,000 plus take a deduction from your state income tax, as well as earn other credits and deductions that you would normally receive for having a child on your federal income tax.

No matter what benefits you receive, these will simply offset the expenses of having a child. The funds available are usually not enough to ever make adopting a child a financial benefit. Some families receive enough benefits so that a parent can stay home with the child, which is usually what the child needs. Children are not meant to be financial assets. However, adopting a child with special needs should not be a financial risk for a family.

ADOPTION ASSISTANCE CHECKLIST

Whenever a family receives adoption assistance, a written adoption assistance agreement between the adoptive parents and the state agency will be provided. These agreements vary from state to state, but a model adoption assistance agreement is one that contains the requirements under Title IV-E and is useful for adoptive families who move across state lines. The agreement should state that a commitment is made regardless of where the adoptive parents live and should specify the kinds of care and services that will be provided. It should be specific enough to ensure future enforcement but flexible enough to allow for new provisions if circumstances change. For example, if your child is receiving physical therapy, the agreement should describe the services in detail and state that if the provider can no longer offer services or if you move, equal services will be provided. Services should be described in very specific terms. It should not read "therapy will be provided" but should read "individual and family therapy will be provided for at least one hour per week by a licensed child psychologist or social worker." The agreement should also state the date on which each benefit will start and the circumstances under which it can be terminated.

Following is a checklist of questions to refer to when reviewing your adoption assistance agreement:

1. Does the agreement clearly state all the responsibilities of the prospective adoptive parents? Are financial reporting and recertification requirements explicit?
2. Is the agreement signed by someone with proper authority to bind the state agency?
3. Are all necessary agencies parties to the agreement?
4. Does the agreement specify the amount of cash assistance to be provided?
5. Does the agreement state all necessary services to be provided?
6. Does the agreement give the date when each benefit and service will begin?
7. Does the agreement clearly list the conditions under which benefits and services may be terminated?
8. Does the agreement specify the conditions under which benefits and services can increase or decrease? Is there any clause that restricts the prospective adoptive parents' authority to negotiate changes in the future?
9. Do the services end when the child turns eighteen or twenty-one?
10. Does the agreement specify what will happen if the adoptive parents die?
11. Does the agreement specify that the agreement itself will still be in effect and that the benefits will remain in effect if the adoptive family moves out of state?
12. Does the agreement provide for Medicaid eligibility?

If you believe your child has special medical or psychological needs that will not be adequately met by the subsidies and services outlined in your agreement, it would be wise to take the child to a specialist of your choice (orthopedist, neurologist, psychiatrist) to obtain the clearest prognosis possible so that you can negotiate the best possible agreement for your child. Even if this means taking your child to a specialist who does not accept Medicaid, in the end, it may save you both money and time.

NEGOTIATING AN AGREEMENT

Federal policy requires that the child's and the family's circumstances be taken into consideration in establishing an adoption assistance agreement. For example, although written state guidelines specify the maximum amount of monthly payments in each age category, the state and the adoptive parents can negotiate the amount. Your goal as adoptive parents should be to provide comprehensive support. Follow these steps:

1. Obtain complete information on the child's family background and medical history, including current health status, psychiatric and psychological evaluations, if necessary, and the current physical, intellectual, and emotional needs of the child. State agencies do not always collect all the essential information about a child, and the information is not always in one place. Nor does the agency always provide prospective adoptive parents all the information available. Federal law, however, requires that the following be in the child's foster care plan:

   - The names and addresses of the child's health and education providers
   - The child's grade-level performance
   - The child's immunization records
   - The child's medical problems
   - The child's medications
   - Other relevant health and educational information

2. Based on the child's medical needs and on his social and educational background, a discussion of services may be needed.
3. Give thorough consideration to your resources and ability to meet the child's needs so that he will successfully be incorporated into your family. Take into account not only your income, but your other expenses, the number of children in your home, and the circumstances of these children.
4. Compile complete information about the federal and state adoption assistance programs available, including service and medical subsidies.
5. Negotiate a support plan that combines all appropriate programs.
6. Negotiate specific guidelines for services to be provided in the event that you move to another state. Although federal law requires federal adoption assistance agreements to state that subsidies remain in effect regardless of where you move, some services may not be specifically addressed in the agreement.

Remember, federal adoption assistance agreements remain in effect regardless of the state in which you live. If you live in South Carolina and your child receives

$200 per month in subsidies and you move to New York City, where the cost of living is much higher, you will still receive only $200 per month.

Enforcement

Most of the disagreements that arise over the negotiation or enforcement of an agreement can be handled on an informal basis. When they cannot, federal law requires that states provide prospective adoptive parents a "fair hearing" before the appropriate state agency to contest the agreement or petition for its enforcement. Some states have special review panels to hear adoption assistance appeals. A fair hearing can also be helpful if a caseworker is not responsive to the adoptive parents' requests. There are separate fair hearings for Medicaid and Title XX services.

Fair hearings are informal occasions, and the rules of evidence do not strictly apply, so many adoptive and prospective adoptive parents represent themselves instead of hiring an attorney. The fair hearing officer can decide about the fact that is in dispute and order the agency to follow state statutes and agency guidelines. We strongly recommend, however, that you hire an attorney to work with you throughout this process. An attorney can help the family by establishing the eligibility of the child for benefits, helping plan the negotiation of the adoption assistance agreement and future changes, and taking legal steps to enforce the agreement if the family does not receive the proper benefits and services. Often additional benefits such as speech therapy, psychological counseling, and equipment for disabilities can be negotiated. Why shortchange yourself or your adopted child? Have an attorney negotiate as much as possible in your favor.

Prospective adoptive parents who are presented with a standard agency form that sets forth the terms should negotiate an individual agreement that meets the child's needs. Except for legal restrictions, there is no requirement that the adoption assistance agreement follow any particular format.

Sometimes foster parents are told that they will not receive adoption assistance if they adopt their foster child, or prospective adoptive parents who want to adopt a particular child are informed that the child will not be eligible for subsidies. In these situations, the prospective adoptive parents can request the agency to reconsider the decision and, if necessary, can demand a fair hearing. Have your attorney provide the state agency with the information necessary to establish the child's eligibility. If the state criteria are too strict, they may be challenged as not conforming to federal law.

Note: If you adopt a child whose parents signed a voluntary consent, you will need to have a judicial determination that the adoption is in the child's best interest or that remaining with the birth family is contrary to the child's welfare. This needs to be done within six months of the parents' signing the consent because you will not be able to go back later and obtain subsidies should the need arise.

Title IV-E for a Child's Blood Relatives

In order for a child who is to be adopted by relatives to meet Title IV-E requirements, the court must usually state that it is against the child's welfare for him to stay in his biological parents' home or that placement in the adoptive home is in his best interest. There is no need to discuss the manner in which the child came into care. The child must also have been AFDC eligible at the time the adoption petition was filed.

LOANS

We do not recommend taking out a loan to adopt a child, except what will be returned to you in tax credits and other benefits right after you adopt the child. Adopting a child should not put you into debt. Children are expensive creatures in and of themselves; your expenditures are going to increase once they arrive in your home. Also, most families cut back on their work schedules once they have children, thus decreasing the family income. Therefore, we suggest that you try to live on what you earn and use your expendable income and savings for the adoption. If your income is going to decrease and your expenses are going to rise after the arrival of a child, then paying off a loan is going to be an added expense that may be difficult to do.

If you must take out a loan, take out a second mortgage or borrow against your 401(k) since this is a secured loan. Some organizations provide unsecured loans specifically for adoption purposes, but these loans have interest rates of 12 percent or more. If you know, for example, that you will receive a tax credit of $10,160 per child and your employer will give you $2,000 toward your adoption once it is finalized, then you may consider taking out a second mortgage that you will immediately pay back once you receive the $12,160. Of course, this amount will not cover the expenses of most international adoptions, but it certainly can make a significant contribution. Moreover, if you adopt two children at the same time and the expenses for the second child are not high, you may find that once you receive the double benefits, it significantly offsets the cost of the adoption.

One family received $10,000 per child for the adoption of two international children as part of an employee benefits package, plus they received additional funds in nonrecurring adoption subsidies. Because they adopted two children and the international fee was only $4,000 more for a second adoption, the benefits from the employer more than offset the extra expenses incurred. Their adoption expenses were nearly all paid for through the husband's employer and the subsidies.

Also, remember that most adoptions do not take place overnight; you will not need to pay for an adoption in one lump sum, even if you work with an agency. The expenses are usually spread over at least a six-month period.

GRANTS AND OTHER RESOURCES

If you spend some time on the Internet, you can find many organizations that provide grants to those adopting. (One example is the Fore Adoption Foundation at *www.foreadoption.com.)* In most instances, however, there are very limited funds available, and few people ever receive these. Of the nearly 1,000 adoptions that we have conducted, only two families ever received such grants. Both families were in ministries.

No one can make a tax-deductible donation to an organization or adoption agency on behalf of a specific adoptive family. However, others can make a tax-deductible donation for the expenses associated with the adoption of specific children. Usually people make donations on behalf of older children or those with special needs. Then the adoptive family can identify a child and adopt him at a reduced fee or at no cost at all.

Your church or house of worship, which probably supports many worthwhile projects, may also view your adopting a child as a community endeavor and not just a family matter and be willing to help with some of the cost. The members of the congregation can make tax-deductible donations to the church or organization, and the funds can then be given to an adoptive family. However, as stated previously, one cannot make a donation to a church or organization on behalf of a specific adoptive family.

People are moved to help when they see a child's face. If you feel that you are called to adopt a child with special needs, for example, and can show people the child or type of child you are seeking to adopt, you can give those who may want to make a difference in the life of a child an opportunity for them to contribute to a child's being placed in a loving home.

In summary, you should use your imagination when looking for ways to pay for your adoption or to obtain ongoing benefits after adoption. Some families, especially those adopting internationally, have garage sales, bake sales, etc. People are especially supportive if you have an identified child because they feel they are helping more than a family: They are helping an orphan. Many people have no idea that federal and state funds are available. In addition, when families are seriously considering adopting, they often find that family members are very supportive, sometimes even financially.

Chapter Nineteen

Healthy Mothers, Healthy Babies

I f you are adopting independently or through a domestic agency, you may be actively involved in the birth mother's prenatal care. The level of medical attention a woman receives while pregnant can greatly influence both her health and the baby's. Not surprisingly, adoptive parents are usually very concerned about the quality of medical care a birth mother receives. Often a birth mother has not had any prenatal care before she contacts a couple. Perhaps she did not know she was pregnant at first, and when she found out, she immediately began to make adoption arrangements before doing anything else.

You and your attorney will often make the initial medical arrangements for prenatal care if a birth mother has not already done so. Here is some advice about how to find an obstetrician.

FINDING AN OBSTETRICIAN

First, try to get as much information as possible both about what kind of obstetrician the birth mother would like to have and about the obstetricians in her area who are sensitive to adoption issues. Find out whether the birth mother prefers a male or a female doctor, and do your best to honor that preference. Contact an adoption support group or the RESOLVE chapter closest to where the birth mother will deliver her baby, and ask for names of physicians who understand what is involved in an adoption and the special needs a birth mother may have before, during, and after the baby's birth.

A physician should be sensitive and recognize that each birth mother has different needs. Some, for example, may show detachment toward the baby in utero, while others may be very interested. One birth mother may want to see the baby's image on the ultrasound screen, while another may not. Some women want to go to prenatal classes. Others do not. After the birth, some birth mothers want to see and care for the baby while in the hospital. Others do not.

If you can't find the right physician through a support group, there are other sources to try. An adoption agency in the birth mother's area may know of some obstetricians who support adoption. Another person to ask is your gynecologist or infertility specialist. Then there's your attorney, who has handled many adoptions and may even have a list of names on hand.

Most birth mothers use Medicaid to receive prenatal care and to cover the costs associated with labor and delivery, as well as the baby's hospital stay and any medical treatment he may receive. Medicaid means that you and the birth mother will have much less say in selecting a physician. At a clinic, a birth mother may see several different health practitioners, each of whom may have varying views on adoption.

Ask the birth mother whether she has any preference about where she receives treatment. The advantage of using a clinic is that they frequently offer prenatal care at no cost or at a minimal cost, based on a sliding scale; also, she and the baby will both be covered in the hospital. Even if your insurance is supposed to cover the expenses of the child, there is sometimes some ambiguity in this area, so it is reassuring to know that in the event of a medical problem, Medicaid will cover the child's medical bills.

To find a prenatal clinic that accepts Medicaid patients, call the state Medicaid office in the state where the birth mother will deliver to get information. In some states, a woman who has no medical coverage can go to a prenatal clinic without paying anything under a plan called "presumptive eligibility." The purpose of this plan is to encourage women to seek prenatal care regardless of their financial status. At the first visit, the clinic staff will determine, based on the woman's financial resources, for what assistance programs she may qualify. In New York state, for example, if a woman qualifies for Medicaid, the clinic staff can assist her in completing the forms right there instead of at a Medicaid office.

Some states have special prenatal programs such as the "Healthy Mothers, Healthy Babies" program. To find the coordinator in your state, visit *www.hmhb. org/index.html.*

Contacting the Obstetrician

Before deciding on an obstetrician, you will need to call and ask some questions. For example:

1. *What are your fees?* The physician may want payment up front to protect himself in case the birth mother changes her mind about placing her baby for adoption. If she does, she may not be able to pay for the services rendered, and the adoptive parents will not want to. Although the physician's viewpoint is understandable, you certainly do not want to end up paying for a woman's medical bills only to have her change her mind. If a physician does ask for payment up front and you truly believe that the birth mother is going to place the

baby with you, then go ahead and pay. But never pay the doctor more because this is an adoption. That is unethical.

2. *What kind of insurance does the office accept?* When it comes to medical insurance, ask the doctor's office the following questions: (a) Do they accept Medicaid payments? (b) Do they expect payment up front before the insurance carrier has reimbursed them? (Some physicians want to be paid up front; the insurance company then reimburses the patient.)

3. *If a woman has no insurance, what is her payment schedule?* If you will be paying for the birth mother's medical expenses, ask if you can set up a payment schedule. These medical expenses cannot be recouped. Have the monies put in your attorney's escrow account; if the woman changes her mind about the adoption, the monies will not be sent to the physician.

   The practice of placing the woman's medical expenses in escrow may be deemed illegal in some instances if your paying the medical expenses is contingent upon her placing her child for adoption. Some authorities believe the practice should be prohibited when payment is contingent on the birth mother's placing the child for adoption. Never pressure a woman to place her baby for adoption by telling her that her medical bills will not be paid if she does not. Payment arrangements are between you and the doctor.

4. *Will the clinic staff or physician give medical treatment to a woman who will be placing her baby for adoption?* Even before making the first appointment, let the obstetrician know right away of the woman's adoption plans. This is better than finding out later that the obstetrician or the support staff has a negative attitude toward adoption. When you call, you may start by saying, "I am a prospective adoptive mother, and I am helping a woman find an obstetrician. This woman is planning to place her baby for adoption through private channels with my husband and me. I want to know whether your staff will care for a pregnant woman placing a baby for adoption." If the person answering the phone says that the obstetrician will accept a woman placing her baby for adoption, ask the following questions:

   - Has the obstetrician treated other women who were placing the baby for adoption through private channels? If the staff says yes, you may want to ask whether everything went well.
   - Does the office have a policy about treating birth mothers? Most offices will not have a written policy, but by asking the question, you let them know that you expect professional protocol to be followed in treating the birth mother.

- Will the obstetrician permit the adoptive parents to be in the delivery room with the birth mother? If you and the birth mother are very sure it is in everyone's best interest for you to take her to prenatal visits and to be present in the delivery room, discuss this with the obstetrician right away. Even if you do not have plans to be in the delivery room, this is still a good question to ask. If the obstetrician says yes, this probably signals that she has positive views about adoption.

You might consider having your attorney's staff screen obstetricians before you or the birth mother calls for an appointment. By doing so, you can be saved some awkward moments on the telephone. After the attorney's staff has done the screening, you can then call the office yourself and simply make an appointment for the birth mother.

In the past few years, there has been a marked improvement in the attitudes of physicians, nurses, social workers, and others who may be involved in caring for the birth mother, but you could still encounter a lack of understanding and discretion. Even though this may be true, the obstetrician's staff should be aware of the birth mother's situation in case she wants to make special prenatal arrangements. For instance, she may not want to attend birthing classes that include discussions on baby care. Whether you want to let the health care staff know that you are the prospective adoptive parent is a matter of personal preference. If you will be accompanying the birth mother to her prenatal visits, you will probably want to say who you are. Be prepared for the possibility that although they support the birth mother, they see you as an intruder.

5. *Does the obstetrician have a female midwife or nurse practitioner on staff?* If the obstetrician is male, the birth mother may feel more comfortable being treated by a female nurse practitioner. Nurse practitioners and midwives often have broader views on women's issues, too, and may be more supportive of women who choose adoption.
6. *At what hospital(s) does the obstetrician deliver babies?* This is an important question because the social services departments of certain hospitals are known for their negative attitude toward adoption.

Determining the Staff's Attitude Toward Adoption

Based on the responses to your questions, you will have some idea about the staff's attitude already. If you are still not sure (and this is not unusual), you may want to go with the birth mother to her first obstetrical appointment.

If you are dealing with a clinic, there may be counselors who will try to talk her out of her decision to place the baby. Be honest with your birth mother and tell her this. Ask her how she would like to handle this situation.

In all fairness, most obstetricians and their staff are knowledgeable about adoption, have a positive attitude about it, and will provide a birth mother with proper health care and respect. There are doctors, however, who look on independent adoption as a quasi-legal activity or, at any rate, an inappropriate choice for a woman to make. A particularly shocking example of this occurred with an adoptive mother named Linda, who took her own mother to the doctor's office for an appointment. The doctor said hello to Linda and her four-month-old baby. When Linda casually mentioned that she had adopted her baby, the doctor responded, "The [birth] parents should be shot."

Some professionals oppose adoption. If the obstetrician you select turns out to be one of them, the earlier you find it out, the better.

PRENATAL CARE

Prenatal health care should be comprehensive and should include the following:

1. *Medical history and complete physical examination.*
2. *Laboratory and diagnostic procedures, including:*

- Blood pressure
- Hemoglobin and hematocrit (to test for iron-deficiency anemia)
- ABO/Rh typing (to determine blood type and Rh factor)
- Sexually transmitted diseases cultures
- Hepatitis B surface antigen
- Urinalysis for bacteria in urine

For high-risk groups:

- Hemoglobin electrophoresis
- Rubella antibodies
- Chlamydia testing
- HIV testing and counseling

3. *Nutrition assessment and counseling and, if appropriate, a referral to the government's Woman, Infant, and Children (WIC) program.* Entry into a WIC program is based upon financial and nutritional status. The guidelines are very broad, and a woman who is well above the poverty level may still be eligible. WIC centers have nutritionists and dietitians who counsel women and give them vouchers for specific food items, like milk, cheese, nutritious cereals, and iron-rich foods.

4. *Health education, including information about fetal development, preventive health care, and preparation for labor and delivery.*
5. *Basic psychological assessment.* In particular, anyone suspected of substance abuse should receive special attention and referrals.

   Although the problems associated with alcohol and drug abuse can be profound, do not expect an obstetrician, especially one in private practice, to do a thorough investigation of a birth mother's possible substance abuse. The most that the average physician will do is to ask the woman whether she uses alcohol or drugs. She will probably just answer "no," even if she does. There are ways, however, through careful, appropriate, and tactful questioning to elicit honest answers from a pregnant woman about her history of drug and alcohol use.
6. *Screening for environmental health hazards common in the particular community or work site (pesticides, radiation, parasitic infections, etc.) where the birth mother lives and/or works.* Many birth defects can be associated with environmental exposures.

THE BABY'S BIRTH AND HOSPITAL STAY

Once you have selected an obstetrician and know the hospital where the baby will be born, either you or your attorney should contact the hospital to find out about its adoption policy. Ask whether you can speak with a social worker. It is likely that a social worker will meet with the birth mother while she is in the hospital.

Here are some questions you will want to ask:

1. *Does the hospital have a policy regarding independent adoption?* If so, is the policy enforced, or do the personnel practice a more flexible policy? Some hospitals could have archaic policies of forbidding the private placement of infants for adoption that are no longer followed. Based on the way the policy is explained by employees, you will probably discover their attitude toward adoption.
2. *Can adoptive parents be in the delivery room if the birth mother authorizes their presence?* (Ask the obstetrician first.)
3. *Can the adoptive parents visit the baby and birth mother in the hospital?*
4. *If so, can the adoptive parents dress and feed the baby if the birth mother permits?*
5. *If the birth mother does not want to see the baby, what arrangements are made for the baby to be fed, dressed, and bathed?* In one hospital, the social workers threatened to call a state agency that deals with child abuse to claim that a birth mother was neglecting the baby. In another case, a nurse forced a birth mother against her will to dress the baby before the woman and child were discharged. Through her tears, this poor woman had to fully dress the infant she did not even want to see.

6. *If the birth mother chooses, can she be placed on a medical/surgical floor after delivery instead of the maternity floor?* Many birth mothers, even those who desire to see the baby, do not want to be on the maternity floor facing questions from other new mothers and nurses.

7. *What hospital personnel are allowed to talk to the birth mother about her decision to adopt, and what are they allowed to say?* Find out whether the hospital has a policy about the kinds of questions and comments—including tactless, unsolicited advice—that nurses, social workers, housekeepers, and other hospital personnel are permitted to make to a birth mother about her decision. Some people feel they have a right to comment about a woman's choice to place a baby for adoption, saying things such as "How can you give away your own baby?" If you sense that the social worker will not prevent unsolicited advice from hospital staff, then ask how the hospital administrator would handle such remarks.

Even more alarming are hospital personnel who know "the perfect couple" to adopt the baby and try to persuade the birth mother to place the baby with a couple other than you. These solicitations can come from anyone, from a physician to the person who delivers meals. Be honest. Warn your birth mother that people may make negative comments or that they may try to get her to place the baby with another couple. Ask her how she would handle such a scenario. Mentally rehearsing her response can help her deal with insensitive people, especially at a time when her emotions are very strong.

8. *Does hospital policy allow direct placement of the baby with the adoptive couple at the hospital?* Some hospitals do not allow anyone except the birth mother or an adoption agency to leave with a baby. Find out whether the adoptive parents and attorney can leave the hospital with the baby if the birth mother has signed the consent forms or whether the birth mother must leave the hospital with the baby.

If the hospital does not allow you or your attorney to leave with the baby and if a birth mother does not wish to see the baby, discuss the possibility of having a friend or relative hold the baby and leave with her or hiring a private-duty nurse to carry the baby out. As the adoptive parents, you can then meet the person carrying the baby outside the hospital.

Financial Arrangements

By law, any woman can walk into a hospital and deliver a baby. She cannot be turned away. Therefore, you are not responsible for paying the hospital bill before the baby's birth. In fact, if the birth mother has no insurance and she is not able to pay, have the hospital send her the bill. There may be special funds that assist those in a low-income category without insurance, and if you do pay the bill, it will be based on the birth mother's income and not yours.

Some hospitals will try to charge extra if an adoptive couple is paying the bill. Make all arrangements through your attorney's office. He or she can find out how much the hospital charges for delivery, the mother's care, and the nursery. Make sure he examines all the bills! We have twice caught hospitals charging an adoptive couple $4,000 more than they should have. Apparently, because no insurance carrier was paying the bill (and therefore questioning it), the hospital billing department sought to collect extra revenue. These are not isolated examples. When a hospital bill is excessive, your attorney can often negotiate to have it reduced.

What if the hospital bills are excessive because of medical complications? A premature baby with many medical complications can run up a medical bill well over $100,000. Even a $20,000 hospital bill can be beyond the means of many couples. (Hospital bills generally run about $1,000 a day for patients.)

How unfortunate that a loving couple with limited means may have to reconsider an adoption if the baby's hospital bill is beyond their financial ability. If the birth mother changed her mind and decided to raise the child, the hospital would have to absorb the bill anyway. If it is impossible for you to pay for the hospital bill, here are some strategies to consider.

First, see whether your health insurance policy will pay for the baby's expenses. Technically, if you are legally bound to pay the bill, then your insurance company is required by law to cover it. This is a gray area, however, and you want to be very sure. You will probably have to make the decision whether to proceed with the adoption before you get a firm (and written) commitment from the insurance company. Some health maintenance organizations (HMOs) will now pay for the infant's medical expenses if the child is born at a participating hospital and is attended by a participating physician.

Second, make sure your insurance company will pay the baby's medical expenses once she is home with you. You are not obligated to tell your insurance company (although most ask) whether the child is adopted. Do not allow the insurance company to stall you. Call your state health insurance commissioner. Document all phone calls. Federal legislation now requires insurance companies to pay for the medical expenses of an adopted child at placement.

Third, see whether the birth mother qualifies for Medicaid. Medicaid funds will cover the hospital bill. A birth mother can usually obtain Medicaid coverage retroactively up to ninety days after birth, depending on the state.

If the birth mother cannot take responsibility for the bills, have her claim herself as an indigent. Her hospital bills may then be absorbed by special state funds designated for this purpose.

Never allow the hospital billing department to send you bills directly.

If the birth mother will be "paying" the bills, have your attorney send her the money to send to the hospital. Carefully document all paperwork. Save all your canceled checks.

Document every transaction you make and what you have paid, no matter how little or how much you have spent.

The Baby's Delivery

The birth of a baby is one of life's most wonderful events. You may want to share in this experience with the birth mother. Of course, many factors can keep you from doing so. But if it is possible to be there, the birth mother may appreciate your support.

Several factors will help determine whether you can be present at the birth, beginning, of course, with the birth mother's preference. She may want the adoptive parent to be there to give support and encouragement, or she may want this to be "her time" with the baby. She may have other support to help her through labor and delivery—the birth father, a family member, or a special friend.

Some hospitals have a policy about nonfamily members being present at the delivery. In others, as soon as hospital staff hear "adoptive parent," red flags start waving, and a "policy" is suddenly established that forbids your presence. If you and the birth mother are determined that you will be there, you will have to be the birth mother's "friend" or coach and simply not reveal your status to hospital personnel. Some hospitals are very cooperative, while others are very uncooperative. If possible, find out what you can expect before the baby's birth.

Do take your comfort level into consideration. If you nearly faint when you have blood drawn, then you may not be a good candidate to view a baby's delivery, especially if it turns into a cesarean section birth. If a birth mother really wants you there, perhaps you can compromise and hold her hand and look at her face during delivery.

The Length of the Hospital Stay

A mother who has given birth vaginally will generally stay in the hospital one to three days. Most newborns are also released after a couple of days. A woman who has had a cesarean section may stay in the hospital a few days longer than the baby. If a baby has a medical problem, such as jaundice, he may remain in the hospital after the mother is released.

Usually these circumstances present no problem. If the baby is released after the birth mother is, she must sometimes come back to the hospital so that the hospital staff will permit the baby's release.

The Baby's Medical Records

Once the baby is born, you should receive all relevant hospital records. Like any other parent, you should know your child's health history. This information may be important for future use.

In most instances, the staff will tell you the baby's Apgar scores. This test, which is administered one and five minutes after birth, measures five things: skin coloration, pulse rate, muscular tone, respiratory rate, and reflex activity, with a possible score of 0, 1, or 2 in each category, with ten being the best score. This test only describes the baby's overall physical condition in the first five minutes of life—it does not predict the baby's long-term outcome.

A baby who is released from the hospital is generally a healthy child. However, do not expect the hospital to send any records home with the birth mother or you. You may want to have a pediatrician, whom you should have already selected, contact the hospital to receive all medical records. It is best if you can have the birth mother sign a release to have all medical records sent to your pediatrician or attorney. Some hospitals will not release the medical information without the birth mother's signature or will insist on adoption documents before they will release the information.

The Release of the Baby and Birth Mother from the Hospital

For the birth mother, going home from the hospital usually means separation from the baby and can be an especially emotional time for her. If you know her address, you may consider sending flowers or another small token of caring to her home. If you do not have her address, have your attorney's office arrange for the delivery. Ask your attorney what is an appropriate amount to spend without appearing cheap but still remaining within the confines of the law.

The baby will need clothes to wear home from the hospital. Bring these to the hospital after the baby is born or send them through your attorney or the birth mother's friend or family member. Shopping for baby clothes can be very difficult since it is one of the last steps in allowing you to hope and believe that this long-wanted baby will truly be yours. These tiny clothes in a very real way symbolize that wonderful moment of bringing the baby home with you for the first time. If you can, we suggest you purchase a lovely new baby outfit and wash it carefully to protect newborn skin before taking it to the hospital—or borrow an outfit that looks brand-new. If it is too difficult for you to do this yourself, have a friend do it for you.

During our involvement in adoptions over the years, we have at times encountered the unexpected in this area of clothes for the baby to wear home from the hospital—including a wonderful adoptive couple who sent used, stained clothes to the birth mother's attorney. The couple reasoned that there would be no "loss" in case the birth mother changed her mind. It was easier for them to focus on the loss of a few dollars for baby clothes than on the possibility that there could be a loss of their dream of bringing home their baby. Fortunately, the attorney was sensitive enough to buy new clothes to send to the hospital.

Have a clean infant car seat to take the baby home. Many hospitals will not allow you to leave without a car seat, and it is illegal for a child to ride in a vehicle without one.

Potential Problems at the Hospital

By this time, you may well be wondering why some hospital staff seem so hostile toward adoption. In all fairness, hospitals are simply trying to stay out of legal difficulties. Hospital attorneys, social workers, and administrators as a rule know little, if anything, about adoption and the legal process. Each state has very different laws, and sometimes even within a state the laws can vary county by county. To expect hospital staff to have a complete grasp of the law may be expecting too much. Hospitals want to maintain a good public image as well and fear that if an adoption situation is handled improperly, they could be sued or, worse, receive bad publicity. Unfortunately, it often happens that in trying to "keep their hands clean," hospitals end up taking away a birth mother's basic rights such as allowing her to be with the baby or insisting that she care for the baby when it is not her desire to do so. Of course, these reasons do not explain all the problems at hospitals. Social workers also have their own agenda. They have been trained to "preserve" the family unit, meaning that some view adoption as the last option for very desperate women. Some social workers feel they must counsel a birth mother and insist she explain her reasons for wanting to place the baby for adoption. No other patient is required to endure such pressure before she makes a personal, nonmedical decision.

Then there are the nurses and other health care professionals who may not want to deal with a birth mother who will probably not be caring for the infant. In the first place, it may mean more work for the nurses. After all, they, instead of the mother, must feed and change the infant. Second, nurses view the maternity floor as a happy place, and they may not want to see someone leave without her baby. Finally, professionals are accustomed to handling every situation according to a routine, and adoption may mean they have to rethink how they will handle a birth mother and child.

HEALTH RISKS

To cover every possible health problem a child could have would require an entire medical book. Yet, as adoptive parents you do want to know the possible genetic and environmental factors that could influence your child's health so that you can make informed decisions. First, you need this information to assess the medical risks and decide whether you can accept a child with these risk factors. Second, if you proceed with the adoption, your child's medical background may be crucial to his well-being.

It is your attorney's responsibility to do a thorough investigation of the birth parents' medical backgrounds and those of their families. Most birth parents will reveal basic health history information (such as a family history of diabetes or heart disease) to a physician or lawyer. Getting a birth mother to admit her drug and alcohol use during pregnancy is a much more difficult task, and yet obtaining this information is absolutely essential. The consequences of substance or alcohol abuse on the child's development are often profound.

A pregnant woman's use of tobacco, alcohol, or drugs is only one of many risk factors associated with defects in the child. Other risk factors that should be assessed include:

1. *A family history of reproductive problems.*
2. *Multiple previous pregnancies within a short time span.*
3. *Medical problems concurrent with the pregnancy, such as sexually transmitted diseases, diabetes, and heart, liver, or kidney disease.*
4. *Obesity, poor eating habits, or signs of poor nutrition.*
5. *Poor living conditions and lack of education.*
6. *Excessive stress.*
7. *Inadequate prenatal care.* About 15 percent of white women have no prenatal visits in the first trimester of pregnancy; whereas about 25 percent of black and Hispanic women have no prenatal care in the first trimester. It is not unusual for birth mothers to wait until the second or third trimester to seek medical care. Many are not aware of their pregnancy or are in denial. Overall, only a small minority of women have no prenatal care.
8. *Repeated exposure to environmental hazards such as lead, pesticides, or x-rays.*
9. *Being younger than fifteen years old.* Teenage mothers are twice as likely to have low birth weight babies, and they have a higher incidence of obstetrical complications. Low birth weight infants are forty times more likely to die during the first eight days of life and twenty times more likely to die during the first year of life than other infants. Those who live often have developmental problems. Teenage mothers are also more likely to have sexually transmitted diseases, because they are more likely to have had multiple sexual partners.

Genetic Diseases

Whether adopted or not, everyone should know his or her genetic background. Indeed, having a thorough genetic history can be essential in preventing certain diseases. Some diseases with a strong genetic component have an adult onset, such as diabetes. Perhaps because there are no signs for many years, 80 percent of those who have this kind of diabetes do not take the precaution of maintaining good eating habits and are overweight. On the other hand, if you know that diabetes runs in your child's family, you can significantly decrease his likelihood of developing the disease by having a home where good nutrition and regular exercise keep the family in good health and body weight in the normal range. Other genetically linked diseases, such as breast and other cancers, should be screened for more frequently if they run in the family.

Some genetic diseases need to be identified and monitored from birth. For example, newborns are given a routine test for phenylketonuria (PKU), a genetically carried disease. When diagnosed, it can easily be treated by altering the child's diet, but if the disease is not identified or treated, the child can develop profound mental retardation.

If possible, have the birth parents or their parents describe their traits and those of other family members (parents, grandparents, siblings) including:

- Physical characteristics
- Educational experience
- Religion
- Nationality and racial background
- Employment history
- Social adjustments (the way they relate to friends, coworkers, community)
- Interests, hobbies, talents, skills, recreational activities
- Intelligence, aptitude, temperament, personality
- Medical history

Hepatitis B and AIDS

The two sexually transmitted diseases adoptive parents need to be aware of are AIDS (Acquired Immune Deficiency Syndrome) and hepatitis B. Babies are now routinely screened for HIV infection, the virus that causes AIDS, and adoptive parents will be told immediately if the screening is positive.

All babies in the United States now also receive hepatitis B immunoglobulin (in case the child has the disease) and HBV vaccine to prevent getting hepatitis B later in life (such as through sexual contact). Studies have shown that immediate treatment beginning two to twelve hours after the baby's birth with injections of hepatitis B immunoglobulin and hepatitis B vaccine is 85 percent to 95 percent effective in preventing hepatitis B virus chronic carrier status in childhood, in which the disease lasts for more than six months.

In 1993, an estimated 7,000 infants were born to women who carried the AIDS virus. Of these 7,000 infants, between 1,000 and 2,000 were HIV-infected, based on a transmission rate of about 15 percent to 30 percent. In 2003, only an estimated 300 newborns contracted the virus from their mother.

Many misconceptions exist about how a mother transmits HIV to her newborn. Since the fetus does not share the mother's blood supply, it is not exposed to the virus in utero. Rather, it is believed that the newborn contracts HIV when coming in contact with his mother's blood during delivery, if her blood enters his body. One way a woman can reduce the risk of having an HIV-infected newborn is by taking the anti-HIV drug Retrovir (also known as zidovudine or AZT) while pregnant. This greatly reduces the amount of HIV in her blood, thus greatly minimizing her risk of transmitting HIV to her baby during delivery.

Poor Nutrition

Malnutrition is a major cause of low birth weight babies. These babies are ten times more likely to be mentally retarded. A lower birth weight can lead to a lower I.Q. This is not surprising, considering that the baby's brain develops the most during the last trimester of pregnancy and the first month after birth. A birth mother who is undernourished can cause irreversible neurological and brain underdevelopment. Lack of oxygen, birth injuries, and respiratory distress, moreover, mostly affect babies who weigh less than five and a half pounds.

Most women should gain at least twenty-four pounds during pregnancy. Studies have shown that a thirty-five pound weight gain produces babies who weigh an average of eight pounds. These larger babies are more active, mentally more alert, and generally healthier than five-pound babies.

BIRTH MOTHERS AND SUBSTANCE ABUSE

Certain medical problems can arise if a birth mother uses drugs, alcohol, or tobacco during her pregnancy. Although the problems associated with these substances are not always apparent at birth, they may, for example, develop into a learning disability when the child reaches age five.

Yet, a birth mother's use of these substances does not guarantee that the child will have problems. Only 30 percent of babies born to mothers who used crack or cocaine, for example, display health or learning problems. Most birth defects are not attributable to maternal drug and alcohol use but to genetic or other factors.

If you suspect that a birth mother is using drugs or alcohol during her pregnancy, find out as much as possible about the effects on the unborn child of the substance she is using and the problems that may arise from this as the child matures.

What You Need to Know

You will want a detailed list of any over-the-counter and prescription medications or illicit drugs a woman has used during her pregnancy. Certain medications, whether prescribed by a doctor or not, can have a detrimental effect on the fetus.

To find out about a birth mother's possible tobacco, drug, and alcohol use, a doctor, lawyer, or adoption counselor needs to ask the appropriate questions. Unfortunately, although the doctor is certainly the most appropriate person to raise this issue, few doctors know how to ask a pregnant woman about her drug history in a way that elicits an accurate response. Sometimes a woman is simply not honest; at other times, she just does not know how to answer a direct yet vague question like "Do you use drugs?" Her idea of what constitutes a "drug" or "drug use" may be different from the doctor's.

If you are involved in an identified adoption, the agency, by law, is responsible for investigating and evaluating the medical condition and background of all children to be adopted and to communicate that information to the adoptive parents. It is up to the agency, therefore, to ask appropriate questions. Certainly an adoption counselor, such as a physician, is in a better position than you or your attorney to raise these sensitive questions. If you are using an agency, make sure that the counselor investigates all avenues to determine any medical problems or history of drug or alcohol use.

In the case of an independent adoption, however, because you cannot depend upon the birth mother's obstetrician, you may have to ask your attorney to collect this sensitive information as part of the woman's medical background. It may be a little more difficult for an attorney to find an appropriate way to ask a woman about her alcohol and drug use. After all, he is representing the couple, and the birth mother may see these questions as a threat. He must, however, carefully and tactfully pose the questions to elicit a truthful response; it is his legal responsibility to obtain all information important to a child's health and to share this information with the adoptive parents. Make it clear to your attorney that you want this information. If you are working with an agency, your attorney should check to make sure the agency has investigated the drug use issue thoroughly.

Of course, you may be the person most likely to see the birth mother on a regular basis. However, it is a very delicate matter for adoptive parents to ask questions that relate to substance abuse. You cannot bluntly pose such a question, but through discussion and some leading questions, you may be able to elicit some honest responses.

In asking a woman whether she is using tobacco, alcohol, or drugs, the following techniques can be helpful. The first is to frame questions about substance abuse within the context of another questionnaire. A medical or dietary intake form, for example, can ask, "What do you like to drink: water, milk, juice, beer, soft drinks, wine, iced tea?" That way, the woman's drinking history is asked matter-of-factly, minimizing any embarrassment.

Another technique is simply to ask the woman about substance abuse, but to keep your tone casual. Ask whether she ever used illicit drugs in the same sentence, if possible, in which you ask her about prescription and over-the-counter drugs. You might ask, "Are you taking any medications or drugs such as aspirin, cold medications, vitamins, or prescription medicines such as Phenobarbital, or other drugs such as cocaine, crystal, speed, barbiturates, or heroin?" Notice that this question moves from over-the-counter medications to prescription medications to illicit drugs. You could ask whether she has ever used stimulants or tranquilizers. Use the specific brand names of the drugs. For example, ask, "Do you take Valium?"

If she answers yes to any of these questions, then in the same casual tone, ask what her approximate maximum use or consumption is. Try to "normalize" immoderate consumption so that she does not feel ashamed. When a woman answers, for example, that she drinks beer, ask "How much do you drink—two or three cans or about one or two six-packs a day?" If she sees that you are comfortable discussing these amounts of alcohol consumption, she is more likely to be honest with you. When asking about consumption, it is important to follow up by asking "Do you ever use more?" The purpose of this question is to determine whether the woman ever binges on alcohol or drugs or both.

If direct questions do not seem appropriate for any reason, asking a woman about how she relaxes, deals with stress, and handles her emotions can be a good way to lead into questions about alcohol and drug use. Ask questions like these: "How do you usually relax when you are tired or stressed?" "Do you find that smoking a cigarette helps you to relax?" "Do you talk with a friend over a drink or take some time out for yourself?"

You can also ask what kinds of drugs she has "tried" in the past. A woman who is too embarrassed to tell you that she is using drugs during her pregnancy may be willing to reveal that she has used them just before pregnancy. If so, this is a strong indicator that she is still using them or at least used them before she found out she was pregnant. Many birth mothers do not know they are pregnant until three to four months into their pregnancy. Even if she states truthfully that she did not use drugs or alcohol after she found out she was pregnant, she may still have used them up to her second trimester. If a woman admits that she has used tobacco, alcohol, and drugs in the past, try to get as much detailed information as possible about previous use.

Physicians are in a position to administer questionnaires about drug use and to include a drug screening as part of a routine urine test. The questionnaire may even state, "Your urine will be tested for diabetes and for drug use. Do you know of any drugs that may be in your urine?" Women often provide very accurate answers to such questionnaires. A skilled physician may know how to ask a woman directly about her drug and alcohol use in a way that gets an honest response.

It is very difficult to get an honest answer from a birth mother. Usually, birth mothers will readily admit tobacco use throughout the pregnancy and will say they drank some alcohol before pregnancy or before they knew they were pregnant. But hardly any women will admit alcohol or drug use after knowing they are pregnant. This may explain why so much is known about how the amount of tobacco used while pregnant has an increased detrimental outcome for the children. It is also well known that increased alcohol consumption while pregnant also increases developmental and behavioral problems in the children. However, it appears that women can drink very little and still have detrimental effects on their children. These seemingly small doses of alcohol during pregnancy causing serious problems in the children may be due to the fact that women greatly underreport their consumption of alcohol. As to the use of drugs, drugs tend to stay in the body for extended periods of time after use, so a "drug test" can reveal drug use even if the woman stopped using them weeks before being tested. Therefore, even for women who do not admit to using drugs or underreport their use, the tests can determine the truth.

Helping Women with Substance Abuse Problems

Physicians, agency caseworkers, and other professionals have an obligation to talk to birth mothers about substance abuse and its consequences for the developing fetus. Many women, when told of the harmful effects that tobacco, alcohol, and drugs can have on the unborn child, will stop using these substances. Such information must be given in a simple and positive manner so that it is clear and well understood. If the risks associated with a certain drug are exaggerated, the birth mother may dismiss the message to quit. For example, it would be inappropriate to insist that a woman stop drinking all caffeinated beverages. Here are examples of positive language: If you stop drinking alcohol now, you will have a better chance of having a healthier baby. You and the baby will feel better if you are sober.

If gentle encouragement is not enough incentive for her to quit smoking, drinking, or using drugs, the woman is addicted and cannot quit without help. She will need to be referred to a treatment center. Making a good referral, however, is not always easy. Some treatment centers will not accept pregnant women. Women who use one drug often abuse another (most people in treatment centers are also smokers, yet smoking as an addiction is seldom addressed).

Ideally, a pregnant woman should receive comprehensive treatment both for her dependency and for her pregnancy. A multidisciplinary approach employing social workers, nurses, doctors, and counselors best meets a woman's needs.

THE SIGNS AND RESULTS OF SUBSTANCE ABUSE
Sometimes simple, careful observation of a birth mother can provide information about possible substance abuse. Here are some of the clues and symptoms associated with various substances:

Tobacco

- Dry coughing, yellow stains on fingers and teeth, "tobacco breath."
- Jitteriness. If you meet with her for an extended period of time, you may notice that after an hour or so she has to use the ladies' room or go outside.
- A sibling who smokes. According to research, the strongest indicator of a teenager's being a smoker is if an older sibling smokes.

Alcohol

- History of a previous low-birth-weight delivery. If a woman had a previous pregnancy, find out the child's weight and whether the birth mother had any problems in delivery, particularly placental abnormalities.
- The smell of alcohol on her breath.
- A family history of alcohol abuse.
- No prenatal care.

Drugs

- Disease. Diseases that are spread through intravenous use, such as hepatitis B and hepatitis C, can be one indication that a woman has used drugs.

- Malnourishment. Drug abusers often eat poorly, leading to malnourishment.
- Nasal inflammation can be evidence of snorting cocaine; needle scars ("track" marks) on the inside of the arm or other places can be evidence of use of illegal intravenous drug use. Some users try to cover up these marks with long sleeves, even in hot weather. Unusually large (dilated) pupils or unusually small (pinpoint) pupils can also be signs of drug use. Drug users sometimes wear sunglasses to hide their abnormal pupil size.

Nicotine

Here are some of the possible effects of nicotine on a newborn infant:

- Low birth weight. Low birth weight babies are forty times more likely than normal weight babies to die before they are one month old. Those who do survive may have health problems, including mental retardation, cerebral palsy, and hearing and visual problems.
- Increased risk of physical abnormalities.
- Malformations such as heart defects, cleft palate, and hernias.
- Central nervous system defects.
- Threefold risk of sudden infant death syndrome (SIDS).

As the child grows, the following problems may arise:

- Hyperactivity and lack of self-control.
- Decreased attention span.
- Irritability.
- Decreased language development.
- Decreased academic ability.

Alcohol

Among the health problems associated with prenatal alcohol use, fetal alcohol syndrome is the most serious. Indeed, prenatal exposure to alcohol is now considered more dangerous to the health of the child than cocaine. Its consequences include:

- Growth retardation (decreased weight, height, and head circumference)
- Specific facial abnormalities (the eyes are almond-shaped, the nose is short and upturned, the upper lip is thin, and the area between the mouth and nose is flattened)

- Decreased intellectual and motor abilities, as well as microencephaly (small head and profound mental retardation)

Long-term problems include such psychosocial problems as poor judgment, short attention span, and inability to pick up social cues and form friendships. These problems are evident into adulthood, even in those with normal IQs. They interfere with learning, and most of the children cannot live or work independently when they reach adulthood. Children who are raised in foster care or adopted do not do better than those raised by their birth families. FAS is the third leading cause of mental retardation after Down syndrome and spina bifida in the United States and the leading cause of mental retardation in the world. Unlike these disabilities, however, FAS is completely preventable.

It is difficult to recognize FAS in a newborn. Small size and abnormal behavior in the newborn can result from any number of factors, including prenatal exposure to cigarettes or drugs. The typical FAS facial features may not be apparent. In an international adoption, the diagnosis may be even more difficult, especially when no maternal history is known, no growth and developmental records are available, and poor growth and development may be attributed to living in an orphanage and poor nutrition.

A physician diagnosing FAS must recognize three problem areas: pre- or postnatal growth deficiency, central nervous system abnormality, and facial signs. When a child has abnormal findings in one or more of these areas with a suspected history of prenatal exposure, the term "fetal alcohol effect" (rather than "fetal alcohol syndrome") or "subclinical FAS" is often used. In other words, while the symptoms are not severe enough to diagnosis a child with the syndrome, they do have significant problems. Research in animals shows that just one-fifth the amount of alcohol needed to produce the obvious problems associated with FAS can cause learning problems in the offspring. Such problems are not noticeable in infancy, but the effects can manifest themselves as the child grows.

Heavy drinking is defined as having two or more drinks per day or fourteen or more per week. A drink is equal to one twelve-ounce beer; one four-ounce glass of wine; or one one-ounce glass of distilled spirits such as vodka, whiskey, or scotch. Problems associated with heavy drinking include:

- Classic FAS
- Partial FAS or "fetal alcohol effect"
- Sleep disturbances
- Jitteriness
- Poor muscle tone

- Poor sucking response
- Minimal brain dysfunction
- Slight malformations
- Behavior problems such as hyperactivity, decreased alertness, disrupted sleep patterns, feeding difficulties, and decreased intellectual capability

As the amount and frequency of alcohol consumption increase, so do the likelihood and extent of medical problems. Even two drinks a day can cause growth retardation. Fetal alcohol effects can occur in babies whose mothers have two to four drinks a day about 10 percent of the time during the pregnancy. This means there are potential problems for the baby if a pregnant woman has two drinks only three or four days a month.

Studies suggest that pregnant women should not consume any alcohol. The American Council on Science and Health (ACSH) recommends that women avoid alcohol completely throughout their pregnancies.

Alcohol can have different effects at different stages of fetal development. In the beginning stages of pregnancy, about six drinks per week are too much, even if the woman stops drinking after she learns that she is pregnant. Alcohol can impair or halt the delivery of oxygen through the umbilical cord. During the first months of pregnancy, even a few minutes of oxygen deprivation can have negative effects on the fetus's brain. Alcohol can also interfere with the passage of nutrients through the placenta to the fetus.

How does one decide whether to adopt a baby who has been prenatally exposed to alcohol? First, it is important to recognize that the likelihood of a birth mother having consumed some alcohol during pregnancy is very high, especially if she is a young woman enduring an unplanned pregnancy. Working with a birth mother who has taken a few drinks at the beginning of her pregnancy is probably not taking an unnecessary risk. With evidence now indicating that the higher the birth mother's level of alcohol intake, the more likely the child will develop learning or other medical problems, adoptive couples will want to know about a birth mother's drinking patterns during her pregnancy. The more you know, the more informed a decision you can make. Perhaps you are willing to accept a child who has been exposed to alcohol, but not if the child has profound problems.

Even if the likelihood of the child's having fetal alcohol syndrome or its effects is low, you should think carefully beforehand about the possibility. If you feel you cannot accept the risk of problems that may not even manifest themselves until the child is in school, then you should not continue dealing with a birth mother whose drinking history is questionable. In some cases, the problems are apparent as soon as the child is born. An infant with profound FAS will probably display at birth the facial characteristics associated with the syndrome. If so, you will need to decide then whether or not you want to rear a child who may also be mentally retarded or have a lower-than-average IQ.

For more information, the National Organization on Fetal Alcohol Syndrome home page at *www.nofas.org* offers information and resources for families affected by FAS. To view pictures of children with FAS and obtain additional resources, visit *www.come-over.to/fasstar.*

Cocaine

Cocaine can pose a great threat to unborn babies, beginning with its tendency to cause a decrease in the mother's overall functioning—which then can lead to even more drug use by the mother and poor prenatal care. Some of the other effects include:

- Threefold risk of premature birth.
- Increased risk of a stroke (caused by increased fetal blood pressure). This is rare but can cause permanent brain damage.
- Smaller head circumference, which may mean the child will have a smaller brain.
- Increased likelihood of low weight at birth. Low birth weight babies are forty times more likely than babies with a normal weight to die before they are one month old. Those who do survive have increased health problems, including mental retardation, cerebral palsy, and hearing and visual problems.
- Tenfold risk of sudden infant death syndrome (SIDS).
- Increased likelihood of genitourinary defects that can cause infections.

As with any drug exposure, the most significant long-term effects of prenatal cocaine exposure are on a child's behavior. As cocaine-exposed children mature, they have a higher risk of developmental and learning problems. Many of these problems can be minimized through a good environment.

It is also vital to remember that the parent's expectation of their child's outcome in and of itself has a tremendous role in their child's growth and well-being. If the parents live in a state of anxiety waiting for signs of problem behaviors and developmental delays, this is a very uneasy environment in which the child will grow up. Negative expectations place a tremendous burden on the child, as he knows on some level his parents' attitude toward him: that he is damaged and will never really be like other children. Perhaps most importantly, parents' negative expectations greatly hinder their own ability to open their heart to the child and love him with a big heart, an optimistic heart that has chosen to hope for the best, and to deal with issues as they come up rather than constantly anticipating the worst.

If you are planning to adopt a baby who has been exposed to cocaine, understand that he may need special attention, particularly during the first eight to ten weeks, when he may be extremely sensitive to stimuli. Even eye contact can overload the child's system, causing him to close his eyes. Often the baby is either crying or in a deep sleep, making it difficult to bond with him. Parents may be convinced that the child simply doesn't love them.

The problem is not psychological, however, but physiological. This means that it is not the baby's emotions, but rather the baby's body that may not be able to tolerate more than the slightest amount of stimulation, including light, sound, touch, smell, sight, and activity. It is somewhat like the baby is born with a migraine that lasts for several weeks. The most loving thing is not to hold your baby all the time, sing to him, and leave his bassinet in the living room so that he doesn't miss out on any of the family action. Rather, if you know that quiet aloneness may be the best thing for him for awhile, you will quietly meet his needs for food and diaper changes and not take it personally that he is not ready to interact with you. He will be ready soon enough, and it will be an extra pleasure when he is ready for more eye contact, more touch, and more time with you. With early intervention, children can develop normally and can even be mainstreamed.

Heroin and Opiates

Heroin and opiates belong to a group of drugs called opioids, which are natural and synthetic drugs that act primarily on the central nervous system. They include such therapeutic medicines as morphine, opium, codeine, meperidine (Demerol), oxycodone (Percodan), and methadone (Dolophine), which is used in treating heroin dependency.

Heroin can be taken in different forms, but mostly it is injected. Pregnancy complications for heroin addicts include early separation of the placenta, premature labor, and ruptured membranes. Toxemia during pregnancy affects 10 percent to 15 percent of addicts, resulting in high blood pressure and even seizures. About half of infants born to heroin-abusing women with no prenatal care have low birth weight, and 80 percent have serious medical problems. The chaotic lifestyles of addicts also increase their chances of contracting AIDS through sex or needle sharing. Heroin readily crosses the placenta. If the mother suddenly stops taking the drug while pregnant, the fetus can experience withdrawal and die. Although opioid exposure before birth is not associated with an increased risk for physical malformations, researchers reported that one in four infants born to mothers in the methadone treatment program they studied had strabismus, a visual disorder in which the infant's eyes cannot focus properly. It was unclear whether heroin or other drugs had caused the disorder.

Between 60 percent and 90 percent of these newborns born to heroin-abusing women develop withdrawal symptoms and require special gentle handling and medication. Like the jittery cocaine babies, it is challenging to care for these babies. Withdrawal symptoms can include high-pitched crying, fever, irregular breathing, and seizures within forty-eight to seventy-two hours after birth. Occasionally, these symptoms do not begin until two to four weeks after birth. Irritability resulting from overarousal usually ends at about one month but can last up to three months or more.

After these babies are a month old, however, only subtle differences can be observed between them and those not exposed to narcotics in utero. Muscle development may be uneven, and coordination may be impaired. Studies are difficult to conduct since mothers often drop out of the studies, and the home environments usually make it difficult to distinguish problems associated with drug exposure from those stemming from poor parenting. Like the cocaine-exposed children, physical and psychological development seems to be within normal ranges, but speech development may be impaired.

PCP

PCP (Phencyclidine) is a synthetic drug with no clinical use. Very little research has been conducted on prenatally exposed infants because women who take PCPs often take other drugs as well.

Like infants born to mothers who use cocaine or heroin, PCP-exposed newborns are jittery, have poor visual coordination, and are difficult to console. Although these babies alternate between restlessness and calm, they do not have withdrawal symptoms. Animal studies suggest that PCP at very high doses may cause birth defects.

Marijuana

There is limited knowledge about the long-term effects marijuana has on the developing fetus. It is known, however, that its primary component easily crosses the placenta. Marijuana use may be associated with low birth weight and birth defects similar to those with fetal alcohol syndrome and depression of the central nervous system in the newborn.

Sedatives and Tranquilizers

All minor tranquilizers have been associated with increased fetal malformations if used during the first trimester of pregnancy. These birth defects are similar to those of babies with fetal alcohol syndrome. Nearly all the infants are also significantly below normal birth weight.

Valium (diazepam). When taken in the first trimester, Valium increases fourfold the likelihood of a cleft palate, lip anomalies, and malformations of the heart and arteries. This risk increases when Valium is combined with smoking and alcohol. If it is taken within the last two to four months of pregnancy, even in low dosages (ten to fifteen milligrams), the infant may suffer from tremors, lethargy, and other symptoms associated with withdrawal in newborns.

Barbiturates. Barbiturates are commonly used drugs that include sedative hypnotics and antiseizure medications. They are associated with birth defects similar to fetal alcohol syndrome. Infants born to mothers who use barbiturates can suffer from tremors, restlessness, high-pitched crying, and convulsions.

Prescription Drugs

Accutane (isotretinoin). Accutane, an antiacne medication, is associated with major abnormalities such as microencephalus (small head with severe mental retardation) and external ear and cardiovascular defects.

Antibiotics. Some antibiotics, including tetracycline and some sulfanilamides, when taken during the last four to five months of pregnancy may cause permanent discoloration of the child's teeth. For the most part, antibiotics are considered safe.

WHAT RISKS CAN YOU ACCEPT?

Before you adopt, you and your spouse will want to decide what conditions you can and cannot accept in a child. Your decisions will also influence the kind of adoption that you will choose. For example, you may be able to accept a problem if it is present right at birth (such as cleft palate) and you know the exact treatment that the child will receive (e.g., surgery and speech therapy). However, you may not be able to accept a child who may develop learning problems later on because the birth mother used cocaine occasionally during her pregnancy. If you are an anxious person and tend to expect the worst, it is probably not fair to you or to the child for you to adopt this kind of child whose problems may manifest themselves when the child starts school. Don't tell yourself that you "should" be able to adopt this kind of child. Rather, be realistic about the fact that we are all human and have our own strengths and weaknesses. Be honest with yourself and with the agency when they ask you what problems you can or cannot accept and to what degree.

You may have to assume on some level that a birth mother may have drunk at least some alcohol, taken some over-the-counter medicines, and perhaps even used illicit drugs. You may have to base your decision on your gut feelings and the actual health of the baby at delivery.

With your spouse, list the medical conditions you could accept and those that you could not. In each case, ask yourselves if you could truly accept a child with this disease. Could you live with the condition and all it may entail? Would you constantly be looking for any sign of the disease, to the child's detriment? For example, a professional psychologist and her husband were told of a birth mother who had a three-generation family history of clinical depression. Knowing this, the couple felt they would be on the lookout for signs of depression at all times, and this would be bad for the child.

Based on the conditions you agree you can accept, ask yourselves next what resources you have that can enable you to handle each condition appropriately. Include financial resources, time, personal strength and patience, support systems, and access to care.

What If You Cannot Accept the Child's Health Status?

The choice is yours. Do not feel guilty if you cannot accept certain medical problems. You have the right to choose, just as the birth mother has the right to select you as parents and then to change her mind. Remember, many couples are willing to adopt newborns with physical problems and mental retardation.

One day a birth mother contacted our office and said that she had a one-week-old baby who had a 95 percent chance of developing muscular dystrophy (MD)—a condition in which the child can have profound disabilities and an early death. The child's MD status could not be determined for sure until he was three months old. We contacted a couple that same day, the couple said they were interested, and that day the child went home with his adoptive parents.

Another couple was ready to adopt a baby through private channels. After the baby was born, the birth mother revealed that she had used cocaine during her pregnancy, having previously stated that she was not using drugs. The couple decided that they did not want to take any chances; yet they felt very guilty because they had visited the baby in the hospital and were concerned about her overall future, especially if the birth mother decided to raise the child herself. An agency was contacted, and the child was immediately placed in a loving home. Fortunately, the baby is perfectly healthy and at this point shows no adverse effects from drug exposure.

Adoption is a positive choice in our society, although it is not always viewed that way. As a prospective adoptive parent, however, you should not make the decision to adopt based on your concern about the negative environment the child may encounter if you do not. This is not a good reason to adopt a child. Children have the right to be loved for themselves, not because someone felt sorry for them. No adoptive parent should be a martyr, and no child should be considered a burden.

If you decide that you cannot go ahead with an adoption, refer the birth mother to another couple or to an agency with the resources to place the baby with a loving couple. Virtually all babies, no matter how severe their condition, can be placed in an adoptive home.

Genetic Illness

Should you proceed with an adoption if genetic illness is in the family? When agreeing to commit yourself to a birth mother, even one who does not use alcohol, tobacco, or drugs, you know that the baby has at least the same risk of medical problems as if you yourself had given birth. None of us lives in a risk-free world, even in the best circumstances. Some risks, however, are known and calculated. If a birth mother tells you that a certain kind of genetic illness has been diagnosed in her family, then you must decide whether you can accept a child who may have the genetic potential for it.

If a baby is to be born with a genetic disease like hemophilia, you must first decide whether you can accept a child who has this disease. If you cannot and you know it, be honest with the birth mother and tell her so. You may know of other couples who are interested in adopting a child with this disease. It is comforting to be able to give a birth mother the name of a couple or an adoption agency. If you are uncertain about accepting a particular medical condition, tell the birth mother that your acceptance depends upon how profound the problem is. You could wait until the child is born or ask for amniocentesis, if appropriate, and then tell the birth mother whether you are interested in adopting the baby. If you can accept the disease, start to research what help you could provide the child to minimize the impact of the disease.

Mental Illness

In some ways, it is harder to accept a child who may develop a disease later in childhood. For some the uncertainty is worse than dealing with the disease itself. You may feel as if you are living with a time bomb, particularly if the child has a genetic predisposition to certain mental illnesses.

One couple had agonized over whether to adopt a baby whose family has a history of schizophrenia. They decided that they would find it very difficult to raise a child who might develop the disease in early adolescence. In some ways, they wished they had not known since their knowledge meant that they would always be looking for a sign of mental illness in the child. This watchfulness could cause them to overreact to any emotional problems the child might have. After much discussion, the couple decided not to adopt this baby.

Very often, the birth mother's genetic history is known, but not the birth father's. Had it been the birth father with a family history of schizophrenia, it is likely that no one would ever have known, and the couple would have adopted the baby. Someone with one manic-depressive parent has about a 20 percent chance of inheriting the disease. If the birth father is very young, he may not even have begun to display the behavior associated with manic depression. No one would know that he would someday have the condition or that he is a genetic carrier.

HOW TO ACCEPT A CHILD WITH A MEDICAL CONDITION

Just as people dream of the ideal biological child, those who are infertile resolve to adopt and then begin to fantasize about the ideal adopted child. If a problem does arise, you can go through another stage of resolution and accept the condition. Some people are better suited than others to deal with a child's medical condition or disability. You may not know how strongly you may feel for a child, and you may find yourself willing to rear a child who has limitations.

Get all the information you can. If a problem does arise during pregnancy or right after birth, your attorney should get hold of the birth mother's and child's medical records so that he and you can discuss the possible problems with the attending physicians.

If you adopt a child with a medical condition or disability, let him know that you accept him. A few years down the road, a child who is different will know it. Accepting a child who has a medical or behavior problem or the potential for one is like accepting any other child—adopted or biological. We accept a child for who he is—not what we want him to become. Having a child with a disability can cause us to become more aware of the things that we unthinkingly say about other people's habits, the way they look, and their choices. To show your child that you accept him, demonstrate that you accept all kinds of people. This can mean that you participate in intercultural events, that you restrict your comments about other people's habits and characteristics, and that you show an interest in a broad range of subjects and ideas.

Know your financial limitations. A child born with an acute medical condition needs care that may not be covered by your insurance. Hospital bills, for instance, can be tremendous. Have your attorney make arrangements so that if you do proceed with the adoption that you are not responsible for the child's medical bills. One way of doing this is to use an adoption agency, which may then be able to apply for Medicaid to finance the child's hospital costs. Another is to get state funds to support the child. For more about financial assistance for special needs children, read Chapter 18 Adoption Expenses.

You may find, however, that your insurance will cover all the child's medical needs. Adopted children can now have the same medical coverage that biological children have. The Omnibus Budget Reconciliation Act of 1993 mandates that as long as your group health insurance from your employer covers dependents, then adopted children are covered by the same standards as soon as they are placed with you. There cannot be restricted coverage because the child has a preexisting condition. This legislation may benefit the child and your pocketbook before the child even comes home. For example, if a newborn baby has surgery while in the hospital and the birth mother is not permitted to sign a consent terminating her rights until three or more days after birth, your insurance company is probably obligated to pay for the baby's surgery.

If a child is covered by Medicaid and has complications after birth requiring expensive medical intervention, check with your insurance company first to see what it will pay for once the consent for adoption is signed. You may want to delay having the birth mother sign a consent while the child is in the hospital if you are not sure your insurance company will pay all medical expenses. Often Medicaid coverage does not extend to the child once the baby is placed for adoption—even if he is still in the hospital. You do not want to be in a situation where you are morally or legally obligated to pay tens of thousands of dollars because you were in health insurance limbo.

Chapter Twenty

Preparing for a Baby's Homecoming

In preparing for a new baby or child's homecoming, one of your first tasks will be to select a pediatrician. If you are adopting internationally, once your child is home, you may want to take her to a clinic that specializes in evaluation of internationally adopted children. Usually such a place will not be close to home, so this will be a special visit.

If you are adopting a child through the social services department, you will want to find a pediatrician who is aware of the special risk factors in your child's life and who will be sensitive and knowledgeable about such.

If you are adopting an infant, contact a pediatrician before the baby is born and explain that you will be adopting and would like to have the child examined soon after placement. The doctor's response should give you a good idea of her attitude about adoption. Most pediatricians understand the situation and do not expect you to have the child's or birth parents' complete medical histories. If you are adopting a newborn infant, also ask whether the pediatrician would be willing to call the hospital physician who treated the baby to discuss the baby's overall health, since the records may not arrive for a few weeks.

If your child is born in another state, you may have to select a pediatrician there for the child's first visit since you may have to stay in the state where the baby is born for a week or more until you receive Interstate Compact approval. Call an adoption support group in that area for a recommendation.

Because some hospitals may not give you a full medical history of the infant, you will need to have him examined within a day or two of his release from the hospital, not to determine whether he is healthy enough to proceed with the adoption, but simply to reassure yourself that all is well. If there are any medical problems, they are almost certain to be minor ones since no infant with a serious illness or condition would be released from the hospital.

INFANT AND CHILD CARE
Like any first-time parent, you will want to know how to care for an infant, baby, or child. Nothing can substitute for experience, and if you have not spent much time

or any time caring for a child, the best thing you can do to prepare for parenthood is to spend more time with the children you know, such as nieces and nephews or neighbors' children. If you feel comfortable, you may eventually want to take care of them on your own. When friends and family members know that you are pursuing adoption, they will probably be more than glad to "help" you in this way!

Most couples get some infant care training in childbirth classes; but more and more hospitals, agencies, and adoption support groups are offering infant care and parenting classes that are separate from childbirth classes. Call a local chapter of RESOLVE or another adoption support group for information.

In addition to taking classes, it is a good idea to buy or borrow from the library a general baby care book such as Penelope Leach's *Your Child from Birth to Five Years Old*. Such books can be found in any general bookstore. If you are adopting an older child, buy a book that addresses what a typical child of that age is like. Most likely, your child will not be a typical child of his particular age if he is coming from an institution or through the foster care system. Reading such a book, however, can give you a base as to what is "normal behavior" for a six-year-old so that you can determine if the child's actions are typical for his age or if his behavior is way out of range. Friends and relatives may have valuable advice in this area, although they have limited experience and have their own biases about you and probably about adopted children. Physicians and teachers, while not without their own biases, have a more balanced view of where your child falls in the range of what a child his age should be doing.

Breastfeeding or Bottle-feeding

You may have heard that adoptive mothers can breastfeed their children. This is true. Because there are many advantages for the child in receiving breast milk as opposed to formula, you may want to consider breastfeeding. Approach it realistically, however. Most women who have nursed an adopted infant did so for less than a month. It is difficult and tiring, and even maximum milk production supplies only 25 percent of the milk your child needs. The rest must come from formula or from purchased breast milk (expensive and not readily available). Of course, getting some human milk, with its natural antibodies, is better than formula alone.

If you decide to pursue this option, your doctor may offer to prescribe hormones—prolactin and oxytocin—to cause milk production. Debra Stewart Peterson suggests in *Breastfeeding the Adopted Baby*, however, that you not take these drugs. She says the baby's regular nursing will send the message to your pituitary gland to produce these hormones naturally, stimulating milk production. Also, some women experience fatigue with these medications.

To prepare for nursing an adopted child, Peterson suggests wearing nipple shells to stimulate the hormone oxytocin, instead of pumping your breasts before the baby is placed with you. Once the baby is with you, start using a supplemental device called Supplemental Nutrition System or Lact-Aid. This delivers formula to the baby by a very small diameter tube that is taped close to your nipple. Every time the child nurses, she is sucking your nipple and the tubing (which gives her formula) at the same time. Her sucking on your nipples will stimulate the hormones that will cause you to produce milk. Lest it remain a mystery how this gentle sucking could stimulate your breasts to produce milk, this is no gentle sucking! These little ones are serious about their calorie intake. Of course, you may find it difficult to get the formula warmed up and attach the tubing to your breasts while your infant is crying for milk, especially in the middle of the night. Peterson writes that the less stressed you are during these weeks of building up your milk supply, the easier it will be for your body to produce milk.

Even if you know ahead of time that you would like to try nursing your infant, you may not want to pump your breasts, wear nipple shells, or take hormones before the child's birth in case the birth mother changes her mind or the adoption does not proceed as quickly as you had anticipated.

Some resources on breastfeeding and adoption include:

www.lalecheleague.org/NB/NBadoptive.html Call 800-LA LECHE
The Adoptive Breastfeeding Resource Web site—*www.fourfriends.com/abrw*
Debra Stewart Peterson's book *Breastfeeding the Adopted Baby*

Infant Equipment

Of course, you will be excited about preparing a nursery. We recommend, however, that you not set up a nursery until you actually have the baby. Just keep the room in reserve, ready for a baby, and if you like, cover the walls in a color scheme that will coordinate with baby decor. We decorated our nursery in yellow wallpaper—just in case we ever had children. When selecting the pattern, we knew we could not stand to look at teddy bears or other baby motifs until we actually had a child.

You may want to ask some friends or family to hold on to a few basic items, such as undershirts and one-piece pajamas, a bassinet or cradle, and a car seat. You could arrange with a friend whose child has outgrown his infant gear and clothing to let you use some of these items until you have your own. As soon as you take the baby home, your friends and family will probably inundate you with gifts. In any case, the only items you will really need to begin with are some warm blankets and a few outfits. The hospital usually sends the child home with formula and diapers, and you will not need a crib until the child is about two or three months old. In fact, if you suddenly get a call to pick up a baby, there's nothing wrong with taking a drawer out of the bureau and lining it with blankets for a cradle.

NAMING THE CHILD

Selecting a name for an adopted child is not very different from selecting a name for a biological child. Sometimes, however, there may be special considerations.

In years past, the birth mother selected the child's name, and the adoptive parents called the child by that name. During the last few decades, however, the birth mother has selected a name to go on the original birth certificate, and the adoptive parents have selected another name that goes on the child's permanent birth certificate. Now, as open adoption becomes more acceptable, a birth mother may request that you give the child a name she has selected, or you may request that she put the name you have selected on the original birth certificate. Why? Because when you communicate with the birth parents, it is easier and less awkward for everyone to refer to the child by the same name. You do not want the birth mother referring to the child as Melinda when you named her Catherine. By keeping the names similar or the same, you preserve the child's original identity instead of taking it away. When older adoptees meet their birth mothers, the first two questions they often ask are "What did you name me?" and "Why did you place me for adoption?"

If your birth mother asks you to give the child a name you do not like, consider using it as a middle name. Sometimes, however, you may need to suggest that she reconsider the name she has chosen. If the birth mother tells you that she is giving the child a name she has always loved, or is naming him after a dear cousin who died, or is selecting a name for some other very strong reason, suggest that she not do so. Encourage her to choose a name that she truly loves but to save the special name for later when she is married and prepared to raise a child. If she gives the child a name that has a strong sentimental association, she may identify the adoption with that person or tragic event. For example, she does not need to be reminded of her adoption plans every time she hears her deceased father's name mentioned.

If your child has an ethnic look that is different from yours—such as if he clearly looks Spanish and you and your spouse are of Norwegian extraction—giving your child a very Nordic family name may cause comment such as "How did such a dark-haired boy get the name Leif?" Try not to select a name that will make the child feel he must continually explain why his name does not "match" his looks.

Once you have selected a name, discuss your choice with the birth mother, if you feel it is appropriate to do so. Perhaps together you can agree on a name for the baby.

When adopting an older child, the circumstances can be quite different. If your child is a toddler, you may want to gradually change your child's name by combining it with the child's original name. As soon as some internationally adopted children realize that they now have an "American" name, they don't want to be called by their original name—just as some internationally adopted children no longer want to speak in their original tongue but prefer English.

If the child is older than a toddler, then you probably want to give the child a choice. For example, an eight-year-old adopted through the social services system very much wanted to change his name. He really liked his new uncle, Herman, so he considered this as his new name. His mother suggested that he take a more common name, and so the child decided on Michael.

Another woman, who is an adoptive mother of children through social services, was also adopted herself. She remembers her adoptive mother renaming her and did not like her new name. Her original name was Sarah, and she was thankful that when she adopted her daughter, her daughter's name happened to be Sarah, which, of course, she did not change.

One mother tells the story of her son from Guatemala:

• • •

My son, who was eight years old at the time we adopted him, was named Enrique and went by its diminutive, "Quique" (KEE-kay). Because we lived in a small Midwestern town, with hardly any Hispanics, I suggested that he use a more "American" sounding name, such as Lu, Louis, or Henry. He rejected all names, especially Lu, because he said there is a dorky cartoon character in Guatemala by that name.

I tried to find a more English version of Quique but couldn't. We just left it at Quique, and that seems to be just fine. At least one person in our small town finally has learned to pronounce it.

People often call him Quiqui (KEE-kee), rather than Quique; so I have to struggle to keep his name real and pure. I have to explain that "Quique" is to "Enrique" what "Bob" is to Robert." Will people continue to bungle his name? Certainly. Will his Spanish name and its Spanish diminutive someday reduce his opportunity to find a job? Probably. But finally I realized that it is his name, and he has a right to it, whether or not the people around him understand Spanish spelling and pronunciation rules.

• • •

Bibliography

BOOKS

Abrams, Richard S. *Will It Hurt the Baby?* Reading, MA: Addison-Wesley, 1990.

Adamec, Christine. *There ARE Babies to Adopt.* New York: Kensington Press, 1996.

Adamec, Christine, and William L. Pierce. *Encyclopedia of Adoption.* New York: Facts on File, 1991.

Crain, Connie, and Janice Duffy. *How to Adopt a Child.* Nashville, TN: Thomas Nelson, 1994.

Fahlberg, Vera. *Common Behavioral Problems.* Michigan Department of Social Services, 1987.

Gilman, Lois. *The Adoption Resource Book.* New York: HarperCollins, 1992.

Hotchner, Tracie. *Pregnancy and Childbirth.* New York: Avon Books, 1984.

Johnston, Patricia Irwin. *Adopting after Infertility.* Indianapolis, IN: Perspective Press, 1992.

Keck, Gregory C., and Regina M. Kupecky. *Adopting the Hurt Child.* Colorado Springs, CO: NavPress, 1998.

Mattes, Jane. *Single Mothers by Choice.* New York: Random House, 1994.

McKelvey, Carol, and JoEllen Stevens. *The Adoption Crisis: The Truth Behind Adoption and Foster Care.* Golden, CO: Fulcrum Publishing, 1994.

Nelson-Erichsen, Jean, and Heino R. Erichsen. *How to Adopt Internationally.* The Woodlands, TX: Los Ninos International Adoption Center, 1993.

O'Hanlon, Tim. *Adoption Subsidy: A Guide for Adoptive Parents.* New Roots, An Adoptive Families Support Group, 1995.

Reynolds, Nancy Thalia. *Adopting Your Child.* North Vancouver, British Columbia, Canada: Self-Counsel Press, 1993.

Sweet, O. Robin, and Patty Bryan. *Adopt International.* New York: Farrar, Straus and Giroux, 1996.

Van Gulden, Holly, and Lida M. Bartels-Rabb. *Real Parents, Real Children: Parenting the Adopted Child.* New York: Crossroads, 1994.

Wine, Judith. *The Canadian Adoption Guide: A Family at Last.* Toronto, Ontario, Canada: McGraw-Hill Ryerson, 1995.

ARTICLES, STUDIES, AND NEWSLETTERS

Adamec, Christine. "Rip-offs." *The Adoption Advocates NEWSletter* Vol. 3, No. 9, September 1995, p. 5.

"All in the Family." *The New Republic,* January 24, 1994, p. 6.

Barth, Richard P. "Adoption of Drug-Exposed Children." University of California School of Social Welfare, Child Welfare Research Center, *Children and Youth Services Review* Vol. 13, 1991, pp. 323–342.

Bartholet, Elizabeth. "Where Do Black Children Belong? The Politics of Race Matching in Adoption." *University of Pennsylvania Law Review* Vol. 139, No. 5, May 1991, pp. 1163–1256.

"Black Women Are Not More or Less Likely to Place a Child for Adoption: An Empirical Analysis of Adoption." *Economic Inquiry* Vol. XXXI, January 1993, pp. 59–70.

Blanton, Terril L., and Jeanne Buckner Deschner. "Biological Mother's Grief: The Post-adoptive Experience in Open Versus Confidential Adoption." *Child Welfare* Vol. 69, No. 6, November/December 1990, pp. 525–535.

Boer, Frits, Versluis den Bieman, J. M. Herma, and Frank C. Verhulst. "International Adoption of Children with Siblings: Behavioral Outcomes." Leiden University, Dept of Child and Adolescent Psychiatry, Netherlands. Published in *American Journal of Orthopsychiatry* Vol. 62, No. 2, April 1994, pp. 252–262.

Bowen, James S. "Cultural Convergences and Divergences, The Nexus Between Putative Afro-American Family Values and the Best Interests of the Child." *Journal of Family Law* Vol. 26, 1988, pp. 487, 502.

Bussiere, Alice, and Ellen C. Sega. "Children with Special Needs." *Adoption Law and Practice.* Matthew Bender and Company, 1994.

Chamberlain, Patricia, Sandra Moreland, and Cathleen Reid. "Enhanced Services and Stipends for Foster Parents: Effects on Retention Rates and Outcomes for Children." *Child Welfare* Vol. 71, No. 5, September/October 1992, pp. 387–401.

Chandra, Anjani, Penelope Maza, and Christine Bachrach. "Adoption, Adoption Seeking, and Relinquishment for Adoption in the United States." Advance Data from *Vital and Health Statistics of the Centers for Disease Control and Prevention* No. 306, May 11, 1999.

Chasnoff, Ira. "Guidelines for Adopting Drug-Exposed Infants and Children." National Association of Perinatal Addiction, Dept. of Research and Education, 1994.

Cocozzeli, Carmelo. "Predicting the Decision of Biological Mothers to Retain or Relinquish Their Babies for Adoption: Implications for Open Adoption."

Child Welfare League of America Vol. LXVIII, No. 5, January/February 1989.

"Common Questions on The Adoption Tax Credit." *National Adoption Reports,* newsletter from the National Council for Adoption, Washington, D.C., September/October 1996, pp. 8, 9.

Cook, Paddy Shannon, et al. "Alcohol, Tobacco, and Other Drugs May Harm the Unborn." U.S. Department of Health and Human Services, 1990.

Crain, Connie. "'What I Need Is a Mom': The Welfare State Denies Homes to Thousands of Foster Children." *Policy Review* Vol. 10, No. 73, Summer 1995, p. 40.

Daly, Kerry J., and Michael Sobol. "Adoption in Canada: A Profile." Taken from a study prepared for the Royal Commission on New Reproductive Technologies. *Transition,* September 1992, pp. 4–5.

Downey, Douglas B. "Understanding Academic Achievement Among Children in Step-Households: The Roles of Parental Resources, Sex of Stepparent, and Sex of Child." *Social Forces* Vol. 73, March 1995, p. 875.

"Fact Sheet on Adoption." National Council for Adoption, 1930 Seventeenth Street, NW, Washington, DC 20009-6297, 202-238-1200.

Flango, Victor E., and Karen R. Flango. "How Many Children Were Adopted in 1992?" *Child Welfare* Vol. LXXIV, No. 5, September/October 1995.

Forde-Mazrui, Kim. "Black Identity and Child Placement: The Best Interests of Black and Biracial Children." *Michigan Law Review* No. 4, February 1994, pp. 925–967.

Foster, Maurice, Esq. "Adoption by Grandparents." *State Court Journal* Vol. 18, No. 1, Summer 1994, pp. 27–31.

Glidden, Laraine M. "Adopted Children with Developmental Disabilities: Post-placement Family Functioning." *Children and Youth Services Review* Vol. 13, No. 5–6, 1991, pp. 363–377.

Goetting, Ann, and Mark G. Goetting. "How Parents Fare After Placement." Western Kentucky University, *Journal of Child and Family Studies* Vol. 2, No. 4, December 1993, pp. 353–369.

Gonzalez, Nilda M., and Magda Campbell. "Cocaine Babies: Does Prenatal Exposure to Cocaine Affect Development?" *Journal of the American Academy of Child and Adolescent Psychiatry* Vol. 33, No. 1, 1994, pp. 16–19.

Groze, Victor, Simeon Haines, Mark Barth, and Richard P. Case. "Barriers in Permanency Planning for Medically Fragile Children: Drug Affected Children and HIV Infected Children." Case Western Reserve University, Mandel School of Applied Social Sciences. *Child and Adolescent Social Work Journal* Vol. 11, No. 1, February 1994, pp. 63–85.

Hayes, Peter. "Transracial Adoption: Politics and Ideology." Iowa State University,

Child Welfare Vol. 72, No. 3, May/June 1993, pp. 301–310.

Hostetter, Margaret, and Dana Johnson. "Medical Concerns for International Adoptees." *Report on Intercountry Adoption,* 1996, pp. 50–51.

Jenista, Jerri Ann. "Adoptions from Africa." *Adoption Medical News* Vol. I, No. 2, November/December 1995, p. 2.

Jenista, Jerri Ann. "Chronic Hepatitis B: Medical Management Issues." *Adoption Medical News* Vol. I, No. 2, November/December 1995.

Jenista, Jerri Ann. "Health Status of the 'New' International Adopted Child. *Adoption Medical News* Vol. II, No. 6, June 1996, p. 3.

Kallgren, Carl A., and Pamela J. Caudill. "Current Transracial Adoption Practices: Racial Dissonance or Racial Awareness?" Pennsylvania State University, *Psychological Reports* Vol. 72, No. 2, April 1993, pp. 551–558.

Kennedy, Randall. "Orphans of Separatism: The Politics of Transracial Adoption." *The American Prospect,* Spring 1994, pp. 38–45.

Kirkland, Judy. *Washington Metropolitan Area RESOLVE Newsletter,* March 1987.

Kraft, Adrienne D., et al. "Some Theoretical Considerations on Confidential Adoptions." *Human Services Press,* 1985, pp. 13–21.

Kroll, Joe. "Waiting Children Still Wait." *Adoptalk,* Summer 1995, p 1.

Laws, Rita. "Between the Lines: How to Read a Waiting Child Description." *Adoptive Families,* September/October 1995, pp. 34–35.

Lewert, George. "Children and AIDS." Columbia Presbyterian Medical Center, Dept. of Social Work Services. *Social Casework* Vol. 69, No. 6, June 1988, pp. 348–354.

Mahoney, Joan. "The Black Baby Doll: Transracial Adoption and Cultural Preservation." *UMKC Law Review* Vol. 59, No. 85, 1991, pp. 487–501.

McDonald, Thomas P., Alice A. Lieberman, Susan Partridge, and Helaine Hornby. "Assessing the Role of Agency Services in Reducing Adoption Disruptions." *Children and Youth Services Review* Vol. 13, No. 5–6, 1991, pp. 425–438.

Melina, Lois. "Prenatal Drug Exposure Affects School-Age Child's Behavior." *Adopted Child* Vol. 15, No. 1, January 1996.

Melina, Lois. "Relative Adoptions Have Benefits, But Also Have Unique Challenges." *Adopted Child* Vol. 12, No. 2, February 1993, pp. 1–4.

National Council for Adoption, Washington, DC. *National Adoption Reports,* July 1996.

North American Council on Adoptable Children, St. Paul, MN. "The New Adoption Tax Credit." *Adoptalk,* Fall 1996, p. 5.

Phillips, B. Lee. "Open Adoption: A New Look at Adoption Practice and Policy in Texas." *Baylor Law Review* Vol. 43, No. 407, 1991, pp. 407–429.

"Recommendations of the U.S. Public Health Service Task Force on the Use of

Zidovudine (AZT) to Reduce Perinatal Transmission of Human Immunodeficiency Virus." The Center for Disease Control and Prevention, *Morbidity and Mortality Weekly Report* Vol. 43, August 5, 1995, p. 194.

Resnick, Michael D. "Studying Adolescent Mothers' Decision-Making About Adoption and Parenting" *Social Work,* January/February 1984.

Rosenthal, James A., and Victor Groze. "Behavioral Problems of Special Needs Adopted Children." *Children and Youth Services Review* Vol. 13, No. 5–6, 1991, pp. 343–361.

Sawyer, Richard J., and Howard Dubowitz. "School Performance of Children in Kinship Care." Academy for Educational Development, Washington, D.C., published in *Child Abuse and Neglect* Vol. 18, No. 7, July 1994, pp. 587–597.

Schneider, Jane. "Assessment of Infant Motor Developments." Presentation at NAPARE conference, New York, August 10, 1988.

Schur, William M. "Adoption Procedure." *Adoption Law and Practice* Vol. 4, No. 1, December 1994, pp. 26–27.

Shinyei, Marilyn E., and Linda Edney. "Open Adoption in Canada." *Transition,* September 1992, pp. 8–10.

U.S. Department of Health and Human Services, Administration on Children, Youth and Families, Children's Bureau. *Adoption and Foster Care Analysis and Reporting System (AFCARS).*

Verhulst, Frank C., Monika Althaus, Versluis den Bieman, and Sophia J. Herma. "Damaging Backgrounds: Later Adjustment of International Adoptees." Children's Hospital, Dept. of Child Psychiatry, Rotterdam, Netherlands. Printed in *Journal of the American Academy of Child and Adolescent Psychiatry* Vol. 31, No. 3, May 1992, pp. 518–524.

Vroegh, Karen S. "Transracial Adoption: How It Is 17 Years Later." *Chicago Child Care Society,* p. 55.

Widermeier, Jeannette. "Adoption Subsidy Q & A." *Adoptalk,* Winter 1996, pp. 7, 12.

Woodmansee, Carol. "Life Book." *Foster Care Connection* Vol. 1, No. 5, October 1995.

Yolton, Kimberly A., and Rosemary Bolig. "Psychosocial, Behavioral, and Developmental Characteristics of Toddlers Prenatally Exposed to Cocaine." University of Tennessee, Dept. of Pediatrics, *Child Study Journal* Vol. 24, No. 1, 1994, pp. 49–68.

Adoption Laws:

State-by-State Questions and Answers

This section provides answers to some of the most commonly asked questions about adoption law, primarily for people adopting independently or through a private agency. We have not attempted to address the laws and regulations relative to adoptions in which the birth parents' rights have been terminated due to abuse or neglect. However, some of the laws we do discuss can be applied to such situations.

Laws are subject to change, and even within a state, there can be county-by-county differences based on the way a judge interprets the law.

Several guides were considered in addressing the questions, including *Adoption Laws: Answers to the Most-Asked Questions*, published by the National Adoption Information Clearinghouse. In addition, scores of attorneys were interviewed, as well as the state adoption specialists and/or staff at ICPC units in nearly every state to determine how the law is actually practiced there.

Can an attorney serve as an intermediary?

This question asks whether an attorney can "find" a birth mother for an adoptive couple. In most states, this is permissible as long as the attorney is not paid for her role as the intermediary; in other words, an attorney can "match" an adoptive couple with a birth mother, but she can not charge for that referral. She can only charge for actual legal services rendered. In several other states, an attorney technically is not even supposed to tell an adoptive couple about a birth mother. In many states that permit intermediaries, an attorney cannot directly place the baby with a couple. He may refer the birth mother to the adoptive couple, and the parties must then communicate with each other, either face-to-face or through letters or telephone calls.

In these states, an attorney cannot operate like an agency. The birth mother cannot place the baby first with the attorney and allow him or her to then select the adoptive parents. The attorney also cannot present information about and pictures of several couples to a birth mother and let her choose the couple.

Also, in many states the attorney cannot charge a fee for assisting a couple with finding a birth mother. Some judges will not even allow an attorney to charge an hourly rate for the services involved in finding and making arrangements to match a birth mother with an adoptive couple. Instead, the attorney may only charge a flat rate related to legal services provided, regardless of whether the couple finds a birth mother or not. Sometimes an attorney who does locate birth mothers for couples will have a higher fee than one who does not.

Is advertising permitted?

In most states and Washington, D.C., you can place an adoption advertisement in a newspaper. Some newspapers may have their own restrictions and may require you to have a letter from your attorney verifying that your interest in adoption is legitimate.

The *Gale Directory of Publications and Broadcast Media* provides a state-by-state listing of newspapers and magazines in the United States and Canada. This can be found in your library's reference section.

Who must consent to the adoption?

In almost all states, if a birth mother does not sign a surrender, then she must at least provide a written consent to the adoption. A surrender is the legal document which terminates a birth parent's rights, while a consent is the birth parent's approval of or agreement to the adoption. A consent or surrender is not necessary in those situations in which her rights are terminated because of mental illness, child abuse, neglect, and so forth. State laws vary on the circumstances in which a birth father's consent is required. A small number of states do not even require a birth parent's written consent before placement; the birth parents must, however, receive notice of the hearing that terminates their parental rights. It is a wise practice, however, to have in writing the birth parents' consent to the adoption (at the very least, that of the birth mother's consent) to avoid any later allegations of wrongdoing or kidnapping.

When a birth parent is under eighteen years of age, a parent or court-appointed guardian may also have to consent to the adoption.

Again, after consent is given, the birth parents usually must be notified of the court hearing that will terminate their rights.

What is the difference between a birth mother's consent to adoption and the surrender or relinquishment of her parental rights?

A document that indicates that the birth mother is consenting to the adoption of her child by the adoptive couple is often referred to as the birth mother's consent to adoption. The birth mother's rights are not terminated by her signing this consent document; it is simply a statement by her that she is agreeable to the placement of her child with the adoptive couple, knowing that the couple will start legal proceedings to adopt the child. It is written evidence that the adoptive couple has physical custody of the child with the birth mother's approval.

A document which, if signed by the birth mother, terminates her parental rights is known as a surrender or relinquishment of parental rights and is often referred to simply as a surrender or relinquishment. Some states allow only an approved adoption agency to "take a surrender" after several hours of counseling with a birth mother and birth father. Obviously, signing such a document is a serious matter, and all attempts must be made to ensure that the birth parents really want to place the baby for adoption and understand fully the consequences of their actions. As an aside, the counseling provided must also inform the birth parents of state financial assistance available to them if they decide to keep the child. Many states allow an attorney or certified social worker to take a surrender without involving an adoption agency.

Some states allow the surrender document to be signed in front of a notary or an attorney, but some require that it be signed in court before a judge. Many states specify that the birth parents rights are terminated immediately upon signing the surrender documents, while other states have a revocation period that allows the birth parents to revoke their surrender of parental rights within a specific amount of time. Such revocation periods are noted where applicable.

Because most of the state laws reviewed referred to the surrender document as a "consent," the section on surrender of parental rights also uses "consent" to describe the termination of parental rights. Many attorneys and agency social workers also refer to the surrender as the consent. In discussing the termination of parental rights with an attorney or ICPC staff, it is wise to confirm that the consent referred to has the same legal effect as the surrender of parental rights.

What is a notice of an adoption hearing?

Notice of the adoption hearing must be given to the birth parents unless they waive their rights to this notice, which some states allow, or they have already signed surrender documents which contain waiver of notice of the adoption hearing. The notice document states that the adoptive couple (usually first names only) desires to adopt "Baby Boy Smith" and a hearing will be held on the matter; the time, date, and place of the hearing are also stated. Some states require that the adoption petition or complaint be served on the birth parent by a process server. Most states, except Virginia, allow all confidential information about the adoptive couple to be "whited out." Usually the birth parents must be given notice within a specified time period (usually between twenty to thirty days) prior to the hearing. How this is given varies from state to state. Sometimes notice is given in person (which means that a process server or law enforcement officer personally hands the legal documents to the birth parent), while other states allow the notice to be provided by certified mail. If the birth parent cannot be found or their identity is not known, notice is given by publication in a newspaper. Exactly what is published depends on the state; the notice is placed in the legal notices section of a newspaper along with notices of foreclosure actions and local zoning board applications and meetings. The basic contents of such a notice are that a baby was born on a certain date to the birth mother, the birth father is alleged to be the father of the child, and if he desires to assert his parental rights to the baby before the adoption is finalized, he must do so within a certain time frame.

Several states, such as North Carolina, allow birth parents seven days after signing a surrender to revoke it. In many states, such as New Jersey and South Carolina, the surrender is not revocable unless the birth parents can show they were coerced into signing or they did not understand the seriousness of their actions because they were taking medications at the time that affected their judgment.

A small number of states require the birth parents to testify in court that they signed the surrender documents with full knowledge and understanding and that it was their intention to place the baby for adoption; until this is done, the surrenders can be revoked within a certain time period (ten to forty-five days). In lieu of the birth parents' attending a court hearing, some states allow the adoptive couple's attorney to present to the judge the signed surrender documents for the judge's inspection and approval.

Again, if an attorney or ICPC staff member discusses adoption law and practice with terms such as "consent" or "surrender," be sure to ask for definitions. It is important to know whether "consent" as used in that attorney's state means termination of parental rights or simply the birth mother's written statement of approval that the adoptive parents have custody of the baby with the intention to adopt him or her. Ask whether there is a time period for revocation; also, ask if the birth parents must go to court to finalize the surrender in front of a judge.

What is a petition or complaint for adoption?

To schedule an adoption hearing in court, the attorney for the couple files with the clerk of the court (usually the family court clerk of court) an adoption petition or complaint, usually in the county in which the couple lives. The petition tells the court of the adoptive couple's desire to adopt the baby placed with them. The identities of the birth mother and birth father are disclosed; if the identity of the birth father is not known or the birth mother refuses to name him, then this is stated.

The petition for adoption also requests that the judge terminate the birth parents' rights, either by legally recognizing the surrender document or based on the legal grounds of abandonment (if they have not already been terminated), and finalize the adoption. The information most often required in a petition is:

- Identifying information about the adoptive parents, including names, ages, and addresses.
- The relationship between the adoptive parents and the child.
- The legal reason that the birth parents' rights are being terminated.
- An explanation of why the adoption is in the child's best interest.
- Proof that the adoptive parents are fit to adopt the child.
- The name of the guardian appointed for the child, if required.
- The name of the adoption agency or certified social worker chosen by the court to conduct postplacement supervision and to provide a written report to the court.

Some states require that only one hearing be held to terminate birth parents' rights and to finalize the adoption. Other states have a two-step process. The first hearing, scheduled ten to ninety days after placement, is known as a preliminary hearing, which allows the judge to terminate the rights of the birth parents (assuming they have no objections) and to review the home study report. The final hearing is scheduled months later and simply allows more time for the placement to be reviewed by the court vis-à-vis the postsupervisory visit reports. The preliminary hearing is the critical one; the rights of the birth parents are terminated, and the adoptive couple acquires "the legal rights of parents" but not the legal title of parents. The purpose of the final hearing has nothing to do with the birth parents' rights because these have already been terminated. Rather, it is to allow the state to further evaluate by home visits the fitness of the adoptive couple as the parents of the child to be adopted. It is at the final hearing that the adoptive couple acquires the legal title of parents.

The judgment of adoption or order of adoption is signed by the judge holding the hearing and is the legal document that states the adoptive couple has legally adopted the child. This document allows the birth certificate to be revised showing the adoptive couple as parents as of the date of birth of the adopted child.

When can consent be taken from birth mother (father), and how long after the consent is signed can it be revoked?

In most states, a birth mother cannot sign a surrender form until after the baby's birth. In states in which she can sign it before the birth, it is not valid until after the birth. In many states, the surrender cannot be signed until seventy-two hours or more after the baby's birth.

In some states, a birth mother can also revoke her surrender within a certain time period (such as ten to thirty days after signing). If this happens, the court usually must then determine what is in the child's best interest.

A birth mother's surrender in some states, such as South Carolina, automatically terminates her rights. In other states, a birth mother signs a surrender, but her rights must also be terminated by a judge (e.g., Colorado).

What are the birth father's rights?

See Chapter 8 for more information on this issue.

What fees can the adoptive parents pay?

In most states, adoptive parents are allowed to pay reasonable fees associated with the adoption so that placing a child is not financially burdensome to a birth mother. However, direct payment to the birth mother for placing a child for adoption is illegal in all states. State laws vary as to the penalty for this crime, but in nearly all states, baby buying is grounds for a birth mother to revoke her consent, even after the adoption is finalized.

In all states, the adoptive parents can pay for medical fees and their own legal fees, and in most states, the adoptive parents can also pay for some living expenses. However, the issue is subject to much interpretation. Often an attorney will, as required by some state laws, have all living expenses preapproved by the judge who will oversee the adoption. Because living expenses for a birth mother can be high (for example, if a birth mother lives at a fancy hotel), most judges place a cap on what is considered "reasonable."

Another rule of thumb for defining reasonable expenses is that after all adoption-related expenses are paid, the birth mother should not have a financial gain. In other words, she should not have extra money in her bank account or a new car in her driveway as a result of placing the baby for adoption.

Where does the final adoption take place?

In most states, you and your baby will attend an adoption finalization. This usually takes place at your county courthouse. If your child was born in your state, your attorney may suggest that the adoption proceedings take place in the county where the child was born, depending upon the presiding judge. For example, one judge may define "reasonable" living expenses that can be paid to the birth mother more broadly than another judge. You may want the more lenient judge to finalize your adoption.

If you are finalizing the adoption in another state (usually the state where the baby was born), you will probably go to court in the county where the baby was born. Note: In some states, you cannot finalize an adoption unless you are a resident.

How are familial and stepparent adoptions different from nonbiological adoptions?

When a relative or stepparent is adopting a child, the laws will often be more lenient, and requirements such as the home study may be less stringent or waived altogether. In general, the legal process is much easier unless the adoption is contested.

Can a nonresident finalize an adoption in the state?

If you adopt a child who is born outside of your state, you may have the option of finalizing the adoption in that state. However, many states do not permit you to adopt unless you are a resident.

Note: If you plan to advertise in a state where you are not a resident and because of your state adoption laws you also need to finalize the adoption there, call an attorney or the ICPC in that state and make sure you are still permitted to finalize there. (For example, if you live in Georgia and you find a birth mother through advertising in another state, you cannot finalize the adoption in Georgia.) To spend the money on advertising only to find out that you cannot finalize in that state is a waste of time and money.

If you just moved to a state, the laws specifying how long you have to live in a state before you can adopt generally do not apply. You can usually proceed with your adoption plans because by the time the adoption is finalized you will have lived in the state long enough to qualify for residency.

ADOPTION AGENCIES AND SUPPORT GROUPS

In an attempt to make this book a complete adoption resource, lists of private adoption agencies and support groups for each state are included. There are also numerous public adoption agencies, and the adoption specialist's office of each state can forward you a list or refer you to the proper state office for more information about state-operated adoption agencies. Since there was no way for us to confirm the professionalism and competency of all the adoption agencies and support groups listed, check with a local adoption support group for references. Also, you or your attorney can call the state office responsible for licensing adoption agencies for background information on any particular agency. Your attorney can also call the person at your local family court who is responsible for processing adoption cases; this person can probably provide a reference to a particular agency.

ALABAMA LAWS RELATED TO ADOPTION:
QUESTIONS AND ANSWERS

Can an attorney serve as an intermediary?

Yes, but he can charge only for legal services rendered either to a birth parent or to the adoptive couple. He or she cannot directly place a child with the adoptive parents.

Is advertising permitted?

No.

Who must consent to the adoption?

1. The birth mother.
2. The birth mother's husband, regardless of paternity, if he and the mother were married and the child was born during the marriage or within 300 days after the marriage was terminated; or before the child's birth if he and the mother had attempted to marry in compliance with the law, although the attempted marriage is invalid, and the child was born during the attempted marriage or within 300 days after termination of cohabitation; or after the child's birth if he and the mother were married or attempted to marry and with his knowledge or consent he was named father on the birth certificate, if he is obligated to pay child support; or if he received the adoptee into his home and openly held out the child as his own.
3. The adoption agency that has legal custody of the adoptee, unless the court orders placement without the agency's consent.
4. The presumed father, if he is known to the court and if he responds within thirty days to the notice he receives.
5. The adoptee, if fourteen years of age or older, unless the adoptee is found not to have the mental capacity to consent.

If the parent of the child to be adopted is a minor, a guardian *ad litem* must be appointed to represent the birth parents' interests as to the child being adopted.

When can consent be taken from the birth mother (father), and how long after the consent is signed can it be revoked?

Consent may take place at any time, except that once signed it may be withdrawn in writing within five days after the signing of the consent or the birth of the child. Consent can be withdrawn if the court finds that it is in the child's best interest within fourteen days after the child's birth or after the signing of consent. Consent can also be withdrawn within one year if it was obtained by fraud, duress, mistake, or undue influence.

Generally, independent adoptions are finalized ninety days after birth, and agency adoptions are finalized 180 days after birth.

What are the birth father's rights?

His rights are the same as the birth mother's, but it is essential to consult your attorney, as each case is different. The unwed birth father's consent can be dispensed with if he signs an affidavit saying that he is not the father or indicating that he has no interest in the child. His consent is also not necessary if he has not provided support or communicated with the child for a period of six months; the birth father's rights are considered terminated after this six-month period by reason of abandonment. While it is not clear from case law whether the birth father must receive notice of the adoption hearing if he does abandon his parental rights, it is wise to ensure the receipt of such notice. The birth father's rights are terminated if he does not respond within thirty days after being provided notice of the adoption proceeding. If he cannot be located or if his identity is unknown, then he can be served by publication; that is, a notice of the adoption proceeding is placed in a newspaper in the town or county of his last known whereabouts. If he does not respond to such publication, then his rights are terminated.

A putative father who files notice with the putative father registry within thirty days of the birth of the child is entitled to notice of adoption hearings. If he does not file within this time period, he is presumed to have given irrevocable implied consent to the adoption.

What fees can adoptive parents pay?

Adoptive parents can pay reasonable fees such as medical, living, and legal expenses with court approval.

Where does the adoption hearing take place?

The hearing can take place in the county in which the adoptive parents live, the child lives, or where the agency that has custody of the child is located.

How are familial and stepparent adoptions different from nonbiological adoptions?

Home studies are very seldom required, and there is no requirement as to disclosure of fees and costs. There is a one-year waiting period for a child in the home before the adoption can proceed. In stepparent and relative adoptions, visitation rights for grandparents may be given at the discretion of the court.

Can a nonresident finalize an adoption in this state?

Yes. After the child is placed in the adoptive home, at least one adoptive parent must be able to be at home with the child for at least sixty days.

ALASKA LAWS RELATED TO ADOPTION: QUESTIONS AND ANSWERS

Can an attorney serve as an intermediary?
Yes.

Is advertising permitted?
Yes.

Who must consent to the adoption?
1. The birth mother.
2. The birth father, if he was married to the mother at the time of conception, or at any time after conception, or if he is the child's father by adoption, or has otherwise legitimated the child.
3. Any person who has custody of the child, or the court if the legal guardian is not empowered to consent.
4. The adoptee, if older than ten years of age, unless the court dispenses with this consent.
5. The spouse of the adoptor.

Written consent must indicate whether the child or parent is a member of an Indian tribe.

When can consent be taken from the birth mother (father), and how long after the consent is signed can it be revoked?
Consent can be taken at any time after the birth. It can be withdrawn in writing before the entry of the decree of the adoption and within ten days after consent is given or after ten days if the court finds it to be in the child's best interest.

What are the birth father's rights?
The birth father's consent to the adoption is required if he has legitimized the child by marrying the mother. It is doubtful that the requirement of marriage to assert birth father rights would hold up in the state Supreme Court or in the U.S. Supreme Court. If the birth father acknowledged the child as his, maintained contact with the child, and supported him or her monetarily, then marrying the birth mother to assert his rights would not be necessary in view of the Supreme Court cases dealing with birth father rights. If the birth father has not had contact with the child for six months, then it is presumed that he has abandoned his parental rights and his consent is not necessary. It is expected that a reasonable investigation will be made to assure that any possible birth fathers are provided notice of the adoption proceedings.

What fees can adoptive parents pay?

Adoptive parents must submit all expenses to the court. The expenses allowed and included in the report to the court are expenses for the child's birth and placement, birth mother's medical care, and adoption services (agency adoption).

Where does the adoption hearing take place?

The hearing may take place in the district in which adoptive parents live, the child lives, or where the agency is located.

How are familial and stepparent adoptions different from nonbiological adoptions?

There are few requirements regarding birth parent notice and the home study. No disclosure of fees is required. Grandparents may have visitation rights if a stepparent or other grandparent has adopted the child.

Can a nonresident finalize an adoption in this state?

Yes.

In addition to state laws, rules must be followed that are written in the Alaska Rules of Court. An adoption attorney should have this rule book.

ARIZONA LAWS RELATED TO ADOPTION: QUESTIONS AND ANSWERS

Can an attorney serve as an intermediary?

Yes, attorneys may assist in direct placement adoptions. However, prior to attorney involvement, the birth parents must have already selected the adoptive parents, or if after attorney involvement, an adoptive couple must be certified by the court as a couple approved to adopt. Also, the adoptive parents must already have an approved home study filed with the court. An attorney can be paid for services in connection with an adoption, provided the court has found her fees to be reasonable and necessary.

Is advertising permitted?

Yes.

Who must consent to the adoption?

1. The birth mother.
2. The agency that has given consent to place the child for adoption.
3. The birth father, if he was married to the birth mother at the time of conception or at any time prior to the child's birth, or if a court has established paternity.

When can consent be taken from the birth mother (father), and how long after the consent is signed can it be revoked?
Consent cannot be taken until seventy-two hours after the baby's birth and is irrevocable, unless obtained by fraud, duress, or undue influence.

What are the birth father's rights?
The law permits the serving of a "Potential Father Notice" on any man identified by the birth mother. This notice can be served at any time that an adoption plan is being considered. The birth father has thirty days after being served the notice to proceed with paternity proceedings. If he fails to respond within thirty days, his consent is not required.

Arizona law also provides for a registry in which a putative father can file a claim as to his paternity of a child to be born. If he does not file a claim within thirty days after the child's birth, then he may not assert any parental interest in the child, unless he can show that he was unable to file such a claim and that he then did file within thirty days after being able to file. The fact that he was not aware of the birth mother's pregnancy is not a valid excuse for not filing a claim.

If the birth father is married to the birth mother, his rights are the same as hers.

What fees can adoptive parents pay?
Reasonable medical, counseling, and legal expenses can be paid. Living expenses can be paid with court approval; a payment exceeding $1,000 for birth mother living expenses must be approved by the court before payment. Expenses are reviewed by the court at the final adoption hearing. The birth mother must also submit an affidavit indicating her understanding that payment of any expenses for her benefit does not obligate her to place her child for adoption.

Where does the adoption hearing take place?
The adoption hearing takes place in the court in the county in which the adoptive parents live.

How are familial and stepparent adoptions different from nonbiological adoptions?
No home study is required, and a stepparent adoption can be expedited depending upon how long the stepparent has been married to the parent and how long the child has been in the home.

Can a nonresident finalize an adoption in this state?
No.

Source: Arizona Revised Statutes Chapter 1, Article 1, Sections 8-101 to 8-132

ARKANSAS LAWS RELATED TO ADOPTION: QUESTIONS AND ANSWERS

Can an attorney serve as an intermediary?
Yes.

Is advertising permitted?
Yes.

Who must consent to the adoption?
1. The birth mother.
2. The birth father, if he was married to the mother at the time the child was conceived or at any time thereafter; if he adopted the child; if he has custody of the child at the time the petition for adoption is filed; or if he has otherwise legitimated the child.
3. Any person who has custody of the child, or the court if the legal guardian is not empowered to consent.
4. The adoptee, if ten years of age or older, unless the court waives this.
5. The spouse of the adoptor.

When can consent be taken from the birth mother (father), and how long after the consent is signed can it be revoked?
Consent may take place at any time after the birth of the child and cannot be withdrawn after the entry of the decree of adoption. Consent may be withdrawn before the entry of the decree of adoption but must be withdrawn within ten calendar days after the consent was given or after the child was born, whichever is later.

What are the birth father's rights?
Adoption law provides that if the birth father is not married to the birth mother his consent is not necessary, and he must file a claim of paternity with the putative father registry located at the Department of Vital Records; a birth father who files such a claim is entitled to notice of any adoption proceedings. The birth father's written consent for the adoption is needed if he was married to the birth mother at the time of conception or any time thereafter, or if he has legitimized the child.

In cases involving a child born to an unmarried mother, a search must be made of possible fathers in the putative father registry. If someone has filed a claim of paternity, he must receive notice of the pending adoption. After being notified, the putative father has a given time, set by the state, to claim an interest in the child.

What fees can adoptive parents pay?
Medical and legal fees can be paid, as well as living expenses. A listing of these expenses must be submitted to the court.

Where does the adoption hearing take place?
The hearing can take place in the county in which the adoptive parents live, the child lives, or where the agency that has custody of child is located.

How are familial and stepparent adoptions different from nonbiological adoptions?
No home study is required. The adoption process is less complicated and, therefore, less expensive.

Can a nonresident finalize an adoption in this state?
Yes. Nonresidents can usually obtain a final decree of adoption within two weeks after the baby's birth.

Note: Arkansas requires prospective adoptive parents to have FBI fingerprint clearance before an adoption hearing.

CALIFORNIA LAWS RELATED TO ADOPTION: QUESTIONS AND ANSWERS

Can an attorney serve as an intermediary?
Yes. In fact, many nonattorneys also serve as intermediaries and operate as independent facilitators. It is important to note that a facilitator must identify herself as an adoption facilitator and that she is not licensed as an adoption agency.

Is advertising permitted?
No, only a licensed intermediary, attorney, or adoption agency can advertise. Many prospective adoptive parents simply advertise in other states or in national publications.

Who must consent to the adoption?
1. The birth mother.
2. The man who is presumed to be the father by marriage or attempted marriage to the mother at the time of birth or within 300 days prior to birth; or had been legitimated as the father by other specified means.
3. Department of Social Services or county adoption agency, where parental consent is not necessary and only if either has legal custody of the adoptee.
4. An adoptee who is over twelve years of age.
5. Consent is not necessary if a birth parent has not supported or communicated with an adoptee for a period exceeding one year.

When can consent be taken from the birth mother (father), and how long after the consent is signed can it be revoked?

The birth mother must be counseled twice by a state-authorized adoption service provider. (There are many in the state.) The first advisement can occur before the child's birth; the birth mother must then be readvised with at least ten days between the first and second session before she can sign a placement agreement that contains the consent. The maximum fee for being advised is $500; however, travel and counseling time can also be added to the fee.

The consent can be given any time after the baby is born and the mother is discharged from the hospital. In an agency adoption, the relinquishment is binding, and in an independent adoption, the birth parents can withdraw consent before thirty days or waive those thirty days.

The waiver must be signed in front of a state social worker, but finding such a social worker can sometimes be difficult. If a state social worker is not available because the birth mother lives in a remote area, she can go before a judge, but this very seldom is necessary. There is no charge for the social worker's service.

Because a preplacement home study is not required for an in-state placement, a social worker will not take a waiver until she knows more about the adoptive parents, and usually the social worker will want to meet the parties involved.

If a child is born in another state, the taking of a consent must follow California procedure, and there must be ten days in between the advisement of counsel and the second advisement before a consent can be taken. The birth mother's consent and waiver can be taken by an attorney who represents her exclusively in lieu of a state-authorized adoption placement provider and a state social worker.

Regarding independent adoptions, any required consents may be withdrawn, until thirty days have passed, at which time the consent becomes permanent. A parent's relinquishment to an adoption agency, filed with the department, is final, and there is no period of time in which she can revoke. It may be rescinded only upon mutual agreement of the relinquishing parents and adoption agency.

Note: Your adoption can become an identified agency adoption in which the agency conducts your home study and takes the birth mother's relinquishment at any time after the child is born. This process can be done without signing an adoption placement agreement and without involvement of the Department of Social Services.

What are the birth father's rights?

The court shall order that relevant persons and agencies make efforts to identify the alleged birth father. Any potential birth father who is identified must be given notice of the hearing. After the birth father, or more than one birth father, is notified, he must claim paternity within thirty days and appear at the hearing, or parental rights will be terminated. If the birth father does appear in court, the court will determine if he is in fact the father and then determine if it is in the child's best interest for the father to retain his parental rights. If so, the father's consent will be required. If not, the court will terminate the father's parental rights.

What fees can adoptive parents pay?
Adoptive parents can pay medical, legal, and reasonable living expenses and must file with the court a report of all expenses paid.

Where does the adoption hearing take place?
The hearing takes place in the county where the adoptive parents live. In the case of adult adoptions, the hearing takes place in the county where the adoptive parent resides or where the adult adoptee resides.

How are familial and stepparent adoptions different from nonbiological adoptions?
The home study is more superficial and is conducted by the county. In a stepparent adoption, the parents must be married at least one year.

In a relative adoption, the birth parents' rights can be terminated by a citation hearing as well as by the same methods as an independent adoption. Consents are revocable, by court order, until the final adoption. No accounting report is required, and no placement agreement is required. Also, there is no requirement for the birth parent to meet with an adoption service provider.

In a stepparent adoption, there is no statutory time limit in which the adoption must be completed, so the process often takes a long time.

If a child is adopted by a stepparent or grandparent and one of the child's parents is deceased, then the deceased parent's parents may be granted visitation rights if it is in the child's best interest.

Can a nonresident finalize an adoption in this state?
No.

Note: There are many facilitators who "find" birth mothers. They market themselves to look like agencies and try to recruit adoptive parents. While doing so, they also find birth mothers, although they cannot advertise to find birth mothers. The facilitators' fees can be very high—as much as $6,000 to $12,000 just to find a birth mother. If a facilitator finds a birth mother, you must also use an attorney and a counselor for the birth mother. Some facilitators do much for the birth mother, and their fee includes making many arrangements such as finding an apartment, making health care visits, and so on.

Birth mothers are often contacted through obstetricians. In California, this method of contacting birth mothers is very different from most states. Since physicians can serve as intermediaries, perhaps this is the reason why so many are willing to tell birth mothers and adoptive parents about each other.

COLORADO LAWS RELATED TO ADOPTION: QUESTIONS AND ANSWERS

Whether independent adoption is legal or not in Colorado is debatable, as the statute is unclear. However, an attorney has outlined a uniform code for family court judges to follow when interpreting the statute. In addition, an independent adoption must become a "designated" adoption, which is essentially an identified agency adoption. A birth mother and adoptive parents can meet without the assistance of an agency, but an agency must become involved by providing counseling to the birth mother, conducting a home study for the prospective adoptive couple, and completing certain forms.

In Colorado, adoptive parents can seek a birth mother through an intermediary such as an attorney, physician, or member of the clergy and can also advertise. (Intermediaries cannot be reimbursed for that specific service.)

If an out-of-state couple finds a birth mother in Colorado, the couple must have their home study comply with Colorado Interstate Compact regulations.

Can an attorney serve as an intermediary?
Yes, although the attorney is not licensed to place children with adoptive parents and cannot charge for such a service.

Is advertising permitted?
Yes.

Who must consent to the adoption?
Both birth parents must consent, unless the birth father has abandoned the child and/or birth mother by lack of support or contact.

When can consent be taken from the birth mother (father), and how long after the consent is signed can it be revoked?
Consents cannot be given until after the child is born, and a personal court appearance is required. The state Department of Social Services must provide counseling to a birth parent before he or she offers a surrender of parental rights.

What are the birth father's rights?
He must have notice of the adoption proceedings if he has not consented to the adoption, and he must file a paternity action within thirty days of receiving notice

that he is the father or likely father. He also must file a paternity action within thirty days of the child's birth if he has received notice prior or at birth that he is the father or likely father.

What fees can adoptive parents pay?
Attorney fees and other fees are permitted if approved by the court. Adoptive couples who have made direct contact with the birth mother may pay limited reasonable living expenses in addition to reasonable telephone and maternity clothing expenses. Only an adoption agency can receive payment in locating or identifying a child for adoption. A statement of all fees must be submitted to the court.

Where does the adoption hearing take place?
The hearing takes place in the county where the adoptive parents live or where the child placement adoption agency is located.

How are familial and stepparent adoptions different from nonbiological adoptions?
No agency involvement is required. The adoption process for a stepparent adoption is very simple. In a familial adoption, the adoptive parents can be named as guardians at the time of placement.

Can a nonresident finalize an adoption in this state?
Yes, if they comply with Colorado law. The birth parents' rights must be terminated through a court hearing. This usually occurs about thirty days after the child is born.

Source: Colorado Revised Statutes, Sections 19-5-20 to 19-5-304

CONNECTICUT LAWS RELATED TO ADOPTION: QUESTIONS AND ANSWERS

Can an attorney serve as an intermediary?
No.

Is advertising permitted?
Yes.

Who must consent to the adoption?
1. The birth parents, unless either has failed to maintain a relationship with the child for a period exceeding one year.
2. The adoptive parents.

When can consent be taken from the birth mother (father), and how long after the consent is signed can it be revoked?

A consent can be taken forty-eight hours after the child's birth and is revocable until the court hearing (about thirty days later) by the filing of a petition by the birth parent to set aside the consent; a court will then consider what is in the best interests of the child to be adopted.

Because most birth mothers and adoptive parents do not want the baby in foster care, some agencies place the baby directly in the adoptive couple's home before the first court hearing. This is considered a "legal risk placement" (i.e., the birth mother can change her mind after the baby is in the adoptive parents' home).

What are the birth father's rights?

If he has been named or claims to be the birth father, he must be notified of the adoption proceedings. He must assert his rights within sixty days of receiving notice, or his rights will be terminated.

What fees can adoptive parents pay?

Expenses allowed are counseling for the birth mother (including transportation), birth mother's living expenses, reasonable telephone costs, and reasonable maternity clothing costs. The cost for living expenses shall not exceed $1,500 unless approved in unusual circumstances by the court.

Where does the adoption hearing take place?

The hearing takes place in the county where the adoptive parents live or where the child placement adoption agency is located.

How are familial and stepparent adoptions different from nonbiological adoptions?

No agency involvement is required. If all necessary persons have consented, the court will waive the investigation and report by the Children and Youth Services.

Can a nonresident finalize an adoption in this state?

Yes.

DELAWARE LAWS RELATED TO ADOPTION: QUESTIONS AND ANSWERS

Independent adoption is illegal in Delaware. Identified adoptions are permitted, however, and most agencies are willing to conduct them.

If the fees for an agency are too high, it is suggested that a Delaware couple contact an attorney and then advertise and finalize an adoption in one of the following nearby states: New York, New Jersey, Pennsylvania, Maryland, Washington, D.C., Virginia, or South Carolina. (In New Jersey, Maryland, and Washington, D.C., an agency must be involved if an out-of-state couple finalizes there.) However, a Delaware agency must conduct your home study.

Can an attorney serve as an intermediary?
No.

Is advertising permitted?
No.

Who must consent to the adoption?
1. Both birth parents.
2. A licensed agency or the Department of Services for Children, Youth and Their Families.

When can consent be taken from the birth mother (father), and how long after the consent is signed can it be revoked?
Consent cannot be given by the birth mother until the child is born but can be given by the birth father before the child's birth. The birth parents or agency can request the court to revoke the consent within sixty days after filing the adoption petition. The court will then decide what is in the best interest of the child.

What are the birth father's rights?
The presumed father's consent is required unless he has abandoned the child.

What fees can adoptive parents pay?
The agency can only charge for services rendered, court costs, and legal fees.

Where does the adoption hearing take place?
The hearing can take place in the county where the adoptive parents reside or where the child placement agency is located.

How are familial and stepparent adoptions different from nonbiological adoptions?
An agency adoption is not required, but a home study is required. The child must be in the home for at least one year.

Can a nonresident finalize an adoption in this state?
No. You must be a resident. However, no specific length of time is required to establish residency.

WASHINGTON, D.C. LAWS RELATED TO ADOPTION: QUESTIONS AND ANSWERS

Can an attorney serve as an intermediary?
No.

Is advertising permitted?
Yes.

Who must consent to the adoption?
1. Both birth parents.
2. The child placement adoption agency, if involved.

When can consent be taken from the birth mother (father), and how long after the consent is signed can it be revoked?
A relinquishment is given in an agency adoption, and a consent is given in an independent adoption. These can both be signed seventy-two hours after the child's birth. A relinquishment can be revoked up to ten days after signing. A consent is irrevocable.

A birth parent must receive counseling prior to signing.

What are the birth father's rights?
As long the birth father has been given notice and it can be shown during a hearing that he has abandoned the child or has not provided support to the child for at least six months, his consent is not required. Also, his consent is not required if the court determines after a hearing that consent is withheld contrary to the best interests of the child. If the birth father cannot be located, the court will waive his consent after a detailed search is conducted.

What fees can adoptive parents pay?
There are no laws regarding permissible fees; however, medical and legal fees can be paid.

Where does the adoption hearing take place?
The Superior Court of D.C. has jurisdiction if the adoptive couple is a legal resident of Washington, D.C. or has lived there for one year, or if the child is in the legal custody of an agency licensed by Washington, D.C.

How are familial and stepparent adoptions different from nonbiological adoptions?
In a stepparent adoption, the court may waive the home study if the noncustodial parent consents to the adoption.

Can a nonresident finalize an adoption in Washington, D.C.?
Yes. However, the adoption must be an agency placement.

Source: District of Columbia Code, Chapter 3, Sections 16-301 to 16-315

FLORIDA LAWS RELATED TO ADOPTION: QUESTIONS AND ANSWERS

Can an attorney serve as an intermediary?
Yes. According to ICPC guidelines, an attorney or physician licensed in Florida can place children within the state.

Attorneys and agencies outside of Florida may place children in the state if they adhere to ICPC guidelines and the Florida Adoption Act.

Is advertising permitted?
Yes. Technically only attorneys and agencies may advertise, but advertising is a well-accepted practice. The law requires that a license number be shown on all adoption-related advertisements in the state. However, in practice a couple can place an ad without an attorney. Many newspapers will require a letter from your attorney.

Who must consent to the adoption?
1. The birth mother.
2. The birth father, if he has acknowledged in writing that he is the child's father or was married to the mother when the child was conceived or born, or if he has supported the child.
3. A consent is not necessary if it can be established that a birth parent has made only marginal efforts to assume parental responsibility.

When can consent be given by the birth mother (father), and how long after the consent is signed can it be revoked?
Consent by a birth mother cannot be given until forty-eight hours after the child is born; a birth father may sign at any time after birth. Once the consent is signed for a baby under six months, it is irrevocable; a consent signed for a child older than six months can be revoked three days after signing or at any time prior to placement. Once placement occurs, it is not revocable.

Unless excused by the court, the law requires an independent, licensed psychologist or social worker to interview the birth parents to ensure that consent was given on a voluntary basis. The same social worker would also conduct the adoptive couple's resident home study before the baby is placed in their home.

What are the birth father's rights?

Florida has a putative father registry, and a birth father must file a notarized claim at any time prior to birth or before the filing of a petition for termination of birth parent rights. The birth father may only challenge the adoption if he has provided meaningful emotional and financial support. The court must either excuse his consent or obtain it. The birth father's consent is not needed if he does not respond in writing to a request for his consent within sixty days.

What fees can adoptive parents pay?

All fees for an attorney or physician intermediary or out-of-state adoption agency must be submitted to the court for prior approval. Payment of living expenses is permitted up to six weeks after the baby's birth. Any fees over $800, except for medical, hospital, or court costs, must be preapproved by the court. A final report of all fees associated with the adoption must be reported to the court.

Where does the adoption hearing take place?

The adoption hearing takes place in the county where the adoptive parents reside or where the child placement agency is located.

How are familial and stepparent adoptions different from nonbiological adoptions?

No home study is required unless requested by the court. If the grandparents have visitation rights, their rights continue if a relative or stepparent adopts the child.

Can a nonresident finalize an adoption in this state?

Yes. There is some confusion as to whether the state's new adoption laws require nonresidents to finalize in Florida.

Source: Florida Statutes, Sections 63.012 to 63.301

GEORGIA LAWS RELATED TO ADOPTION: QUESTIONS AND ANSWERS

Can an attorney serve as an intermediary?

No.

Is advertising permitted?

No, and you may not post fliers either. Networking in Georgia is limited to those you know. We recommend getting out your school yearbook and professional, church denomination, and volunteer membership directories and send letters to as many people as possible.

Georgia residents who advertise in another state cannot finalize the adoption in Georgia; they must finalize in the state where they advertised. Therefore, make sure nonresidents can finalize in that state before you advertise.

Who must consent to the adoption?
1. The birth mother.
2. The child placement agency, if involved.
3. The birth father, unless he has abandoned the child, cannot be found, or has failed to support or communicate with the child or mother for longer than one year, or if he failed to support or communicate with the mother during her pregnancy.

When can consent be taken from the birth mother (father), and how long after the consent is signed can it be revoked?
Consent cannot be obtained until twenty-four hours after the child's birth. In both an agency and independent adoption, the birth parents have ten days after signing the consent to withdraw consent.

What are the birth father's rights?
Georgia law requires that a known or unknown birth father whose consent is not required has a right to a notice. The birth father of a child born out of wedlock must be served with notice of the hearing. If he does not respond within thirty days to notice of adoption, his parental rights will be terminated, and he cannot legally object to the adoption. If his location is not known, a petition will be filed with the court to terminate his rights and allow the adoption to occur. The court will then make a decision to proceed with the adoption based on whether the birth father has established a familial bond with the child or if reasonable efforts were made to locate him. Publication for the unknown birth father must be done.

Judges very seldom permit a birth mother to not name the birth father. In one scenario, an adoption took more than one year to finalize because the birth mother would not name a birth father who had threatened her life.

Parental rights can also be terminated because of a felony and imprisonment that has a negative effect on the parent-child relationship.

A birth father who has registered with the putative father registry is entitled to notice of adoption proceedings.

What fees can adoptive parents pay?
Only medical and legal expenses for the birth mother and child are permitted. Any other payment is considered an inducement. Only in an agency adoption can living expenses be paid. A report of payments must be filed with the court. Every

attorney must also file a report of all fees paid or promised to the attorney for all services rendered.

Where does the adoption hearing take place?

The hearing takes place in the court in the county where the adoptive parents reside.

How are familial and stepparent adoptions different from nonbiological adoptions?

Some courts do not require a home study. The child's biological parents must give written permission for a relative or stepparent to adopt the child.

If the grandparents have court-ordered visitation rights previous to an adoption, they may file an objection to an adoption by another blood relative. The court will then decide if the child should be adopted by the other relative. If the court approves the adoption, the grandparent's visitation rights remain.

Can a nonresident finalize an adoption in this state?

No. You must be a resident of Georgia for at least six months before filing to adopt.

HAWAII LAWS RELATED TO ADOPTION: QUESTIONS AND ANSWERS

Can an attorney serve as an intermediary?

Yes.

Is advertising permitted?

No. Only attorneys can advertise.

Who must consent to the adoption?

1. The birth mother.
2. The presumed birth father.

When can consent be taken from the birth mother (father), and how long after the consent is signed can it be revoked?

Consent can be taken at any time after the sixth month of pregnancy and is considered irrevocable once the child is placed, unless placement is not in the child's best interest.

The birth parents may have to appear in court unless the consent is taken before the court hearing and is accepted by the court without a personal appearance.

What are the birth father's rights?

The birth father's consent is required if he was married to the birth mother (or attempted to marry her) at the time of child's birth or if the child was born within 300 days after their marriage ended; or if he has received the child in his home as his own child or acknowledges paternity in writing or agreed to his name being placed on the child's birth certificate; or if by court order or written promise, he agrees to support the child.

Also, notice to a birth father is required if he is not a "legal," "court approved," or a "presumed" father but is a father who has filed a petition for paternity within the first thirty days of the child's birth, or before the birth mother consented to the adoption, or before the placement of the child with the adoptive parents.

Notice to a birth father is not required if he was not married to the birth mother at time of conception or birth and the court upon good cause finds that the birth father has not shown by a concerted effort interest or responsibility for the child to be adopted.

A birth father's consent is not necessary if it can be shown that he deserted the minor child to be adopted for a period of ninety days or he has not supported the child or had contact with the child for a period of one year.

What fees can adoptive parents pay?

The law does not address this matter.

Where does the adoption hearing take place?

The hearing may take place in the family court where the adoptive parents live, where the child was born, or where the child placement agency is located.

How are familial and stepparent adoptions different from nonbiological adoptions?

The law does not address this issue.

Can a nonresident finalize an adoption in this state?

Yes.

IDAHO LAWS RELATED TO ADOPTION: QUESTIONS AND ANSWERS

Can an attorney serve as an intermediary?

Yes.

Is advertising permitted?

No.

Who must consent to the adoption?
The birth parents.

When can consent be taken from the birth mother (father), and how long after the consent is signed can it be revoked?
The birth mother can give consent any time after the child's birth; if birth parents petition for revocation, they must reimburse the adoptive couple for expenses paid. A revocation period is not addressed in statute.

What are the birth father's rights?
The birth father may claim rights if he registers with the Registry of Vital Statistics of the Department of Health and Welfare. This claim must occur before the child is placed or before the commencement of any legal action to terminate the parental rights of the birth mother. If he fails to file, he can never try to establish paternity, and his parental rights may be terminated. The Department of Health and Welfare, the adoption agency, or the adoption attorney must notify him of his need to register so that if he desires, he can give his intent to support the child and exercise his rights. If the birth father cannot be located, an attempt must be made to notify him through publication at least ten days before parental rights are terminated or the child is placed with an agency.

What fees can adoptive parents pay?
Payment of medical, legal, and some living expenses is permitted but cannot exceed $2,000 without court approval.

Where does the adoption hearing take place?
The hearing usually takes place in the District Court in the county where the adoptive parents reside.

How are familial and stepparent adoptions different from nonbiological adoptions?
A home study may be required if requested by the court. There is no state residency requirement.

Can a nonresident finalize an adoption in this state?
No. You must live in the state for at least six consecutive months.

Source: Idaho Code, Sections 16-1501 to 16-1513

ILLINOIS LAWS RELATED TO ADOPTION: QUESTIONS AND ANSWERS

Can an attorney serve as an intermediary?
Many attorneys do, but technically they should not.

Is advertising permitted?
Technically it is not permitted, but it is done extensively.

Who must consent to the adoption?
1. The birth mother.
2. The birth father, if married to the birth mother, or if the child was born out of wedlock and he has lived with the child for six months and has openly stated that he is the child's father, or has maintained substantial and continuous contact with the child during a six-month period of the prior year; if the child is placed less than six months after birth and the birth father has held himself out as the birth father within thirty days of birth and has likely paid or made good faith effort to pay for the expenses of birth and further financial support of the child within thirty days of birth; if he has registered with the putative father registry and commenced a paternity action within thirty days of birth or within ten days of it being possible to register in cases where the birth father can show that he could not register through no fault of his own.

When can consent be taken from the birth mother (father), and how long after the consent is signed can it be revoked?
Consent cannot be given until seventy-two hours after the child's birth. However, the birth father's consent can be given before the birth, and he can revoke his consent within seventy-two hours of the birth if he notifies the representative to whom he had given consent. Rights are terminated via written consents taken in the presence of a notary public or, preferably, in the presence of a judge. Consent is irrevocable.

The consents must include confirmation that three hours of counseling were offered to the birth parents.

What are the birth father's rights?
Illinois has a putative father registry, and a birth father (generally) must register within thirty days of birth and initiate a parentage action. He can also establish his rights by marrying the birth mother, holding himself out as the birth father, and by having substantial contact with the birth mother, and by paying for expenses and support.

What fees can adoptive parents pay?

Adoptive parents can pay reasonable living expenses, legal expenses, and medical expenses, as needed. No fees can be paid for placing a child.

Where does the adoption hearing take place?

The hearing may take place in the county where the adoptive parents reside, where the birth parents reside, where the baby was born, or where the child placement agency is located.

How are familial and stepparent adoptions different from nonbiological adoptions?

The process is faster (four to six weeks), and the home study and criminal check are not mandatory. If a home study is conducted, there is minimal investigation. Grandparents have visitation rights if the adoption is by close relatives and occurs after the death of both parents.

Can a nonresident finalize an adoption in this state?

Yes, but only if the child is placed by an agency; otherwise, adoptive parents must have lived in the state for six months.

Source: Illinois Revised Statutes, Sections 750-50-.01 to 750-5-24

INDIANA LAWS RELATED TO ADOPTION: QUESTIONS AND ANSWERS

Can an attorney serve as an intermediary?

Yes, intermediaries are permitted to place children for adoption.

Is advertising permitted?

Yes.

Who must consent to the adoption?

1. The birth mother.
2. The birth father, if married to the birth mother, or if the birth father's paternity is established by the court.
3. The parents of a birth parent who is under eighteen years old, if the court decides that it is in the adoptee's best interest to get their consent.

When can consent be taken from the birth mother (father), and how long after the consent is signed can it be revoked?

Consent can be given twenty-four hours after the child's birth. It can be revoked within thirty days of being given if the court determines it is in the child's best interest (which is very difficult to prove). The adoption usually takes place three to four months after the consent is signed, but it can take up to one year. Every county is different.

What are the birth father's rights?

Birth fathers are entitled to receive a notice of the adoption, either before or after the birth. If the birth mother identifies the birth father and provides his address, he must receive the notice. If the birth mother does not name him or provide his address, he must file with the putative father registry any time during the pregnancy or up to thirty days after the child's birth or the filing of the adoption petition in order to assert his rights. A birth father's or putative father's consent is irrevocably implied without any court action if thirty days after receiving actual notice he fails to file a paternity action or in the case where he files, he fails to establish paternity within a reasonable time frame.

What fees can adoptive parents pay?

Reasonable expenses are permitted for the birth mother's medical needs and legal fees. Reasonable living expenses during her pregnancy and up to six weeks later can also be paid. Total expenses cannot exceed $3,000 unless approved by the court. Lost wages must be offset by payment of living expenses and unemployment compensation benefits.

Where does the adoption hearing take place?

The hearing may take place in the county where the adoptive parents reside, where the adoptee lives, or where the child placement agency is located.

How are familial and stepparent adoptions different from nonbiological adoptions?

These adoptions are handled the same way as nonrelative adoptions, except that written approval of an adoption agency or the Department of Public Welfare is not necessary. Grandparents may be given visitation rights when adopted by a stepparent.

Can a nonresident finalize an adoption in this state?

No, unless they are adopting a special needs child.

Source: Indiana Code, Sections 31-19-1-1 to 31-19-25-14

IOWA LAWS RELATED TO ADOPTION: QUESTIONS AND ANSWERS

Can an attorney serve as an intermediary?

Yes, attorneys can place children in adoptive homes.

Is advertising permitted?
Yes.

Who must consent to the adoption?
The birth parents must consent; except if it can be shown that a birth parent has failed to support the child or has abandoned the child, then the birth parent's consent is not necessary. Also, if the birth parent is a chronic substance abuser or has committed more than one act of domestic abuse, then that birth parent's consent is not necessary.

When can consent be taken from the birth mother (father), and how long after the consent is signed can it be revoked?
The consent cannot be taken until seventy-two hours after the child's birth. The birth parent can revoke consent within ninety-six hours after signing. This means the child must be at least eight days old before the consent is irrevocable.

At least three hours of counseling must be made available to birth parents who request it.

What are the birth father's rights?
If a birth father cannot be located or refuses to give consent, the court will determine if the adoption is in the child's best interest without such a consent.

Iowa has a putative father registry, and a man seeking birth father rights must register before or after the child's birth, but no later than the filing of a petition to terminate his parental rights to the child to be adopted.

What fees can adoptive parents pay?
The adoptive parents must file with the court a statement of all money paid.

Where does the adoption hearing take place?
The hearing takes place in the county where the adoptive parents reside.

How are familial and stepparent adoptions different from nonbiological adoptions?
Family relations may be distant, and the adoption can still be considered a relative adoption. The child does not necessarily have to live in the home for at least six months, as is the case with other adoptions, in order for the adoption to be finalized.

Grandparents may be given visitation rights when a grandchild is adopted by a stepparent, as long as the grandparents already have a substantial relationship with the child and it is in the child's best interest.

Can a nonresident finalize an adoption in this state?
No.

Source: Iowa Code Sections 600.1 to 600.24. 24

KANSAS LAW RELATED TO ADOPTION:
QUESTIONS AND ANSWERS

Can an attorney serve as an intermediary?

A reading of the statute would seem to indicate that an attorney cannot act as an intermediary, but the custom in the state is that as long as attorneys only charge for legal services then attorneys can act as intermediaries.

Is advertising permitted?

Possibly. Even though the existing statute forbids it, there has been some allowance of advertising. People are advertising in Kansas newspapers.

By law, only adoption agencies can advertise in newspapers; however, attorneys can place advertisements in the yellow pages.

Who must consent to the adoption?

Both birth parents.

When can consent be taken from the birth mother (father), and how long after the consent is signed can it be revoked?

Consents (for independent adoptions) and relinquishments (for agency adoptions) cannot be obtained until twelve hours after the baby's birth and are irrevocable. Consents must be acknowledged before a judge. The birth parents' rights in an independent adoption are terminated at a court hearing that takes place thirty to sixty days after the adoption petition is filed. The birth father can sign a consent or relinquishment before the birth, but he can revoke it seventy-two hours after birth.

What are the birth father's rights?

The birth father's consent is not necessary if he is not a "presumed" father, if his relationship has not been established by the court, or if he is not married to the birth mother. If he voluntarily agrees to place the child for adoption, the birth mother must file a petition to terminate his parental rights. A birth father's parental rights may be involuntarily terminated for failure to support the birth mother during the last six months of pregnancy, unfitness, abandonment of the child, abandonment of the mother despite knowledge of her pregnancy, rape, or nonsupport of the child for at least two years. (The proceeding terms, as appropriate, also apply to birth mothers.)

The court must make efforts to determine who the father is based on certain factors (e.g., if he has provided for the child or was married to the mother at time of conception). If these factors cannot be found and he does not claim his rights to the child, his rights can be terminated.

What fees can adoptive parents pay?

Legal, medical, living expenses, and counseling fees associated with the adoption can be paid, and these fees must be approved by the court.

Health insurers are required to offer adoptive parents the option to purchase coverage for the birth mother's delivery expenses.

Where does the adoption hearing take place?

The hearing can take place in the county where the adoptive parents live, the child lives, or where the adoption agency is located.

How are familial and stepparent adoptions different from nonbiological adoptions?

Home studies are not necessary in stepparent adoptions, and the court may waive the need for one when grandparents are adopting. All other issues remain the same.

Can a nonresident finalize an adoption in this state?

Yes.

KENTUCKY LAWS RELATED TO ADOPTION: QUESTIONS AND ANSWERS

Can an attorney serve as an intermediary?

Yes, in a stepparent or relative adoption and only upon written approval of the Secretary of Human Resources in a private adoption.

Is advertising permitted?

No. Prospective adoptive parents cannot advertise in newspapers or other publications, but they can post fliers and distribute business cards.

Who must consent to the adoption?

1. The birth mother.
2. The birth father, if he is married to and lives with the birth mother, or if not married to the birth mother but his paternity has been determined by a court order, or if an affidavit of paternity is filed.

When can consent be given by the birth mother (father), and how long after the consent is signed can it be revoked?

Consent cannot be given until seventy-two hours after birth. The consent can only be revoked if done within twenty days after the adoptive parents have been approved by the Cabinet for Human Resources or twenty days after placement if approval provided prior to birth.

What are the birth father's rights?

The birth father's consent is needed if paternity has been determined by the court or an affidavit of paternity is filed with the court. He generally must assert his paternity within sixty days after birth. The birth father will lose his parental rights if he has abandoned the child for ninety days or has not cared for or protected the child for at least six months.

What fees can adoptive parents pay?

Adoptive parents can pay for medical, legal, counseling, and living expenses, subject to court review and approval. An adoption agency is permitted to charge reasonable fees.

Where does the adoption hearing take place?

The hearing takes place in the county where the adoptive parents live.

How are familial and stepparent adoptions different from nonbiological adoptions?

Home studies may not be necessary in a stepparent or close relative adoption. The law does not specifically address these types of adoptions.

Can a nonresident finalize an adoption in this state?

No. Only residents and nonresidents who have lived in Kentucky for at least one year can adopt.

Source: Kentucky Revised Statutes Annotated, Sections 199.470 to 199.590

LOUISIANA LAWS RELATED TO ADOPTION: QUESTIONS AND ANSWERS

Can an attorney serve as an intermediary?

Yes.

Is advertising permitted?

The statute covering advertising indicates that only licensed child placement agencies or Louisiana-based crisis pregnancy centers can advertise relative to adoption plans.

Who must consent to the adoption?

1. The birth mother.
2. The birth father.
3. The parents or guardians of any birth parents who are under the age of eighteen at the time of surrender (applies to independent adoptions only).

When can consent be taken from the birth mother (father), and how long after the consent is signed can it be revoked?

In both agency and private adoptions, a consent cannot be given by a birth mother until the child is five days old. Consent is essentially irrevocable. A birth father can sign at any time prior to birth or after, but his consent is irrevocable only on the fifth day after birth.

Birth parents' rights are terminated at a court hearing, but the birth parents' appearance is not required.

What are the birth father's rights?

The birth father of a child born out of wedlock must consent to the adoption before the mother's termination or relinquishment, unless he has signed a valid surrender. In Louisiana, legal fathers, fathers who have formally acknowledged or legitimized the child (even if they are not the biological father), or fathers who register with the putative father registry must provide a Consent or Surrender of Parental Rights, except in cases in which the birth father has failed to support the child or has failed to communicate with or visit the child for six months.

What fees can adoptive parents pay?

Medical, hospital, and legal fees can be paid. A statement of fees paid must be included in the adoption petition.

Where does the adoption hearing take place?

The hearing may take place in the county where the adoptive parents reside.

How are familial and stepparent adoptions different from nonbiological adoptions?

No home study is required. The adoption can be finalized quickly, and no written termination of parental rights is necessarily required. In stepparent adoptions in which the former spouse has died, the grandparents may be granted limited visitation rights.

Can a nonresident finalize an adoption in this state?

Yes.

Source: Louisiana Revised Statutes Annotated Sections 9:400, Ch. C. Title XII and 40:74 to 40.79

MAINE LAWS RELATED TO ADOPTION: QUESTIONS AND ANSWERS

Can an attorney serve as an intermediary?

Yes.

Is advertising permitted?
Adoption agencies can advertise in accordance with rules set forth by the State Social Services Department.

Who must consent to the adoption?
The birth mother and the birth father (if married to the birth mother).

When can consent be taken from the birth mother (father), and how long after the consent is signed can it be revoked?
The law is not clear, but it appears consent can be given any time after the child's birth. Parental consent in an independent adoption is executed before a judge. The consent can be revoked up to three days after the consent is signed; after three days the consent becomes final and irrevocable. In an agency adoption, consent is not given until seventy-two hours after birth and is signed before a notary, filed with the probate court, and is irrevocable.

What are the birth father's rights?
The birth father must provide a consent if his name is on the birth certificate, his whereabouts are known, and he is involved in the child's life. Otherwise, his consent is not needed. If the birth father has been given notice of the adoption, he has twenty days to petition the court to establish his paternity. The judge will then decide whether to give the birth father parental rights, based on the birth father's ability and willingness to support the child.

What fees can adoptive parents pay?
Reasonable living expenses, counseling for birth mother and birth father, transportation costs, medical costs, agency fees, and legal fees can be paid.

Where does the adoption hearing take place?
The hearing can take place in the county where the adoptive parents live, where the child lives, or where the adoption agency is located.

How are familial and stepparent adoptions different from nonbiological adoptions?
When a blood relative is adopting, no home study is required.

Can a nonresident finalize an adoption in this state?
Yes.

Source: Maine Revised Statutes Annotated Title 19, Sections 1101 to 1144, Title 22, 2706-A to 2766, 4171 to 4176, and 8201 to 8204

MARYLAND LAWS RELATED TO ADOPTION: QUESTIONS AND ANSWERS

Can an attorney serve as an intermediary?
No.

Is advertising permitted?
Yes.

Who must consent to the adoption?
1. Birth mother.
2. Birth father who is married to the birth mother; is named on the birth certificate; is identified by the birth mother or birth father; or who has held himself out as the birth father and the birth mother agrees.
3. Adopting agency that placed the child.

When can consent be taken from the birth mother (father), and how long after the consent is signed can it be revoked?
Consent cannot be taken until the child's birth. The birth parents can revoke their consent up to thirty days after signing or until the final adoption decree is entered, whichever occurs first. A final adoption decree can be challenged up to six months after finalization for reasons of fraud or duress.

What are the birth father's rights?
His consent is not required in cases in which the child is abandoned by the birth father or the adoption is in the best interest of the child, provided, however, the child has not been in the birth father's custody for at least one year; the child has been in the adoptive couple's custody for six months; the adoptive couple has bonded with the child; and the birth father has no contact with the child or has not supported or cared for the child.

What fees can adoptive parents pay?
Payments for reasonable medical, hospital, and legal services are permitted. In an independent adoption, the birth parents will be advised of their right to receive legal counsel and adoption counseling; the court may order the adoptive parents to pay all or some of these costs. A description of all fees paid must be filed with the court.

Where does the adoption hearing take place?
The law does not address this issue. According to ICPC, the petition for adoption is filed in the county where the adoptive parents live.

How are familial and stepparent adoptions different from nonbiological adoptions?

Familial adoptions are treated just like an independent adoption, including a home study.

Can a nonresident finalize an adoption in this state?

Yes, but only if an agency receives consent from the birth parents.

Source: Maryland Codes Annotated Family Law Sections 5-301 to 5-330 and 5-4A-01 to 5-4A-07

MASSACHUSETTS LAWS RELATED TO ADOPTION: QUESTIONS AND ANSWERS

Independent adoption is illegal in Massachusetts; however, an agency-identified adoption is permissible. Adoptive parents may participate in independent adoptions in other states. The other state's laws and guidelines would then govern the process.

Can an attorney serve as an intermediary?

An attorney can serve as intermediary provided the adoptive family has a home study done by a Massachusetts agency and the child is surrendered to an agency.

Is advertising permitted?

No.

Who must consent to the adoption?

1. The birth mother and the child placement agency.
2. The birth father if he is married to the birth mother.

When can consent be taken from the birth mother (father), and how long after the consent is signed can it be revoked?

Consent cannot be taken until four days after the child is born and is irrevocable.

What are the birth father's rights?

Notice must be sent to the birth father who files a declaration of paternity with the Department of Social Services. Consent of the birth father is not necessary if notice of the adoption proceedings is served on him and he does not object within thirty days or if the court finds that it is in the child's best interest not to require the consent in view of the birth father's lack of ability, capacity, fitness, and readiness to take parental responsibility or if the child has been in an adoption agency's custody at least one year.

What fees can adoptive parents pay?

Payments for reasonable living, medical, hospital, and legal services are permitted.

Where does the adoption hearing take place?

The hearing takes place in the county where the child or the adoptive parents live.

How are familial and stepparent adoptions different from nonbiological adoptions?

No home study or agency involvement is required, thereby saving time and expenses.

Can a nonresident finalize an adoption in this state?

Yes, but only if an agency receives consent from the birth parents.

Source: Massachusetts General Laws Chapter 210, Section I to 11 A

MICHIGAN LAWS RELATED TO ADOPTION: QUESTIONS AND ANSWERS

Can an attorney serve as an intermediary?

Yes, but the attorney cannot be reimbursed for this service.

Is advertising permitted?

Yes. Some newspapers may accept classified ads with a letter from an attorney or agency.

Who must consent to the adoption?

1. Both birth parents must consent unless they have released the child to an adoption agency, or the birth father's consent is not required for the reason(s) outlined below.
2. If an agency has custody of the child, the agency must consent.

When can consent be taken from birth mother (father), and how long after the consent is signed can it be revoked?

A consent must be given before a judge who must explain their parental rights to the birth parents. A consent is not needed if the child is released to an adoption agency and the rights of the birth parents are thereafter terminated by court proceedings, notice of which they must receive. Consent must be given within a reasonable time frame; if this is not done, the court may determine if the withholding of consent is "arbitrary and capricious." If the birth parents select the adoptive parents, then approval must be granted by the probate court as to the placement.

A birth parent may petition the court to revoke his or her consent prior to the child being placed with the adoptive couple, at which point the consent becomes irrevocable.

What are the birth father's rights?

If the alleged birth father's consent cannot be obtained, the adoption cannot take place until his rights are terminated. The birth mother can terminate her own parental rights while waiting for him to do so. The birth father's rights can be terminated if these requirements are met:

- He does not respond to notice of the adoption.
- He denies interest in custody of the child.
- He fails to appear at the adoption hearing and denies interest in the child.
- His identity or location are unknown and reasonable efforts have been made to find him, and he has not provided for or cared for the child for at least ninety days.
- If the birth father requests custody, the court shall determine his ability to care for the child and if it is in the child's best interest.

What fees can adoptive parents pay?

Adoptive parents can pay for the birth mother's medical expenses, counseling, legal fees, travel, and reasonable living expenses. Fees and charges must be approved by the court.

Where does the adoption hearing take place?

The hearing can take place in the court of the county where the adoptive parents live or where the child lives.

How are familial and stepparent adoptions different from nonbiological adoptions?

There are no specific provisions in the law for relative adoptions. In a stepparent adoption, a parent who does not have legal custody of the child but whose rights have not been terminated must consent to the adoption.

Can a nonresident finalize an adoption in this state?

Yes.

MINNESOTA LAWS RELATED TO ADOPTION: QUESTIONS AND ANSWERS

Can an attorney serve as an intermediary?

No.

Is advertising permitted?

Yes.

Who must consent to the adoption?
1. The birth parents.
2. If a birth parent is a minor, consent of the minor's parent or guardian is also required.

When can consent be taken from the birth mother (father), and how long after the consent is signed can it be revoked?
Consent cannot be signed until seventy-two hours after birth. Case law appears to suggest that the consent is irrevocable unless fraud, duress, or undue influence can be shown in addition to showing that it would be in the child's best interest to revoke the consent. A consent must be signed before an agency or a judge. If a birth mother refuses counseling by an agency, she must sign the consent in front of a judge.

What are the birth father's rights?
A birth father is the presumed father if his name is on the birth certificate, he has substantially supported the child, or has been identified as the father. The presumed birth father must have his rights terminated through a consent or in court after providing him notice of the hearing and showing that he has abandoned the child over a certain period of time. If a nonpresumed birth father wants to retain his rights, he must file a paternity action within thirty days after the birth of the child or within thirty days of receiving notice from the birth father registry with which he must register.

The unwed birth father must be served a notice of the adoption placement and hearing, but this can be waived if the child was conceived as a result of rape or incest or if locating him might cause physical or severe emotional harm to the birth mother or child.

What fees can adoptive parents pay?
Adoptive parents can pay for legal, medical, counseling, and reasonable living expenses. No expenses can be paid beyond six weeks after birth.

Where does the adoption hearing take place?
The hearing takes place in the court of the county where the adoptive parents live.

How are familial and stepparent adoptions different from nonbiological adoptions?
Familial adoptions are not different from nonfamilial adoptions. In stepparent adoptions, the court can waive the home study requirement. Also, the consent requires just two witnesses and a notary public; no agency or judge is required to

take the consent. In a stepparent adoption, the residence requirement of living in Minnesota for one year may also be waived.

Can a nonresident finalize an adoption in this state?

No. The adoptive parents must have lived in Minnesota for at least one year and with the child for three months. The court can waive this requirement.

Special Note: If the biological parents request that the child be placed with an adoptive family of the same or similar religious or ethnic background, the agency shall do so if a family is available.

Source: Minnesota Code Annotated Sections 259:10 to 259:49

MISSISSIPPI LAWS RELATED TO ADOPTION: QUESTIONS AND ANSWERS

Can an attorney serve as an intermediary?

Yes.

Is advertising permitted?

Yes.

Who must consent to the adoption?

Both birth parents must consent if married to each other. Consent is not necessary if it can be shown that the parent has abandoned or deserted the child to be adopted. Also, no consent is needed if it can be established that the parent is mentally, morally, or otherwise unfit to raise the child.

When can consent be taken from the birth mother (father), and how long after the consent is signed can it be revoked?

Consent cannot be given until the child is three days old and is irrevocable, unless it can be shown that a consent was signed by way of fraud, under duress or undue influence, and it would be in the best interests of the child to revoke the consent.

What are the birth father's rights?

If the birth father is not married to the birth mother, he does not have a right to object to the adoption, unless within thirty days of birth he demonstrates a full commitment to being a parent.

What fees can adoptive parents pay?

Reasonable fees approved by the court may be charged for the preadoption investigation. Also, medical, legal, and, in some instances, living expenses can be paid.

Where does the adoption hearing take place?
The hearing takes place in the court of the county where the adoptive parents live or where the child lives.

How are familial and stepparent adoptions different from nonbiological adoptions?
The residency requirement is waived.

Can a nonresident finalize an adoption in this state?
No. Adoptive parents must have resided in the state for ninety days before filing the adoption petition.

Source: Mississippi Code Annotated Sections 93-17-1 to 93-17-223

MISSOURI LAWS RELATED TO ADOPTION: QUESTIONS AND ANSWERS

Can an attorney serve as an intermediary?
Yes.

Is advertising permitted?
Yes.

Who must consent to the adoption?
The birth parents and the court must consent.

When can consent be taken from the birth mother (father), and how long after the consent is signed can it be revoked?
Written consent can be given either before or after birth, but it is only valid when the consent is reviewed and accepted by a judge. The consent should be filed immediately after it is signed. Judges will consider a birth parent who wants to revoke consent up to the first court hearing, which usually takes place about one to two weeks after the consent is filed.

Some judges require the child to be placed in foster care before being placed with the adoptive couple and before the parental rights are terminated. Because many birth mothers and adoptive parents are opposed to this, a court must be selected that will permit direct placement of the child into the couple's home. It appears that using an experienced attorney to resolve this situation is critical.

What are the birth father's rights?
If the birth father's identity is unknown or cannot be determined, then his consent is not needed. Either birth mother or birth father can waive in writing the need to provide consent. Also, no consent is required if either birth parent willfully

abandoned the child or neglected to provide the child with care and protection for a period of sixty days (if the child is under one year of age) or for a period of six months (if the child is over one year of age). In addition, consent from either parent is not required if that parent is served with the adoption complaint and either does not file an answer with the court or does not appear at the court hearing.

There is a birth father registry, and the birth father must file either before birth or within fifteen days after birth a notice of intent to claim paternity.

What fees can adoptive parents pay?
Legal, medical, and reasonable living expenses can be paid. All statements of payment must be submitted to the court. The court may refuse to allow the adoption if payments were unreasonable or if the adoptive parents did not report all expenses paid.

Where does the adoption hearing take place?
It can take place in the juvenile court in the county where the adoptive parents live or where the child lives.

How are familial and stepparent adoptions different from nonbiological adoptions?
The court may waive the home study requirement in a stepparent adoption.

Can a nonresident finalize an adoption in this state?
Yes. If you are not from Missouri but adopt a child there, however, a Missouri adoption agency must review your home study (conducted in your state), and the court must verify the home study. The cost for a Missouri agency to review your home study is usually about $2,000.

Source: Missouri Revised Statutes, Chapter 453, Sections 453.005 to 453.503

MONTANA LAWS RELATED TO ADOPTION: QUESTIONS AND ANSWERS

Can an attorney serve as an intermediary?
No.

Is advertising permitted?
No. Nor is any public solicitation permitted, such as posting fliers or sending letters, except to people that you know.

Who must consent to the adoption?
1. Both birth parents.
2. The executive head of an agency (if an agency adoption).

When can consent be taken from the birth mother (father), and how long after the consent is signed can it be revoked?

Consent cannot be given until seventy-two hours after the child's birth and is irrevocable once an order of termination has been issued; the birth mother must have received counseling prior to signing. If the birth mother changes her mind, the court will consider the best interests of the child up until the time the adoption is finalized.

What are the birth father's rights?

If he is named on the birth certificate with his consent or if he is otherwise named, his consent is required. If he acknowledges paternity in a writing filed with the Department of Health and Environmental Sciences in the district court in his home county, then his consent is also required. If he contests the adoption, he must present his case to the court. A birth father's rights may be terminated without his consent if he is served with a notice thirty days before the child's expected date of delivery and he fails to file a notice of intent to claim paternity before the child's birth. If the birth father's whereabouts are not known, then his rights can be terminated if he has not provided support for the mother or shown any interest in the child or otherwise provided for the child's care during a time period of ninety days before the adoption hearing. If the birth father's identity is unknown, then his rights can be terminated if he has not supported the birth mother during her pregnancy or provided support for the child after the birth.

The state has a birth father registry, and the birth father must file within seventy-two hours after birth his intent.

What fees can adoptive parents pay?

Legal, medical, and other reasonable expenses can be paid. In an independent adoption, all fees and expenses must be submitted in an itemized statement to the court.

Where does the adoption hearing take place?

The adoption hearing takes place in the District Court in the county where the adoptive parents reside.

How are familial and stepparent adoptions different from nonbiological adoptions?

The home study report may be waived by the court. In relative adoptions, the pre-adoption investigation and report that is required of all adoptions may be waived.

Can a nonresident finalize an adoption in this state?

No. You must be residing in the state at the time of petition.

Source: Montana Code Annotated Title Sections 42-2-101 to 42-2-503

NEBRASKA LAWS RELATED TO ADOPTION: QUESTIONS AND ANSWERS

Can an attorney serve as an intermediary?

This is open to interpretation; the attorney general opinion states that an attorney can legally assist birth parents and adoptive parents in meeting each other. Also, although it is unlawful for anyone to place a child for adoption without a license, this does not prevent an attorney from assisting a birth parent in selecting an adoptive couple.

Is advertising permitted?

No.

Who must consent to the adoption?

1. Both birth parents must consent if married to each other.
2. The birth mother must consent if the child was born out of wedlock.

When can consent be taken from the birth mother (father), and how long after the consent is signed can it be revoked?

Consent in a private placement must be done in front of the birth mother's attorney and at least one other witness. The consent is irrevocable when signed; however, until the final adoption, the birth mother can revoke her consent, which then forces a judge to consider whether remaining with the adoptive couple or being returned to the birth mother is in the best interests of the child. Relinquishment to an agency is irrevocable after the agency accepts full responsibility for the child.

What are the birth father's rights?

The unmarried father's rights are not recognized unless he files a notice to claim paternity within five days after the baby's birth or within five days after receiving notice of the adoption proceedings. If he wants custody of the child, the court will determine if he can properly care for the child and if it would be in the child's best interest. If it can be shown that the birth father has abandoned the child for at least six months, then his rights can also be terminated.

What fees can adoptive parents pay?

There are no special provisions in the law, but adoptive parents can pay for living, medical, counseling, and one-time legal expenses.

Where does the adoption hearing take place?

The hearing takes place in the court of the county where the adoptive parents live.

How are familial and stepparent adoptions different from nonbiological adoptions?

In stepparent adoptions, the home study is sometimes waived.

Can a nonresident finalize an adoption in this state?

No.

Source: Nebraska Revised Statutes Sections 43-101 to 43-160

NEVADA LAWS RELATED TO ADOPTION: QUESTIONS AND ANSWERS

If you live in Nevada but adopt in another state or if you live in another state and adopt a child from Nevada, you must pay the ICPC fee of $1,000.

Can an attorney serve as an intermediary?

Yes, but no fee can be charged for the service.

Is advertising permitted?

No.

Who must consent to the adoption?

1. Both birth parents.
2. An agency, if involved.

When can consent be taken from the birth mother (father), and how long after the consent is signed can it be revoked?

The birth father can sign a consent before the child's birth if he is not married to the birth mother. The birth mother's consent cannot be given until seventy-two hours after birth. Consent cannot be revoked, and consents must be taken in front of a licensed social worker, preferably a Department of Child and Family Services caseworker.

What are the birth father's rights?

His consent is required. If he wants to parent the child and comes forward in a timely fashion, he has the right to parent unless it can be shown that it would not be in the child's best interests.

What fees can adoptive parents pay?

Reasonable living expenses can be paid, and an affidavit of all medical fees and other expenses paid must be submitted to the court.

Unlike other states, Nevada has a law that makes it illegal for the birth parent to receive money for medical expenses or other necessary expenses from an adoptive parent if she has no true intention of placing the child for adoption. Certainly every birth mother has the right to change her mind; she just cannot use adoption plans as a means of having her bills paid for by an adoptive couple.

Where does the adoption hearing take place?
The hearing takes place in the District Court where the adoptive parents live or where the child lives.

How are familial and stepparent adoptions different from nonbiological adoptions?
The court may waive the home study requirement.

Can a nonresident finalize an adoption in this state?
No. You must have resided in Nevada for six months before the adoption.

Source: Nevada Revised Statutes Vol. 11, Sections 127.005 to 127.420

NEW HAMPSHIRE LAWS RELATED TO ADOPTION: QUESTIONS AND ANSWERS

Can an attorney serve as an intermediary?
Yes.

Is advertising permitted?
Yes.

Who must consent to the adoption?
1. Both birth parents must consent if married to each other.
2. The involved agency must consent.
3. If the birth mother is under eighteen years old, then her parents may be required to sign a consent.

When can consent be taken from the birth mother (father), and how long after the consent is signed can it be revoked?
Consent cannot be taken until seventy-two hours after the child's birth. Consent can be withdrawn until the final decree if the court finds that it is in the best interests of the child not to remain with the adoptive couple but to be returned to the birth parent.

What are the birth father's rights?
A birth father has the right to a hearing to prove paternity if he is named by the birth mother, has filed a notice with the Office of Child Support and Enforcement that he is the father, or if he is living with the birth mother or child and providing support. He must request such a hearing within thirty days after receiving notice of the adoption proceeding, and if he does not do so, then he forfeits all parental rights to the child.

If the birth father is not married to the birth mother and has not met the above paternity requirements, then his consent is not required.

What fees can adoptive parents pay?

The adoptive parents must file a statement with the court listing all legal fees and medical expenses paid, as well as living expenses paid for the birth parents.

Where does the adoption hearing take place?

The hearing takes place in the Probate Court where the adoptive parents or adoptee lives.

How are familial and stepparent adoptions different from nonbiological adoptions?

The court may waive the home study requirement.

Can a nonresident finalize an adoption in this state?

No. There is a six-month residency requirement for the adoptive parent or the child, unless the child is in the legal care of a licensed adoption agency in New Hampshire. If that is the case, then the adoption can be finalized in the county in which the agency maintains its main office.

Source: New Hampshire Revised Statutes Sections 170-B: 1 to 170- B: 26

NEW JERSEY LAWS RELATED TO ADOPTION: QUESTIONS AND ANSWERS

Can an attorney serve as an intermediary?

Yes, but he or she cannot be paid for such services.

Is advertising permitted?

Yes.

Who must consent to the adoption?

Both birth parents must consent.

When can consent be taken from the birth mother (father), and how long after the consent is signed can it be revoked?

In an agency adoption, a surrender of parental rights can be taken seventy-two hours after the child's birth and is irrevocable. In a nonagency independent adoption, the birth mother can appear before a judge and have her rights terminated. If she does not do that, then her parental rights are not terminated until the first court hearing, which is usually held sixty to ninety days after the adoption petition is filed. Each birth parent must receive notice of this first hearing. During this time, the birth parents can revoke their consent and have the child returned to them. New Jersey, unlike other states, does not consider whether it would be in the child's best interests to remain with the adoptive couple unless the parental rights have been terminated.

What are the birth father's rights?

If the birth father cannot be determined or if the birth mother refuses to name him and the court is unable to determine who he is, his consent is not needed, and his parental rights are terminated at the first hearing held two to three months after the adoption is filed. In an independent adoption, notice must be sent by certified mail to a known birth father of the adoption hearing. Some judges want the birth father served with the notice by a process server. If the known birth father does not respond within thirty days and does not appear at the first hearing, then his rights are terminated. The adoption is finalized approximately seven months after the first hearing.

In an agency adoption, the adoption complaint is filed six months after placement, and a final hearing is held within thirty days after filing of the complaint. If the birth father has not signed an agency surrender, then his rights can be terminated at the final hearing if he has received notice of the hearing and has not responded. An agency can terminate his rights sooner by scheduling a termination hearing at any time after the birth and providing him notice of the hearing. As long as he does not object in writing or appear at the hearing, his rights are terminated.

In both agency or private adoptions, a birth parent's rights can be terminated by the court if it can be established that the birth parent has abandoned his or her rights to the child. This can be established by showing that the birth parent had no contact with or provided no emotional or monetary support for the child during the six-month period prior to placement.

What fees can adoptive parents pay?

Legal, medical, counseling, and living expenses can be paid. However, all expenses must be submitted to the court before the final adoption. In an independent adoption, judges only permit limited expenses to be paid and may not approve certain items.

Where does the adoption hearing take place?

The hearing takes place in the court of the county where the adoptive parents or birth parents reside or where the agency is located.

How are familial and stepparent adoptions different from nonbiological adoptions?

The court can waive a home study if the child has resided with the adoptive parent for a period of at least six months.

Can a nonresident finalize an adoption in this state?

Yes, but only through an agency.

Source: New Jersey Revised Statutes Sections 9:3-38 to 9 3-54

NEW MEXICO LAWS RELATED TO ADOPTION: QUESTIONS AND ANSWERS

A home study must be conducted thirty days before a child can be placed in your home in an interstate independent adoption. If you plan to advertise outside of the state, be sure to have a home study very near completion before placing an advertisement. Also, your attorney must obtain a court order that permits a child from another state to come into your home.

Can an attorney serve as an intermediary?

No.

Is advertising permitted?

Yes.

Who must consent to the adoption?

1. The birth mother.
2. The birth father if he is married to or attempted to marry the birth mother, or if the child was born within 300 days after the marriage ended, or if he has stated he is the father and established a personal and financial relationship with the child.
3. The adoption agency involved, if applicable. Consent is not required if either birth parent has left the child with a third party (the adoptive couple, for example) and has not supported the child or communicated with the child for a period of three months if the child is under the age of six years. If the child is over the age of six years, then the time period is six months.

When can consent be taken from the birth mother (father), and how long after the consent is signed can it be revoked?

Consent cannot be given until forty-eight hours after the child's birth and must be taken in front of a judge. Consent cannot be withdrawn unless it was obtained by fraud. A consent can be taken by an adoption agency or by a person appointed by the court to take a consent.

If the surrender is not taken before a judge, then the birth parent must be represented by counsel.

What are the birth father's rights?

His rights are limited, as described previously. If he has not registered with a putative father registry within ninety days of the child's birth, then his consent is not needed. In addition, consent is not required of a parent who has left the child to be adopted unidentified for a period of fourteen days.

What fees can adoptive parents pay?
Medical, legal, and living expenses can be paid. All expenses paid must be filed by the adoptive parents with the court.

Where does the adoption hearing take place?
The hearing takes place in the court of the county where the adoptive parents live, where the child lives, or where the agency is located.

How are familial and stepparent adoptions different from nonbiological adoptions?
If the child has lived with a relative (up to the fifth degree of relation) for at least one year, then the home study can be waived. Grandparent visitation rights apply to adoption by a stepparent or relative, a person designated in the deceased parent's will, or a person who served as a godparent.

Can a nonresident finalize an adoption in this state?
Yes, if the child to be adopted is a resident of New Mexico or has been born in New Mexico and is less than six months old and placed by an adoption agency.

NEW YORK LAWS RELATED TO ADOPTION: QUESTIONS AND ANSWERS
In New York, a birth mother must have separate representation from the adoptive parents; therefore, she must have her own attorney whose fees can be paid by the adoptive parents.

Can an attorney serve as an intermediary?
No. Generally, this practice is considered an illegal placement under Social Services Law. It does not matter if the attorney located the birth mother in or out of state.

Is advertising permitted?
Yes.

Who must consent to the adoption?
1. The birth mother.
2. The birth father, if the child is born or conceived in wedlock.

When can consent be taken from the birth mother (father), and how long after the consent is signed can it be revoked?
Consent cannot be signed until the child is born. Generally, in a private placement

in which the consent is not taken in court, a birth parent has up to forty-five days to revoke a consent. The parent must attempt to revoke the consent by notification to the court where the adoption proceeding takes place. If the attempt is timely, then it will open the door legally for the court to conduct a "best interests" hearing to determine whether the child should remain with the adoptive couple or return to the objecting birth parent. If consents are taken by an agency, the birth parents have up to thirty days to revoke a consent. However, in an independent adoption, if a judge receives consent from the birth parents, their rights are terminated at that point and are irrevocable even if it is only a few days after placement.

The birth father can also sign an irrevocable consent before the birth.

What are the birth father's rights?

If the child is born in wedlock, the birth father has the same rights as the birth mother. If a child is born out of wedlock and the birth father has maintained substantial and continuous contact with the child and has financially supported the child, then his consent is needed. If the birth father was not involved during the six months before placement and is named by the birth mother, he must receive a notice. In addition, if a birth father files an acknowledgment of paternity with the putative father registry, then he shall be entitled to notice of the adoption. He is then entitled to a "best interests" hearing if he contests the adoption. In New York, the best interests of the child are paramount, and if the birth father has not shown the prerequisite concern for the child, he may not upset the adoption placement. It is not sufficient for him to suggest that he was not aware of the pregnancy or birth of the child.

What fees can adoptive parents pay?

In a private adoption, the adoptive parents must give the court a statement of all fees and expenses paid. New York judges usually permit the adoptive parents to pay more living expenses than is generally permitted in other states. The attorney must also give an affidavit of all fees received.

The adoptive parents' health insurer must cover the baby's medical expenses as soon as he or she is born.

Where does the adoption hearing take place?

The hearing takes place in the Family Court or Surrogate Court in the county where the adoptive parents reside or where the placement agency is located.

How are familial and stepparent adoptions different from nonbiological adoptions?

Legally, they are handled in the same way. In a stepparent adoption, if the noncustodial birth parent is unwilling to consent, then you need to be able to prove that they abandoned the child for at least six months before the adoption can proceed.

Can a nonresident finalize an adoption in this state?

Yes, if the child is born in the state and the adoptive parents are certified as approved parents by the court.

Source: New York Domestic Relations Law Sections 109 to 117 and New York Social Services Law 372 to 373 (1997)

NORTH CAROLINA LAWS RELATED TO ADOPTION: QUESTIONS AND ANSWERS

Can an attorney serve as an intermediary?

In a direct placement, a birth parent must personally select the prospective adoptive parent, but the birth parent may obtain assistance from another person or entity or an adoption facilitator in locating or evaluating a prospective adoptive parent. Information about the adoptive parent must be given to the birth parent by the adoptive parent or the adoptive parent's attorney. This information must include the home study and may include additional information if requested by the birth parent. An intermediary is allowed as long as that person is not compensated for services.

Is advertising permitted?

No. You may not post fliers either. Networking is limited to those you know.

Who must consent to the adoption?

1. The birth mother.
2. The birth father, if he is married to the birth mother or has established paternity.

When can consent be taken from the birth mother (father), and how long after the consent is signed can it be revoked?

A consent to adopt an unborn child or one who is less than three months old may be revoked within seven days. A consent to the adoption of an older child may be revoked within seven days.

What are the birth father's rights?

If named, the birth father must consent to the adoption. If the birth father has not consented to the adoption and fails to respond to a notice of adoption proceedings within fifteen days after being notified, his consent is not required. He has thirty days to respond to a petition of adoption filed in court. If he does not respond, then his consent is not needed, and the adoption can go forward.

If the birth father wants to contest the adoption of a child born out of wedlock, he must establish paternity by filing a petition for legitimization. Paternity can also be established if he has provided substantial financial support or consistent care to the child and mother.

What fees can adoptive parents pay?

Adoptive parents can pay for medical, traveling, and counseling services that are directly related to the adoption, as well as ordinary living expenses (for no longer than six weeks after delivery) and legal expenses during the pregnancy. An affidavit of all moneys paid in connection with the adoption must be presented to the court.

Where does the adoption hearing take place?

The adoption hearing takes place in the court of the county where the adoptive parents live, where the child lives, or where the child placement agency is located.

How are familial and stepparent adoptions different from nonbiological adoptions?

The child must have resided primarily with the stepparent and the legal parent for at least six months. The state residency and probationary period are waived in stepparent and grandparent adoptions. Grandparents' visitation rights are still in effect after the adoption. Grandparents may also seek visitation rights if it is in the child's best interest.

Can a nonresident finalize an adoption in this state?

No. Only those who have lived in North Carolina for at least six months can adopt.

NORTH DAKOTA LAWS RELATED TO ADOPTION: QUESTIONS AND ANSWERS

In general, if you adopt a child in a state in which independent adoption is legal, to finalize the adoption there you must use an agency in that state to meet North Dakota's ICPC regulations. However, check with an attorney to confirm this information since North Dakota does use The Uniform Adoption Act, which does not require the use of an agency, as its adoption statute appears to.

Can an attorney serve as an intermediary?

No.

Is advertising permitted?

No.

Who must consent to the adoption?

Both birth parents.

When can consent be taken from the birth mother (father), and how long after the consent is signed can it be revoked?

Consent can be withdrawn before the adoption decree is final if it is in the child's best interests.

What are the birth father's rights?

He must give consent if he receives the child into his home and claims the child as his biological child or if he acknowledges paternity in a document filed with the Division of Vital Statistics. Consent is not needed from either birth parent if it can be shown that the child to be adopted has been abandoned by a birth parent or that a birth parent has not communicated with or supported the child for at least one year. Also, consent is not necessary if the birth parent is unavailable, absent with no explanation, incapable, or has failed to establish a substantial relationship with the child. A court that finds these conditions will terminate the birth parent's parental rights.

What fees can adoptive parents pay?

A full accounting must be given to the court of all fees paid for medical care (both prenatal and postnatal care of the birth mother and child) as well as placement and agency fees.

Where does the adoption hearing take place?

The adoption hearing takes place in the court of the county where the adoptive parents live or the child lives or where the child placement agency is located.

How are familial and stepparent adoptions different from nonbiological adoptions?

In a stepparent adoption, the court does not need an accounting of expenses.

Can a nonresident finalize an adoption in this state?

Yes.

Source: North Dakota Century Code Sections 14-15-10 to 14-15-23

OHIO LAWS RELATED TO ADOPTION: QUESTIONS AND ANSWERS

Can an attorney serve as an intermediary?

Yes.

Is advertising permitted?

No. If a prospective adoptive parent does advertise, the Department of Human Services will contact you and ask you not to do so, although they will not prosecute. It is recommended that you advertise instead in newspapers along the Pennsylvania and West Virginia borders since these publications are often available in Ohio.

Who must consent to the adoption?

1. The birth mother.

2. The birth father if the child was conceived or born while he was married to the birth mother, or if he claims to be the father and establishes a relationship with the child before placement, or if he has acknowledged the child in writing before placement, signed the birth certificate, or filed an objection to the adoption before the placement.

When can consent be taken from the birth mother (father), and how long after the consent is signed can it be revoked?

Consent can be taken seventy-two hours after the child's birth and is irrevocable unless the birth parents attempt to withdraw before the filing of an interlocutory order or the final adoption decree; any such withdrawal will be successful after the filing of the final decree only if the court finds it is in the child's best interest to do so. An adoption cannot be finalized until the child has lived in the adoptive parents' home for at least six months.

What are the birth father's rights?

If the birth father has abandoned the birth mother during the pregnancy or if he has failed to provide for the child, his consent is not required. If after thirty days of the child's placement he does not file a paternity case or an objection to the adoption, his parental rights are terminated. As with all birth fathers, he must receive notice of the adoption proceedings.

What fees can adoptive parents pay?

Only medical and legal expenses and agency fees are permitted. Temporary maintenance of the birth mother is also permitted. The adoptive parents must submit a statement to the court of all fees and expenses paid.

Where does the adoption hearing take place?

The adoption hearing takes place in the court of the county where the adoptive parents live, where the child was born, where the birth parents live, or where the placement agency is located.

How are familial and stepparent adoptions different from nonbiological adoptions?

If a child is adopted by a stepparent, this does not curtail the court's power to award visitation rights to grandparents. A home study is not required in a stepparent or grandparent adoption.

Can a nonresident finalize an adoption in this state?

Yes.

Source: Ohio Revised Code Annotated Sections 3101.01 to 3107.44

OKLAHOMA LAWS RELATED TO ADOPTION: QUESTIONS AND ANSWERS

Can an attorney serve as an intermediary?
Yes.

Is advertising permitted?
Yes.

Who must consent to the adoption?
1. Both birth parents, if sixteen years or older.
2. If the birth mother or father is younger than sixteen, then a guardian or parent must also give written consent.
3. The child placement agency, if it has custody of the child.

When can consent be taken from the birth mother (father), and how long after the consent is signed can it be revoked?
The birth parents can appear before the judge and consent in writing to the adoption and a termination of their parental rights seventy-two hours after the birth of the child. A birth parent may also provide in writing a consent to a person authorized to do so; however, such a consent can be withdrawn up to fifteen days after signing if the court finds it is in the child's best interest. An agency surrender can be signed in front of the agency caseworker, and the birth parent need not go to court. This type of consent is irrevocable at the time of signing.

What are the birth father's rights?
The birth father's consent is not required if he fails to acknowledge his paternity and does not support the mother during pregnancy; or if he fails to prove that he is the father or fails to exercise parental duties toward the child within ninety days of the birth; or if he waives his right to notice of the adoption hearing; or if he does not appear at the adoption hearing after receiving notice or file an objection within thirty days of receiving notice.

Consent is also not necessary from a birth parent who willfully fails to communicate and maintain a significant relationship with or who fails or refuses to support a child for twelve months.

What fees can adoptive parents pay?
Medical and legal expenses are permitted. Living expenses can be paid in a private adoption with court preapproval.

Where does the adoption hearing take place?

The hearing can take place in the court of the county where the adoptive parents live, where the birth parents live, or where the placement agency is located.

How are familial and stepparent adoptions different from nonbiological adoptions?

Generally, in a stepparent adoption no home study is required. A stepparent adoption can be finalized in about three to four weeks. Grandparent visitation rights are permitted in stepparent adoptions or relative adoptions only if at least one of the biological parents is deceased and it is in the child's best interest. In a relative adoption, a home study is required, and the steps for a nonbiological adoption are followed.

Can a nonresident finalize an adoption in this state?

Yes, but only if the child is a resident of Oklahoma.

OREGON LAWS RELATED TO ADOPTION: QUESTIONS AND ANSWERS

Can an attorney serve as an intermediary?

Yes.

Is advertising permitted?

Yes, if the adoptive parents have an Oregon-approved home study.

Who must consent to the adoption?

The birth parents.

When can consent be taken from the birth mother (father), and how long after the consent is signed can it be revoked?

A birth mother can sign the consent after birth when she has recovered from the effects of delivery. The consent is irrevocable once a certificate of irrevocability has been filed with the court.

What are the birth father's rights?

Unless the birth father has supported the birth mother and the child (by monetary means and/or emotional relationship) or he files with the putative father registry indicating that he is the father, he is not entitled to notice of any adoption proceedings and cannot contest the adoption. The birth father is also entitled to notice if he resided with the minor child at any time during the sixty days prior to the filing of an adoption complaint or at any time during the sixty days after the child's birth. The birth father's rights can also be terminated if it can be established that he has not maintained a relationship with the child for a certain period of time.

What fees can adoptive parents pay?

Medical, legal, and reasonable living expenses can be paid. The adoptive parents must submit to the court an itemized list stating all fees and expenses paid.

No fees can be paid or accepted for finding a child or an adoptive parent, unless it is the reasonable fee of a licensed adoption agency. The Children's Services Division may charge up to $750 for a home study.

Where does the adoption hearing take place?

The adoption hearing can take place in the court of the county where the adoptive parents live, where the child's birth parents live, or where the placement agency is located.

How are familial and stepparent adoptions different from nonbiological adoptions?

No home study is required in a stepparent adoption or a relative adoption if the child has resided with the stepparent or relative for six months before filing the petition.

Can a nonresident finalize an adoption in this state?

Yes, if the birth mother is a resident. The adoptive parent, birth parent, or child must reside in Oregon continuously for six months prior to the date of the adoption petition.

Source: Oregon Revised Statutes Section 109.305 to 109.500 and 432.405 to 432.430

PENNSYLVANIA LAWS RELATED TO ADOPTION: QUESTIONS AND ANSWERS

Can an attorney serve as an intermediary?

Yes. However, an attorney cannot accept any fees or charge on an hourly basis for this service.

Is advertising permitted?

Yes.

Who must consent to the adoption?

1. The birth parents.
2. The birth mother's husband, if he was married to her at any time within one year before the child's birth, unless he proves not to be the child's biological father.

A birth parent's consent is not required if he or she has had no contact with a newborn for a period of four months or for a period of six months for an older child.

When can consent be taken from the birth mother (father), and how long after the consent is signed can it be revoked?

Consents can be given seventy-two hours after the child's birth. All consents must be confirmed by a court hearing, which occurs at least fifty days after the consents are taken. The consents are filed with the court at least forty days after they are signed; the court then schedules a hearing to confirm consents at least ten days later. The birth parents must receive notice of this hearing, and they can revoke their consents up until the court hearing. Generally, this hearing occurs two to four months after the baby's birth, making Pennsylvania a "legal risk" state.

Birth fathers can sign consents, even before birth.

What are the birth father's rights?

He can sign a consent before or after the birth, and his rights essentially end when the birth mother's rights are terminated at the termination hearing. In general, if the birth father does not sign a consent, his rights can be terminated as a "putative father" as long as he is not married to the birth mother, has failed to acknowledge paternity, and does not appear in court to oppose the adoption.

He must still receive notice of the termination proceedings whether he signs a consent or not.

What fees can adoptive parents pay?

No living expenses can be paid in an agency or independent adoption. In an independent adoption, only medical and hospital expenses are permitted. In an agency adoption, reasonable administrative costs and counseling fees are permitted.

The court may also require the adoptive parents to pay for the birth parents' legal fees and the child's guardian. An itemized statement of all money paid must be made in the adoption report.

Where does the adoption hearing take place?

The hearing can take place in the court of the county where the adoptive parents live, where the birth parents live, or where the placement agency is located.

How are familial and stepparent adoptions different from nonbiological adoptions?

They are handled the same way other adoptions are conducted, except that a home study may be waived in a stepparent adoption. The attorney can request that the hearing to confirm the consent also be the final hearing, instead of waiting for the final hearing to be held at a later date.

Can a nonresident finalize an adoption in this state?
Yes. For nonresidents to finalize in Pennsylvania, they must have proof that they have no history of child abuse or child-related crimes.

Source: Pennsylvania Consolidated Statutes Title 23, Section 2101 and Title 55, Sections 33501. 1 to 3350.14

RHODE ISLAND LAWS RELATED TO ADOPTION: QUESTIONS AND ANSWERS

In an independent adoption, even if the child is brought into the state, the Department of Children and Their Families must be notified within fifteen days. Failure to notify could result in the court ordering the child to be removed from the adoptive parents' home.

A home study must be conducted within fifteen days of a child's placement. If you plan to advertise in another state, you may not need to have a home study completed at the time of placement; however, the state in which the child is born will require a completed home study, as well as Interstate Compact approval, before the child is permitted to leave the state.

The religious preference of the biological parents is honored, as much as is practically possible, when placing a child.

Can an attorney serve as an intermediary?
Yes.

Is advertising permitted?
Technically not, but ads are placed.

Who must consent to the adoption?
1. The birth parents.
2. The birth parents' guardian or court-appointed guardian if the birth parent is a minor.

When can consent be taken from the birth mother (father), and how long after the consent is signed can it be revoked?
Consent cannot be given sooner than fifteen days after the child's birth. No law discusses revocation, but case law suggests it is only possible due to fraud, duress, or misrepresentation.

What are the birth father's rights?
Unless the birth father has neglected to provide care for the child for at least one year, is excessively using drugs or alcohol, is unfit based on conduct or mental illness, or has abandoned or deserted the child, his consent is required.

What fees can adoptive parents pay?

The law does not address this issue. However, paying legal, medical, and reasonable living expenses is permitted.

Where does the adoption hearing take place?

The law does not address where the adoption hearing takes place, but it is usually conducted in the county where the adoptive parents live.

How are familial and stepparent adoptions different from nonbiological adoptions?

A specific statute deals with stepparent adoption. Relative adoptions are not significantly different from nonbiological adoptions.

Can a nonresident finalize an adoption in this state?

Yes, but only in an agency adoption.

Source: General Laws of Rhode Island Sections 15-7-2 to 15-7-22

SOUTH CAROLINA LAWS RELATED TO ADOPTION: QUESTIONS AND ANSWERS

If you advertise in South Carolina and are not a state resident, you must petition the South Carolina Family Court to take a child out of state.

Nonresidents may adopt a child who has special needs or in cases where there has been public notoriety concerning the child or the child's family. They may also adopt if they are a relative; or if one of the adoptive parents is in the military in South Carolina; or there are unusual or exceptional circumstances making adoption by a nonresident in the child's best interest. If you personally meet with a birth mother and she selects you as the adoptive parent, then the courts will usually permit adoption under the "unusual or exceptional circumstances" clause. (See the following discussion.)

Can an attorney serve as an intermediary?

Yes. A person who facilitates an adoption is not required to be licensed.

Is advertising permitted?

Yes.

Who must consent to the adoption?

1. The birth mother.
2. The birth father, if he is married to the birth mother or if he states that he is the biological parent and has either lived with the birth mother for six months or

more before the child was born or has paid medical and other expenses during the mother's pregnancy.

When can consent be taken from the birth mother (father), and how long after the consent is signed can it be revoked?

Consent cannot be given until the child is born and the birth mother has basically recovered from the effects of delivery; once given, it cannot be withdrawn unless it was given involuntarily or obtained under duress or through coercion. The final adoption decree makes the consent irrevocable.

What are the birth father's rights?

Essentially, the birth father must have supported the birth mother during her pregnancy if his consent is to be required. If he has not done so for at least the last six months during her pregnancy or if he has not supported the child during the last six months before placement, he must only be given notice of the adoption; his surrender is not required.

What fees can adoptive parents pay?

The following expenses can be paid: medical expenses, reasonable living expenses for a limited period of time, fees for investigation and report, fees for those required to take the surrender, reasonable attorney fees and the fee of the guardian appointed by the court, and reasonable fees to a child-placement agency.

Where does the adoption hearing take place?

The adoption hearing may take place in the court of the county where the adoptive parents live, where the child was born, or where the child placement agency is located.

How are familial and stepparent adoptions different from nonbiological adoptions?

A home study is not required.

Can a nonresident finalize an adoption in this state?

Yes. The final adoption hearing is held in the county in which the baby was born.

Special Note: South Carolina was known for years as the "adoption capital" of the nation; its laws were not highly structured or restrictive. It was not until *Time* magazine put South Carolina on its front cover and intimated that it was the country's baby market that the South Carolina legislature enacted the "special needs" requirement. Now, South Carolina law states that a child cannot be placed with an out-of-state adoptive parent unless there are unusual or exceptional circumstances. However, what has developed since the 1989 enactment of the law is a flexible approach in allowing out-of-state couples to adopt children born or residing in South Carolina.

The ambiguous nature of the law in South Carolina is an example that demonstrates the need for an experienced adoption attorney.

Source: South Carolina Code of Laws Sections 20-7-1650 to 20-7-1895

SOUTH DAKOTA LAWS RELATED TO ADOPTION: QUESTIONS AND ANSWERS

Can an attorney serve as an intermediary?
No.

Is advertising permitted?
Yes.

Who must consent to the adoption?
1. The birth mother.
2. The birth father, if he is married to the birth mother or if he states the child is his and asserts paternity within sixty days after the birth.

When can consent be taken from the birth mother (father), and how long after the consent is signed can it be revoked?
Consent can be taken any time before or after the child's birth but is not valid until after birth. Birth parents can revoke consent up until termination of their parental rights, which can occur only five days after birth at a court hearing attended by the birth mother. The birth father does not have to go to court but can have his rights terminated by power of attorney.

What are the birth father's rights?
If he is known and identified by the birth mother, his consent is required. If he is unknown, newspaper notices must be placed in an effort to locate him as a "John Doe" birth father. If a known birth father has abandoned the child for a period of one year, then his rights can be terminated without his consent.

What fees can adoptive parents pay?
Only fees and expenses approved by the court and fees charged by a child placement agency are permitted. If any other adoption-related moneys are paid without approval from the court, you could be charged with a felony.

Where does the adoption hearing take place?
The adoption hearing takes place in the court of the county where the adoptive parents live or where the child lives.

How are familial and stepparent adoptions different from nonbiological adoptions?
In a stepparent adoption, a judge may, but is not compelled to, order a home study.

Can a nonresident finalize an adoption in this state?
Yes.

TENNESSEE LAWS RELATED TO ADOPTION: QUESTIONS AND ANSWERS

Can an attorney serve as an intermediary?
Yes, but no fee can be charged.

Is advertising permitted?
Yes.

Who must consent to the adoption?
1. The birth mother.
2. The birth father, if he is married to the birth mother or if he listed on the birth certificate or named by the birth mother and has claimed paternity.

When can consent be taken from the birth mother (father), and how long after the consent is signed can it be revoked?
A surrender can be taken seventy-two hours after birth, and if a petition to adoption has not been filed, a birth mother has ten days to revoke the consent.

In cases of conflict, the courts are instructed to favor (not merely consider) the child's best interest.

What are the birth father's rights?
If the birth father is named by the birth mother and his whereabouts are unknown, a diligent search must be made to find him and notify him of the adoption. If he cannot be found, then he must be informed of the adoption through public notice (usually placed in a newspaper).

The court is allowed to exclude the birth father if the child is born out of wedlock and the birth father has failed to register with the putative father registry within thirty days of the child's birth and to file change of address information within ten days of any such change. If he is registered, this will subject him to court-ordered child support and medical payments. If he fails to register, his rights can be terminated. After receiving notice of the birth, the birth father must file a legitimation complaint within thirty days, and if he does not, then his rights can be terminated.

The birth father is also required to pay pregnancy-related expenses and child support as soon as he is informed of the birth mother's pregnancy or the child's birth. If he does not do so, then his rights can be terminated.

What fees can adoptive parents pay?

Only an adoption agency can receive fees for serving as an intermediary. Reasonable medical and legal fees and living expenses can be paid. The adoptive parents must give the court a statement of any fees paid or received.

Where does the adoption hearing take place?

The adoption hearing takes place in the court of the county where the adoptive parents live, where the adoptee lives, or where the child placement agency is located.

How are familial and stepparent adoptions different from nonbiological adoptions?

The home study and the six-month waiting period before finalization are waived.

Can a nonresident finalize an adoption in this state?

No. You must have lived in Tennessee for at least one year before filing the petition to adopt. This requirement is waived for those serving in the military who were residents of Tennessee for one year before entering the military.

Note: The birth parents must be given notice of the availability of counseling. If the birth parent cannot afford counseling, the adoptive couple must pay for the counseling.

Source: Tennessee Code Annotated Sections 36-1-102 to 36-1-206

TEXAS LAWS RELATED TO ADOPTION: QUESTIONS AND ANSWERS

In Texas, a preadoption report is given to the adoptive parents, which provides the health, social, educational, and genetic history of the child and the child's biological family.

Can an attorney serve as an intermediary?

No.

Is advertising permitted?

Yes.

Who must consent to the adoption?

1. Both birth parents.
2. A managing conservator, if appointed; a conservator is a person or agency who retains all the rights and powers of a parent to the exclusion of other parents.

When can consent be taken from the birth mother (father), and how long after the consent is signed can it be revoked?

Consent cannot be taken until forty-eight hours after the birth and is irrevocable if the consent designates the Department of Human Services as managing conservator.

The consent must specifically state that it cannot be revoked; otherwise, birth parents have up to eleven days to revoke the consents. During this period of time, the adoptive couple or adoption agency must file the adoption petition in order that the birth parents' rights are terminated.

Termination of rights can also be done by court appearance by the birth parents within ten days of filing.

What are the birth father's rights?

There is no consent required of a birth father who has abandoned the child with no means of identification or who does not file an admission of paternity within a reasonable time frame. If the birth father cannot be found, his rights can be terminated by publication of notice of the adoption proceedings; termination will occur after a certain time period has elapsed if he does not respond. Texas law also states if a birth parent leaves a child in the custody of another, not intending to return and without providing adequate support for the child, then consent is not required, and that birth parent's rights can be terminated.

If a birth father is out of the picture, you may want to file his termination of parental rights before the birth. Also, his rights cannot be terminated until five days after publication of the notice begins. In this way, once the child is born, the paperwork is completed.

What fees can adoptive parents pay?

Medical, legal, and reasonable counseling fees are permitted. In an independent adoption, no living expenses can be paid; such fees can only be paid through an adoption agency.

Where does the adoption hearing take place?

The adoption hearing may take place in the court of the county where the adoptive parents live, the child lives, or where the placement agency is located.

How are familial and stepparent adoptions different from nonbiological adoptions?

In a relative or stepparent adoption, the preadoption report on the child's background and status is not required.

Can a nonresident finalize an adoption in this state?

Yes.

UTAH LAWS RELATED TO ADOPTION: QUESTIONS AND ANSWERS

Can an attorney serve as an intermediary?
Yes.

Is advertising permitted?
Yes.

Who must consent to the adoption?
1. The birth mother.
2. The birth father, if he is married to the birth mother or if he has demonstrated a significant commitment to the child.
3. The child placement agency, if involved.

When can consent be taken from the birth mother (father), and how long after the consent is signed can it be revoked?
Consent cannot be taken until at least twenty-four hours after the birth. The consent is irrevocable once signed.

What are the birth father's rights?
Although 1995 legislation reduced birth fathers' rights, their rights must still be terminated by the court. No consent is needed if the birth father has not established paternity by filing an action in court, provided support for the birth mother during her pregnancy or for the child after delivery, or made an effort to maintain a parental relationship with the child.

What fees can adoptive parents pay?
Attorneys or other intermediaries cannot charge for locating a birth mother. A statement of all fees for legal, medical, and living expenses paid must be filed with the court before the final adoption.

Where does the adoption hearing take place?
The hearing may take place in the court of the county where the adoptive parents live.

How are familial and stepparent adoptions different from nonbiological adoptions?
Generally, no home study is required in stepparent and familial adoptions. In a stepparent adoption, the child must reside with the petitioning parent for more than twelve months, instead of the six months required in other adoptions.

Can a nonresident finalize an adoption in this state?
No. However, residency can be established.

Source: Utah Code Annotated Sections 78-30-1 to 78-30-9

VERMONT LAWS RELATED TO ADOPTION: QUESTIONS AND ANSWERS

Can an attorney serve as an intermediary?
Yes.

Is advertising permitted?
Yes.

Who must consent to the adoption?
1. The birth parents, if married to each other.
2. The birth mother, if the child is born out of wedlock or if the husband is not the child's biological father.
3. The child placement agency, if involved.

When can consent be taken from the birth mother (father), and how long after the consent is signed can it be revoked?
Consent cannot be taken until thirty-six hours after birth. The consent is given before a probate judge and can be revoked up to twenty-one days.

What are the birth father's rights?
A birth father has full paternal rights. His rights cannot be terminated unless he provides a consent or it can be shown that he has abandoned his rights to the child to be adopted. Vermont law also states that a birth father's rights can be waived if he does not acknowledge paternity at the time of the adoption hearing or if he has executed a notarized statement denying paternity or disclaiming any interest in the child to be adopted with an acknowledgment that his statement is irrevocable when signed.

He has thirty days after receiving notice of an adoption hearing to respond.

What fees can adoptive parents pay?
Payment of medical, legal, and some living expenses are permitted. The Department of Social and Rehabilitation Services may charge a fee of up to $535 for conducting a home study.

Where does the adoption hearing take place?
The adoption hearing takes place in the court of the county where the adoptive parents live. If they do not live in the state, the hearing takes place where the child placement agency is located.

How are familial and stepparent adoptions different from nonbiological adoptions?
In a stepparent adoption, the process is simple and an out-of-court consent is permitted. In a relative adoption, no home study is required under the present law.

Can a nonresident finalize an adoption in this state?

Yes, but only an agency adoption.

VIRGINIA LAWS RELATED TO ADOPTION: QUESTIONS AND ANSWERS

In Virginia in a private placement adoption, the birth family and the adoptive family must exchange identifying information.

Can an attorney serve as an intermediary?

Yes.

Is advertising permitted?

Yes.

Who must consent to the adoption?

1. Both birth parents.
2. The child placement agency, if involved.

When can consent be taken from the birth mother (father), and how long after the consent is signed can it be revoked?

In an agency adoption, consent can be taken ten days after the child's birth and can be revoked fifteen days after signed, or twenty-five days after birth, or until adoptive placement, whichever is later.

In an independent adoption, a consent hearing takes place within ten days of filing the petition or as soon as is practical but not sooner than ten days after birth. The hearing can take place in the county where the adoptive parents live, where the birth mother lives, or where the child was born. If the birth parents live outside of Virginia, the consent hearing may take place in the birth parents' state of residence, as long as the proceedings are first instituted in a Virginia court so that the Virginia court has jurisdiction over them.

Parental consent is revocable before the final adoption if it was given under fraud or duress or if both the adoptive parents and birth parents agree to revoke it.

A birth father who is not married to the birth mother at the time of the child's conception or birth does not need to give a consent in court. He must be provided notice of the adoption proceedings, or he can sign a consent that waives further notice of adoption proceedings.

If the birth parents place a child and both birth mother and father do not show up in court (without good cause and after being given notice), the court may grant the adoption petition without their consent if the court finds it is in the child's best interests to do so. (Virtually all birth mothers do go to court, however.)

What are the birth father's rights?

When a birth father's consent is required and he has not consented, he must be given notice of the termination hearing and/or the adoption hearing. The hearing may be held after the birth mother's hearing. If the birth father does not respond within twenty-one days after personal notice of the hearing or ten days after an Order of Publication (notice of the adoption proceedings placed in the legal notices section of the newspaper), then the hearing can be held, and his rights can be terminated.

If the birth father's consent is required but the court can also determine that the consent is withheld contrary to the child's best interests or cannot be obtained, the court will approve of the adoption as long as notice was provided to the birth father. Many judges will not permit a birth mother to refuse to name the birth father except in extreme situations such as rape.

What fees can adoptive parents pay?

Medical, legal, and transportation costs are permitted. Reasonable living expenses, including maternity clothes, can be paid if the birth mother's physician states that she cannot work. All fees must be disclosed to the court.

Where does the adoption hearing take place?

The adoption hearing takes place in the court of the county where the adoptive parents live or where the child placement agency is located.

How are familial and stepparent adoptions different from nonbiological adoptions?

Generally, in a stepparent adoption, a hearing may not be required and is up to the court's discretion. In consensual stepparent adoptions, home studies are not necessarily required. In addition, relatives up to the fourth degree are now given special relative adoption status. These include the child's great aunt and uncle. In general, in a familial adoption no postplacement supervision is required. Also, no hearing is required before the court for qualified relative adoptions.

Can a nonresident finalize an adoption in this state?

Yes, but only in an agency or agency-identified adoption.

Source: Code of Virginia Annotated Sections 63.1-220 to 63.1-238.5

WASHINGTON LAWS RELATED TO ADOPTION: QUESTIONS AND ANSWERS

Can an attorney serve as an intermediary?

Yes.

Is advertising permitted?

Yes, but only through a Washington licensed agency and with verification of a completed home study in compliance with Washington law. Those outside of Washington cannot advertise in Washington newspapers.

Who must consent to the adoption?

1. Both birth parents.
2. The child placement agency, if involved.

When can consent be taken from the birth mother (father), and how long after the consent is signed can it be revoked?

In general, consents can be taken before birth, but the order terminating rights cannot be entered with the court until forty-eight hours after the birth or signing, whichever is later. The birth mother must appear in court to testify as to her consent. The birth father does not have to appear, but his consent can be brought before the court. Once entered into the court, the birth mother's and the birth father's consents are irrevocable.

What are the birth father's rights?

The birth father must consent or be given notice by serving him with summons or notice personally, and he has twenty days to respond or he waives his right to object. He can also be provided notice by publishing a notice of the adoption proceedings in the legal notices of a newspaper if his whereabouts are unknown. He does have an opportunity to object and have a hearing on his parenting abilities to show the court that it would be in the child's best interests to be parented by him. His rights can be terminated if it can be shown that he failed to perform his parental obligations, showing a substantial lack of regard for them.

What fees can adoptive parents pay?

The legal and agency fees must be reasonable and should be based on time spent in conducting preadoption home studies and preparing the report. Living expenses must be approved by the court. At the adoptive parent's request, this fee can be reviewed.

Where does the hearing take place?

The hearing takes place in the court of the county where the adoptive parents live or where the child lives.

How are familial and stepparent adoptions different from nonbiological adoptions?

They are essentially the same, except that the home study may be streamlined or waived.

Can a nonresident finalize an adoption in this state?
Yes.

Source: Revised Code of Washington Sections 26.33.020 to 26.33.410

WEST VIRGINIA LAWS RELATED TO ADOPTION: QUESTIONS AND ANSWERS

Can an attorney serve as an intermediary?
Yes, as long as fees are related to services rendered.

Is advertising permitted?
Yes.

Who must consent to the adoption?
1. Both birth parents.
2. If a birth parent is under eighteen, the court must approve the consent and appoint a guardian.

When can consent be taken from the birth mother (father), and how long after the consent is signed can it be revoked?
Consent cannot be given until seventy-two hours after the child's birth and may be revoked within ten days if the adoptive parents are in-state residents or up to twenty days if they are from out of state, unless the term "irrevocable" is written onto the consent.

The consent shall be taken by a judge, notary, or person designated by the court. If the birth parent is a minor, the consent shall be executed before a judge.

It is generally recommended that an out-of-state couple adopting a child born in West Virginia provide documentation, such as consents, that complies with both West Virginia law and the state laws of the adoptive parents.

What are the birth father's rights?
Notice of the adoption proceedings is given to any birth father who has exercised parental duties, unless the child is more than six months old and the birth father has not asserted his parental rights.

What fees can adoptive parents pay?
Payment of legal, medical, and adoption agency fees or fees to other persons is limited to cover fees-for-services only. All fees must be approved by the court.

Where does the adoption hearing take place?
The adoption hearing takes place in the court of the county where the adoptive parents live.

How are familial and stepparent adoptions different from nonbiological adoptions?

The preadoption home study is not required in a relative adoption. Closeness in age cannot be the sole factor in denying an adoption in stepparent adoptions.

In some stepparent adoptions, some grandparent visitations may be granted.

Can a nonresident finalize an adoption in this state?

No.

WISCONSIN LAWS RELATED TO ADOPTION: QUESTIONS AND ANSWERS

Private adoption is allowed in Wisconsin, but an agency must conduct a home study and provide counseling to the birth parents.

In an interstate independent adoption, an agency must serve as the child's guardian from the time the child is placed with the adoptive couple to the time the adoption is finalized (about six months after consent is signed). Also, an agency must provide counseling to a birth mother in an independent adoption. Contact the ICPC office for written procedural information.

Can an attorney serve as an intermediary?

No, but the attorney is allowed to pass names along such as a friend might do, as long as no fees are charged.

Is advertising permitted?

No.

Who must consent to the adoption?

The birth parents must consent.

When can consent be taken from the birth mother (father), and how long after the consent is signed can it be revoked?

A birth mother must have her rights terminated in court after the birth; there is no revocation period. A birth father who is not married to the birth mother and who does not appear in court with her may sign a written consent in front of a notary, and his consent is thereafter filed with the court at the time of the birth mother's hearing. Once the hearing takes place, he cannot revoke his consent. The hearing is normally held within thirty days of the filing of the petition for termination of parental rights of the birth parents.

What are the birth father's rights?

Generally, a birth father has the right to be notified of the court hearing. This can be done by notifying him personally or by publication of the adoption proceedings in the legal notices section of the newspaper if his whereabouts are unknown. If he appears and contests the adoption, he can be represented by an attorney at public expense.

What fees can adoptive parents pay?

A birth mother can be reimbursed for medical, legal, and agency expenses. With court approval, a birth mother may also be reimbursed for maternity clothing, travel, and child care. She must get a statement from her employer and her physician stating that she cannot work.

Living expenses up to $1,000 can be paid if necessary to protect the health and welfare of the mother and unborn baby.

Where does the adoption hearing take place?

The adoption hearing takes place in the court of the county where the adoptive parents live or where the child lives.

How are familial and stepparent adoptions different from nonbiological adoptions?

A child may be placed with a relative without a court order. Generally, in a stepparent or relative adoption, the termination of parental rights and adoption can take place at the same hearing; in other adoptions, there is a six-month waiting period from termination of rights to the adoption finalization. Also, a screening is conducted instead of a full home study.

Can a nonresident finalize an adoption in this state?

No.

WYOMING LAWS RELATED TO ADOPTION: QUESTIONS AND ANSWERS

Can an attorney serve as an intermediary?

Yes. However, attorneys generally do not bring birth parents and adoptive parents together. Because the population of Wyoming is only 400,000 and it is the ninth largest state, such a service is difficult to offer in such a sparsely populated area.

Is advertising permitted?

Yes.

Who must consent to the adoption?

1. Both birth parents, if the birth father is known.
2. The head of the child placement agency, if involved.

When can consent be given by the birth mother (father), and how long after the consent is signed can it be revoked?

Consent cannot be given until the child is born. Once signed, the consent is irrevocable.

What are the birth father's rights?

The birth father's consent is not needed if the birth mother does not know his name, or if he has been given notice of the hearing and has not responded within thirty days after receiving notice of the child's birth, or if he has abandoned or deserted the child, or if he has failed to contribute to the support of the child for one year or more, or if he has failed to pay at least 70 percent of court-ordered support for a period of two years. A putative father also has no right to contest the adoption unless he has asserted paternity or registered with the birth father registry.

If he does object to the adoption and has shown an interest and responsibility for the child within thirty days after being notified of the birth, then the court will decide whether his objections are valid and his assertions of paternity timely, as well as what would be in the best interests of the child.

What fees can adoptive parents pay?

Medical, legal, and living expenses can be paid. An accounting of them must be given to the court.

Where does the adoption hearing take place?

The adoption hearing takes place in District Court. Adoptions are usually finalized in about six months.

How are familial and stepparent adoptions different from nonbiological adoptions?

A medical report is not required in a stepparent adoption.

Can a nonresident finalize an adoption in this state?

No. According to ICPC guidelines, a petitioner must be a resident of Wyoming for at least sixty days.

Source: Wyoming Statutes Sections 1-22-101 to 10220116 and 1-22-201 to 1-22-203

Appendix B

Adoption Organizations:

State-by-State Listings

This appendix lists the names, addresses, and telephone numbers of each state's adoption specialist, state bar association, and Interstate Compact on the Placement of Children unit, as well as adoption attorneys, private adoption agencies, and adoption support groups. How each can be of assistance to you is briefly discussed as follows.

STATE ADOPTION SPECIALIST

The adoption specialist is usually in the state's social services office (or Office of Children's Protective Services). Sometimes this person also serves in the office of the Interstate Compact on the Placement of Children (see following). This specialist should have a comprehensive view of the state's adoption system and may provide statistical data, names of licensed agencies, details about adoption statutes, subsidized adoption programs, and other information.

The specialist's staff may also be able to recommend attorneys who are thorough and who submit paperwork in a timely manner.

If you feel that an agency or attorney is not handling your case ethically or properly, you can call the state specialist to question the procedure. Do not report any unethical practices to this office because complaints of this nature should be directed to the attorneys' ethics office of the state bar association or the state Supreme Court. Complaints concerning agencies should be directed to the adoption agency licensing office in the state's Department of Social Services.

STATE BAR ASSOCIATION

Most bar associations will refer you to attorneys who practice family and adoption law. Be aware that an attorney listed as practicing family law most likely handles divorces and custody contests resulting from divorces but not adoptions. If the attorney indicates that he or she does handle adoptions, make sure the attorney has experience handling your type of adoption since many attorneys have only handled agency or stepparent adoptions. When you receive a referral, check the attorney's credentials with another source (e.g., a member of an adoption support group or RESOLVE).

The state bar association may also give information about appropriate legal fees.

In discussing your specific adoption with an attorney, do not hesitate to ask the attorney detailed questions, such as whether he will interact directly with a birth mother in a private adoption (and if he has done so in the past) or with the agency social worker in an agency adoption. Also, will the attorney review agency surrender documents or international adoption decrees before an adoption is finalized? Many attorneys who indicate they do adoptions simply mean they will file the court documents at the time you are ready for court. The involvement of these attorneys is quite limited and can be inadequate; for example, many couples tell us that a particular attorney was "an adoption attorney," and yet, the same attorney never assisted with picking the baby up from the hospital nor in interacting with the hospital social worker prior to delivery or the discharge of the birth mother from the hospital.

INTERSTATE COMPACT ON THE PLACEMENT OF CHILDREN (ICPC)

Because adoptive couples and birth parents often live in different states, the need to regulate the interstate movement of children was recognized as early as the 1950s. The Interstate Compact on the Placement of Children provides such a mechanism and also outlines the procedure for the orderly transfer of children across state lines. The ICPC states that each state must have an office (or a separate unit of its social services agency) to monitor the individuals, organizations, or other entities involved in the placement of children in other states.

These include:

- The birth mother and birth father
- The adoption agency
- Any other person having custody of the child, including grandparents and other relatives
- Any corporation or association
- A court
- The state or the appropriate agency, or a subdivision of a state agency

The ICPC does not involve the placement of a child by a family member into the home of another close relative, unless the child is in the custody of the state social services department. It only covers children placed through the foster care system, court-ordered placements of children, and children placed for adoption into the homes of nonrelatives.

Within the legal language of the ICPC, the birth mother of a child to be placed is called the "sending agency," and the state from which the child comes is called the "sending state." (Note: If a birth mother's rights have been terminated and an adoption agency is involved, then the agency is known as the sending agency.) The sending ICPC office or unit retains jurisdiction over the child when he or she crosses a state line to the "receiving state." Keeping jurisdiction means that the ICPC unit receives supervisory reports and other regular reports detailing the child's adjustment to the new home and general progress. Generally, this information comes from the postplacement supervisory visits, which are similar to a home study but occur after the child is placed into the adoptive family's home. It also means that if the sending ICPC unit or sending agency (birth mother or adoption agency) believes that the adoptive family is not providing a home in "the best interests" of the child, then the sending ICPC unit or sending agency has the right to petition the court to have the child removed from the home and returned to either the birth parent or the agency.

The sending ICPC unit must be given the adoptive couple's approved home study before the child is placed with the adoptive parents. Until an adoption is finalized, the sending agency is technically responsible for the legal and financial protection of the child.

States began participating in the ICPC beginning in 1960. New Jersey was the last state to join in 1990. All states now participate in the ICPC and have enacted similar ICPC laws within their states' statutory scheme for adoption.

While ICPC laws in each state are generally the same, certain guidelines vary. For example, some states require that the home study include a criminal and child abuse clearance provided by the appropriate state law enforcement agency, while others simply request a letter stating that the couple has no criminal history from the couple's hometown police department.

Connecticut residents are required to use only an "approved" agency in the state in which the child is born. In fact, many states' ICPC guidelines mandate that a couple's home study be completed only by an approved adoption agency and not by a certified social worker, who is normally allowed in several states to provide home studies for in-state adoptions.

If you are adopting a child from out of state, it is critical that your attorney know the regulations for both the sending and the receiving states. Sometimes the guidelines for each state can appear contradictory. For example, in Virginia the adoptive and birth parents must know each other's names and addresses, while another state may require that all information be kept confidential. Also, sometimes the ICPC guidelines or state laws can change. Therefore, your attorney should talk with the correct personnel in the ICPC units for exact regulations and procedures.

Your attorney should do this even if you have retained an attorney in the sending state. Unless your attorney has dealt extensively with the attorney in the sending state, he or she should not simply assume the other attorney knows their own state adoption laws and ICPC regulations.

Each state has a compact administrator, as well as one or more deputy administrators, who are responsible for day-to-day tasks. The deputy compact administrator generally handles all telephone calls and correspondence and grants the necessary approval to place a child with an out-of-state couple.

Contacting the right person at the ICPC office and having your attorney(s) quickly submit the correct paperwork is very important when the child you are about to adopt is in another state. Until all the required documents are submitted to and approved by the ICPC offices of both the sending and receiving states, the adoptive couple is not allowed to cross state lines with the child. For example, if you are from New York and you locate a baby born in Utah, you will most likely go to Utah once the infant is discharged from the hospital. However, you cannot leave the state with the child until the ICPC offices in both Utah and New York give you permission. If the paperwork is not processed properly, you could find yourself living in a hotel for a couple of weeks with your new baby while you wait for approval from the ICPC offices. Of course, you want an attorney or adoption agency that will process all paperwork very quickly so that you can return home as soon as possible.

Do not depend on the ICPC personnel to fully assist you. Many ICPC offices are very helpful and do take the time to provide information; most are particularly helpful in dealing with attorneys who want a list of that state's ICPC requirements. However, many of the units are understaffed; your lawyer should develop a good relationship with the adoption attorney in the state where the baby is born so that he or she can monitor the flow of paper and any new requests for information put forth by the ICPC offices.

ADOPTION ATTORNEYS

The adoption attorneys listed are either members of the American Academy of Adoption Attorneys or attorneys who have conducted a significant number of adoptions and are well versed in adoption law. In some states in which the population is very low, an attorney may conduct only a few adoptions, but the attorney should still be very knowledgeable. None of the attorneys are endorsed by the authors. Call a local RESOLVE support group or adoption support group members to determine if other people have used the attorney. Also, you can telephone the ICPC office and ask for names of attorneys who practice adoption law regularly in that state.

ALABAMA

Adoptive/Foster Family Support Groups

Agape
P.O. Box 850663
Mobile, AL 36685
Phone: (251) 625-1133
Toll-Free: (800) 239-1020
E-mail: patricekenney@juno.com

Adoption Support Group
1204 Misty Lane
Tuscaloosa, AL 35405
Phone: (205) 391-9385
Fax: (205) 342-9855
E-mail: tcfapa2002@yahoo.com

Alabama Foster & Adoptive Parent Association
1091 County Road 1659
Cullman, AL 35058
Phone: (256) 796-7351
Fax: (775) 667-8282
E-mail: Frogmh@aol.com
Web site: www.afapa.org

Children's Aid Society
1500 Old County Road
Daphne, AL 36526
Phone: (251) 626-2864
E-mail: peboyd@mindspring.com

Greater Birmingham Foster and Adoptive Parents Association
P.O. Box 11926
Birmingham, AL 35202-1926
Phone: (205) 655-1543
Fax: (205) 655-1543
E-mail: Bamabison@aol.com

Single Adoptive Parents Support Group
2407 Titonka Road
Birmingham, AL 35244
Phone: (205) 733-0976
E-mail: catkins@dhhs.state.nh.us

Licensed Private Adoption Agencies

Angel Adoptions
P.O. Box 702
Helena, AL 35080
Phone: (205) 621-0316
Fax: (205) 621-0379
Toll-Free: (800) 523-5720
E-mail: angeladoptions@msn.com

Agape
P.O. Box 850663
Mobile, AL 36685
Phone: (251) 625-1133
Toll-Free: (800) 239-1020
E-mail: patricekenney@juno.com

Al-Hajj, Inc.
4249 Lomac Street, Suite C
Montgomery, AL 36106
Phone: (334) 215-7338

Alabama Baptist Children's Homes and Family Ministries, Inc.
P.O. Box 361767
Birmingham, AL 35236-1767
Phone: (205) 982-1112
Fax: (205) 982-9992
Toll-Free: (888) 720-8805
Web site: www.abchome.org

Association for Guidance, Aid, Placement and Empathy (AGAPE), Inc.
P.O. Box 230472
2813 Mastin Lake Road, Suite 200
Montgomery, AL 36123
Phone: (334) 272-9466
Fax: (334) 272-0378
E-mail: info@agape-nal-inc.org
Web site: www.agape-nal-inc.org

Camellia Therapeutic Foster Agency
P.O. Box 788
2310 Crawford Road
Phoenix City, AL 36867
Phone: (334) 448-2999

Catholic Family Services
1010 Church Street NW
Huntsville, AL 35804
Phone: (256) 536-0073
Fax: (256) 534-3141
E-mail: cfshsv@knology.net

Catholic Family Services, Inc.
733 37th Street East
Tuscaloosa, AL 35405
Phone: (205) 553-9045

Catholic Family Services, Inc.
2164 11th Avenue South
Birmingham, AL 35205
Phone: (205) 324-6561

Catholic Social Services of Mobile
P.O. Box 759
Mobile, AL 36601
Phone: (251) 434-1550
Fax: (251) 434-1549
E-mail: kklogan@cssmobile.org
– Intercountry Program
– Child Placement

Catholic Social Services of Montgomery
4455 Narrow Lane Road
Montgomery, AL 36116-2953
Phone: (334) 288-8890
Fax: (334) 288-9322
E-mail: information@cssalabama.org
Web site: www.cssalabama.org

Children of the World
110 South Section Street
Fairhope, AL 36562
Phone: (334) 990-3550
Fax: (251) 990-3494
E-mail: adoption@childrenofthe world.com
Web site: www.childrenoftheworld.com
– Intercountry Program
– Child Placement

Children's Aid Society
181 West Valley Avenue,
Suite 300
Homewood, AL 35209
Phone: (205) 943-5343
Fax: (205) 252-3828
E-mail: cas@childrensaid.org
Web site: www.childrensaid.org

Family Adoption Services, Inc.
529 Beacon Parkway West,
Suite 108
Birmingham, AL 35209
Phone: (205) 290-0077
Fax: (205) 290-0758
Toll-Free: (800) 877-4177
E-mail: info@familyadoptionser
vices.com
Web site: www.
familyadoptionservices.com
– Intercountry Program
– Home Study

Lifeline Children's Services
2908 Pump House Road
Birmingham, AL 35243
Phone: (205) 967-0919

Southern Social Works, Inc.
P.O. Box 8084
Anniston, AL 36202
Phone: (256) 237-4990
Fax: (256) 240-9808
E-mail: sosocwrks@aol.com
Web site: www.
southernsocialworks.com
– Intercountry Program
– Home Study

Special Beginnings, Inc.
1301 Azalea Road
Mobile, AL 36695
Phone: (334) 666-6703
Fax: (334) 343-7173
Toll-Free: (888) 666-6703
Web site: www.
specialbeginnings.org
– Intercountry Program
– Child Placement

Specialized Alternatives for
Families Youth of America
(SAFY)
4770 Woodmere Boulevard, Suite C
Montgomery, AL 36106-3084
Phone: (334) 270-3181

United Methodist Children's
Home
P.O. Box 8084
Selma, AL 36702
Phone: (334) 875-7283
Fax: (334) 875-5161
E-mail: umchalwf@bellsouth.net
Web site: www.umch.net

Villa Hope International
Adoption
6 Office Park Circle, Suite 218
Birmingham, AL 35223
Phone: (205) 870-7359
Fax: (205) 871-6629
E-mail: villahope@villahope.org
Web site: www.villahope.org
– Intercountry Program
– Child Placement

**Local/Regional Offices
of the State (Public)
Adoption Agency**
Web site: www.dhr.state.al.us/
counties.htm

**Birth Family and Search
Support Groups**

Alabama Department of
Human Resources
P.O. Box 687
1003 South Mulberry Avenue
Butler, AL 36904-0687
Phone: (205) 459-9700
Fax: (205) 459-2452
E-mail: lwels@dhr.state.al.us
Web site: www.dhr.state.al.us/
counties.htm

Orphan Voyage of AL
1610 Pinehurst Boulevard
Sheffield, AL 35660
Phone: (205) 383-7377

**State Adoption Exchange/
Photolisting of Children
Waiting For Adoption**

Families 4 Alabama's Kids
P.O. Box 190047
Birmingham, AL 35219-0047
Fax: (205) 271-1770
Toll-Free: (866) 425-5437
Web site: www.adoptuskids.
org/states/AL

**State Adoption
Specialist/Manager**

Alabama Department of
Human Resources
Sandy Holmes
50 North Ripley Street
Montgomery, AL 36130-4000
Phone: (334) 242-1374
Fax: (334) 242-0939
E-mail: sholmes2@dhr.state.al.us
Web site: www.dhr.state.al.us/
page.asp?pageid=306

**State Foster Care
Specialist/Manager**

Alabama Department of
Human Resources
Linda Campbell
P.O. Box 30400
Montgomery, AL 36130-4000
Phone: (334) 242-8449
Fax: (334) 242-0939
E-mail: lcampbell@dhr.state.al.us
Web site: www.dhr.state.al.us/
Page.asp?pageid=331

**State Interstate Compact on
the Placement of Children
(ICPC) Administrator**

Alabama Department of
Human Resources
50 North Ripley Street
Montgomery, AL 36130
Phone: (334) 242-9500
Fax: (334) 242-0939
E-mail: fwilson@dhr.state.al.us
Web site: www.dhr.state.al.us

State Licensing Specialist

Alabama Department of Human Resources
Faye Wilson
50 North Ripley Street
Montgomery, AL 36130
Phone: (334) 242-9500
E-mail: fwilson@dhr.state.al.us
Web site: www.dhr.state.al.us

State Complaints Office

Alabama Department of Human Resources
Family Services Division
50 North Ripley Street
Montgomery, AL 36130
Phone: (334) 242-9500

Not-for-profit/Nonprofit

National Children's Advocacy Center
Administrative Offices
210 Pratt Avenue
Huntsville, AL 35801
Phone: (256) 533-0531
Fax: (256) 534-6883
E-mail: webmaster@ncac-hsv.org
Web site: www.ncac-hsv.org

The Family and Child Training System (FACTS)
P.O. Box 1021
Montgomery, AL 36102-1021
Phone: (344) 262-5993
Toll-Free: (877) 232-5437
Web site: www.factstraining.org

ALASKA

Adoptive/Foster Family Support Groups

Adoptive Parents Embracing Sanity (APES)
2837 Wendy's Way
Anchorage, AK 99517-1402
Phone: (907) 243-6561

Alaska Attachment and Bonding Associates
P.O. Box 872188
Wasilla, AK 99687-2188
Phone: (907) 376-0366
Fax: (907) 376-3840
E-mail: Eleanor@mtaonline.net
Web site: www.akattachment.org

Alaska Foster Parent Training Center
815 2nd Avenue, Suite 101
Fairbanks, AK 99701
Phone: (907) 479-7307
Fax: (907) 749-4666
After hours: (907) 452-4566
E-mail: sward@nwresource.org
Web site: www.afptc.org

Anchorage Adoptive Parents Association
Anchorage, AK
Phone: (907) 278-8516

Booth Memorial Youth and Family Services
3600 East 20th Avenue
Anchorage, AK 99508
Phone: (907) 279-0522

Catholic Social Services (CSS)
3710 E. 20th Avenue, Suite 1
Anchorage, AK 99508
Phone: (907) 276-5590
Fax: (907) 276-5539
Toll-Free: (888) 625-7315
E-mail: pregnancy@css.ak.org
Web site: www.cssalaska.org

North American Council on Adoptable Children State Representative
1018 26th Avenue
Fairbanks, AK 99701
Phone: (907) 452-5397
E-mail: info@nacac.org
Web site: www.nacac.org

Toughlove
3000 East 16th Avenue
Anchorage, AK 99501
Phone: (907) 566-0656

Licensed Private Adoption Agencies

Adopt An Angel Child
308 G Street, Suite 225
Anchorage, AK 99501

Adoption Advocates International
218 Martin Drive
Fairbanks, AK 99712
Phone: (907) 457-3832
E-mail: aai@adoptionadvocates.org
Web site: www. adoptionadvocates.org/alaska
– Intercountry Program
– Child Placement

Alaska International Adoption Agency
308 G Street, Suite 225
Anchorage, AK 99501
Phone: (907) 677-2888
E-mail: info@akadoptions.com
Web site: www.akadoptions.com
– Intercountry Program
– Child Placement

Catholic Social Services (CSS)
3710 E. 20th Avenue, Suite 1
Anchorage, AK 99508
Phone: (907) 276-5590
Fax: (907) 276-5539
Toll-Free: (888) 625-7315
E-mail: pregnancy@css.ak.org
Web site: www.cssalaska.org
– Intercountry Program
– Home Study

Circle of Hope International Adoption Agency
1217 Georgeson Loop
Sitka, AK 99835-7014
Phone: (907) 966-2606
– Intercountry Program
– Child Placement

Fairbanks Counseling and Adoption
912 Barnette Street
Fairbanks, AK 99701
Phone: (907) 456-4729
Fax: (907) 456-4623
E-mail: melody@fcaalaska.org
– Intercountry Program
– Home Study

World Association for Children and Parents (WACAP)
4704 Kenai Avenue
Anchorage, AK 99508

Local/Regional Offices of the State (Public) Adoption Agency

Department of Health and Social Services State Office
Office of Children's Services
P.O. Box 110630
130 Seward Street, Room 4F
Juneau, AK 99811-0630
Phone: (907) 465-3170
Fax: (907) 465-3397

Alaska Department of Health and Social Services
Anchorage Regional Office
550 West 8th Avenue, Suite 304
Anchorage, AK 99501-3553
Phone: (907) 269-4000
Fax: (907) 269-3901
Toll-Free: (800) 478-4444
Web site: www.state.ak.us/local/akdir1.html

Alaska Department of Health and Social Services
Vintage Park
3025 Clinton Drive, Second Floor
Juneau, AK 99801
Phone: (907) 465-3235
Fax: (907) 465-1669
Web site: www.hss.state.ak.us/dfys/

State Adoption Exchange/ Photolisting of Children Waiting For Adoption

Alaska Adoption Exchange
Phone: (206) 441-6822
Toll-Free: (800) 704-9133
E-mail: akae@nwresource.org
Web site: www.akae.org

State Adoption Specialist/Manager

Alaska Department of Health and Social Services
Linda West
P.O. Box 110630
350 Main Street, 4th Floor
Juneau, AK 99811-0630
Phone: (907) 465-2145
Fax: (907) 465-3397
E-mail: Linda_west@health.state.ak.us
Web site: www.hss.state.ak.us/ocs/Adoptions/default.htm

State Foster Care Specialist/Manager

Alaska Office of Children's Services
Izabel Bowers
P.O. Box 110630
Juneau, AK 99811-0630
Phone: (907) 465-2218
Fax: (907) 465-3656
E-mail: izabel_bowers@health.state.ak.us
Web site: www.hss.state.ak.us/ocs/FosterCare/default.htm

State Interstate Compact on the Placement of Children (ICPC) Administrator

Alaska Department of Health and Social Services
P.O. Box 110630
130 Seward Street, Room 4F
Juneau, AK 99811-0630
Phone: (907) 465-3191
Fax: (907) 465-3397

E-mail: marcia_pickering@health.state.ak.us
Web site: www.hss.state.ak.us/dfys

State Licensing Specialist

Alaska Department of Health and Social Services
Division of Family and Youth Services
P.O. Box 110630
130 Seward Street, Room 4F
Juneau, AK 99811-0630
Phone: (907) 465-2817
Fax: (907) 465-3397
Web site: www.hss.state.ak.us/dfys

ARIZONA

Adoptive/Foster Family Support Groups

Adoptive Parents of Yavapai County
3005 Sequoya Lane
Prescott, AZ 86301
Phone: (602) 445-6519

Aid to Adoption of Special Kids (AASK)
2320 North 20th Street
Phoenix, AZ 85006
Phone: (602) 254-2275
Fax: (602) 212-2564
Toll-Free: (800) 568-2614
E-mail: info@aask-az.org
Web site: www.AASK-AZ.org

Arizona Adoptive Families Support Group
10926 North 128th Place
Scottsdale, AZ 85259
Phone: (480) 451-9831

Arizona Association for Foster & Adoptive Parents
4757 E. Greenway Road., Suite 107 B
PMB 165
Phoenix, AZ 85032
Phone: (602) 488-2374
Fax: (602) 485-1810
Web site: www.azafap.org

Arizona Families for Children
1011 North Craycroft, Suite 470
Tucson, AZ 85711
Phone: (520) 327-3324
Fax: (520) 881-0768

Arizona's Children Association (AzCA)
2700 South Eighth Avenue
Tucson, AZ 85713
Phone: (520) 622-7611
Fax: (520) 624-7042
Toll-Free: (800) 947-7611
E-mail: fchaffee@arizonaschildren.org
Web site: www.arizonaschildren.org

Children with AIDS Project of America
P.O. Box 23778
Tempe, AZ 85285
Phone: (480) 774-9718
Fax: (480) 921-0449
Toll-Free: (800) 866-AIDS
Web site: www.aidskids.org

Families First
501 East Thomas Road, Suite 100
Phoenix, AZ 85012
Phone: (602) 493-1722
Fax: (602) 212-2564
Web site: www.aask-az.org

Post-Adoptive Families Together
P.O. Box 12685
Tucson, AZ 85732-2685
Phone: (520) 907-3949

Licensed Private Adoption Agencies

Adoption Journeys of Arizona, Inc.
4065 East Roberts Place
Tucson, AZ 85711
Phone: (520) 327-0899
Fax: (520) 327-0899
E-mail: www.adoptionjourneys.org
– Intercountry Program
– Child Placement

Aid to Adoption of Special Kids (AASK)
2320 North 20th Street
Phoenix, AZ 85006
Phone: (602) 254-2275
Fax: (602) 212-2564
Toll-Free: (800) 568-2614
E-mail: info@aask-az.org
Web site: www.AASK-AZ.org

Arizona Family Adoption Services, Inc.
346 East Palm Lane
Phoenix, AZ 85004-1531
Phone: (602) 254-2271
Fax: (602) 254-1581
E-mail: info@azadoptions.com
Web site: www.azadoptions.com
– Intercountry Program
– Home Study

Arizona's Children Association (AzCA)
2700 South Eighth Avenue
Tucson, AZ 85713
Phone: (520) 622-7611
Fax: (520) 624-7042
Toll-Free: (800) 947-7611
E-mail: fchaffee@arizonaschildren.org
Web site: www.arizonaschildren.org

Birth Hope Adoption Agency, Inc.
3225 North Central Avenue, Suite 1217
Phoenix, AZ 85012
Phone: (602) 277-2868

Black Family and Children's Services, Inc.
2323 North Third Street, Suite 202
Phoenix, AZ 85004
Phone: (602) 256-2948
Fax: (602) 276-1984

Building Arizona Families
6027 N. 132nd Drive
Litchfield Park, AZ 85340
Phone: (623) 936-4729
Fax: (623) 936-4729
Toll-Free: (800) 340-9665
E-mail: info@BuildingArizona Families.com
Web site: www. BuildingArizonaFamilies.com

Casey Family Program
1600 North Country Club
Tucson, AZ 85716
Phone: (520) 323-0886
Fax: (520) 323-6819

Catholic Community Services in Western Arizona
690 East 32nd Street
Yuma, AZ 85365
Phone: (520) 341-9400
Toll-Free: (888) 514-3482
Web site: www.ccs-soaz.org/ccswa.htm

Catholic Community Services of Southeastern Arizona
P.O. Box 1777
Bisbee, AZ 85603
Phone: (520) 432-2285
Toll-Free: (800) 338-2474
Web site: www.ccs-soaz.org/csssea.htm

Catholic Social Services of Central and Northern Arizona
1825 West Northern Avenue
Phoenix, AZ 85021
Phone: (602) 997-6105
Web site: www.diocesephoenix.org/css/

Catholic Social Services of
Central and Northern Arizona
430 North Dobson Road, Suite 110
Mesa, AZ 85201
Phone: (480) 964-8771

Catholic Social Services of
Southern Arizona, Inc. (CCS)
140 West Speedway, Suite 130
Tucson, AZ 85703-7687
Phone: (520) 623-0344
Fax: (520) 770-8578
Toll-Free: (800) 234-0344
Web site: www.ccs-soaz.org/css.
htm

Child Hope and Aid International
1645 North Alvernon Way
Tucson, AZ 85712
Phone: (520) 881-7474

Christian Family Care Agency
1700 East Fort Lowell, Suite 101
Tucson, AZ 85719
Phone: (520) 296-8255
Fax: (520) 296-8773
E-mail: stephanie@christianfam
ilycare.org
Web site: www.cfcare.org
– Intercountry Program
– Home Study

Commonwealth Adoptions
International, Inc.
1585 E. River Road, Suite 121
Tucson, AZ 85718
Phone: (520) 327-7574
Fax: (520) 327-8640
E-mail: info@commonwealthad
option.org
Web site: www.
commonwealthadoption.org
– Intercountry Program
– Child Placement

Dillon Southwest
3014 North Hayden Road, Suite
101
Scottsdale, AZ 85251
Phone: (480) 945-2221

Fax: (480) 945-3956
E-mail: info@dillonsouthwest.org
Web site: www.dillonsouthwest.
org
– Intercountry Program
– Child Placement
– Home Study

Family Service Agency
1530 East Flower Street
Phoenix, AZ 85014
Phone: (602) 264-9891
E-mail: fsaphoenix@aol.com
Web site: www.fsaphoenix.org

Hand in Hand International
Adoptions
931 East Southern Avenue, Suite
108
Mesa, AZ 85204
Phone: (480) 892-5550
Fax: (480) 892-7322
E-mail: arizona@hihiadopt.org
Web site: www.hihiadopt.org
– Intercountry Program
– Child Placement

Home Builders For Children, Inc.
3014 North Hayden Road
Scottsdale, AZ 85251
Phone: (480) 429-5344
Fax: (480) 945-3956
Web site: www.homes4children.
org

LDS Family Services
5049 East Broadway Boulevard,
Suite 126
Tucson, AZ 85711
Phone: (520) 745-0459
Fax: (520) 512-0647

MAPS Arizona
7000 North 16th Street, Suite
120 #438
Phoenix, AZ 85020
Phone: (602) 277-9243
Fax: (602) 279-9469
Web site: www.mapsadopt.org
– Intercountry Program
– Child Placement

Oasis Adoption Services, LLC.
11795 North Via De La Verbenita
Tucson, AZ 85737
Phone: (520) 579-5578
Fax: (520) 579-5578
E-mail: cb@oasisadoption.com
Web site: www.oasisadoption.
com

**Birth Family and Search
Support Groups**

Adoption Counseling Home
11260 North 92nd Street, #1046
Scottsdale, AZ 85260
Phone: (602) 614-9222
Fax: (602) 614-0241

Adult Adoptees Support Group
7757 East Marquise Drive
Tucson, AZ 85715
Phone: (602) 885-6771

Arizona's Children Association
(AzCA)
2700 South Eighth Avenue
Tucson, AZ 85713
Phone: (520) 622-7611
Fax: (520) 624-7042
Toll-Free: (800) 947-7611
E-mail: fchaffee@arizonaschild
ren.org
Web site: www.arizonaschildren.
org

Catholic Community Services
of Southern Arizona, Inc.
(CCS)
140 West Speedway, Suite 130
Tucson, AZ 85705-7687
Phone: (520) 623-0344
Fax: (520) 770-8578
Toll-Free: (800) 234-0344
Web site: www.ccs-soaz.org/css.
htm

Concerned United Birthparents (CUB)
2613 North Saratoga Street
Tempe, AZ 85381

Flagstaff Adoption Search and Support Group
P.O. Box 1031
Flagstaff, AZ 86002
Phone: (520) 779-3817

Past Present Future
7290 West Shaw Butte Drive
Peoria, AZ 85345
Phone: (602) 486-3042

Search Triad, Inc.
Box 10181
Phoenix, AZ 85064
Phone: (480) 834-7417
E-mail: searchtriad@att.net
Web site: http://searchtriad.org

T.R.I.A.D.
Box 12806
Tucson, AZ 85732-2806
Phone: (520) 881-8250

State Adoption Exchange/ Photolisting of Children Waiting For Adoption

Arizona Department of Economic Security
P.O. Box 17951
Tucson, AZ 85731
Phone: (520) 327-3324
Toll-Free: (877) 543-7633
Web site: www.de.state.az.us/ dcyf/adoption/meet.asp

State Adoption Specialist/Manager

Arizona Department of Economic Security
Angela Cause
P.O. Box 6123-940A
Phoenix, AZ 85007
Phone: (602) 542-5499
Fax: (602) 542-3330
E-mail: acause@azdes.gov
Web site: www.de.state.az.us/ dcyf/adoption/default.asp

State Confidential Intermediary Service

Arizona Confidential Intermediary Program
Arizona Judicial Branch
1501 West Washington, Suite 104
Phoenix, AZ 85007
Phone: (602) 364-0575
Fax: (602) 364-0358
TDD: (602) 542-9545
Toll-Free: (800) 732-8193
E-mail: cip@supreme.sp.state. az.us
Web site: www.supreme.state. az.us/cip

State Foster Care Specialist/Manager

Arizona Department of Economic Security
Belva Stites
P.O. Box 6123–940A
1789 West Jefferson
Phoenix, AZ 85005
Phone: (602) 542-2431
Fax: (602) 542-3330
E-mail: bstites@azdes.gov
Web site: www.azdes.gov/dcyf/ adoption/

State Interstate Compact on the Placement of Children (ICPC) Administrator

Arizona Department of Economic Security
P.O. Box 6123-030C-1
Phoenix, AZ 85005
Phone: (602) 235-5499
E-mail: Ruby.Pittman@mail. de.state.az.us

State Licensing Specialist

Office of Licensing Certification and Regulation
Patrick Reed
1951 West Camelback Road, Suite 400

Phoenix, AZ 85015
Phone: (602) 347-6346
Phone: (602) 347-6340
Fax: (502) 336-9603
Toll-Free: (888) 229-1814
E-mail: PatrickReed@azdes.gov

Not-for-profit/Nonprofit

Childhelp USA
15757 North 78th Street
Scottsdale, AZ 85260
Phone: (480) 922-8212
Fax: (480) 922-7061
TDD: (800) 2-A-CHILD
Toll-Free: (800) 4-A-CHILD
Web site: www.childhelpusa.org

Professional Association

National Association of Foster Care Reviewers
1501 West Washington Avenue, Suite 128
Phoenix, AZ 85007
Phone: (602) 542-9409
E-mail: info@nafcr.org
Web site: www.nafcr.org

ARKANSAS

Adoptive/Foster Family Support Groups

AFACT and North American Council on Adoptable Children
17 McKee Circle
North Little Rock, AR 72116
Phone: (501) 372-3300
Fax: (501) 372-8060
E-mail: bjean@metroplan.org

Adopt America Network and North American
Council on Adoptable Children Representative
1314 North Boston Avenue
Russellville, AR 72801
Phone: (501) 967-9337

Families Are Special, Inc.
805 Claremont Avenue
Sherwood, AR 72120
Phone: (501) 983-9069
Fax: (501) 758-4704
E-mail: NLRMYC@aol.com
Web site: www.
arkansasadopttoday.org

Miracles
1008 Barbara
Jacksonville, AR 72076

River Valley Adoption Group
1005 West 18th Terrace
Russellville, AR 72801
Phone: (501) 967-1641

Searcy Children's Homes, Inc.
900 North Main Street
Searcy, AR 72143
Phone: (501) 268-3243
Fax: (501) 278-4773
E-mail: searchychildrenshomes@
mail.com

**Licensed Private
Adoption Agencies**

Adoption Advantage, Inc.
1116 Garland Street
Little Rock, AR 72201
Phone: (501) 376-7778

Adoption Advantage, Inc.
13720 Col. Glenn Road
Little Rock, AR 72210
Phone: (501) 376-7778
Fax: (501) 376-7775
Toll-Free: (877) 349-9334
E-mail: info@adoptionadvantage.
com
Web site: www.
adoptionadvantage.com

Adoption Services, Inc.
2500 North Tyler Street
Little Rock, AR 72207
Phone: (501) 664-0340
Fax: (501) 664-9186

Bethany Christian Services
1100 North University Avenue,
Suite 66
Little Rock, AR 72207-6344
Phone: (501) 664-5729
Fax: (501) 664-5740
E-mail: bcslittlerock@bethany.
org
Web site: www.bethany.org/
arkansas
– Intercountry Program
– Child Placement

Children's Home, Inc.
P.O. Box 7257
Sherwood, AR 72124
Phone: (501) 268-4330
Fax: (501) 835-5301
E-mail: sherwood-chi@sbcglobal.
net

**Children's Home, Inc. Church
of Christ**
5515 Old Walcott Road
Paragould, AR 72450
Phone: (870) 239-4031

Children's Homes, Inc.
900 North Main Street
Searcy, AR 72143
Phone: (501) 268-4330
Fax: (501) 278-4773
E-mail: sherwood-chi@sbcglobal.
net
Web site: www.childrenshomes.
org

Dillon International, Inc.
P.O. Box 94698
North Little Rock, AR 72190
Phone: (501) 791-9300
E-mail: dillonarkansas@dillonad
opt.com
Web site: www.dillonadopt.com
– Intercountry Program
– Child Placement

Families Are Special, Inc.
805 Claremont Avenue
Sherwood, AR 72120
Phone: (501) 983-9069

Fax: (501) 758-4704
E-mail: NLRMYC@aol.com
Web site: www.
arkansasadopttoday.org

Family Life Connections
P.O. Box 2645
700 West B Street
Russellville, AR 72811
Phone: (479) 968-5400
Fax: (479) 968-1990
E-mail: sanford@csw.net

Gladney Center for Adoption
P.O. Box 94615
North Little Rock, AR 72190-4615
Phone: (501) 791-3206
E-mail: info@gladney.org
Web site: www.gladney.org
– Intercountry Program
– Child Placement

**Holt International Children's
Services**
5016 Western Hills Avenue
Little Rock, AR 72204
Phone: (501) 568-2827
Fax: (501) 568-2827
E-mail: info@holtinternational.
org
Web site: www.holtintl.org
– Intercountry Program
– Child Placement

Integrity, Inc.
6124 Northmoor Drive
Little Rock, AR 72204
Phone: (501) 614-7200
Fax: (501) 614-7254
E-mail: vgrantham@integrityinc.
org
– Intercountry Program
– Child Placement
– Home Study

International Families, Inc.
28 Shenandoah Way
Cabot, AR 72023
Phone: (501) 605-9928

Searcy Children's Homes, Inc.
900 North Main Street
Searcy, AR 72143
Phone: (501) 268-3243
Fax: (501) 278-4773
E-mail: searcychildrenshomes@
mail.com

Southern Christian Home
P.O. Box 649
Morrilton, AR 72110
Phone: (501) 354-2428
Fax: (501) 354-2429
Web site: www.schome.com

Ventures for Children International
1621 Starr Drive
Fayetteville, AR 72701
Phone: (479) 582-0305
Fax: (208) 248-7181
E-mail: info@venturesforchildren.
org
Web site: www.
venturesforchildren.org
– Intercountry Program
– Child Placement

Western Arkansas Youth Shelter
P.O. Box 48, Highway 96
Cecil, AR 72930
Phone: (501) 667-2946

Local/Regional Offices of the State (Public) Adoption Agency

Arkansas Department of Human Services (ADHS)
Alden Roller
P.O. Box 1437, Slot S565
Little Rock, AR 72203-1437
Phone: (501) 682-8460
Fax: (501) 682-8094
TDD: (501) 682-1442
Toll-Free: (888) 736-2820
E-mail: alden.roller@mail.state.
ar.us
Web site: https://170.94.232.16/
wa_FC_ADOPTION/FCA_Inquiry.
asp

State Adoption Exchange/ Photolisting of Children Waiting For Adoption

Arkansas Adoption Resource Exchange
P.O. Box 1437, Slot S565
Little Rock, AR 72203-1437
Phone: (501) 682-8460
Fax: (501) 682-8094
TDD: (501) 682-1442
Toll-Free: (888) 736-2820
E-mail: alden.roller@mail.state.
ar.us
Web site: www.accessarkansas.
org/dhs/adoption/adoption.html

State Adoption Specialist/Manager

Arkansas Department of Human Services (ADHS)
Alden Roller
P.O. Box 1437, Slot S565
Little Rock, AR 72203-1437
Phone: (501) 682-8460
Fax: (501) 682-8094
TDD: (501) 682-1442
Toll-Free: (888) 736-2820
E-mail: alden.roller@mail.state.
ar.us
Web site: https://170.94.232.16/
wa_FC_ADOPTION/FCA_Inquiry.
asp

State Foster Care Specialist/Manager

Arkansas Department of Human Services
Edward Wallace
P.O. Box 1437
Slot #S565
Little Rock, AR 72203-1437
Phone: (501) 682-1569
Fax: (501) 682-5272
E-mail: ed.wallace@mail.state.
ar.us
Web site: www.state.ar.us/dhs/
chilnfam/FosterFamilies.htm

State Interstate Compact on the Placement of Children (ICPC) Administrator

Arkansas Department of Human Services
Division of Children and Family Services
P.O. Box 1437 Slot S567
Little Rock, AR 72203-1437
Phone: (501) 682-8556
Fax: (501) 682-8561
E-mail: marty.nodurfth@mail.
state.ar.us
Web site: www.state.ar.us/dhs/
chilnfam

State Licensing Specialist

Arkansas Department of Human Services
Greg Gilliland
Child Welfare Agency Licensing Unit
115 Market Street
Hot Springs, AR 71901
Phone: (501) 321-0966

State Reunion Registry

Arkansas Department of Human Services
P.O. Box 1437, Slot S565
Little Rock, AR 72203-1437
Phone: (501) 682-8460
Fax: (501) 682-8094
TDD: (501) 682-1442
Toll-Free: (888) 736-2820
E-mail: alden.roller@mail.state.
ar.us
Web site: https://170.94.232.16/
wa_FC_ADOPTION/FCA_Inquiry.
asp

Arkansas Mutual Consent Voluntary Adoption Registry
P.O. Box 1437 Slot S565
Little Rock, AR 72203-1437
Phone: (501) 682-8462
E-mail: judy.ford@mail.state.ar.us
Web site: www.state.ar.us/dhs/
adoption/mcvar.htm

State Liaison Officers

Arkansas Department of Human Services
Division of Children & Family Services
P.O. Box 1437, Slot 830
Little Rock, AR 72203-1437

CALIFORNIA

Adoptive/Foster Family Support Groups

AASK Adopt A Special Kid
7700 Edgewater Drive
Suite 320, Building B
Oakland, CA 94621
Phone: (510) 553-1748
Fax: (510) 553-1747
Toll-Free: (888) 680-7349
E-mail: andrea@adopta
specialkid.org
Web site: www.
adoptaspecialkid.org

AFTER Adoptive Parent Education #4
124 River Road
Salinas, CA 93908-9601
Phone: (831) 649-3033
Fax: (831) 649-4843
E-mail: carolyn@kinshipcenter.
org
Web site: www.afteradoption.
org

AFTER Adoptive Parent Education #5
BAAS Meeting Room
465 Fairchild Street, Suite 215
Mountain View, CA 94303
Phone: (408) 573-8222
Web site: www.afteradoption.
org

AFTER- Adoptive Parent Support Group
115 East Gish Road, Suite 246
San Jose, CA 95112
Phone: (408) 573-8222

Toll-Free: (877) 332-3837
E-mail: louise@rainbow-family.
org
Web site: www.afteradoption.
org

Adoption Connection
1710 Scott Street
San Francisco, CA 94115-3004
Phone: (415) 359-2494
Fax: (415) 359-2490
Toll-Free: (800) 972-9225
E-mail: families@adoptionconne
ction.org
Web site: www.
adoptionconnection.org
– Intercountry Program
– Adoptive Parent/Family Preparation
– Agency Able to Place Children with United States Citizens Living Abroad
– Education/Preparation
– Home Study
– Information/Referral

Adoption Horizons
10 West 7th Street, Suite F
Eureka, CA 95501
Phone: (707) 444-9909
Fax: (707) 442-6672
Toll-Free: (800) 682-3678
E-mail: adoption@sbcglobal.net
Web site: www.adoption-horizons.org
– Intercountry Program
– Adoptive Parent/Family Preparation
– Agency Able to Place Children with United States Citizens Living Abroad
– Child Placement
– Education/Preparation
– Information/Referral

Adoption Information Center (AIC)
643 West 6th Street
San Pedro, CA 90731
Phone: (310) 732-1023

Fax: (310) 732-1019
E-mail: LAadoptions@yahoo.com
Web site: www.
adoptioninfocenter.com

Adoption Paths
P.O. Box 2746
Santa Cruz, CA 95063-2746
Phone: (831) 476-7252
E-mail: info@adoptionpaths.com
Web site: www.adoptionpaths.
com

Adoption Support Group of Santa Monica
1452 26th Street #103
Santa Monica, CA 90404
Phone: (310) 829-1438
Fax: (310) 476-1963
E-mail: marlourussell@hotmail.
com
Web site: www.
marlourussellphd.com

Aspira Foster & Family Services
333 Gellert Boulevard, Suite 203
Daly City, CA 94015-2614
Phone: (805) 654-6800
Fax: (805) 654-6803
E-mail: doug@mossbeachhomes.
com
Web site: www.aspiranet.org or www.mossbeachhomes.com

Bay Area Single Adoptive Parent Group
385 South 14th Street
San Jose, CA 95112
Phone: (408) 292-1638

Bethany Christian Services – North Region
3048 Hahn Drive
Modesto, CA 95350-6503
Phone: (209) 522-5121
Fax: (209) 522-1499
Toll-Free: (800) 454-0454
E-mail: bcsmodesto@bethany.org
Web site: www.bethany.org/
modesto

Black Adoption Research Center
125 2nd Street
Oakland, CA 94607
Phone: (510) 839-3678

Black Linkage for Adopted Children
840 West Neldome Street
Altadena, CA 91001
Phone: (626) 296-3506
Fax: (213) 483-8109

California Department of Social Services – Fresno County
2135 Fresno Street, Suite 401
Fresno, CA 93721
Phone: (559) 262-4402
Fax: (559) 262-4435

California Department of Social Services – Placer County
11716 Enterprise Drive
Auburn, CA 95603
Phone: (530) 889-6700
Fax: (530) 889-6735
E-mail: tbardakj@placer.ca.gov
Web site: www.placer.ca.gov

California Department of Social Services – Shasta County
P.O. Box 496005
Redding, CA 96049-6005
Phone: (530) 225-5791
Fax: (530) 225-5884
E-mail: adoptions@co.shasta.ca.us
Web site: www.adoptions.co.shasta.ca.us

California State Foster Parent Association, Inc.
P.O. Box 22772
San Diego, CA 92192
Phone: (858) 552-0691

Children's Bureau of Southern California (CBSC)
11815 Riverside Drive
North Hollywood, CA 91607
Phone: (818) 985-8154
Fax: (818) 985-7045
Toll-Free: (800) 730-3933
E-mail: cstogel@all4kids.org
Web site: www.all4kids.org

Chrysalis House, Inc. (CHI)
4035 North Fresno Street, Suite 101
Fresno, CA 93726
Phone: (559) 229-9862
Fax: (559) 229-9863
E-mail: contact-us@chrysalishouse.com
Web site: www.chrysalishouse.com
– Intercountry Program
– Adoptive Parent/Family Preparation
– Agency Able to Place Children with United States Citizens Living Abroad
– Child Placement
– Education/Preparation
– Information/Referral

Families Adopting in Response (FAIR)
P.O. Box 51436
Palo Alto, CA 94303
Phone: (650) 856-3513
Fax: (650) 494-2971
E-mail: lansing@fairfamilies.org
Web site: www.fairfamilies.org

Families with Adopted Children from Eastern Europe
11260 Overland Avenue, Unit 20F
Culver City, CA 90230
Phone: (310) 204-0323
E-mail: mason@loop.com

Families for Attachment Resources
Polinsky Children's Center
9400 Ruffin Court

San Diego, CA 92123-5399
Phone: (619) 690-2840

FamiliesFirst
2100 Fifth Street
Davis, CA 95616
Phone: (530) 753-0220
Fax: (530) 785-3390
Toll-Free: (800) 698-4968
E-mail: nscott@familiesfirstinc.org
Web site: www.familiesfirstinc.org

Family Connections Adoptions (FCA)
7257 N. Maple, Suite 101
Fresno, CA 93720
Phone: (559) 325-9388
Fax: (559) 325-9373
E-mail:dianewagers@fcadoptions.org
Web site: www.fcadoptions.org

Five Acres
760 West Mountain View Street
Altadena, CA 91101
Phone: (626) 798-6793
Fax: (626) 585-1664
Toll-Free: (800) 696-6793
Web site: www.5acres.org

Foster Family Network
P.O. Box 627
Chapter 82, CA FPA, Inc.
Pinole, CA 94564
Phone: (510) 724-6942

Future Families Adoption and Foster Care and Family Services
Future Families Office
1671 The Alameda, Suite 201
San Jose, CA 95126
Phone: (408) 298-8789
Fax: (408) 298-8870
Toll-Free: (800) 922-5437
E-mail: contactme@futurefamilies.org
Web site: www.futurefamilies.org

Grandma's Angels
6703 St. Clair Avenue
North Hollywood, CA 91606
Phone: (818) 759-1312
E-mail: gbangels@aol.com
Web site: www.grandmasangels.
org

Hand in Hand – An Adoptive Family Support Group
4707 Tenbury Lane
Rocklin, CA 95677
Phone: (916) 806-2240
After hours: (916) 771-4446
E-mail: pstewart@surewest.net

HelP. O.ne Child
Union Presbyterian Church
858 University Avenue
Los Altos, CA 94024
Phone: (650) 917-1210
Fax: (650) 917-5796
Toll-Free: (888) 543-4673
Web site: www.helponechild.org

Holy Family Services Adoption & Foster Care (HFS)
402 South Marengo Avenue
Pasadena, CA 91101-3113
Phone: (626) 432-5680
Fax: (626) 578-7321
Toll-Free: (800) 464-ADOPT
E-mail: HFSAdopt@aol.com
Web site: www.
holyfamilyservices.org

Independent Adoption Center
391 Taylor Boulevard, Suite 100
Pleasant Hill, CA 94523
Phone: (925) 827-2229
Fax: (925) 603-0820
Toll-Free: (800) 877-6736
E-mail: staff@adoptionhelp.org
Web site: www.adoptionhelp.org

Kids & Families Together
856 E. Thompson Boulevard
Ventura, CA 93001-2918
Phone: (805) 643-3734
Fax: (805) 643-0271
E-mail: David@kidsandfamilies.org

Web site: www.kidsandfamilies.
org

Kinship Center
1520 Brookhollow Drive, Suite 41
Santa Ana, CA 92705
Phone: (909) 518-8282
Fax: (714) 979-8135
E-mail: kfelder@kinshipcenter.org

LDS Family Services – San Jose
6980 Santa Teresa Boulevard,
Suite 140
San Jose, CA 95119
Phone: (408) 361-0133
Fax: (408) 361-0132
E-mail: fam-ca-sanjose@
ldschurch.org
Web site: www.
ldsfamilyservices.org

Lilliput Children's Services
1610 Arden Way, #273
Sacramento, CA 95815
Phone: (916) 923-5444
Fax: (916) 923-2365
E-mail: adopt@lilliput.org
Web site: www.lilliput.org

National Council for Single Adoptive Parents
P.O. Box 567
Mount Hermon, CA 95041
Toll-Free: (888) 490-4600
E-mail: info@ncsap.com
Web site: www.ncsap.org

North County Adoptive Parent Association
P.O. Box 235244
Encinitas, CA 92023
Phone: (760) 635-7920
E-mail: rferr@sdcoe.k12.ca.us
Web site: www.adoptionrocks.org

North County Lifeline-Post Adoption Program
200 Michigan Avenue
Vista, CA 92084
Phone: (760) 726-4900

E-mail: ptrunell@nclifeline.org
Web site: www.nclifeline.org

Olive Crest Adoption Services
2130 East Fourth Street,
Suite 200
Santa Ana, CA 92705
Phone: (714) 543-5437
Fax: (714) 543-5463
Toll-Free: (800) 550-2445
Web site: www.olivecrest.org

Open Door Society and North American
Council on Adoptable Children
Representative
170 East Highland, Room E
Sierra Madre, CA 91204
Phone: (818) 355-5920

Open Door Society of Los Angeles
10841 Acama Street
Toluca Lake, CA 91602
Phone: (818) 760-8509
E-mail: speclot@sbcglobal.net

Optimist Community Services (OYHFS)
7330 North Fiogueroa Street
Los Angeles, CA 90041
Phone: (323) 341-5561
Fax: (323) 257-6418
Toll-Free: (800) 454-5561
E-mail: silorlando@oyhfs.org
Web site: www.oyhfs.org

PACT, an Adoption Alliance
4179 Piedmont Avenue, Suite 330
Oakland, CA 94611
Phone: (510) 243-9460
Fax: (510) 243-9970
Toll-Free: (800) 750-7950
E-mail: info@pactadopt.org
Web site: www.pactadopt.org

Parents & Children Together (PACT)
643 West 6th Street
San Pedro, CA 90731
Phone: (310) 732-1023
Fax: (310) 732-1019

Parents for Parents
1928 Dartmoor Drive
Lemongrove, CA 91945
Phone: (619) 463-1389
Fax: (619) 464-0115

Placer County Foster/Adopt Parents Support Group
11716 Enterprise Drive
Auburn, CA 95603
Phone: (530) 823-7278
Fax: (530) 886-6735

Post Adoption Services Project
749 F Street
Arcata, CA 95521
Phone: (707) 826-9178
Fax: (707) 822-5756
After hours: (707) 822-5756
E-mail: cinsav@aol.com
Web site: www.
postadoptservices.com

Private Adoption- Where to Begin?
P.O. Box 405
Boulder Creek, CA 95006

RESOLVE of Greater Los Angeles Support Group
P.O. Box 8453
Calabasas, CA 91372
Phone: (818) 222-1335
Fax: (818) 222-1336
Toll-Free: (866) 888-7452
E-mail: office@resolvela.org
Web site: www.resolvela.org

RESOLVE of Northern California
312 Sutter Street, #405
San Francisco, CA 94108
Phone: (415) 788-3002
Fax: (415) 788-6774
E-mail: resolvenc@aol.com
Web site: www.resolvenc.org

Rauline Atkins
2248 South Cloverdale Avenue
Los Angeles, CA 90020

Phone: (323) 935-4276
Fax: (323) 965-1015
E-mail: rauline@fosterparents.
com or raulinem@aol.com

Room for One More
c/o Ward A.M.E Church
1177 West 25th Street
Los Angeles, CA 90007
Phone: (626) 359-3680

San Diego County Foster Parent Association
13451 Starridge Street
Poway, CA 92064
Phone: (619) 748-4502
Fax: (619) 748-2458
E-mail: FstrMom4U@aol.com

Sierra Adoption Services
8928 Volunteer Lane, #240
Sacramento, CA 95826
Phone: (916) 368-5114
Fax: (916) 368-5157
E-mail: vmarchus@
sierraadoption.org
Web site: www.sierraadoption.
org

Single Adoptive Parents
South Bay Chapter
385 South 14th Street
San Jose, CA 95112
Phone: (408) 292-1638

Southern California Foster Family and Adoption Agency (SCFFAA)
155 North Occidental Boulevard
Los Angeles, CA 90026
Phone: (213) 365-2900
Fax: (213) 365-0228
Toll-Free: (888) 888-1183
E-mail:robynlharrod90035@
yahoo.com
Web site: www.scffaa.org

Stars of David International, Inc.
Jewish Adoption Information
Exchange

107 Mandala Court
Walnut Creek, CA 94596
Phone: (925) 932-3078
E-mail: MikeREllen@aol.com
Web site: www.starsofdavid.org

Stars of David International, Inc.
Jewish Family Service – Orange
County Chapter
250 Baker Street East, Suite G
Costa Mesa, CA 92626-4500
Phone: (714) 939-1111
Fax: (714) 939-1772
E-mail: starsdavid@aol.com
Web site: www.starsofdavid.org

Stars of David International, Inc.
Jewish Family Service of San
Diego
3715 6th Avenue
San Diego, CA 92103-4316
Phone: (619) 291-0473
Fax: (619) 291-2419
Web site: www.starsofdavid.org

Stepping Stones Foster Parent Association
24414 Marigold Avenue
Harbour City, CA 90710
Phone: (310) 539-0268
Fax: (310) 534-8120

Supporting Parents Adopting At-Risk Kids (SPAARK)
P.O. Box 2914
Sacramento, CA 95812
Phone: (916) 941-8180

Sycamores Adoption Agency
625 Fair Oaks Avenue, Suite 300
South Pasadena, CA 91030
Phone: (626) 395-7100, ext. 4505
Fax: (626) 799-4596
Toll-Free: (888) 243-2645
E-mail: BethGallegos@
sycamores.org
Web site: www.sycamores.org

The Institute for Black Parenting Adoption Support Group
1299 E. Artesia Boulevard, Suite 200
Carson, CA 90746
Phone: (310) 900-0949
E-mail: jroman@blackparenting.org
Web site: www.instituteforblackparenting.org

United Community Caregivers
9849 Glade Avenue
Chatsworth, CA 91311
Phone: (818) 998-4481
Fax: (818) 998-4204
Web site: www.fosterparents.com

Wide Smiles
P.O. Box 5153
Stockton, CA 95205

Yuba-Sutter Foster Adoptive Parent Association
2785 Plute Road
Marysville, CA 95901
Phone: (530) 743-8437

Licensed Private Adoption Agencies

A Better Way, Inc.
3200 Adeline Street
Berkeley, CA 94703
Phone: (510) 601-0203
Fax: (510) 601-4002
E-mail: abetterway@california.com

AASK Adopt A Special Kid
7700 Edgewater Drive, Suite 320, Bulding B
Oakland, CA 94621
Phone: (510) 553-1748
Fax: (510) 553-1747
Toll-Free: (888) 680-7349
E-mail: andrea@adoptaspecialkid.org
Web site: www.adoptaspecialkid.org

ACCEPT (An Adoption and Counseling Center)
339 South San Antonio Road, Suite 1A
Los Altos, CA 94022
Phone: (650) 917-8090
Fax: (650) 917-8093
E-mail: info@acceptadoptions.org
Web site: www.acceptadoptions.org
– Intercountry Program
– Child Placement

Across the World Adoptions (ATWA)
399 Taylor Boulevard, Suite 102
Pleasant Hill, CA 94523
Phone: (925) 356-6260
Fax: (925) 827-9396
Toll-Free: (800) 610-5607
E-mail: adopt@atwakids.org
Web site: www.adopting.com/atwa/

Adopt A Child
2500 West Manchester Boulevard
Inglewood, CA 90305
Phone: (323) 750-5855

Adopt International
121 Springdale Way
Redwood City, CA 94062
Phone: (650) 369-7300
Fax: (650) 369-7400
E-mail: adoptinter@aol.com
Web site: www.adopt-intl.org
– Intercountry Program
– Child Placement

Adopt International
160 Santa Clara Avenue, Suite 2
Oakland, CA 94610
Phone: (510) 653-8600
Fax: (510) 653-8603
E-mail: adoptinter@aol.com
Web site: www.adopt-intl.org
– Intercountry Program
– Child Placement

Adoption Connection
1710 Scott Street
San Francisco, CA 94115-3004
Phone: (415) 359-2494
Fax: (415) 359-2490
Toll-Free: (800) 972-9225
E-mail: families@adoptionconnection.org
Web site: www.adoptionconnection.org
– Intercountry Program
– Adoptive Parent/Family Preparation
– Agency Able to Place Children with United States Citizens Living Abroad
– Education/Preparation
– Home Study
– Information/Referral

Adoption Horizons
10 West 7th Street, Suite F
Eureka, CA 95501
Phone: (707) 444-9909
Fax: (707) 442-6672
Toll-Free: (800) 682-3678
E-mail: adoption@sbcglobal.net
Web site: www.adoption-horizons.org
– Intercountry Program
– Adoptive Parent/Family Preparation
– Agency Able to Place Children with United States Citizens Living Abroad
– Child Placement
– Education/Preparation
– Information/Referral

Adoption Network of Catholic Charities
98 Bosworth Street, 3rd Floor
San Francisco, CA 94112
Phone: (415) 406-2387
Fax: (415) 406-2386
Web site: www.cccyo.org

Adoption Options, Inc.
4025 Camino Del Rio South,
Suite 300
San Diego, CA 92108-4108
Phone: (619) 542-7772
Fax: (619) 542-7773
Toll-Free: (877) 542-7772
E-mail: info@adoption-options.
org
Web site: www.adoption-
options.org
– Intercountry Program
– Child Placement

Adoptions Unlimited, Inc.
4091 Riverside Drive
Suites 115 and 116
Chino, CA 91710
Phone: (909) 902-1412
Fax: (909) 902-1414
E-mail: auca@aol.com
Web site: www.adopting.
com/aui/
– Intercountry Program
– Child Placement

**Alternative Family Services
Adoption Agency**
25 Division Street, Suite 201
San Francisco, CA 94103
Phone: (415) 626-2700
Fax: (415) 626-2760

Angels' Haven Outreach
25134 Avenida Rotella
Santa Clarita, CA 91355
Phone: (661) 259-2943
Fax: (661) 799-3318
E-mail: sherry@angels-haven.com
Web site: www.angels-haven.com
– Intercountry Program
– Adoptive Parent/Family
Preparation
– Child Placement
– Education/Preparation
– Information/Referral

**Aspira Foster & Family
Services**
333 Gellery Boulevard, Suite 203

Daly City, CA 94015-2614
Phone: (805) 654-6800
Fax: (805) 654-6803
E-mail: doug@mossbeachhomes.
com
Web site: www.aspiranet.org or
www.mossbeachhomes.com

Bal Jagat Children's World, Inc.
9311 Farralone Avenue
Chatsworth, CA 91311
Phone: (818) 709-4737
Fax: (818) 772-6377
E-mail: bjcw@earthlink.net
Web site: www.baljagat.org
– Intercountry Program
– Child Placement

**Bay Area Adoption Services,
Inc.**
465 Fairchild Drive, Suite 215
Mountain View, CA 94043
Phone: (650) 964-3800
Fax: (650) 964-6467
E-mail: info@baas.org
Web site: www.baas.org
– Intercountry Program
– Child Placement

**Bethany Christian Services
- North Region**
3048 Hahn Drive
Modesto, CA 95350-6503
Phone: (209) 522-5121
Fax: (209) 522-1499
Toll-Free: (800) 454-0454
E-mail: bcsmodesto@bethany.org
Web site: www.bethany.org/
modesto

**Bethany Christian Services
– South Region**
16700 Valley View Avenue,
Suite 210
La Mirada, CA 90638
Phone: (714) 994-0500
Fax: (714) 994-0515
E-mail: bcslamirada@bethany.org
Web site: www.bethany.org/
lamirada

Bethany Christian Services, Inc.
14125 Telephone Avenue,
Suite 12
Chino, CA 91710-5771
Phone: (909) 465-0057
Fax: (909) 628-8294
E-mail: bcschino@bethany.org
Web site: www.bethany.org/
downey

Better Life Children Services
1337 Howe Avenue, Suite 107
Sacramento, CA 95825
Phone: (916) 641-0661
Fax: (916) 614-0664

**Black Adoption Placement and
Research Center**
7801 Edgewater Drive, Suite 2000
Oakland, CA 94621-2002
Phone: (510) 430-3600
Fax: (510) 430-3615
Toll-Free: (800) 299-3678
E-mail: family@baprc.org
Web site: www.baprc.org

**Catholic Charities Adoption
Agency**
349 Cedar Street
San Diego, CA 92101-3197
Phone: (619) 231-2828
Fax: (619) 232-3807

Children's Bureau
3910 Oakwood Avenue
Los Angeles, CA 90004-3487
Phone: (323) 953-7356
Fax: (323) 661-7306
E-mail: cbsc@earthlink.net
Web site: www.all4kids.org

Chrysalis House, Inc. (CHI)
4035 North Fresno Street,
Suite 101
Fresno, CA 93726
Phone: (559) 229-9862
Fax: (559) 229-9863
E-mail: contact-
us@chrysalishouse.com
Web site: www.chrysalishouse.
com

– Intercountry Program
– Adoptive Parent/Family Preparation
– Agency Able to Place Children with United States Citizens Living Abroad
– Child Placement
– Education/Preparation
– Information/Referral

East West Adoptions, Inc.
2 Parnassus Road
Berkeley, CA 94708
Phone: (510) 644-3996
Fax: (603) 908-8473
E-mail: info@eastwestadopt.com
Web site: http://users.lmi.net/ewadopt
– Intercountry Program
– Child Placement

Ettie Lee Youth and Family Services
7637 Citrus Avenue
Fontana, CA 92336
Phone: (909) 823-5662

Families First
6507 4th Avenue, Suite 400
Sacramento, CA 95817
Phone: (916) 641-9595
Fax: (916) 641-9599
Web site: www.familiesfirstinc.org

Families First
2291 West March Lane, Suite C-101
Stockton, CA 95207
Phone: (209) 954-3000
Toll-Free: (800) 310-7799

Families United, Inc.
P.O. Box 865
Folsom, CA 95763
Phone: (916) 863-5457
Fax: (916) 863-5459
Toll-Free: (800) 597-1667

Families United, Inc.
1125 Missouri Street, Suite 302
Fairfield, CA 94533
Phone: (707) 428-4086
Fax: (707) 428-4124

Families United, Inc.
475 Oro Dam Boulevard, Suite E
Oroville, CA 95965
Phone: (530) 532-0321
Fax: (530) 532-0767

Families United, Inc.
1210 South Main Street
Lakeport, CA 95453
Phone: (707) 263-9553
Fax: (707) 263-4332

Families for Children
2990 Lava Ridge Court, Suite 170
Roseville, CA 95661-3077
Phone: (916) 789-8688
Fax: (916) 789-7008
Toll-Free: (800) 955-2455
E-mail: ffc@families4children.com
Web site: www.families4children.com

Families for Children
560 First Street, B-201
Benicia, CA 94510
Phone: (707) 748-4150
Fax: (707) 748-4159

Family Builders By Adoption
528 Grand Avenue
Oakland, CA 94610
Phone: (510) 272-0204
Fax: (510) 272-0277
E-mail: kids@familybuilders.org
Web site: www.familybuilders.org

Family Connection Adoptions
Southern California Office
2181 El Camino Real, #206
Oceanside, CA 92054
Phone: (760) 941-4240
Fax: (760) 941-0016

Family Connections Adoptions
Main Office
1120 Tully Road
Modesto, CA 95352
Phone: (209) 524-8844
Fax: (209) 578-9823
Web site: www.fcadoptions.org
– Intercountry Program
– Adoptive Parent/Family Preparation
– Agency Able to Place Children with United States Citizens Living Abroad
– Child Placement
– Education/Preparation
– Home Study

Family Connections Adoptions
1401 Lel Camino Avenue, #102
Sacramento, CA 95815
Phone: (916) 568-5966
Fax: (916) 568-6005
E-mail: fcadoptsac@msn.com
– Intercountry Program
– Child Placement

Family Linkage Adoptions
290 I.O.O.F. Avenue
Gilroy, CA 95020
Phone: (408) 846-2135

Family Network, Inc.
307 Webster Street
Monterey, CA 93940
Phone: (831) 655-5077
Fax: (831) 655-3811
Toll-Free: (800) 888-0242
E-mail: geofamnet@aol.com
Web site: www.adopt-familynetwork.com
– Intercountry Program
– Child Placement

Five Acres
760 West Mountain View Street
Altadena, CA 91101
Phone: (626) 798-6793
Fax: (626) 585-1664
Toll-Free: (800) 696-6793
Web site: www.5acres.org

Future Families Adoption and Foster Care and Family Services
Future Families Office
1671 The Alameda, Suite #201
San Jose, CA 95126-2222
Phone: (408) 298-8789
Fax: (408) 298-8870
Toll-Free: (888) 922-5437
E-mail:contactme@
futurefamilies.org
Web site: www.futurefamilies.org
– Intercountry Program
– Adoptive Parent/Family Preparation
– Agency Able to Place Children with United States Citizens Living Abroad
– Education/Preparation
– Home Study
– Information/Referral

Genesis Adoption Agency
7475 North Palm Avenue,
Suite 107
Fresno, CA 93711
Phone: (559) 439-5437
E-mail: khastie@genesiskids.org

God's Families International Adoption Services
P.O. Box 320
Trabuco Canyon, CA 92679
Phone: (714) 858-7621
Fax: (714) 858-5431
E-mail: director@godsfamilies.
org
Web site: www.godsfamilies.org
– Intercountry Program
– Child Placement

Hand in Hand Foundation
200 Helen Court
Santa Cruz, CA 95065
Phone: (831) 476-1866
Fax: (831) 476-9287

Heartsent Adoptions, Inc.
15 Altarinda Road, Suite 100
Orinda, CA 94563

Phone: (925) 254-8883
Fax: (925) 254-8866
E-mail: heartsent@earthlink.net
Web site: www.heartsent.org
– Intercountry Program
– Child Placement

Heartsent Adoptions, Inc.
7940 California Avenue, Suite 2
Fair Oaks, CA 95628
Phone: (916) 965-8881
Fax: (916) 965-8893
E-mail: heartsent@earthlink.net
Web site: www.heartsent.org
– Intercountry Program
– Child Placement

Holt International Children's Services
3807 Pasadena Avenue, Suite 115
Sacramento, CA 95821
Phone: (916) 487-4658
Fax: (916) 487-7068
E-mail: info@holtintl.org
Web site: www.holtintl.org

Holy Family Services – Counseling and Adoption
1403 South Main Street
Santa Ana, CA 92707-1790
Phone: (714) 835-5551
Fax: (714) 973-4971
Web site: www.hfs.org
– Intercountry Program
– Child Placement

Holy Family Services – Counseling and Adoption
1441 North D Street
San Bernardino, CA 92405-4738
Phone: (909) 885-4882
Fax: (626) 578-7321
Web site: www.hfs.org
– Intercountry Program
– Child Placement

Holy Family Services – Counseling and Adoption
80 East Hillcrest Avenue,
Suite 210
Thousand Oaks, CA 91360

Phone: (805) 374-6797
Web site: www.hfs.org
– Intercountry Program
– Child Placement

Holy Family Services Adoption & Foster Care
402 South Marengo Avenue
Pasadena, CA 91101-3113
Phone: (626) 432-5680
Fax: (626) 578-7321
Toll-Free: (800) 464-ADOPT
E-mail: HFSAdopt@aol.com
Web site: www.
holyfamilyservices.org

Hope 4 Kids Adoption
P.O. Box 1235
Capestrano, CA 92693
Phone: (949) 496-9430
Fax: (949) 496-3042
E-mail: info@hope4kids.com
Web site: www.hope4kids.com

Independent Adoption Center
Central Office, Headquarters
391 Taylor Boulevard, Suite 100
Pleasant Hill, CA 94523
Phone: (925) 827-2229
Fax: (925) 603-0820
Toll-Free: (800) 877-6736
E-mail: staff@adoptionhelp.org
Web site: www.adoptionhelp.org
– Intercountry Program
– Child Placement
– Adoptive Parent/Family Preparation
– Agency Able to Place Children with United States Citizens Living Abroad
– Home Study

Indian Child and Family Services
1200 Nevada Street, Suite 202
Redlands, CA 92374
Phone: (909) 793-1709
Fax: (909) 793-1789
Toll-Free: (800) 969-7237

Infant of Prague
6059 North Palm Avenue
Fresno, CA 93704
Phone: (559) 447-3333
Fax: (559) 447-3322
Web site: www.infantofprague.
org

Inner Circle Foster Care and Adoption Services
7120 Hayvenhurst Avenue,
Suite 204
Van Nuys, CA 91406
Phone: (818) 988-6300
Fax: (818) 988-7087
E-mail: jillr@fosterfamily.org
Web site: www.fosterfamily.org

International Christian Adoptions
41745 Rider Way, #2
Temecula, CA 92590
Phone: (909) 695-3336
Fax: (909) 308-1753
E-mail: ICA1@gte.net
Web site: www.4achild.com
— Intercountry Program
— Child Placement

Kern Bridges Adoption Agency
1615 V Street
Bakersfield, CA 93301
Phone: (661) 322-0421
Fax: (661) 322-8448
Web site: www.kernbridges.com

Kinship Center
124 River Road
Salinas, CA 93908
Phone: (831) 455-4706
Fax: (831) 495-4789
E-mail: kinship@redshift.com
Web site: www.kinshipcenter.org

Kinship Center
1520 Brookhollow Drive, Suite 41
Santa Ana, CA 92705
Phone: (714) 979-2365
Fax: (714) 979-8135
E-mail: kinship@redshift.com
Web site: www.kinshipcenter.org

LDS Family Services
California North Agency
6060 Sunrise Vista Drive,
Suite 1160
Citrus Heights, CA 95610
Phone: (916) 725-5032

Latino Family Institute, Inc.
1501 Cameron Avenue, Suite 240
West Covina, CA 91790
Phone: (626) 472-0123

Life Adoption Services
440 West Main Street
Tustin, CA 92780
Phone: (714) 838-5433
Fax: (714) 838-1160
E-mail: lifeadoption@fea.net
Web site: www.lifeadoption.com
— Intercountry Program
— Child Placement

McKinley Children's Center
762 West Cypress
San Dimas, CA 91773
Phone: (909) 599-1227
E-mail: Support@mckinleyCC.org
Web site: www.mckinleycc.org

Nightlight Christian Adoptions
801 East Chapman Avenue,
Suite 106
Fullerton, CA 92831
Phone: (714) 278-1020
Fax: (714) 278-1063
E-mail: info@Nightlight.org
Web site: www.Nightlight.org
— Intercountry Program
— Adoptive Parent/Family
Preparation
— Agency Able to Place Children
with United States Citizens Living
Abroad
— Child Placement
— Education/Preparation
— Home Study
— Information/Referral
— Post-placement Supervision
Prior to Adoption Finalization

North Bay Adoptions
444 Tenth Street, 3rd Floor
Santa Rosa, CA 95401
Phone: (707) 570-2940
Fax: (707) 570-2940
Web site: www.
northbayadoptions.com
— Intercountry Program
— Child Placement

Oakland Family Service
CA
E-mail: ofs@ofs-family.org
Web site: www.ofs-family.org

Olive Crest Adoption Services
2130 East Fourth Street,
Suite 200
Santa Ana, CA 92705
Phone: (714) 543-5437
Fax: (714) 543-5463
Toll-Free: (800) 550-2445
Web site: www.olivecrest.org

Optimist Community Services (OYHFS)
7330 North Fioguroa Street
Los Angeles, CA 90041
Phone: (323) 341-5561
Fax: (323) 257-6418
Toll-Free: (800) 454-5561
E-mail: silorlando@oyhfs.org
Web site: www.oyhfs.org

Partners For Adoption
4527 Montgomery Drive, Suite A
Santa Rosa, CA 95409
Phone: (707) 539-9068
Fax: (707) 539-9466
E-mail: mclause@aaapia.org
Web site: www.aaapia.org
— Intercountry Program
— Adoptive Parent/Family
Preparation
— Agency Able to Place Children
with United States Citizens Living
Abroad
— Child Placement
— Education/Preparation
— Home Study
— Information/Referral

Penny Lane Adoption Agency
9140 Van Nuys Boulevard,
Suite 108
Panorama City, CA 91402
Phone: (818) 894-3384
Fax: (818) 894-3384
Web site: www.pennylane.org

Share Homes
307 East Kettleman Lane
Lodi, CA 95240
Phone: (209) 334-6376

Sierra Adoption Services
8928 Volunteer Lane, Suite 240
Sacramento, CA 95826
Phone: (916) 368-5114
Fax: (916) 368-5157
E-mail:vmarchus@sierraadoption.
org
Web site: www.sierraadoption.
org
– Intercountry Program
– Adoptive Parent/Family
Preparation
– Education/Preparation
– Home Study
– Post-placement Supervision
Prior to Adoption Finalization

**Southern California Foster
Family and Adoption Agency
(SCFFAA)**
155 North Occidental Boulevard
Los Angeles, CA 90026
Phone: (213) 365-2900
Fax: (213) 365-0228
Toll-Free: (888) 888-1183
E-mail: robynlharrod90035@
yahoo.com
Web site: www.scffaa.org

**Special Families Foster Care
and Adoptions**
3002 Armstrong Street
San Diego, CA 92111
Phone: (858) 277-9550
Fax: (858) 277-3998

St. Patrick's Home for Children
6525 53rd Avenue
Sacramento, CA 95828
Phone: (916) 386-1603
Fax: (916) 386-0654

Sycamores Adoption Agency
625 Fair Oaks Avenue, Suite 300
South Pasadena, CA 91030
Phone: (626) 395-7100, ext. 4505
Fax: (626) 799-4596
Toll-Free: (888) 243-2645
E-mail: BethGallegos@
sycamores.org
Web site: www.sycamores.org

**True to Life Children's
Services**
1800 North Gravenstein Highway
Sebastopol, CA 95472
Phone: (707) 823-7300
Fax: (707) 823-3410
E-mail: info@tlc4kids.org
Web site: www.tlc4kids.org

**The Adoption Network
Catholic Charities CYO**
98 Bosworth Street, 3rd Floor
San Francisco, CA 94112
Phone: (415) 406-2387
Fax: (415) 406-2386
E-mail: hhurrell@cccyo.org
Web site: www.cccyo.org
– Intercountry Program
– Agency Able to Place Children
with United States Citizens Living
Abroad
– Home Study

**Valley Teen Ranch Foster
Family and Adoption Agency**
2610 West Shaw, Suite 105
Fresno, CA 93711
Phone: (559) 437-1144
Fax: (559) 438-5004
– Intercountry Program
– Home Study
– Post-placement Supervision
Prior to Adoption Finalization

**Vista Del Mar Child and Family
Services**
3200 Motor Avenue
Los Angeles, CA 90034
Phone: (310) 836-1223
Fax: (310) 836-3863
Toll-Free: (888) 228-4782
E-mail: adoptions@vistadelmar.org
Web site: www.vistadelmar.org
– Intercountry Program
– Child Placement

**Birth Family and Search
Support Groups**

**Adoptees Birthparents
Association**
2027 Finch Court
Simi Valley, CA 93063
Phone: (805) 583-4306

Adoption Connection
1710 Scott Street
San Francisco, CA 94115-3004
Phone: (415) 359-2494
Fax: (415) 359-2490
Toll-Free: (800) 972-9225
E-mail: families@adoptionconne
ction.org
Web site: www.
adoptionconnection.org
– Intercountry Program
– Adoptive Parent/Family
Preparation
– Agency Able to Place Children
with United States Citizens Living
Abroad
– Education/Preparation
– Home Study
– Information/Referral

Adoption Reality
2180 Clover Street
Simi Valley, CA 93065
Phone: (805) 526-2289

**Adoption Reunion Support
Group**
1115 Sunset Drive
Vista, CA 92083
Phone: (619) 726-1924

Adoption Support Group of
Santa Monica
1452 26th Street, #103
Santa Monica, CA 90404
Phone: (310) 829-1438
Fax: (310) 476-1963
E-mail: marlourussell@hotmail.
com
Web site: www.
marlourussellphd.com

Adoption Triad Support Group
1755 Diamond Mountain Road
Calistoga, CA 94515
Phone: (707) 943-5877

American Adoption Congress
State Representative
54 Wellington Avenue
San Anselmo, CA 94960-2502
Phone: (415) 453-0902
E-mail: Ellen@coopadopt.com

Americans for Open Records
P.O. Box 401
Palm Desert, CA 92261

Bay Area Birthmothers
Association
1546 Great Highway, #44
San Francisco, CA 94122
Phone: (415) 564-3691
E-mail: unlockingheart@hotmail.
com
Web site: www.unlockingthe
heart.com/A_resources.htm

Central Coast Adoption
Support Group
1718 Longbranch
Grover City, CA 93433
Phone: (805) 481-4086

Concerned United
Birthparents, Inc. (CUB)
14820 Figueras Rd.
LaMirada, CA 90638
Phone: (714) 521-4204
Fax: (714) 521-4204
Toll-Free: (800) 822-2777
E-mail: info@CUBbirthparents.org

Web site: www.cubirthparents.
org

Hand in Hand
391 Teasdale Street
Thousand Oaks, CA 91360
Phone: (714) 951-1689

Korean American Adoptee
Adoptive Family Network
P.O. Box 5585
El Dorado Hills, CA 95762
Phone: (916) 933-1447
E-mail: KAANet@aol.com
Web site: http://members.aol.
com/kaanet

Los Angeles County Adoption
Search Association
P.O. Box 1461
Roseville, CA 95661
Phone: (916) 784-2711

Mendo Lake Adoption Triad
620 Walnut Avenue
Ukiah, CA 95482
Phone: (707) 468-0648

PURE, Inc.
P.O. Box 638
Westminster, CA 92683
Phone: (714) 892-4098

ReConnections of California
41669 Zinfandel Avenue
Temecula, CA 92591
Phone: (909) 695-1152
E-mail: lisarick@aol.com

Santa Cruz Birthmother
Support
P.O. Box 1780
Freedom, CA 95019
Phone: (831) 728-3876

Search Finders of California
P.O. Box 24595
San Jose, CA 95154
Phone: (408) 356-6711

Searchers Connection
7709 Skyhill Drive
Los Angeles, CA 90068
Phone: (213) 878-0630

South Coast Adoption
Research and Support
P.O. Box 39
Harbor City, CA 90710
Phone: (213) 833-5822

Stephen S. Wise Adoption
Support Center
15500 Stephen S. Wise Drive
Los Angeles, CA 90077
Phone: (310) 889-2209
Fax: (310) 472-9395

**State Adoption Exchange/
Photolisting of Children
Waiting For Adoption**

California Kids Connection
528 Grand Avenue
Oakland, CA 94610
Phone: (510) 272-0204
Fax: (510) 272-0277
E-mail: kidsconnection@family
builders.org
Web site: www.
CAKidsConnection.com

**State Adoption
Specialist/Manager**

California Department of
Social Services
Patricia Aguiar
744 P Street, MS 19-69
Sacramento, CA 95814
Phone: (916) 651-7464
Fax: (916) 324-3044
Toll-Free: (800) 543-7487
E-mail: Pat.Aguiar@dss.ca.gov
Web site: www.childsworld.
ca.gov/CFSDAdopti_309.htm

State Foster Care Specialist/Manager

California Department of Social Services
Patricia Aguiar
744 P Street MS 19-69
Sacramento, CA 95814
Phone: (916) 651-7464
Fax: (916) 324-3044
Toll-Free: (800) 543-7487
E-mail: Pat.Aguiar@dss.ca.gov
Web site: www.childsworld.
ca.gov/FosterCare_310.htm

State Interstate Compact on the Placement of Children (ICPC) Administrator

California Department of Social Services
744 P Street, MS 3-90
Sacramento, CA 95814
Phone: (916) 651-8111
Fax: (916) 323-9266
E-mail: jackie.rodriguez@dss.
ca.gov
Web site: www.childsworld.
ca.gov

State Licensing Specialist

California Department of Social Services
Jo Frederick
744 P Street, MS 17-17
Sacramento, CA 95814
Phone: (916) 657-2346
Fax: (916) 657-3783
Web site: http://ccld.ca.gov/
default.htm

State Reunion Registry

California Department of Social Services
Adoption Branch
744 P Street, MS 3-31
Sacramento, CA 95814
Phone: (916) 322-3778
Web site: www.childsworld.
ca.gov

Statewide Adoption Recruitment Line

California Statewide Adoption Recruitment Line
CA
Toll-Free: (800). KI DS.4. U S

Statewide Foster Care Recruitment Line

California Statewide Foster Care Recruitment Line
CA
Toll-Free: (800). KI DS.4. U S

State Complaints Office

California Department of Social Services
Children's Services Branch
744 P Street, M/S 19-90
Sacramento, CA 95814
Phone: (916) 445-2832

Advocacy

Chadwick Center for Children and Families
3020 Children's Way, MC 5016
San Diego, CA 92123
Phone: (858) 966-8572
Phone: (858) 576-1700, x 4972
Fax: (858) 966-8018
E-mail: chadwickcenter@chsd.
org
Web site: www.charityadvantage.
com/chadwickcenter

Independent Adoption Center Headquarters
391 Taylor Boulevard, Suite 100
Pleasant Hill, CA 94523
Phone: (925) 827-2229
Fax: (925) 603-0820
Toll-Free: (800) 877-6736
E-mail: staff@adoptionhelp.org
Web site: www.adoptionhelp.org

Parents Anonymous, Inc.
675 West Foothill Boulevard,
Suite 220

Claremont, CA 91711-3475
Phone: (909) 621-6184
Fax: (909) 625-6304
E-mail: parentsanonymous@pare
ntsanonymous.org
Web site: www.
parentsanonymous.org

Children's Bureau funded

National Abandoned Infants Assistance
Resource Center
1950 Addison Street
Suite 104, No. 7402
Berkeley, CA 94720-7402
Phone: (510) 643-8390
Fax: (510) 643-7019
E-mail: aia@uclink.berkeley.edu
Web site: http://aia.berkeley.edu

National Center on Substance Abuse and Child Welfare
4940 Irvine Boulevard, Suite 202
Irvine, CA 92612
Phone: (714) 505-3525
Fax: (714) 505-3626
E-mail: ncsacw@samhsa.gov
Web site: www.ncsacw.samhsa.
gov

Federally Funded Foundation

Independent Adoption Center Headquarters
391 Taylor Boulevard, Suite 100
Pleasant Hill, CA 94523
Phone: (925) 827-2229
Fax: (925) 603-0820
Toll-Free: (800) 877-6736
E-mail: staff@adoptionhelp.org
Web site: www.adoptionhelp.org

National Council for Single Adoptive Parents
P.O. Box 567
Mount Hermon, CA 95041
Toll-Free: (888) 490-4600
E-mail: info@ncsap.com
Web site: www.ncsap.org

Research

Chadwick Center for Children and Families
3020 Children's Way, MC 5016
San Diego, CA 92123
Phone: (858) 966-8572
Phone: (858) 576-1700, x 4972
Fax: (858) 966-8018
E-mail: chadwickcenter@chsd.org
Web site: www.charityadvantage.com/chadwickcenter

Resource Center

Korean American Adoptee Adoptive Family Network
P.O. Box 5585
El Dorado Hills, CA 95762
Phone: (916) 933-1447
E-mail: KAANet@aol.com
Web site: www.KAANet.com

COLORADO

Adoptive/Foster Family Support Groups

Adoption Alliance Special Needs Adult, Pre-Teen Support Groups/New Mentoring Program
2121 South Oneida Street, Suite 420
Denver, CO 80224
Phone: (303) 584-9900
Fax: (303) 584-9007
E-mail: mtem@adoptall.com
Web site: www.adoptall.com
– Intercountry Program
– Child Placement

Adoptive Families Support Group of S/W Colorado
214 Far View Road
Durango, CO 81303
Phone: (970) 259-1495
E-mail: tskemp@frontier.net

Adoptive Families of Boulder
P.O. Box 2118
Boulder, CO 80306
Phone: (303) 939-8375

Adoptive Families of Colorado Springs
2625 Tuckerman Court
Colorado Springs, CO 80918
Phone: (719) 590-7126

Adoptive Families of Denver
4243 East Geddes Avenue
Littleton, CO 80122
Phone: (720) 529-6784
E-mail: dpiercesr@msn.com
– Intercountry Program
– Adoptive Parent/Family Preparation
– Agency Able to Place Children with United States Citizens Living Abroad
– Information/Referral

Adoptive Family Resources
Family Institute of Colorado
1155 Sherman Street, Suite 201
Denver, CO 80203
Phone: (303) 881-7630
Fax: (303) 942-1217
E-mail: jan@adoptivefamilyresources.org
Web site: www.adoptivefamilyresources.org

Adoptive Parent Support Group for Developmentally Disabled
3635 West 77th
Westminster, CO 80234
Phone: (303) 428-4266

Advocates for Black Adoption
4715 Crystal Street
Denver, CO 80239
Phone: (303) 375-1531

Arapahoe Advocates for Children
3000 South Jamaica Court, #175
Aurora, CO 80114-4601

Attachment Center at Evergreen
P.O. Box 2764
27618 Fireweed
Evergreen, CO 80437-2764
Phone: (303) 674-1910
Web site: www.attachmentcenter.org

Brett and Diane Maddy
24 Sheep Mountain Court
Livermore, CO 80536
Phone: (970) 867-4205

Colorado Coalition of Adoptive Families
P.O. Box 270398
Louisville, CO 80027-0398
Phone: (303) 620-5150
E-mail: cocafcave@yahoo.com
Web site: www.cocaf.org

Colorado Parents for All Children
P.O. Box 2850
Frisco, CO 80443
Phone: (719) 668-3780

Colorado Parents for All Children (CPFAC)
13478 West Auburn Avenue
Lakewood, CO 80228
Phone: (303) 763-7382

Denver Adoptive Mothers Club
1881 South Meade Street
Denver, CO 80219
Phone: (303) 935-3847

Families with Children from Vietnam
7258 Nebraska Way
Longmont, CO 80504
Phone: (303) 702-1984

Family Attachment Institute
P.O. Box 1731
Evergreen, CO 80437
Phone: (303) 674-0547

Friends of Russian and Ukrainian Adoption
Phone: (303) 756-6446

Jewish Children's Adoption Network
P.O. Box 147016
Denver, CO 80214-7016
Phone: (303) 573-8113
Fax: (303) 893-1447
E-mail: jcan@qwest.net
Web site: www.users.qwest.net/~jcan

Larimer County Foster/ Adoptive Parent Association
8320 Firethorn Drive
Loveland, CO 80538
Phone: (970) 669-3047
Fax: (970) 669-0674
E-mail: Toddg@verinet.com
Web site: www.lcfpa.org

Single Adoptive Families Everywhere
6451 South Lakeview
Littleton, CO 80120
Phone: (303) 730-1044

Licensed Private Adoption Agencies

AAC Adoption and Family Network
P.O. Box W
735 East Highway 56
Berthoud, CO 80513
Phone: (970) 532-3576
Fax: (303) 442-2231
E-mail: aacadopt@frii.com
Web site: www.aacadoption.com
– Intercountry Program
– Child Placement

ABBA Family Services
10995 Independence Circle East
Parker, CO 80134
Phone: (303) 333-8652
Fax: (303) 333-5081

Adoption Choice Center
729 South Cascade Avenue, #2
Colorado Springs, CO 80903
Phone: (719) 444-0198
Fax: (719) 444-0186

Adoption Journey
5612 North 71st Street
Longmont, CO 80503
Phone: (303) 530-9124

Adoption Services, Inc.
1108 North Star Drive
Colorado Springs, CO 80906
Phone: (719) 632-9941

Adoptions Advocacy and Alternatives
2500 South College Avenue
Fort Collins, CO 80527
Phone: (970) 493-5868
Fax: (970) 472-0352
E-mail: jfgallagher@aol.com

Angeldance International
2237 West 30th Avenue
Denver, CO 80211
Phone: (303) 561-1199

Bethany Christian Services of Colorado
9185 East Kenyon Avenue, Suite 190
Denver, CO 80237
Phone: (303) 221-0734
Fax: (303) 221-0960
Toll-Free: (800) 986-4484
E-mail: info@bethany.org
Web site: www.bethany.org
– Intercountry Program
– Child Placement

Catholic Charities and Community Services
2525 West Alameda Avenue
Denver, CO 80219
Phone: (303) 742-0828

Catholic Charities of Colorado Springs, Inc.
228 North Cascade
Colorado Springs, CO 80903

Catholic Social Services, Inc.
Family Counseling Center
429 West Tenth Street, Suite 101
Pueblo, CO 81003
Phone: (719) 544-4234
E-mail: jmazur@pueblocharities.org

Children's Haven of Hope
19682 East Union Drive
Aurora, CO 80015
Phone: (303) 699-4710
Fax: (720) 870-8755

Chinese Children Adoption International
6920 South Holly Circle, Suite 100
Englewood, CO 80112
Phone: (303) 850-9998
Fax: (303) 850-9997
E-mail: ccai@chinesechildren.org
Web site: www.chinesechildren.org
– Intercountry Program
– Child Placement

Christian Family Services
1399 South Havana Street, Suite 204
Aurora, CO 80012
Phone: (303) 337-6747
Fax: (303) 368-4661
E-mail: pam@christianfamilyservices.us

Colorado Adoption Center
1136 East Stuart Street, Suite 4201
Fort Collins, CO 80525
Phone: (970) 493-8816

Colorado Christian Home
2950 Tennyson Street
Denver, CO 80212
Phone: (303) 433-2541

Colorado Christian Services
1100 West Littleton Boulevard, Suite 105
Littleton, CO 80120

Phone: (303) 761-7236
Fax: (303) 761-7237
Toll-Free: (800) 988-0600
E-mail: ccserv@qwest.net
Web site: www.
christianservices.org

Covenant International
940 Wadsworth Boulevard
Lakewood, CO 80214-4590
Phone: (719) 360-0371

**Designated Adoption Services
of Colorado, Inc.**
1420 Vance Street, Suite 202
Lakewood, CO 80215
Phone: (303) 232-0234

Family Ties Adoption Agency
7257 Rogers Street
Arvada, CO 80007
Phone: (303) 420-3660

**Friends of Children of Various
Nations**
1562 Pearl Street
Denver, CO 80203
Phone: (303) 837-9438
Fax: (303) 837-9848
– Intercountry Program
– Child Placement

**Hand in Hand International
Adoptions**
453 East Wonderview Avenue
PMB #333
Estes Park, CO 80517
Phone: (970) 586-6866
Fax: (970) 577-9452
E-mail: colorado@hihiadopt.org
Web site: www.hihiadopt.org
– Intercountry Program
– Child Placement

Hands Across the Ocean
3401 South Clermont Street
Denver, CO 80222
Phone: (720) 971-7885
E-mail: hatoadopt@aol.com

Hope and Home
620 Southpointe Court, Suite 185
Colorado Springs, CO 80906
Phone: (719) 575-9887
Fax: (719) 575-0553
E-mail: info@hopeandhome.org

**International Adoption
Network**
5300 East Florida
Denver, CO 80222

Kid's Crossing, Inc.
414 Broadway
Pueblo, CO 81004
Phone: (719) 545-3882

Kid's Crossing, Inc.
1440 East Fountain Boulevard
Colorado Springs, CO 80910
Phone: (719) 632-4569

LDS Family Services
3263 Fraser Street, Suite 3
Aurora, CO 80011
Phone: (303) 371-1000

Littlest Angels International
2191-2225 Drive,
Cedaredge, CO 81413
Phone: (970) 856-6177
Fax: (970) 928-2020
Toll-Free: (800) 875-4253
E-mail: ltlst@aol.com
Web site: www.Littlestangelsint
ernational.com
– Intercountry Program
– Child Placement

Loving Homes
212 West 13th Street
Pueblo, CO 81003
Phone: (719) 545-6181
E-mail: lhomes@aol.com

Loving Homes
10800 East Bethany
Aurora, CO 80014
Phone: (303) 671-6884
E-mail: lhomes@aol.com

**Lutheran Family Services of
Colorado**
3800 Automation Way, Suite 200
Ft. Collins, CO 80525
Phone: (970) 266-1788
Fax: (970) 266-1799
E-mail: Newhomesn@lfsco.org
Web site: www.lfsco.org

**Lutheran Family Services of
Colorado**
363 South Harlan Street,
Suite 200
Denver, CO 80226
Phone: (303) 922-3433
Fax: (303) 922-7335
E-mail: Newhomesc@lfsco.org
Web site: www.lfsco.org

MAPS of Colorado
P.O. Box 42
Silverthorne, CO 80498
Phone: (970) 262-2998
E-mail: deborah@deborahhage.
com
Web site: www.mapsadopt.org

One Light Adoptions, Inc.
Boulder, CO 80302
Phone: (303) 442-8880
Fax: (303) 442-8889
Toll-Free: (888) 442-8885
E-mail: info@onelightadoptions.
org
Web site: www.
onelightadoptions.org
– Intercountry Program
– Child Placement

Parent Resource Center
2930 Austin Bluffs Parkway,
Suite 102
Colorado Springs, CO 80918
Phone: (719) 599-7772

Rainbow House International
167 – 47th Avenue Court
Greeley, CO 80634
Phone: (303) 830-2108
– Intercountry Program
– Child Placement

Small Miracles
5555 Denver Tech Center
Parkway
Suite B-2100
Englewood, CO 80111
Phone: (303) 220-7611
Fax: (303) 694-2622
E-mail: smallmiracles@smallmir
acles.org
Web site: www.smallmiracles.org

Top of the Trail
543 South Second
Montrose, CO 81401
Phone: (970) 249-4131
Fax: (970) 249-4218
E-mail: tot@montrose.net

Whole Family
8231 S. Marshall Court
Littleton, CO 80128-5864
Phone: (303) 851-8149

**Youth Oasis Uplifting
Nurturing Guidance Services
(Y.O.U.N.G.S.)**
3302 East LaSalle Street
Colorado Springs, CO 80909
Phone: (719) 634-7395

**Birth and Family Search
Support Groups**

**Adoptees and Birthparents
Together**
5213 Miners Creek Court
Ft. Collins, CO 80525

Adoptees in Search
P.O. Box 17822
Denver, CO 80226
Phone: (303) 232-6302
E-mail: AISDenver@aol.com

Birthparents Group
P.O. Box 16512
Colorado Springs, CO 80935

**Concerned United
Birthparents (CUB)**
P.O. Box 2137
Wheat Ridge, CO 80304-2137

Phone: (303) 825-3430
E-mail: cubdenver@aol.com

**Concerned United
Birthparents (CUB)**
2538 Keller Farm Drive
Boulder, CO 80304
Phone: (303) 447-8112

Re-Unite
P.O. Box 7945
Aspen, CO 81612
Phone: (970) 927-2400

Search and Support of Denver
805 South Ogden
Denver, CO 80209
Phone: (303) 778-8612

**State Adoption Exchange/
Photolisting Children
Waiting For Adoption**

Adoption Exchange (The)
Main Office
14232 East Evans Avenue
Aurora, CO 80014
Phone: (303) 755-4756
Fax: (303) 755-1339
Toll-Free: (800) 451-5246
E-mail: kids@adoptex.org
Web site: www.adoptex.org

**Jewish Children's Adoption
Network**
P.O. Box 147016
Denver, CO 80214-7016
Phone: (303) 573-8113
Fax: (303) 893-1447
E-mail: jcan@qwest.net
Web site: www.users.qwest.
net/~jcan

**State Adoption
Specialist/Manager**

**Colorado Department of Social
Services**
1575 Sherman Street
Denver, CO 80203-1714
Phone: (303) 866-3197
Fax: (303) 866-5563
E-mail: Sharen.Ford@state.co.us

**State Foster Care
Specialist/Manager**

Colorado State Department of
Social Services
Division of Child Welfare
1575 Sherman Street
Denver, CO 80203
Phone: (303) 866-3546
Fax: (303) 866-4629
E-mail: Mary.Griffin@state.co.us

**State Interstate Compact on
the Placement of Children
(ICPC) Administrator**

Colorado Department of Social
Services
Division of Child Welfare
1575 Sherman Street
Denver, CO 80203
Phone: (303) 866-2998
Fax: (303) 866-4629
Web site: www.cdhs.state.co.us/
cyf/cwelfare/cwweb.html

State Licensing Specialist

Colorado Department of Social
Services
Division of Child Care
1575 Sherman Street
Denver, CO 80203
Phone: (303) 866-5958
Fax: (303) 866-4453
Toll-Free: (800) 799-5876
E-mail: marlene.romero@state.
co.us
Web site: www.cdhs.state.co.us/
childcare/licensing.htm

State Reunion Registry

Colorado Adoption Family
Resource Registry
Colorado Department of
Social Services
1575 Sherman Street
Denver, CO 80203

Colorado Voluntary Adoption Registry
Colorado Department of Public Health and Environment
4300 Cherry Creek Drive South (HSVR-VR-A1)
Denver, CO 80246-1530
Phone: (303) 692-2188
Web site: www.cdphe.state.co.us/hs/aboutadoptionregistry.html

Statewide Adoption Recruitment Line

Colorado Statewide Adoption Recruitment Line
Phone: (303) 755-4756
Toll-Free: (800) 451-5246
E-mail: suzanne@adoptex.org

Statewide Foster Care Recruitment Line

Colorado Statewide Foster Care Recruitment Line
Phone: (303) 866-4603
Toll-Free: (866) 229-7605
E-mail: cheryl.jacobson@state.co.us
– Intercountry Program
– Adoptive Parent/Family Preparation
– Agency Able to Place Children with United States Citizens Living Abroad
– Child Placement
– Education/Preparation

Adoption Options
2600 South Parker Road,
Suite 2-320
Aurora, CO 80014
Phone: (303) 695-1601
Fax: (303) 695-1626
E-mail: clawson@adoption-options.com
Web site: www.myoptions.org
– Intercountry Program
– Adoptive Parent/Family Preparation
– Agency Able to Place Children

with United States Citizens Living Abroad
– Child Placement
– Education/Preparation
– Home Study
– Information/Referral
– Post-placement Supervision Prior to Adoption Finalization

Licensed Private Adoption Agencies for Intercountry Adoptions

Adoption Homestudy Agency of Colorado
4685 West Princeton Avenue
Denver, CO 80236
Phone: (720) 214-0606
Fax: (303) 794-8803
E-mail: marj@adoptionhomestudy.org
Web site: www.adoptionhomestudy.org
– Intercountry Program
– Adoptive Parent/Family Preparation
– Agency Able to Place Children with United States Citizens Living Abroad
– Child Placement
– Education/Preparation

Adoption Options
2600 South Parker Road,
Suite 2-320
Aurora, CO 80014
Phone: (303) 695-1601
Fax: (303) 695-1626
E-mail: clawson@adoption-options.com
Web site: www.myoptions.org
– Intercountry Program
– Adoptive Parent/Family Preparation
– Agency Able to Place Children with United States Citizens Living Abroad
– Child Placement
– Education/Preparation
– Home Study

– Information/Referral
– Post-placement Supervision Prior to Adoption Finalization

Hope's Promise
309 Jerry Street, Suite 202
Castle Rock, CO 80104
Phone: (303) 660-0277
Fax: (303) 660-0297
E-mail: adopt@hopespromise.com
Web site: www.hopespromise.com
– Intercountry Program
– Adoptive Parent/Family Preparation
– Agency Able to Place Children with United States Citizens Living Abroad
– Child Placement
– Education/Preparation
– Home Study
– Information/Referral

CONNECTICUT

Adoptive/Foster Family Support Groups

Attachment Disorder Parents Network of Connecticut
85 Westwood Avenue
Plainville, CT 06062
Phone: (860) 669-2750

Casey Family Services
789 Reservoir Avenue
Bridgeport, CT 06606
Phone: (203) 372-3722
Fax: (203) 372-3558
Toll-Free: (800) 332-6991
Web site: www.caseyfamilyservices.org

Casey Family Services Gothic Park
43 Woodland Street
Hartford, CT 06105
Phone: (860) 727-1030
Toll-Free: (800) 732-6921
Web site: www.caseyfamilyservices.org

Child Adoption Resource
Association, Inc.
2 Union Plaza, Suite 300
New London, CT 06320
Phone: (860) 444-0553
Fax: (860) 444-6527
After hours: (860) 848-1422
E-mail: director@adoptacarakid.
org
Web site: www.adoptacarakid.org
— Intercountry Program
— Child Placement

Connecticut Association of
Foster and Adoptive Parents,
Inc.
2189 Silas Deane Highway,
Suite 2
Rocky Hill, CT 06067
Phone: (860) 258-3400
Fax: (860) 258-3410
Toll-Free: (800) 861-8838
Web site: www.cafap.com

Downey Side
2264 Silas Deane Highway,
Suite 100
Rocky Hill, CT 06067-2333
Phone: (860) 257-1694
Fax: (860) 257-1698
Toll-Free: (800) US-Child
E-mail: downeysidect@yahoo.com
Web site: www.downeyside.org

Downey Side Parents
2264 Silas Deane Highway,
Suite 200
Rocky Hill, CT 06067-2333
Phone: (860) 257-1694
Fax: (860) 257-1698
E-mail: RockyHillCT@downey
side.org
Web site: www.Downeyside.com

Family and Children's Agency,
Inc.
9 Mott Avenue
Norwalk, CT 06850
Phone: (203) 855-8765
Fax: (203) 838-3325

Toll-Free: (800) 676-4066
E-mail: adoption@fcagency.org
Web site: www.
familyandchildrensagency.org
— Intercountry Program
— Adoptive Parent/Family
Preparation
— Agency Able to Place Children
with United States Citizens Living
Abroad
— Child Placement
— Education/Preparation
— Home Study
— Homeland Tours
— Information/Referral

LDS Family Services
34 Jerome Street, Suite 319
Bloomfield, CT 06002
Fax: (603) 889-4358
Toll-Free: (800) 735-0149
E-mail: fam-nh@ldschurch.org
Web site: www.
ldsfamilyservices.org

Latin America Parents Asso-
ciation of Connecticut, Inc.
P.O. Box 523
Unionville, CT 06085-0523
Phone: (203) 270-1424
E-mail: joet@highcaliber.com
Web site: www.lapact.
homestead.com

North American Council
on Adoptable Children
Representative
506 Taylor Road
Enfield, CT 06082
Phone: (203) 749-9123

Stars of David International,
Inc.
Bridgeport Area Chapter
Jewish Family Service
2370 Park Avenue
Bridgeport, CT 06604
Phone: (203) 366-5438
Fax: (203) 366-1580
Web site: www.starsofdavid.org

**Licensed Private
Adoption Agencies**

A Child Among Us Center for
Adoption Inc.
2410 New London Turnpike
South Glastonbury, CT 06073
Phone: (860) 657-2467
Fax: (860) 659-5786
Toll-Free: (800) 360-2220
Web site: www.achildamongus.
org

Adoption Center at Jewish
Family Service
740 North Main Street
West Hartford, CT 06117
Phone: (860) 236-1927
Fax: (860) 236-6483
E-mail: helish@jfshartford.org
Web site: www.jfshartford.org
— Intercountry Program
— Child Placement

Boys Village Youth and Family
Services, Inc.
528 Wheelers Farm Road
Milford, CT 06460
Phone: (203) 877-0300
Fax: (203) 876-0076
Toll-Free: (888) 922-5528
E-mail: sylviak@boysvill.org
Web site: www.boysvill.org

Casey Family Services
Bridgeport Division
789 Reservoir Avenue
Bridgeport, CT 06606
Phone: (203) 372-3722
Fax: (203) 372-3558
Web site: www.
caseyfamilyservices.org

Casey Family Services
Hartford Division
43 Woodland Street
Hartford, CT 06105
Phone: (860) 727-1030
Fax: (860) 727-9355
Web site: www.
caseyfamilyservices.org

Catholic Charities of Fairfield County
238 Jewett Avenue
Bridgeport, CT 06606
Phone: (203) 372-4301
E-mail: adoption@ccfc-ct.org
Web site: www.ccfc-ct.org
– Intercountry Program
– Child Placement

Catholic Charities of the Diocese of Norwich
331 Main Street
Norwich, CT 06360
Phone: (860) 889-8346
Fax: (860) 889-2658
E-mail: jjsmey1@snet.net

Catholic Charities, Catholic Family Services
Archdiocese of Hartford
467 Bloomfield Avenue
Bloomfield, CT 06002
Phone: (860) 242-9577
Fax: (860) 286-2800

Catholic Charities, New Haven District Office
478 Orange Street
New Haven, CT 06502
Phone: (203) 787-2207
Fax: (203) 773-3626
Toll-Free: (800) 538-4448
E-mail: adoptionnewhaven@cccfs.org

Child Adoption Resource Association, Inc.
2 Union Plaza, Suite 300
New London, CT 06320
Phone: (860) 444-0553
Fax: (860) 444-6527
After hours: (860) 848-1422
E-mail: director@adoptacarakid.org
Web site: www.adoptacarakid.org
– Intercountry Program
– Child Placement

Children's Center
1400 Whitney Avenue
Hamden, CT 06514
Phone: (203) 248-2116
Fax: (203) 786-6408
– Intercountry Program
– Child Placement

Community Residences, Inc.
732 West Street, Suite 2
Plainville, CT 06489
Phone: (860) 621-7600
Fax: (860) 628-8190
Toll-Free: (888) 737-7775
E-mail: kannis@criinc.org
Web site: www.criinc.org

Connection, Inc.
955 South Main Street
Middletown, CT 06457
Phone: (860) 343-5500
Fax: (860) 343-5517

Curtis Home Foundation
380 Crown Street
Meriden, CT 06450
Phone: (203) 237-9526
Fax: (203) 630-2121

DARE Family Services, Inc.
1184 Burnside Avenue
East Hartford, CT 06108
Phone: (860) 291-8688
Fax: (860) 291-2689
E-mail: darect@juno.com

Family Services of Central Connecticut, Inc.
92 Vine Street
New Britain, CT 06052
Phone: (860) 223-9291
Fax: (860) 223-3111

Franciscan Family Care Center, Inc.
271 Finch Avenue
Meriden, CT 06450
Phone: (203) 237-8084
Fax: (203) 639-1333

Healing the Children Northeast, Inc.
P.O. Box 129
21 Main Street
New Milford, CT 06776
Phone: (860) 355-1828
Fax: (860) 350-6634
Web site: www.htcne.org

Highland Heights St. Francis Home for Children, Inc.
P.O. Box 1224
651 Prospect Street
New Haven, CT 06505
Phone: (203) 777-5513

International Alliance for Children, Inc.
2 Ledge Lane
New Milford, CT 06776
Phone: (860) 354-3417

Jewish Family Service of New Haven
1440 Whalley Avenue
New Haven, CT 06515
Phone: (203) 389-5599
Fax: (203) 389-5904
E-mail: contact@jfsnh.org
Web site: www.jfsnh.org
– Intercountry Program
– Home Study

Jewish Family Services Inc.
2370 Park Avenue
Bridgeport, CT 06604
Phone: (203) 366-5438
Fax: (203) 366-1580
Web site: www.jfsnh.org

Lutheran Social Services of New England
2139 Silas Deane Highway, #201
Rocky Hill, CT 06067
Phone: (860) 257-9889
Fax: (860) 257-0340
Toll-Free: (800) 286-9889
E-mail: LSSadoptct@aol.com
Web site: www.adoptlss.org
– Intercountry Program
– Child Placement

North American Family
Institute
10 Waterchase Drive
Rocky Hill, CT 06067
Phone: (860) 529-1522
Fax: (860) 529-1802

Quinebaug Valley Youth and
Family Services
P.O. Box 378
Wauregan, CT 06387
Phone: (860) 564-6100
Toll-Free: (800) 953-0295

Rainbow Adoptions
International, Inc.
80 Garden Street
Wethersfield, CT 06109
Phone: (860) 721-0099
Fax: (860) 257-4376
E-mail:
rainbow@rainbowadoptions.org
Web site: www.
rainbowadoptions.org
– Intercountry Program
– Child Placement

United Services, Int.
P.O. Box 378
303 Putnam Road
Wauregan, CT 06387
Fax: (203) 564-6110
Toll-Free: (800) 953-0295
E-mail: qupabbrown@usmhs.org
Web site: www.usmhs.org

Village for Families
and Children, Inc.
Phone: (860) 297-0555
Web site: www.
villageforchildren.org/index.html

Wellspring Foundation
P.O. Box 370
21 Arch Bridge Road
Bethlehem, CT 06751
Phone: (203) 266-7235
Fax: (860) 266-5830

Wide Horizons for Children
776 Farmington Avenue
West Hartford, CT 06119
Phone: (860) 570-1740
Fax: (860) 570-1745
E-mail: info@whfc.org
Web site: www.whfc.org
– Intercountry Program
– Child Placement

**Birth Family and Search
Support Groups**

Adoption Answers Support
Kinship (AASK)
8 Homestead Drive
So. Glastonbury, CT 06073-2804
Phone: (860) 657-4005

Adoption Healing
F2 Hadik Parkway
South Norwalk, CT 06854
Phone: (203) 866-8988

Birthparent Support Group
9 Whitney Road
Columbia, CT 06237
Phone: (203) 228-0076

Concerned United
Birthparents
P.O. Box 558
Bethel, CT 06801
Phone: (203) 633-3130

Ties That Bind
P.O. Box 3119
Milford, CT 06460
Phone: (203) 874-2023

**State Adoption Exchange/
Photolisting of Children
Waiting For Adoption**

Connecticut Department of
Children and Families
Office of Foster and Adoption
Services
505 Hudson Street
Hartford, CT 06106
Phone: (860) 550-6578
Fax: (860) 566-6726

Toll-Free: (888) 543-4376
Web site: www.state.ct.us/dcf/
AdoptPics/photohome.htm

**State Adoption
Specialist/Manager**

Connecticut Department of
Children and Families
Office of Foster and Adoption
Services
505 Hudson Street
Hartford, CT 06106
Phone: (860) 550-6350
Fax: (860) 556-6726
E-mail: doreen.jordon@po.state.
ct.us

Connecticut Department of
Children and Families
505 Hudson Street
Hartford, CT 06106
Phone: (860) 550-6350
Fax: (860)-556-6726

**State Foster Care
Specialist/Manager**

Connecticut Department of
Children and Families
Office of Foster and Adoption
Services
505 Hudson Street
Hartford, CT 06106
Phone: (860) 550-6350
Fax: (860) 566-6726
E-mail: derith.mcgann@po.state.
ct.us
Web site: www.state.ct.us/dcf/
foster.htm

**State Interstate Compact on
the Placement of Children
(ICPC) Administrator**

Connecticut Department of
Children and Families
Office of Foster and Adoption
Services
505 Hudson Street
Hartford, CT 06106
Phone: (860) 550-6469

Fax: (860) 566-6726
E-mail: Sandra.Matlack@po.
state.ct.us
Web site: www.state.ct.us/dcf

State Licensing Specialist

Connecticut Department of
Children and Families
505 Hudson Street
Hartford, CT 06106
Phone: (860) 550-6306
Fax: (860) 566-6726
E-mail: thomas.dematteo@state.
ct.us

State Reunion Registry

Connecticut Department of
Children and Families
Office of Foster and Adoption
Services
505 Hudson Street
Hartford, CT 06106
Phone: (860) 550-6578
Fax: (860) 550-6726
Web site: www.state.ct.us/dcf/
foster.htm

Licensed Private
Adoption Agencies for
Domestic Adoptions

Downey Side
2264 Silas Deane Highway,
Suite 100
Rocky Hill, CT 06067-2333
Phone: (860) 257-1694
Fax: (860) 257-1698
Toll-Free: (800) US-Child
E-mail: downeysidect@yahoo.com
Web site: www.downeyside.org

Family and Children's Agency,
Inc.
9 Mott Avenue
Norwalk, CT 06850
Phone: (203) 855-8765
Fax: (203) 838-3325
Toll-Free: (800) 676-4066
E-mail: adoption@fcagency.org

Web site: www.familyand
childrensagency.org
– Intercountry Program
– Adoptive Parent/Family
Preparation
– Agency Able to Place Children
with United States Citizens Living
Abroad
– Child Placement
– Education/Preparation
– Home Study
– Homeland Tours
– Information/Referral

LDS Family Services
34 Jerome Street, Suite 319
Bloomfield, CT 06002
Fax: (603) 889-4358
Toll-Free: (800) 735-0149
E-mail: fam-nh@ldschurch.org
Web site: www.
ldsfamilyservices.org

Licensed Private
Adoption Agencies for
Intercountry Adoptions

Family and Children's Agency
Inc.
9 Mott Avenue
Norwalk, CT 06850
Phone: (203) 855-8765
Fax: (203) 838-3325
Toll-Free: (800) 676-4066
E-mail: adoption@fcagency.org
Web site: www.
familyandchildrensagency.org
– Intercountry Program
– Adoptive Parent/Family
Preparation
– Agency Able to Place Children
with United States Citizens Living
Abroad
– Child Placement
– Education/Preparation
– Home Study
– Homeland Tours
– Information/Referral

DELAWARE

Adoptive/Foster Family
Support Groups

Adoptive Families Information
and Support and North Ameri-
can Council on Adoptable
Children Representative
523 Ashland Ridge Road
Hockessin, DE 19707
Phone: (302) 239-0727
Web site: www.nacac.org

Adoptive Families with Infor-
mation and Support
P.O. Box 7405
Wilmington, DE 19803-7405
Phone: (302) 571-8784
E-mail: afis@delanet.com and
mwolfe@delanet.com

Children and Families First
1019 Mattlind Way
Milford, DE 19963
E-mail: info@ccde.org
Web site: www.cffde.org

Deaf Adoptive Parents'
Network
20 North Skyward Drive
Newark, DE 19713
Phone: (302) 652-1640

Delaware Adoptive Parents
Support Group
9 Maple Avenue
Newark, DE 19711-4793
Phone: (302) 738-9113

Donna Walton
8 North Brandwine Road
Milford, DE 19963
Phone: (302) 422-0182
E-mail: laurensmom96@aol.com

Child and Home Study
Associates
242 North James Street, Suite 202
Wilmington, DE 19804
Phone: (302) 475-5433
E-mail: chsadopt@aol.com
Web site: www.chsadoptions.org
– Intercountry Program
– Adoptive Parent/Family
Preparation
– Education/Preparation
– Home Study
– Information/Referral
– Post-placement Supervision
Prior to Adoption Finalization

**Licensed Private
Adoption Agencies**

Adoption House
3411 Silverside Road,
Suite 101 Webster
Wilmington, DE 19180
Phone: (302) 477-0944
Fax: (302) 477-0955
E-mail: adopt@adopthouse.org
Web site: www.adoptionhouse.org

Adoptions From The Heart, Inc.
18-A Trolley Square
Wilmington, DE 19806
Phone: (302) 658-8883
Fax: (302) 658-8873
E-mail: adoption@adoptionsfrom
theheart.org
Web site: www.
adoptionsfromtheheart.org
– Intercountry Program
– Child Placement

Bethany Christian Services
Suite 201G, Commonwealth
Building
260 Chapman Road
Newark, DE 19702
Phone: (302) 369-3470
Fax: (302) 369-1315
Toll-Free: (800) 215-0702
Web site: www.bethany.org
– Intercountry Program
– Child Placement

Catholic Charities, Inc.
Wilmington Diocese
2601 West Fourth Street
Wilmington, DE 19805
Phone: (302) 655-9624
Fax: (302) 655-9733
Web site: www.cdow.org

Catholic Charities, Inc.
1155 West Walker Road
Dover, DE 19904
Phone: (302) 674-1600

Children and Families First
2005 Baynard Boulevard
Wilmington, DE 19802
Phone: (302) 658-5177
Fax: (302) 658-5170
Web site: www.cffde.org

Children's Choice of Delaware,
Inc.
1151 Walker Road, Suite 100
Dover, DE 19904-6539
Phone: (302) 678-0404

LDS Family Services
500 West Chestnut Hill Road
Newark, DE 19713
Phone: (302) 456-3782

Madison Adoption Associates
1009 Woodstream Drive
Wilmington, DE 19810
Phone: (302) 475-8977
Fax: (302) 529-1976
E-mail: adoptnow@aol.com
Web site: www.
madisonadoption.com
– Intercountry Program
– Child Placement

Welcome House Adoption
Program (of Pearl S. Buck
International)
2401 Pennsylvania Avenue #504
Wilmington, DE 19806
Phone: (302) 656-7711
Fax: (302) 656-7710
Toll-Free: (800) 220-2825
Web site: www.pearl-s-buck.org

**Local/Regional Offices
of the State (Public)
Adoption Agency**

Delaware Department of Ser-
vices for Children, Youth and
Their Families
1825 Faulkland Road
Wilmington, DE 19805
Phone: (302) 633-2655
E-mail: adoption.dscyf@state.
de.us
Web site: www.state.de.us/kids/
adoption.htm

**Birth Family and Search
Support Groups**

Adoption Forum of Delaware
20 Weates Drive
Penn Acres, DE 19720
Phone: (302) 633-4743

Finders Keepers
P.O. Box 748
Bear, DE 19701-0748
Phone: (302) 834-8888
E-mail: SEARCHDE@aol.com

**State Adoption Exchange/
Photolisting of Children
Waiting For Adoption**

Delaware Adoption Registry
1825 Faulkland Road
Wilmington, DE 19805

**State Adoption
Specialist/Manager**

Delaware Department of Ser-
vices for Children, Youth and
Their Families
1825 Faulkland Road
Wilmington, DE 19805-1195
Phone: (302) 633-2655
Fax: (302) 633-2652
E-mail: frank.perfinski@state.
de.us
Web site: www.state.de.us/kids/
adoption.htm

State Foster Care Specialist/Manager

Delaware Department of Services to Children, Youth and Their Families
Delaware Division of Family Services
1825 Faulkland Road
Wilmington, DE 19805
Phone: (302) 633-2665
Fax: (302) 633-2652
E-mail: jbates@state.de.us
Web site: www.state.de.us/kids/fs.htm

State Interstate Compact on the Placement of Children (ICPC) Administrator

Delaware Department of Services for Children, Youth and Their Families
Office of Case Management
1825 Faulkland Road
Wilmington, DE 19805
Phone: (302) 633-2698
Fax: (302) 633-2652
Web site: www.state.de.us/kids/dfsocm.htm

State Licensing Specialist

Delaware Department of Services for Children, Youth and Their Families
Office of Child Care Licensing
Barrett Building
821 Silver Lake Blvd, Suite 103
Dover, DE 19904
Phone: (302) 739-5487
Fax: (302) 739-6589
Toll-Free: (800) 822-2236
Web site: www.state.de.us/kids/occlhome.htm

State Reunion Registry

Delaware Adoption Registry
1825 Faulkland Road
Wilmington, DE 19805

Statewide Adoption Recruitment Line

Delaware Statewide Adoption Recruitment Line
Toll-Free: (800) 464-4357

DISTRICT OF COLUMBIA

Adoptive/Foster Family Support Groups

ASIA Family and Friends
7720 Alaska Avenue NW
Washington, DC 20012
Phone: (202) 726-7193
E-mail: info@asia-adopt.org
Web site: www.asia-adopt.org

Families for Private Adoptions
P.O. Box 6375
Washington, DC 20015-0375
Phone: (292) 722-0338
Web site: www.ffpa.org

Licensed Private Adoption Agencies

Adoption Center of Washington, Inc.
1726 M Street NW, Suite 1101
Washington, DC 20036
Phone: (202) 452-8278
Fax: (202) 452-8280
Toll-Free: (800) 452-3878
E-mail: info@adoptioncenter.com
Web site: www.adoptioncenter.com
– Intercountry Program
– Child Placement

Adoption Service Information Agency, Inc. (ASIA)
7720 Alaska Avenue NW
Washington, DC 20012
Phone: (202) 726-7193
Fax: (202) 722-4928
E-mail: ASIAadopt@aol.com
Web site: www.asia-adopt.org

Adoptions Together Inc.
419 7th Street NW, Suite 201
Washington, DC 20004
Phone: (202) 628-5017
E-mail: adoptionworks@adoptionstogether.org
Web site: www.adoptionstogether.org

Barker Foundation, Inc.
4400 MacArthur Boulevard NW, Suite 200
Washington, DC 20818
Phone: (202) 363-7511
Toll-Free: (800) 673-8489
E-mail: info@barkerfoundation.org
Web site: www.barkerfoundation.org

Catholic Charities Archdiocese of Washington, D.C.
1438 Rhode Island Avenue NE
Washington, DC 20018
Phone: (202) 526-4100
Web site: www.catholiccharities.org

Catholic Charities Archdiocese of Washington, D.C.
Pregnancy and Adoption Services
The James Cardinal Hickey Center
924 G Street NW
Washington, DC 20001
Phone: (202) 772-4327
Fax: (202) 772-4409
E-mail: banksd@catholiccharitiesdc.org
Web site: www.catholiccharitiesdc.org

Family and Child Services, Inc.
929 L Street NW
Washington, DC 20001
Phone: (202) 289-1510
Fax: (202) 371-0863
Web site: www.familyandchildservices.org

International Families, Inc.
5 Thomas Circle NW
Washington, DC 20005
Phone: (202) 667-5779
Fax: (202) 667-5922
E-mail: ifichild@aol.com
Web site: www.ifichild.com

Lutheran Social Services of
the National Capital Area
4406 Georgia Avenue NW
Washington, DC 20011-7124
Phone: (202) 723-3000
Fax: (202) 723-3303
E-mail: greenberg@lssnca.org
Web site: www.lssnca.org
– Intercountry Program
– Child Placement

Progressive Life Center
1123 11th Street NW
Washington, DC 20001
Phone: (202) 842-4570

**Local/Regional Offices
of the State (Public)
Adoption Agency**

Child and Family Services
Agency of DC
400 6th Street, SW, 5th Floor
Washington, DC 20024
Phone: (202) 442-6000
Fax: (202) 727-6505
E-mail: cfsa@dc.gov
Web site: http://cfsa.dc.gov

**Regional/District
Public Agencies**

District of Columbia Child and
Family Services Agency
400 6th Street SW, 5th Floor
Washington, DC 20024
Phone: (202) 442-6000
Fax: (202) 442-6498

**Birth Family and Search
Support Groups**

American Adoption Congress
P.O. Box 42730
Washington, DC 20036
Phone: (202) 483-3399
Web site: www.american
adoptioncongress.org

Center for Child Protection
and Family Support
714 G Street, SE
Washington, DC 20003
Phone: (202) 544-3144
Fax: (202) 547-3601
E-mail: ccpfs@centerchildprote
ction.org
Web site: www.
centerchildprotection.org

**State Adoption Exchange/
Photolisting of Children
Waiting For Adoption**

District of Columbia Department of Human Services
2700 Martin Luther King
Avenue SE
801 East Building
Washington, DC 20020

**State Adoption
Specialist/Manager**

District of Columbia Child and
Family Services
400 6th Street SW
Washington, DC 20024
Phone: (202) 727-4733
Fax: (202) 727-7709
E-mail: Wjohnson1@cfsa-dc.org

**State Interstate Compact on
the Placement of Children
(ICPC) Administrator**

Department of Human
Services
District of Columbia Child and
Family Services Agency
609 H Street NE
Washington, DC 20002

Phone: (202) 698-4637
Fax: (202) 727-6881

State Licensing Specialist

Department of Health
– Licensing and Regulatory
Administration
Human Social Services Facility
Division
825 North Capital Street NE
Washington, DC 20002
Phone: (202) 442-5929
Fax: (202) 442-9430

National Adoption Information
Clearinghouse
330 C Street SW
Washington, DC 20447
Phone: (703) 352-3488
Fax: (703) 385-3206
Toll-Free: (888) 251-0078
E-mail: naic@caliber.com
Web site: http://naic.acf.hhs.gov

FLORIDA

**Adoptive/Foster Family
Support Groups**

A Bond of Love – Tallahassee
Families
Touched by Adoption
6732 Pasadena Drive
Tallahassee, FL 32311
Phone: (850) 671-5793
Fax: (850) 671-5793
E-mail: abondoflove@hotmail.com

AdoptNet
130 NW 28th Street
Gainesville, FL 32607-2511
Phone: (352) 377-6455

Adoption Council of Tampa Bay
4102 West Linbaugh Avenue, #200
Tampa Bay, FL 33624
E-mail: AllanABC@aol.com

Adoption Support Network

Phone: (941) 721-7670
Fax: (941) 721-8950
After hours: (941) 720-5014
E-mail: mmurphy@sarasota-ymca.org
Web site: www.sarasota-ymca.org

Daniel Memorial Adoption Information Center and North American Council on Adoptable Children Representative

4203 Southpoint Boulevard
Jacksonville, FL 32216
Phone: (904) 353-0679
Fax: (904) 353-3472
E-mail: brooks@danielkids.org
Web site: www.danielkids.org

Family Connection

4514 Oak Fair Boulevard, #143
Tampa, FL 33610
Phone: (813) 661-4028
E-mail: lawhitt@sylviathomascenter.org
Web site: www.sylviathomascenter.org

Florida Foster and Adoptive Parents Association

P.O. Box 34
1333 East 3rd Avenue
Mount Dora, FL 32757
Phone: (352) 735-0446
E-mail: StevensNA@aol.com

Heritage For Black Children, Inc.

4823 Silver Star Road, Suite 110
Orlando, FL 32808
Phone: (407) 292-7722
Fax: (407) 292-6540
After hours: (407) 299-5770
E-mail: heritageasap@wmconnect.com

Heart to Heart Adoption Service, Inc.

2940 Fontana Place
Royal Palm Beach, FL 33411

Phone: (561) 383-8590
Fax: (561) 383-8618

Parents Adoption Lifeline

319 Cordova Road
West Palm Beach, FL 33401
Phone: (561) 837-5054
Phone: (561) 308-0290
Fax: (561) 833-5412
After hours: (561) 833-2849
E-mail: jnl@bellsouth.net
Web site: www.adoptionlifeline.org

People Adopting Children Everywhere

3521 Swallow Drive
Melbourne, FL 32935
Phone: (321) 253-0456

Pinellas Council on Adoptable Children

3861 38th Street South
St. Petersburg, FL 33711
Phone: (727) 866-7829
Fax: (727) 866-8963

SNAP and North American Council on Adoptable Children Representative

15913 Layton Court
Tampa, FL 33647
Phone: (813) 971-4752

Stars of David International, Inc.

Jewish Adoption Information Exchange
21300 Ruth and Baron Coleman Boulevard
Boca Raton, FL 33428
Phone: (561) 852-3380
Fax: (561) 852-3332
E-mail: starsdavid@aol.com
Web site: www.starsofdavid.org

Licensed Private Adoption Agencies

A Bond of Love Adoption Agency, Inc.

1800 Siesta Drive
Sarasota, FL 34239
Phone: (941) 957-0064
Fax: (941) 957-0064
Toll-Free: (800) 225-4543
E-mail: abladopt@aol.com
Web site: www.abondoflove.net

Adoption Advocates, Inc.

11407 Seminole Boulevard
Largo, FL 33778
Phone: (727) 391-8096
Fax: (727) 399-0026
E-mail: Adoptme@gte.net
Web site: http://adoptionadvocatesinc.com

Adoption Agency of Central Florida

1681 Maitland Avenue
Maitland, FL 32751
Phone: (407) 831-2154

Adoption By Choice

St. Andrew's Square
4102 West Linebaugh Avenue, Suite 200
Tampa, FL 33624
Phone: (813) 960-2229
Fax: (813) 969-2339
Toll-Free: (800) 421-2229
E-mail: info@abcadopt.com
Web site: www.abcadopt.com

Adoption Placement, Inc.

1840 North Pine Island Road
Plantation, FL 33322
Phone: (954) 474-8494
Fax: (954) 474-2251
E-mail: api@adoptionplacement.com
Web site: www.adoptionplacement.com
– Intercountry Program
– Child Placement

Adoption Resources of Florida
662 Key Royale Drive
Holmes Beach, FL 34217
Phone: (813) 251-3388
Phone: (941) 779-1632
Fax: (813) 251-4187
E-mail: cghuston@aol.com
Web site: www.mapsadopt.org
– Intercountry Program
– Child Placement

Adoption Source, Inc.
6401 Congress Avenue, Suite 205
Boca Raton, FL 33487
Phone: (561) 912-9229
Fax: (561) 912-9912
– Intercountry Program
– Child Placement

Advocates for Children and Families
16831 NE 6th Avenue
North Miami Beach, FL 33162-2408
Phone: (305) 653-2474
Fax: (305) 653-2746
Toll-Free: (800) 348-0467
E-mail: info@adoptionflorida.org
Web site: www.adoptionflorida.org

All About Adoptions, Inc.
701 West Cypress Creek Road, Suite 302
Ft. Lauderdale, FL 33309
Phone: (954) 202-7889
Fax: (954) 771-3047
E-mail: miamiadopt@aol.com

An Angel's Answer Adoption Agency
98 SE 6th Avenue, #3
Del Ray, FL 33483
Phone: (561) 276-0660

Catholic Charities
P.O. Box 8246
900 54th Street
West Palm Beach, FL 33407
Phone: (561) 842-2406

Fax: (561) 863-5379
Web site: www.diocesepb.org/catholic/charity.html

Catholic Charities
11 First Street SE
Ft. Walton Beach, FL 32548
Phone: (850) 244-2825
Fax: (850) 244-2963
E-mail: cathcharfwb@earthlink.net

Catholic Charities
Diocese of St. Petersburg
2021 East Busch Boulevard
Tampa, FL 33612
Phone: (813) 631-4393
Fax: (813) 631-4395
E-mail: jwoody@ccdosp.org
Web site: www.catholiccharities.org

Catholic Charities Bureau
134 East Church Street, Suite 2
Jacksonville, FL 32202-3130
Phone: (904) 354-4846
Fax: (904) 354-4718
Web site: www.ccbjaf.org

Catholic Charities Bureau
225 West King Street
St. Augustine, FL 32084
Phone: (904) 829-6300
Fax: (904) 829-0494
E-mail: rstringer@ccbstaug.org
– Intercountry Program
– Child Placement

Catholic Charities of Northwest Florida, Inc.
222 East Government Street
Pensacola, FL 32502
Phone: (850) 436-6410
Fax: (850) 436-6419
E-mail: cathchar@bellsouth.net
– Intercountry Program
– Child Placement

Catholic Charities of the Diocese of Venice, Inc.
4930 Fruitville Road
Sarasota, FL 34232-2206

Phone: (941) 379-9111
Fax: (941) 379-3611
E-mail: srqcnslg@juno.com

Catholic Social Services
1771 North Semoran Boulevard
Orlando, FL 32807
Phone: (407) 658-1818

Catholic Social Services
817 Dixon Boulevard, #16
Cocoa, FL 32922
Phone: (407) 636-6144
Fax: (321) 631-4209
E-mail: seitz@aol.com
– Intercountry Program
– Home Study

Children's Home Society of Florida
2400 Ridgewood Avenue, Suite 32
Daytona Beach, FL 32119
Phone: (904) 304-7600
Fax: (904) 304-7620
Toll-Free: (800) 737-5756
E-mail: Donna.Marietta@chsfl.org
Web site: www.chsfl.org

Children's Home Society of Florida
P.O. Box 5616
3027 San Diego Road
Jacksonville, FL 32247-5616
Phone: (904) 348-2811
Fax: (904) 348-2818
E-mail: rjohnson@chsfl.org
Web site: www.chsfl.org

Children's Home Society of Florida
3535 Lawton Road, Suite 260
Orlando, FL 32803
Phone: (407) 895-5800
Fax: (407) 895-5801
E-mail: kim.brien@chsfl.org
Web site: www.chsfl.org

Children's Home Society of Florida
Family Builders
3001 W. Silver Springs Boulevard
Building C
Ocala, FL 34475
Phone: (352) 620-7398
Phone: (352) 620-7398
Web site: www.chsfl.org

Children's Home Society of Florida
P.O. Box 19136
5375 North 9th Avenue
Pensacola, FL 32523
Phone: (850) 494-5990
Fax: (850) 494-5981
E-mail: cynthia.blacklaw@chsfl.org
Web site: www.chsfl.org

Children's Home Society of Florida
800 NW 15th Street
Miami, FL 33136-1495
Phone: (305) 324-1262
Fax: (305) 326-7430
E-mail: carla.penn@chsfl.org
Web site: www.chsfl.org

Children's Home Society of Florida
415 Avenue A, Suite 101
Fort Pierce, FL 34950
Phone: (561) 489-5601
Fax: (561) 489-5604
Toll-Free: (800) 235-2229
E-mail: larry.wilms@chsfl.org
Web site: www.chsfl.org

Christian Family Services
2720 SW 2nd Avenue
Gainesville, FL 32607
Phone: (352) 378-6202

Commonwealth Adoptions International, Inc.
13902 North Dale Mabry Highway,
Suite 102
Tampa, FL 33618
Phone: (813) 269-4646

Fax: (813) 269-7722
E-mail: tampa.cai@verizon.net
Web site: www.commmonwealthadoption.org

Everyday Blessings
13129 St. Francis Lane
Thonotosassa, FL 33592
Phone: (813) 982-9226
Fax: (813) 986-0298
E-mail: everybless@aol.com
Web site: www.everybless.org
– Intercountry Program
– Child Placement

Family Creations, Inc.
5550 26th Street West, Suite 8A
Bradenton, FL 34207
Phone: (941) 727-9630
Toll-Free: (866) 322-9630
E-mail: familycreationsadoption@msn.com
Web site: www.familycreationsinc.com
– Intercountry Program
– Child Placement

Florida Baptist Children's Home
7748 SW 95th Terrace
Miami, FL 33156
Phone: (305) 271-4121
Fax: (305) 271-8891
E-mail: fbchomes.org

Florida Baptist Children's Home
8415 Buck Lake Road
Tallahassee, FL 32317-9522
Phone: (850) 878-1458

Florida Baptist Children's Home
1000 Chemstrand Road
Cantonment, FL 32533-8916
Phone: (850) 494-9530

Florida Baptist Family Ministries
1015 Sikes Boulevard
Lakeland, FL 33815

Florida Home Studies and Adoption, Inc.
5930 Palmer Boulevard
Sarasota, FL 34232
Phone: (941) 342-8189
Fax: (941) 371-3125
Fax: (941) 371-3125
E-mail: susan@flhomestudies.com
E-mail: info@flhomestudies.com

Gift of Life, Inc.
4437 Park Boulevard
Pinellas Park, FL 33781-3540
Phone: (727) 549-1416
Fax: (727) 548-8174
Toll-Free: (800) 216-5433
Web site: www.giftoflifeinc.org

Gorman Family Life Center, Inc.
dba Life for Kids
315 North Wymore Road
Winter Park, FL 32789
Phone: (407) 629-5437
Fax: (407) 629-5812
Toll-Free: (888) 629-5437
E-mail: lifeforkids@yahoo.com
Web site: www.lifeforkids.com
– Intercountry Program
– Home Study

Intercountry Adoption Center, Inc.
7204 13th Avenue West
Bradenton, FL 32409
Phone: (941) 761-1345
Fax: (941) 761-1239
E-mail: iac.fl@verizon.net
Web site: www.intercountryadopt.com
– Intercountry Program
– Child Placement

International Children's Foundation
11030 North Kendall Drive,
Suite 200
Miami, FL 33176
Phone: (305) 275-8810
Fax: (305) 275-6802

Jewish Adoption and Foster Care (JAFCO)
4200 North University Drive
Sunrise, FL 33351
Phone: (954) 749-7230
Fax: (954) 749-7231
E-mail: info@jafco.org
Web site: www.jafco.org

Jewish Family Services
300 41st Street, Suite 216
Miami Beach, FL 33145
Phone: (305) 672-8080

Jewish Family and Community Services, Inc. (a.k.a. First Coast Adoption Professionals)
6261 Dupont Station
Jacksonville, FL 32217
Phone: (904) 448-1933
E-mail: iyoung@jfcsjax.org

Mid-Florida Adoption Reunions
P.O. Box 3475
Belleview, FL
Phone: (352) 237-1955

Mother and Child Reunion
2219 SW Mt. Vernon Street
Port St. Lucie, FL 34953
Phone: (561) 878-9101

National Organization for Father Adoption Reform
Phone: (941) 637-7477

O.A.S.I.S. (National Headquarters)
P.O. Box 53-0761
Miami Shores, FL 33153
Phone: (305) 948-8933

Organized Adoption Search Info Services, Inc.
Phone: (305) 948-8933

Orphan Voyage
Phone: (904) 398-4269

Orphan Voyage of FL/Paton House
1122 Marco Place
Jacksonville, FL 32207-4043

Orphan Voyage of Jacksonville
Phone: (904) 292-9200

Searches International
1600 West 64th Street
Hialeah, FL 33012-6106

Triad Search and Support Group
3408 Neptune Drive
Orlando, FL 32804
Phone: (407) 843-2760

Triad-Central Florida
2359 Summerfield Road
Orlando, FL 32837
Phone: (407) 850-9141
Fax: (407) 850-9687

Lifelink Child and Family Services Corporation
1031 South Euclid Street
Sarasota, FL 34237
Phone: (941) 957-1614
E-mail: alladopt@lifelink.org
Web site: www.lifelink.org
− Intercountry Program
− Child Placement

New Beginnings Family and Children's Services
1301 Seminole Boulevard, Suite 111
Largo, FL 33773
Phone: (727) 584-5262
Fax: (727) 584-6322
E-mail: newbeginn@aol.com
Web site: www.new-beginnings.org
− Intercountry Program
− Child Placement

One World Adoption Services, Inc.
400 Fairway Drive, Suite 107
Deerfield, FL 33441
Phone: (954) 596-2223

Open Door Adoption Agency
220 Alba Avenue
Quincy, FL 32351
Phone: (850) 627-1420
Web site: www.opendooradoption.com

Southeastern Network of Youth and Family Services
3780 Via Del Rey, Suite C
Bonita Springs, FL 34134
Phone: (239) 949-4414
Fax: (239) 949-4911

Suncoast International Adoptions, Inc.
12651 Walsingham Road, Suite C
Largo, FL 33774
Phone: (727) 596-3135
Fax: (727) 593-0106
E-mail: suncoastadoption@aol.com

State Adoption Exchange/ Photolisting of Children Waiting For Adoption

Child Adoption Program
Florida Department of Children and Families
1317 Winewood Boulevard, Building 7
Tallahassee, FL 32399-0700
Fax: (850) 488-0751
Toll-Free: (800) 372-3678
Web site: www.myflorida.com/cf_web/myflorida2/healthhuman/adoption/

Florida Adoption Information Center
Daniel Memorial, Inc.
4203 Southpoint Boulevard
Jacksonville, FL 32216

State Adoption Specialist/Manager

Florida Department of Children and Families
Florida's Adoption Exchange
1317 Winewood Boulevard
Building 7, Room 208
Tallahassee, FL 32399-0700

Phone: (850) 921-2177
Fax: (850) 488-0751
E-mail: carol_hutcheson@dcf.
state.fl.us
Web site: http://www5.myflorida.
com/cf_web/myflorida2/health
human/adoption/

State Foster Care Specialist/Manager

Florida Department of Children and Families
1317 Winewood Boulevard,
Building 7
Tallahassee, FL 32399-0700
Phone: (850) 921-3005
Fax: (850) 488-0751
E-mail: Gay_Frizzell@dcf.state.
fl.us

State Interstate Compact on the Placement of Children (ICPC) Administrator

Florida Department of Children and Families
1317 Winewood Boulevard,
Building 7
Tallahassee, FL 32399-0700
Phone: (941) 342-8189

St. Vincent Adoption Center
18601 SW 97th Avenue
Miami, FL 33157
Phone: (305) 445-5714

Suncoast International Adoptions, Inc.
12651 Walsingham Road, Suite C
Largo, FL 33774
Phone: (727) 596-3135
Fax: (727) 593-0106
E-mail: suncoastadoption@aol.com
– Intercountry Program
– Child Placement

Tedi Bear Adoptions, Inc.
P.O. Box 3651
Ponte Vedra Beach, FL 32004
Phone: (904) 280-1644
Fax: (904) 280-1646

E-mail: info@tedibearadoptions.
org
– Intercountry Program
– Child Placement

The Children's Home, Inc.
10909 Memorial Highway
Tampa, FL 33615
Phone: (813) 855-4435, ext. 2037
Fax: (813) 864-1325
E-mail: efisher@tampachi.org
Web site: www.
thechildrenshomeinc.com

Universal Aid for Children
Cypress Village East
167 SW 6th Street
Pompano Beach, FL 33060
Phone: (954) 785-0033
Fax: (954) 785-7003
E-mail: uacadopt@aol.com
Web site: www.uacadoption.org
– Intercountry Program
– Child Placement

Universal Aid for Children
1435 South Miami Avenue
Miami, FL 33130
Phone: (305) 577-8977

Regional/District Public Agencies

Florida Department of Children and Families
Office of Family Safety
1317 Winewood Boulevard,
Building 6
Tallahassee, FL 32399-0700
Phone: (850) 921-1928
E-mail: vicki_mccrary@dcf.state.
fl.us

Florida Department of Children and Families
1317 Winewood Boulevard,
Building 7
Tallahassee, FL 32399-0700
Phone: (850) 921-2594
Fax: (850) 488-0751

State Reunion Registry

Florida Adoption Reunion Registry (FARR)
Florida Department of Health and
Rehabilitation Services
1317 Winewood Boulevard,
Building 7
Tallahassee, FL 32399-0700
Phone: (850) 488-8000
Toll-Free: (800) 962-3678

GEORGIA

Adoptive/Foster Family Support Groups

Adoption Services, Inc. Parent Support Group S.T.A.R.T. Parenting (Support the Adoptive Route to Parenting)
P.O. Box 155
Pavo, GA 31778
Phone: (912) 859-2654

Alliance of Single Adoptive Parents
687 Kennolia Drive SW
Atlanta, GA 30310-2363
Phone: (404) 755-3280

BREAK Project
3070 Pritchards Mill Terrace
Douglasville, GA 30135-6604
Phone: (770) 920-0120

Beth Shumake
2769 Waters Edge Drive
Gainesville, GA 30504-3971

Brantley County Adoptive Parent Support Group
Phone: (912) 462-5656

Central Savannah River Area Council on Adoptable Children (CSRA-COAC)
2 Peachtree St. NE, Suite 8-102
Atlanta, GA 30303
Toll-Free: (800) 603-1322

Cradle of Love/Jewish Family and Career Services
Stars of David International, Inc.
265 Village Parkway
Marietta, GA 30062
Phone: (770) 955-8550
E-mail: info@jfcs-atlanta.org
Web site: www.starsofdavid.org

Early County Adoption Support Group
P.O. Box 747
Blakely, GA 31723
Phone: (912) 723-4331

Families By Choice
195 Ashton Drive
Macon, GA 31220
Phone: (912) 474-6348
Fax: (912) 743-0964

Families with Children from China
4502 Lake Ivanhoe Drive
Tucker, GA 30084
Phone: (770) 939-8500
E-mail: caugh@aol.com
Web site: http://catalog.com/fwcfc

Flint River Adoptive Parent Support Group
Spalding County DFCS
411 East Solomon Street
Griffin, GA 30223
Phone: (770) 228-1386
Toll-Free: (800) 299-2038

Foster Parent Association Group
P.O. Box 155
Douglasville, GA 30133
Phone: (770) 942-0219
Fax: (770) 489-8382

Georgia Council on Adoptable Children (GA COAC)
3559 London Road
Atlanta, GA 30341
Phone: (770) 986-0760

Lowndes Area Adoption Support Group
P.O. Box 372
Valdosta, GA 31603-0372
Phone: (229) 247-8030
E-mail: burk611@bellsouth.net

Lutheran Ministries of Georgia
Heart to Heart Adoption Services
756 W. Peachtree Street NW
Atlanta, GA 30308
Phone: (404) 607-7126
Fax: (404) 875-9258
E-mail: lmofga@mindspring.com
Web site: www.lmg.org

North American Council on Adoptable Children
P.O. Box 7727
Atlanta, GA 30357

One Church, One Child Program, Inc.
P.O. Box 115238
Atlanta, GA 30310
Phone: (404) 766-0383
Toll-Free: (800) 662-3651

Parents of Adopted Children
5622 Fairmont Highway SE
Calhoun, GA 30701

Roots Adoptive Parent Support Group
1777 Phoenix Parkway, Suite 108
Atlanta, GA 30349
Phone: (770) 907-7770
Fax: (770) 907-7726
Web site: www.rootsadopt.org

Single Women Adopting Children
865 Whitehall Way
Roswell, GA 30076
Phone: (770) 640-0495

Sowega Six Adoptive Parents Group
345 Duke-Wells Road
Bainbridge, GA 31717
Phone: (912) 248-2420

Special Needs Adoption Parent Support
345 Westerhall Court
Atlanta, GA 30328
Phone: (770) 399-6157

Stars of David
3300 Arborwood Drive
Alpharetta, GA 30202
Phone: (770) 992-3422
E-mail: starsdavid@aol.com
Web site: www.starsofdavid.org

Licensed Private Adoption Agencies

AAA Partners in Adoption
E-mail: mclause@aaapia.org
Web site: www.aaapia.org

Adoption Planning, Inc.
17 Executive Park Drive, Suite 490
Atlanta, GA 30329
Phone: (404) 248-9105
Fax: (404) 248-0419
Toll-Free: (800) 367-3203
E-mail: wecare@adoption planning.org
Web site: www. adoptionplanning.org

Adoption Services, Inc.
P.O. Box 278
1065 West Harris Street
Pavo, GA 31778
Phone: (229) 859-2654
Fax: (229) 859-2412

All God's Children, Inc
1671 Meriweather Drive, Suite 101
Bogart, GA 30622
Phone: (706) 316-2421
Fax: (706) 316-2423
E-mail: info@agcadoption.org
Web site: www.agccadoption.orp

Baptist Children's Home and Family Ministries, Inc.
505 Waterworks Road
Palmetto, GA 30268
Phone: (770) 463-3800
Toll-Free: (800) 252-0872
Web site: www.gbchfm.org

Bethany Christian Services
15 Dunwoody Park Drive,
Suite 200
Atlanta, GA 30338
Phone: (770) 455-7111
Fax: (770) 455-7118
Toll-Free: (800) 238-4269
E-mail: mboston@bethany.org
Web site: www.bethany.org/
atlanta
– Intercountry Program
– Child Placement

Bethany Christian Services
5210 Armour Road, Suite 200A
Columbus, GA 31904
Phone: (706) 576-5766
Fax: (770) 395-1692

Catholic Social Services, Inc.
Pregnancy, Parenting and
Adoption Program
680 West Peachtree Street NW
Atlanta, GA 30308
Phone: (404) 881-6571
Fax: (404) 888-7816
Web site: www.cssatlanta.com

Community Connections, Inc.
6552 James B. Rivers Drive
Stone Mountain, GA 30083

Eastern European Adoption Network of Georgia
415 Dunhill View Court
Alpharetta, GA 30005
Phone: (770) 740-9353
Fax: (770) 740-0283
Web site: http://geocities.com/
diane12102000/EEANGA.html

Edgewood Baptist Church, Inc.
New Beginning Adoption and
Counseling Agency
1316 Wynnton Court, Suite A
Columbus, GA 31906
Phone: (706) 571-3346

Elina International Adoption Services, Inc.
310 Saddle Creek Drive
Roswell, GA 30076
Phone: (770) 650-0730
Fax: (770) 587-9185
E-mail: info@elinaadoption.org
Web site: www.elinaadoption.org
– Intercountry Program
– Child Placement

Extended Families and Educational Services
3079 Campbellton Road SW
Atlanta, GA 30311-5400
Phone: (404) 756-0148

Families First
P.O. Box 7998
1105 West Peachtree Street NE
Atlanta, GA 30357
Phone: (404) 853-2867
Fax: (404) 688-9760
E-mail: peggy@familiesfirst.org
Web site: www.familiesfirst.org

Family Counseling Center/ CSRA, Inc.
603 Ellis Street
Augusta, GA 30901
Phone: (706) 722-6512

Family Values Network, Inc.
7277 Wood Hollow Way Stone
Mountain, GA 30087

Father Flanagan's Boys Home, Inc.
2591 Candler Road
Decatur, GA 30032

Forsyth County Child Advocacy Center, Inc.
104 Kelly Mill Road
Cumming, GA 30040

Gateway Community Service Board
415 Bonaventure Road
Thunderbolt, GA 31405

Genesis Adoptions
E-mail: genesis@abraxis.com
Web site: www.
GenesisAdoptions.org
– Intercountry Program
– Child Placement

Georgia Association for Guidance, Aid, Placement and Empathy (AGAPE), Inc.
3094 Mercer University Drive,
Suite 200
Atlanta, GA 30341
Phone: (404) 452-9995

Georgia Baptist Children's Home and Family Ministries North Area (Palmetto)
505 Waterworks Road
Palmetto, GA 30268
Phone: (770) 463-3800
Toll-Free: (800) 252-0872
Web site: www.gbchfm.org

Georgia Mentor
2799 Lawrenceville Highway,
Suite 201
Decatur, GA 30033
Phone: (770) 496-5500
Fax: (770) 496-0101
E-mail: lori.campbell@thementor
network.com
Web site: www.
thementornetwork.com

Georgia Youth Advocate Program, Inc.
343 Telfair Street
Augusta, GA 30901
Toll-Free: (800) 722-3912
Web site: www.gyap.org

Giving Tree, Inc.
1842 Clairmont Road
Decatur, GA 30033
Phone: (404) 633-3383
Fax: (404) 633-3348
E-mail: theresa@thegivingtree.org
Web site: www.thegivingtree.org

Heritage Adoption Services
6555 Abercorn Street, Suite 200
Savannah, GA 31405
Phone: (912) 355-9179
Fax: (912) 355-1499

Hope for Children, Inc.
24 Perimeter Center East,
Suite 2400
Atlanta, GA 30346
Phone: (770) 391-1511
Fax: (770) 391-1556
Toll-Free: (800) 522-2913
E-mail: josh_holt@hopeww.org
Web site: www.hopeforchildren.org
– Intercountry Program
– Child Placement

Illien Adoptions International, Inc.
1250 Piedmont Avenue NE
Atlanta, GA 30309
Phone: (404) 815-1599
Fax: (404) 876-0483
E-mail: illienusa@aol.com
Web site: www.illienadopt.com
– Intercountry Program
– Child Placement

Independent Adoption Center
3774 Lavista Road, Suite 100
Tucker, GA 30084
Phone: (404) 321-6900
Fax: (404) 321-6600
Toll-Free: (800) 877-6736
Web site: www.adoptionhelp.org

Jewish Family Services, Inc.
Cradle of Love Adoption
Counseling and Services
4549 Chamblee-Dunwoody Road
Atlanta, GA 30338-6210
Phone: (770) 955-8550

LDS Family Services
4823 North Royal Atlanta Drive
Tucker, GA 30084
Phone: (404) 939-2121

Lutheran Ministries of Georgia, Inc.
756 West Peachtree Street NW
Atlanta, GA 30308
Phone: (404) 607-7126
Fax: (404) 875-9258
E-mail: lmgadoption@
mindspring.com
Web site: www.lmg.org/
programs/adoptions.htm

Open Door Adoption Agency, Inc.
P.O. Box 4
403B North Broad Street
Thomasville, GA 31799-0004
Phone: (229) 228-6339
Fax: (229) 228-4726
Toll-Free: (800) 868-6339
Web site: www.
opendooradoption.com
– Intercountry Program
– Child Placement

ROOTS, Inc.
1777 Phoenix Parkway, Suite 108
College Park, GA 30349
Phone: (770) 907-7770
Fax: (770) 907-7726
E-mail: radopt@hotmail.com
Web site: www.rootsadopt.com

World Partners Adoption, Inc.
2205 Summit Oaks Court
Lawrenceville, GA 30043
Phone: (770) 962-7860
Fax: (770) 513-7767
Toll-Free: (800) 350-7338
E-mail: WPAdopt@aol.com
Web site: www.
worldpartnersadoption.org
– Intercountry Program
– Child Placement

Birth Family and Search Support Groups

Adoptee Birthparent Connection
P.O. Box 851
Rosewell, GA 30077
Phone: (770) 642-9063

Adoptee's Search Network
3317 Spring Creek Drive
Conyers, GA 30208

Adoption Angles and Extensions
4565 Pond Lane
Marietta, GA 30066

Atlanta Birthparent/Adoptee
Hammond Park Community
Center
6005 Glenridge Drive
Atlanta, GA 30328
Phone: (770) 422-6486

Bridges in Adoption Connection
6810 Wright Road
Atlanta, GA 30328

Families First
P.O. Box 7948, Station C 1105
West Peachtree Street NE
Atlanta, GA 30357
Phone: (404) 853-2800

State Adoption Exchange/ Photolisting of Children Waiting For Adoption

Georgia State Adoption Exchange
Two Peachtree Street NW,
Suite 8-407
Atlanta, GA 30303-3142
Phone: (404) 657-3479
Toll-Free: (800) 603-1322

State Adoption Specialist/Manager

Georgia Department of Human Resources Division of Children and Family Services
Office of Adoptions
Two Peachtree Street NW, Suite 8-400
Atlanta, GA 30303-3142
Phone: (404) 657-3558
Fax: (404) 657-9498
Toll-Free: (888) 460-2467
E-mail: gmgreer@dhr.state.ga.us

State Foster Care Specialist/Manager

Georgia Department of Human Resources
Division of Children and Family Services
State Foster Care Unit 2
Peachtree Street NW, 18th Floor
Atlanta, GA 30303-3142
Phone: (404) 657-3459
Fax: (404) 657-3415
E-mail: bbwright@dhr.state.ga.us

State Interstate Compact on the Placement of Children (ICPC) Administrator

Georgia Department of Human Resources
Division of Family and Children Services
Office of Adoptions
Two Peachtree Street NW
Atlanta, GA 30303-3142
Phone: (404) 657-3564
Toll-Free: (888) 460-2467
Web site: www.adoptions.dhr.state.ga.us

Georgia Department of Human Resources
Office of Regulatory Services
Two Peachtree Street NW
Atlanta, GA 30303-3142
Phone: (404) 657-5560
Fax: (404) 657-5708

E-mail: jccato@dhr.state.ga.us
Web site: www.ors.dhr.state.ga.us/

State Reunion Registry

Georgia Adoption Reunion Registry
Families First/Office of Adoptions
Two Peachtree Street NW, Suite 323
Atlanta, GA 30303-3142
Phone: (404) 657-3555
Toll-Free: (888) 328-0055
Web site: www.adoptions.dhr.state.ga.us/reunion.htm

Statewide Adoption Recruitment Line

Georgia Statewide Adoption Recruitment Line
Toll-Free: (877)-210-KIDS

Statewide Foster Care Recruitment Line

Georgia Statewide Foster Care Recruitment Line
Toll-Free: (877)-210-KIDS

HAWAII

Adoptive/Foster Family Support Groups

Casey Family Program
98-1688 Laauhuahua Place
Pearl City, HI 96782
Phone: (808) 454-1653
Fax: (808) 533-1018
E-mail: nmatsumoto@hawaii.rr.com

Kauai Adoption and Permanency Alliance
2970 Kele Street, Suite 203
Lihue Kauai, HI 96746
Phone: (808) 240-2844
Phone: (808) 245-1815
Fax: (808) 245-5325
After hours: (808) 645-0126

E-mail: pchock@cfs-hawaii.org; kamika@hawaii.rr.com

Resolve of HI-Kafuai Site
3721-A Omao Road
Koloa, HI 96756
Phone: (808) 742-8885

Resources for Life
59-349 Olomana Road
Kamuela, HI 96743
Phone: (808) 880-1412

Stars of David International, Inc.
Shaloha Chapter
P.O. Box 61595
Honolulu, HI 96839
Phone: (808) 988-1989
Fax: (808) 988-1989
E-mail: wolffwrite@aol.com
Web site: www.starsofdavid.org

Licensed Private Adoption Agencies

Adopt International
820 Mililani Street, Suite 401
Honolulu, HI 96813
Phone: (808) 523-1400
Fax: (808) 969-6665
Toll-Free: (800) 969-6665
E-mail: adoptinter@aol.com
Web site: www.adopt-intl.org
— Intercountry Program
— Child Placement

Adoption Choices
210 Ward Avenue, Suite 324
Honolulu, HI 96814
Toll-Free: (800) 898-6028

Casey Family Program
1848 Nuuanu Avenue
Honolulu, HI 96817
Phone: (808) 521-9531
Web site: www.casey.org

Casey Family Program
96 Puuhonu Place
Hilo, HI 96720
Phone: (808) 935-2876

Catholic Charities Family
Services
200 North Vineyard Boulevard,
Suite 200
Honolulu, HI 96817
Phone: (808) 536-1794
Fax: (808) 535-0187
– Intercountry Program
– Child Placement

Child and Family Services
200 North Vineyard Boulevard,
Building B
Honolulu, HI 96817
– Intercountry Program
– Child Placement

Crown Child Placement
International, Inc.
P.O. Box 3990
Malini, HI 96789
Phone: (808) 946-0443
Toll-Free: (800) 860-0035
– Intercountry Program
– Child Placement

Hawaii International Child
Placement and Family
Services, Inc.
1168 Waimanu Street
Honolulu, HI 96814
Phone: (808) 589-2367
Fax: (808) 593-2247
E-mail: adopt@h-i-c.org
Web site: www.h-i-c.org
– Intercountry Program
– Child Placement

LDS Family Services Hawaii
Honolulu Agency
1500 South Beretania Street,
Suite 403
Honolulu, HI 96826
Phone: (808) 945-3690
Fax: (808) 945-2811
E-mail: fam-hi@ldschurch.org

Queen Liliuokalani Children's
Center
1300 Halona Street
Honolulu, HI 96817
Phone: (808) 847-1302

**Regional/District
Public Agencies**

Department of Human
Services
Social Service Division,
East Hawaii
75 Aupuni Street, Suite 112
Hilo, HI 96720
Phone: (808) 933-0689

Department of Human
Services
Social Service Division, Kauai
3060 Eiwa Street,
Room 104
Lihue, HI 96766-1890
Phone: (808) 274-3300

Department of Human
Services
Social Service Division, Maui
1955 Main Street, Suite 300
Wailuku, HI 96793
Phone: (808) 243-5256

Department of Human
Services
Social Service Division, Oahu
420 Waiakamilo Road,
Suite 300B
Honolulu, HI 96817-4941
Phone: (808) 832-5451

Department of Human
Services
Social Service Division,
West Hawaii
Captain Cook State Civic Center,
Box 230
Captain Cook, HI 96704
Phone: (808) 323-4581

**Birth Family and Search
Support Groups**

Access Hawaii and Concerned
United Birthparents
P.O. Box 1120
Hilo, HI 96721
Phone: (808) 965-7185

Adoption Circle of Hawaii
P.O. Box 61723
Honolulu, HI 96839-1723
Phone: (808) 591-3834

Adoption Support Group
P.O. Box 8377
Honolulu, HI 96815

Committee on Adoption
Reform and Education
55 Niuiki Circle
Honolulu, HI 96815
Phone: (808) 377-2345

Concerned United Birthparents
P.O. Box 37838
Honolulu, HI 96837

Concerned United Birthparents
15-2682 He'e Street
Pahoa, HI 96778

**State Adoption Exchange/
Photolisting of Children
Waiting For Adoption**

Central Adoption Exchange of
Hawaii
810 Richards Street, Suite 400
Honolulu, HI 96813
Phone: (808) 586-5698
Fax: (808) 586-4806

**State Adoption
Specialist/Manager**

Hawaii Department of Human
Services
810 Richards Street, Suite 400
Honolulu, HI 96813
Phone: (808) 586-5698
Fax: (808) 586-4806
E-mail: lkazama@dhs.hawaii.gov
Web site: www.state.hi.us/dhs/
index.html

State Foster Care Specialist/Manager

Hawaii Department of Human Services
Child Welfare Services Division
810 Richards Street, Suite 400
Honolulu, HI 96813
Phone: (808) 586-5698
Fax: (808) 586-4806

State Interstate Compact on the Placement of Children (ICPC) Administrator

Hawaii Department of Human Services
810 Richards Street, Suite 400
Honolulu, HI 96813
Phone: (808) 586-5699
Fax: (808) 586-4806

State Licensing Specialist

Hawaii Department of Human Services
810 Richards Street, Suite 400
Honolulu, HI 96813
Phone: (808) 586-5698
Fax: (808) 586-4806
Web site: www.state.hi.us/dhs/

State Reunion Registry

Family Court Central Registry
Court Management Services
777 Punchbowl Street
P.O. Box 3498
Honolulu, HI 96811
Phone: (808) 539-4424
Web site: www.state.hi.us/jud

Statewide Adoption Recruitment Line

Hawaii Statewide Adoption Recruitment Line
Toll-Free: (808) 441-0999

Statewide Foster Care Recruitment Line

Hawaii Statewide Foster Care Recruitment Line
Toll-Free: (800) 995-7949

IDAHO

Adoptive/Foster Family Support Groups

Families Involved in Adoption
P.O. Box 612
Priest River, ID 83856

Families Together
2714 – 8th Avenue
Lewiston, ID 83501

Families of M.A.C. (Multicultural and Adopted Children)
2820 Shamrock
Nampa, ID 83686
Phone: (208) 463-4040
E-mail: seward@worldnet.att.net
Web site: www.familiesofmac.com

North American Council on Adoptable Children
1301 Spokane Street
Post Falls, ID 83854
Phone: (208) 773-5629
E-mail: info@nacac.org
Web site: www.nacac.org

Licensed Private Adoption Agencies

Bannock Youth Foundation
P.O. Box 246
Pocatello, ID 83206
Phone: (208) 667-1898

CASI Foundation For Children
2308 North Cole Road, Suite E
Boise, ID 83704
Phone: (208) 376-0558
Fax: (208) 376-1931
Toll-Free: (800) 376-0558
E-mail: info@adoptcasi.org
Web site: www.adoptcasi.org

– Intercountry Program
– Child Placement

Idaho Youth Ranch Adoption Services
P.O. Box 8538
Boise, ID 83704
Phone: (208) 377-2613
Fax: (208) 377-2819
E-mail: lcorpus@youthranch.org
Web site: www.youthranch.org

Idaho Youth Ranch Adoption and Foster Care Services
2201 Government Way, Suite J
Coeur D'Alene, ID 83814
Phone: (208) 667-1898
E-mail: adoptionsnorth@youthranch.org
Web site: www.youthranch.org

LDS Family Services, Inc.
1169 Call Creek Place, Suite B
Pocatello, ID 83201
Phone: (208) 232-7780
Fax: (208) 232-7782
E-mail: fam-id-pocatello@ldschurch.org

Lutheran Community Services Northwest
2201 Government Way, Suite J
Coeur d'Alene, ID 83814
Phone: (360) 354-7867

Birth Family and Search Support Groups

American Adoption Congress State Representative
4348 Maverick Way
Boise, ID 83709
Phone: (208) 362-2281
E-mail: MTYMO@aol.com

Search Finders of Idaho
P.O. Box 7941
Boise, ID 83707
Phone: (208) 375-9803

Triad Endeavors
P.O. Box 249
Pinehurst, ID 83850

**State Adoption Exchange/
Photolisting of Children
Waiting For Adoption**

Idaho Department of Health
and Welfare
Division of Family and Community
Services
P.O. Box 83720
450 West State Street
Boise, ID 83720-0036
Phone: (208) 334-5700
Fax: (208) 334-6664
Toll-Free: (800) 926-2588
Web site: www2.state.id.us/
dhw/Adoption/index.htm

**State Adoption
Specialist/Manager**

Idaho Department of Health
and Welfare
Division of Family and Community
Services
P.O. Box 83720
450 West State Street, 5th Floor
Boise, ID 83720-0036
Phone: (208) 334-5700
Fax: (208) 334-6664
Web site: www2.state.id.us/
dhw/Adoption

**State Foster Care
Specialist/Manager**

Idaho Department of Health
and Welfare
Division of Family and Community
Services
P.O. Box 83720
450 West State Street, 5th Floor
Boise, ID 83720-0036
Phone: (208) 334-5695
Fax: (208) 334-6664
E-mail: harmerm2@idhw.state.
id.us
Web site: www2.state.id.us/
dhw/Adoption

**State Interstate Compact on
the Placement of Children
(ICPC) Administrator**

Idaho Department of Health
and Welfare
Division of Family and Community
Services
P.O. Box 83720
450 West State Street
Boise, ID 83720
Phone: (208) 334-5500
Fax: (208) 334-6699

State Licensing Specialist

Idaho Department of Health
and Welfare
Division of Family and Community
Services
P.O. Box 83720
450 West State Street
Boise, ID 83720-0036
Phone: (208) 334-5702
Fax: (208) 334-6664
E-mail: vandusen@idhw.state.
id.us

State Reunion Registry

Voluntary Adoption Registry,
Vital Records Section
Center for Vital Statistics and
Health Policy
P.O. Box 83720
450 West State Street
Boise, ID 83720-0036
Phone: (208) 334-5990
Web site: www2.state.id.us/
dhw/vital_stats/adopt/var.htm

ILLINOIS

**Adoptive/Foster Family
Support Groups**

Adoption Information Center
120 West Madison, Suite 800
Chicago, IL 60602
Phone: (312) 346-1516
Fax: (312) 346-0004
E-mail: www.adoptinfo-il.org

Adoptive Families Today
P.O. Box 1726
Barrington, IL 60011
Phone: (847) 382-0858
Fax: (847) 382-0831
E-mail: adopadvo@aol.com
Web site: www.
adoptivefamiliestoday.org

Akokanan Adoptive Parents
Coalition
5539 West Jackson Boulevard
Chicago, IL 60644
Phone: (773) 722-7900
After hours: (773) 261-9170

All-Adopt Support Group
727 Ramona Place
Godfrey, IL 62035
Phone: (618) 466-8926

Attachment Disorder Network
17572 West Bridle Trail Road
Gurnee, IL 60031
Phone: (847) 855-8676
Fax: (847) 855-8702
E-mail: nancyadn@earthlink.net
Web site: www.radzebra.org

Beatrice Caffrey Youth
Services
5401 South Wentworth, #201
Chicago, IL 00006-0609
Phone: (773) 285-8644
Fax: (773) 285-8633

Bridge Communication
221 North LaSalle, Suite 1100
Chicago, IL 60601
Phone: (312) 377-2748
Fax: (312) 220-0004
Web site: www.
bridgecommunications.org

Chicago Area Families for
Adoption
PMB 108
1212 Naper Boulevard, Suite 119
Naperville, IL 60540-8360
Phone: (708) 235-3994
Fax: (630) 839-7580
After hours: (630) 585-4680

E-mail: info@caffa.org
Web site: www.caffa.org

Child International
4121 Crestwood
Northbrook, IL 60062
Phone: (847) 272-2511

Friends of the Cradle
2049 Ridge Avenue
Evanston, IL 60201
Phone: (847) 475-5800
Fax: (847) 475-5871
Web site: www.cradle.org

Illinois Coalition for TRUTH in Adoption
1904 West Dickens Avenue
Chicago, IL 60614
Phone: (773) 235-7632
E-mail: Iltreesurgeon@aol.com
Web site: www.prairienet.
org/icta

Illinois Council on Adoptable Children (COAC)
6119 North Hawthorne
Rosemont, IL 60018
Phone: (847) 698-3668
Fax: (630) 629-1926

Illinois Foster Parent Association
665 Silver Creek Road
Woodstock, IL 60098
Phone: (217) 448-4191
Web site: www.
illinoisfosterparent.org

New Family
1365 Wiley Road, Suite 153
Schaumburg, IL 00006-0173
Phone: (847) 755-0576
Fax: (847) 755-0822

North American Council on Adoptable Children Representative
487 Bradford Place
Bolingbrook, IL 60440
Phone: (312) 633-3425
Web site: www.nacac.org

Pamark Support Group
1037 South Des Plaines Avenue,
Unit 306
Forest Park, IL 60130
Phone: (708) 378-3300
Fax: (708) 366-8319
After hours: (708) 366-8318
E-mail: pamarkii@cs.com

Royal Family Support Group
7428 Washington Street,
Unit 505
Forest Park, IL 60130
Phone: (773) 620-3874
Fax: (708) 488-1669
E-mail:
gervaiseassociates@yahoo.com

Special Needs Adoption Support Group
Lifelink/Bensenville Home
Society
331 York Road
Bensenville, IL 60106
Phone: (630) 766-5800
Fax: (630) 521-8844
E-mail: alladopt@lifelink.org
Web site: www.lifelinkadoption.org

Stars of David International, Inc.
Chicago Area Chapter
3175 Commercial Avenue,
Suite 100
Northbrook, IL 60062-1915
Phone: (847) 509-9929
Fax: (847) 509-9545
Toll-Free: (800) 782-7349
E-mail: StarsDavid@aol.com
Web site: www.starsofdavid.org

We Care Parent Support Group
132 North Karlov
Chicago, IL 60624
Phone: (773) 863-5694
After hours: (773) 722-6312
E-mail: PFFC@Softhome.net

Licensed Private Adoption Agencies

Adoption World
211 East Ontario Street,
Suite 1010
Chicago, IL 00006-0611
Phone: (312) 664-8933
– Intercountry Program
– Child Placement

Adoption-Link, Inc.
1145 Westgate, Suite 104
Oak Park, IL 60301
Phone: (708) 524-1433
Fax: (708) 524-9691
Web site: www.
adoptionlinkillinois.com

Aunt Martha's Youth Services
233 West Joe Orr Road
Chicago Heights, IL 60411-1744
Phone: (708) 754-1044

Aurora Catholic Social Services
1700 North Farnsworth Avenue,
Suite 18
Aurora, IL 60505
Phone: (708) 892-4366

Baby Fold
612 Oglesby Road, Suite A
Normal, IL 61761
Phone: (309) 454-1770
Fax: (309) 454-9257
E-mail: kblum@thebabyfold.org

Bethany Christian Services
9718 South Halsted Street
Chicago, IL 60628-1007
Phone: (773) 233-7600
Fax: (773) 233-7617
E-mail: bcschicago@bethany.org
Web site: www.bethany.org
– Intercountry Program
– Child Placement

Catholic Charities, Chicago Archdiocese
651 West Lake
Chicago, IL 60661
Phone: (312) 655-7000
E-mail: ccadoptions@earthlink.net
Web site: http:/www.
catholiccharities.net/
workingadoption.htm
– Intercountry Program
– Child Placement

Center for Family Building, Inc.
1740 Ridge Avenue, Suite 208
Evanston, IL 60201
Phone: (847) 869-1518
Fax: (847) 869-4108
E-mail: info@centerforfamily.com
Web site: www.centerforfamily.
com

Chicago Child Care Society
5467 South University Avenue
Chicago, IL 60615
Phone: (773) 643-0452
Web site: www.cccsociety.org

Chicago Youth Centers
10 West 35th Street
Chicago, IL 60616
Phone: (312) 225-8200
Fax: (312) 225-9008
Web site: www.
chicagoyouthcenters.org

Children's Home and Aid Society of Illinois
Rockford, IL 61104
Phone: (815) 962-1043
Fax: (815) 962-1272
Toll-Free: (888) 248-4335
E-mail: adopt@nw.chasi.org
Web site: www.chasisystems.org

Children's Home and Aid Society of Illinois
125 South Wacker Drive,
14th Floor
Chicago, IL 60606
Phone: (312) 424-0200
Web site: www.chasi.org

Counseling and Family Service
330 SW Washington
Peoria, IL 61602
Phone: (309) 676-2400

Cradle
2049 Ridge Avenue
Evanston, IL 60201
Phone: (847) 475-5800
Fax: (847) 475-5871
Toll-Free: (800) 272-3534
E-mail: cradle@cradle.org
Web site: www.cradle.org
– Intercountry Program
– Child Placement

Evangelical Child and Family Agency
1530 North Main Street
Wheaton, IL 60187
Phone: (630) 653-6400
Toll-Free: (800) 526-0844
E-mail: EvanCFA@aol.com
Web site: www.evancfa.org
– Intercountry Program
– Child Placement

Family Counseling Clinic, Inc.
505 East Hawley Street,
Suite 100
Mundlein, IL 60060
Phone: (847) 566-7121
Fax: (847) 566-7310
– Intercountry Program
– Child Placement

Family Resource Center
5828 North Clark Street
Chicago, IL 60660
Phone: (773) 334-2300
Fax: (773) 334-8228
Toll-Free: (800) 676-2229
E-mail: adoption@adoptillinois.org
Web site: www.adoptillinois.org
– Intercountry Program
– Child Placement

Family Service Agency of Adams County
915 Vermont Street
Quincy, IL 62301
Phone: (217) 222-8254

Family Service Center of Sangamon County
1308 South Seventh Street
Springfield, IL 62703
Phone: (217) 528-8406
Fax: (217) 528-8542
Web site: www.service2families.
com
– Intercountry Program
– Child Placement

Glenkirk
2501 North Chestnut
Arlington Heights, IL 60004
Phone: (847) 998-8380
E-mail: adopt@glenkirk.org
Web site: www.glenkirk.org/
services/adoption.html

Hobby Horse House
Jacksonville, IL 62651-1102
Phone: (217) 243-7708
– Intercountry Program
– Child Placement

Hope for the Children
1530 Fairway Drive
Rantoul, IL 61866
Phone: (217) 893-4673
Fax: (217) 893-3126
E-mail: h4tc@soltec.net
Web site: www.hope4children.org

Illinois Baptist Children's Home
4243 Lincolnshire Drive
Mt. Vernon, IL 62864
Phone: (618) 242-4944
E-mail: carladonoho@bchfs.com
Web site: www.bchfs.com/
mtvernon.html

Illinois Children's Christian Home
P.O. Box 200
St. Joseph, IL 61873
Phone: (217) 469-7566

Jewish Children's Bureau of Chicago
1 South Franklin Street
Chicago, IL 60606
Phone: (312) 444-2090
Web site: www.jcbchicago.org

Journeys of the Heart Adoption Services

P.O. Box 28
Glen Ellyn, IL 60138
Phone: (630) 469-4367
Fax: (630) 469-4382
E-mail: JOHChicago@aol.com
Web site: www.
journeysoftheheart.net
– Intercountry Program
– Child Placement

Lifelink Adoption Services

4500 Spring Creek Road
Rockford, IL 00006-1114
Phone: (815) 639-0967
Web site: www.lifelinkadoption.
org

Lifelink/Bensenville Home Society

331 South York Road
Bensenville, IL 60106
Phone: (630) 521-8281
E-mail: alladopt@lifelink.org
Web site: www.lifelinkadoption.
org
– Intercountry Program
– Child Placement

Lutheran Social Services of Illinois

Chicago South Office
11740 South Western Avenue
Chicago, IL 60643
Phone: (773) 371-2700
Fax: (773) 239-5296
Web site: www.lssi.org

New Life Social Services

6316 North Lincoln Ave
Chicago, IL 60659
Phone: (773) 478-4773
Fax: (773) 478-7646
E-mail: info@nlss.org
Web site: www.nlss.org
– Intercountry Program
– Child Placement

Saint Mary's Services

717 West Kirchoff Road
Arlington Heights, IL 60005

Phone: (847) 870-8181
Fax: (847) 870-8323
Web site: http://homepage@
interaccess.com/~stmary/home.
htm

Sunny Ridge Family Center, Inc.

2 South 426 Orchard Road
Wheaton, IL 60187
Phone: (630) 668-5117
Fax: (630) 668-5144
E-mail: tjackson@sunnyridge.org
Web site: www.sunnyridge.org
– Intercountry Program
– Child Placement

United Methodist Children's Home

2023 Richview Road
Mt. Vernon, IL 62864
Phone: (618) 242-1070
E-mail: audreyb@umchome.org

Uniting Families Foundation

P.O. Box 755
95 West Grand Avenue, Suite 206
Lake Villa, IL 60046
Phone: (847) 356-1452
Fax: (847) 356-1584
E-mail: UnitingFam@aol.com
Web site: http://members.aol.
com/UnitingFam/index.html
– Intercountry Program
– Child Placement

Volunteers of America of Illinois

224 N. Des Plaines Street,
Suite 500
Chicago, IL 60661
Phone: (312) 707-9477
Web site: www.voaillinois.com

Birth Family and Search Support Groups

AAC/CUB

835 Ridge Avenue, #208
Evanston, IL 60202
Phone: (708) 328-1686

Adoption Search and Support Group

638 South Randolph
Macomb, IL 61455
Phone: (309) 837-9174

Adoption Triangle

Department of Children and
Family Services
200 South Wyman, Suite 200
Rockford, IL 61101-1232
Phone: (815) 987-7117

Adoption Triangle

c/o Children's Home and Aid
Society
1819 South Neil, Suite D
Champaign, IL 61820
Phone: (217) 359-8815

American Adoption Congress

1400 North State Parkway
Chicago, IL 60610
Phone: (312) 642-3617
Web site: www.
americanadoptioncongress.org

Concerned United Birthparents (CUB)

702 East Algonquin Road
Apartment K111
Arlington Heights, IL 60005
Phone: (847) 439-7644
Fax: (847) 439-8799
E-mail: Bonniebis@aol.com
Web site: www.cubirthparents.org

Family Counseling Center/ Catholic Social Services

Birth Mother Support Group
P.O. Box 6629
Champaign, IL 61826-6629
Phone: (217) 352-6565
E-mail: swilson@ccdop.org

Grandparent Support Circle

3333 West Arthrington, #150
Chicago, IL 60624
Phone: (708) 652-1618

Healing Hearts
P.O. Box 606
Normal, IL 61761
Phone: (309) 452-9849

Hidden Birthright
100 Cumberland
Rochester, IL 62563-9238

Lost Connection
2661 North Illinois Street, Suite 147
Belleville, IL 62221
Phone: (618) 235-9409

Midwest Adoption Center
3166 Des Plaines River Road
Des Plaines, IL 60018
Phone: (708) 298-9096

Search Connection
P.O. Box 2425
Brideview, IL 60455
Phone: (708) 430-9133

Truth Seekers in Adoption
4536 Forest
Downers Grove, IL 60515
Phone: (630) 434-8742

**State Adoption Exchange/
Photolisting of Children
Waiting For Adoption**

Adoption Information Center
of Illinois (AICI)
120 West Madison Street,
Suite 800
Chicago, IL 60602
Phone: (312) 346-1516
Fax: (312) 346-0004
Toll-Free: (800) 572-2390
E-mail: aici@adoptinfo-il.org
Web site: www.adoptinfo-il.org

**State Adoption
Specialist/Manager**

Illinois Department of Children
and Family Services
Division of Foster Care and
Permanency Services
100 West Randolph Street,

Suite 6-100
Chicago, IL 60601
Phone: (312) 814-6858
Fax: (312) 814-3255
E-mail: jdorn@idcfs.state.il.us
Web site: www.state.il.us/dcfs

**State Foster Care
Specialist/Manager**

Illinois Department of Children
and Family Services
Division of Foster Care and
Permanency Services
406 East Monroe Street
Station 25
Springfield, IL 62701
Phone: (217) 524-2422
Fax: (217) 524-3966
Web site: www.state.il.us/dcfs

**State Interstate Compact on
the Placement of Children
(ICPC) Administrator**

Illinois Department of Children
and Family Services
Division of Foster Care and
Permanency Services
406 East Monroe Street
Springfield, IL 62701-1498
Phone: (217) 785-2680
Fax: (217) 785-2459

State Licensing Specialist

Illinois Department of Children
and Family Services
Division of Foster Care and
Permanency Services
406 East Monroe Street
Springfield, IL 62701-1498
Phone: (217) 785-2688
Web site: www.state.il.us/dcfs

State Reunion Registry

Illinois Adoption Registry
Illinois Department of Public
Health
535 West Jefferson Street
Springfield, IL 62761

Phone: (217) 557-5159
Toll-Free: (877) 323-5299
E-mail: mailus@idph.state.il.us
Web site: www.idph.state.il.us/
vital/iladoptreg.htm

INDIANA

**Adoptive/Foster Family
Support Groups**

Adoption Discussion Group of
Wayne County
3401 Glen Hills Drive
Richmond, IN 47374
Fax: (765) 966-5641

Adoption Support Connection
21518 Buntzel Bach Road
Guilford, IN 47022
Phone: (812) 487-2108

Adoptive Family Network
306 Sharon Road
West Lafayette, IN 47906

Adult Adoptee Support Group
3615 Eagle Valley Court
Greenwood, IN 46143

Black Adoption Committee
1631 Kessler Boulevard,
West Drive
Indianapolis, IN 46228
Phone: (317) 253-7660
Fax: (317) 259-7628
E-mail: mosesgray@aol.com

Chosen Children Adoption
Services, Inc.
3203 Julian Drive
New Albany, IN 47150
Phone: (812) 945-6021

Coleman Adoption Services,
Inc.
615 North Alabama, Suite 219
Indianapolis, IN 46204
Phone: (317) 638-0965
E-mail: info@colemanadopt.org

Families Adopting Children Together (FACT)
P.O. Box 151
Rural Route 1
Gentryville, IN 47537
Phone: (812) 925-3341

Foster Parents for Early Permanency
2108 Ashwood Lane
Bloomington, IN 47401-9769
Phone: (812) 334-0171

Greater Love Adoption Decision, Inc.
5000 First Avenue
Evansville, IN 47710
Phone: (812) 424-4523

Guardian Angel Adoption Center
2633 East 136th
Carmel, IN 46032
Phone: (317) 581-1620

Indiana Foster Care and Adoption Association
509 East National, Suite A
Indianapolis, IN 46227
Phone: (317) 524-2600
Fax: (317) 524-2609
Toll-Free: (800) 468-4228
Web site: www.ifcaa.org

Kidsfirst Adoption Center, LLC
9135 North Meridian Street, Suite A6
Indianapolis, IN 46260
Phone: (317) 843-2300

Regina Robinson
1770 West 53rd Avenue
Merrillville, IN 46410

Licensed Private Adoption Agencies

A Loving Choice Adoption Agency
6917 Ridgeland Avenue
Hammond, IN 46324
Phone: (219) 989-8088

Web site: www.a-loving-choice. com

Adoption Resource Services, Inc.
218 South Third Street, #2
Elkhart, IN 46516
Phone: (574) 293-0229
Fax: (574) 293-2210
Toll-Free: (800) 288-2499
E-mail: rcmarco@yahoo.com

Adoption Support Center, Inc.
6331 North Carrolton Avenue
Indianapolis, IN 46220
Phone: (317) 255-5916
Toll-Free: (800) 274-1084
– Intercountry Program
– Child Placement

Adoptions of Indiana, Inc. (AD-IN, Inc.)
1980 East 116th Street, Suite 325
Carmel, IN 46032
Phone: (317) 574-8950
Fax: (317) 574-8971
Toll-Free: (888) 573-0122
E-mail: msterchi@ad-in.org
Web site: www.ad-in.org

Americans for African Adoptions, Inc.
8910 Timberwood Drive
Indianapolis, IN 46234-1952
Phone: (317) 271-4567
Fax: (317) 271-8739
E-mail: info@africanadoptions.org
Web site: www.africanadoptions. org
– Intercountry Program
– Child Placement

Baptist Children's Home and Family Ministries, Inc.
354 West Street
Valparaiso, IN 46383
Phone: (219) 462-4111
Fax: (219) 464-9540
Web site: www. baptistchildrenshome.org

Bethany Christian Services
5650 Caito Drive
Indianapolis, IN 46226-1346
Phone: (317) 568-1000
Fax: (317) 541-4646
E-mail: bcsindianapolis@bethany. org
Web site: www.bethany.org/ indiana
– Intercountry Program
– Child Placement

Center for Family Building, Inc.
8231 Hohman Avenue, Suite 200, #3
Munster, IN 46321
Phone: (219) 836-0163
E-mail: info@centerforfamily.com
Web site: www.centerforfamily. com

Childplace, Inc.
2420 Highway 62
Jeffersonville, IN 47130
Phone: (812) 282-8248
Fax: (812) 282-3291
Toll-Free: (800) 787-9084
Web site: www.childplace.org

Children Are the Future
504 Broadway, Suite 725
Gary, IN 46402
Phone: (219) 881-0750

Children's Bureau of Indianapolis, Inc.
615 North Alabama Street, Suite 426
Indianapolis, IN 46204
Phone: (317) 264-2700
Fax: (317) 264-2714
E-mail: cbinfo@childrensbureau. org
Web site: www.childrensbureau. org

Coleman Adoption Agency
615 North Alabama Street,
Suite 219
Indianapolis, IN 46204
Phone: (317) 368-0965
Fax: (317) 638-0973
Toll-Free: (800) 886-3434
E-mail: priscillak@colemanadopt.
org
Web site: www.colemanadopt.org

Compassionate Care
P.O. Box 12B
Highway 69 West, Route 3,
Wilder Center
Oakland City, IN 47660
Phone: (812) 749-4152
Fax: (812) 749-8190
Toll-Free: (800) 749-4153
E-mail: comcare@gibsoncounty.
net
Web site: www.
compassionatecareadopt.org

**Families Thru International
Adoption**
dba China's Children
400 Bentee Wes Court
Evansville, IN 47715
Phone: (812) 479-9900
Fax: (812) 479-9901
Toll-Free: (888) 797-9900
E-mail: adopt@ftia.org
Web site: www.ftia.org
— Intercountry Program
— Child Placement

Family and Children's Services
655 South Hebron Avenue
Evansville, IN 47714
Phone: (812) 424-4523

G.L.A.D.
P.O. Box 9105
Evansville, IN 47724
Phone: (812) 424-4523
Fax: (812) 424-3180
E-mail: glad@sigecom.net

**Hand In Hand International
Adoptions**
210 A North Orange Street
Albion, IN 46701
Phone: (260) 636-3566
Fax: (260) 636-2554
E-mail: Indiana@hihiadopt.org
Web site: www.hihiadopt.org
— Intercountry Program
— Child Placement

Independent Adoption Center
5224 South East Street,
Suite C10
Indianapolis, IN 46227
Phone: (317) 788-1039
Fax: (317) 788-1094
Toll-Free: (800) 877-6736
E-mail: kathyw@adoptionhelp.org
Web site: www.adoptionhelp.org

**Indiana One Church, One Child
Program, Inc.**
850 North Meridian Street
Indianapolis, IN 46204
Phone: (317) 684-2181
Toll-Free: (800) 323-1660

Indiana Youth Advocate Program
4755 Kingsway Drive, Suite 314
Indianapolis, IN 46205
Phone: (317) 475-9294
Fax: (317) 475-0081
Toll-Free: (800) 471-4795
E-mail: kmc303@comcast.net
Web site: www.nyap.org

LDS Family Services
3333 Founders Road, Suite 200
Indianapolis, IN 46268-1397
Phone: (317) 872-1749
Toll-Free: (877) 872-1749

Loving Option
P.O. Box 172
206 South Main Street
Bluffton, IN 46714
Phone: (260) 824-9077

**Lutheran Child and Family
Services**
1525 North Ritter Avenue
Indianapolis, IN 46219
Phone: (317) 359-5467
Fax: (317) 322-4095
E-mail: wpierce@lutheranfamily.
org
Web site: www.lutheranfamily.org

Open Arms Christian Homes
P.O. Box 37A
Route 2
Bloomfield, IN 47424
Phone: (812) 659-2533

**Specialized Alternatives for
Families and Youth of America
(SAFY)**
2100 Goshen Road
Ft. Wayne, IN 46808
Phone: (260) 422-3672
Web site: www.safy.org

St. Elizabeth's
2500 Churchman Avenue
Indianapolis, IN 46203
Phone: (317) 787-3412
Toll-Free: (800) 499-9113
E-mail: stelizabeths@stelizabe
ths.org
Web site: www.stelizabeths.org

St. Elizabeth's Regional Maternity Center
601 East Market Street
New Albany, IN 47150
Phone: (812) 949-7305
Fax: (812) 941-7008
E-mail: dbarber43@aol.com
Web site: www.stelizabeth.org

**Sunny Ridge Family Center,
Inc.**
900 Ridge Road, Suite H
Munster, IN 46321
Phone: (219) 836-2117
Fax: (219) 836-2621
Web site: www.sunnyridge.org
— Intercountry Program
— Child Placement

The Villages
2405 North Smith Pike
Bloomington, IN 47404
Phone: (812) 332-1245
Toll-Free: (800) 874-6880
Web site: www.villages.org

**Local/Regional Offices
of the State (Public)
Adoption Agency**

Indiana Division of Family and
Children
P.O. Box 227
1145 Bollman Street
Decatur, IN 46733
Phone: (260) 724-9169
Fax: (219) 724-9632
Toll-Free: (800) 262-2347
Web site: www.in.gov/fssa/
children/dfc/directory/index.html

Indiana Division of Family and
Children
401 East Miller Drive
Bloomington, IN 47401
Phone: (812) 336-6351
Web site: www.in.gov/fssa/
children/dfc/directory/index.html

**Birth Family and Search
Support Groups**

Adoptee Identity Doorway/
Reunion Registry of Indiana
P.O. Box 361
South Bend, IN 46624
Phone: (219) 272-3520

Adoptees Birthparents and
Siblings Enlightenment
Network of Thorntown
(A.B.S.E.N.T.)
711 W. Plum Street
Thorntown, IN 46071-1249
Phone: (765) 436-7257

Adoption Triangle NW Indiana
7361 Wilson Place
Merryillville, IN 46410
Phone: (219) 736-5515

Coping with Adoption
61 Country Farm Road
Peru, IN 46970
Phone: (765) 472-7425

Lafayette Adoption Search/
Support Organization
5936 Lookout Drive
West Lafayette, IN 47906
Phone: (765) 567-4139

Reflections
7401 Washington Avenue
Evansville, IN 47715-4513

Search Committee
Madison County Historical Society
P.O. Box 523
Anderson, IN 46016
Phone: (765) 641-2442
E-mail: HWLeedom@aol.com

**State Adoption Exchange/
Photolisting of Children
Waiting For Adoption**

Indiana Adoption Resource
Exchange
509 East National Avenue
Indianapolis, IN 46277
Web site: www.state.in.us/fssa/
adoption/index.html

**State Adoption
Specialist/Manager**

Indiana Division of Family and
Children
Bureau of Family Protection and
Preservation
402 West Washington Street
3rd Floor, W-364
Indianapolis, IN 46204
Phone: (317) 233-1743
Fax: (317) 232-4436
Toll-Free: (888) 204-7466
Web site: www.in.gov/fssa/
adoption/index.html

**State Foster Care
Specialist/Manager**

Indiana Family and Social Ser-
vices Administration
Warren County Department of
Families and Children
20 West 2nd Street
Williamsport, IN 47993
Phone: (765) 762-6125
Fax: (765) 762-8017
E-mail: measter@fssa.state.in.us
Web site: www.state.in.us/fssa/
adoption/index.html

**State Interstate Compact on
the Placement of Children
(ICPC) Administrator**

Indiana Division of Family and
Children
Bureau of Family Protection and
Preservation
402 Washington Street,
Room W-364
Indianapolis, IN 46201
Phone: (317) 232-4769
Fax: (317) 232-4436
E-mail: ningle@fssa.state.in.us
Web site: www.state.in.us/fssa/
adoption

State Licensing Specialist

Indiana Division of Family and
Children
402 West Washington Street,
Room W-364
Indianapolis, IN 46201
Phone: (317) 232-3476

State Reunion Registry

Indiana Adoption History
Registry
Indiana State Department of
Health, Vital Statistics
2 North Meridian Street
Section B-4
Indianapolis, IN 46204
Phone: (317) 233-7253
Phone: (317) 233-7279

IOWA

Adoptive/Foster Family Support Groups

Adoptive Families of Greater Des Moines
1690 Northwest Drive
Des Moines, IA 50310

Allison Area Foster Parent Support Group
2004 11th Street SE
Waverly, IA 50677
Phone: (319) 352-2197
Fax: (319) 252-8581
E-mail: magnall_ifapa@msn.com

Avalon Center
114 4th Street NW
Mason City, IA 50401
Phone: (641) 422-0070
Fax: (641) 422-0060
E-mail: leah@avaloncenter.us
Web site: www.avaloncenter.us
– Intercountry Program
– Home Study

Black Hawk County Foster Parent Support Group
800 Blackhawk Road
Waterloo, IA 50701-9213
Phone: (319) 236-0863

Black Hawk Foster Parent Support Group
1459 West 2nd Street
Waterloo, IA 50701
Phone: (319) 234-0835

Boone and Story County Foster Parent Support Group
P.O. Box 1628
Ames, IA 50010
Phone: (515) 233-6011

Boone/Story County Adoption Support Group
817 Keeler
Boone, IA 50036
Phone: (515) 433-7836

Charlton Valley Foster Parents
P.O. Box 78
Rural Route 8
Bloomfield, IA 52537
Phone: (515) 642-3334

Child Connect Foster Parent Support Group
705 Douglas, Suite 652
Sioux City, IA 51101
Phone: (712) 255-9061
E-mail: mlnitzschke@cableone.net

Children and Families of Iowa
1111 University Avenue
Des Moines, IA 50314
Phone: (515) 288-1981
Fax: (515) 288-9109
E-mail: agencyinfo@cfiowa.org
Web site: www.cfiowa.org

Children and Families of Iowa
Fort Dodge Office
1728 Central Avenue, #10
Fort Dodge, IA 50501-4200
Phone: (641) 573-2193

Climbing Hill Support Group
3047 – 290th Street
Hornick, IA 51206
Phone: (712) 874-3415

Council Bluffs Foster and Adoptive Parents
436 South First
Council Bluffs, IA 51503
Phone: (712) 323-0983

Dallas County Adoption Support Group
Madison/Warren Counties
Adoption Support Group
1111 University Avenue
Des Moines, IA 50314
Phone: (641) 288-1981, ext. 332
Fax: (641) 246-1245
E-mail: ruthannj@cfiowa.org
Web site: www.cfiowa.org

Delaware County Foster Parent Association
Rural Route 1
Ryan, IA 52330

Des Moines/Henry/Louisa Support Group
2155 – 120th Street
Windfield, IA 52659
Phone: (319) 254-2223

Dubuque County Foster Parent Association
1270 Kelly Lane
Dubuque, IA 52003

Eastern IA Foster and Adoptive Parent Association
1612 – 9th Street NW
Clinton, IA 52732
Phone: (319) 242-2644

Family Connections and North American
Council on Adoptable Children
Representative
66684 110th Street
McCallsburg, IA 50154

Floyd, Chickasaw, Mitchell County Foster Parent Association
P.O. Box 65
Marble Rock, IA 50653-0065
Phone: (641) 228-2350

Forest Ridge Foster Parent Group
P.O. Box 515
Estherville, IA 51334-0515
Phone: (712) 362-7026
Fax: (712) 362-7254

Forever Families
24096 Road L34
Underwood, IA 51576
Phone: (712) 328-9490
E-mail: timhack@aol.com

Fort Dodge Area/Webster County Support Group
95 Forest Boulevard
Humboldt, IA 50548-1811
Phone: (641) 573-3880

Foster and Adoptive Parents Association of Greater Des Moines
502 South Columbus Street
Pleasantville, IA 50225-9363
Phone: (641) 274-4648

HARMONY Foster and Adoptive Parent Support Group
P.O. Box 174
Rural Route 2
Woodbine, IA 51579

Humboldt Foster/Adoptive Support Group
301 5th Street, North
Humboldt, IA 50548
Phone: (515) 332-1003

Iowa City Area Adoptive Families
2840 Brookside
Iowa City, IA 52245
Phone: (319) 351-9079

Iowa Connects
149 – 35th Place
Runnells, IA 50237
Phone: (515) 966-2565
Fax: (515) 462-2024
E-mail: iaconnects@aol.com
Web site: http://hometwon.aol.com/iaconnects/myhomepage.html

Iowa Foster and Adoptive Parents Association (IFAPA)
6864 NE 14th Street, Suite 5
Ankeny, IA 50021
Phone: (515) 965-9245
Fax: (515) 289-2080
Toll-Free: (800) 277-8145
E-mail: ifapa@ifapa.org
Web site: www.ifapa.com

JAMS
8124 Main
Reasnor, IA 50323
Phone: (641) 793-2361

Jackson/Jones Co Foster and Adoptive Parent Association
16186 308th Avenue
Bellevue, IA 52031
Phone: (563) 672-3622

Jasper County Support Group
5351 Liberty Avenue
Newton, IA 50208

Kris and Greg Vierkant
1722 East Clark
Charles City, IA 50616
Phone: (641) 228-7971

Lutheran Social Services
1812 – 24th Avenue West
Spencer, IA 51301
Phone: (712) 262-9171

Lutheran Social Services
4240 Hickory Lane
Sioux City, IA 51106
Phone: (712) 276-1073

Marshall County/Quakerdale Support Group
P.O. Box 8
c/o Catherine Hurd
New Providence, IA 50206
Phone: (515) 488-2410

Mike and Becky Wetter
304 – 29th SW
Mason City, IA 50401
Phone: (641) 423-4188

Muscatine Foster/Adoptive Parent Group
2038 Captains Court
Muscatine, IA 52761
Phone: (319) 263-8357

North Central Foster Parent Association
2315 Rake Avenue
Garner, IA 50438
Phone: (641) 923-2618

Northeast Iowa Foster Parent Support Group
1622 4th Street
Boone, IA 50036-3714
Phone: (319) 387-0646

Osky Cluster Foster and Adoptive Parent Group
2386 LaVeen Avenue
Oskaloosa, IA 52577
Phone: (515) 673-7296

Ours Through Adoption
2618 Arlington Avenue
Davenport, IA 52803
Phone: (319) 322-6469

Quad Cities Special Needs Adoption Group
509 Fulton Street
Grand Mound, IA 52571
Phone: (319) 847-1316

Rhonda Neher
26505 K Avenue
Grundy Center, IA 50638
Phone: (319) 824-3286

SW Corner Foster Parent Support Group
103 West Lowell Avenue
Shenandoah, IA 51601
Phone: (712) 246-4733
Toll-Free: (800) 484-6678 (code 9281)

SW IA Adoption Support Group
25375 Ivory Road
Glenwood, IA 51534
Phone: (712) 527-5053

Scott County Foster Parent Association
4022 Greenway Drive
Davenport, IA 52804
Phone: (319) 386-6497

Special Needs Adoption Support Group
111 West 15th Street
Davenport, IA 52803
Phone: (563) 322-7419

T.L.C – Foster and Adoptive Parent Association
208 South Walnut
Lamoni, IA 50140
Phone: (641) 783-2446

Tanager Place – Cedar Rapids
2309 C Street, SW
Cedar Rapids, IA 52404
Phone: (319) 365-9164
Fax: (319) 365-6411
E-mail: info@tanagerplace.org
Web site: www.tanagerplace.org

Warren County Foster Parent Association
Warren County DHS
P.O. Box 729
Indianola, IA 50125

Wayland Area Adoptive Parent Support Group
310 East Main Street
Wayland, IA 52654
Phone: (319) 256-6881
E-mail: mcshumaker@farmtel.net

West Central Iowa Support Group for Foster/Adoptive Parents
420 West 19th Street
Carroll, IA 51401
Phone: (712) 792-9281

West Iowa Adoptive Families
Phone: (712) 676-2288
Phone: (712) 263-5709
E-mail: jclausen@pionet.net

Western Polk County Foster and Adoptive Support Group
6114 Windsor Drive
Des Moines, IA 50312
Phone: (641) 274-2291

Licensed Private Adoption Agencies

4 R Kids
3632 Pierce Street
Sioux City, IA 51104
Phone: (712) 258-8033

Adoption Connection, Ltd.
The Iowa Center for Adoption
315 North Ankeny Boulevard
Ankeny, IA 50021
Phone: (515) 965-8029

Adoption International, Inc.
8450 Hickman Road, Suite 22
Clive, IA 50325
Phone: (515) 727-5840
Fax: (515) 727-5841
E-mail: adoptchild@msn.com
– Intercountry Program
– Child Placement

American Home Finding Association
P.O. Box 656
217 East 5th Street
Ottumwa, IA 52501
Phone: (515) 682-3449

Avalon Center
114 4th Street NW
Mason City, IA 50401
Phone: (641) 422-0070
Fax: (641) 422-0060
E-mail: leah@avaloncenter.us
Web site: www.avaloncenter.us
– Intercountry Program
– Home Study

Baptist Children's Home and Family Ministries
808 SW Ankeny Road
Ankeny, IA 50021-9718
Phone: (515) 964-0986

Bethany Christian Services
Des Moines
8525 Douglas Avenue, Suite 34
Des Moines, IA 50322-3300
Phone: (515) 270-0824
Fax: (515) 270-0605
Toll-Free: (800) 238-4269
E-mail: bcsdesmoines@bethany.org
Web site: www.bethany.org/desmoines
– Intercountry Program
– Child Placement

Catholic Charities Diocese of Des Moines
P.O. Box 723
601 Grand Avenue
Des Moines, IA 50309
Phone: (515) 244-3761

Fax: (515) 237-5070
Toll-Free: (800)-CARE-002
E-mail: mdewitte@dmdiocese.org
Web site: www.dmdiocese.org

Child Connect
705 Douglas Street, Suite 652
Sioux City, IA 51101
Phone: (712) 255-9061

Children and Families of Iowa
Des Moines Office
1111 University Avenue
Des Moines, IA 50314
Phone: (515) 288-1981
Fax: (515) 288-9109
E-mail: agencyinfo@cfiowa.org
Web site: www.cfiowa.org

Children and Families of Iowa
Fort Dodge Office
1728 Central Avenue, Suite 101
Fort Dodge, IA 50501
Phone: (515) 573-2193

Children and Families of Iowa
Creston Office
214 West Montgomery
Creston, IA 50801
Phone: (515) 782-5607

Children's Square U.S.A. Child Connect
P.O. Box 8C
North 6th and Avenue East
Council Bluffs, IA 51502-3008
Phone: (712) 322-3700

Coleman Counseling
601 Humboldt Avenue
Bode, IA 50519
Phone: (515) 379-2101
Fax: (515) 379-2312
– Intercountry Program
– Home Study

Crittenton Center
P.O. Box 295
303 West 24th Street
Sioux City, IA 51102-0295
Phone: (712) 255-4321
Web site: www.crittentoncenter.org

Families of North East Iowa
P.O. Box 806
Maquoketa, IA 52060
Phone: (319) 652-4958

Families, Inc.
P.O. Box 130
101 West Main Street
West Branch, IA 52358
Phone: (319) 643-2532
Fax: (319) 643-5708
E-mail: families@Lcom.net

Family Connections
P.O. Box 374
Schleswig, IA 51461
Phone: (712) 676-2288
Fax: (712) 676-2288
Toll-Free: (888) 723-4887
E-mail: jclausen@pionet.net
Web site: www.family-connections-services.com

Family Resources Adoption Network
1429 LaSalle Avenue
New Hampton, IA 50659
Phone: (641) 394-5800
Fax: (641) 394-5800
E-mail: familyresources@netins.net
Web site: www.familyres.net
– Intercountry Program
– Child Placement

Family Resources Adoption Network
1429 LaSalle Avenue
New Hampton, IA 50659
Phone: (641) 394-5800
Fax: (641) 394-5800
E-mail: familyresources@netins.net
Web site: www.familyres.net
– Intercountry Program
– Child Placement

Family Resources, Inc.
Burlington Office
218 North 3rd Street, Suite 706
Burlington, IA 52601
Toll-Free: (800) 756-1050

First Resources Corporation
Ottumwa Office
835 West Main
Ottumwa, IA 52501
Phone: (515) 856-5382

Four Oaks, Inc.
Cedar Rapids Office
5400 Kirkwood Boulevard SW
Cedar Rapids, IA 52404
Phone: (319) 364-0259
Fax: (319) 364-1162
Web site: www.fouroaks.org

Gift of Love International Adoptions, Inc.
7405 University Boulevard, Suite 8
Des Moines, IA 50325
Phone: (515) 255-3388
Fax: (515) 279-3017
Toll-Free: (877) 282-8015
E-mail: adoption@giftoflove.org
Web site: www.giftoflove.org
– Intercountry Program
– Child Placement

Healing the Children
412 East Church Street
Marshalltown, IA 50158
Phone: (515) 753-7544

Hillcrest Family Services
Cedar Rapids Office
4080 1st Avenue NE, Suite 102A
Cedar Rapids, IA 52402
Phone: (319) 362-3149
Fax: (319) 362-8923
Web site: www.hillcrest-fs.org

Hillcrest Family Services
Dubuque Office
4080 1st Avenue NE, Suite 102A
Cedar Rapids, IA 52402
Phone: (319) 362-3149

Fax: (319) 362-8923
Web site: www.hillcrest-fs.org

Hillcrest Family Services
Maquoketa Office
714 West Platt
Maquoketa, IA 52060
Phone: (563) 652-4958

Holt International Children's Services
P.O. Box 488
103 West Main Street
LeGrand, IA 50142
Phone: (641) 479-2054
– Intercountry Program
– Child Placement

Integrative Health Services, Inc.
P.O. Box 118
223 West Welsh Street
Williamsburg, IA 52361
Phone: (319) 668-2050

Keys to Living
463 Northland Avenue
Cedar Rapids, IA 52402-6237
Phone: (319) 377-2161

LDS Family Services
P.O. Box 65713
3301 Ashworth Road
West Des Moines, IA 50265
Phone: (515) 226-0484

Lutheran Services in Iowa
105 South 7th Street
Denison, IA 51442
Phone: (712) 263-9341
Fax: (712) 263-6061
Toll-Free: (866) 409-2351
Web site: www.lssia.org
– Intercountry Program
– Child Placement

Lutheran Social Service of Iowa
Cedar Rapids Office
5005 Bowling Street SW, Suite B
Cedar Rapids, IA 52404
Phone: (319) 366-2374

Lutheran Social Services in Iowa
3125 Cottage Grove
Des Moines, IA 50311
Phone: (515) 271-4946
Web site: www.lssia.org

New Horizons Adoption Agency Inc.
103 East State Street, Suite 623
Mason City, IA 50402
Phone: (641) 421-7332
Toll-Free: (800) 314-3370
E-mail: nhaa@means.net
Web site: www.
nhadoptionagency.com
– Intercountry Program
– Child Placement

West Iowa Family Services
P.O. Box 178
11 North 7th Street
Denison, IA 51442
Phone: (712) 263-8445
Fax: (712) 263-8445
E-mail: jclausen@pionet.net
Web site: www.family-
connections-services.com

Young House, Inc.
P.O. Box 845
724 North 3rd
Burlington, IA 52601
Phone: (319) 752-4000
Fax: (319) 758-6650
E-mail: jshelman@younghouse.org
Web site: www.younghouse.org

**Local/Regional Offices
of the State (Public)
Adoption Agency**

Iowa Department of Human Services
Web site: www.dhs.state.ia.us/
locations/locations.asp

**Birth Family and Search
Support Groups**

Concerned United Birthpar-
ents (CUB)
National Headquarters
P.O. Box 8151
Des Moines, IA 50306
Phone: (515) 265-4622
Fax: (515) 263-9541
Toll-Free: (800) 822-2777
E-mail: KKC720@aol.com
Web site: www.cubirthparents.org

Concerned United Birthpar-
ents (CUB)
790 Lilly Lane
Boone, IA 50036
Phone: (515) 432-9356
Web site: www.cubirthparents.org

Concerned United Birthparents (CUB)
500 Kimberly Lane
Des Moines, IA 50317

Iowa Reunion Registry
P.O. Box 8
Blairsburg, IA 50034-0008

**State Adoption Exchange/
Photolisting of Children
Waiting For Adoption**

Iowa Department of Human Services
Adoption Resource Exchange
Division of Adult, Children and Family Services
Hoover Building, 5th Floor
1305 East Walnut
Des Moines, IA 50319-0114
Phone: (515) 281-5358
Fax: (515) 281-4597
E-mail: ccarey@dhs.state.ia.us
Web site: www.dhs.state.ia.us/
ACFS/ACFS.asp

Iowa's KidSake Special Needs Adoption Project
6864 NE 14th Street, Suite 5
Ankeny, IA 50021

Phone: (515) 289-4649
Toll-Free: (800) 243-0756
E-mail: info@iakids.org
Web site: www.iakids.org

**State Adoption
Specialist/Manager**

Iowa Department of Human Services
Adult, Children and Family Services
Hoover State Office Building, 5th Floor
1305 East Walnut
Des Moines, IA 50319-0114
Phone: (515) 281-5358
Fax: (515) 281-4597
E-mail: ccarey@dhs.state.ia.us
Web site: www.dhs.state.ia.us/
ACFS/ACFS.asp

**State Foster Care
Specialist/Manager**

Iowa Department of Human Services
Division of Adult, Children and Family Services
Hoover State Office Building, 5th Floor
1305 East Walnut
Des Moines, IA 50319-0114
Phone: (515) 281-5358
Fax: (515) 281-4597
E-mail: ccarey@dhs.state.ia.us

**State Interstate Compact on
the Placement of Children
(ICPC) Administrator**

Iowa Department of Human Services
Adult, Children and Family Services
Hoover State Office Building, 5th Floor
Des Moines, IA 50319
Phone: (515) 281-5730
Fax: (515) 281-4597
Web site: www.dhs.state.ia.us/
ACFS/ACFS.asp

State Licensing Specialist

Iowa Department of Human Services
Adult, Children, and Family Services
Hoover State Office Building,
5th Floor
Des Moines, IA 50319
Phone: (515) 281-6802
Fax: (515) 281-4597
Web site: www.dhs.state.ia.us/
ACFS/ACFS.asp

State Reunion Registry

Iowa Mutual Consent Voluntary Adoption Registry
Iowa Department of Public Health, Bureau of Vital Records
Lucas State Office Building,
1st Floor
321 East 12th Street
Des Moines, IA 50319-0075
Phone: (515) 281-4944
Web site: www.idph.state.ia.us/
pa/vr.htm

Statewide Adoption Recruitment Line

Iowa Statewide Adoption Recruitment Line
Phone: (515) 289-4649
Toll-Free: (800) 243-0756
E-mail: kidsake@iakids.org

Statewide Foster Care Recruitment Line

Iowa Statewide Foster Care Recruitment Line
Phone: (515) 289-4567
Toll-Free: (800) 277-8145
E-mail: kidsake@iakids.org

KANSAS

Adoptive/Foster Family Support Groups

Adoption Concerns Triangle
411 SW Greenwood Avenue
Topeka, KS 66606
Phone: (785) 235-6122
E-mail: waugh5@aol.com
Web site: www.freeyellow.
com/members6/
adoptionconcernstriangle

Adoption Option
7211 West 98 Terrace
#100
Overland Park, KS 66212
Phone: (785) 642-7900

Adoption with Wisdom and Honesty
905 Duffy Road
Hutchison, KS 67501-1955
Phone: (316) 662-3854
Fax: (316) 245-5099
E-mail: rap@pvi.org

Barb Hansen
3 Anderson Court
Newton, KS 67114-1409
Phone: (316) 283-9529

Becky Merrill
P.O. Box 462
Riverton, KS 66770
Phone: (316) 848-3796

Bev Regier
4828 NE 24th Street
Newton, KS 67114-9453
Phone: (316) 283-1016

Caring and Sharing Grandparents
2201 South Bonebrake
Hutchinson, KS 67501
Phone: (316) 663-4134
Fax: (316) 663-4134

Cheryl Walters
2226 Shalimar Drive
Salina, KS 67401
Phone: (785) 827-7052

Cindy Beeson
2439 Edgemont
Arkansas City, KS 67005
Phone: (316) 442-6736

Foster Children of Johnson County, Inc.
11835 Roe PMB #106
Leawood, KS 66211
Phone: (913) 768.1840
E-mail: pamrob@comcast.net

Harold and Julie Thorne
P.O. Box 14
Hoisington, KS 67544
Phone: (316) 653-4340
E-mail: hlthorne@yahoo.com

International Families of Mid-America
6708 Granada Road
Prairie Village, KS 66208
Phone: (913) 722-5697

Jan Hula
604 East 11th
Pittsburg, KS 66762
Phone: (316) 231-7681

Janet S. O'Dell
308 North Elm
McPherson, KS 67460
Phone: (316) 241-0382

KEE Kids
421 Wetmore Street
Wichita, KS 67209-1318
Phone: (316) 721-4122

Kansas Families for Kids-Teen Voices
4744 Roundtree Court
Shawnee, KS 66226
Phone: (913) 422-4797
E-mail: slshikles@earthlink.net

Kris Goossen
P.O. Box 165
Potwin, KS 67123
Phone: (316) 752-3700

Linda Plett
810 East Center Street
Inman, KS 67546
Phone: (316) 585-2586

Marian Wilson
921 East 13th
Winefield, KS 67156
Phone: (316) 221-9475

Mike and Penny Dorrell
1222 Millington
Winfield, KS 67156
Phone: (316) 221-2098

Prairie View
1901 East First
Newton, KS 67114
Phone: (316) 744-3701

Sharon Gagnon
5205 Skyline Road
Hutchinson, KS 67502
Phone: (316) 665-6255

Special Needs Adoption
Project
University of Kansas Medical
Center
Children's Rehabilitation Unit
3901 Rainbow Boulevard,
#5017
Kansas City, KS 66103
Phone: (913) 588-5745

Teresa LaCoss
9 Lake Drive
Mulvane, KS 67110
Phone: (316) 777-0460

Vern and Ann Friesen
7250 Troy Road
Manhattan, KS 66502-8328
Phone: (785) 539-2041
E-mail: FriesenA@aol.com

**Licensed Private
Adoption Agencies**

Adoption Centre of Kansas,
Inc.
1831 Woodrow Avenue
Wichita, KS 67203
Phone: (316) 265-5289
Fax: (316) 265-3953
Toll-Free: (800) 804-3632
E-mail: casemanager@adoption
centre.com
Web site: www.adoptioncentre.
com

Adoption Option
7211 West 98th Terrace,
#100
Overland Park, KS 66212
Phone: (913) 642-7900
Fax: (913) 897-0154

Adoption and Beyond, Inc.
16236 Metcalf Avenue
Overland Park, KS 66085
Phone: (913) 381-6919
Fax: (913) 381-6909
E-mail: adopt@adoption-beyond.
org
Web site: www.adoption-
beyond.org
— Intercountry Program
— Child Placement

Adoption and Counseling
Services
18090 Nieman Road
Overland Park, KS 66210
Phone: (913) 339-6776
— Intercountry Program
— Home Study

Adoption and Fertility
Resources
Kansas Location
10925 Antioch Road, Suite 103
Overland Park, KS 66210
Phone: (816) 781-8550
Fax: (816) 792-3219

Adoption of Babies and Chil-
dren, Inc. (ABC Adoption)
9230 Pflumm Road
Lenexa, KS 66215-3346
Phone: (913) 894-2223
Fax: (913) 894-2839
Toll-Free: (800) 406-2909
E-mail: abcadoption@msn.com
Web site: www.abcadoption.org
— Intercountry Program
— Child Placement

American Adoptions
9101 West 110th Street, Suite 200
Overland Park, KS 66210
Fax: (913) 383-1615
Toll-Free: (800) 236-7846
E-mail: adoptions@americanado
ptions.com
Web site: www.
americanadoptions.com

Catholic Charities
425 North Topeka
Wichita, KS 67202
Phone: (316) 263-0507
Fax: (316) 263-5259
Toll-Free: (866) 222-3555
Web site: www.
wkscatholiccharities.org

Catholic Community Services
2220 Central Avenue
Kansas City, KS 66102
Phone: (913) 621-1504
Fax: (913) 621-4507
E-mail: mschimberg@catholiccha
ritiesks.org
Web site: www.
catholiccharitiesks.org

Christian Family Services of
the Midwest, Inc.
10500 Barkley, Suite 216
Overland Park, KS 66212
Phone: (913) 383-3337
Fax: (913) 381-2547
E-mail: mlbcfs@abac.com
Web site: www.cfskc.org

Family Life Services of
Southern Kansas
305 South Summit
Arkansas City, KS 67005-2848
Phone: (316) 442-1688

Heartland International
Adoptions
1831 Woodrow Avenue
Wichita, KS 67203-2932
Phone: (316) 265-5289

Inserco, Inc.
5120 East Central, #A
Wichita, KS 67208
Phone: (316) 681-3840

Kaw Valley Center
4300 Brenner Road
Kansas City, KS 66104
Phone: (913) 334-0294

Special Additions, Inc.
P.O. Box 10
19055 Metcalf Avenue
Stilwell, KS 66085
Phone: (913) 681-9604
Fax: (913) 681-0748
E-mail: specialadd@aol.com
Web site: www.specialad.org
– Intercountry Program
– Child Placement

Sunflower Family Services
1503 Vine Street, Suite E
Hays, KS 67601
Phone: (913) 625-4600
Toll-Free: (800) 555-4614
E-mail: teresaw@sunflower
family.org
Web site: www.sunflowerfamily.
org

The Villages, Inc.
2219 SW 29th Street
Topeka, KS 66611-1908
Phone: (785) 267-5900

Local/Regional Offices of the State (Public) Adoption Agency

Kansas Children's Service
League
Kansas City – Black Adoption
Program and Services
P.O. Box 17-1273
630 Minnesota Street, Suite 210
Kansas City, KS 66117
Phone: (913) 621-2016
E-mail: tlong@kcsl.org
Web site: www.kcsl.org

Kansas Children's
Service League
Wichita
P.O. Box 517
1365 North Custer
Wichita, KS 67201
Phone: (316) 942-4261
E-mail: tlong@kcsl.org
Web site: www.kcsl.org

Kansas Children's
Service League
Manhattan
217 Southwind Place
Manhattan, KS 66503
Phone: (785) 539-3193
E-mail: tlong@kcsl.org
Web site: www.kcsl.org

Birth Family and Search Support Groups

Adoption Concerns Triangle
1427 North Harrison
Topeka, KS 66608

Getting To Know You Search
and Support Group
1770 South Roosevelt
Wichita, KS 67218
Phone: (316) 682-5190
E-mail: HEARTS121@aol.com

State Adoption Specialist/Manager

Kansas Department of Social
and Rehabilitation Services
Children and Family Policy Division
Docking State Office Building, 5th
Floor South
915 SW Harrison
Topeka, KS 66612
Phone: (785) 296-0918
Fax: (785) 368-8159
E-mail: pal@SRSKANSAS.org
Web site: www.SRSKANSAS.org

State Interstate Compact on the Placement of Children (ICPC) Administrator

Kansas Department of Social
and Rehabilitation Services
Children and Family Policy Division
Docking State Office Building,
5th Floor
Topeka, KS 66612
Phone: (785) 296-4648

State Licensing Specialist

Kansas Department of Health
and Environment
Child Care Licensing and
Regulation
Curtis State Office Building
1000 SW Jackson, Suite 200
Topeka, KS 66612-1274
Phone: (785) 296-8892
Fax: (785) 296-7025
E-mail: jchase@kdhe.state.ks.us

KENTUCKY

Adoptive/Foster Family Support Groups

APAK and North American
Council on Adoptable Children
400 Chippewa Drive
Frankfort, KY 00004-0601
Phone: (502) 695-5104

Adoption Support for Kentucky
Lexington, KY 40507
Phone: (859) 257-3196
Fax: (859) 257-3918
Toll-Free: (877) 440-6376
E-mail: adoptky@uky.edu
Web site: www.uky.edu/
SocialWork/trc/adopt.html

Adoptive and Foster Parent Association
1414 Grapevine Road
Madisonville , KY 42431-3515
Phone: (912) 826-1851
Fax: (912) 275-6111

Families with Children From China
3602 Trail Creek Place
Louisville, KY 00004-0241
Phone: (502) 429-8328
E-mail: pmcdonogh@aol.com

Fayette County Adoptive Parents Support Group
1843 Donco Court
Lexington, KY 40505
Phone: (859) 299-2749
E-mail: sturgeon@infionline.net

Friends Through Adoption
4938 Open Meadow Drive
Independence, KY 00004-1051

Friends of Black Children
3050 West Broadway
Louisville, KY 00004-0211
Phone: (502) 778-2631

Parents and Adoptive Children of Kentucky
139 Highland Drive
Madisonville, KY 00004-2431
Phone: (502) 825-2158

Licensed Private Adoption Agencies

A Helping Hand Adoption Agency
501 Darby Creek Road, Suite 17
Lexington, KY 40509

Phone: (859) 263-9964
Fax: (859) 263-9957
Toll-Free: (800) 525-0871
E-mail: info@worldadoptions.org
Web site: www.worldadoptions.org
— Intercountry Program
— Child Placement

Access Adoptions, Inc.
880 Edgewood Drive
Lexington, KY 40515
Phone: (859) 271-9078

Adopt! Inc.
135 Lackawanna Road
Lexington, KY 40503
Phone: (859) 276-6249
Fax: (859) 276-5570
E-mail: info@adoptinc.org
Web site: www.adoptinc.org

Adoption Assistance, Inc.
510 Maple Avenue
Danville, KY 00004-0422
Phone: (859) 236-2761
E-mail: adoption@adoptionassistance.com
Web site: www.adoptionassistance.com
— Intercountry Program
— Home Study

Adoption and Home Study Specialists, Inc.
10507 Timberwood Circle, Suite 216
Louisville, KY 40223
Phone: (502) 423-7713

Adoptions of Kentucky
One Riverfront Plaza, Suite 1708
Louisville, KY 42642
Phone: (502) 585-3005
Fax: (502) 585-5369
Toll-Free: (800) 542-5245
Web site: www.adoptionsofkentucky.com

Bluegrass Christian Adoption Services
1517 Nicholasville Road, Suite 405
Lexington, KY 40503
Phone: (859) 276-2222
Fax: (859) 277-7999
E-mail: mary@mail.bluegrassadoption.org
Web site: www.iglou.com/kac/bluegrass.html

Catholic Charities
2911 South Fourth Street
Louisville, KY 40208
Phone: (502) 637-9786
Fax: (502) 637-9780
E-mail: jpallo@archlou.org
Web site: www.iglou.com/kac/cathcharities.html

Catholic Social Service Bureau
1310 West Main Street
Lexington, KY 40508
Phone: (859) 253-1993
Fax: (859) 254-6284
E-mail: Lhainley@cdlex.org
Web site: www.iglou.com/kac/cathsocsvcbureau.html

Childplace, Inc.
4500 Westport Road
Louisville, KY 40207
Phone: (502) 363-1633
Toll-Free: (800) 787-9084
E-mail: nathans@childplace.org
Web site: www.childplace.org

Children's Home of Northern Kentucky
200 Home Road
Covington, KY 41011
Phone: (859) 261-8768
Fax: (859) 291-2431
E-mail: shamilton.cinoh@juno.com
Web site: www.iglou.com/kac/childrenshome.html
— Intercountry Program
— Child Placement

Cumberland River Region
MH-MR Board
1203 American Greeting Road
Corbin, KY 40702
Phone: (606) 528-7010

Ed Necco and Associates, Inc.
544 East Main Street
Bowling Green, KY 42101
Phone: (270) 781-8112
Fax: (270) 781-8114
Toll-Free: (866) 838-2029
Web site: www.enakids.com

Holly Hill Children's Home
Route 1, Box 21
Washington Terrace
California, KY 41007
Phone: (859) 635-0500
Fax: (859) 498-2606
Web site: www.familyconnection
inc.org/hopehill/index.html

Holston Family Services
503 Maple Street
Murray, KY 42071
Phone: (270) 759-5007
Web site: www.holstonhome.org

Home of the Innocents
10936 Dixie Highway
Louisville, KY 40272
Phone: (502) 995-4415
Fax: (502) 995-4420
Web site: www.
homeoftheinnocents.org

Jewish Family and Vocational Service
3587 Dutchmans Lane
Louisville, KY 40205
Phone: (502) 452-6341
Fax: (502) 452-6718
E-mail: jfvs@jfvs.com
Web site: www.jfvs.com
– Intercountry Program
– Home Study

Kentucky Adoption Services, Inc.
4501 Bridge Ridge Court
Owensboro, KY 42303
Phone: (270) 689-2598
Fax: (270) 684-6748
Toll-Free: (866) KIDS4KY
E-mail: adopt@kentuckyadoption
services.org
Web site: www.
kentuckyadoptionservices.org
– Intercountry Program
– Child Placement

Kentucky Baptist Homes for Children
10801 Shelbyville Road
Louisville, KY 40243
Phone: (502) 568-9117
Toll-Free: (800) 928-5242
E-mail: adoption@kbhc.org
Web site: www.kbhc.org
– Intercountry Program
– Child Placement

LDS Family Services, Inc.
1000 Hurstbourne Lane
Louisville, KY 40224
Phone: (502) 429-0077
Fax: (317) 872-1756
E-mail: fam-in@ldschurch.org
Web site: ldsfamilyservices.org

Mary Hurst
1015 Dorsey Lane
Louisville, KY 40223
Phone: (502) 245-1576

Mary Kendall Family Services
2508 New Hartford Road
Owensboro, KY 42303
Phone: (270) 683-3724
Toll-Free: (877) 887-4481
E-mail: drrankin@kyumh.org
Web site: www.kyumh.org

New Beginnings Family Services
1939 Goldsmith Lane
Louisville, KY 40218
Phone: (502) 485-0722

SAFY of Kentucky
71 Cavalier Boulevard, Suite 103
Florence, KY 41042
Toll-Free: (888) 525-7239

Shoemakers Christian Homes for Children and Adolescents
1939 Goldsmith Lane, Suite 136
Louisville, KY 40218
Phone: (502) 485-0722

Specialized Alternatives for Families and Youth of Kentucky
3150 Custer Drive, Suite 103
Lexington, KY 40517
Phone: (859) 971-2585
Fax: (859) 971-7594
Toll-Free: (888) 722-6333
E-mail: safy@safy.org
Web site: www.safy.org

St. Elizabeth's Regional Maternity Center
11103 Park Road
Louisville, KY 40220
Phone: (502) 412-0990
Fax: (812) 941-7008
Web site: www.stelizabethsl.org

St. Joseph's Children's Home
2823 Frankfort Avenue
Louisville, KY 40206
Phone: (502) 893-0241
Fax: (502) 896-2394
E-mail: Elizabet@stjoseph
childrenshome.org
Web site: www.sjkids.org

Treatment Foster Care and Adoption Services
308 Maple Street
Hazard, KY 41701
Phone: (606) 398-7245

Villages
4021 Preston Highway
Louisville, KY 40213
Phone: (502) 361-7010

Western United Methodist
Family Services
739 Washington Street
Paducah, KY 42003
Phone: (270) 443-9004
Fax: (270) 443-3128
Toll-Free: (877) 998-5437
E-mail: umfs@bellsouth.net

**Birth Family and Search
Support Groups**

Concerned United Birthparents
9233 Encino Court
Louisville, KY 40223
Phone: (502) 423-1438
E-mail: sherszew@aol.com
Web site: www.cubirthparents.org

**State Adoption Exchange/
Photolisting of Children
Waiting For Adoption**

Kentucky Department for
Community Based Services
Cabinet for Families and Children
275 East Main Street, 3CE
Frankfort, KY 00004-0621
Phone: (502) 564-2147
Fax: (502) 564-5995
Toll-Free: (800) 232-5437
E-mail: charla.pratt@mail.state.
ky.us
Web site: http://cfc.state.ky.us/
help/foster_care.asp

Special Needs Adoption Program (SNAP)
Department of Community-Based
Services
1350 East New Circle Road
Lexington, KY 00004-0505
Phone: (502) 595-4303
Toll-Free: (800) 432-9346
Web site: http://cfc.state.ky.us/
cbs-snap/search.asp

**State Adoption
Specialist/Manager**

Commonwealth of Kentucky
Cabinet for Families and Children
275 East Main Street, 3CE
Frankfort, KY 40621
Phone: (502) 564-2147
Fax: (502) 564-9554
E-mail: charla.pratt@mail.state.
ky.us
Web site: http://cfc.state.ky.us/
help/adoption.asp

**State Foster Care
Specialist/Manager**

Kentucky Department for
Community Based Services
Cabinet for Families & Children
275 East Main Street, 3C-E
Frankfort, KY 40621
Phone: (502) 564-2147
Fax: (502) 564-5995
E-mail: charla.pratt@mail.state.
ky.us

**State Interstate Compact on
the Placement of Children
(ICPC) Administrator**

Commonwealth of Kentucky
Cabinet For Families and Children
275 East Main Street, 4th Floor
Frankfort, KY 00004-0601
Phone: (502) 564-4826

State Licensing Specialist

Cabinet for Health Services
– Office of Inspector General
Division of Licensing and
Regulation
275 East Main Street, 4th Floor
Frankfort, KY 00004-0601
Phone: (502) 564-2800
E-mail: rebecca.cecil@mail.state.
ky.us
Web site: http://chs.state.
ky.us/oig/

State Reunion Registry

Program Specialist
Department for Social Services
275 East Main Street
Sixth Floor, West
Frankfort, KY 00004-0621
Phone: (502) 564-2147

LOUISIANA

**Adoptive/Foster Family
Support Groups**

Adoptive Couples Together
P.O. Box 1311
Kenner, LA 70063

F.A.I.R. Visions, Inc.
610 South 16th Street
Monroe, LA 71202
Phone: (318) 340-0230
E-mail: kirp50@juno.com

GNOFAP
7425 Edward Street
New Orleans, LA 70126
Phone: (504) 246-2402

Institute for Black Parenting
10001 Lake Forest Boulevard,
Suite 311
New Orleans, LA 70127
Phone: (504) 245-9386
Fax: (504) 245-0956
Toll-Free: (866) 245-4427
Web site: www.instituteforblack
parenting.org

Louisiana Adoption Advisory
Board (LAAB), Inc.
205 Elephant Walk Boulevard
Caremo, LA 70520
Phone: (337) 896-5571

Louisiana Adoption Advisory
Board (LAAB), Inc.
3727 Roman Street
Metairie, LA 70001
Phone: (504) 835-7518
Fax: (504) 837-4768
Web site: www.laab.org

Natchitoche River
P.O. Box 486
Provencal, LA 71468
Phone: (318) 472-8701
Fax: (318) 472-9205

New Orleans Support Group
1500 Deslonde Street
New Orleans, LA 70117
Phone: (504) 944-8126

North American Council on Adoptable Children
3528 Vincennes Place
New Orleans, LA 70125
Phone: (504) 866-4449
Web site: www.nacac.org

Pride and Hope Ministry
31314 Jerry Moses Road
Angie, LA 70426
Phone: (985) 986-2808

Washington Parish Foster and Adoptive Association
31298 Jerry Moses Road
Angie, LA 70426
Phone: (985) 986-2808

Licensed Private Adoption Agencies

Acorn Adoption, Inc.
3350 Ridgelake Drive, Suite 259
Metairie, LA 70002
Phone: (504) 838-0080
Toll-Free: (888) 221-1370
E-mail: acornadoption@msn.com
Web site: www.acornadoption.org

Adoption Options of LA, Inc.
aka Global Adoptions, Inc.
1724 North Burnside, Suite 7
Gonzales, LA 70737
Phone: (225) 644-1033

Beacon House Adoption Services, Inc.
15254 Old Hammond Highway, Suite C-2
Baton Rouge, LA 70816
Phone: (225) 272-3221

Toll-Free: (888) 987-6300
E-mail: beacon01@bellsouth.net
Web site: www.beaconhouseadoption.com
– Intercountry Program
– Child Placement

Catholic Charities Archdiocese of New Orleans
E-mail: ccano@archdiocese-no.org
Web site: www.catholiccharities-no.org

Catholic Community Services Counseling, Maternity, and Adoption Department
1900 South Acadian Thruway
Baton Rouge, LA 70808
Phone: (225) 336-8708

Children's Bureau of New Orleans
210 Baronne Street, Suite 722
New Orleans, LA 70112
Phone: (504) 525-2366

D. Missy Everson, LCSW, DCSW – A Professional Corporation
2020 East 70th Street, Suite #205
Shreveport, LA 71105
Phone: (318) 798-7664
Fax: (318) 861-1710
E-mail: dmeapc@aol.com
Web site: www.adoptinla.com

Holy Cross Child Placement Agency, Inc.
910 Pierremont Road, Suite 356
Shreveport, LA 71106
Phone: (318) 865-3199
Fax: (318) 219-8260
E-mail: domahea@aol.com

Jewish Family Service of Greater New Orleans
3330 West Esplanade Avenue South, Suite 600
Metairie, LA 70002-3454
Phone: (504) 831-8475

LDS Social Services
Pratt Center
2000 Old Spanish Trail, Suite 115
Slidell, LA 70458
Phone: (504) 649-2774

Louisiana Baptist Children's Home
P.O. Box 4196
Monroe, LA 71211
Phone: (318) 343-2244
E-mail: home@lbch.org
Web site: www.lbch.org

Mercy Ministries of America
P.O. Box 3028
West Monroe, LA 71210
Phone: (318) 388-2040
Fax: (318) 322-5310
Web site: www.mercyministries.com

St. Elizabeth Foundation
8054 Summa Avenue, Suite A
Baton Rouge, LA 70809
Phone: (225) 769-8888
Fax: (225) 769-6874
Toll-Free: (800) 738-5683
Web site: www.saintelizabethfoundation.org

St. Gerard's Adoption Network, Inc.
P.O. Box 769
Eunice, LA 70535
Phone: (318) 457-1111

Sunnybrook Children's Home, Inc.
2101 Forsythe Avenue
Monroe, LA 71201
Phone: (318) 329-8161

Volunteers of America of North Louisiana
701 Stubbs Avenue
Monroe, LA 71201
Phone: (318) 322-2272
E-mail: bjohnston@voanorthla.org
Web site: www.voanorthla.com

Birth Family and Search Support Groups

Adoption Connection of LA
7301 West Judge Perez #311
Arabi, LA 70032
Phone: (504) 277-0030

Adoption Connection of Louisiana Adoptees Birthright Committee
P.O. Box 6921
Metairie, LA 70010

Adoption Search Organization
8154 Longwood Drive
Denhan Springs, LA 70726

Lost and Found
18343 Weatherwood Drive
Baton Rouge, LA 70817
Phone: (225) 769-2456

Louisiana Adoption Resource Exchange (LARE)
P.O. Box 3318
Baton Rouge, LA 70821
Toll-Free: (800) 259-3428
Web site: www.adopt.org/la/

State Adoption Specialist/Manager

Louisiana Department of Social Services
Office of Community Services
P.O. Box 3318
333 Laurel Street
Baton Rouge, LA 70821
Phone: (225) 342-4086
Fax: (225) 342-9087
E-mail: bdaniels@dss.state.la.us
Web site: www.dss.state.la.us/offocs/index.htm

State Foster Care Specialist/Manager

Louisiana Department of Social Services
Office of Community Services
P.O. Box 3318
Baton Rouge, LA 70821

Phone: (225) 342-4006
Fax: (225) 342-9087
E-mail: jpittma1@dss.state.la.us
Web site: www.dss.state.la.us/offocs/index.htm

State Interstate Compact on the Placement of Children (ICPC) Administrator

Louisiana Department of Social Services
Office of Community Services
P.O. Box 3318
Baton Rouge, LA 70821
Phone: (225) 342-2297

State Licensing Specialist

Louisiana Department of Social Services Bureau of Licensing
P.O. Box 3078
Baton Rouge, LA 70821-3078
Phone: (225) 922-0015
Fax: (225) 922-0014
Web site: www.dss.state.la.us/offos/html/licensing.html

Louisiana Voluntary Adoption Registry
P.O. Box 3318
Baton Rouge, LA 70821
Toll-Free: (800) 259-2456
Web site: www.dss.state.la.us/offocs/html/registry.html

MAINE

Adoptive/Foster Family Support Groups

Adoption Triad Support Group
93 Silver Street
Waterville, ME 04901
Phone: (207) 873-3525
E-mail: jfranck@mainechildrenshome.org

Adoptive Families Peer Support Group
P.O. Box 52
Sherman Station, ME 04777
Phone: (207) 365-4895

Adoptive Families of Maine
P.O. Box 350
Portage, ME 04708
Phone: (207) 435-8018

Adoptive Families of Maine and North American Council on Adoptable Children
156 Essex Street
Bangor, ME 04401
Phone: (207) 941-9500

Adoptive Parent Peer Support for Cumberland and York Counties
1st Parish Congregational Church
School Street
Gorham, ME 04038
Phone: (207) 642-3978

Adoptive and Foster Families of Maine
Old Town, ME 04468
Phone: (207) 827-2331
Fax: (207) 827-1974
Toll-Free: (800) 833-9786
E-mail: bette@affm.net
Web site: www.affm.net

Adoptive and Foster Families of Maine Peer Support Group
Department of Human Services
396 Griffin Road
Bangor, ME 04401
Phone: (207) 827-1874

Casey Family Services
Portland, ME 04101
Phone: (207) 772-4110
Toll-Free: (800) 559-1115
E-mail: hstephenson@caseyfamilyservices.org

Child Welfare Training Institute
University of Southern Maine
295 Water Street
Augusta, ME 04330
Phone: (207) 345-9739
Fax: (207) 626-5210
E-mail: carol.brocker@state.
me.us

Lewiston/Auburn Post
Adoption Support Group
95 Lane Road
Mechanic Falls, ME 04256
Phone: (207) 345-9739

Maine Adoption Placement
Services
Adoption Support Group
181 State Street
Bangor, ME 04401
Phone: (207) 941-9500
Fax: (207) 941-8942
E-mail: mapsbangor@mapsadopt.
org
Web site: www.mapsadopt.org

Multi-Cultural Family Group
87 Spring Street
Portland, ME 04103

Northern Maine Adoption
Support Network
RFD #2
P.O. Box 3320
Houlton, ME 04730
Phone: (207) 532-7584

Racial Diversity Group
Phone: (207) 839-3824

Spirit of Adoption
Phone: (207) 892-3433

**Licensed Private
Adoption Agencies**

Adopt Cambodia
P.O. Box 399
Woolwich, ME 04579
Phone: (207) 442-7612
– Intercountry Program
– Child Placement

C.A.R.E. Development
P.O. Box 936
Bangor, ME 04401
Phone: (207) 945-4240
Fax: (207) 990-3660
E-mail: info@caredev.org

FACT
Bangor, ME
E-mail: info@familiesandchildren.
org

Families and Children Together
(F.A.C.T)
304 Hancock Street, Suite 2B
Bangor, ME 04401
Phone: (207) 941-2347
Fax: (207) 990-3316
E-mail: info@familiesandchildren.
org
Web site: www.
familiesandchildren.org

Good Samaritan Agency
100 Ridgewood Drive
Bangor, ME 04401
Phone: (207) 942-7211
Fax: (207) 990-0851
Toll-Free: (800) 249-1811
E-mail: goodsam@midmaine.com
– Intercountry Program
– Child Placement

International Adoption
Services Centre, Inc.
P.O. Box 56
Gardiner, ME 04345
Phone: (207) 582-8842
Fax: (207) 582-9027
Toll-Free: (888) 68-ADOPT
E-mail: IASC@adelphia.net
– Intercountry Program
– Child Placement

Maine Adoption Placement
Service (MAPS)
International Office
277 Congress Street
Portland, ME 04101
Phone: (207) 775-4101
Fax: (207) 775-1019

E-mail: info@mapsadopt.org
Web site: www.mapsadopt.org
– Intercountry Program
– Child Placement

Maine Children's Home for
Little Wanderers
11 Mulliken Court
Augusta, ME 04330
Phone: (207) 622-1552
Fax: (207) 621-8376
Web site: www.mint.net/
mainechildrenshome

SMART Child and Family
Services
P.O. Box 1360
Windham, ME 04062
Phone: (207) 893-0386
Fax: (207) 893-2086
E-mail: officeatsmart@aol.com
Web site: www.smartagency.org

St. Andre's Home, Inc.
283 Elm Street
Biddeford, ME 04005
Phone: (207) 282-3351
Fax: (207) 282-8733
E-mail: saintandre@aol.com

**Birth Family and Search
Support Groups**

Adoption Support of
Penobscot Bay
Taylor's Point
Tenant's Harbor, ME 04860

Care Development of Maine
970 Illinois Avenue
Bangor, ME 04401
Phone: (207) 945-4240
E-mail: khirsch@caredev.org

Chinese and American Friend-
ship Association of Maine
P.O. Box 10372
Portland, ME 04104
Phone: (207) 871-7437

Maine Adoption Placement
Services
306 Congress Street
Portland, ME 04101
Phone: (207) 772-3678

Mid-Coast Adoptive Families
77 Orchard Hill Road
Dresden, ME 04342
Phone: (207) 666-3416

Rainbow Connection
25 Campion Street
Cape Elizabeth, ME 04107
Phone: (207) 767-1767
E-mail: freetobeyou@aol.com

**State Adoption Exchange/
Photolisting of Children
Waiting For Adoption**

Northern New England
Exchange
221 State Street
State House
Augusta, ME 04333-0011
Phone: (207) 287-5060
Fax: (207) 287-5282
Web site: www.adopt.org/me/

**State Adoption
Specialist/Manager**

Maine Department of Human
Services
Bureau of Child and Family
Services
State House Station #11
221 State Street
Augusta, ME 04333-0011
Phone: (207) 287-5060
Fax: (207) 287-5282
E-mail: Virginia.
s.marriner@maine.gov
Web site: www.adopt.org/me/

**State Interstate Compact on
the Placement of Children
(ICPC) Administrator**

Maine Department of Human
Services
Bureau of Child and Family Services
221 State Street
Augusta, ME 04333-0011
Phone: (207) 287-5060
Fax: (207) 287-5282
E-mail: Charles.P.Gagnon@state.
me.us

State Licensing Specialist

Maine Department of Human
Services
Bureau of Child and Family
Services
221 State Street, Station 11
Augusta, ME 04333-0011
Phone: (207) 287-5060
Fax: (207) 287-5282
Web site: www.state.me.us/dhs

State Reunion Registry

Maine State Adoption Reunion
Registry
Office of Vital Records
221 State Street
Augusta, ME 04333-0011
Phone: (207) 287-3181
Web site: www.state.me.us/dhs/
DHSaddresses.htm

**Statewide Adoption
Recruitment Line**

Maine Statewide Adoption
Recruitment Line
Phone: (207) 582-8842
Toll-Free: (877) 505-0545
E-mail: affme@aol.com
Web site: www.afamilyforme.org

**Statewide Foster Care
Recruitment Line**

Maine Statewide Foster Care
Recruitment Line
Phone: (207) 582-8842
Toll-Free: (877) 505-0545
E-mail: affme@aol.com
Web site: www.afamilyforme.org

MARYLAND

**Adoptive/Foster Family
Support GroupsAdoption
Support Group**
15 Ridge View Drive
Westminster, MD 21157
Phone: (410) 876-3068
Fax: (410) 876-5317
E-mail: beckipearson@hotmail.com

Adoptive Families and Friends
1815 Beaver Creek Lane
Frederick, MD 21702
E-mail: Dwasserba@aol.com
Web site: www.members.aol.
com/Dwasserba/i nfo.html

Adoptive Families and Friends
3936 Southview Court
Jefferson, MD 21755
Phone: (301) 473-8477

Adoptive Families on the Move
8255 Streamwood Drive
Pikesville, MD 21208
Phone: (410) 496-6861

Adoptive Family and Friends
728 Jefferson Pike
Knoxville, MD 21758
Phone: (301) 834-7233

**Allegany County Department
of Social Services**
P.O. Box 1420
Cumberland, MD 21501-1420
Phone: (301) 729-1727
Fax: (301) 784-7211
E-mail: cplatter@dhr.state.md.us

Baltimore Adopted Support Parent Group
531 East Coldspring Lane
Baltimore, MD 21212
Phone: (410) 323-6468

Barker Foundation Parents of Adopted Adolescents Group
7945 MacArthur Boulevard, Suite 206
Cabin John, MD 20818
Phone: (301) 229-8300
Fax: (301) 229-0074
Toll-Free: (800) 673-8489
E-mail: info@barkerfoundatiion.org
Web site: www.barkerfoundation.org

Center for Adoption Support and Education/Adoptive Parent Connection (C.A.S.E.)
11120 New Hampshire Avenue, Suite 205
Silver Spring, MD 20904
Phone: (301) 593-9200
Fax: (301) 593-9203
E-mail: caseadopt@adoptionsupport.org
Web site: www.adoptionsupport.org

Cherry Hill Grandparent Support Group
901 Cherry Hill Road, Apt. 371
Baltimore, MD 21225-1355
Phone: (410) 355-0384
Fax: (410) 355-0384

DC Metro Foster and Adoptive Parent Association
7204 Loch Raven Road
Temple Hills, MD 20748
Phone: (301) 449-1061
Fax: (301) 449-5911

DSS Adoptive Parents
2310 ½ Madison Avenue
Baltimore, MD 21217
Phone: (410) 383-8840
Fax: (410) 545-7472

FAB Support Group
4513 Old Philadelphia Road
Aberdeen, MD 21001
Phone: (410) 569-7269
E-mail: pegsflor@aol.com

FCC Central Maryland
11850 Blue Freeway
Columbia, MD 21044
Phone: (410) 740-2164

Faith Christian Full Gospel Church
500 East Lincoln Avenue
Salisbury, MD 21804
Phone: (410) 241-7475
E-mail: overseerdouglas@aol.com

Families Adopting Children Everywhere and North American Council on Adoptable Children Representative
P.O. Box 28058
Baltimore, MD 21239
Phone: (410) 488-2656
E-mail: Famadopt2000@aol.com
Web site: www.face2000.org

Families with Children from China – Central Maryland
P.O. Box 2392
Columbia, MD 21045

International Children's Alliance (ICA)
8807 Colesville Drive, 3rd Floor
Silver Spring, MD 20910
Phone: (301) 495-09710
Fax: (301) 495-9790
E-mail: Info@adoptica.org
Web site: www.adoptica.org

Latin America Parents Association of the National Capital Region
P.O. Box 4403
Silver Spring, MD 20904-4403
Phone: (301) 431-3407
E-mail: info@lapa.com
Web site: www.lapa.com

Maryland Adoption
12600 War Admiral Way
Gaithersburg, MD 20878
Phone: (301) 258-2664
E-mail: Callahanea@aol.com

Maryland Department of Social Services
12578 Garrett Highway
Oakland, MD 21550
Phone: (301) 533-3000
Fax: (301) 334-5413
E-mail: Barnett@dhr.state.md.us
Web site: www.dhr.state.md.us/garrett.htm

Maryland Department of Social Services
201 Baptist Street, Suite 27
Salisbury, MD 21802-2298
Phone: (410) 543-6885
Fax: (410) 219-2828
E-mail: Cwilson@dhr.state.md.us
Web site: www.dhrstate.md.us/wicomico.htm

Maryland League of Foster and Adoptive Parents
11 East Mt. Royal Avenue, Suite 2B
Baltimore, MD 21202
Phone: (410) 385-2715
Fax: (410) 685-2364

National Mentor Healthcare, Inc.
7127 Ambassador Road
Baltimore, MD 21244
Phone: (410) 944-5055
Fax: (410) 944-5581

One Church One Child
31 Norwood Road
Silver Spring, MD 20905
Phone: (301) 384-2601

Open Adoption Discussion Group
22310 Old Hundred Road
Barnesville, MD 20838
Phone: (301) 972-8579
E-mail: msaasta@hotmail.com

Prince George's County Foster Parent Association
805 Brightseat Road
Landover, MD 20785-4723
Phone: (301) 249-2748

Prince George's County Foster Parent Association
11809 Cleaver Drive
Mitchville, MD 20721
Phone: (301) 249-2748
Fax: (301) 249-8756
E-mail: beasleystewart@hotmail.com

Project Oz Adoptions, Inc.
10363 Southern Maryland Boulevard, #102
Dunkirk, MD 20754
Phone: (410) 286-5454
Fax: (410) 286-8440
Toll-Free: (866) 236-7869
E-mail: adopt@projectoz.com
Web site: www.projectoz.com

Stars of David International, Inc.
5750 Park Heights Avenue
Baltimore, MD 21215
Phone: (410) 466-9200
Fax: (410) 664-0551
E-mail: jfs@jfs.org
Web site: www.starsofdavid.org

Support Group for Adoptive Foster Parents
11 East Mount Royal Avenue, Suite 2B
Baltimore, MD 21202
Phone: (410) 385-2715

United House of Prayer For All People
3401 Edgewood Road
Baltimore, MD 21215
Phone: (410) 367-3100
Fax: (410) 542-5500
After hours: (410) 542-5300

Licensed Private Adoption Agencies

Adoption Alliances - JFS
6 Park Center Court, Suite 211
Owings Mills, MD 21117
Phone: (410) 581-1031
Fax: (410) 356-0103
E-mail: M.Hettleman@jfs.org
Web site: www.jfs.org

Adoption Options/JSSA
6123 Montrose Road
Rockville, MD 20852-4880
Phone: (301) 816-2700
Fax: (301) 770-8471
E-mail: blutton@jssa.org
– Intercountry Program
– Child Placement

Adoption Resources Center, Inc.
6630 Baltimore National Pike, Suite 205-A
Baltimore, MD 21228
Phone: (410) 744-6393
Fax: (410) 744-1533
E-mail: info@adoptsource.org
Web site: www.adoptionresource.org
– Intercountry Program
– Child Placement

Adoption Service Information Agency, Inc.
8555 16th Street, Suite 600
Silver Spring, MD 20910
Phone: (301) 587-7068
Fax: (301) 587-3869
Web site: www.asia-adopt.org
– Intercountry Program
– Child Placement

Adoptions Forever, Inc.
5830 Hubbard Drive
Rockville, MD 20852
Phone: (301) 468-1818
Fax: (301) 881-7871
E-mail: adopt@adoptionsforever.com

Web site: www.adoptionsforever.com
– Intercountry Program
– Child Placement

Adoptions Together, Inc.
5740 Executive Drive, Suite 107
Baltimore, MD 21228
Phone: (410) 653-3446
Fax: (410) 869-8419
E-mail: adoptionworks@adoptionstogether.org
Web site: www.adoptionstogether.org
– Intercountry Program
– Child Placement

Barker Foundation, Inc.
7945 MacArthur Boulevard, Room 206
Cabin John, MD 20818
Phone: (301) 229-8300
Fax: (301) 229-0074
Toll-Free: (800) 673-8489
Toll-Free: (800) 821-3104
E-mail: info@barkerfoundation.org
Web site: www.barkerfoundation.org
– Intercountry Program
– Child Placement

Bethany Christian Services
2130 Priest Bridge Drive, Suite 9
Crofton, MD 21114
Phone: (410) 721-2835
Fax: (410) 721-5523
E-mail: bcscrofton@bethany.org
Web site: www.bethany.org/maryland
– Intercountry Program
– Child Placement

Board of Child Care
3300 Gaither Road
Baltimore, MD 21244
Phone: (410) 922-2100
Fax: (410) 922-7830
Web site: www.boardofchildcare.org

Burlington United Methodist Family Services, Inc.
P.O. Box 422
St. Paul's United Methodist Church
10711 South Second Street
Oakland, MD 21532
Phone: (301) 334-1285
Fax: (301) 334-6352
E-mail: bumfs@qcnet.net

CASI Foundation for Children
3415 Olandwood Court, #201
Olney, MD 20832
Phone: (301) 570-9600
Fax: (301) 570-9233
E-mail: info@adoptcasi.org
Web site: www.adoptcasi.org

Catholic Charities
1 East Mt. Royal Avenue
Baltimore, MD 21202
Phone: (410) 659-4050
Fax: (410) 659-4060
Toll-Free: 800-CARE-002
E-mail: families@catholiccharities-md.org
Web site: www.catholiccharities-md.org

Catholic Charities Archdiocese of Washington D.C.
11160 Veirs Mill Road, Suite 700
Wheaton, MD 20902
Phone: (301) 942-1856

Center for Adoptive Families (Adoptions Together, Inc.)
5750 Executive Drive, Suite 107
Baltimore, MD 21228
Phone: (410) 869-0620
Fax: (410) 869-8419
E-mail: jklotz@adoptions together.org
Web site: www.centerforadoptiv efamilies.org

Children's Choice
1103 Butterworth Court
Stevensville, MD 21666
Phone: (410) 643-9290

Fax: (410) 643-9293
E-mail: childschoice@toad.net
Web site: www.childrenschoice. org

Cradle of Hope Adoption Center, Inc.
8630 Fenton Street, Suite 310
Silver Spring, MD 20910
Phone: (301) 587-4400
Fax: (301) 588-3091
E-mail: cradle@cradlehope.org
Web site: www.cradlehope.org

Creative Adoptions, Inc.
10750 Hickory Ridge Road, Suite 109
Columbia, MD 21044
Phone: (301) 596-1521
Fax: (301) 596-0346
E-mail: cai@creativeadoptions.org
Web site: www. creativeadoptions.org
– Intercountry Program
– Child Placement

Daisyfields Foundation, Forever After
5670-B The Alameda
Baltimore, MD 21239
Phone: (410) 464-2215
Fax: (410) 464-2556

Datz Foundation
16220 Frederick Road
Gaithersburg, MD 20877
Phone: (301) 258-0629
Fax: (301) 921-6689
E-mail: datz@patriot.net
Web site: www.datzfound.com

Diakon Lutheran Social Ministries
Maritime Center 1 at Pointe Breeze
2200 Broening Highway, Suite 110
Baltimore, MD 21224
Phone: (410) 633-6990
Fax: (410) 633-7943

E-mail: hoyler@diakon.org
Web site: www.diakon.org/adoption/index.shtml

Family Building Center
606 Baltimore Avenue, Suite 400
Towson, MD 21204-4903
Phone: (410) 296-5126
Fax: (410) 296-5128

Family and Child Services of Washington, D.C., Inc.
5301 76th Avenue
Landover Hills, MD 20784
Phone: (301) 459-4121
Fax: (202) 371-0863
Web site: www. familyandchildservices.org

Family and Children's Society
204 West Lanvale Street
Baltimore, MD 21217
Phone: (410) 669-9000
Fax: (410) 728-2972

Frank Adoption Center
9 East Church Street
Frederick, MD 21701
Phone: (301) 682-5025
Fax: (301) 682-5026
– Intercountry Program
– Child Placement

Holy Cross Child Placement Agency, Inc.
St. John's Episcopal Church
6701 Wisconsin Avenue
Chevy Chase, MD 20815
Phone: (301) 907-6887
Fax: (202) 237-2846
– Intercountry Program
– Child Placement

International Children's Alliance
8807 Colesville Road, 3rd Floor
Silver Spring, MD 20910
Phone: (301) 495-9710
Fax: (301) 495-9790
E-mail: jennifer@adoptica.org
Web site: www.adoptica.org
– Intercountry Program
– Child Placement

International Families, Inc.
613 Hawkesburg Lane
Silver Spring, MD 20904
Phone: (301) 622-2406
E-mail: ifichild@aol.com
Web site: www.ifichild.com
– Intercountry Program
– Child Placement

International Social Service
700 Light Street
Baltimore, MD 21230-3850
Phone: (410) 230-2734
Fax: (410) 230-2741
E-mail: sjoyce@iss.usa.org
Web site: www.lirs.org
– Intercountry Program
– Child Placement

LDS Family Services
172 Thomas Johnson Drive, #200
Frederick, MD 21702
Phone: (301) 694-5896
Fax: (301) 662-8737
E-mail: fam-md@ldschurch.org
Web site: www.lds.org

Lutheran Social Services of the National Capital Area
Zion Evangelical Lutheran Church
7410 New Hampshire Avenue
Tacoma Park, MD 20912
Phone: (301) 434-0080
Fax: (202) 723-3303
E-mail: greenberg@lssnca.org
Web site: www.lssnca.org
– Intercountry Program
– Child Placement

Project Oz Adoptions, Inc.
10363 Southern Maryland
Boulevard, #102
Dunkirk, MD 20754
Phone: (410) 286-5454
Fax: (410) 286-8440
Toll-Free: (866) 236-7869
E-mail: adopt@projectoz.com
Web site: www.projectoz.com
– Intercountry Program
– Child Placement

Rainbow Christian Services
6000 Davis Boulevard
Camp Springs, MD 20746
Phone: (301) 899-3200

World Child, Inc. Adoption and Assistance
9300 Colombia Boulevard
Silver Spring, MD 20910
Phone: (301) 588-3000
Fax: (301) 585-7879
Web site: www.worldchild.org
– Intercountry Program
– Child Placement

World Child, Inc.
207 Brooks Avenue
Gaithersburg, MD 20877
Phone: (301) 977-8339
Fax: (301) 608-2425
E-mail: info@worldchild.org
Web site: www.worldchild.org
– Intercountry Program
– Child Placement

Birth Family and Search Support Groups

Adoptee Birthfamily Connection
P.O. Box 115
Rocky Ridge, MD 21778
Phone: (301) 271-3037

Adoptions Together
5750 Executive Drive, Suite 107
Baltimore, MD 20903
Phone: (301) 869-0620
Fax: (301) 869-8419
Web site: www.centerforadoptiv
efamilies.org

Barker Foundation Adult Adoptee Support Group
7945 MacArthur Boulevard, Suite 206
Cabin John, MD 20818
Phone: (301) 229-8300

Concerned United Birthparents, Baltimore Area (CUB)
327 Dogwood Road
Millersville, MD 21108
Phone: (410) 544-0083
E-mail: margymc@aol.com
Web site: www.cubirthparents.
org

Searchlight, Inc.
P.O. Box 441
Glen Dale, MD 20769
Phone: (410) 262-8894

State Adoption Exchange/ Photolisting of Children Waiting for Adoption

Maryland Adoption Resource Exchange (MARE)
311 West Saratoga Street
Baltimore, MD 21201
Phone: (410) 767-7359
Toll-Free: (800) 392-3678
E-mail: mare@dhr.state.md.us
Web site: www.adoptuskids.
org/states/md

State Adoption Specialist/Manager

Maryland Department of Human Resources
311 West Saratoga Street
Baltimore, MD 21201
Phone: (410) 767-7506
Fax: (410) 333-0922
E-mail: spettawa@dhr.state.
md.us
Web site: www.dhr.state.md.us/
adopt.htm

State Foster Care Specialist/Manager

Maryland Department of Human Resources
Social Services Administration
311 West Saratoga Street
Baltimore, MD 21201
Phone: (410) 767-7713
Fax: (410) 333-6556
E-mail: shargrov@dhr.state.
md.us
Web site: www.dhr.state.md.us/
foster/index.html

State Interstate Compact on the Placement of Children (ICPC) Administrator

Maryland Department of Human Resources
311 West Saratoga Street
Baltimore, MD 21201
Phone: (410) 767-7506
Fax: (410) 333-0922
E-mail: spettwa@dhr.state.md.us

State Licensing Specialist

Maryland Department of Human Resources
Grace Turner
311 West Saratoga Street
Baltimore, MD 21201
Phone: (410) 767-7903
E-mail: gturner@dhr.state.md.us

State Reunion Registry

Maryland Mutual Consent Voluntary Adoption Registry
311 West Saratoga Street
Baltimore, MD 21201-3251
Phone: (410) 767-7423
Toll-Free: (800) 392-3678
E-mail: msmith11@dhr.state.md.us
Web site: www.dhr.state.md.us/
voladopr.htm

Children's Bureau funded

Collaboration to AdoptUSKids
Adoption Exchange Association
8015 Corporate Drive
Baltimore, MD 21236
Phone: (410) 933-5700
Fax: (303) 933-5716
Toll-Free: (888) 200-4005
E-mail: info@adoptuskids.org
Web site: www.adoptuskids.org

National Institute of Child Health and Human Development
31 Center Drive
Bldg 31, Room 2A32, MSC 2425
Bethesda, MD 20892-2425
Toll-Free: (800) 370-2943
E-mail: NICHDClearinghouse@
mail.nih.gov
Web site: www.nichd.nih.gov

Resource Center

Collaboration to AdoptUSKids
Adoption Exchange Association
8015 Corporate Drive
Baltimore, MD 21236
Phone: (410) 933-5700
Fax: (303) 933-5716
Toll-Free: (888) 200-4005
E-mail: info@adoptuskids.org
Web site: www.adoptuskids.org

Maternal and Child Health Bureau
Parklawn Building Room 18-05
5600 Fishers Lane
Rockville, MD 20857
Phone: (301) 443-2170
Fax: (301) 443-1797
E-mail: ctibbs@hrsa.gov
Web site: www.mchb.hrsa.gov/

Service provider

Collaboration to AdoptUSKids
Adoption Exchange Association
8015 Corporate Drive
Baltimore, MD 21236
Phone: (410) 933-5700

Fax: (303) 933-5716
Toll-Free: (888) 200-4005
E-mail: info@adoptuskids.org
Web site: www.adoptuskids.org

International Social Services – American Branch
700 Light Street
Baltimore, MD 21230
Phone: (410) 230-2734
Fax: (410) 230-2741
E-mail: issusa@lirs.org
Web site: www.iss-usa.org

MASSACHUSETTS

Adoptive/Foster Family Support Groups

A Program of Children's Friend
20 Hamilton Street
Worcester, MA 01604-2202
Phone: (508) 791-4488
Fax: (508) 753-9625

A Red Thread Adoption Services
681 Washington Street, Suite 12
Norwood, MA 02062
Phone: (781) 762-22428
Fax: (781) 762-2561
Toll free: (888) 871-9699
E-mail: info@redthreadadopt.org
Web site: www.redthreadadopt.
org

Adoption Counselors, Inc
130 Temple Street
West Newton, MA 02465
Phone: (617) 969-7025

Adoption Choices/Jewish Family Service of Metrowest
475 Franklin Street, Suite 101
Framingham, MA 01702
Phone: (508) 875-3100
Fax: (508) 875-4373
Toll-Free: (800) 872-5232
E-mail: deldridge@jfsmw.org
Web site: www.adoptionchoices.
info

Adoption Resource Center
380 Massachusetts Avenue
Acton, MA 01720
Phone: (978) 264-3813
Fax: (978) 263-3088
E-mail: MRowlinson@cfys.org
Web site: www.CFYS.org

Adoptive Families Together, Inc.
418 Commonwealth Avenue
Boston, MA 02215-2801
Phone: (617) 929-3800
Fax: (617) 929-3850
E-mail: noffarrell@verizon.net
Web site: www.adoptivefamilies.
org

Boston Single Mothers By Choice
P.O. Box 600027
Newtonville, MA 02160-0001
Phone: (617) 964-9949

Canton Area Adoptive Families Together
104 Rockland Street
Canton, MA 02021
Phone: (718) 828-8797

Center for Family Connections
350 Cambridge Street
Cambridge, MA 02141
Phone: (617) 547-0909
Fax: (617) 497-5952
Toll-Free: (800) 546-6328
Web site: www.kinnect.org

Children's Aid and Family Service of Hampshire County, Inc. (CAFS)
8 Trumbull Road
Northampton, MA 01060
Phone: (413) 584-5690
Fax: (413) 586-9436
E-mail: admin@cafshc.org
Web site: http://users.rcn.
com/cafs

Families for Russian and Ukrainian Adoptions
New England Area
669 Main Street
Lancaster, MA 01523
Phone: (978) 368-1966
E-mail: info@fruanewengland.org
Web site: www.fruanewengland.
org

Family Center Pre and Post Adoption Consulting Team
366 Somerville Avenue
Somerville, MA 02143
Phone: (617) 628-8815

Home for Little Wanderers
271 Huntington Avenue
Boston, MA 02115
Phone: (617) 267-3700
Fax: (617) 267-8142
Toll-Free: (888) 466-3321
E-mail: pwisnewski@thehome.
org
Web site: www.thehome.org

Latin American Adoptive Families
211 Turner Road
Falmouth, MA 02536
Phone: (508) 459-4525
Web site: www.marisol.com/
laaf/laafhome.htm

Massachusetts Coalition for Adoption, Inc.
504 Dudley Street
Roxbury, MA 02119
Phone: (617) 445-6655
Fax: (617) 445-4796
E-mail: kstevens@csrox.org

ODS Adoption Community of New England
1750 Washington Street
Holliston, MA 01746-2234
Phone: (508) 429-4260
Fax: (508) 429-2261
Toll free (800 93ADOPT
E-mail: info@odsacone.org
Web site: www.odsma.org

ParentaLinks at Center for Family Connections
350 Cambridge Street
Cambridge, MA 02141
Phone: (617) 547-0909
Fax: (617) 497-5952
After hours: (617) 547-0909
E-mail: cffc@kinnect.org
Web site: www.kinnect.org

Raising Our Children's Children
89 Ruthuen Street
Dorchester, MA 02121
Phone: (617) 541-3561

Single Parents for the Adoption of Children Everywhere
6 Sunshine Avenue
Natick, MA 01760
Phone: (508) 655-5426

Stars of David of Massachusetts
8 Brook Way
Westboro, MA 01581
Phone: (508) 752-2512
E-mail: starsdavid@aol.com
Web site: www.starsofdavid.org

Licensed Private Adoption Agencies

A Full Circle Adoptions
39 Main Street
Northampton, MA 01060
Phone: (413) 587-0007
Fax: (413) 584-1624
Toll-Free: (888) 452-3678
Toll-Free: (800) 452-3678
E-mail: adoption@fullcircleadop
tions.com
Web site: www.
fullcircleadoptions.org

A Red Thread Adoption Services
681 Washington Street, Suite 12
Norwood, MA 02062
Phone: (781) 762-2428
Fax: (781) 762-2561
Toll-Free: (888) 871-9699

E-mail: info@redthreadadopt.org
Web site: www.redthreadadopt.
org

Act of Love Adoptions
6 Huron Drive
Natick, MA 01760
Toll-Free: (800) 277-5387

Adoption Choices/Jewish Family Service of Metrowest
475 Franklin Street, Suite 101
Framingham, MA 01702
Phone: (508) 875-3100
Fax: (508) 875-4373
Toll-Free: (800) 872-5232
E-mail: deldridge@jfsmw.org
Web site: www.
adoptionchoicesinfo.org

Adoption Resource Associates
262 Upland Road
Cambridge, MA 02140
Phone: (617) 492-8888

Adoption Resource Center at Brightside
Brightside for Families and Children
2112 Riverdale Street
West Springfield, MA 01089
Phone: (413) 788-7366
Fax: (413) 827-4377
Toll-Free: (877) 777-7774
E-mail: info@brightsideadoption.
org
Web site: www.
brightsideadoption.org
– Intercountry Program
– Child Placement

Adoption Resources
1340 Centre Street
Newton Centre, MA 02159
Phone: (617) 332-2218
Fax: (617) 332-2695
Toll-Free: (800) 533-4346
E-mail: adoptionresources.org
– Intercountry Program
– Child Placement

Adoption With Love, Inc.
188 Needham Street, Suite 250
Newton, MA 02464
Phone: (617) 964-4357
Fax: (617) 964-2676
Toll-Free: (800) 722-7731
E-mail: acohen@awlonline.org
Web site: www.
adoptionswithlove.org

AdoptionLink
15 Lenox Street
Springfield, MA 01108
Phone: (413) 737-2601
Fax: (413) 737-0323
Toll-Free: (800) 942-3947
E-mail: info@jfslink.org
Web site: www.jfslink.org

Adoptive Families Together, Inc.
20 Harvard Drive
Hingham, MA 02043
Phone: (781) 749-1106
Toll-Free: (617) 929-3850
E-mail: linda@adoptivefamilies.
org
Web site: www.adoptivefamilies.
org

Alliance for Children, Inc.
55 William Street, Suite G10
Wellesley, MA 02481
Phone: (781) 431-7148
Fax: (781) 431-7474
E-mail: info@allforchildren.org
Web site: www.allforchildren.org

American-International Children's Alliance, Inc.
P.O. Box 858
Marblehead, MA 01945
Phone: (781) 631-7900
Fax: (603) 658-6579
Toll-Free: (866) 862-3678
E-mail: aica@comcast.net
Web site: www.adopting.
com/aica

Angel Adoptions, Inc.
11 Dix Street
Waltham, MA 02453

Phone: (781) 899-9222
Fax: (781) 893-8022
E-mail: adoption@angel-
adoptions.org
Web site: www.angel-adoptions.
org

Beacon Adoption Center, Inc.
66 Lake Buel Road
Great Barrington, MA 01230
Phone: (413) 528-2749
Fax: (413) 528-4311
E-mail: mmccurdy@bcn.net
Web site: www.michaelmccu rdy.
com/beacon.htm

Berkshire Center for Families and Children
480 West Street
Pittsfield, MA 01201
Phone: (413) 448-8281

Bethany Christian Services
1538 Turnpike Street
North Andover, MA 01845
Phone: (508) 683-5676
E-mail: bcsrhodeisland@bethany.
org
Web site: www.bethany.org

Boston Adoption Bureau, Inc.
14 Beacon Street, Suite 620
Boston, MA 02108
Phone: (617) 277-1336
Fax: (617) 227-6308
Toll-Free: (800) 338-2224
E-mail: bostonadop@aol.com

Brightside, Inc.
480 West Street
Pittsfield, MA 01201
Phone: (413) 496-9491

Cambridge Family and Children's Services
929 Massachusetts Avenue
Cambridge, MA 02139
Phone: (617) 876-4210
Toll-Free: (800) 906-4163
E-mail: adoption@helpfamilies.org
Web site: www.helpfamilies.org

Catholic Charities of
Cambridge and Somerville
270 Washington Street
Somerville, MA 02143
Phone: (617) 625-1920

Catholic Social Services
P.O. Box M-South Station
Fall River, MA 02724
Phone: (401) 624-0970

Child and Family Service
800 Purchase Street, 4th Floor
New Bedford, MA 02740
Phone: (508) 990-0894
Fax: (413) 586-9436
E-mail: mcaron@cfservices.org

Children's Friend, Inc.
21 Cedar Street
Worcester, MA 01609
Phone: (508) 753-5425
Fax: (508) 757-7659

Children's Legal Services, Inc.
18 Tremont Street, Suite 527
Boston, MA 02108
Phone: (617) 227-3232

Children's Services of Rox-
bury, Inc.
2406 Washington Street
Roxbury, MA 02119
Phone: (617) 445-6655
Fax: (617) 542-2369

China Adoption With Love, Inc
251 Harvard Street, Suite 17
Brookline, MA 02446
Fax: (617) 232-8288
Toll-Free: (800) 888-9812
E-mail: cawli@aol.com
Web site: www.chinaadoption.
org
– Intercountry Program
– Child Placement

Communities for People, Inc.
418 Commonwealth Avenue
Boston, MA 02215
Phone: (617) 267-1031

Concord Family and Youth
Services, Inc.
380 Massachusetts Avenue
Acton, MA 01720
Phone: (978) 263-3006
Fax: (978) 264-3855
Web site: www.cfys.org

DARE Family Services
2 Electronics Avenue
Danvers, MA 01923
Phone: (978) 750-0751
Fax: (978) 750-0749

DARE Family Services
17 Poplar Street
Roslindale, MA 02131
Phone: (617) 469-2311
Fax: (617) 469-3007

Family and Children's Services
of Catholic Charities
53 Highland Avenue
Fitchburg, MA 01420
Phone: (978) 343-4879

Florence Crittenton League
119 Hall Street
Lowell, MA 01854-9671
Phone: (978) 452-9671
Fax: (978) 970-0070
E-mail: info@fcleague.org
Web site: www.fcleague.org

Gift of Life Adoption Services,
Inc.
1087 Newman Avenue
Seekonk, MA 02771
Phone: (508) 761-5661
Web site: www.giftoflife.cc

Home for Little Wanderers
271 Huntington Avenue
Boston, MA 02115
Phone: (617) 267-3700
Fax: (617) 267-8142
Toll-Free: (888) 466-3321
E-mail: pwisnewski@thehome.
org
Web site: www.thehome.org

Hope Adoptions, Inc.
21 Cedar Street
Worcester, MA 01609
Phone: (508) 753-5425

Jewish Family Services of
Worcester
646 Salisbury Street
Worcester, MA 01609
Phone: (508) 757-5579
E-mail: info@jfsworcester.org
Web site: www.jfsworcester.org

Jewish Family and Children's
Services Adoption Resources
1340 Centre Street
Newton, MA 02159
Phone: (617) 332-2218

Love the Children of
Massachusetts
2 Perry Drive
Duxbury, MA 02332
Phone: (781) 934-0063

Lutheran Social Services of
New England, Inc.
74 Elm Street, 2nd Floor
Worcester, MA 01609-2833
Phone: (508) 791-4488
Fax: (508) 753-8051
Toll-Free: (800) 286-9889
E-mail: LSSadoptma@aol.com
Web site: www.adoptlss.org

New Bedford Child and Family
Services
1061 Pleasant Street
New Bedford, MA 02740
Phone: (508) 996-8572
E-mail: crocha@cfservices.org
Web site: www.cfservices.org

Red Thread Adoption Ser-
vices, Inc.
13 Devon Road
Norwood, MA 02062
Toll-Free: (888) 871-9699
E-mail: redthreadadopt@aol.com

Special Adoption Family Services
418 Commonwealth Avenue
Boston, MA 02215-2801
Phone: (617) 572-3678
Fax: (617) 572-3611

United Homes for Children
1147 Main Street, Suite 209-210
Tewksbury, MA 01876
Phone: (978) 640-0089
Fax: (978) 640-9652

Wide Horizons For Children, Inc.
38 Edge Hill Road
Waltham, MA 02451
Phone: (781) 894-5330
Fax: (781) 899-2769
E-mail: info@whfc.org
Web site: www.whfc.org

Birth Family and Search Support Groups

Adoption Connection
351 Lowell Street
Peabody, MA 01960
Phone: (978) 532-1261
E-mail: suedarke@aol.com
Web site: www.adoptionconnection.qpg.com

Adoption Resource Center
350 Cambridge Street
Cambridge, MA 02141
Phone: (617) 547-0909
E-mail: cfsc@kinnect.org

Adoptive Families Together, Inc.
100 Lorraine Drive
East Bridgewater, MA 02333-2029
Phone: (508) 350-9811
E-mail: theresamcnulty@hotmail.com
Web site: www.adoptivefamilies.org
– Intercountry Program

Bright Futures Adoption Center, Inc.
5 Broadview Street
Acton, MA 01720
Phone: (978) 263-5400
Fax: (978) 266-1909
Toll-Free: (877) 652-6678
E-mail: adopt@comap.com
Web site: www.bright-futures.org

Cape Cod Adoption Connection
P.O. Box 336
Brewster, MA 02631
Phone: (508) 896-7332

Center For Family Connections (CFFC)
350 Cambridge Street
Cambridge, MA 02141
Phone: (617) 547-0909
Fax: (617) 497-5952
Toll-Free: (800) 546-6328
E-mail: cffc@kinnect.org
Web site: www.kinnect.org

Concerned United Birthparents (CUB)
Harvard Square
P.O. Box 396
Cambridge, MA 02238-0396
Phone: (617) 328-3005
E-mail: LIBSTEVE@aol.com
Web site: www.cubirthparents.org

Family Center/PACT
366 Somerville Avenue
Somerville, MA 02144
(619) 628-8815

TRY Resource Center
P.O. Box 989
214 State Street
Northampton, MA 01061-0989
Phone: (413) 584-6599
E-mail: try@try.org
Web site: www.try.org

State Adoption Specialist/Manager

Massachusetts Department of Social Services
24 Farnsworth Street
Boston, MA 02210
Phone: (617) 748-2267
Fax: (617) 261-7437
Toll-Free: (800) 543-7508
E-mail: Leo.farley@state.ma.us
Web site: www.mass.gov

State Foster Care Specialist/Manager

Massachusetts Department of Social Services
24 Farnsworth Street
Boston, MA 02110
Phone: (617) 748-2267
Fax: (617) 261-7437
Toll free: (800) 543-7508
E-mail: Leo.farley@state.ma.us
Web site: www.mass.gov

State Interstate Compact on the Placement of Children (ICPC) Administrator

Massachusetts Department of Social Services
Central Office 24 Farnsworth Street
Boston, MA 02110
Phone: (617) 748-2345
E-mail: Beryl.Domingo@state.ma.us

State Licensing Specialist

Massachusetts Office of Child Care Services
Kime McDowell
1 Ashburton Place, Room 1105
Boston, MA 02218
Phone: (617) 988-6600
Web site: www.qualitychildcare.org

State Reunion Registry

Adoption Search Coordinator
24 Farnsworth Street
Boston, MA 02210
Phone: (617) 748-2240

**Statewide Adoption
Recruitment Line**

Massachusetts Statewide
Adoption Recruitment Line
Toll-Free: (800)-KI DS-508

**Statewide Foster Care
Specialist/Manager**

Massachusetts Department of
Social ServicesLeo Farley
24 Farnsworth Street
Boston, MA 02210
Phone: (617) 748-2267
Fax: (617) 261-7437
Toll free: (800) 543-7508
E-mail: Leo.farley@state.ma.us
Web site: www.mass.gove/
portal/index.jsp?

MICHIGAN

**Adoptive/Foster Family
Support Groups**

A.D.O.P.T.
6939 Shields Court
Saginaw, MI 48603
Phone: (517) 781-2089

**Adopt America Network and
North American Council on
Adoptable Children**
3051 Siebert Road
Midland, MI 48640
Phone: (517) 832-8117

**Adoption Identity Movement
of Michigan, Inc.**
P.O. Box 812
Hazel Park, MI 48030
Phone: (248) 548-6291

Adoption Resource Group
1524 Ravineside Drive
Houghton, MI 49931-2700
Phone: (906) 482-5954

**Adoptive Family Support
Network**
233 East Fulton, Suite 108
Grand Rapids, MI 49503
Phone: (616) 458-7945
Fax: (616) 458-7545
E-mail: adoptive@afsn.org
Web site: www.afsn.org

**Adult Adoptee and Birthparent
Support Group**
21700 Northwestern Highway
Suite 1490
Southfield, MI 48075
Phone: (248) 423-2770
Fax: (248) 423-2783
Web site: www.lssm.org

**Anishnabek Community Family
Services (ACFS)**
2864 Ashmun Street
Sault Ste. Marie, MI 49783
Phone: (906) 632-5250
Fax: (906) 632-5266
E-mail: cmcpherson@saulttribe.net
Web site: www.saulttribe.org

Bethany Christian Services
6995 West 48th Street
Fremont, MI 49412-0173
Phone: (231) 924-3390
Fax: (231) 924-2848
E-mail: sjordan@bethany.org
Web site: www.bethany.org/
fremont_mi

CFS of NW Michigan
3785 Veterans Drive
Traverse City, MI 49684
Phone: (616) 946-2104
Fax: (231) 946-0451

Caring Network
1441 South Westnidge
Kalamazoo, MI 49008
Phone: (269) 381-1234
Fax: (616) 381-2932

**Catholic Social Services of
Marquette, Upper Peninsula**
347 Rock Street
Marquette, MI 49855
Phone: (906) 227-9121
Fax: (906) 228-2469
E-mail: lkearney@dioceseofmar
quette.org

Child and Parent Services, Inc.
30600 Telegraph Road
Suite 2215
Bingham Farms, MI 48025
Phone: (248) 646-7790
Fax: (248) 646-4544
Toll-Free: (800) 248-0106
E-mail: cathyeisenberg@aol.com
Web site: www.
childandparentservices.com

Christian Family Services
17105 West 12 Mile Road
Southfield, MI 48076
Phone: (248) 557-8390
Fax: (248) 557-6427
E-mail: cfspyo@aol.com
Web site: www.cfspyo.org

**Clinton County Council for the
Prevention of Child Abuse and
Neglect**
13109 Scavey Road, Suite 4
DeWitt, MI 48820
Phone: (517) 668-0185
Fax: (517) 668-0446
After hours: (517) 646-6983
E-mail: klooster@edzone.net

DAAPSS
713 East F Street
Iron Mountain, MI 49801
Phone: (906) 779-1477

El Centro of Bethany
339 East 16th , Suite 201
Holland, MI 49423
Phone: (269) 396-3391
Fax: (616) 396-1103

Families for International Children
P.O. Box 9974
Wyoming, MI 49509
E-mail: soltysiakP@aol.com
Web site: www.fficgr.org

Families on the Move and North American
Council on Adoptable Children
18727 Avon
Detroit, MI 48219
Phone: (313) 532-0012
Fax: (313) 532-1345
E-mail: vedadthompkins@aol.com

Family Service and Children's Aid (FSCA)
P.O. Box 6128
330 West Michigan Avenue
Jackson, MI 49201
Phone: (517) 787-7920
Fax: (517) 787-2440
E-mail: adoption@strong-families.org
Web site: www.strong-families.org

Foster and Adoptive Family Resource and Support Center
1321 West Michigan Avenue
Battle Creek, MI 49017
Phone: (616) 660-0448
Fax: (616) 660-0449
E-mail: FostAdoptSupport@aol.com

Foster/Adoptive Family Resource Center
23891 Bedford Road
Battle Creek, MI 49017
Phone: (616) 721-8120
Fax: (616) 660-0449

Ing Co Parent Group
809 West Willow Highway
Grand Ledge, MI 48837
Phone: (517) 627-9231

International Adoption Association, Inc.
(DBA Adoption Pros)
517 Baldwin Street
Jenison, MI 49428
Phone: (616) 457-6537
Fax: (616) 457-1260
Toll-Free: (800) 546-4046
E-mail: iaainc@aol.com
Web site: www.adoptionspros.com

Jewish Family Service Alliance for Adoption
24123 Greenfield Road
Southfield, MI 48075
Phone: (248) 559-0117
Fax: (248) 559-5403
E-mail: dstpeter@jfsdetroit.org

Kinship Care Services
Calhoun Intermediate School District
17111 G Drive North
Marshall, MI 49068
Phone: (269) 789-2434
Fax: (269) 789-9584
E-mail: kingp@calhounisd.org
Web site: www.calhounisd.org/sapekinshipcare.htm

MPASS
901 West Memorial Drive
Houghton, MI 49931
Phone: (906) 482-9404

Mason County Foster/Adoptive Association
6052 East Interlochen Road
Fountain, MI 49410
Phone: (616) 462-3566

Michigan Association of Single Adoptive Parents
7412 Coolidge
Centerline, MI 48015
Phone: (810) 758-6909

Michigan Family Independence Agency
235 South Grand Avenue
Lansing, MI 48909

Michigan Foster and Adoptive Parents Association
9786 Sommerset Road
Detroit, MI 48224
Phone: (313) 372-2279
Fax: (313) 272-1403
E-mail: lilliousion@aol.com

Midland County Foster Adoptive Network
3100 Shreeve
Midland, MI 48664
Phone: (989) 835-8738
Fax: (989) 835-4702

Morning Star Adoption Center (MSAC)
15635 West Twelve Mile Road
Southfield, MI 48076
Phone: (248) 483-5484
Fax: (248) 483-6309
Toll-Free: (866) 236-7866
E-mail: msac@bignet.net

North American Council on Adoptable Children Representative
23891 Bedford Road
Battle Creek, MI 49017
Phone: (616) 660-0448

Orchards Adoptive Parent Support Group
30215 Southfield Road, Suite 100
Southfield, MI 48076
Phone: (248) 258-1278

Post Adoption Resources
21700 Northwestern Highway, Suite 1490
Southfield, MI 48075-4901
Phone: (248) 423-2770

Post-Adoption Support Services
805 Leonard NE
Grand Rapids, MI 49302
Phone: (616) 451-2021

Resources for Open Adoption
721 Hawthorne
Royal Oak, MI 48067
Phone: (248) 543-0097
E-mail: brenr@openadoptionins
ight.org
Web site: www.r2pless.com

Singles for Adoption
619 Norton Drive
Kalamazoo, MI 49001
Phone: (616) 381-2581

Spaulding for Children/ National Resource
Center for Special Needs
Adoption
16250 Northland Drive, Suite 120
Southfield, MI 48075
Phone: (248) 443-7080
Fax: (248) 443-7099
E-mail: sfc@spaulding.org
Web site: www.spaulding.org/
adoption/NRC-adoption.html

Stars of David
4458 Apple Valley Lane
West Bloomfield, MI 48323
Phone: (810) 737-3874
E-mail: starsdavid@aol.com
Web site: www.starsofdavid.org

Stars of David International, Inc.
7423 Westbury
West Bloomfield, MI 48322
Phone: (248) 661-3978
E-mail: rosa7423@hotmail.com
Web site: www.starsofdavid.org

The Children's Center of Wayne County
90 Selden
Detroit, MI 48201
Phone: (313) 832-3555
Fax: (313) 262-0901
E-mail: kgarrett@childrensctr.net
Web site: www.
thechildrenscenter.org

The Connection
171 Dawson Street
Sandusky, MI 48471
Phone: (810) 648-0112
Fax: (810) 648-3699

Wayne, Oakland and Macomb County
18066 Greenlawn
Detroit, MI 48221
Phone: (348) 797-3334
Fax: (313) 342-4191
E-mail: crogersd@aol.com

Licensed Private Adoption Agencies

Adoption Associates, Inc
13535 State Road
Grand Ledge, MI 48837-9626
Phone: (517) 627-0805
E-mail: adopt@adoptassoc.com
Web site: www.adoptassoc.com

Adoption Associates, Inc.
1338 Baldwin Street
Jenison, MI 49428
Phone: (616) 667-0677
Fax: (616) 667-0920
E-mail: adopt@adoptassoc.com
Web site: www.adoptassoc.com

Adoption Associates, Inc.
3609 Country Club Drive
St. Clair Shores, MI 48082-2952
Phone: (810) 294-1990
Fax: (616) 667-0920
E-mail: adopt@adoptassoc.com
Web site: www.adoptassoc.com

Adoption Associates, Inc.
800 Thomas L. Parkway
Suite 1
Lansing, MI 48917
Phone: (517) 327-1388
E-mail: adopt@adoptassoc.com
Web site: www.adoptassoc.com

Adoption Consultants
32781 Middlebelt Road
Farmington, MI 48334
Phone: (248) 737-0336
Fax: (248) 737-0349
E-mail: aciadopt@core.com
Web site: www.aciadoption.com

Adoptions of the Heart, Inc.
4295 Summerwind Avenue NE
Grand Rapids, MI 49525
Phone: (616) 365-9811
Fax: (616) 365-9325
E-mail: adoptaid@iserv.net
Web site: www.iserv.net/
~adoptaid

Alliance for Adoption/Jewish Family Service
24123 Greenfield Road
Southfield, MI 48075
Phone: (248) 559-0117
Fax: (248) 559-5403
E-mail: dstpeter@jfsdetroit.org

Alternatives for Children and Families
P.O. Box 3038
609 South Saginaw Street, Suite 505
Flint, MI 48502
Phone: (810) 235-0683
Fax: (810) 235-4619

Americans for International Aid and Adoption
2151 Livernois, Suite 200
Troy, MI 48083
Phone: (248) 362-1207
Fax: (248) 362-8222
Web site: www.aiaaadopt.org

Bethany Christian Services
5985 West Main Street, Suite 104
Kalamazoo, MI 49009-8708
Phone: (269) 372-8800
Fax: (269) 372-8855
E-mail: bcskalamazoo@bethany.
org
Web site: www.bethany.org/
kalamazoo

Bethany Christian Services
P.O. Box 294
901 Eastern Avenue NE
Grand Rapids, MI 49501-0294
Phone: (612) 224-7479
Fax: (616) 224-7589
E-mail: bcsgrandrapids@bethany.
org
Web site: www.bethany.org

Catholic Family Services
1819 Gull Road
Kalamazoo, MI 49098
Phone: (269) 381-9800
Fax: (269) 381-2932

Child and Family Services of Michigan, State Office
P.O. Box 348
2157 University Park Drive
Okemos, MI 48805
Phone: (517) 349-6226
Fax: (517) 349-0969
Toll-Free: (800) 878-6587
E-mail: cfsm@cfsm.org
Web site: www.cfsm.org

Child and Parent Services, Inc.
30600 Telegraph Road, Suite 2215
Bingham Farms, MI 48025
Phone: (248) 646-7790
Fax: (248) 646-4544
Toll-Free: (800) 248-0106
Web site: www.
childandparentservices.com

Children's Hope Adoption Services
P.O. Box 467
Mt. Pleasant, MI 48804
Phone: (989) 775-8229
Fax: (989) 775-8208

Christ Child House
15751 Joy Road
Detroit, MI 48228
Phone: (313) 584-6077
Fax: (313) 584-1148
Web site: www.christchild
house.org

Christian Care Maternity Ministries
214 North Mill Street
St. Louis, MI 48880
Phone: (517) 681-2172

Christian Cradle, Inc.
4590 Oakwood Drive
Okemos, MI 48664
Phone: (517) 351-7500
Fax: (517) 351-4810
Toll-Free: (800) 891-2584

D.A. Blodgett Services for Children and Families
805 Leonard Street NE
Grand Rapids, MI 49503-1184
Phone: (616) 451-2021
Fax: (616) 451-8936
Web site: www.dablodgett.org

Eagle Village , Inc.
4507 170th Avenue
Hersey, MI 49639
Phone: (231) 832-2234
Fax: (231) 832-2470
Toll-Free: (800) 748-0061
Web site: www.eaglevillage.org

Eastern European Adoption Services
INC 22233 Genesis
Woodhaven, MI 48183
Phone: (734) 479-2348
Fax: (734) 479-6330
– Intercountry Program
– Child Placement

Eastern European Adoption Services
177 Biddle
Wyandotte, MI 48192
Phone: (734) 246-9802
Fax: (734) 246-9802

Ennis Center for Children
129 East 3rd Street
Flint, MI 48502
Phone: (810) 233-4031
Fax: (810) 233-0008
E-mail: support@enniscenter.org
Web site: www.enniscenter.org

Ennis Center for Children
3650 Dixie Highway
Waterford, MI 48329
Phone: (248) 618-1260
Fax: (248) 618-1266
E-mail: support@enniscenter.org
Web site: www.enniscenter.org

Evergreen Children's Services
10421 West Seven Mile Road
Detroit, MI 48221
Phone: (313) 862-1000
Fax: (313) 862-6464
E-mail:
dredmand@evergreenserv.org
Web site: www.evergreenserv.
org

Family Adoption Consultants
P.O. Box 50489
421 West Crosstown Parkway
Kalamazoo, MI 49005
Phone: (269) 343-3316
Fax: (269) 343-3359
E-mail: melissa@facadopt.org
Web site: www.facadopt.org

Family Counseling and Children's Services of Lenewee County
220 North Main Street
Adrian, MI 49221
Phone: (517) 265-5352
Fax: (517) 263-6090
E-mail: fccsoflenawee@hotmail.
com
Web site: www.fccservices.org

Family MatchMakers, Inc.
2544 Martin SE
Grand Rapids, MI 49507
Phone: (616) 243-1803
Fax: (616) 243-1803
Web site: www.
familymatchmakers.org

Family Service and Children's Aid (FSCA)
P.O. Box 6128
330 West Michigan Avenue
Jackson, MI 49201
Phone: (517) 787-7920
Fax: (517) 787-2440
E-mail: adoption@strong-families.org
Web site: www.strong-families.org

Family and Children's Services, Inc.
535 Emmett Street East
Battle Creek, MI 49017
Phone: (269) 965-3247
Fax: (269) 966-4135
E-mail: battlecreek@csfm.org
Web site: www.cfsm.org

Family and Children's Services, Inc.
1608 Lake Street
Kalamazoo, MI 49001
Phone: (269) 344-0202
Fax: (269) 344-0285
E-mail: anneh@csfm.org
Web site: www.cfsm.org

Forever Families, Inc.
42400 West Grand River Avenue, Suite 101
Novi, MI 48375
Phone: (248) 344-9606
Fax: (248) 344-9604
E-mail: info@forever-families.org
Web site: www.forever-families.org

Hands Across the Water
2890 Carpenter Road, Suite 600
Ann Arbor, MI 48108
Phone: (734) 477-0135
Fax: (734) 477-0213
E-mail: hatw.nelson@att.net
Web site: www.hatw.org

HelpSource
201 North Wayne Road
Westland, MI 48185-3689

Phone: (734) 722-0423
Fax: (734) 641-8524
Web site: www.helpsourceagency.com

Homes for Black Children
511 East Larned Street
Detroit, MI 48226
Phone: (313) 961-4777
Fax: (313) 961-2994
E-mail: hbchildren@aol.com
Web site: www.homesforblackchildren.org

Interact Family Services
1260 Woodkrest Drive
Flint, MI 48532

International Adoption Association
517 Baldwin Avenue
Jenison, MI 49428
Phone: (616) 457-6537
Fax: (616) 457-1260
E-mail: iaainc@aol.com
Web site: www.adoptionpros.com

Judson Center
4925 Packard Street, Suite 200
Ann Arbor, MI 48108
Phone: (734) 528-1720
Fax: (734) 528-1695

Keane Center for Adoption
930 Mason
Dearborn, MI 48124
Phone: (313) 277-4664
Fax: (313) 278-1767
E-mail: cbrail@provide.net
Web site: www.keaneadoption.org

Lula Belle Stewart Center
11000 West McNichols, Suite 115
Detroit, MI 48221
Phone: (313) 862-4600
Fax: (313) 864-2233

Lutheran Adoption Service
21700 Northwestern Highway, Suite 1490
Southfield, MI 48075-4919
Phone: (248) 423-2770

Fax: (248) 423-2783
Web site: www.lssm.org/service/adoption/adoption.asp

Lutheran Adoption Service
Kalamazoo Branch
3234 South Westnedge Avenue
Kalamazoo, MI 49008
Phone: (269) 345-5776
Fax: (269) 345-4011
E-mail: jcare@lssm.org

Lutheran Adoption Service
Ann Arbor Branch
2500 Packard Road
Ann Arbor, MI 48104
Phone: (734) 971-1944
Fax: (734) 971-2137
E-mail: jcare@lssm.org
Web site: www.lasadoption.org

Methodist Children's Home Society
26645 West 6 Mile Road
Detroit, MI 48240
Phone: (313) 531-4060
Fax: (313) 531-9962
E-mail: lkoger@provide.net
Web site: www.resa.net/earlyon/agency/methodistchildren.html

Michigan Indian Child Welfare Agency
1345 Monroe Avenue NW, Suite 220
Grand Rapids, MI 49505
Phone: (616) 454-9221
Fax: (616) 454-3142
Toll-Free: (800) 880-2089

Michigan Indian Child Welfare Agency
6425 South Pennsylvania Avenue, Suite 3
Lansing, MI 48911
Phone: (517) 393-3256
Fax: (517) 393-0838
Toll-Free: (800) 346-4292
E-mail: heximerl@aol.com

Oakland Family Service
114 Orchard Lake Road
Pontiac, MI 48341
Phone: (248) 858-7215
Fax: (248) 858-8227
E-mail: ofs@ofs-family.org

Orchards Children's Services
42140 Van Dyke Road, Suite 206
Sterling Heights, MI 48314
Phone: (810) 997-3886
Fax: (810) 997-0629
E-mail: adopt@orchards.org
Web site: www.orchard.org

Sault Tribe Binogii Placement Agency
2864 Ashmun Street, 3rd Floor
Sault St. Marie, MI 49783
Phone: (906) 632-5250
Fax: (906) 632-5266
E-mail: patch2@sootribe.org
Web site: www.sootribe.org

Spaulding for Children
16250 Northland Drive, Suite 120
Southfield, MI 48075
Phone: (248) 443-0300
Fax: (248) 443-2845
E-mail: sfc@Spaulding.org
Web site: www.spaulding.org

Spectrum Human Services, Inc.
23077 Greenfield Road, Suite 500
Southfield, MI 48075
Phone: (248) 552-8020
Fax: (248) 552-1135
E-mail:
rswaninger@spectrumhuman.org
Web site: www.spectrumhuman.org

St. Francis Family Services
17500 West 8 Mile Road
Southfield, MI 48075
Phone: (248) 552-0750
Fax: (248) 552-9019

St. Vincent-Sarah Fisher Center
27400 West 12 Mile Road
Farmington Hills, MI 48334
Phone: (248) 626-7527
Fax: (248) 539-3584
E-mail: svs@aol.com
Web site: www.svsfcenter.org

Teen Ranch, Inc.
2861 Main Street
Marlette, MI 48453
Phone: (989) 635-7511
Fax: (989) 635-3324
E-mail: lponder@teenranch.com
Web site: www.teenranch.com
— Intercountry Program
— Home Study

Whaley Children's Center
1201 North Grand Traverse Street
Flint, MI 48503
Phone: (810) 234-3603
Fax: (810) 232-3416
Web site: www.whaleychildren.org

Birth Family and Search Support Groups

A.P.A.R.T. (Adoptees and Parents Alone Rejoicing Together)
1175 Roberts Road
Stockbridge, MI 49285
Phone: (517) 851-7129

Adoptee's Search for Knowledge
P.O. Box 762
East Lansing, MI 48826-0762
Phone: (517) 321-7291

Adoption Circle Support Group
4925 Packard
Ann Arbor, MI 48108-1521
Phone: (313) 971-9781

Adoption Connections of Battle Creek
P.O. Box 293
8072 Kingsbury
Cloverdale, MI 49035-0293
Phone: (616) 623-8060

Adoption Identity Movement (AIM)
Southeast Michigan Area
P.O. Box 812
Hazel Park, MI 48030
Phone: (248) 548-6291
E-mail: DGeorgeW@aol.com

Adoption Insight
P.O. Box 171
Portage, MI 49081
Phone: (616) 327-1999

Adoption Support Group
21700 Northwestern Highway, Suite 1490
Southfield, MI 48075-4901
Phone: (810) 423-2770

Birth Bond
1015 East Columbia Street
Mason, MI 48854

Bonding by Blood, Unlimited
5845 Waterman Road
Foess Family Farm
Vassar, MI 48768-9790
Phone: (517) 823-8248

Catholic Services of Macomb County
P.O. Box 380290
15945 Canal Road
Clinton Township, MI 48038
Phone: (586) 416-2300
Fax: (586) 416-2311
Toll-Free: (888) BABYDUE
Web site: www.csmacomb.org/adoption.htm

Child and Family Services of Michigan, State Office
P.O. Box 348
2157 University Park Drive
Okemos, MI 48805
Phone: (517) 349-6226
Fax: (517) 349-0969
Toll-Free: (800) 878-6587
E-mail: christy@cfsm.org
Web site: www.cfsm.org

Child and Parent Services, Inc.
30600 Telegraph Road,
Suite 2215
Bingham Farms, MI 48025
Phone: (248) 646-7790
Fax: (248) 646-4544
Toll-Free: (800) 248-0106
E-mail: cathyeisenberg@aol.com
Web site: www.
childandparentservices.com

**Concerned United
Birthparents (CUB)**
524 Westchester Drive
Saginaw, MI 48603
Phone: (517) 792-5876
Web site: www.cubirthparents.org

Kalamazoo Birthparent Support Group
P.O. Box 2183
Portage, MI 49081
Phone: (616) 324-0634

**Lutheran Adoption Service
(LAS)**
21700 Northwestern Highway,
Suite 1490
Southfield, MI 48075-4901
Phone: (248) 423-2770
Fax: (248) 423-2783
E-mail: Kmasc@lssm.org
Web site: www.LSSM.org/
service/adoption

Mid-Michigan Adoption
Identity
13636 Podunk Road
Cedar Springs, MI 49319

Post-Adoption Support
Services
Route #1, Box 360
Bellaire Road
Baraga, MI 48809

Tri-County Genealogical
Society
21715 Britanny
Eastpointe, MI 48021-2503
Phone: (810) 774-7953

**State Adoption
Specialist/Manager**

Michigan Family
Independence Agency
Bill Johnson
P.O. Box 30037
Lansing, MI 48909
Phone: (517) 373-3513
Fax: (517) 335-4019
E-mail: Johnsonb3@michigan.
gov
Web site: www.michigan.gov/
fia/1,1607,7-124-5452_7116---
,00.html

**State Foster Care
Specialist/Manager**

Michigan Family Independence Agency (FIA)
Mary Chaliman
235 South Grand Avenue, Suite 514
Lansing, MI 48909
Phone: (517) 335-4652
Fax: (517) 241-7047
E-mail: chalimanm2@michigan.
gov
Web site: www.michigan.gov/
fia/1,1607,7-124-5452_7117---
,00.html

**State Interstate Compact on
the Placement of Children
(ICPC) Administrator**

Michigan Family
Independence Agency
P.O. Box 30037
Lansing, MI 48909
Phone: (517) 373-6918
E-mail: MurrayD2@Michigan.gov

State Licensing Specialist

Department of Consumer and
Industry Services
Bureau of Regulatory Services
Miriam Bullock
7109 West Saginaw
2nd Floor, Box 30650
Lansing, MI 48909-8150

Phone: (517) 373-8383
Fax: (517) 335-6121
E-mail: mbullo@michigan.gov
Web site: www.commerce.state.
mi.us/brs/cwl/home.htm

State Reunion Registry

Central Adoption Registry
P.O. Box 30037
Lansing, MI 48909
Phone: (517) 373-3513
Fax: (517) 335-4019
Web site: www.mfia.state.mi.us/
CFSAdmin/adoption/registry.html

Federally Funded

National Resource Center for
Special Needs Adoption
16250 Northland Drive, Suite 120
Southfield, MI 48075
Phone: (248) 443-0306 or
(248) 443-7080
Fax: (248) 443-7099
E-mail: nrc@nrcadoption.org
Web site: www.nrcadoption.org

**Licensed Private
Adoption Agencies**

Adoption Associates, Inc
13535 State Road
Grand Ledge, MI 48837-9626
Phone: (517) 627-0805
E-mail: adopt@adoptassoc.com
Web site: www.adoptassoc.com

Adoption Associates, Inc.
1338 Baldwin Street
Jenison, MI 49428
Phone: (616) 667-0677
Fax: (616) 667-0920
E-mail: adopt@adoptassoc.com
Web site: www.adoptassoc.com

Adoption Associates, Inc.
3609 Country Club Drive
St. Clair Shores, MI 48082-2952
Phone: (810) 294-1990
Fax: (616) 667-0920
E-mail: adopt@adoptassoc.com
Web site: www.adoptassoc.com

Adoption Associates, Inc.
800 Thomas L. Parkway,
Suite 1
Lansing, MI 48917
Phone: (517) 327-1388
E-mail: adopt@adoptassoc.com
Web site: www.adoptassoc.com

Adoption Consultants
32781 Middlebelt Road
Farmington, MI 48334
Phone: (248) 737-0336
Fax: (248) 737-0349
E-mail: aciadopt@core.com
Web site: www.aciadoption.com

Adoptions of the Heart, Inc.
4295 Summerwind Avenue NE
Grand Rapids, MI 49525
Phone: (616) 365-9811
Fax: (616) 365-9325
E-mail: adoptaid@iserv.net
Web site: www.iserv.net/
~adoptaid

Alliance for Adoption/Jewish Family Service
24123 Greenfield Road
Southfield, MI 48075
Phone: (248) 559-0117
Fax: (248) 559-5403
E-mail: dstpeter@jfsdetroit.org

Alternatives for Children and Families
P.O. Box 3038
609 South Saginaw Street, Suite 505
Flint, MI 48502
Phone: (810) 235-0683
Fax: (810) 235-4619

Americans for International Aid and Adoption
2151 Livernois, Suite 200
Troy, MI 48083
Phone: (248) 362-1207
Fax: (248) 362-8222
E-mail: www.aiaaadopt.org

Anishnabek Community Family Services (ACFS)
2864 Ashmun Street
Sault Ste. Marie, MI 49783
Phone: (906) 632-5250
Fax: (906) 632-5266
E-mail: cmcpherson@saulttribe.net
Web site: www.saulttribe.org

Bethany Christian Services
P.O. Box 294
901 Eastern Avenue NE
Grand Rapids, MI 49501-0294
Phone: (612) 224-7479
Fax: (616) 224-7589
E-mail: bcsgrandrapids@bethany.org
Web site: www.bethany.org

Child and Family Services
1352 Terrane Street
Muskeyon, MI 49442
Phone: (616) 726-3582

Child and Family Services of Northeast Michigan, Inc.
P.O. Box 516
1044 US-23 North
Alpena, MI 49707
Phone: (989) 356-4567
Fax: (989) 354-6100
Toll-Free: (800) 779-0396
E-mail: cfsalp@freeway.net
Web site: www.cfsnemi.org

Child and Family Services of Northwestern Michigan, Inc.
3785 Veterans Drive
Traverse City, MI 49684
Phone: (231) 946-8975
Fax: (231) 946-0451
E-mail: clemmen@cfsmail.org
Web site: www.cfsnwmi.org

Child and Family Services of Southwest Michigan
2450 M 139
Benton Harbor, MI 49022-6445
Phone: (269) 983-5545
Fax: (269) 983-4920
Toll-Free: (888) 237-1891

Child and Family Services of Western Michigan, Inc.
412 Century Lane
Holland, MI 49423
Phone: (616) 396-2301
Fax: (616) 396-8070
E-mail: www.cfswm.org

Child and Family Services of the Upper Peninsula, Inc.
705 Sharon Avenue, Suite 1
Houghton, MI 49931
Phone: (906) 482-4488
Fax: (906) 482-4401
E-mail: dhoganson1952@hotmail.com
Web site: www.cfsm.org

Child and Family Services, Capital Area
4287 Five Oaks Drive
Lansing, MI 48911
Phone: (517) 882-4000
Fax: (517) 882-3506
E-mail: info@childandfamily.org
Web site: www.childandfamily.org

Children's Hope Adoption Services
P.O. Box 467
Mt. Pleasant, MI 48804-0469
Phone: (989) 775-8229
Fax: (989) 775-8208

Christ Child House
15751 Joy Road
Detroit, MI 48228
Phone: (313) 584-6077
Fax: (313) 584-1148

Christian Care Maternity Ministries
214 North Mill Street
St. Louis, MI 48880
Phone: (517) 681-2172

Christian Cradle, Inc.
4590 Oakwood Drive
Okemos, MI 48664
Phone: (517) 351-7500
Fax: (517) 351-4810
Toll-Free: (800) 891-2584
E-mail: cciadopt@ia4u.net
Web site: www.christiancradle.
org

Christian Family Services
17105 West 12 Mile Road
Southfield, MI 48076
Phone: (248) 557-8390
Fax: (248) 557-6427
E-mail: cfspyo@aol.com
Web site: www.cfspyo.org

D.A. Blodgett Services for Children and Families
805 Leonard Street NE
Grand Rapids, MI 49503-1184
Phone: (616) 451-2021
Fax: (616) 451-8936
Web site: www.dablodgett.org

Developmental Disabilities
420 West 5th Avenue
Flint, MI 48503
Phone: (810) 257-3714

Eagle Village, Inc.
4507 170th Avenue
Hersey, MI 49639
Phone: (231) 832-2234
Fax: (231) 832-2470
Toll-Free: (800) 748-0061
E-mail: www.eaglevillage.org

Eastern European Adoption Services
INC 22233 Genesis
Woodhaven, MI 48183
Phone: (734) 479-2348
Fax: (734) 479-6330

Ennis Center for Children
3650 Dixie Highway
Waterford, MI 48329
Phone: (248) 618-1260
Fax: (248) 618-1266

E-mail: support@enniscenter.org
Web site: www.enniscenter.org

Evergreen Children's Services
10421 West Seven Mile Road
Detroit, MI 48221
Phone: (313) 862-1000
Fax: (313) 862-6464
E-mail: dredmand@
evergreenserv.org
Web site: www.evergreenserv.org

Family Adoption Consultants
P.O. Box 50489
421 West Crosstown Parkway
Kalamazoo, MI 49005
Phone: (269) 343-3316
Fax: (269) 343-3359
E-mail: melissa@facadopt.org
Web site: www.facadopt.org

Family Counseling and Children's Services of Lenewee County
220 North Main Street
Adrian, MI 49221
Phone: (517) 265-5352
Fax: (517) 263-6090
E-mail: fccsoflenawee@hotmail.
com
Web site: www.fccservices.org

Family MatchMakers, Inc.
2544 Martin SE
Grand Rapids, MI 49507
Phone: (616) 243-1803
Fax: (616) 243-1803
E-mail: www.familymatchmakers.
org

Family Service and Children's Aid
P.O. Box 6128
330 West Michigan Avenue
Jackson, MI 49201
Phone: (517) 787-7920
Fax: (517) 787-2440
E-mail: adoption@strong-
families.org
Web site: www.strong-families.
org

Family and Children's Services, Inc.
535 Emmett Street East
Battle Creek, MI 49017
Phone: (269) 965-3247
Fax: (269) 966-4135
E-mail: battlecreek@csfm.org
Web site: www.cfsm.org

Forever Families, Inc.
42400 West Grand River Avenue
Suite 101
Novi, MI 48375
Phone: (248) 344-9606
Fax: (248) 344-9604
E-mail: info@forever-families.org
Web site: www.forever-families.
org

Hands Across the Water
2890 Carpenter Road,
Suite 600
Ann Arbor, MI 48108
Phone: (734) 477-0135
Fax: (734) 477-0213
e-mail: hatw.nelson@att.net
Web site: www.hatw.org

HelpSource
201 North Wayne Road
Westland, MI 48185-3689
Phone: (734) 722-0423
Fax: (734) 641-8524
E-mail: www.helpsourceagency.
com

Homes for Black Children
511 East Larned Street
Detroit, MI 48226
Phone: (313) 961-4777
Fax: (313) 961-2994
E-mail: hbchildren@aol.com
Web site: www.
homesforblackchildren.org

Interact Family Services
1260 Woodkrest Drive
Flint, MI 48532

International Adoption Association
517 Baldwin Avenue
Jenison, MI 49428
Phone: (616) 457-6537
Fax: (616) 457-1260
E-mail: iaainc@aol.com
Web site: www.adoptionpros.com

Judson Center
4925 Packard Street,
Suite 200
Ann Arbor, MI 48108
Phone: (734) 528-1720
Fax: (734) 528-1695

Keane Center for Adoption
930 Mason
Dearborn, MI 48124
Phone: (313) 277-4664
Fax: (313) 278-1767
E-mail: cbrail@provide.net
Web site: www.keaneadoption.org

LDS Family Services
– Farmington Hills
37634 Enterprise Court
Farmington Hills, MI 48331
Phone: (248) 553-0902
Fax: (248) 553-2632
Toll-Free: (800) 250-2923
E-mail: kstewart@ldsfs.net
Web site: www.providentliving.org/familyservices/strength

Lula Belle Stewart Center
11000 West McNichols,
Suite 115
Detroit, MI 48221
Phone: (313) 862-4600
Fax: (313) 864-2233

Lutheran Adoption Service
2976 Ivanrest,
Suite 140
Grandville, MI 49418-1440
Phone: (616) 532-8286
Fax: (616) 532-8919

Lutheran Adoption Service
Ann Arbor Branch
2500 Packard Road
Ann Arbor, MI 48104
Phone: (734) 971-1944
Fax: (734) 971-2137
E-mail: jcare@lssm.org
Web site: www.lasadoption.org

Lutheran Adoption Service
Kalamazoo Branch
3234 South Westnedge Avenue
Kalamazoo, MI 49008
Phone: (269) 345-5776
Fax: (269) 345-4011
E-mail: jcare@lssm.org

Lutheran Adoption Service
(LAS)
21700 Northwestern Highway,
Suite 1490
Southfield, MI 48075-4901
Phone: (248) 423-2770
Fax: (248) 423-2783
E-mail: Kmasc@lssm.org
Web site: www.LSSM.org/service/adoption

Michigan Indian Child Welfare Agency
1345 Monroe Avenue NW
Suite 220
Grand Rapids, MI 49505
Phone: (616) 454-9221
Fax: (616) 454-3142
Toll-Free: (800) 880-2089

Michigan Indian Child Welfare Agency
6425 South Pennsylvania Avenue,
Suite 3
Lansing, MI 48911
Phone: (517) 393-3256
Fax: (517) 393-0838
Toll-Free: (800) 346-4292
E-mail: heximerl@aol.com

Oakland Family Service
114 Orchard Lake Road
Pontiac, MI 48341

Phone: (248) 858-7215
Fax: (248) 858-8227
E-mail: ofs@ofs-family.org

Orchards Children's Services
42140 Van Dyke Road,
Suite 206
Sterling Heights, MI 48314
Phone: (810) 997-3886
Fax: (810) 997-0629
E-mail: adopt@orchards.org
Web site: www.orchard.org

Orchards Children's Services
30215 Southfield Road
Southfield, MI 48076
Phone: (248) 258-2099
Fax: (248) 258-0487
E-mail: adopt@orchards.org
Web site: www.orchard.org

Sault Tribe Binogii Placement Agency
2864 Ashmun Street
3rd Floor
Sault St. Marie, MI 49783
Phone: (906) 632-5250
Fax: (906) 632-5266
E-mail: patch2@sootribe.org
Web site: www.sootribe.org

Spaulding for Children
16250 Northland Drive,
Suite 120
Southfield, MI 48075
Phone: (248) 443-0300
Fax: (248) 443-2845
E-mail: sfc@Spaulding.org
Web site: www.spaulding.org

Spectrum Human Services, Inc.
23077 Greenfield Road,
Suite 500
Southfield, MI 48075
Phone: (248) 552-8020
Fax: (248) 552-1135
E-mail:
rswaninger@spectrumhuman.org
Web site: www.spectrumhuman.org

St. Francis Family Services
17500 West 8 Mile Road
Southfield, MI 48075
Phone: (248) 552-0750
Fax: (248) 552-9019

St. Vincent-Sarah Fisher Center
27400 West 12 Mile Road
Farmington Hills, MI 48334
Phone: (248) 626-7527
Fax: (248) 539-3584
E-mail: svs@aol.com
Web site: www.svsfcenter.org

Teen Ranch Family Services
2861 Main Street
Marlette, MI 48453
Phone: (989) 635-7511
E-mail: www.teenranch.com

Teen Ranch, Inc.
4672 Marlette Road
Clifford, MI 48727
Phone: (989) 635-7511
Fax: (989) 635-3324
Toll-Free: (800) 732-2441
E-mail: kpatriquin@teenranch.com
Web site: www.teenranch.com

Teen Ranch, Inc.
4672 Marlette Road
Clifford, MI 48727
Phone: (989) 635-7511
Fax: (989) 635-3324
Toll-Free: (800) 732-2441
E-mail: kpatriquin@teenranch.com
Web site: www.teenranch.com

The Children's Center of Wayne County
90 Selden
Detroit, MI 48201
Phone: (313) 832-3555
Fax: (313) 262-0901
E-mail: kgarrett@childrensctr.net
Web site: www.thechildrenscenter.org

Whaley Children's Center
1201 North Grand Traverse Street
Flint, MI 48503
Phone: (810) 234-3603
Fax: (810) 232-3416
E-mail: www.whaleychildren.org

MINNESOTA

Adoptive/Foster Family Support Groups

Adoption Connections
15716 30th Street
Brownton, MN 55312
Phone: (320) 328-5967
E-mail: fullhaus@hutchtel.net

Adoption Miracle International, Inc.
19108 Kingswood Terrace
Minnetonka, MN 55345
Phone: (952) 470-6141
Fax: (612) 677-3453
E-mail: info@adoptionmiracle.org
Web site: www.adoptionmiracle.org
– Intercountry Program
– Adoptive Parent/Family Preparation
– Child Placement
– Education/Preparation
– Home Study
– Information/Referral
– Post-placement Supervision Prior to Adoption Finalization

Adoptive Family Network
4720 East 34th Street
Minneapolis, MN 55406
Phone: (612) 721-5209

African American Adoption Agency
2356 University Avenue, Suite 220
St. Paul, MN 55114
Phone: (651) 659-0460
Fax: (651) 644-5306
Toll-Free: (888) 840-4084
E-mail: afadopt@afadopt.org
Web site: www.afadopt.org

Aitkin County Support Group
Minnesota Adoption Support and Preservation
3286 37th Street NW
Maple Lake, MN 55358
Phone: (320) 963-6055
Toll-Free: (877) 699-5937

Bulgarian Family Support
19826 Dakota Avenue
Prior Lake, MN 55372
Phone: (952) 447-5449

Carver County
970 Raymond Avenue, Suite 106
St. Paul, MN 55114-1149
Phone: (952) 442-2850

Catholic Charities/Seton Services
1276 University Avenue
St. Paul, MN 55104-4101
Phone: (651) 641-1180
Fax: (651) 641-1005
E-mail: croller@ccspm.org
Web site: www.ccspm.org
– Intercountry Program
– Adoptive Parent/Family Preparation
– Agency Able to Place Children with United States Citizens Living Abroad
– Education/Preparation
– Information/Referral

Child Link International (CLI)
6508 Stevens Avenue South
Richfield, MN 55423
Phone: (612) 861-9048
Fax: (612) 869-2004
E-mail: ChildLink1@aol.com
Web site: www.child-link.com
– Intercountry Program
– Adoptive Parent/Family Preparation
– Child Placement
– Education/Preparation
– Information/Referral

Chippewa-Kandiyohi-Meeker-Swift Counties Support Group
MN
Phone: (507) 283-9693
Toll-Free: (877) 349-6353

Chosen Ones Adoption Agency
1622 East Sandhurst Drive
Maplewood, MN 55109
Phone: (651) 770-5508
Fax: (651) 330-7582
E-mail: emhchosen1@aol.com
Web site: www.chosen1s.org
– Intercountry Program
– Adoptive Parent/Family
Preparation
– Agency Able to Place Children
with United States Citizens Living
Abroad
– Child Placement
– Education/Preparation
– Home Study
– Homeland Tours
– Information/Referral
– Post-placement Supervision
Prior to Adoption Finalization

Downey Side
560 Dunnell Court, Suite 201
Owatonna, MN 55060
Phone: (507) 446-8503
Fax: (507) 446-8505
Web site: www.downeyside.org

Duluth Adoptive Parents Support Group
Duluth, MN
Phone: (218) 525-0808

Duluth Families with Children from China
Duluth, MN
Phone: (218) 525-4906

East Central
3286 37th Street N.W.
Maple Lake, MN 55358
Phone: (320) 963-6055
Toll-Free: (877) 699-5937
E-mail: djpribyl@lakedalelink.net

Families Helping Families in Adoption
Anoka County, MN
Phone: (612) 767-9076

Families Under Severe Stress
2230 Como Avenue
St. Paul, MN 55108
Phone: (651) 646-3036

Families of Multi-Racial Adoptions
10 Woodview Drive
Mankato, MN 56001
Phone: (507) 345-1850

Granite Falls Support Group
Granite Falls, MN
Phone: (320) 564-5656

HOPE Adoption and Family Services International, Inc.
5850 Omaha Avenue North
Oak Park Heights, MN 55082
Phone: (651) 439-2446
Fax: (651) 439-2071
E-mail: hope@hopeadoptionservices.org
Web site: www.hopeadoptionservices.org
– Intercountry Program
– Adoptive Parent/Family
Preparation
– Education/Preparation
– Home Study
– Information/Referral
– Post-placement Supervision
Prior to Adoption Finalization

Hand in Hand International Adoptions
1360 University Avenue West,
#176
St. Paul, MN 55104
Phone: (651) 917-0384
Fax: (651) 649-0896
E-mail: minnesota@hihiadopt.org
Web site: www.hihiadopt.org

Harambee Project
1800 Glenwood Avenue North
Minneapolis, MN 55405
Phone: (612) 374-4139
E-mail: harambee@
redeemermpls.org
Web site: www.redeemermpls.org

Hennepin County
970 Raymond Avenue, Suite 106
St. Paul, MN 55114
Phone: (651) 644-3036
Fax: (612) 938-6534

Hennepin County Foster Care Association
3347 Georgia Avenue North
Crystal, MN 55427
Phone: (763) 537-7615

Honduran Adoptive Families
Phone: (651) 698-5887

Kanabec/MilleLacs County's Adoption Support Group
Courthouse
Milaca, MN 56353
Phone: (320) 983-8208
E-mail: nancy.elmquist@co.mille-lacs.mn.us

Large Adoptive Families Together Expanding Resources (LAFTER)
418 South Fairview Drive
Luverne, MN 56156
Phone: (507) 283-4551
E-mail: Maeflye@aol.com
Web site: www.lafter.org

Love Has No Boundaries
911 Albion Avenue
Fairmont, MN 56031
Phone: (507) 235-8748

Lutheran Social Services of
Minnesota (LSS of Minnesota)
2414 Park Avenue
Minneapolis, MN 55404
Phone: (612) 879-5230
Fax: (612) 871-0354
Toll-Free: (888) 205-3769
E-mail: adoption@lssmn.org
Web site: www.
minnesotaadoption.org
– Intercountry Program
– Adoptive Parent/Family
Preparation

MN ASAP
3286 37th Street NW
Maple Lake, MN 55358
Phone: (320) 963-6055
E-mail: djpribyl@lakedalelink.net

**Minnesota Adoption Resource
Network (MARN)**
430 Oak Grove Street, Suite 404
Minneapolis, MN 55403
Phone: (612) 861-7115
Fax: (612) 861-7112
Toll-Free: (877) 966-2727
E-mail: info@mnadopt.org
Web site: www.mnadopt.org/ OR
www.mnasap.org

**Minnesota Adoption Support
and Preservation**
219 Lake Elmo Avenue
Lake Elmo, MN 55042
Phone: (651) 770-1247
Toll-Free: (651) 770-7571
E-mail: buuggme@aol.com

**Minnesota Foster Care
Association**
Phone: (612) 333-2943

**Minnesota Kinship Caregivers
Association**
3027 Ensign Avenue North
New Hope, MN 55427
Phone: (763) 732-1142

**Multiracial Single Parent
Group**
Phone: (651) 603-0245

**New Horizons Adoption
Agency, Inc. (NHAA)**
Frost Benco Building
Highway 254
Frost, MN 56033
Phone: (507) 878-3200
Fax: (507) 878-3132
E-mail: nhaa@means.net
Web site: www.
nhadoptionagency.com
– Intercountry Program
– Adoptive Parent/Family
Preparation

**New Life Family Services
(NLFS)**
1515 East 66th Street
Richfield, MN 55423
Phone: (612) 866-7643
Fax: (612) 798-0965
Toll-Free: (888) 690-4673
E-mail: anderson.amy@nlfs.org
Web site: www.
newlifefamilyservices.com

Ninos de Paraguay
7801 Bush Lake Drive
Bloomington, MN 55438
Phone: (952) 829-0938

**North American Council on
Adoptable Children**
Waconia, MN 55387
Phone: (952) 442-2586
Fax: (952) 442-2828
Web site: www.nacac.org

North Central
63370 County Road 557
Bearville/Cook, MN 55723
Phone: (218) 376-4650
Toll-Free: (877) 454-KIDS
E-mail: hayskids@frontiernet.net

**North Suburban Ours for a
United Response**
2723 Crown Hill Court
White Bear Lake, MN 55110
Phone: (612) 442-2586

Northeast
1829 Morningside Avenue
Duluth, MN 55803
Phone: (218) 525-0664
Toll-Free: (866) 302-2211
E-mail: Kvisina@charter.net

**Northland Families Through
Adoption**
518 Lagarde Road
Wrenswall, MN 55797

Northwest
10894 190th Street N.E.
Thief River Falls, MN 56701
Phone: (218) 681-1761
Toll-Free: (877) 373-0433
E-mail: jhesse@wiktel.com

**Northwest Adoptive Families
Association and the North
American Council on Adopt-
able Children Representative**
970 Raymond Avenue, Suite 106
St. Paul, MN 35114
Phone: (651) 644-3036
Fax: (651) 644-9848
Web site: www.nacac.org

**Northwest Minnesota Families
Through Adoption**
P.O. Box 135
Crookston, MN 56716

**Parents of (Asian) Indian
Children**
Phone: (612) 944-7114

**Parents of Latin American
Children**
16665 Argon Street NW
Anoka, MN 55304
Phone: (612) 494-9290

Partners for Adoption
621 County Road
10 South East
Watertown, MN 55388
Phone: (612) 955-2046

Partners in Adoption
607 West Main Street
Marshall, MN 56258
Phone: (507) 532-1260
Web site: www.aaapia.org

Peruvian Adoptive Families
2717 Cedar Lane
Burnsville, MN 55337
Phone: (651) 439-6749

Professional Association of
Treatment Homes (PATH)
500 Alworth Building
306 West Superior Street
Duluth, MN 55802
Phone: (218) 722-6106
Fax: (218) 722-8356
E-mail: tireland@pathinc.org
Web site: www.pathinc.org

Rainbow Families
Phone: (612) 370-6651

Rochester Area Adoptive
Families Together
962 Elton Hills Court NW
Rochester, MN 55901
Phone: (507) 281-4807

Single Parents
664 Gaston Avenue
Shoreview, MN 55126
Phone: (651) 484-6697

Southeast
56966 Juneau Road
Mankato, MN 56001
Phone: (507) 292-8886
Toll-Free: (888) 450-5059
E-mail: laughlin7@lakes.com

Southwest
418 S. Fairview Dr.
Luverne, MN 56156
Phone: (507) 283-9693
Toll-Free: (877) 349-6353
E-mail: maeflye@aol.com

Special Parents Adoption
Network (SPAN)
304 Darrell Court
Stillwater, MN 55082
Phone: (651) 351-2778
E-mail: denisertift@aol.com

Statewide American Indian
Community
101 West McAndrews, Suite 112
Burnsville, MN 55337
Phone: (952) 892-7846
Toll-Free: (877) 392-0270
E-mail: MNCOFAS@aol.com

Teresa Julkowski
1610 Liberty Street
Mora, MN 55051
Phone: (320) 679-2467
E-mail: dtjulkowski@hotmail.com

Washington County
2119 Lake Elmo Avenue
Lake Elmo, MN 55042
Phone: (651) 770-1247
Fax: (651) 770-7571
E-mail: buuggme@aol.com

West Central
415 7th Ave. E.
Alexandria, MN 56308
Phone: (320) 763-3144
Toll-Free: (800) 728-1736
E-mail: adopt@rea-alp.com

**Licensed Private
Adoption Agencies**

Adoption Miracle
International, Inc.
19108 Kingswood Terrace
Minnetonka, MN 55345
Phone: (952) 470-6141
Fax: (612) 677-3453
E-mail: info@adoptionmiracle.org
Web site: www.adoptionmiracle.
org

African American Adoption
Agency
2356 University Avenue, Suite
220
St. Paul, MN 55114
Phone: (651) 659-0460
Fax: (651) 644-5306
Toll-Free: (888) 840-4084
E-mail: afadopt@afadopt.org
Web site: www.afadopt.org

Bethany Christian Services
3025 Harbor Lane North, Suite
316
Plymouth, MN 55447
Phone: (763) 553-0344
Fax: (763) 553-0117
Toll-Free: (866) 321-1964
E-mail: bcsplymouth@bethany.
org
Web site: www.bethany.org/
plymouth
– Intercountry Program
– Adoptive Parent/Family
Preparation

Caritas Family Services
157 Roosevelt Road
St. Cloud, MN 56301
Phone: (320) 650-1660
Fax: (320) 253-7464
Toll-Free: (800) 830-8254
Web site: www.stcdio.org/cc

Catholic Charities/Seton
Services
1276 University Avenue
St. Paul, MN 55104-4101
Phone: (651) 641-1180
Fax: (651) 641-1005
E-mail: croller@ccspm.org
Web site: www.ccspm.org
– Intercountry Program
– Adoptive Parent/Family
Preparation
– Agency Able to Place Children
with United States Citizens Living
Abroad

Child Link International
6508 Stevens Avenue South
Richfield, MN 55423
Phone: (612) 861-9048
Fax: (612) 869-2004
E-mail: ChildLink1@aol.com
Web site: www.child-link.com
– Intercountry Program
– Adoptive Parent/Family
Preparation
– Child Placement
– Education/Preparation
– Information/Referral

Children's Home Society and Family Services
1605 Eustis Street
St. Paul, MN 55108-1219
Phone: (651) 646-6393
Fax: (651) 646-0436
Toll-Free: (800) 952-9302
Web site: www.chsfs.org
– Intercountry Program
– Education/Preparation

Children's Home Society of Minnesota
1605 Eustis Street
St. Paul, MN 55108-1798
Phone: (651) 646-6393
Fax: (651) 646-0436
Toll-Free: (800) 942-9302
Web site: www.chsm.com

Chosen Ones Adoption Agency
1622 East Sandhurst Drive
Maplewood, MN 55109
Phone: (651) 770-5508
Fax: (651) 330-7582
E-mail: emhchosen1@aol.com
Web site: www.chosen1s.org
– Intercountry Program
– Adoptive Parent/Family
Preparation
– Agency Able to Place Children
with United States Citizens Living
Abroad

Crossroads Adoption Services
4600 West 77th Street, Suite 204
Minneapolis, MN 55435
Phone: (952) 831-5707
Fax: (952) 831-5129
E-mail: kids@crossroads
adoption.com
Web site: www.
crossroadsadoption.com
– Intercountry Program
– Information/Referral

Downey Side
560 Dunnell Court, Suite 201
Owatonna, MN 55060
Phone: (507) 446-8503
Fax: (507) 446-8505
Web site: www.downeyside.org

European Children's Adoption Services
6050 Cheshire Lane North
Plymouth, MN 55446
Phone: (763) 694-6131
Fax: (763) 694-6104
E-mail: zina@ecasus.org
Web site: www.ecasus.org
– Intercountry Program
– Agency Able to Place Children
with United States Citizens Living
Abroad

Family Alternatives
416 East Hennepin Avenue
Minneapolis, MN 55414
Phone: (612) 379-5341
Fax: (612) 379-5328

Family Resources
2903 Euclid Avenue
Anoka, MN 55303
Phone: (763) 422-8590
Fax: (763) 323-8050
E-mail: familyresources@msn.
com
Web site: www.familyres.net
– Intercountry Program
– Child Placement

HOPE Adoption and Family Services International, Inc.
5850 Omaha Avenue North
Oak Park Heights, MN 55082
Phone: (651) 439-2446
Fax: (651) 439-2071
E-mail: hope@hopeadoptionser
vices.org
Web site: www.
hopeadoptionservices.org
– Intercountry Program

Hand in Hand International Adoptions
1360 University Avenue West,
#176
St. Paul, MN 55104
Phone: (651) 917-0384
Fax: (651) 649-0896
E-mail: minnesota@hihiadopt.org
Web site: www.hihiadopt.org
– Intercountry Program
– Adoptive Parent/Family
Preparation

Holy Family Adoption Agency
525 Thomas Avenue
St. Paul, MN 55103
Phone: (651) 220-0090

International Adoption Services
4940 Viking Drive, Suite 388
Edina, MN 55435
Phone: (952) 893-1343
Fax: (952) 893-9193
E-mail: info@ias-ww.com
Web site: www.ias-ww.com
– Intercountry Program
– Child Placement

LDS Social Services
6120 Earl Brown Drive, Suite 210
Brooklyn Center, MN 55430
Phone: (763) 560-0900

Love Basket, Inc.
3902 Minnesota Avenue
Duluth, MN 55802
Phone: (218) 720-3097
Fax: (218) 722-0195

Web site: www.lovebasket.org
– Intercountry Program
– Child Placement

Lutheran Social Services of Minnesota (LSS)

2414 Park Avenue
Minneapolis, MN 55404
Phone: (612) 879-5230
Fax: (612) 871-0354
Toll-Free: (888) 205-3769
E-mail: adoption@lssmn.org
Web site: www.
minnesotaadoption.org
– Intercountry Program
– Adoptive Parent/Family
Preparation

New Horizons Adoption Agency, Inc. (NHAA)

Frost Benco Building
Highway 254
Frost, MN 56033
Phone: (507) 878-3200
Fax: (507) 878-3132
E-mail: nhaa@means.net
Web site: www.
nhadoptionagency.com
– Intercountry Program
– Adoptive Parent/Family
Preparation

New Life Family Services (NLFS)

1515 East 66th Street
Richfield, MN 55423
Phone: (612) 866-7643
Fax: (612) 798-0965
Toll-Free: (888) 690-4673
E-mail: anderson.amy@nlfs.org
Web site: www.
newlifefamilyservices.com

North Homes, Inc.

1880 River Road
Grand Rapids, MN 55744-4085
Phone: (218) 327-3000
Fax: (218) 327-1871
Toll-Free: (888) 430-3055
E-mail: thomasc@uslink.net

Permanent Family Resource Center

1220 Tower Road
Fergus Falls, MN 56537
Phone: (218) 998-3400
Fax: (218) 739-4989
E-mail: email@permanentfamily.
org
Web site: www.permanentfamily.
org

Reaching Arms International, Inc.

3701 Winnetka Avenue North
New Hope, MN 55427
Phone: (763) 591-0791
Fax: (763) 591-9701
E-mail: raiadopt@raiadopt.org
Web site: www.raiadopt.org
– Intercountry Program
– Child Placement

Summit Adoption Home Studies, Inc.

1389 Summit Avenue
St. Paul, MN 55105
Phone: (651) 645-6657
Fax: (651) 645-6713
E-mail: summitadopt@uswest.net
Web site: www.summitadoption.
com
– Intercountry Program
– Adoptive Parent/Family
Preparation
– Home Study
– Post-placement Supervision
Prior to Adoption Finalization

Upper Midwest American Indian Center

1035 West Broadway
Minneapolis, MN 55411
Phone: (612) 522-4436
Fax: (612) 522-8855

Wellspring Adoption Agency

111 3rd Avenue South, # 370
Minneapolis, MN 55401
Phone: (612) 333-0691
Fax: (612) 332-1839

Birth Family and Search Support Groups

Catholic Charities/Seton Services

1276 University Avenue
St. Paul, MN 55104-4101
Phone: (651) 641-1180
Fax: (651) 641-1005
E-mail: croller@ccspm.org
Web site: www.ccspm.org
– Intercountry Program
– Adoptive Parent/Family
Preparation
– Agency Able to Place Children
with United States Citizens Living
Abroad
– Education/Preparation
– Information/Referral

Chosen Ones Adoption Agency

1622 East Sandhurst Drive
Maplewood, MN 55109
Phone: (651) 770-5508
Fax: (651) 330-7582
E-mail: emhchosen1@aol.com
Web site: www.chosen1s.org
– Intercountry Program
– Adoptive Parent/Family
Preparation
– Agency Able to Place Children
with United States Citizens Living
Abroad
– Child Placement
– Education/Preparation
– Home Study
– Homeland Tours
– Information/Referral
– Post-placement Supervision
Prior to Adoption Finalization

Concerned United Birthparents (CUB)

6429 Mendelsohn Lane
Edina, MN 55343
Phone: (612) 938-5866
E-mail: sayspazz@aol.com
Web site: www.cubirthparents.
org

HOPE Adoption and Family
Services International, Inc.
5850 Omaha Avenue North
Oak Park Heights, MN 55082
Phone: (651) 439-2446
Fax: (651) 439-2071
E-mail: hope@hopeadoption
services.org
Web site: www.
hopeadoptionservices.org
– Intercountry Program
– Adoptive Parent/Family
Preparation
– Education/Preparation
– Home Study
– Information/Referral
– Post-placement Supervision
Prior to Adoption Finalization

Lutheran Social Services of
Minnesota (LSS)
2414 Park Avenue
Minneapolis, MN 55404
Phone: (612) 879-5230
Fax: (612) 871-0354
Toll-Free: (888) 205-3769
E-mail: adoption@lssmn.org
Web site: www.
minnesotaadoption.org
– Intercountry Program
– Adoptive Parent/Family
Preparation
– Agency Able to Place Children
with United States Citizens Living
Abroad
– Child Placement
– Education/Preparation
– Home Study
– Information/Referral
– Post-placement Supervision
Prior to Adoption Finalization

Minnesota Reunion Registry/
Liberal Education for Adoptive
Families
23247 Lofton Court North
N. Scandia, MN 55073-9752
Phone: (612) 436-2215

**State Adoption Exchange/
Photolisting of Children
Waiting For Adoption**

Minnesota Adoption Resource
Network, Inc.
430 Oak Grove Street
Minneapolis, MN 55403
Phone: (612) 861-7115
Fax: (612) 861-7112
E-mail: info@mnadopt.org
Web site: www.mnadopt.org

**State Adoption
Specialist/Manager**

Minnesota Department of
Human Services
Connie Caron
Human Services Building
444 Lafayette Road
St. Paul, MN 55155-3831
Phone: (651) 282-3793
Fax: (651) 297-1949
E-mail: connie.caron@state.mn.us
Web site: www.dhs.state.mn.us/
childint/programs/Adoption/
default.htm

**State Foster Care
Specialist/Manager**

Minnesota Department of
Human Services
Kris Johnson
Human Services Building
444 Lafayette Road North
St. Paul, MN 55155-3832
Phone: (651) 297-2711
Fax: (651) 297-1949
E-mail: kris.johnson@state.mn.us
Web site: www.dhs.state.mn.us/
childint/programs/fostercare/
default.htm

**State Interstate Compact on
the Placement of Children
(ICPC) Administrator**

Minnesota Department of
Human Services
Human Services Building
444 Lafayette Road North
St. Paul, MN 55155
Phone: (651) 296-2487
Fax: (612) 297-1949
E-mail: erin.sullivan-
sutton@state.mn.us
Web site: www.dhs.state.mn.us/
childint/programs/Adoption/
compact.htm

State Licensing Specialist

Minnesota Department of
Human Services
Human Services Building
444 Lafayette Road North
St. Paul, MN 55155
Phone: (651) 296-3971
Fax: (651) 297-1490

State Reunion Registry

Adoption Archive
Human Services Building
444 Lafayette Road North
St. Paul, MN 55155
Phone: (651) 296-2795

**Statewide Adoption
Recruitment Line**

Minnesota Statewide Adop-
tion Recruitment Line
Toll-Free: (866) 665-4378

**Statewide Foster Care
Recruitment Line**

Minnesota Statewide Foster
Care Recruitment Line
Toll-Free: (866) 665-4378

Training

National Council on Family Relations

3989 Central Avenue, NE, Suite 550
Minneapolis, MN 55421-3921
Fax: (763) 781-9348
Toll-Free: (888) 781-9331
E-mail: info@ncfr.org
Web site: www.ncfr.com

North American Council on Adoptable Children

970 Raymond Avenue, Suite 106
St. Paul, MN 55114
Phone: (651) 644-3036
Fax: (651) 644-9848
E-mail: info@nacac.org
Web site: www.nacac.org

MISSISSIPPI

Adoptive/Foster Family Support Groups

Harden House Adoption Support and Protection Program

P.O. Box 1576
110 North Gaither Street
Fulton, MS 38843
Phone: (601) 862-7318
E-mail: hardenad@nexband.com
Web site: www.hardenhouse.org

Mississippi Adoption Foster Parent Group

P.O. Box 4055
Brandon, MS 39047
Phone: (601) 829-1095

Mississippi DHS

48 Old Settlement Road
Tylertown, MS 39667
Phone: (601) 876-4479

North American Council on Adoptable Children Representative

100 Byram Drive, Apt. 11B
Jackson, MS 39272-9399
Phone: (601) 922-3989

South Mississippi Foster Parents Association

P.O. Box 919
Escatawpa, MS 39552
Phone: (228) 990-4336
E-mail: karaskloset@aol.com

Southwest Mississippi Adoption Support Group

27 Guitar Lane
Foxworth, MS 39483
Phone: (601) 736-6835

Southwest Mississippi Foster and Adoptive

Parent Support Group
901 Union Road
Tylertown, MS 39667
Phone: (601) 876-6978
E-mail: magnum03@netdoor.com

Licensed Private Adoption Agencies

Acorn Adoptions, Inc.

113 South Beach Boulevard, Suite D
Bay St. Louis, MS 39520
Toll-Free: (888) 221-1370
E-mail: acornadoption@msn.com
Web site: www.acornadoption.org

Bethany Christian Services

2618 Southerland Street
Jackson, MS 39216-4825
Phone: (601) 366-4282
Fax: (601) 366-4287
Toll-Free: (800) 331-5876
E-mail: bcsjackson@bethany.org
Web site: www.bethany.org/mississippi
– Intercountry Program
– Child Placement

Bethany Christian Services

116 Lawrence Drive, Suite 3
Columbus, MS 39702-5319
Phone: (662) 327-6740
Toll-Free: (800) 331-5876
E-mail: bcscolumbus@bethany.org

Web site: www.bethany.org/mississippi
– Intercountry Program
– Child Placement

Bethany Christian Services

7 Professional Parkway, Suite 103
Hattiesburg, MS 39402-2637
Phone: (601) 264-4984
Fax: (601) 264-2648
Toll-Free: (800) 331-5876
E-mail: bcshattiesburg@bethany.org
Web site: www.bethany.org/mississippi
– Intercountry Program
– Child Placement

Catholic Charities, Inc.

530 George Street
Jackson, MS 39202
Phone: (601) 960-8649
Fax: (601) 960-8657
Toll-Free: (800) 844-8655
E-mail: stephanie.harris@catholiccharitiesjackson.org
Web site: www.catholiccharitiesjackson.org

Catholic Social and Community Services

P.O. Box 1457
Biloxi, MS 39533-1457
Phone: (228) 374-8316

Mississippi Children's Home Society

P.O. Box 1078
1900 North West Street
Jackson, MS 39215
Phone: (601) 352-7784
Toll-Free: (800) 388-6247
E-mail: adoption@mchscares.org
Web site: www.mchsfsa.org/adoption.html
– Intercountry Program
– Child Placement

New Beginnings of Tupelo
1445 East Main Street
Tupelo, MS 38804
Phone: (662) 842-6752
Fax: (662) 840-7176
Toll-Free: (800) 264-2229
E-mail: crt@nbi.cc
Web site: www.nbi.cc
– Intercountry Program
– Home Study

World Child, Inc.
338 Lake Harbor Drive
Ridgeland, MS 39157

Birth Family and Search Support Groups

Adoption Information Network
P.O. Box 4154
Meridian, MS 39304
Phone: (601) 482-7556

State Adoption Exchange/ Photolisting of Children Waiting For Adoption

Mississippi Adoption
Resource Exchange
750 North State Street
P.O. Box 352
Jackson, MS 39205
Phone: (601) 359-4407
Toll-Free: (800) 821-9157
Web site: www.mdhs.state.
ms.us/fcs_adopt.html#children

State Adoption Specialist/Manager

Mississippi Department of
Human Services
Phoebe Clark
750 North State Street
Jackson, MS 39202
Phone: (601) 359-4981
Fax: (601) 359-4226
E-mail: pclark@mdhs.state.ms.us
Web site: www.mdhs.state.
ms.us/fcs_adopt.html

State Foster Care Specialist/Manager

Mississippi Department of
Human Services
Katherine Hardy
P.O. Box 352
750 North State Street
Jackson, MS 39205
Phone: (601) 359-4995
Fax: (601) 359-4978
Web site: www.mdhs.state.
ms.us/fcs_foster.html

MISSOURI

Adoptive/Foster Family Support Groups

Adoption Exchange PARTNER
Program
100 North Euclid Avenue, Suite 504
St. Louis, MO 63108
Phone: (314) 367-3343
Fax: (314) 367-3363
Toll-Free: (877) 723-6781
After hours: (314) 961-9756
(Laurie Murphy)
E-mail: larhonda@adoptex.org
Web site: www.adoptex.org

Adoption Today
5350 Casa Royale Drive
St. Louis, MO 63129-3007
Phone: (314) 894-4586

Adoption Triad Support
Network (ATSN)
144 Westwoods Drive
Liberty, MO 64068-1188
Phone: (913) 362-4230
E-mail: jennifer@our-reunion.net

Adoption by Family Therapy
dba Adoption for Families
91 Havilah Lane
Lampe, MO 65681-9542
Phone: (417) 882-7700
Fax: (417) 779-2128
Toll-Free: (888) 449-2229

E-mail: swampler@mchsi.com
Web site: www.
adoptionforfamilies.com
– Intercountry Program
– Adoptive Parent/Family
Preparation
– Child Placement
– Education/Preparation
– Home Study
– Information/Referral
– Post-placement Supervision
Prior to Adoption Finalization

Adoptive Parents of Southwest Missouri
4925 Royal Drive
Springfield, MO 65804
Phone: (417) 887-5788

Children and Adults with
Attention-Deficit/Hyperactiv-
ity Disorder (CHADD)
P.O. Box 25173
St. Louis, MO 65801
Phone: (314) 963-5259

Citizens for Missouri's Chil-
dren and North American
Council on Adoptable Children
Representative
701 South Skinner Boulevard,
Apartment 303
St. Louis, MO 63105-3326
Phone: (314) 647-2003

Crittenton Center for Child
and Family
Development Support Group
Mabee Building
10918 Elm Avenue
Kansas City, MO 64134
Phone: (816) 767-4110

Downey Side
216 S. Meramec
Clayton, MO 63105
Phone: (314) 863-4577
Fax: (314) 863-4570
Toll-Free: (800) US-CHILD
E-mail: stlouismo@downeyside.org
Web site: www.downeyside.org

Family Resource Center
3309 South Kingshighway
St. Louis, MO 63116
Phone: (314) 534-9350
Fax: (314) 353-3813

Foster Friends
1816 Lackland Hill Parkway, Suite 200
St. Louis, MO 63146
Phone: (314) 817-2285
E-mail: mohlemiller@slarc.org

Foster and Adoptive Care Coalition (FACC)
111 North 7th Street, 6th Floor
St. Louis, MO 63101
Phone: (314) 340-7722
Fax: (314) 340-7754
Toll-Free: (800) 367-8373
E-mail: melaniescheetz@foster-adopt.org
Web site: www.foster-adopt.org

Foster and Adoptive Parents of Mid-Missouri
7701 Cedar Hills Road
Ashland, MO 65010
Phone: (573) 657-9652
Fax: (573) 657-9656

Jasper County DFS Office
P.O. Box 1353
601 Commercial
Joplin, MO 64802
Phone: (417) 629-3050
Fax: (417) 629-3209
Toll-Free: (887) 212-8720
– Intercountry Program
– Adoptive Parent/Family Preparation
– Agency Able to Place Children with United States Citizens Living Abroad
– Child Placement
– Education/Preparation
– Home Study
– Information/Referral

LIGHT House
7110 Wyandotte
Kansas City, MO 64114
Phone: (816) 361-2233
Fax: (816) 361-8333
E-mail: info@lighthouse-inc.org
Web site: www.lighthouse-inc.org

Lara L. Deveraux Counseling and Adoption Services
7911 Forsyth, 2nd Floor
Clayton, MO 63015
Phone: (314) 725-7605
Fax: (314) 721-2602
E-mail: lldeveraux@yahoo.com
– Intercountry Program
– Adoptive Parent/Family Preparation
– Child Placement
– Education/Preparation
– Home Study
– Information/Referral
– Post-placement Supervision Prior to Adoption Finalization

Lutheran Family and Children's Services of Missouri
8631 Delmar Boulevard
University City, MO 63124
Phone: (314) 787-5100
Fax: (314) 534-1588
Toll-Free: (800) 727-0218
Web site: www.lfcsmo.org
– Intercountry Program
– Adoptive Parent/Family Preparation
– Education/Preparation
– Home Study
– Information/Referral
– Post-placement Supervision Prior to Adoption Finalization

Midwest Foster Care and Adoption Association, Inc.
3210 Lee's Summit Road
Independence, MO 64055
Phone: (816) 350-0215
Phone: (866) 794-KIDS
E-mail: mfcaa@mail.com

Web site: www.mfcaa.org
– Intercountry Program
– Adoptive Parent/Family Preparation
– Education/Preparation

Missouri Foster Care and Adoption Association
3737 Harry S. Truman Boulevard
St. Charles, MO 63301
Phone: (636) 250-3367
After hours: (636) 250-3367
E-mail: judyb327@aol.com

Missouri Statewide Foster Care Recruitment Line
Phone: (314) 367-3343
Fax: (314) 367-3363
Toll-Free: (800) 554-2222
E-mail: larhonda@adoptex.org

Parkland Foster and Adoptive Families Support Group
408 North Allen Street
Bonne Terre, MO 63628
Phone: (573) 701-7365
Fax: (573) 756-6007
After hours: (573) 358-3512
E-mail: milcar@jcn.net

SW Missouri Foster/Adopt Support Group
P.O. Box 277
Cape Fair, MO 65624
Phone: (417) 538-4362

Single Adoptive Parents Support Group
1800 Fairview Road
Columbia, MO 65203
Phone: (573) 445-1262
E-mail: batkin7@hotmail.com

St. Louis Attachment Network (SLAN)
1170 Timber Run Drive
St. Louis, MO 63146
Web site: www.stlattachnet.freehosting.net

St. Louis County Adoptive Parent and Foster Parent Support Group
11097 St. Charles Rock Road
Pattonville Learning Center
St. Louis, MO 63074
Phone: (314) 426-3944

Stars of David International, Inc.
1608 Stone Hollow Road
Wildwood, MO 63038-2417
Phone: (314) 207-6682
E-mail: starsdavid@aol.com
Web site: www.starsofdavid.org

Licensed Private Adoption Agencies

Action for Adoption
1015 Locust Street
St. Louis, MO 63101
Phone: (816) 490-0198

Adopt Kids, Inc.
109 West Jefferson, Suite 203
Kirkwood, MO 63122
Phone: (314) 965-2203

Adoption Advocates
3100 Broadway, Suite 218
Kansas City, MO 64111
Phone: (816) 753-1881
– Intercountry Program
– Child Placement

Adoption Counseling, Inc.
1420 West Lexington Avenue
Independence, MO 64052
Phone: (816) 507-0822

Adoption Option
Seaport Professional Complex
144 Westwoods Drive
Liberty, MO 64068
Phone: (816) 224-1525

Adoption and Beyond, Inc.
401 West 89th Street
Kansas City, MO 64114
Phone: (816) 822-2800
E-mail: adopt@adoption-beyond.org

Web site: www.adoption-beyond.org
– Intercountry Program
– Child Placement

Adoption and Counseling Services for Families
8301 State Line, Suite 216
Kansas City, MO 64111
Phone: (816) 942-8440

Adoption and Fertility Resources
144 Westwoods Drive
Liberty, MO 64068
Phone: (816) 781-8550
Fax: (816) 792-3219

Adoption by Family Therapy
dba Adoption for Families
91 Havilah Lane
Lampe, MO 65681-9542
Phone: (417) 882-7700
Fax: (417) 779-2128
Toll-Free: (888) 449-2229
E-mail: swampler@mchsi.com
Web site: www.adoptionforfamilies.com
– Intercountry Program
– Adoptive Parent/Family Preparation

Affordable Adoption Solutions, Inc.
221 ½ Madison Street
Jefferson City, MO 65101
Phone: (573) 632-6646
Fax: (573) 659-8815

Alternatives Opportunities, Inc.
dba Gateway Youth and Family Services
222 East Water
Springfield, MO 65806
Phone: (417) 869-8911

American Adoption
306 East 12th Street, Suite 908
Kansas City, MO 64106
Toll-Free: (800) 875-2229

E-mail: adoptions@americanadoptions.com
Web site: www.americanadoptions.com

Annie Malone Children and Family Service Center
2612 Annie Malone Drive
St. Louis, MO 63113
Phone: (314) 531-0120

BFT Holding Corporation
dba Bringing Families Together, LLC.
7151 North Lindbergh Boulevard
Hazelwood, MO 63042
Phone: (314) 731-3969
Fax: (314) 731-3906
E-mail: TonyaE@BringingFamiliesTogether.com
Web site: www.bringingfamiliestogether.com
– Intercountry Program
– Agency Able to Place Children with United States Citizens Living Abroad
– Home Study

Bethany Christian Services
1 McBride and Son Corporate Center Drive, Suite 210
Chesterfield, MO 63054
Phone: (636) 536-6363
Fax: (636) 536-6262
E-mail: bcschesterfield@bethany.org
Web site: www.bethany.org/missouri
– Intercountry Program
– Child Placement

Boys and Girls Town of Missouri
13160 County Road 3610
St. James, MO 65559
Phone: (573) 265-3251

Butterfield Youth Services
11 West Eastwood
Marshall, MO 65340
Phone: (660) 886-2253

Catholic Charities of Kansas City/St. Joseph, Inc.
1112 Broadway
Kansas City, MO 64105
Phone: (816) 221-4377
Fax: (800) 221-9116
Toll-Free: (800) 875-4377
E-mail: jthompson@ccharities.com
Web site: www.catholiccharities-kcsj.org
– Intercountry Program
– Adoptive Parent/Family Preparation
– Home Study
– Information/Referral
– Post-placement Supervision Prior to Adoption Finalization

Catholic Services for Children and Youth
20 Archbishop May Drive
St. Louis, MO 63119
Phone: (314) 792-7400
Fax: (314) 792-7438
E-mail: jjames@ccstl.org

Central Baptist Family Services
1015 Locust Street, Suite 900
St. Louis, MO 63101
Phone: (314) 241-4345
Fax: (314) 241-4330

Children of the World, Inc.
16 North Central Avenue
Clayton, MO 63105
Phone: (314) 721-4070
Fax: (314) 721-2602
E-mail: rrivera264@aol.com
Web site: www.childrenoftheworldnet.com

Children's Home Society of Missouri
9445 Litzsinger Road
Brentwood, MO 63144
Phone: (314) 968-2350
Fax: (314) 968-4239
Web site: www.chsmo.com

Children's Hope International
9229 Lackland Road
St. Louis, MO 63114
Phone: (314) 890-0086
Fax: (314) 427-4288
E-mail: adoption@childrenshopeint.org
Web site: www.ChildrensHope.com

Christian Family Life Center
620 N. McKnight Road, #2A
St. Louis, MO 63105
Phone: (314) 862-6300
Fax: (314) 862-2540
Web site: www.cflcenter.org
– Intercountry Program
– Child Placement

Christian Family Services
7955 Big Bend Boulevard
Webster Groves, MO 63119
Phone: (314) 968-2216
Fax: (314) 968-2335
E-mail: parents@cfserve.org
Web site: www.cfserve.org

Christian Family Services of the Midwest, Inc.
5703 North Flora
Gladstone, MO 64118
Phone: (816) 452-2077

Christian Salvation Services
4390 Lindell Boulevard, Suite 200
St. Louis, MO 63108
Phone: (314) 535-5919
Fax: (314) 535-1353
E-mail: cssusm@swbell.net
Web site: www.csstpe.org.tw
– Intercountry Program
– Adoptive Parent/Family Preparation

Crittenton St. Luke's Health Care System
10918 Elm Avenue
Kansas City, MO 64134
Phone: (816) 765-6600

Dillon International, Inc.
1 First Missouri Center, Suite 115
St. Louis, MO 63141
Phone: (314) 576-4100
Fax: (314) 453-9975
E-mail: dillonkids@aol.com
Web site: www.dillonadopt.com
– Intercountry Program
– Child Placement

Edgewood Children's Home
330 North Gore Avenue
Webster Groves, MO 63119
Phone: (314) 968-2060

Farm, Inc. (THE)
dba KYDS,INC
3549 Broadway
Kansas City, MO 64111
Phone: (816) 931-4703

Faith House
5355 Page
St. Louis, MO 63112
Phone: (314) 367-5400

Family Builders, Inc.
203 Huntington Road
Kansas City, MO 64113
Phone: (816) 822-2169

Family Care Center
14377 Woodlake Drive, Suite 308
Chesterfield, MO 63017
Phone: (314) 576-6493
Fax: (314) 576-7319
E-mail: fcc@birch.net

Family Resource Center
3309 South Kingshighway
St. Louis, MO 63116
Phone: (314) 534-9350
Fax: (314) 353-3813

Friends of African-American Families and Children Service Center
3920 Lindell Boulevard, Suite 102
St. Louis, MO 63108
Phone: (314) 535-2453
Fax: (314) 535-3100

Future, Inc.
643 Wynn Place
St. Louis, MO 63021
Phone: (314) 391-8868

General Protestants Children's
Home
12685 Olive Street
Creve Coeur, MO 63141
Phone: (314) 434-5858

Heart of America Family
Services
3100 NE 83rd Street, Suite 1401
Kansas City, MO 64119
Phone: (816) 436-0486
– Intercountry Program
– Child Placement

Hope N. Heller, Ph.D. Adoption
Services, Inc.
11330 Olive Boulevard, Suite 225
St. Louis, MO 63141
Phone: (314) 567-7500
Fax: (314) 567-8512
Web site: www.hopenhellerphd.
com
– Intercountry Program
– Adoptive Parent/Family
Preparation

James A. Roberts Agency
Penn Tower Building
3100 Broadway, Suite 64111
Kansas City, MO 61104
Phone: (816) 753-3333

LDS Family Services
517 West Walnut, Suite 2
Independence, MO 64050
Phone: (816) 461-5512
Fax: (816) 461-4907
E-mail: fam-mo-
independence@ldschurch.org
Web site: www.
ldsfamilyservices.org

LIGHT House
7110 Wyandotte
Kansas City, MO 64114
Phone: (816) 361-2233
Fax: (816) 361-8333

E-mail: info@lighthouse-inc.org
Web site: www.lighthouse-inc.org

Lara L. Deveraux Counseling
and Adoption Services
7911 Forsyth, 2nd Floor
Clayton, MO 63015
Phone: (314) 725-7605
Fax: (314) 721-2602
E-mail: lldeveraux@yahoo.com
– Intercountry Program
– Adoptive Parent/Family
Preparation

Love Basket, Inc.
10306 State Highway 21
Hillsboro, MO 63050
Phone: (636) 797-4100
Fax: (636) 789-4978
E-mail: LoveBasket@LoveBasket.
org
Web site: www.lovebasket.org
– Intercountry Program
– Child Placement

Lutheran Family and Children's
Services of Missouri
8631 Delmar Boulevard
St. Louis, MO 63124-1990
Phone: (314) 534-1515 or
(314) 787-5100
Fax: (314) 534-1588
Toll-Free: (800) 727-0218
Web site: www.lfcsmo.org
– Intercountry Program
– Adoptive Parent/Family
Preparation

Mattie Rhodes Memorial
Society
5001 Independence Avenue
Kansas City, MO 64124
Phone: (816) 471-2536

Missouri Alliance for Children
and Families L.L.C.
724 Heisinger
Jefferson City, MO 65109
Phone: (573) 556-8090
Toll-Free: (573) 632-2761
E-mail: ltennyson@ma-cf.org

Missouri Baptist Children's
Home/MBCH
Children and Family Ministries
11300 St. Charles Rock Road
Bridgeton, MO 63044
Phone: (314) 739-6811
Fax: (314) 739-6325
Web site: www.mbch.org

New Family Connection
201 North Kingshighway
St. Charles, MO 63301
Phone: (636) 949-0577
– Intercountry Program
– Child Placement

Niles Children's Home
1911 East 23rd Street
Kansas City, MO 64127
Phone: (816) 241-3448

Our Little Haven
4326 Lindell Boulevard
St. Louis, MO 63108
Phone: (314) 533-2229

Presbyterian Children's
Services, Inc.
dba Farmington Children's Home
608 Pine Street
Farmington, MO 63640
Phone: (573) 756-6744
Fax: (573) 756-5579
Toll-Free: (800) 747-1855
E-mail: cindylively@care4kids.org
Web site: www.
presbyterianchildren.org/fch.html

Professional Adoption
Resources
P.O. Box 11
Troy, MO 63379
Phone: (636) 528-2499

Reaching Out Thru Interna-
tional Adoption, Inc.
1889 Summitview Drive
St. Charles, MO 63303
Phone: (636) 255-0554
Fax: (636) 255-0554
E-mail: wieschhaus@yahoo.com

Web site: www.adoptachild.us
– Intercountry Program
– Child Placement

Respond, Inc.
4411 North Newstead Avenue
St. Louis, MO 63115
Phone: (314) 383-4243

Safe Cradle Adoption Agency
11715 Administration Drive,
Suite 101
Creve Coeur, MO 63146
Phone: (314) 991-2580

Salvation Army Hope Center
3740 Marine Avenue
St. Louis, MO 63118
Phone: (314) 773-0980

Seek International
4583 Chestnut Park Plaza, Suite
205
St. Louis, MO 63129-3100
Phone: (314) 416-9723
Fax: (314) 416-7880
– Intercountry Program
– Child Placement

**Small World Adoption
Foundation, Inc. (SWAF)**
15480 Clayton Road, Suite 300
Ballwin, MO 63011
Phone: (636) 207-9229
Fax: (636) 207-9055
E-mail: staff@swaf.com
Web site: www.swaf.com
– Intercountry Program
– Adoptive Parent/Family
Preparation
– Child Placement

Special Additions, Inc.
701 Berkshire Drive
Belton, MO 64012
Phone: (816) 421-3737

Spofford – Cornerstone
9700 Grandview Road
Kansas City, MO 64134
Phone: (816) 508-3400

St. Louis Christian Home, Inc.
dba Echo
3033 North Euclid Avenue
St. Louis, MO 63115
Phone: (314) 381-3100

**Universal Adoption Services
(UAS)**
1905 Cole Drive
Jefferson City, MO 65109
Phone: (573) 634-3733
E-mail: uas@earthlink.net
– Intercountry Program
– Adoptive Parent/Family
Preparation
– Agency Able to Place Children
with United States Citizens Living
Abroad
– Education/Preparation
– Home Study

**Urban Behavioral Healthcare
Institute (UBH)**
1104 South Jefferson Avenue
St. Louis, MO 63104
Phone: (314) 577-5000
Fax: (314) 577-5003
E-mail: lstaylor@urbanbehav.com
Web site: www.urbanbehav.com

**Birth Family and Search
Support Groups**

Adoption Search of Missouri
9434 Bristol Avenue
St. Louis, MO 63117

Birthmom Support Group
P.O. Box 505
Springfield, MO 65801
Phone: (417) 889-4207

**Concerned United Birthpar-
ents (CUB)**
7000 Jackson
Kansas City, MO 63142

**Lutheran Family and Children's
Services of Missouri**
8631 Delmar Boulevard
St. Louis, MO 63124-1990

Phone: (314) 534-1515 or
(314) 787-5100
Fax: (314) 534-1588
Toll-Free: (800) 727-0218
Web site: www.lfcsmo.org
– Intercountry Program
– Adoptive Parent/Family
Preparation
– Education/Preparation
– Home Study
– Information/Referral
– Post-placement Supervision
Prior to Adoption Finalization

Missouri Adoption Reform
708 B Demaret Drive
Columbia, MO 65202
Phone: (573) 814-3469

Searcher's Forum
830 Marshall Avenue
Webster Grove, MO 63119-2003

**Universal Adoption Services
(UAS)**
1905 Cole Drive
Jefferson City, MO 65109
Phone: (573) 634-3733
E-mail: uas@earthlink.net
– Intercountry Program
– Adoptive Parent/Family
Preparation
– Agency Able to Place Children
with United States Citizens Living
Abroad
– Education/Preparation
– Home Study

**State Adoption Exchange/
Photolisting of Children
Waiting For Adoption**

Missouri Adoption Exchange
100 Euclid Avenue, Suite 504
St. Louis, MO 63108
Phone: (314) 367-3343
Toll-Free: (800) 554-2222
E-mail: russ@adoptex.org
Web site: www.dss.mo.gov

Missouri Adoption Photolisting
P.O. Box 1527
221 West High Street
Jefferson City, MO 65102-1527
Phone: (573) 751-4815
TDD: (800) 735-2966
TDD: (800) 735-2466
Toll-Free: (800) 554-2222
E-mail: r adopt@dss.mo.gov
Web site: www.dss.mo.gov/cd/
adopt/index.htm

**State Adoption
Specialist/Manager**

Missouri Department of Social
Services
Cindy Wilkinson
615 Howerton Court
P.O. Box 88
Jefferson City, MO 65103-0088
Phone: (573) 751-3171
Fax: (573) 526-3971
E-mail: cindy.r.wilkinson@dss.
mo.us
Web site: www.dss.mo.gov/cd/
adopt.htm

**State Foster Care
Specialist/Manager**

Missouri Department of Social
Services
Cindy Wilkinson
615 Howerton Court
P.O. Box 88
Jefferson City, MO 65103-0088
Phone: (573) 751-3171
Fax: (573) 526-3971
E-mail: cindy.r.wilkinson@dss.
mo.us
Web site: www.dss.mo.gov/cd/
cfpp.htm

**State Interstate Compact on
the Placement of Children
(ICPC) Administrator**

Missouri Department of Social
Services
P.O. Box 88
615 Howerton Court

Jefferson City, MO 65103
Phone: (573) 751-2981
E-mail: Mary.C.Kliethermes@dss.
mo.gov
Web site: www.dss.mo.gov

State Licensing Specialist

Missouri Department of Social
Services
P.O. Box 88
615 Howerton Court
Jefferson City, MO 65103
Phone: (573) 751-4954
Web site: www.dss.mo.gov

State Reunion Registry

Missouri Division of Family
Services
P.O. Box 88
615 Howerton Court
Jefferson City, MO 65103
Phone: (573) 751-3171
Toll-Free: (800) 554-2222
Web site: www.dss.mo.gov/cd/
adopt/adoir.htm

**Statewide Adoption
Recruitment Line**

Missouri Statewide Adoption
Recruitment Line
Phone: (314) 367-3343
Toll-Free: (800) 554-2222

**Statewide Foster Care
Recruitment Line**

Missouri Statewide Foster
Care Recruitment Line
Phone: (314) 367-3343
Toll-Free: (800) 554-2222

MONTANA

**Adoptive/Foster Family
Support Groups**

Adoptive Parent Support
Group
500 South Lamborn
Helena, MT 59601

Phone: (866) 457-4859
E-mail: SusanB@intermountain.
org

Casey Family Program
2510 South 7th West
Missoula, MT 59801
Phone: (406) 543-3632

Dan Fox Home for Kids
P.O. Box 7617
Missoula, MT 59807
Phone: (406) 721-2754

**Family Support in Adoption
Association and North Ameri-
can Council on Adoptable
Children Representative**
7049 Fox Lane
Darby, MT 59829
Phone: (406) 349-2488

Global Adoption Services
P.O. Box 790
Eureka, MT 59917
Phone: (406) 252-1444

Hearts and Homes
P.O. Box 8265
Bozeman, MT 59773
Phone: (406) 284-3095
E-mail: heartsnhomes1@yahoo.
com

**Intermountain Children's
Home Path Program**
500 South Lamborn
Helena, MT 59601
Phone: (440) 442-7920

Larry Loberg
1343 Beaverhead Drive
Helena, MT 59602-7604
Phone: (406) 846-2229

**Montana State Foster/
Adoptive Parent Association**
8450 Mourning Dove Drive
Missoula, MT 59808
Phone: (406) 728-7173
E-mail: twelvellewellyns@aol.
com

Montana State Foster/
Adoptive Parents Association
1740 Augsburg Drive
Billings, MT 59105
Phone: (406) 245-7543
E-mail: mblendu@aol.com
Web site: www.geocities.com/
msf/apa

Yellowstone Valley Foster and
Adoption Association
1740 Augsburg Drive
Billings, MT 59105
Phone: (406) 245-7543

**Licensed Private
Adoption Agencies**

A New Arrival
P.O. Box 445
204 South Main Street
Twin Bridges, MT 59754
Phone: (406) 684-5312
Fax: (406) 684-5315
E-mail: info@anewarrival.com
Web site: www.anewarrival.com
– Intercountry Program
– Child Placement

Catholic Social Services for
Montana
1048 North 30th Street
Billings, MT 59101
Phone: (406) 252-3399
Fax: (406) 252-9173
Toll-Free: (800) 222-9388
(in-state only)
E-mail: beckyh@180com.net

Catholic Social Services
of Montana
P.O. Box 907
25 South Ewing
Helena, MT 59624
Phone: (406) 442-4130
Fax: (406) 442-4192
E-mail: Rosemary@catholicsocial
servicesofmontana.org
Web site: www.catholicsocialser
vicesofmontana.org

LDS Family Services
2620 Colonial Drive, Suite D
Helena, MT 59601
Phone: (406) 443-1660
E-mail: fam-mt@ldschurch.org
Web site: www.
ldsfamilyservices.org
– Intercountry Program
– Child Placement

Lutheran Social Services
P.O. Box 1345
Great Falls, MT 59403
Phone: (406) 761-4341

**State Foster Care
Specialist/Manager**

Montana Department of Public
Health and Human Services
Child and Family Services
Division
Betsy Stimatz
P.O. Box 8005
Helena, MT 59604-8005
Phone: (406) 444-1675
Fax: (406) 444-5956
E-mail: bstimatz@state.mt.us
Web site: http://vhsp.dphhs.
state.mt.us/dph_r3.htm

**State Interstate Compact on
the Placement of Children
(ICPC) Administrator**

Montana Department of Public
Health and Human Services
Child and Family Services Division
P.O. Box 8005
Helena, MT 59604-8005
Phone: (406) 444-5917
Fax: (406) 444-5956
E-mail: kmorese@state.mt.us

**State Licensing
Specialist/Manager**

Montana Department of Public
Health and Human Services
Child and Family Services Division
Lynda Korth
P.O. Box 8005
Helena, MT 59604-8005

Phone: (406) 444-5900
E-mail: lkorth@state.mt.us
Web site: www.dphhs.state.mt.us

NEBRASKA

**Adoptive/Foster Family
Support Groups**

Fos-Adopt Support Group
6001 Sunrise Road
Lincoln, NE 68510
Phone: (402) 489-1295

Nebraska Foster and Adoptive
Parent Association
212 Haymarket Square
808 P Street
Lincoln, NE 68508
Phone: (402) 476-2273
E-mail: nfapa@alltel.net
Web site: www.nfapa.org

North American Council
on Adoptable Children
Representative
712 West Koenig
Grand Island, NE 68801
Phone: (308) 382-4495
Fax: (308) 385-0407
E-mail: oldmill@kdsi.net

Stars of David International,
Inc.
Jewish Family Services – Omaha
Chapter
333 South 132nd Street
Omaha, NE 68154
Phone: (402) 330-2024
Fax: (402) 333-5497
E-mail: starsdavid@aol.com
Web site: www.starsofdavid.org

Tri-City Coalition for
Post-Adoption Supports
and Services
712 West Koenig
Grand Island, NE 68801
Phone: (308) 382-4495
Fax: (308) 385-0407
After hours: (308) 382-4495
E-mail: oldmill@kdsi.net

Voices for Children in Nebraska
7521 Main Street
Omaha, NE 68127
Phone: (402) 597-3100
Fax: (402) 597-2705
E-mail: voices@uswest.net
Web site: www.
voicesforchildren.com

**Licensed Private
Adoption Agencies**

Adoption Links Worldwide
5017 Leavenworth Street
Omaha, NE 68106
Phone: (402) 556-2367
Fax: (402) 556-2401
Toll-Free: (800) 66 CHILD
E-mail: alww@alww.org
Web site: www.alww.org
– Intercountry Program
– Child Placement

Catholic Charities Children's
Services
3300 North 60th Street
Omaha, NE 68104
Phone: (402) 554-0520
E-mail: catholiccharities@ccom
aha.org
Web site: www.ccomaha.org
– Intercountry Program
– Home Study

Child Saving Institute
115 South 46th Street
Omaha, NE 68132
Phone: (402) 553-6000
Fax: (402) 553-2428
Toll-Free: (888) 588-6003
Web site: www.childsaving.org

Holt International Children's
Services
10685 Bedford Avenue, Suite 300
Omaha, NE 68134
Phone: (402) 934-5031
Fax: (402) 934-5034
E-mail: info@holtintl.org
Web site: www.holtintl.org

Jewish Family Services
333 South 132nd Street
Omaha, NE 68154
Phone: (402) 330-2024

Lutheran Family Services of
Nebraska, Inc.
124 South 24th Street, Suite 200
Omaha, NE 68102
Phone: (402) 342-7007
Fax: (402) 978-5637
Toll-Free: (800) 267-9876
E-mail: ltempleplotz@lfsneb.org
Web site: www.lfsneb.org
– Intercountry Program
– Child Placement

Nebraska Children's Home
Society
4939 South 118th Street
Omaha, NE 68137
Phone: (402) 451-0787
Fax: (402) 898-7750
E-mail: adopt@nchs.org
Web site: www.nchs.org

Nebraska Christian Services,
Inc.
2600 South 124th Street
Omaha, NE 68144
Phone: (402) 334-3278
Fax: (402) 697-5147
E-mail: ccarterburn@hotmail.com

**Birth Family and Search
Support Groups**

Adoption Triad
Midwest-Omaha
3711 N. 108th Street
Omaha, NE 68134
Phone: (402) 493-8047
Phone: (402) 890-3706

Alice Beyke ISC
1850 South Baltimore
Hastings, NE 68901
Phone: (402) 462-6349

Concerned United
Birthparents (CUB)
9621 Parker Street
Omaha, NE 68114
Phone: (402) 397-6394
Web site: www.cubirthparents.org

Concerned United
Birthparents (CUB)
4075 West Airport Road
Grand Island, NE 68803
Phone: (308) 384-3571
Fax: (308) 389-3900
Web site: www.cubirthparents.org

Midwest Adoption Triad
P.O. Box 37273
Omaha, NE 68137
Phone: (402) 493-8047

**State Adoption Exchange/
Photolisting of Children
Waiting For Adoption**

Nebraska Adoption Resource
Exchange
Protection and Safety Division
P.O. Box 95044
Lincoln, NE 68509-5044
Phone: (402) 471-9331
E-mail: mary.dyer@hhss.state.
ne.us
Web site: www.hhs.state.ne.us/
adp/ad pxchan.htm

**State Adoption
Specialist/Manager/**

State Interstate Compact on
the Placement of Children
(ICPC) Administrator
Nebraska Department of Health
and Human Services
Protection and Safety Division
Mary Dyer
P.O. Box 95044
Lincoln, NE 68509-5044
Phone: (402) 471-9331
Fax: (402) 471-9034
E-mail: mary.dyer@hhss.state.
ne.us

Web site: www.hhs.state.ne.us/
adp/adpindex.htm

State Foster Care Specialist/Manager

Nebraska Department of Health and Human Services
Becky Henderson
P.O. Box 95026
301 Centennial Mall South
Lincoln, NE 68505-5026
Phone: (402) 471-9333
Fax: (402) 471-9034
E-mail: becky.henderson@hhss.
state.ne.us
Web site: www.hhs.state.ne.us/
chs/foc/focindex.htm

State Reunion Registry

Nebraska Department of Health and Human Services
P.O. Box 95044
Lincoln, NE 68509
Phone: (402) 471-9254

NEVADA

Adoptive/Foster Family Support Groups

Adoption Exchange
1516 East Tropicana Avenue,
Suite 240
Las Vegas, NV 89120
Phone: (702) 436-6335
Fax: (702) 436-6304
Web site: www.adoptex.org

Catholic Charities of Southern Nevada
2077 East Sahara Avenue, Suite B
Las Vegas, NV 89104
Phone: (702) 385-3351
Fax: (702) 388-8723
E-mail: adoption@catholic
charities.com
Web site: www.catholiccharities.
com

Court Appointed Special Advocate (CASA) Program
601 North Pecos Road, Room #50
Las Vegas, NV 89101
Phone: (702) 455-4306

FAS Support Group of Southern Nevada
1643 Hinson Street
Las Vegas, NV 89102-3808
Phone: (702) 643-7574
Fax: (702) 367-2047
E-mail: coy4125@aol.com

Foster Care and Adoption Association of Nevada
3426 Wild Filly Lane
Las Vegas, NV 89030
Phone: (702) 636-9007
Fax: (702) 636-9028
E-mail: dblazzard@aol.com

Adoptive/Foster Family Support Groups

Foster Parents of Southern Nevada
P.O. Box 570127
Las Vegas, NV 89129-0127
Phone: (702) 396-0585
E-mail: THEHENRYSO8@cox.net
Web site: www.fpsn.saff.org

Nevada Children's Center
2929 South Decatur Boulevard
Las Vegas, NV 89102
Phone: (702) 221-4900
Phone: (702) 349-7085
After hours: (702) 461-8836
E-mail: NNVCC@aol.com

Sierra Association of Foster Families
8700 Osage Road
Reno, NV 89506
Phone: (775) 677-9381
Fax: (775) 677-9379

Licensed Private Adoption Agencies

Catholic Charities of Southern Nevada
2077 East Sahara Avenue,
Suite B
Las Vegas, NV 89104
Phone: (702) 385-3351
Fax: (702) 388-8723
E-mail: adoption@catholic
charities.com
Web site: www.catholiccharities.
com
– Intercountry Program

Catholic Community Services of Northern Nevada
P.O. Box 5099
500 East 4th Street
Reno, NV 89513
Phone: (775) 322-7073
Web site: http://heather.
greatbasin.com/~ccsn n2/i ndex.
htm

LDS Family Services
513 South Ninth Street
Las Vegas, NV 89101
Phone: (702) 385-1072

New Hope Child and Family Agency
440 Ridge Street, Suite 4
Reno, NV 89501
Phone: (775) 323-0122
Fax: (775) 323-4543
E-mail: info@newhopekids.org
Web site: www.newhopekids.org

Premier Adoption Agency
590 West Mesquite Boulevard,
Suite 202B
Mesquite, NV 89027
Phone: (702) 346-4922
Fax: (702) 346-0330
Toll-Free: (800) 876-0187
Web site: www.premieradoption.
org

**Birth Family and Search
Support Groups**

Adoptees Search Connection
9713 Quail Springs Street
Las Vegas, NV 89117

**State Adoption Exchange/
Photolisting of Children
Waiting For Adoption**

Nevada Adoption Exchange
1516 East Tropicana Avenue,
Suite 240
Las Vegas, NV 89119
Phone: (702) 455-4024
Phone: (775) 337-4502
Phone: (775) 687-4943, est. 233
Phone: (702) 436-6335
Fax: (702) 436-63304
Web site: http://dcfs.state.nv.us/
page50.html

**State Adoption
Specialist/Manager/
Licensing Specialist**

Nevada Department of Human
Resources
Division of Child and Family
Services
Wanda Scott
4220 South Maryland Parkway
Building B, Suite 300
Las Vegas, NV 89119
Phone: (702) 486-7633
Fax: (702) 486-7626
E-mail: wlscott@dcfs.state.nv.us
Web site: http://dcfs.state.nv.us/
page33.html

**State Foster Care
Specialist/Manager**

Nevada Department of Human
Resources
Division of Child and Family
Services
Rebecca Richard-Maley
711 East 5th Street
Carson City, NV 89701-5092
Phone: (775) 684-4450

Fax: (775) 684-4457
E-mail: B.RICHARD-MALEY@
dcfs.state.nv.us
Web site: http://dcfs.state.nv.us/
page25.html

**Interstate Compact on
the Placement of Children
(ICPC) Administrator**

Nevada Department of Human
Resources
Division of Child and Family
Services
711 East 5th Street
Carson City, NV 89701
Phone: (775) 684-4400
Fax: (775) 684-4456
E-mail: mdunn@dcfs.state.nv.us
Web site: http://dcfs.state.nv.us/
page20.html

NEW HAMPSHIRE

**Adoptive/Foster Family
Support Groups**

AFT
224 Crescent Way
Portsmouth, NH 03801
Phone: (603) 591-7967
E-mail: eliolori@msn.com

Casey Family Services
Building 2
105 Loudon Road
Concord, NH 03301
Phone: (603) 224-8909
Web site: www.
caseyfamilyservices.org

New Hampshire Foster and
Adoptive Parent
P.O. Box 2802
Concord, NH 03302
Phone: (603) 224-8909
Fax: (603) 224-2584
E-mail: Lstanley@caseyfamily
services.org
Web site: www.nhfapa.org

New Hampshire Foster and
Adoptive Parent Association
and North American Council
on Adoptable Children Representative
9 Webster Street
Nashua, NH 03060
Phone: (603) 577-8932
Web site: http://nhfapa.org

Ours for a United Response of
New England
347 Candia Road
Chester, NH 03036
Phone: (617) 967-4648

**Licensed Private
Adoption Agencies**

Adoptive Families for Children
26 Fairview Street
Keene, NH 03431
Phone: (603) 357-4456
Fax: (603) 352-8543
E-mail: adfams@msn.com
– Intercountry Program
– Child Placement

Bethany Christian Services of
New England
P.O. Box 320
Candia, NH 03034-0320
Phone: (603) 483-2886
Fax: (603) 483-0161
Web site: www.bethany.org
– Intercountry Program
– Child Placement

Casey Family Services
Building 2
105 Loudon Road
Concord, NH 03301
Phone: (603) 224-8909
Web site: www.
caseyfamilyservices.org

**Child and Family Services of
New Hampshire**
99 Hanover Street
Manchester, NH 03105
Phone: (603) 668-1920

Fax: (603) 668-6260
Toll-Free: (800) 640-6486
E-mail: info@cfsnh.org
Web site: www.cfsnh.org

Creative Advocates for Children and Families
P.O. Box 1703
Manchester, NH 03105
Phone: (603) 623-5006
E-mail: suzannesrjk@aol.com

LDS Family Services
547 Amherst Street, Suite 404
Nashua, NH 03063-4000
Phone: (603) 889-0148
Fax: (603) 889-4358
Toll-Free: (800) 735-0419
E-mail: fam-nh@ldschurch.org
Web site: www.
ldsfamilyservices.org

Lutheran Social Services of New England
261 Sheep Davis Road, Suite A-1
Concord, NH 03301
Phone: (603) 224-8111
Fax: (603) 224-5473
Toll-Free: (800) 244-8119
E-mail: adoption@lssnorth.org
Web site: www.adoptlss.org
– Intercountry Program
– Child Placement

New Hampshire Catholic Charities, Inc.
P.O. Box 686
215 Myrtle Street
Manchester, NH 03105-0686
Phone: (603) 669-3030
Fax: (603) 626-1252
Toll-Free: (800) 562-5249
Web site: www.
catholiccharitiesnh.org
– Intercountry Program
– Child Placement

New Hope Christian Services
210 Silk Farm Road
Concord, NH 03301
Phone: (603) 225-0992
Fax: (603) 225-7400
E-mail: NewhopeAd@aol.com
Web site: www.peekaboo.net/
nh/adopt
– Intercountry Program
– Child Placement

Wide Horizons for Children
P.O. Box 476
Milford, NH 03055
Phone: (603) 672-3000
Fax: (603) 672-7182
E-mail: vpeterson@whfc.org
Web site: www.whfc.org
– Intercountry Program
– Home Study

Birth Family and Search Support Groups

Birthmothers Support Group
P.O. Box 1483
Dover, NH 03021
Phone: (603) 343-2341
E-mail: birthmothersofnh@yahoo.com

Casey Family Services
Building 2
105 Loudon Road
Concord, NH 03301
Phone: (603) 224-8909
Fax: (603) 224-2584
E-mail: info@caseyfamily
services.org
Web site: www.
caseyfamilyservices.org

Circle of Hope
P.O. Box 127
Somersworth, NH 03878
Phone: (603) 692-5917

Pieces of Yesterday
P.O. Box 1703
Manchester, NH 03105

Wide Horizons for Children
P.O. Box 476
Milford, NH 03055
Phone: (603) 672-3000
Fax: (603) 672-7182
E-mail: vpeterson@whfc.org
Web site: www.whfc.org
– Intercountry Program
– Home Study

State Adoption Specialist/Manager

New Hampshire Department of Health and Human Services
Division for Children, Youth and Families
Catherine Atkins
129 Pleasant Street
Concord, NH 03301
Phone: (603) 271-4707
Fax: (603) 271-4729
E-mail: catkins@dhhs.state.nh.us
Web site: www.dhhs.state.
nh.us/DHHS/FCADOPTION/
default./htm

State Foster Care Specialist/Manager and Licensing Specialist

New Hampshire Department of Health and Human Services
Division of Children, Youth and Families
Gail Degoosh
129 Pleasant Street
Concord, NH 03301-6522
Phone: (603) 271-4711
Fax: (603) 271-4729
E-mail: gdegoosh@dhhs.state.
nh.us
Web site: www.dhhs.state.
nh.us/DHHS/FCADOPTION/
default./htm

NEW JERSEY

Adoptive/Foster Family Support Groups

Adoption Information Service, Inc.
12 Roberts Street
Rockaway, NJ 07866
Phone: (973) 586-1552

Adoption Parent Organization
Mercer
P.O. Box 8882
Hamilton, NJ 08650

Adoptive Parents Organization
of Central New Jersey
P.O. Box 8882
Hamilton, NJ 08650
Phone: (609) 588-9693

Adoptive Single Parents of
New Jersey
73 Tristan Road
Clifton, NJ 07013
Phone: (908) 766-6281

Camden County FACES
130 South Mansfield Boulevard
Cherry Hill, NJ 08034
Phone: (609) 784-1081

Central New Jersey Singles
Network of Adoptive Parents
P.O. Box 1012
Flemington, NJ 08822
Phone: (908) 782-5500

Concerned Parents for Adop-
tion and North American
Council on Adoptable Children
State Representative
12 Reed Drive North
Princeton Junction, NJ 08550
Phone: (609) 799-3269
E-mail: lebfromnj@aol.com

Concerned Persons for
Adoption
P.O. Box 179
Whippany, NJ 07981
Phone: (908) 273-5694

E-mail: info@cpfanj.org
Web site: www.cpfanj.org

Faces of South Jersey
884 Rambler Avenue
Runnemede, NJ 08078

Friends of Love the Children
24 Roland Road
Murray Hill, NJ 07974

Jersey Shore Families by
Adoption
24 Redwood Drive
Toms River, NJ 08753

Latin America Adoptive Par-
ents Association of Northern
New Jersey
P.O. Box 245
Mt. Arlington, NJ 07856
Phone: (201) 438-9214

New Jersey Adoptive Parents
Support Group
9 Brighton Road
Mt. Holly, NJ 08060
Phone: (609) 863-1166

New Jersey Adoptive Parents'
Support Group
P.O. Box 951
Cherry Hill, NJ 08003
E-mail: Kfmoon@aol.com

Rainbow Families
670 Oakley Place
Oradell, NJ 07649
Phone: (201) 261-1148

Singles Network of Adoptive
Parents
8 North Whittesbog Road
Browns Mills, NJ 08015
Phone: (609) 893-7875

Stars of David Chaverim
(Friends)
681 Cornwallis Drive
Mt. Laurel, NJ 08055
Phone: (856) 866-0055
E-mail: marlkress@aol.com

Stars of David International,
Inc.
Brunswick Area Chapter
61 David Court
Dayton, NJ 08810
Phone: (732) 445-2269
Fax: (732) 445-3571
Web site: www.starsofdavid.org

TREND (Teaching, Respon-
sibility, Education Network,
Diversity)
322 Center Square Road
Woolwich Township, NJ 08085
Phone: (856) 467-2185
Web site: www.joycemedia.
com/trend

Licensed Private Adoption Agencies

A Loving Choice Adoption
Associates
P.O. Box 7612
85 Spruce Drive
Shrewsbury, NJ 07702
Phone: (732) 224-0924
Fax: (732) 842-1740
E-mail: alovingchoice@comcast.
net

Adoptions From the Heart
451 Woodland Avenue
Cherry Hill, NJ 08002
Phone: (856) 665-5655
Fax: (856) 665-5855
E-mail: adoption@adoptionsfrom
theheart.org
Web site: www.
adoptionsfromtheheart.org
– Intercountry Program
– Child Placement

Associated Catholic Charities
Archdiocese of Newark
499 Belgrove Drive, Suite 2
Kearny, NJ 07032
Phone: (201) 246-7378
Fax: (201) 991-3771

Bethany Christian Services
445 Godwin Avenue
Midland Park, NJ 07432
Phone: (201) 444-7775
Fax: (201) 444-5420
E-mail:
bcsmidlandpark@bethany.org
Web site: www.bethany.org/
newjersey
– Intercountry Program
– Child Placement

Better Living Services
P.O. Box 2969
560 Springfield Avenue, Suite C
Westfield, NJ 07090-2969
Phone: (908) 654-0277
Fax: (908) 654-0414

**Catholic Family and
Community Services**
Adoption and Counseling
Services
476 17th Avenue
Paterson, NJ 07501
Phone: (973) 523-9595
Fax: (973) 523-0930
– Intercountry Program
– Child Placement

Children of the World
685 Bloomfield Avenue, Suite 201
Verona, NJ 07044
Phone: (973) 239-0100
Fax: (973) 239-3443
Web site: www.childrenofthe
worldadoptioNorthcom
– Intercountry Program
– Child Placement

**Children's Aid and Family
Services, Inc.**
60 Evergreen Place
East Orange, NJ 07018
Phone: (973) 673-6454
Web site: www.cafsnj.org

**Children's Choice of New
Jersey, Inc.**
151 Fries Mill Road,
Suite 205-206
Turnersville, NJ 08012

Phone: (856) 228-5223
Toll-Free: (800) 220-8320

Family Options
19 Bridge Avenue
Red Bank, NJ 07701
Phone: (732) 936-0770
Toll-Free: (800) 734-7143
Fax: (732) 936-0094
E-mail: infofamopt@aol.com
Web site: www.
familyoptionsadoptions.org
– Intercountry Program
– Child Placement

**Growing Families Worldwide
Adoption**
Fax: (856) 228-6522
Web site: www.childrenschoice.
org
– Intercountry Program
– Child Placement

**Children's Home Society of
New Jersey**
635 South Clinton Avenue
Trenton, NJ 08611-1831
Phone: (609) 695-6274
Fax: (609) 394-5769
E-mail: kwestbrook@chsofnj.org
Web site: www.chsofnj.org

Christian Homes for Children
214 State Street
Hackensack, NJ 07601-5534
Phone: (201) 342-4235
Fax: (201) 342-0246
– Intercountry Program
– Child Placement

Downey Side, Inc.
1901 North Olden Avenue, Suite
45
Ewing, NJ 08618
Phone: (609) 538-8200
Fax: (609) 538-8335
E-mail: ewingnj@downeyside.org
Web site: www.downeyside.org

Family and Children's Services
1900 Route 35
Oakhurst, NJ 07755-2758
Phone: (732) 531-9111
Fax: (732) 531-8507
Web site: www.fcsmonmouth.org

**Golden Cradle Adoption Ser-
vices, Inc.**
1050 North Kings Highway, Suite
201
Cherry Hill, NJ 08034
Phone: (856) 667-2229
Fax: (856) 667-5437
E-mail: adoptions@goldencradle.
org
Web site: www.goldencradle.org
– Intercountry Program
– Child Placement

**Growing Families Worldwide
Adoption Agency, Inc.**
178 South Street
Freehold, NJ 07728
Phone: (732) 431-4330
Fax: (732) 431-4358
– Intercountry Program
– Child Placement

**Holt International Children's
Services**
340 Scotch Road, 2nd Floor
Trenton, NJ 08628
Phone: (609) 882-4972
Fax: (609) 883-2398
E-mail: info@holtintl.org
Web site: www.holtintl.org
– Intercountry Program
– Child Placement

**Homestudies and Adoption
Placement Services (HAPS),
Inc.**
668 American Legion Drive
Teaneck, NJ 07666
Phone: (201) 836-5554
Fax: (201) 836-0204
E-mail: marie@haps.org
Web site: www.haps.org
– Intercountry Program
– Child Placement

Jewish Family Services of
Central New Jersey
655 Westfield Avenue
Elizabeth, NJ 07208
Phone: (908) 352-8375
Fax: (908) 352-8858

Jewish Family Services of
Metro West
256 Columbia Turnpike, Suite 105
Florham Park, NJ 07932-0825
Phone: (973) 765-9050

Jewish Family & Children's
Services of Southern NJ
1301 Springdale Road, Suite 150
Cherry Hill, NJ 08003-2729
Phone: (856) 424-1333
Fax: (973) 765-0195
Web site: www.jfs-mekzonj.org

Jewish Family Services of
Monmouth County
705 Summerfield Avenue
Asbury Park, NJ 07712
Phone: (732) 774-6886
Fax: (732) 774-8809
Web site: www.jscsmonmouth.
org

Lutheran Social Ministries of
New Jersey
6 Terri Lane, Suite 300
Burlington, NJ 08016-4905
Phone: (609) 386-7171
Fax: (609) 386-7191
E-mail: mrose@lsmnj.org
Web site: www.lsmnj.org

Reaching Out Thru
International Adoption
312 South Lincoln Avenue
Cherry Hill, NJ 08002
Phone: (856) 321-0777
Fax: (856) 321-0809
E-mail: reachoutnj@aol.com
Web site: www.adoptachild.us
– Intercountry Program
– Child Placement

Seedlings, Inc.
375 Route 10 East
Whippany, NJ 07981-2104
Phone: (973) 884-7488
Fax: (973) 884-8648
Web site: www.seedlings-inc.org
– Intercountry Program
– Child Placement

Small World Agency
New Jersey Branch Office
257 West Broad Street
Palmyra, NJ 08065-1463
Phone: (856) 829-2769

**State Adoption
Specialist/Manager**

New Jersey Department of
Human Services
Division of Youth and Family
Services
50 East State Street
5th Floor, CN 717
Trenton, NJ 08625-0717
Phone: (609) 984-6080
Fax: (609) 984-5449
E-mail: dbender@dhs.state.nj.us
Web site: www.state.nj.us/
humanservices/adoption/adopt.
html

**State Foster Care
Specialist/Manager**

New Jersey Department of
Human Services
Division of Youth
and Family Services
50 East State Street
Trenton, NJ 08625
Phone: (609) 943-5559
Fax: (609) 984-0482

New Jersey Division of Youth
and Family Services
Office of Program Support and
Permanency
P.O. Box 717
50 East State Street
Trenton, NJ 08625-0717

Phone: (609) 292-3035
Fax: (609) 984-0507
E-mail: dyounkin@dhs.state.nj.us
Web site: www.njfostercare.org

**State Interstate Compact on
the Placement of Children
(ICPC) Administrator**

New Jersey Department of
Human Services
Division of Youth and Family
Services
P.O. Box 717
50 East State Street, 7th Floor SE
Capital Center
Trenton, NJ 08625
Phone: (609) 292-0010
Web site: www.state.nj.us/
humanservices/adoption/adopt.
html

State Licensing Specialist

New Jersey Department of
Human Services
Division of Youth and Family
Services
P.O. Box 717
Trenton, NJ 08625-0717
Phone: (609) 292-8255
E-mail: amontes@dhs.state.nj.us
Web site: www.state.nj.us/
humanservices/adoption/
resourceframe.html

State Reunion Registry

New Jersey Division of Youth
and Family Services
Adoption Registry Coordinator
P.O. Box 717
Trenton, NJ 08625-0717
Phone: (609) 984-6800
Fax: (609) 984-5449
E-mail: dhelb@dhs.state.nj.us
Web site: www.state.nj.us/
humanservices/adoption/
registryframe.html

Statewide Adoption Recruitment Line

New Jersey Statewide
Adoption Recruitment Line
Toll-Free: (800)-9-ADOPT

Statewide Foster Care Recruitment Line

New Jersey Statewide
Foster Care
Recruitment Line
Toll-Free: (877)-NJ-Foster

NEW MEXICO

CYFD/PSD
P.O. Drawer 5160
PERA Building, #219
Santa Fe, NM 87502
Phone: (505) 827-3991
Fax: (505) 827-8480

Adoptive/Foster Family Support Groups

Adoption Alliance/ACT
1719 Santa Fe River Road
Santa Fe, NM 87501
Phone: (505) 995-8346
Fax: (505) 988-5177

Adoption Exchange
New Mexico Office
2929 Coors Boulevard NW, Suite 100E
Albuquerque, NM 87120
Phone: (505) 247-1769
Fax: (505) 888-5978
E-mail: elipton@adoptex.org
Web site: www.Adoptex.org

All Our Kids Adoption Support Group
3500 Indian School Road NE
Albuquerque, NM 87106
Phone: (505) 858-3028

CYFD/PSD
La Familia
707 Broadway Boulevard NE, #103
Albuquerque, NM 87102-2300
Phone: (505) 766-9361

New Mexico Treatment Foster Parents Association
358 Sedillo Road
Tijeras, NM 87059
Phone: (505) 286-1294
E-mail: grward@earthlink.net

Valencia County PSD
P.O. Box 220
Los Lunas, NM 87031

Licensed Private Adoption Agencies

A.M.O.R. Adoptions, Inc.
3700 Coors Boulevard NW, Suite F
Albuquerque, NM 87120
Phone: (505) 831-0888
Toll-Free: (877) 712-2667
Fax: (505) 831-2800
Web site: www. AMORADoptions.com
– Intercountry Program
– Child Placement

Adoption Assistance Agency
2800 Eubank NE
Albuquerque, NM 87122
Toll-Free: (888) 422-3678
Fax: (501) 821-4111
Web site: www. adoptionassistanceagency.org

Adoption Plus
11811 Menaul NE, Suite 5
Albuquerque, NM 87112
Phone: (505) 262-0446
Fax: (505) 298-6653

Catholic Charities
501 South 4th Street
Santa Rosa, NM 88435
Phone: (505) 472-5938
Toll-Free: (800) 313-6023

Fax: (505) 472-4938
Web site: catholiccharitiesasf.org

Chaparral Maternity and Adoptions
1503 University Boulevard NE
Albuquerque, NM 87102
Phone: (505) 243-2586
Fax: (505) 243-0446

Child-Rite/AASK
P.O. Box 1448
Taos, NM 87529
Phone: (505) 758-0343
E-mail: lcarlson@childrite.org

Christian Child Placement Services
1356 NM 236
Portales, NM 88130
Phone: (505) 356-4232
Fax: (505) 356-0760
E-mail: charlesa@nmcch.org
Web site: www.nmcch.org
– Intercountry Program
– Home Study

Families for Children
6209 Hendrex NE
Albuquerque, NM 87110
Phone: (505) 881-4200

Family Matters
3301-R Coors NW, Suite 286
Albuquerque, NM 87120
Phone: (505) 344-8811
Fax: (505) 343-1919
E-mail: rdabusines@aol.com

LDS Family Services
3807 Atrisco Drive NW, Suite C
Albuquerque, NM 87120
Phone: (505) 836-5947

La Familia Placement Services
707 Broadway NE, Suite 103
Albuquerque, NM 87102
Phone: (505) 766-9361
Web site: www.la-familia-inc.org

New Mexico Parent & Child
Resources, Inc.
3500 Indian School Road NE
Albuquerque, NM 87106
Phone: (505) 858-3028
Fax: (505) 268-4973
E-mail: adesiderio@nmpcr.org
Web site: www.nmpcr.org

New Mexico Parent & Child
Resources, Inc.
3500 Indian School NE
Albuquerque, NM 87106
Phone: (505) 268-4973
Fax: (505) 268-5056
E-mail: adesiderio@nmpcr.org
Web site: www.nmpcr.org

Rainbow House International
19676 Highway 314
Belen, NM 87002
Phone: (505) 861-1234
Fax: (505) 864-8420
E-mail: rainbow@rhi.org
Web site: www.rhi.org
– Intercountry Program
– Child Placement

**Birth Family and Search
Support Groups**

Operation Identity
13101 Blackstone NE
Albuquerque, NM 87111
Phone: (505) 293-3144

**State Adoption Exchange/
Photolisting of Children
Waiting For Adoption**

New Mexico Adoption
Exchange
New Mexico Children, Youth and
Families Department
2929 Coors Boulevard, Suite 100E
Albuquerque, NM 87120
Phone: (505) 247-1769
Fax: (505) 888-5978
E-mail: Kathy@adoptex.org
Web site: www.state.nm.us/
cyfd/adopt_categories.htm

**State Adoption
Specialist/Manager**

Central Adoption Unit
PERA Building, Room 225B
P.O. Drawer 5160
Santa Fe, NM 87502-5160
Phone: (505) 841-7949
Fax: (505) 841-7932
E-mail: amlucero@cyfd.state.
nm.us
Web site: www.state.nm.us/
cyfd/foster.htm

New Mexico Department of
Children, Youth and Families
Protective Services Division
P.O. Drawer 1560
Santa Fe, NM 87502
Fax: (505) 827-8480
Phone: (505) 827-3991
E-mail: lsmcnall@cyfd.state.
nm.us
Web site: www.state.nm.us/
cyfd/adopt.htm

**State Foster Care
Specialist/Manager**

New Mexico Department of
Children, Youth and Families
Protective Services Division
P.O. Drawer 1560
Santa Fe, NM 87502
Fax: (505) 827-8480
Phone: (505) 827-3991
E-mail: lsmcnall@cyfd.state.nm.us
Web site: www.state.nm.us/
cyfd/adopt.htm

**State Interstate Compact on
the Placement of Children
(ICPC) Administrator**

New Mexico Children, Youth
and Families Department
PERA Building, Room 225B
P.O. Drawer 5160
Santa Fe, NM 87502-5160
Phone: (505) 827-8457
Fax: (505) 827-8433

State Licensing Specialist

New Mexico Children, Youth
and Families Department
PERA Building, Room 225B
P.O. Drawer 5160
Santa Fe, NM 87502-5160
Phone: (505) 827-8428
Fax: (505) 827-8480
E-mail: jrounsville@cyfd.state.
nm.us

**Statewide Adoption
Recruitment Line**

New Mexico Statewide
Adoption Recruitment Line
Toll-Free: (800) 432-2075

NEW YORK

**Adoptive/Foster Family
Support Groups**

A.D.O.P.T.
P.O. Box 430
Rural Route 1
Jeffersonville, NY 12748
Phone: (914) 482-5339
E-mail: cdayton@catskill.net

ABC Variety House Foster and
Adoptive Parents Association
438 East 120th Street, #2C
New York, NY 10035
Phone: (212) 860-3192

ACE: A Chance to Exhale
876 Central Parkway
Schenectady, NY 12309
Phone: (518) 347-1417
E-mail: acediversity@aol.com

Adoption Group of Orange
County
P.O. Box 156
Chester, NY 10918-0156
Phone: (845) 427-3955

Adoption Resource Network, Inc.
P.O. Box 178
Pittsford, NY 14534
Phone: (585) 586-9586
E-mail: Lisa_Maynard@arni.org
Web site: www.arni.org

Adoptive Families Association
1000 Coddington Road
Ithaca, NY 14850
Phone: (607) 277-8372

Adoptive Families Association of Tompkins County
1000 Coddington Rd
Ithaca, NY 14850
Phone: (607) 277-8372

Adoptive Families Coalition, Inc.
P.O. Box 603
Glenmont, NY 12077
Phone: (518) 448-5295
Web site: www.timesunion.com/communities/afc

Adoptive Families of Chemung County
750 State Route 414
Beaver Dams, NY 14812
Phone: (607) 936-4706
E-mail: lwakeman@hotmail.com

Adoptive Families of Older Children, Inc. (AFOC)
149-32A Union Turnpike
Flushing, NY 11367
Phone: (718) 380-7234
E-mail: info@adoptolder.org
Web site: www.adoptolder.org

Adoptive Families of Westchester
11 Bristol Place
Yonkers, NY 10710
Phone: (914) 779-1509

Adoptive Family Network of Central New York
112 Windsor Drive
North Syracuse, NY 13212

Phone: (315) 458-7379
E-mail: tbhopkins@att.net

Adoptive Family Network of Central New York
P.O. Box 52
Jamesville, NY 13078
Phone: (315) 469-1945
E-mail: Bctaz1@aol.com
Web site: www.adoptivefamily.org

Adoptive Parents Committee, New York State
Web site: www.adoptiveparents.org

Adoptive and Foster Parents of Eastern New York
655 Wyona Street
Brooklyn, NY 11207
Phone: (718) 257-6020

Allegany County Foster Parent Association
7324 Country Road
Caneadea, NY 14717
Phone: (716) 365-2187

Angel Guardian Home Foster and Adoptive
Parents Association
241 Greene Avenue
Brooklyn, NY 11238-1304
Phone: (718) 398-4301

Angels Support Network
14 Baylor Circle
Rochester, NY 14624
Phone: (716) 594-9051
E-mail: angelsr5@aol.com

Brookwood Child Care FAPA
131-51 226th Street
Laurelton, NY 11413

Camp Mu Ji Gae, Inc.
c/o Parsons Child and Family Center
60 Academy Road
Albany, NY 12208
Phone: (518) 426-2607

Capital District Foster and Adoptive Parents
Support Group
4 Arden Road
Scotia, NY 12302
Phone: (518) 370-0589

Capitol District - Albany, Troy, Schenectady, Saratoga Upstate NY
Single Adoptive Parents
38 Shaker Drive Boulevard
Loudonville, NY 12211
Phone: (518) 489-4322

Catholic Adoptive Parents Association, Inc.
(CAPA)
74-07 Kessel Street
Forest Hills, NY 11375-1488
Phone: (718) 793-6276

Catholic Home Bureau Foster and Adoptive
Parents Association
P.O. Box 117
Yonkers, NY 10704
Phone: (914) 375-3746

Cayuga County Foster Parents
RD3 Rt 41A
Moravia, NY 13118
E-mail: mrmom13118@yahoo.com

Cayuga County Foster and Adoptive Parent Association
1248 Sherwood Road
Aurora, NY 13026
Phone: (315) 364-5272
E-mail: raffs5@baldcom.net

Center Kids: The Family Project of the Lesbian and Gay Community Services Center of NY
208 West 13th Street
New York, NY 10011
Phone: (212) 620-7310
Fax: (212) 924-2657
E-mail: centerkids@gaycenter.org
Web site: www.gaycenter.org

Central New York Friends of
Love the Children
P.O. Box 6797
Syracuse, NY 13217
Phone: (315) 656-8015

Champlain Valley Adoptive
Families, Inc.
6 Grace Avenue
Plattsburgh, NY 12901
Phone: (518) 563-5224

Chautauqua County Foster/
Adoptive Parent Association,
Inc.
5290 Spooner Road
Ashville, NY 14710
E-mail: ccfapa@cecomet.net
Web site: http://foster.
adoption.50megs.com

Chautauqua County Foster/
Adoptive Parent Association,
Inc.
2125 Mann Road
Clymer, NY 14724-9631
Phone: (716) 769-7587
E-mail: ccfapa@cecomet.net
Web site: http://foster.
adoption.50megs.com

Chemung County Foster and
Adoptive Parents
723 West First Street
Elmira, NY 14905
Phone: (607) 734-8472

Chenango County Adoptive
Families Association
23 County Road 10A
Norwich, NY 13815
Phone: (607) 334-5596
E-mail: barnesfamily@
frontiernet.net

Chenango County LINK Family
6 Orchard Street
Afton, NY 13730
Phone: (607) 639-3665

Child Development Support
Corp Foster and Adoptive
Parents Association
681 Sterling Place
Apartment 1 R
Brooklyn, NY 11216
Phone: (718) 398-3903

Children with Special Needs
Parents Association, Inc.
1461 East 59th Street
Brooklyn, NY 11234
Phone: (718) 531-6974

Clinton County FAPA
7 Chestnut Street
Champlain, NY 12919
Phone: (518) 298-2804
E-mail: agehrig@primelink1.net

Clinton County FAPA
1029 Route 228
Plattsburgh, NY 12901
Phone: (518) 643-6849
E-mail: anna3md@aol.com

Coalition for Hispanic FS
Foster Parent Association
315 Wetckoff Avenue, 4th Floor
Brooklyn, NY 11237
Phone: (718) 497-6090

Columbia County Resource
Parents
P.O. Box 352
Ghent, NY 12075
Phone: (518) 392-1667

Committed Parents for Black
Adoption
Building 1 B, #8A
900 Baychester
Bronx, NY 10475
Phone: (718) 671-6772

Concerned Foster and Adoptive Parents Support Group
1256 Ocean Avenue
Brooklyn, NY 11230
Phone: (718) 859-5108

Cortland County Foster and
Adoptive Parents Association
5488 Cuyler Hill Road
Truxton, NY 13158
Phone: (607) 842-6522
E-mail: kathygibbs14@yahoo.com

Crystal Baker
131 Jersey Street
GC
Staten Island, NY 10301
Phone: (718) 981-6229

DFCS Foster and Adoptive
Parents Association
413 Clermont Avenue
Brooklyn, NY 11238
Phone: (718) 636-1829

Dare to Care
Foster/Adoptive Parent
Association of Broome County
640 Underwood Road
Vestal, NY 13850
Phone: (607) 748-5127
After hours: (607) 748-5127
E-mail: ampurdy5127@aol.com

Delaware County Foster and
Adoptive Parents
RD 2 Box 198
Walton, NY 13856
Phone: (607) 865-4107

Dutchess County Foster
Parents
27 Gray Street
Poughkeepsie, NY 12603
Phone: (914) 454-7578

Edwin Gould FAPA, Inc.
15-19 West 110th Street
Apartment 33
New York, NY 10026
Phone: (212) 426-5150
E-mail: Egfapa@aol.com

Episcopal Social Services
Parent Group
710 Tinton Avenue #5E
Bronx, NY 10455
Phone: (718) 585-2137

Erie County Foster and Adoptive Parents
Support Group
164 Broadmoor Drive
Tonawanda, NY 14150
Phone: (716) 694-8170

FANS
232 Bramble Court
Williamsville, NY 14221
Phone: (716) 688-8915

FAPA Of Nassau County
337 Weidner Avenue
Oceanside, NY 11572
Phone: (516) 763-2745
E-mail: NassauCountyFAPA@aol.com

Families Through Adoption
10172 Campbell Road
Sauquoit, NY 13456
Phone: (315) 733-6984
E-mail: davesne@adelphia.net

Families with Children from China Southern Tier
11809 Theresa Drive
Corning, NY 14830
Phone: (607) 936-3876

Families with Children from China
Ithaca Chapter (Southern Tier)
1421 Mecklenberg Road
Ithaca, NY 14850
Phone: (607) 255-7274
E-mail: pm11@cornell.edu

Families with Children from China of Greater New York
P.O. Box 237065
Ansonia Station
New York, NY 10023
Phone: (212) 579-0115
E-mail: GreaterNYFCC@aol.com
Web site: www.fccny.org

Families with Children from Vietnam–Rochester
1303 Hatch Road
Webster, NY 14580

Phone: (585) 787-9038
E-mail: dwikiera@aol.com

Families and Children Together for Support (FACTS)
4104 Allendale Parkway
Blasdell, NY 14219
Phone: (716) 648-7960
E-mail: FACTS4Fam@aol.com

Families for the Children/ Adirondack Region
303 Coy Road
Greenfield Center, NY 12833
Phone: (518) 893-7699

Families for the Future, Inc
One Sheldon Drive
Ballston Lake, NY 12019-2557
Phone: (518) 399-8676

Families of Children Adopted from Paraguay
61 Jane Street, #10 D
New York, NY 10014
Phone: (212) 243-2067

Families with Children from China–Rochester
7 Caywood Avenue
Fairport, NY 14450
Phone: (716) 223-9229
E-mail: makmd@rochester.rr.com

Family Focus Adoption Services
54-40 Little Neck Parkway
Little Neck, NY 11362
Phone: (718) 224-1919
Fax: (718) 225-8360

Focus Parent Support Group– Dutchess County
26 Howard Road
Poughkeepsie, NY 12603
Phone: (845) 485-4671

Forestdale Foster Parents Association
116-07 167th Street
Jamaica, NY 11434
Phone: (718) 276-0006

Foster Parents Advisory Council of Suffolk County
31 Hastings Drive
Stony Brook, NY 11790
Phone: (631) 689-9301
After hours: (631) 871-7233
Fax: (631) 689-9301
Web site: www.F-Pac.org

Foster Parents Advisory Council of Suffolk County (F-PAC)
91 Tree Road
Centereach, NY 11720
Phone: (516) 471-3689
E-mail: FPACPREZ@aol.com

Foster Parents Organization of Madison County
P.O. Box 242
South Main Street
Munnsville, NY 13409
Phone: (315) 495-6556

Foster and Adoptive Families Support Services, Inc.
2 Lowell Road
New Hartford, NY 13413
Phone: (315) 724-2989
E-mail: dac2547@aol.com

Foster and Adoptive Family Support Services, Inc. –Herkimer County
Travis Road
Hornesville, NY 13475
Phone: (315) 858-2146
E-mail: share1969@yahoo.com

Foster and Adoptive Family Support Services, Inc.–Madison County
303 West Road
Oneida, NY 13421
Phone: (315) 661-4921
E-mail: rmoyer1@twcny.rr.com

Foster and Adoptive Parents Association
52 Secor Lane
Pelham Manor, NY 10803
Phone: (914) 712-0903

Foster and Adoptive Parents
Association of Cattaraugus
County
3675 Five Mile Road
Allegany, NY 14706
Phone: (716) 372-3965

Foster and Adoptive Family
Support Services, Inc.
Madison County
303 West Road
Oneida, NY 13421
Phone: (315) 661-4921
Web site: www.fafss.org

Foster and Adoptive Family
Support Services, Inc.
Herkimer County
5419 Graham Road
Utica, NY 13502
Phone: (315) 732-2481
E-mail: clingercat@adelphia.net
Web site: www.fafss.org

Foster and Adoptive Family
Support Services, Inc.
Oneida County
2 Lowell Drive
New Hartford, NY 13413
Phone: (315) 724-2989
Fax: (315) 724-4407
E-mail: dac2547@aol.com
Web site: www.fafss.org
– Intercountry Program
– Education/Preparation
– Information/Referral

Foster and Adoptive Parent
Association
21 St. James Place, #10L
Brooklyn, NY 11205
Phone: (718) 783-6540

Foster and Adoptive Parents
Advisory
Committee of Edwin Gould
Services for Children
15-19 West 110th Street #33
New York, NY 10026
Phone: (212) 426-5150

Fax: (212) 426-1667
E-mail: EGFAPA@aol.com

Foster and Adoptive Parents
Association of the Society for
Children and Families
P.O. Box 402
Staten Island, NY 10310-0402
Phone: (718) 720-5907

Foster and Adoptive Parents
Group of Brookwood Children
Care
131-51 226th Street
Laurelton, NY 11413
Phone: (718) 978-0978

Foster and Adoptive Parents
Organization of New York
536 East 37th Street, #7
Brooklyn, NY 11203
Phone: (718) 282-7413

Foster/Adoptive Parent Association of Oswego County, Inc.
120 Kingdom Road
Oswego, NY 13126
Phone: (315) 342-2824

Friends in Adoption
6 Chelsey Place, Suite 215
Clifton Park, NY 12065
Phone: (518) 371-9910
E-mail: fia@vermontel.net

Friends in Adoption Support
Group
134 Darroch Road
Delmar, NY 12054
Phone: (518) 439-3957

Friends in Adoption of Long
Island Support Group
3 Brenda Lane
Manorville, NY 11949
Phone: (631) 878-6511

Friends of Children From Asia
3164 Route 43
Averill Park, NY 12018
Phone: (518) 674-5802
E-mail: gvfalco@aol.com

Gateway-Longview Foster
Parents
202 North Barry Street
Olean, NY 14760
Phone: (716) 373-0139

Gathering International
Families Together (GIFT)
2229 Walnut Avenue
Ronkonoma, NY 11779
Phone: (212) 978-9524

Genesee County Foster and
Adoptive Parents Association
9374 South Street Road
LeRoy, NY 14482
Phone: (716) 768-7464

Good Sheperd/McMahon
Association for Foster and
Adoptive Parents
144 Sutter Avenue
Brooklyn, NY 11212
Phone: (718) 498-9857

Graham Windham Foster Parent Association
4144 Gunther Avenue
Bronx, NY 10466
Phone: (719) 325-9154

Grandparents Advocacy
Project
1595 Metropolitan Avenue, #6 G
Bronx, NY 10462
Phone: (718) 863-4776

Greater Rochester Committee
for Single Adoptive Parents
100 Hollywood Avenue
Rochester, NY 14618
Phone: (716) 271-5996

Greene County Foster and
Adoptive Parents Association
380 Cairo Junction Road
Catskill, NY 12414

Montgomery County Foster
and Adoptive Parents
Association
12 Prospect Street
Fultonville, NY 12072
Phone: (518) 853-4477

Nassau County Foster and
Adoptive Parents Association
3373 Weidner Avenue
Oceanside, NY 11572
Phone: (516) 763-2745

New Alternatives For Children
Foster and Adoptive Parent
Support Group
108-19 Guy R Brewer Boulevard
Jamaica, NY 11433

New Beginnings Single Parent
Support Group
11 Lynn Place
Bethpage, NY 11714
Phone: (516) 938-7252
E-mail: mreichar@optonline.net

New Life for Children, Inc.
P.O. Box 11164
Rochester, NY 14611
Phone: (716) 436-6075

New York Council on
Adoptable Children
589 Eighth Avenue, 15th Floor
New York, NY 10018
Phone: (212) 714-2788
E-mail: coac@erols.com
Web site: www.coac.org

New York Singles Adopting
Children-Long Island
60-41 251 Street
Little Neck, NY 11362-2433
Phone: (718) 229-7240
E-mail: nysac@aol.com

New York State Citizens'
Coalition for Children
Region VII Co-Coordinator
219 Edgewater Avenue
Bayport, NY 11705

New York State Citizens'
Coalition for Children and
North American Council on
Adoptable Children Represen-
tative
306 East State Street, Suite 220
Ithaca, NY 14850
Phone: (607) 272-0034
Fax: (607) 272-0035
E-mail: office@nysccc.org
Web site: www.nysccc.org

New York State Foster and
Adoptive Parents Association,
Inc.
134-39 224th Street
Laurelton, NY 11413
Toll-Free: (800) 332-7014

Niagara Adoption Support
Network Services
323 Tremont Street
North Tonawanda, NY 14120
Phone: (716) 695-8230
E-mail: niagaraadoption@yahoo.
com

Niagara County Foster and
Adoptive Parents Association
6901 Walmore Road
Niagara Falls, NY 14304
Phone: (716) 731-5087

North Chautauqua County
Foster Parents Association
5695 East Main Road
Brocton, NY 14716-9737
Phone: (716) 792-9001

North Country Adoption
Parent Group, Inc.
820 Rees Street
Clayton, NY 13624
Phone: (315) 686-2245
E-mail: TFlynt@aol.com

North Country Adoption
Support Group
250 Arsenal Street
Watertone, NY 13601
Phone: (315) 639-3124

Onondaga County Foster/
Adoptive Parents Association
3305 Cedarvale Road
Nedrow, NY 13120
Phone: (315) 492-1882
E-mail: debisouthard@cs.com

Open Door Society of Long
Island
40 Pennsylvania Avenue
Medford, NY 11763
Phone: (516) 758-5571

Otsego Adopt, Inc.
P.O. Box 323
Springfield Center, NY 13468
Phone: (315) 858-0304

Otsego County Foster Parent
Support Group
197 Main Street
Cooperstown, NY 13326
Phone: (607) 547-4355

Otsego County Special Needs
Adoption Information and
Referral
P.O. Box 712
Morris, NY 13808
Phone: (607) 263-5093

Ours Through Adoption
51 Ketchum Place
Buffalo, NY 14213
Phone: (716) 886-1837

PACES
P.O. Box 1223
Amherst, NY 14226
Phone: (716) 824-3967

Parents Helping Parents
54 Meyers Road
Kingston, NY 12401

Parents of Dunbar, Inc.
P.O. Box 89
Syracuse, NY 13205
Phone: (315) 476-4269

Parson International Adoption
Advisory Board
6955 Suzanne Court
Schenectady, NY 12303
Phone: (518) 355-8705

Passage Adoption Support
Group
3785 Colin Court
North Tonawanda, NY 14120
Phone: (716) 694-9847

Pius XII Foster and Adoptive
Parents Association
66 Judith Drive
Stormville, NY 12582
Phone: (914) 221-0753

Positively Kids, Inc.
17 Prospect Drive
Queensbury, NY 12804
Phone: (518) 798-0915
E-mail: Posikids@aol.com

Private Adoption Support
3785 Colin Court
North Tonawanda, NY 14120
Phone: (716) 694-9807

Private Adoption Support
Group/Western New York
142 Brush Creek Road
Williamsburg, NY 14221
Phone: (716) 689-8991

Proud Parents, Inc.
35 Baker Road
Hopwell Junction, NY 12533
Phone: (845) 223-7663

Putnam County Foster Parent
Association
43 Marie Road
Carmel, NY 10512
Phone: (914) 225-5708

Putnam County Foster and
Adoptive Parent Group
8 Iris Court
Carmel, NY 10512
Phone: (845) 225-1836
E-mail: frankatini@aol.com

Rensselaer County Foster
Parents
Rural Route 1, Box 116A
Womanock Road
Stephentown, NY 12168
Phone: (518) 733-6393

Rochester African-American
Adoption Group
2126 Lehigh Station Road
Pittsford, NY 14534
Phone: (585) 334-9699

Rochester Attachment
Network
227 Aldine Street
Rochester, NY 14619-1204
Phone: (716) 527-0514

Rockland County Foster and
Adoptive Parents Association
1 Jacqueline Road
Chestnut Ridge, NY 10952
Phone: (914) 356-0922

SAFFE (Support for Adoptive
and Foster Families To Excel)
1868 Atwater Road
King Ferry, NY 13081
Phone: (315) 364-5161
E-mail: hlittle@baldcom.net

SHINE
1337 East Main Street
Rochester, NY 14609
Phone: (716) 293-2223

Salvation Army FAPA
275 Cherry Street, #17B
New York, NY 10002
Phone: (212) 227-8266

Saratoga County Foster
Parents Support Group
P.O. Box 91
Victory Mills, NY 12884
Phone: (518) 695-4174

Seamen's Society FAPA
1537 Manor Road
Staten Island, NY 10314
Phone: (718) 667-6525

Seneca County Foster and
Adoptive Parent Group
P.O. Box 690
Waterloo, NY 13165-0690
Phone: (315) 539-5609

Seneca County Foster/
Adoptive Parents
Support Group
3402 Woodworth Road
Geneva, NY 14456
Phone: (315) 781-2762

Single Mothers By Choice
P.O. Box 1642
Gracie Square Station
New York, NY 10028
Phone: (212) 988-0993
E-mail: mattes@pipeline.com

Single Parents for Adoption
73 Cleveland Avenue
Buffalo, NY 14223
Phone: (716) 873-4173

South Shore Adoptive Parents
Group
1551 Manatuck Boulevard
Bayshore, NY 11706
Phone: (516) 968-4079
E-mail: wdrumm9601@aol.com

Southern Chautauqua County
Foster Parents Association
5290 Spooner Road
Ashville, NY 14710
Phone: (716) 782-4280

Southern Tier Adoptive
Families (STAF)
P.O. Box 930
Vestal, NY 13851
Phone: (607) 785-7003
Web site: www.tier.net/staf

St. Augustine Parent Group
34 Kerns Avenue
Buffalo, NY 14211
Phone: (716) 891-5545

St. Catherine's Foster Parent Support Group
40 North Maine Avenue
Albany, NY 12203

St. Christopher–Ottilie Foster and Adoptive Parent Group/ Queens
110-14 173rd Street
St. Albans, NY 11433
Phone: (718) 526-2391

St. Christopher–Ottilie Foster and Adoptive Parents Group/ Kings
290 Willoughby Avenue
#1L
Brooklyn, NY 11205
Phone: (718) 638-8543

St. Christopher–Ottilie Foster and Adoptive Parents Group/ Nassau
188-40A 71st Crescent, #3C
Fresh Meadows, NY 11365
Phone: (718) 454-6316

St. Christopher Jennie Clarkson Foster and Adoptive Parents Association, Inc.
4 Dennison Street
White Plains, NY 10606
Phone: (914) 328-0848

St. Lawrence County Foster Parents Association
320 Pine Street
Ogdensburg, NY 13669
Phone: (315) 393-1261
Web site: http://web.northnet. org/slcfosterparents/

St. Lawrence County Helping Hands Foster Parent Support Group
1079 Little Bow Road
Governor, NY 13642
Phone: (315) 287-3826

St. Vincent's Foster and Adoptive Parents Association
237 East 93rd Street
Brooklyn, NY 11212
Phone: (718) 346-3615

Stars of David International, Inc.
Jewish Family Service of Rockland County
900 Route 45, Suite 2
New City, NY 10956-1140
Phone: (914) 354-2121
Fax: (914) 354-2928
Web site: www.starsofdavid.org

Stars of David International, Inc.
Jewish Child Care Association of NY
120 Wall Street
New York, NY 10005
Phone: (212) 558-9907

Stars of David International, Inc.
Long Island Chapter
19 Tiffany Road
Oyster Bay, NY 11771
Phone: (516) 922-9481
E-mail: Hjtd@aol.com
Web site: www.starsofdavid.org

Stars of David International, Inc.
Jewish Family Service of Buffalo and Erie County
70 Barker Street
Buffalo, NY 14209-2013
Phone: (716) 883-1914
Fax: (716) 883-7637
E-mail: starsdavid@aol.com
Web site: www.starsofdavid.org

Stars of David International, Inc.
FEGS–Long Island Chapter
6900 Jericho Turnpike, Suite 306
Syosset, NY 11791
Phone: (516) 364-8040
Fax: (516) 496-9156

E-mail: starsdavid@aol.com
Web site: www.starsofdavid.org

Stars of David/Albany Region
Jewish Family Services
877 Madison Avenue
Albany, NY 12208
Phone: (518) 482-8856

Steuben County Foster and Adoptive Parents
73 Antlers Inn Road
Wayland, NY 14572
Phone: (845) 728-9365
E-mail: Taustin260@aol.com

Sullivan County Foster and Adoptive Parents Association
1181 Horseshoe Lake Road
Swan Lake, NY 12783
Phone: (914) 583-5037

Supporting Our Families Interested in Adoption
2001 Niagara Falls Boulevard, Suite 5
West Amherst, NY 14228
Phone: (716) 691-3300
Phone: (716) 741-3046
E-mail: niagaraadoption@yahoo. com

Tioga County Foster Parents
9512 State Route 176
Endicott, NY 13760
Phone: (607) 748-5362
E-mail: RMPT33@aol.com

Tompkins County Adoption Support Group
23 Woodland Road
Ithaca, NY 14850
Phone: (607) 539-7656
E-mail: MAcerra@ithaca.edu

Tompkins County Foster and Adoptive Parents Association
351 Hayts Road
Ithaca, NY 14850
Phone: (607) 273-8656
E-mail: bandaidlady1056@msn. com

Tompkins County Foster and Adoptive Parents Association
108 Homestead Road
Ithaca, NY 14850
Phone: (607) 272-5746

Transracial Adoptive Families of Columbia County
1316 Woods Road
Germantown, NY 12526
Phone: (518) 537-5395

Tri County Families of Korean Children
111 Benneywater Road
Port Jervis, NY 12771
Phone: (914) 355-3711

Ulster County Foster Parents
10 Woodland Avenue
Kingston, NY 12401-4128
Phone: (914) 340-4024

United Metropolitan Foster and Adoptive Parents Association
151 Main Street
Staten Island, NY 10307
Phone: (718) 317-8761

Upstate New York Singles Adopting Children
21 Concord Drive
Saratoga Springs, NY 12866
Phone: (518) 581-0891
E-mail: nysac@aol.com

Washington County Foster Parents
3360 State Route 196
Fort Ann, NY 12827
Phone: (518) 632-5496

Wayne County Foster Parents
2953 Marion Wallworth Road
Marion, NY 14505
Phone: (315) 926-1518

We Care Foster and Adoptive Parents Association, Inc.
45 Storey Lane
Yonkers, NY 10710
Phone: (914) 963-8469
E-mail: Awilda39@aol.com

Westchester County Foster and Adoptive Parents Association, Inc.
121 South 13th Avenue
Mount Vernon, NY 10550
Phone: (914) 667-9596

Licensed Private Adoption Agencies

ABSW Child Adoption, Counseling and Referral Service
1969 Madison Avenue
New York, NY 10035
Phone: (212) 831-5181

ARISE Child and Family Services
1065 James Street
Syracuse, NY 13203
Phone: (315) 472-3171

Abbott House
100 North Broadway
Irvington, NY 10533
Phone: (914) 591-3200
E-mail: info@abbotthouse.net
Web site: www.abbotthouse.net/

Adoption S.T.A.R. (Support, Training, Advocacy and Resources), Inc.
2001 Niagara Falls Boulevard, Suite 5
West Amherst, NY 14228
Phone: (716) 691-3300
Fax: (716) 691-1066
E-mail: info@adoptionstar.com
Web site: www.adoptionstar.com

Adoption and Counseling Services, Inc.
307 South Townsend Street
Syracuse, NY 13202
Phone: (315) 471-0109

Advocates for Adoption, Inc.
362 West 46th Street
New York, NY 10036
Phone: (212) 957-3938

Angel Guardian Home
6301 12th Avenue
Brooklyn, NY 11219
Phone: (718) 232-1500

Arnetz Adoption Program
Jewish Child Care Association
120 Wall Street, 12th Floor
New York, NY 10005
Phone: (212) 558-9949
Fax: (212) 558-9993
E-mail: arnetz@jccany.org
Web site: www.jccany.org

Association to Benefit Children
404 East 91st Street
New York, NY 10128
Phone: (212) 369-2010
Fax: (212) 426-9488
E-mail: info@a-b-c.org
Web site: www.a-b-c.org

Baker Victory Services
780 Ridge Road
Lackawanna, NY 14218
Phone: (716) 828-9510

Berkshire Farms Center and Family Services for Youth
39 Columbia Street
Albany, NY 12207
Phone: (518) 465-4304

Bethany Christian Services
Warwick Reformed Church
16 Maple Avenue
Warwick, NY 10990
Phone: (845) 987-1453
E-mail: bcswarwickny@bethany.org
Web site: www.bethany.org/warwick_ny/
– Intercountry Program
– Child Placement

Brookwood Child Care
25 Washington Street
Brooklyn, NY 11201
Phone: (718) 596-5555
Fax: (718) 596-7564
Web site: www.brookwoodchildcare.org

Buffalo Urban League, Inc.
224 Northland Avenue
Buffalo, NY 14208
Phone: (716) 854-7625

Cardinal McCloskey Services
2 Holland Avenue
White Plains, NY 10603
Phone: (914) 997-8000
Fax: (914) 997-2166
Web site: www.
cardinalmccloskey.org

Catholic Charities of Buffalo
525 Washington Street
Buffalo, NY 14203
Phone: (716) 856-4494
Fax: (716) 855-1312
Web site: www.ccwny.org

Catholic Charities of Cortland
33-35 Central Avenue
Cortland, NY 13045
Phone: (607) 756-5992

Catholic Charities of
Ogdensburg
6866 State Highway 37
Ogdensburg, NY 13669-0296
Phone: (315) 393-2660

Catholic Charities of Oneida
and Madison Counties
1408 Genesee Street
Utica, NY 13502
Phone: (315) 724-2158

Catholic Charities of Oswego
108 E. 6th Street
Oswego, NY 13126
Phone: (315) 343-9540

Catholic Charities of
Plattsburgh
4914 South Catherine Street
Plattsburgh, NY 12901
Phone: (518) 561-0470

Catholic Charities of Rome
212 West Liberty Street
Rome, NY 13440
Phone: (315) 337-8600

Catholic Charities of Syracuse
1654 West Onondaga Street
Syracuse, NY 13204
Phone: (315) 424-1840

Catholic Family Center
87 North Clinton Avenue
Rochester, NY 14604
Phone: (585) 546-7200
Web site: www.cfcrochester.org

Catholic Home Bureau for
Dependent Children
1011 First Avenue, 6th Floor
New York, NY 10022
Phone: (212) 371-1000
Fax: (212) 755-4233

Catholic Social Services of
Broome County
232 Main Street
Binghamton, NY 13905
Phone: (607) 729-9166
Toll-Free: (800) CARE-002
Fax: (607) 729-2062
E-mail: kford@ccbc.net
Web site: www.
catholiccharitiesbc.org

Child Development Support
Corporation
52-358 Classon Avenue
Brooklyn, NY 11238
Phone: (718) 230-0056

Child and Family Adoption, Inc.
102 Vineyard Avenue
Highland, NY 12528
Phone: (845) 691-4520

Child and Family Services of
Erie
844 Delaware Avenue
Buffalo, NY14209-2008
Phone: (716) 882-0555
Fax: (716) 882-1451
Web site: www.childfamilybny.
org

Children At Heart Adoption
Services, Inc.
145 North Main Street
Mechanicville, NY 12118-1619

Phone: (518) 664-5988
Fax: (518) 664-1220
Web site: www.childrenatheart.
com
– Intercountry Program
– Child Placement

Children of the World Adoption
Agency, Inc.
27 Hillvale Road
Syosset, NY 11791-6916
Phone: (516) 935-1235
Fax: (516) 933-8532
E-mail: cwaa@attglobal.net
Web site: http://cwaany.org
– Intercountry Program
– Child Placement

Children's Aid Society
Adoption and Foster Home
Division
150 East 45th Street
New York, NY 10017
Phone: (212) 949-4961
Phone: (914) 693-0600
Web site: www.childrensvillage.
org

Children's Home of
Poughkeepsie
91 Fulton Street
Poughkeepsie, NY 12601
Phone: (845) 452-1420

Children's Village
2090 Adam Clayton Powell
Boulevard, 9th Floor
New York, NY 10027
Phone: (212) 932-9009

Children's Village Echo Hills
Dobbs Ferry, NY 10522

Coalition for Hispanic Family
Services
315 Wyckoff Avenue, 4th Floor
Brooklyn, NY 11237
Phone: (718) 497-6090
Fax: (718) 497-9495

Community Counseling and Mediation
185 Montague Street, 7th Floor
Brooklyn, NY 11201
Phone: (718) 875-7751

Community Maternity Services
27 North Main Avenue
Albany, NY 12203
Phone: (518) 482-8836
Fax: (518) 482-5805
Web site: www.cccms.com

Concord Family Services
1221 Bedford Avenue
Brooklyn, NY 11216-2928
Phone: (718) 398-3499

Downey Side Families for Youth
P.O. Box 2139
500 West 32nd Street
New York, NY 10116-2139
Phone: (212) 714-2200
Fax: (212) 714-9518
Web site: www.downeyside.org

Dunbar Association, Inc.
1453 South State Street
Syracuse, NY 13205
Phone: (315) 476-4269

Edwin Gould Services for Children and Families
41 East 11th Street
New York, NY 10003
Phone: (212) 598-0050
Fax: (212) 598-0796
Web site: www.egsc.org

Episcopal Social Service
305 Seventh Avenue, 3rd Floor
New York, NY 10001-6008
Phone: (212) 886-5649

Family Connections
P.O. Box 5555
156 Port Watson Street
Cortland, NY 13045
Phone: (607) 756-6574

Family Focus Adoption Services
54-40 Little Neck Parkway, Suite 4
Little Neck, NY 11362
Phone: (718) 224-1919
Fax: (718) 225-8360

Family and Children's Services of Broome County
257 Main Street
Binghamton, NY 13905
Phone: (607) 729-6206

Family Service of Utica
401 Columbia Street Suite 201
Utica, NY 13502
Phone: (315) 735-2236

Family Service of Westchester, Inc.
1 Summit Avenue
White Plains, NY 10606
Phone: (914) 948-8004
E-mail: fsw@fsw.org
Web site: www.fsw.org

Family Support Systems Unlimited
2530 Grand Concourse
Bronx, NY 10458
Phone: (718) 220-5400

Family Tree Adoption Agency
2 Crestmont Drive
Clifton Park, NY 12065
Phone: (518) 371-1336
Toll-Free: (800) 272-3678
Fax: (518) 371-4262
E-mail: ftaa@aol.com
Web site: www.familytreeadoption.com
– Intercountry Program
– Child Placement

Family & Children's Services of Ithaca
204 North Cayuga Street
Ithaca, NY
Phone: (607) 273-7494

Family and Children's Services of Schenectady
246 Union Street
Schenectady, NY 12305
Phone: (518) 393-1369

Forestdale, Inc.
67-35 112th Street
Forest Hills, NY 11375
Phone: (718) 263-0740
Fax: (718) 575-3931
E-mail: edoffice@forestdaleinc.org
Web site: www.forestdaleinc.org

Gateway-Longview
605 Niagara Street
Buffalo, NY 14201
Phone: (716) 882-8468

Godsend International Adoption and Placement Agency, Inc.
578 Cloverhill Drive
Rochester, NY 14618
Phone: (716) 442-2800

Graham's Gift
4983 East River Road
Grand Island, NY 14072
Phone: (716) 775-6715

Graham-Windham Child Care
33 Irving Place
New York, NY 10003
Phone: (212) 529-6445
Fax: (212) 614-9811

Green Chimneys
P.O. Box 719
Doansburg Road
Brewster, NY 10509-0719
Phone: (914) 279-2996

Hale House Center, Inc.
155 West 122nd Street
New York, NY 10027

Happy Families International Center, Inc.
3 Stone Street
Cold Spring, NY 10516

Phone: (845) 265-9272
Fax: (845) 265-4731
Web site: www.happyfamilies.
org
— Intercountry Program
— Child Placement

Harlem-Dowling Children Services
2090 Adam Clayton Powell, Jr.
Boulevard
7th Avenue
New York, NY 10027
Phone: (212) 749-3656
Fax: (212) 678-1094

Heart of America Adoption Center, Inc.
8676 West 96th Street, Suite 250
Overland Park, NY 66212
Phone: (810) 598-1808

Heart to Heart Adoption Service, Inc.
16 Aron Court
New Hempstead, NY 10977
Phone: (845) 362-1002

Heartshare Human Services
191 Joralemon Street
Brooklyn, NY 11201-4306
Phone: (718) 422-4285
Web site: www.heartshare.com

Hillside Children's Center
Buffalo-Westen Region
712 Main Street
Buffalo, NY 14202
Phone: (716) 848-6405

Hillside Children's Center
1337 East Main Street
Rochester, NY 14609
Phone: (585) 654-4528

Ibero American Action League Inc.
817 East Main Street
Rochester, NY 14605
Phone: (585) 256-8900

Jewish Board of Family and Children Services
120 West 57th Street
New York, NY 10019
Phone: (212) 582-9100
E-mail: admin@jbfcs.org
Web site: www.jbfcs.org

Jewish Family Services of Erie County
70 Barker Street
Buffalo, NY 14209
Web site: www.jfsbuffalo.org

Jewish Family Services of Rochester
441 East Avenue
Rochester, NY 14607
Phone: (585) 461-0110
Fax: (585) 461-9658
E-mail: smeyerowitz@
jfsrochester.org
Web site: www.jfsrochester.org

Karing Angels International Adoptions, Inc.
302 Virginia Avenue
Oceanside, NY 11572-5433
Phone: (516) 764-9563
Fax: (516) 678-8044
E-mail: KaringAngelsIntl@aol.
com
Web site: www.KaringAngelsIntl.
org
— Intercountry Program
— Child Placement

LDS Social Services of New York
22 IBM Road, Suite 205-B
Poughkeepsie, NY 12601
Phone: (914) 462-1288
Fax: (914) 462-1291

Lakeside Family and Children's Services
25 Chapel Street
Brooklyn, NY 11201
Phone: (718) 709-0882
Web site: www.lakesidefamily.org

Leake and Watts Children's Home
463 Hawthorne Avenue
Yonkers, NY 10705
Phone: (914) 375-8700
E-mail: vcarvajal@
leakeandwatts.org
Web site: www.leakeandwatts.org

Little Flower Children's Services
186 Joralemon Street
Brooklyn, NY 11201
Phone: (718) 875-3500
Fax: (718) 625-6102
Web site: www.littleflowerny.org

Louise Wise Services
55 West 125th Street, 12th Floor
New York, NY 10027
Phone: (646) 981-1711
Web site: www.louiswise.org

Lutheran Service Society of New York
P.O. Box 1963
6680 Main Street
Williamsville, NY 14231-1963
Phone: (716) 631-9212

Lutheran Social Services, Inc.
27 Park Place, 5th Floor
New York, NY 10007
Phone: (212) 784-8935

McMahon Services for Children
7 West Burnside Avenue
Bronx, NY 10453
Phone: (718) 561-4340

Miracle Makers, Inc.
510 Gates Avenue
Brooklyn, NY 11216
Phone: (718) 483-3107

New Alternatives for Children
37 West 26th Street
New York, NY 10010
Phone: (212) 696-1550

New Beginnings Family and Children's Services, Inc.
141 Willis Avenue
Mineola, NY 11501
Phone: (516) 747-2204
Fax: (516) 747-2505
E-mail: newbeginn@aol.com
Web site: www.new-beginnings.org

New Hope Family Services
3519 James Street
Syracuse, NY 13206
Phone: (315) 437-8300

New Life Adoption Agency
711 East Genesee Street,
Suite 210
Syracuse, NY 13210
Phone: (315) 422-7300
Fax: (315) 475-7727
E-mail: newlife@newlife
adoption.org
Web site: www.newlifeadoption.org
– Child Placement

New Life International, Inc.
2245 Ocean Parkway, Apt. 5L
Brooklyn, NY 11223
Phone: (718) 787-1284
E-mail: abelev00@yahoo.com

New York Council on Adopt-able Children
589 Eight Avenue, 15th Floor
New York, NY 10018
Phone: (212) 714-2788

New York Foundling Hospital
590 Avenue of the Americas
New York, NY 10011
Phone: (212) 727-6810
Fax: (212) 886-4048
Web site: www.Nyfoundling.org

Ohel Children's Home and Family Services
4510 16th Avenue, 4th Floor
Brooklyn, NY 11204
Phone: (718) 851-6300

Parsons Child and Family Center
60 Academy Road
Albany, NY 12208
Phone: (518) 426-2600
Fax: (518) 447-5234

Pius XII Youth/Family Services
188 West 230 Street
Bronx, NY 10463
Phone: (718) 562-7855

Protestant Board of Guardians
1368 Fullon Street, 2nd Floor
Brooklyn, NY 11216
Phone: (718) 636-8103

Salvation Army
Hearts and Homes
677 South Salina Street
Syracuse, NY 13202
Phone: (315) 479-1324
Toll-Free: (866) 324-1324
Fax: (315) 479-3617
Web site: www.salvationarmysyr.org

Salvation Army Foster Home
132 West 14th Street
New York, NY 10011
Phone: (212) 807-6100

Seamen's Society for Children and Families
25 Hyatt Street, 4th Floor
Staten Island, NY 10301
Phone: (718) 447-7740
Fax: (718) 720-2321
E-mail: 0250ww@dfa.state.ny.us

Sheltering Arms Children's Services
4 West 125th Street
New York, NY 10027
Phone: (646) 442-0400

Small World Charity, Inc.
36 West 37th Street, Suite 501
New York, NY 10018
Phone: (212) 629-4008

Spence-Chapin Services to Families and Children
6 East 94th Street
New York, NY 10128-0698
Phone: (212) 369-0300
Fax: (212) 722-0675
E-mail: info@spence-chapin.org
Web site: www.spence-chapin.org
– Intercountry Program
– Child Placement

St. Augustine Center
1437 Main Street
Buffalo, NY 14209
Phone: (716) 881-3700

St. Christopher Ottilie
Third Avenue and Eighth Street
P.O. Box 1324
Brentwood, NY 11717
Phone: (631) 273-2733
Web site: www.stchristopher-ottilie.org

St. Dominic's Home
343 East 137th Street
Bronx, NY 10454
Phone: (718) 993-5765

St. Mary's Child and Family Services
6301 12th Avenue
Brooklyn, NY 11219
Phone: (718) 232-1500

St. Vincent's Services
205 Montague Street
Brooklyn, NY 11202
Phone: (718) 522-3700
Toll-Free: (888) 522-3700

Urban League of Rochester, Inc.
265 North Clinton Avenue
Rochester, NY 14605
Phone: (585) 325-6530

Voice for International Development and Adoption
354 Allen Street
Hudson, NY 12534

Phone: (518) 828-4527
Fax: (518) 828-0688
E-mail: vidaadopt@aol.com
vida@berk.com
Web site: www.vidaadopt.org
– Intercountry Program
– Child Placement

You Gotta Believe!
1728 Mermaid Avenue, Suite 166
Brooklyn, NY 11224
Phone: (718) 372-3003
Toll-Free: (800) 601-1779
Fax: (718) 372-3033
E-mail: ygbpat@msn.com
Web site: www.yougottabelieve.
org

Birth Family and Search Support Groups

Adoption Circle Long Island
421 Jackson Street
Oceanside, NY 11572

Adoption Crossroads/Council for Equal Rights in Adoption
444 East 76th Street
New York, NY 10021
Phone: (212) 988-0110
E-mail: cera@mail.idt.net
Web site: www.
adoptioncrossroads.org

Also Known As, Inc.
P.O. Box 6037
FDR Station
New York, NY 10150
Phone: (212) 386-9201
Web site: www.akaworld.org

Angels Support Network, Inc.
14 Baylor Circle
Rochester, NY 14624
Phone: (716) 234-1864
E-mail: ANGELSR5@AOL.COM

B.I.R.T.H
7 Cheryle Place
Massappequa, NY 11758

Birth Mothers of Minors (B.M.O.M.S.)
P.O. Box 40
New York, NY 10010
Phone: (212) 532-7059
Fax: (305) 252-2653
E-mail: analee@bellsouth.net;
ake4u@yahoo.com

Birthmothers, Adoptees, Adoptive Parents
United in Support
P.O. Box 299
Victor, NY 14564
Phone: (716) 924-0410

Birthparent Support Network
P.O. Box 34
Old Bethpage, NY 11804
Phone: (516) 931-5925

Birthparent Support Network
11 Rockledge Road
White Plains, NY 10603
Phone: (914) 949-1546

Birthparent Support Network
37 Sylvia Lane
Plainview, NY 11803
Phone: (516) 370-5392

Birthparents and Kids in Desperate Search (B.K.I.D.S.)
P.O. Box 43
Erin, NY 14838
Phone: (607) 739-2957

Concerned United Birthparents (CUB)
16 Gillett Lane
Cazenovia, NY 13035
Phone: (315) 655-9137
E-mail: SANDY21751@aol.com
Web site: www.cubirthparents.
org

KinQuest, Inc.
89 Massachusetts Avenue
Massapequa, NY 11758
Phone: (516) 541-7383

Manhattan Birthparent's Group
P.O. Box 599
New York, NY 10159-0599
Phone: (212) 252-8921
Fax: (212) 252-8921
E-mail: judy.kelly@att.net

Missing Connection
P.O. Box 712
Brownville, NY 13615
E-mail: Jan905@aol.com

Post Adoption Center for Education and Support of WNY (P.A.C.E.S.)
P.O. Box 1223
Amherst, NY 14226-7223
Phone: (716) 824-3967
E-mail: kblake@adelphia.net

Post Adoption Center of Western New York
104 Cazenovia
Buffalo, NY
Phone: (716) 824-3967

Reunions: The Next Step
305 East 40th Street, #12V
New York, NY 10016
Phone: (212) 867-1918

Triad United Support
P.O. Box 299
Victor, NY 14564

State Adoption Exchange/ Photolisting of Children Waiting For Adoption

Children Awaiting Parents (CAP)
595 Blossom Road,
Suite 306
Rochester, NY 14160
Toll-Free: (800) 345-5437
E-mail: adopme@dfa.state.ny.us
Web site: www.ocfs.state.ny.us/
adopt/services.htm

State Adoption Specialist/Manager

New York State Department of
Family Assistance
Office of Children and Family
Services/State Adoption Service
52 Washington Street,
Room 323 North
Rensselaer, NY 12144
Phone: (518) 474-9406
Toll-Free: (800) 345-5437
Fax: (518) 486-6326
E-mail: anne.furman@dfa.state.
ny.us
Web site: www.dfa.state.ny.us/
adopt/adoption.htm

State Foster Care Specialist/Manager

New York State Office of
Children and Family Services
52 Washington Street
South Building, Room 103
Rensselaer, NY 12144-2796
Phone: (518) 474-9582
Fax: (518) 473-2410
E-mail: nancy.martinez@dfa.
state.ny.us

State Interstate Compact on the Placement of Children (ICPC) Administrator

New York Department of
Family Assistance
Office of Children and Family
Services
40 North Pearl Street
Riverview Center, 6th Floor
Albany, NY 12243
Phone: (518) 474-9506
Fax: (518) 486-6326
E-mail: anne.furman@dfa.state.
ny.us

State Licensing Specialist

New York Department of
Family Assistance
Office of Children and Family
Services
52 Washington Street
Riverview Center, 6th Floor
Rensselaer, NY 12144
Phone: (518) 474-9447
Toll-Free: (800) 345-5437
Fax: (518) 486-6326
E-mail: bruce.bushart@dfa.state.
ny.us
Web site: www.dfa.state.ny.us/
adopt/adagcy.htm

State Reunion Registry

NY State Department of Health
Adoption Registry
P.O. Box 2602
Albany, NY 12220-2602
Phone: (518) 474-9600
Web site: www.health.state.
ny.us/nysdoh/consumer/
vr.htm#adoption

National Organization

Evan B. Donaldson Adoption
Institute
525 Broadway, 6th Floor
New York, NY 10012
Phone: (212) 925-4089
Fax: (775) 796-6592
E-mail: info@adoptioninstitute.org
Web site: www.
adoptioninstitute.org

NORTH CAROLINA

Adoptive/Foster Family Support Groups

Adoption Connection–A
Support Group for Adoptive
Families
610 Coliseum Drive
Winston-Salem, NC 27106
E-mail: phamisa@aol.com

Adoptive Parents Together
P.O. Box 35458
1516 Elizabeth Avenue
Charlotte, NC 28235
Phone: (704) 825-2716
Fax: (704) 376-0904
E-mail: annd@thefamilycenter.
net

Another Choice for Black
Children
3028 Beaties Ford Road
Charlotte, NC 28216
Phone: (704) 394-1124
Toll-Free: (800) 774-3534
Fax: (704) 394-3843
E-mail: ruthacfbc@aol.com
Web site: www.anotherchoice.
net

Capital Area Families for
Adoption
2725 Townedge Court
Raleigh, NC 27612
Phone: (919) 782-3836
Fax: (919) 783-9418
E-mail: cafa@rtpnet.org
Web site: www.rtpnet.org/cafa

Chatham County DDS/
Adoption and Foster Care Unit
P.O. Box 489
Pittsboro, NC 27312
Phone: (919) 957-0646
Fax: (919) 542-6355
Web site: www.dhhs.state.nc.us/
dss/cty_cnr/dir.htm

Families with Children from
Vietnam–NC
10009 Whiitestone Road
Raleigh, NC 27615
Web site: www.fcvn.org/
trianglenc.htm

Family Connections Network/
CHS of NC
P.O. Box 1905
Elizabeth City, NC 27906-1905
Phone: (252) 339-6341
Fax: (252) 338-8654

Family Resources
348 Lake Point Lane
Bellows Creek, NC 27009-9207
Phone: (910) 644-1664
Fax: (336) 641-1664

Forever Families of North
Carolina
182 Worley Cove Road
Leicester, NC 28748
Phone: (828) 683-6720

Grafted Families
113 Drawbridge Court
Moorsville, NC 28117
Phone: (704) 660-3909
E-mail: lucarini@juno.com

New Hanover County DSS
P.O. Drawer 1559
Wilmington, NC 28402
Phone: (910) 341-4701

North Carolina Center for
Adoption Education
8821 Oconee Court
Chapel Hill, NC 27516
Phone: (919) 967-5010
Fax: (919) 942-0015

Pittsburgh County Community
Collaborative for Adoption and
Foster Care Enhancement
213-A Ragsdale Building
Greenville, NC 27858
Phone: (252) 328-2480
Fax: (252) 328-0302
E-mail: kenyong@mail.ecu.edu

Roots and Wings
3614 Cardinal Ridge Drive
Greensboro, NC 27410-8345
Phone: (908) 813-8252
Web site: www.adopt-usa.com/
rootsandwings

Single Adoptive Parent
Support Groups
102 South 26th Street
Morehead City, NC 28557
Phone: (919) 247-7071

Southern Piedmont Adoptive
Families of America
P.O. Box 221946
Charlotte, NC 28222-1946
Phone: (704) 399-1616
Toll-Free: (877) 772-3292
Web site: www.spafa.org

Stars of David International,
Inc.
Jewish Family Service
8210 Creedmoor Road, Suite 104
Raleigh, NC 27613
Phone: (919) 676-2200
E-mail: starsdavid@aol.com
Web site: www.starsofdavid.org

Triad Adoptive Parent Support
Group and North American
Council on Adoptable Children
133 Penny Road
High Point, NC 27260
Phone: (910) 886-8230

**Licensed Private
Adoption Agencies**

A Child's Hope
Two Hannover Square, Suite 1860
Raleigh, NC 27601
Phone: (919) 839-8800
E-mail: ach@hermcb.com
Web site: www.achildshope.com

A Way for Children Home
Study Specialists
1811 Sardis Road
Charlotte, NC 28270
Phone: (704) 576-6033
E-mail: awayforchildren@earth
link.net

ADOPTIONS By Julia Childers
118 North College Avenue, Suite 2
Newton, NC 28658
Phone: (828) 465-7005
E-mail: juliachilders@msn.com

AGAPE of N.C., Inc.
302 College Road
Greensboro, NC 27410
Phone: (336) 855-7107
Toll-Free: (800) 330-9449

Adoption Options
118 South Colonial Avenue, Suite
300
Charlotte, NC 28207
Phone: (702) 344-8003
E-mail: Sraburn@aol.com

Alexander Children's Center
P.O. Box 220632
6220 Thermal Road
Charlotte, NC 28222
Phone: (704) 362-8466

Amazing Grace Adoptions
1215 Jones Franklin Road, Suite
205
Raleigh, NC 27606
Phone: (919) 858-8998
E-mail: Agadopt@bellsouth.net

Another Choice for Black
Children
3028 Beatties Ford Road
Charlotte, NC 28216
Phone: (704) 394-1124
Toll-Free: (800) 774-3534
E-mail: ruthacfbc@aol.com

Bethany Christian Services
P.O. Box 470036
Charlotte, NC 28247-0036
Phone: (704) 541-1833
Fax: (704) 541-1833
E-mail: bcscharlotte@bethany.org
Web site: www.bethany.org/
ncarolina

Caring for Children, Inc.
P.O. Box 19113
50 Reddick Road
Asheville, NC 28815
Phone: (828) 298-0186
Fax: (828) 236-2877
E-mail: caring4children@charter.
net

Carolina Adoption Services, Inc.
301 North Elm Street
Greensboro, NC 27401-2028
Phone: (336) 275-9660
Fax: (336) 273-9804
E-mail: cas@carolinaadoption.org
Web site: http://
carolinaadoption.org

Catholic Social Services
1123 South Church Street
Charlotte, NC 28203-4003
Phone: (704) 370-6155
Fax: (704) 370-3377
Web site: www.cssnc.org
– Intercountry Program
– Child Placement

Children's Home Society of North Carolina, Inc.
P.O. Box 14608
604 Meadow Street
Greensboro, NC 27415
Phone: (336) 274-1538
Toll-Free: (800) 632-1400
E-mail: info@chsnc.org
Web site: www.chsnc.org

Christian Adoption Services
624 Matthews-Mint Hill Road, Suite 134
Matthews, NC 28105
Phone: (704) 847-0038
Fax: (704) 841-1438
E-mail: cas@perigee.net
Web site: www.christianadopt.org
– Intercountry Program
– Child Placement

Christian World Adoption
303 7th Avenue East
Hendersonville, NC 28792
Phone: (828) 693-7007
Fax: (828) 693-8113
Toll-Free: (888) 972-3678
Web site: www.cwa.org
– Intercountry Program
– Child Placement

Datz Foundation, Inc.
125 South Union Street, #20
Concord, NC 28026
Phone: (919) 839-8800
Toll-Free: (800) 829-LOVE
E-mail: markeckman@hotmail.com
Web site: www.datzfound.com
– Intercountry Program
– Child Placement

Faith Works Unlimited, Inc.
P.O. Box 14847
Raleigh, NC 27620
Phone: (919) 833-5220
E-mail: fwuinc@bellsouth.net
Web site: www.homestead.com

Family Services, Inc.
610 Coliseum Drive
Winston-Salem, NC 27106-5393
Phone: (336) 722-8173
E-mail: rnagaishi@familyserv.org

Frank Adoption Center
2840 Plaza Place, Suite 325
Raleigh, NC 27612
Phone: (919) 510-9135
Toll-Free: (800) 597-9135
Fax: (919) 510-9137
E-mail: info@frankadopt.org
Web site: www.frankadopt.org
– Intercountry Program
– Child Placement

Gladney Center
235 Commerce Street
Greenville, NC 27858
Phone: (252) 355-6267
E-mail: info@gladney.org
Web site: www.gladney.org
– Intercountry Program
– Child Placement

Grandfather Home
P.O. Box 98
Hickory Nut Gap Road
Banner Elk, NC 28604
Phone: (828) 898-5465
E-mail: j.swinkola@grandfather home.org

Home Study Services of N.C., Inc.
4021 Iverson Street
Raleigh, NC 27604
Phone: (919) 272-6953

Homestudies, LLC
P.O. Box 147
55 Glenway Street
Belmont, NC 28012
Phone: (704) 829-0792
Web site: www.theadoptionguide.com

Independent Adoption Center
3725 National Drive, Suite 219
Raleigh, NC 27612
Phone: (919) 789-0707
Toll-Free: (800) 877-6736
Fax: (919) 789-0708
Web site: www.adoptionhelp.org

LDS Family Services
5624 Executive Center Drive, Suite 109
Charlotte, NC 28212-8832
Phone: (704) 535-2436
Toll-Free: (800) 532-8878
Fax: (704) 535-8116
E-mail: fam-nc@ldschurch.org
Web site: www.ldsfamilyservices.org

Lutheran Family Services in the Carolinas, Inc.
P.O. Box 12287
112 Cox Avenue
Raleigh, NC 27605
Phone: (919) 832-2620
E-mail: caroledavis@lfscarolinas.org

Mandala Adoption Services
6601 Turkey Farm Road
Chapel Hill, NC 27514
Phone: (919) 942-5500
Fax: (919) 942-0248
E-mail: mandalaadopt@earthlink.net
– Intercountry Program
– Child Placement

Methodist Home for Children
P.O. Box 10917
1300 St. Mary's Street, Suite 300
Raleigh, NC 27605-0917
Phone: (919) 828-0345
Toll-Free: (888) 305-4321
Fax: (919) 755-1833
Web site: www.mhfc.org

Nathanson Adoption Services of North Carolina, Inc.
6060 J.A. Jones Drive, Suite 504
Charlotte, NC 28287
Phone: (704) 553-9506
Fax: (704) 553-6143
E-mail: helene@nathansonadopt.com
Web site: www.NathansonAdopt.com

Nazareth Children's Home
P.O. Box 1438
855 Crescent Road
Rockwell, NC 28138
Phone: (704) 279-5556
E-mail: ccone@nazch.com

Newlife Christian Adoptions
500 Benson Road, Suite 202
Garner, NC 27529
Phone: (919) 779-1004

Omni Community Services
3717 National Drive, Suite 100
Raleigh, NC 27612
Toll-Free: (800) 851-8905
E-mail: lkellenberger@omnivisions.com
Web site: www.omnivisions.com

Saint Mary International Adoptions, Inc.
528 East Boulevard, Suite 105
Charlotte, NC 28203
Phone: (704) 375-6531
E-mail: stmaryadoption@hotmail.com
Web site: www.smiaadopt.com

Yahweh Center, Inc.
P.O. Box 10399
Wilmington, NC 28404-0399
Phone: (910) 675-3533
E-mail: croberts@yahwehcenter.org

Adoption Information Exchange (AIE)
P.O. Box 1917
Matthews, NC 28106
Phone: (704) 537-5919
E-mail: MzChrisLee@aol.com

Adoption Issues and Education
P.O. Box 8314
Greenville, NC 27835

Jean Taylor
P.O. Box 1792
Smithfield, NC 27577-1792

L. Giddens Adoption Information Exchange
8539 Monroe Road
Charlotte, NC 28212
Phone: (704) 532-6827

North Carolina Adoption Connections
P.O. Box 4153
Chapel Hill, NC 27515
Phone: (919) 967-5010

State Adoption Exchange/ Photolisting of Children Waiting For Adoption

North Carolina Kids Adoption and Foster Care Network
Center for Study of Social Issues
P.O. Box 26170
Greensboro, NC 27402-6170
Phone: (919) 733-3801
E-mail: Web site: www.dhhs.state.nc.us/dss/adopt

State Adoption Specialist/Manager

North Carolina Department of Health and Human Services
Division of Social Services
2409 Mail Service Center
Raleigh, NC 27699-2409
Phone: (919) 733-2085
Fax: (919) 733-5230
E-mail: Amelia.Lance@ncmail.net
Web site: www.dhhs.state.nc.us/dss/adopt

State Foster Care Specialist/Manager

North Carolina Department of Health and Human Services
Division of Social Services,
Children's Services Section
2408 Mail Service Center
325 North Salisbury Street, Room 756
Raleigh, NC 27699-2408
Phone: (919) 733-5125
Fax: (919) 715-6714
E-mail: joann.lamm@ncmail.net
Web site: www.dhhs.state.nc.us/dss

State Interstate Compact on the Placement of Children (ICPC) Administrator

North Carolina Department of Health and Human Services
Division of Social Services,
Children's Services Section
325 North Salisbury Street
Raleigh, NC 27603-5905
Phone: (919) 733-9464
E-mail: linda.wrightson@ncmail.net
Web site: www.dhhs.state.nc.us/dss/c_srv/cserv_comp.htm

NORTH DAKOTA

Adoptive/Foster Family Support Groups

Adopt America Network–
VFSC and North American
Council on Adoptable Children
Representative
P.O. Box 9859
Fargo, ND 58103
Phone: (701) 235-6433

Devils Lake Area Foster/Adopt
Support Group
Phone: (701) 662-7050

Fargo Area Foster/Adopt
Support Group
Phone: (701) 241-5761

Grand Forks Area Foster/
Adopt Support Group
Phone: (701) 795-3050

Jamestown Area Foster/Adopt
Support Group
FAST (Foster/Adopt Support
Team)
534 87th Avenue SW
Jamestown, ND 58401
Phone: (701) 252-7512

NACAC Representative
P.O. Box 389
Fargo, ND 58107
Phone: (701) 235-7341
Fax: (701) 235-7359
E-mail: Ljohnson@lssnd.org
Web site: www.lssnd.org

NACAC Subsidy
Representative
7316 Ellis Lane
Horace, ND 58047
Phone: (701) 277-2741
E-mail: cloudynd@msn.com

PATH
10921 36 Street SE
Valley City, ND 58072
Phone: (701) 845-0678

Licensed Private Adoption Agencies

AASK (Adults Adopting Spe-
cial Kids–a ND Collaborative
for Special Needs Adoption)
P.O. Box 389
1325 South 11th Street
Fargo, ND 58103
Phone: (701) 235-7341
Toll-Free: (877) 551-6054
Fax: (701) 235-7359
E-mail: ljohnson@lssnd.org
Web site: www.lssnd.org

Adoption Option
412 Demers Avenue
Grand Forks, ND 58201
Phone: (701) 772-7577
Toll-Free: (800) 627-8220
Web site: www.lssnd.org

Adoption Option
Village Family Service Center
1201 25th Street South
Fargo, ND 58106-9859
Phone: (701) 235-6433
Toll-Free: (800) 627-8220
Fax: (701) 235-9693

Adoption Option
511 ½ 2nd Street North
Williston, ND 58801
Phone: (701) 774-0749

Adoption Option
308 2nd Avenue SW
Minot, ND 58701
Phone: (701) 852-3328

Adoption Option
411 North 4th Street, Suite 10
Bismarck, ND 58501
Phone: (701) 255-1165
Toll-Free: (800) 627-8220
Web site: www.thevillagefamily.
org
– Intercountry Program
– Home Study

Adoption Option
1325 11th Street South
Fargo, ND 58107-0389
Phone: (701) 235-7341

Catholic Family Service
1809 South Broadway, Suite W
Minot, ND 58701
Phone: (701) 852-2854
Fax: (701) 852-6573
E-mail: sdokken@cfsnd.org
Web site: www.cfsnd.org

Christian Family Life Services
203 South 8th Street
Fargo, ND 58103
Phone: (701) 237-4473
Fax: (701) 235-1703

Christian Family Life Services
203 South 8th Street
Fargo, ND 58103
Phone: (701) 237-4473
Fax: (701) 280-9062

LDS Social Services
P.O. Box 3100
Bismarck, ND 58502
Phone: (612) 560-0900

Birth Family and Search Support Groups

Lutheran Social Services of
North Dakota
P.O. Box 389
Fargo, ND 58107-0389
Phone: (701) 235-7341

State Adoption Exchange/ Photolisting of Children Waiting For Adoption

North Dakota Department of
Human Services
Child and Family Services
Division
State Capitol Building
600 East Boulevard Avenue
Bismarck, ND 58505
Phone: (701) 328-3538
Toll-Free: (800) 245-3736

Fax: (701) 328-2359
Web site: www.adopt.org

State Adoption Specialist/Manager

North Dakota Department of Human Services
State Capitol Building
600 East Boulevard Avenue
Bismarck, ND 58505
Phone: (701) 328-4805
Toll-Free: (800) 245-3736
Fax: (701) 328-3538
E-mail: sohofj@state.nd.us
Web site: www.state.nd.us/
humanservices

State Foster Care Specialist/Manager

North Dakota Department of Human Services
Children and Family Services
(Dept. 325)
State Capitol Building
600 East Boulevard Avenue
Bismarck, ND 58505
Phone: (701) 328-4934
Fax: (701) 328-3538
E-mail: sosnyd@state.nd.us
Web site: www.state.nd.us/
humanservices

State Interstate Compact on the Placement of Children (ICPC) Administrator

North Dakota Department of Human Services
State Capitol Building
600 East Boulevard Avenue
Bismarck, ND 58505
Phone: (701) 328-4152
Fax: (701) 328-2359
Web site: www.state.nd.us/
humanservices

State Licensing Specialist

North Dakota Department of Human Services
State Capitol Building
600 East Boulevard Avenue
Bismarck, ND 58505
Phone: (701) 328-3538
Fax: (701) 328-2359
E-mail: sohofj@state.nd.us

OHIO

Adoptive/Foster Family Support Groups

ACT Group, Advocates for Children Today
3965 Ganyard
Brunswick, OH 44212
Phone: (330) 225-1088

ACTION, Inc., Adoptive Parent Support Group
6000 Philadelphia Drive
Dayton, OH 45415
Phone: (937) 277-6101
Fax: (937) 277-2962
After hours: (937) 277-6101
E-mail: ACTIONadpt@aol.com
Web site: www.ACTION-
adoption.org

Adopt America Network Support Group
2074 Northridge Drive
Toledo, OH 43611
Phone: (419) 729-9813
Fax: (419) 534-2995
E-mail: Niecemimi2@aol.com
Web site: www.
adoptamericanetwork.org

Adopt America Network of Ohio
340 Bank Street
Painesville, OH 44077
Phone: (440) 352-3780
Web site: www.
adoptamericanetwork.org

Adoption Cluster/Support Group
Phone: (216) 881-3084

Adoption Network Cleveland
1667 East 40th Street
Cleveland, OH 44103
Phone: (216) 881-7511
Fax: (216) 881-7510
E-mail: betsie@adoptionnetwork.
org
Web site: www.
adoptionnetwork.org

Adoptive Families Support Association
P.O. Box 29337
Parma, OH 44129
Phone: (216) 491-4638
Fax: (440) 884-9436
Web site: http://community.
cleveland.com/cc/afsa

Adoptive Family Support Association
P.O. Box 91247
Cleveland, OH 44101-3247
Phone: (216) 881-7511

Adoptive Parent Support Group
2272 Harrisburg Pike
Grove City, OH 43123
Phone: (614) 871-1164

Adoptive Parenting Support
2612 San Rae Drive
Kettering, OH 45419
Phone: (513) 299-2110

Adoptive Parents Together
3955 Euclid Avenue
Cleveland, OH 44115
Phone: (216) 431-4500

Adult Adoptee Support Group
5776 Willowcove Drive
Cincinnati, OH 45239-6660

Attachment Disorders Parents Network
P.O. Box 176
Cortland, OH 44410

Attachment and Bonding Center of Ohio
12608 State Road, Suite 1
Cleveland, OH 44133
Phone: (440) 230-1960
Web site: http://abcofohio.net

Beech Acres Foster and Adoptive Parents
6881 Beechmont Avenue
Cincinnati, OH 45230
Phone: (513) 232-3201
E-mail: mepling@beechacres.org
Web site: www.beechacres.org

Birth Mothers Sharing
3355 Scioto Road
Cincinnati, OH 45244

Catholic Charities, Diocese of Toledo
P.O. Box 985
1933 Spielbusch Avenue
Toledo, OH 43697-0985
Phone: (419) 244-6711
Fax: (494) 244-4791
Web site: www.
catholiccharitiesnwo.org

Celebrate Adoption
11223 Cornell Park Drive
Cincinnati, OH 45242
Phone: (513) 489-1616
Fax: (513) 489-4213

Central Ohio Families with Children from China (COFCC)
P.O. Box 554
Hillard, OH 43026-0554
Phone: (513) 351-5412
Web site: www.crystalsys.
com/cofcc

Charting the Course
770 Stinson Drive
Columbus, OH 43214
Phone: (614) 459-2833
Fax: (614) 459-1422
E-mail: barbv@netwalk.com

Concern for Children, Inc
746 Grove Avenue
Kent, OH 44240
Phone: (330) 678-0090

Concern for Children, Inc.
6425 Somerset Drive
North Olmstead, OH 44070
Phone: (216) 734-7580

Cuyahoga County Foster Parent Association
1348 West 59th Street
Cleveland, OH 44102
Phone: (216) 631-4846

Dayton Area Minority Adoptive Parents, Inc. and North American Council on Adoptable Children State Representative
191 Coddington Avenue
Xenia, OH 45385-5439
Phone: (937) 372-5269
Fax: (937) 372-8894
E-mail: rmoore@dayton.net
Web site: www.damap.org

National Down Syndrome Association of Greater Cincinnati
1821 Summit Road, Suite 102
Cincinnati, OH 45237-2818
Phone: (513) 761-5400
Fax: (513) 761-5401
Web site: www.dsagc.com

Down Syndrome Association of Greater Cincinnati– Adoption Awareness Program
9666 Rexford Drive
Cincinnati, OH 45241
Phone: (513) 554-4485
Fax: (513) 554-4486

E-mail: rsteele @zoomtown.com
Web site: www.dsagc.com

Elaine Thompson
1041 Rosealee Avenue
Elyria, OH 44035-2945
Phone: (440) 365-6629

FACT (Families for Acceptable Care and Treatment)
565 Children Drive West
Columbus, OH 43205
Phone: (614) 228-5523

Families Blessed by Adoption, Ross County
74 Clinton Road
Chillicothe, OH 45601
Phone: (740) 775-6784

Families Woven from the Heart
5278 Wooster Road West
Norton, OH 44203
Phone: (330) 825-7814
After hours: (330) 825-7814
E-mail: aanohio@msn.com
Web site: http://groups.msn.
com/fwfh

Families with Children from China
5141 Morningsun Road
Oxford, OH 45056
Phone: (513) 769-7733
E-mail: bgambill-1@cinergy.com

Foreign Adoptive Children– Eastern Suburbs
11875 Laurel Road
Chesterland, OH 44026
Phone: (440) 729-2535

Foster Parent Association
1863 Barnett Court East
Columbus, OH 43227
Phone: (614) 235-1582
E-mail: Annettscott@aol.com

Friends Through International Adoption
Phone: (513) 832-0442

Good Samaritan Hospital School of Nursing
375 Dixmyth Avenue
Cincinnati, OH 45220-2489
Phone: (513) 872-3727
E-mail: dee_daniels@trihealth.com

Group for Adopted Children and Their Families
11370 Springfield Pike
Cincinnati, OH 45246

Group of Black Adoptive Parents
1055 Grayview Court
Cincinnati, OH 45224
Phone: (513) 541-4166

Heights Parent Center Adoption Support Group
1700 Crest Road
Cleveland Heights, OH 44121
Phone: (216) 321-0079
E-mail: loliver@heightsparent center.org
Web site: www. heightsparentcenter.org

Hope Support Services, Inc.
4071 Killary
Dublin, OH 43016
Phone: (614) 761-0947

House of Samuel, Inc.
1532-A Blaine Avenue
Cambridge, OH 43725
Phone: (740) 439-5634
Fax: (740) 439-0505
E-mail: jim@uplinkusa.net

Jeff and Cate Fopma-Leimbach
8969 Fontainbleau
Cincinnati, OH 45231
Phone: (513) 522-6161

Jewish Community Center, Adoptive Parent Support Group
26001 South Woodland Road
Beachwood, OH 44122
Phone: (216) 831-0700

Joanna Henry
8899 Walnut Street
Lakeview, OH 43331
Phone: (937) 843-5401

Korean Family Connection
Phone: (513) 321-4097
Web site: http://kfcc.tripod.com

Latin American Families
3568 Stoneboat Court
Maineville, OH 45039
Phone: (513) 677-1732

Life RAFFT (Raising Adoptive and Foster Families Together)
13760 Old State Road
Middlefield, OH 44024
Phone: (440) 286-3991

Life Raft
12480 Ravenwood Drive
Chardon, OH 44024
Phone: (216) 285-9141

Miami Valley Adoption Coalition
4923 Timberlawn Court
Greenville, OH 45331
Phone: (937) 537-1021
E-mail: mschaaf@wcoil.com

Mum's the Word
381 Bartley Avenue
Mansfield, OH 44903
Phone: (419) 524-0564

New Roots
P.O. Box 14953
Columbus, OH 43214
Phone: (614) 470-0846
Fax: (614) 293-2400
Web site: www.simplyliving. org/newroots

North American Council on Adoptable Children Represen-tative
1371 Virginia Avenue
Columbus, OH 43212
Phone: (614) 299-0177
E-mail: TimOHanlon@aol.com

Ohio Family Care Association
P.O. Box 82185
Columbus, OH 43202
Phone: (614) 268-7776
Fax: (614) 262-7004
E-mail: ofca@aol.com
Web site: www. ohiofamilycareassoc.org

Ohio Family Care Association
2931 Indianola Avenue
Columbus, OH 43202
Phone: (614) 299-9261

Open Adoption Support Group
541 Brandywynne Court
Dayton, OH 45406
Phone: (513) 275-9628

Our Children of Stark County
1223 11th Street NW
Canton, OH 44703
Phone: (330) 454-7715

Parenting Adopted Children
2070 Valley Park Circle
Broadview Heights, OH 44147
Phone: (216) 237-1197

Parents Supporting Parents
19306 Boerger Road
Marysville, OH 43040
Phone: (937) 349-7105

Parents of Adopted Children
773 Andover Road
Mansfield, OH 44907
Phone: (419) 756-5301

RESOLVE of Ohio
P.O. Box 141277
Columbus, OH 43214-6277
Phone: (216) 468-2365
Toll-Free: (800) 414-6446
Web site: www.resolveofohio.org

Rainbow Families of Toledo
1920 South Shore Boulevard
Oregon, OH 43618
Phone: (419) 693-9259

Single Parents by Adoption
2547 Talbott Avenue
Cincinnati, OH 45211
Phone: (513) 661-5170

Special Needs Adoption
Support Group
Phone: (419) 534-3350

Stark County Family Council
Adoption Support Group
1205 Grove Street NE
North Canton, OH 44721
Phone: (330) 494-2327

Summit County Children Services Post
Adoption Educational Support Group
264 South Arlington Street
Akron, OH 44306
Phone: (330) 379-2028
Fax: (330) 379-1924

Together Forever Families
165 Sterncrest Drive
Moreland Hills, OH 44022
Phone: (440) 542-4562
Fax: (440) 542-4802

**Licensed Private
Adoption Agencies**

A Child's Waiting Adoption
Program
3490 Ridgewood Road
Akron, OH 44333
Phone: (330) 665-1811
Toll-Free: 866-YES-ADOPT
Fax: (330) 668-1889
E-mail: achildswaiting@aol.com
Web site: www.achildswaiting.com

A Place to Call Home, Inc
36 Central Station Place
Johnstown, OH 43031
Phone: (740) 967-2167
Fax: (740) 967-0785

A.C.T.I.O.N.
6000 Philadelphia Drive
Dayton, OH 45415
Phone: (937) 277-6101
Fax: (937) 277-2962

Adolescent Oasis, Inc.
320 Linwood Street, Suite 1A
Dayton, OH 45405
Phone: (937) 228-2810

Adopt America Network
AASK Midwest
1025 North Reynolds Road
Toledo, OH 43615-4753
Fax: (419) 534-2995
E-mail: adoption@adoptamerica
network.org
Web site: www.
adoptamericanetwork.org

Adoption Center, Inc.
12151 Ellsworth Road
North Jackson, OH 44451
Phone: (330) 547-8255
Fax: (330) 547-3327

Adoption Circle
2500 East Main Street, Suite 103
Columbus, OH 43209
Phone: (614) 237-7222
Toll-Free: (800) 927-7222
Fax: (614) 237-8484
E-mail: info@Adoptioncircle.org
Web site: www.adoptioncircle.org

Adoption Connection
11223 Cornell Park Drive
Cincinnati, OH 45242
Phone: (513) 489-1616
Toll-Free: (866) 489-1616
Fax: (513) 489-4213
E-mail: jfladen@jfscinti.org
Web site: www.
adoptioncincinnati.org

Adoption Home Study Services of Ohio
358 Edna Street
Alliance, OH 44601
Phone: (330) 823-8986

Adoption Link, Inc.
3642 East Ermon Road
Yellow Springs, OH 45387
Phone: (937) 767-2466

Adoption Professionals, Inc.
585 East State Street
Salem, OH 44460

Adoption by Gentle Care
389 Library Park South
Columbus, OH 43215-1501
Phone: (614) 469-0007
Fax: (614) 621-2229
Web site: www.adoptgentlecare.com

Adriel School, Inc
414 North Detroit Street
West Liberty, OH 43357
Phone: (937) 465-0010
Fax: (937) 465-8690

Advantage Adoption and
Foster Care, Ltd.
43 East 4th Street
Mansfield, OH 44902
Phone: (419) 528-4411

Agape for Youth, Inc.
7755 Paragon Road
Centerville , OH 45459
Phone: (937) 439-4406
Fax: (937) 439-2908

Alliance Human Services, Inc.
530 South Main Street, Suite 1763
Akron, OH 44331
Phone: (330) 434-3790

American International
Adoption Agency
7045 County Line Road
Williamsfield, OH 44093
Phone: (330) 876-5656
Fax: (330) 876-8003
E-mail: Aiaagency@aol.com
Web site: http://aiaagency.com/first.htm
– Intercountry Program
– Child Placement

Applewood Centers, Inc.
2525 East 22nd Street
Cleveland, OH 44115
Phone: (216) 696-5800
Fax: (216) 459-9821
Web site: www.
applewoodcenters.org

Bair Foundation
275 Martinel Drive
Kent, OH 44240
Phone: (330) 673-6339

Beacon Agency
1836 Euclid Avenue, Suite 500
Cleveland, OH 44115
Phone: (216) 574-0300
Fax: (216) 274-0301

Beech Acres
6881 Beechmont Avenue
Cincinnati, OH 45230
Phone: (513) 231-6630
Fax: (513) 231-6837

Beech Brook
3737 Lander Road
Pepper Pike, OH 44124
Phone: (216) 831-2255

Bellefaire Jewish Children's Bureau
22001 Fairmount Boulevard
Shaker Heights, OH 44118
Phone: (216) 932-2800

Berea Children's Home and Family Services
202 East Bagley Road
Berea, OH 44017
Phone: (440) 234-2006
Toll-Free: (800) 639-4974
Fax: (440) 234-8319
E-mail: jpracko@bchfs.org
Web site: www.bchfs.org

Buckeye Ranch
5665 Hoover Road
Columbus, OH 43123
Phone: (614) 875-2371

Building Blocks Adoption Service, Inc.
P.O. Box 1028
52 Public Square
Medina, OH 44258
Phone: (330) 725-5521
Toll-Free: (866) 321-ADOPT
Fax: (800) 668-2478
E-mail: denise@bbas.org
Web site: www.bbas.org
– Intercountry Program
– Child Placement

Care to Adopt
7741 Pfeiffer Road
Cincinnati, OH 45242
Toll-Free: (888) 242-5094
Fax: (513) 793-1885
Phone: (513) 793-1885
E-mail: caretoadopt@yahoo.com
Web site: www.caretoadopt.com

Caring Hearts Adoption Agency, Inc.
771 Martin Street, Suite 2
Greenville, OH 45331
Phone: (937) 316-6168
Fax: (937) 548-7414
E-mail: adopt@caringheartsado
ption.org
Web site: www.
caringheartsadoption.org

Caring for Kids, Inc.
Orchard Plaza, Suite C
2633 State Route 59
Ravenna, OH 44266
Toll-Free: (800) 254-1725

Catholic Area Regional Agency
P.O. Box 1740
Warren, OH 44482
Phone: (330) 393-4254

Catholic Charities Services Corp./Parmadale
1111 Superior Avenue
Cleveland, OH 44114
Phone: (216) 696-6525

Catholic Charities Diocese of Toledo
1933 Spielbusch Avenue
Toledo, OH 43624
Phone: (419) 244-6711
Fax: (419) 244-4791
Web site: www.
catholiccharitiesnwo.org

Catholic Charities Family Center of Elyria
628 Poplar Street
Elyria, OH 44035
Phone: (440) 366-1106
E-mail: lorain@d
ioceseofcleveland.org
Web site: www.cleveland
catholiccharities.org

Catholic Charities Services Corporation
6753 State Road
Parma, OH 44134
Phone: (440) 845-7700
Fax: (440) 843-5603
E-mail: sxfay@dioceseof
cleveland.org
Web site: www.clevelandcatholic
charities.org

Catholic Charities of Ashtabula County
4200 Park Avenue, 3rd Floor
Ashtabula, OH 44004
Phone: (440) 992-2121
Fax: (440) 992-5974
E-mail: adoption@catholic
charitiesashtabula.org
Web site: www.catholiccharities
ashtabula.org

Catholic Community Services of Warren
1175 Laird Avenue NE, 3rd Floor
Warren, OH 44483
Phone: (216) 393-4254
Fax: (216) 393-4050

Catholic Social Service of Cuyahoga County
7800 Detroit Avenue
Cleveland, OH 44102-2814
Phone: (216) 631-3499
Fax: (216) 631-3654

Catholic Social Services of Southwest Ohio
100 East Eighth Street
Cincinnati, OH 45202
Phone: (513) 241-7745
Fax: (513) 241-4333

Catholic Social Services of the Miami Valley
922 Riverview Avenue
Dayton, OH 45407-2424
Phone: (937) 223-7217
Toll-Free: (800) 300-2937
Fax: (937) 222-6750
E-mail: porterj@cssmv.org
Web site: www.cssmv.org

Catholic Social Services, Inc.
197 East Gay Street, 2nd Floor
Columbus, OH 43215-3229
Phone: (614) 221-5891
Fax: (614) 228-1125
Web site: www.colscss.org

Center for Child and Family Development
8 Main Street
Zanesville, OH 43702
Phone: (740) 453-9089

Cherub International Adoption Services, Inc.
1827 West Tamarron Court
Springboro, OH 45066
Phone: (937) 748-4812
Fax: (937) 748-4889

Children's Home of Cincinnati
5050 Madison Road
Cincinnati, OH 45227
Phone: (513) 272-2800
Fax: (513) 272-2807

Christian Children's Home of Ohio
P.O. Box 765
Wooster, OH 44691
Phone: (330) 345-7949
Toll-Free: (800) 643-9073
Fax: (330) 345-5218

Cleveland Christian Home, Inc.
11401 Lorain Avenue
Cleveland, OH 44111
Phone: (216) 671-0971
Fax: (216) 416-0088

Community Services of Stark County, Inc.
6464 Promway Avenue NW
North Canton, OH 44720
Phone: (330) 305-9696

Directions for Youth and Families Crittenton Center
1414 East Broad Street
Columbus, OH 43205
Phone: (614) 251-0130
Fax: (614) 251-1177

Diversion Foster Care
2215 North Main Street
Findlay, OH 45856
Phone: (419) 422-4770
Toll-Free: (800) 824-3007
Fax: (419) 422-8117
E-mail: tjsas@bright.net

European Adoption Consultants
9800 Boston Road
North Royalton, OH 44133
Phone: (440) 237-3554
Toll-Free: (800) 533-0098
E-mail: EACAdopt@aol.com
Web site: www.eaci.com
– Intercountry Program
– Child Placement

Families Thru International Adoption
9918 Carver Road, Suite 102
Cincinnati, OH 45242
Phone: (513) 794-1515

– Intercountry Program
– Child Placement

Family Adoption Consultants
8536 Crow Drive, Suite #240
Macedonia, OH 44056
Phone: (216) 468-0673
Fax: (330) 468-0678
Web site: www.facadopt.org ,
www.adoption-global.org
– Intercountry Program
– Child Placement

Family Services of Summitt County
212 East Exchange Street
Akron, OH 44304
Phone: (330) 376-9494
Fax: (330) 376-4525
E-mail: jjudy@familyservs.org
Web site: www.familyservs.org

Focus on Youth, Inc.
2718 East Kemper Road
Cincinnati, OH 45241
Phone: (513) 771-4710
Toll-Free: (800) 873-6576
Fax: (513) 771-4768
Web site: www.focusonyouth.com

Hannah's Hope Adoption Cathedral Ministries, Inc.
5225 Alexis Road
Sylvania, OH 43560
Phone: (419) 882-8463

Harbor House Adoptions
P.O. Box 357
119 East Fayette Street
Celina, OH 45822
Phone: (419) 586-5941
Fax: (419) 586-8961
E-mail: life@harborhouse.org
Web site: www.harborhouse.org

House of Samuel, Inc.
1532-A Blaine Avenue
Cambridge, OH 43725
Phone: (740) 439-5634
Fax: (740) 439-0505
E-mail: jim@uplinkusa.netImpact

Adoption Ministries
905 Farnsworth Road
Waterville, OH 43566
Phone: (419) 878-8546

Inner Peace Homes, Inc.
P.O. Box 895
136 South Main Street
Bowling Green, OH 43402
Phone: (419) 354-6525

LDS Family Services, Inc.
4431 Marketing Place
Groveport, OH 43125
Phone: (614) 836-2466
Web site: www.
ldsfamilyservices.org

Lighthouse Youth Services, Inc.
1501 Madison Road
Cincinnati, OH 45206
Phone: (513) 221-3350
Fax: (513) 221-3665
Web site: www.lys.org

Lutheran Children's Aid and Family Services
4100 Franklin Boulevard
Cleveland, OH 44113
Phone: (216) 281-2500

Mathis Care
1191 Galbraith Road
Cincinnati, OH 45231
Phone: (513) 522-7390
Fax: (513) 522-9844

Mid-Western Children's Home
P.O. Box 48
4581 Long Spurling Road
Pleasant Plain, OH 45162
Phone: (513) 877-2141
Fax: (513) 877-2145

New Hope Adoptions International, Inc.
101 West Sandusky Street, Suite 311
Findlay, OH 45840
Phone: (419) 423-0760
Fax: (419) 423-8977
E-mail: nhopeadopt@aol.com

Web site: www.bright.net/
~newhope/
— Intercountry Program
— Child Placement

New Start Foundation, Inc.
119 Main Street
Chardon, OH 44024
Phone: (440) 286-1155

Northeast Ohio Adoption Services
5000 East Market Street Suite 26
Warren, OH 44484
Phone: (330) 856-5582
Toll-Free: (800) 686-6627
Fax: (330) 856-5586
E-mail: cdeal@noas.com
Web site: www.noas.com

Ohio Youth Advocate Program
3780 Ridge Mill Drive
Hilliard, OH 43026
Phone: (614) 777-8777

Options for Families and Youth
5131 West 140th Street
Brook Park, OH 44142
Phone: (216) 267-7070
Fax: (216) 267-7075
E-mail: ofymrush@aol.com

Private Adoption Services, Inc.
3411 Michigan Avenue
Cincinnati, OH 45208
Phone: (513) 871-5777
Fax: (513) 871-8582

Spaulding Adoption Program Beech Brook
3737 Lander Road
Pepper Pike, OH 44124
Phone: (216) 831-0638
Fax: (216) 831-1442

Specialized Alternatives for Families and Youth
10100 Elida Road
Delphos, OH 45833
Phone: (419) 532-7239
Toll-Free: (800) 532-7239
Fax: (419) 695-0004

Web site: www.safy.org

St. Aloysius Orphanage
4721 Reading Road
Cincinnati, OH 45237
Phone: (513) 242-7600
Fax: (513) 242-2845

St. Joseph Children's Treatment Center
650 St. Paul Avenue
Dayton, OH 45410
Phone: (937) 254-3562

Twelve, Inc.
619 Tremont Avenue SW
Massillon, OH 44647
Phone: (330) 837-3555
Toll-Free: (888) 513-8706
Fax: (330) 837-0513

United Methodist Children's Home
1033 High Street
Worthington, OH 43085-4054
Phone: (614) 885-5020
Fax: (614) 885-4058
Web site: www.umchohio.org

V. Beacon, Inc.
1718 Indianwood, Suite A
Maumee, OH 43537
Phone: (419) 887-1629

Westark Family Services, Inc.
42 First Street NE
Massillon, OH 44646
Phone: (330) 832-5043
Fax: (330) 830-2540
E-mail: wfsnmaier@sssnet.com
and wfs325@assnet.com

World Family Adoption Studies
723 Garrett Drive
Columbus, OH 43214
Phone: (614) 459-8606

Youth Engaged for Success
5300 Salem Bend Drive
Trotwood, OH 45426
Phone: (937) 837-4200
Fax: (937) 837-4700

Youth Services Network
3817 Wilmington Pike
Kettering, OH 45429
Phone: (937) 294-4400
Toll-Free: (800) 686-8114
Fax: (937) 294-4440
E-mail: adoption@ysn.org
Web site: www.ysn.org

**State Adoption Exchange/
Photolisting of Children
Waiting For Adoption**

Adoption Network
302 Overlook Park Drive
Cleveland, OH 44110
Phone: (216) 261-1511

Adoption Network
1667 East 40th Street, Suite B-1
Cleveland, OH 44103
Phone: (216) 881-7511
Fax: (216) 881-7510
E-mail: betsie@adoptionnetwork.org
Web site: www.AdoptionNetwork.org

Adoption Triangle Unity
4144 Packard Road
Toledo, OH 43613-1938
Phone: (419) 244-7072

Birthparent Support
3423 Bluerock Road
Cincinnati, OH 45239
Phone: (513) 741-0929

Birthright
6779 Manchester Road
Clinton, OH 44216

Concerned United Birthparent
Perrysburg Branch
2544 Bonnie Lane
Maumee, OH 43537

Concerned United Birthparent
Toledo Branch
6704 Inglewood
Holland, OH 43610

Ohio Adoptee Searches
P.O. Box 856
Waynesville, OH 45068-0856
Phone: (513) 897-2120
Fax: (513) 897-1423
E-mail: Jdehaven@aol.com

Sunshine Reunions
1175 Virginia Avenue
Akron, OH 44306Birth

**Family and Search
Support Groups**

Adopt America Network
1025 North Reynolds Road
Toledo, OH 43615

Adopt America Network
AASK Midwest
1025 North Reynolds Road
Toledo, OH 436154753
Phone: (419) 534-3350
Fax: (419) 534-2995
E-mail: adoption@adoptamerica
network.org
Web site: www.
adoptamericanetwork.org

Adopt Ohio
Family Services
255 East Main Street, 3rd Floor
Columbus, OH 43215-5222
Phone: (614) 466-9274
E-mail: tuckt@odjfs.state.oh.us

**State Adoption
Specialist/Manager**

**Ohio Department of Job and
Family Services**
Office of Family and Child
Services
255 East Main Street, 3rd Floor
Columbus, OH 43215
Phone: (614) 466-9274
Fax: (614) 728-2604
E-mail: harrib06@odjfs.state.
oh.us
Web site: http://jfs.ohio.gov/
oapl/index.htm

**State Foster Care
Specialist/Manager**

**Ohio Department of Job and
Family Services**
Office for Children and Families
65 East Main Street, 5th Floor
Columbus, OH 43215
Phone: (614) 466-9274
Fax: (614) 466-0164
Web site: http://jfs.ohio.gov/

**State Interstate Compact on
the Placement of Children
(ICPC) Administrator**

**Ohio Department of Job and
Family Services**
Office for Children and Families
65 East State Street, 5th Floor
Columbus, OH 43215
Phone: (614) 466-4258
Fax: (614) 466-0164
Web site: www.state.oh.us/odjfs

State Licensing Specialist

**Ohio Department of Job and
Family Services**
Office for Children and Families
255 East Main Street, 3rd Floor
Columbus, OH 43215-5222
Phone: (614) 466-9274
Fax: (614) 466-0164
Web site: www.state.oh.us/
odhs/oapl/bk19.htm

State Reunion Registry

Ohio Adoption Registry
Ohio Department of Health–Vital
Statistics
P.O. Box 15098
35 East Chestnut Street
Columbus, OH 43215-0098
Phone: (614) 644-5635
Web site: www.odh.state.oh.us/
Birth/adopt.htm

Statewide Adoption Recruitment Line

Ohio Statewide Adoption Recruitment Line
Toll-Free: (800) 755-4769

Service provider

Adopt America Network
National Headquarters
Toledo, OH 43615
Phone: (419) 534-3350
Toll-Free: (800) 246-1731
Fax: (419) 534-2995
E-mail: adoption@adoptamerica network.org
Web site: www.adoptamericanetwork.org

National organizations

National Center for Adoption Law and Policy
303 East Broad Street
Columbus, OH 43215
Web site: http://msass.cwru.edu

National Center for Adoption Law and Policy
303 East Broad Street
Columbus, OH 43215
Phone: (614) 236-6730
Fax: (614) 236-6956
E-mail: adoption@law.capital.edu
Web site: www.law.capital.edu/adoption

Foundation

Dave Thomas Foundation for Adoption
4288 West Dublin Granville Road
Dublin, OH 43017
Toll-Free: (800) ASK-DTFA
Fax: (614) 766-3871
E-mail: adoption@wendys.com
Web site: www.davethomasfoundationforadoption.com

OKLAHOMA

Statewide Foster Care Recruitment Line

Adoptive Parents of Central Oklahoma
1237 Mountain Brook Drive
Norman, OK 73072
Phone: (405) 364-8488

Babb Enterprises and North American Council on Adoptable Children Representative
448 Claremont
Norman, OK 73069
Phone: (405) 329-9294

Cleveland County Adoption Support Group
222 Oliphant Avenue
Norman, OK 73026
Phone: (405) 360-8193
E-mail: melisens@yahoo.com

Licensed Private Adoption AgenciesAdoption Affiliates
6136 East 32nd Place
Tulsa, OK 74135
Phone: (918) 664-2275
Toll-Free: (800) 253-6307
E-mail: stacyaai@aol.com
Web site: www.connectinghearts.org

Adoption Center of Northeastern Oklahoma
6202 South Lewis, Suite Q
Tulsa, OK 74136
Phone: (918) 748-9200
Fax: (918) 748-0369

Adoption Choices
5350 S. Western Avenue, Suite 617
Oklahoma City, OK 73109
Phone: (405) 632-7999
Fax: (405) 632-7995
Toll-free: (800) 898-6028
E-mail: info@adoptionchoices.org
Web site: www.adoptionchoices.org

Baptist Children's Home
16301 South Western Avenue
Oklahoma City, OK 73170
Phone: (405) 691-7781
E-mail: blantont@obhc.org
Web site: www.obhc.org

Bethany Adoption Service
3940 North College
Bethany, OK 73008
Phone: (405) 789-5423
Fax: (405) 787-6913
E-mail: jackpetty@prodigy.net

Bless This Child, Inc.
Route 4, Box 1005
Checotah, OK 74426
Phone: (918) 473-7045
Fax: (512) 329-9285
E-mail: blessthischild@ipa.net
Web site: www.blessthischild.com
– Intercountry Program
– Child Placement

Catholic Charities
P.O. Box 6429
739 North Denver Avenue
Tulsa, OK 74106
Phone: (918) 585-8167
E-mail: catholiccharities@tulsacoxmail.com
Web site: www.geocities.com/catholiccharitiestulsa

Chosen Child Adoption Agency
P.O. Box 55424
Tulsa, OK 74155-5424
Phone: (218) 298-0082
Fax: (218) 298-0082

Christian Homes
802 North 10th Street
Duncan, OK 73533
Phone: (405) 252-5131
E-mail: attention@christianhomes.com
Web site: www.christianhomes.com
– Intercountry Program
– Child Placement

Christian Services of Oklahoma
2221 East Memorial Road
Oklahoma, OK 73013
Phone: (405) 478-3362
Toll-Free: 888 409 6650
E-mail: christianservicesofoklaho
ma@yahoo.com
Web site: www.christian-
adoption.org

Crisis Pregnancy Outreach
11323 South Vine Street
Jenks, OK 74037
Phone: (918) 296-3377
Fax: (918) 296-9993
Toll-Free: (888) 648-0869
E-mail: cheryljobauman@
earthlink.net
Web site: www.cpotulsa.org

**Deaconess Home Pregnancy
and Adoption Services**
5300 North Meridian Avenue,
Suite 9
Oklahoma City, OK 73112
Phone: (405) 949-4200
Fax: (405) 945-9673
Toll-Free: (800) 567-6631
E-mail: adoptioninfo@deacones
sokc.org
Web site: www.deaconesshome.
com
– Home Study

Dillon International, Inc.
3227 East 31st Street, Suite 200
Tulsa, OK 74105
Phone: (918) 749-4600
Fax: (918) 749-7144
E-mail: info@dillonadopt.com
Web site: www.dillonadopt.com
– Intercountry Program
– Child Placement

Eagle Ridge
601 NE 63rd
Oklahoma City, OK 73105
Phone: (405) 840-1359

Elizaveta Foundation
6517 South Barnes Avenue
Oklahoma City, OK 73159

Fresh Start
2115 North Boston Place
Tulsa, OK 74106
Phone: (918) 592-0539

Heritage Family Services
5110 South Yale Avenue
Tulsa, OK 74135
Phone: (918) 491-6767
Fax: (918) 491-6717
E-mail: heritagefs@aol.com
Web site: www.
heritagefamilyservices.org

**LDS Social Services of
Oklahoma**
4500 South Garnett, Suite 425
Tulsa, OK 74146
Phone: (918) 665-3090
E-mail: fam-ok@ldschurch.org
Web site: www.
ldsfamilyservices.org

McAlester Counseling Center
501 E. Delaware
McAlester, OK 74501
Phone: (918) 423-1998

Natasha's Story, Inc.
1554 South Yorktown Place
Tulsa, OK 74104
Phone: (918) 747-3617

**Oklahoma Department of
Human Services**
1115 SE 66th Street
Oklahoma City, OK 73149
Phone: (405) 604-8800
Fax: (405) 604-8945
Toll-Free: (866) 231-8394

Oklahoma Home Study
1820 Threestars Road
Edmond, OK 73034
Phone: (405) 341-7959

Pathways International, Inc.
1616 East 19th, Suite 101B
Edmond, OK 73013
Phone: (405) 216-0909
– Intercountry Program
– Child Placement

SAFY of America
1209 Sovereign Row
Oklahoma City, OK 73108
Phone: (405) 942-5570
Web site: www.safy.org

Small Miracles International
1148 South Douglas Boulevard
Midwest City, OK 73130
Phone: (405) 732-7295
Fax: (405) 732-7297
E-mail: MORR@smiint.org
Web site: www.smiint.org
– Intercountry Program
– Child Placement

Small Miracles International
1148 South Douglas Boulevard
Midwest City, OK 73130
Phone: (405) 732-7295
E-mail: smi@ionet.net
Web site: www.smint.org
– Intercountry Program
– Child Placement

**Offices of the State (Public)
Adoption Agency**

Oklahoma Department of
Human Service
Deborah Goodman, State
Adoption Specialist/Manager
907 South Detroit, Suite 750
Tulsa, OK 74120
Phone (405) 521-2475 Tuesday/
Thursday
Phone: (405) 581-2401
Fax: (918) 592-9149
E-mail: Deborah.
Goddman@okdhs.org
Web site: www.okdhs.org/adopt

**State Interstate Compact on
the Placement of Children
(ICPC) Administrator**

Oklahoma Department of
Human Services
Linda Foster
P.O. Box 25352
2400 North Lincoln Boulevard
Oklahoma City, OK 73125

Phone: (405) 522-2471
Fax: (405) 521-2433
E-mail: Linda.Foster@okdhs.org

**State Licensing Specialist/
Manager and ICPC**

Oklahoma Department of
Human Services
Margaret DeVault
Division of Child Care
P.O. Box 25352
2400 North Lincoln Boulevard
Oklahoma City, OK 73125
Phone: (405) 521-3561
Toll-Free: (800) 347-2276
E-mail: Margaret.
Devault@okdhs.org

Foster Care

Oklahoma Department of
Human Services
Amy White
P.O. Box 25352
2400 North Lincoln Boulevard
Oklahoma City, OK 73125
Phone: (405) 521-3561
Phone: (918) 599-8894
Fax: (918) 592-9149
E-mail: annwhilte@okdhs.org
Web site: www.okdhs.org/
fostercare

Margaret Linnemann
State Foster Care Specialist/
Manager
E-mail: Margaret.
linnemann@okdhs.org

State Reunion Registry

Adoption Reunion Registry
Oklahoma Department of Human
Services
P.O. Box 25352
2400 North Lincoln Boulevard
Oklahoma City, OK 73125
Phone: (405) 521-2475
E-mail: margaret.devault@okdhs.
org
Web site: www.okdhs.org/adopt/
reunion.htm

**Statewide Adoption
Information Line**
Phone: (918) 588-1735
Toll-Free: (877) 657-9438

Adopt Older Kids Support
Group
3443 South Mingo
Tulsa, OK 74135
Phone: (918) 449-1391
E-mail: adptolderkids@aol.com

**Adoptive Parents of Central
Oklahohma**
1237 Mountain Brook Drive
Norman, OK 73072
Phone: (405) 364-8488

**Babb Enterprises and North
American Council on Adopt-
able Children**
4113 S. Eastern Avenue
Moore, OK 73160-7635
Phone: (405) 329-9294

**Christian Services of
Oklahoma**
2221 Easter Memorial Road
Edmond, OK 73013
Phone: (405) 478-3362
Toll-free: (888) 409-6650
E-mail: christianservicesofoklaho
ma@yahoo.com
Web site: www.christian-
adoption-org

**Cleveland County Adoption
Support**
222 Oliphant Avenue
Norman, OK 73026
Phone: (405) 360-8193
E-mail: melisens@yahoo.com

Cradle of Lawton
902 NW Kingswood Road
Lawton, OK 73505
Fax: (580) 536-2478
E-mail: Jan.howenstine@juno.
com
Web site: http://user.rli.net/
cradle/

Crisis Pregnancy Outreach
(CPO)
11323 South Vine Street
Jenks, OK 74037
Phone: (918) 296-3377
Fax: (918) 296-9993
Toll-Free: (888) 648-0869
E-mail: cheryljobauman@
earthlink.net
Web site: www.cpotulsa.org

North American Council on
Adoptable Children
P.O. Box 25
Harrah, OK 73045
Phone: (405) 454-1179
Fax: (405) 454-1179
E-mail: rlaws@tds.net

OREGON

**Adoptive/Foster Family
Support Groups**

Adoptive Families Unlimited
1061 Sharon Way
Eugene, OR 97401

Adoptive Families' Support
Group Emanuel Hospital
355 NW Division
Gresham, OR 97030
Phone: (503) 674-3610

Adoptive/Foster – Kids in
Common (KIC)
DHS
St. John's Branch
Phone: (503) 731-4646

Adoptive/Foster Families
Supportive Adolescent Project
(Independent Living Project) DHS
Midtown Branch
Portland, OR
Phone: (503) 731-3147

Adoptive/Foster Support Group
IHOP – Corner of Stark & 242nd
Avenue
Portland, OR
Phone: (503) 666-9369

African-American Support
Group
Portland, OR
Phone: (503) 281-6536

Attachment Disorder Parents
Network (ADPN)
Phone: (503) 652-1402

Boise Elliot School
620 North Fremont
Portland, OR 97227-1230
Phone: (503) 916-6171

Deschutes County Foster/
Adopt Support Group
P.O. Box 559
La Pine, OR 97739
Phone: (541) 536-1355

Families for Children from
China –Oregon & SW
Washington
P.O. Box 5642
Portland, OR 97208
Phone: (503) 295-6322
E-mail: fcc-oregon.org
Web site: www.fcc-oregon.org

Foster & Adoptive Parent
Association
Life in Christ Center
3095 Cherrie Heights Road
The Dalles, OR 97058
Phone: (541) 298-5136

Harney Branch
809 West Jackson
Burns, OR 97720
Phone: (541) 573-2086

Klamath Adoptive Parent Sup-
port Group
P.O. Box 1749
Klamath Falls, OR 97601
Phone: (541) 883-5570

**North American Council
on Adoptable Children
Representative**

NAFA
P.O. Box 25355
Portland, OR 97298-0355
Phone: (503) 243-1356

DHS
1425 NE Irving
Building 400
Portland, OR 97232

Services to Children &
Families
P.O. Box 467
North Bend, OR 97459-0040
Phone: (541) 269-5961

Southern Oregon Adoptive
Families
1156 Conestoga Street
Grand Pass, OR 97527-5381

St. Johns YWCA
8010 North Charleston
Portland, OR 97203
Phone: (503) 721-6779

Stars of David International,
Inc.
Jewish Family and Child Services
1130 SW Morrison, #316
Portland, OR 97205
Phone: (503) 226-7079
Fax: (503) 226-1130
E-mail: starsdavid@aol.com
Web site: www.starsofdavid.org

Support Group for Adopted
Children (Ages 6–10)
Kinship House and Casey Family
Programs
Phone: (503) 460-2796

**Licensed Private
Adoption Agencies**

Adoptions of Southern Oregon
409 Pine Street, Suite 309
Klamath Falls, OR 97601

Phone: (541) 273-9326
Fax: (541) 273-9327

All God's Children International
4114 NE Fremont, Suite 1
Portland, OR 97212
Phone: (503) 282-7652
Fax: (503) 282-2582
Toll-Free: (800) 214-6719
E-mail: info@allgodschildren.org
Web site: www.allgodschildren.org
– Intercountry Program
– Child Placement

Associated Services for Inter-
national Adoption (ASIA)
5935 Willow Lane
Lake Oswego, OR 97035-5344
Phone: (503) 697-6863
Fax: (503) 697-6957
E-mail: staff@asiadopt.org
Web site: www.asiadopt.org
– Intercountry Program
– Child Placement

Boys and Girls Aid Society of
Oregon
18 SW Boundary Court
Portland, OR 97239
Phone: (503) 222-9661
Fax: (503) 224-5960
Toll-Free: (800) 932-2734
Web site: http://boysandgirlsaid.
org

Catholic Charities, Inc.
Pregnancy Support & Open
Adoption Services
447 NE 47th Avenue, Suite 100
Portland, OR 97213-2324
Phone: (503) 238-5196
Fax: (503) 238-0818
E-mail: psa@catholiccharitiesor
egon.org
Web site: www.catholic
charitiesoregon.org

Children's Hope International
Oregon Regional Office
133 SW 2nd
Troutdale, OR 97060

Phone: (503) 665-1589
Fax: (503) 665-7865
E-mail: cascade@childrensHope.
com
Web site: www.childrenshop.
com/Oregon/index.htm

China Adoption Services
P.O. Box 19699
Portland, OR 97280
Phone: (503) 245-0976
E-mail: info@chinadopt.org
− Intercountry Program
− Child Placement

Christian Community Placement Center
P.O. Box 7361
Salem, OR 77303
Phone: (503) 588-5647

Christian Family Adoptions
6040 SE Belmont Street
Portland, OR 97215
Phone: (503) 232-1211
Fax: (503) 232-4756
E-mail: mail@christianfamilyado
ptions.org
Web site: www.
christianfamilyadoptions.org

Columbia Adoption Services, Inc.
1445 Rosemont Road
West Linn, OR 97068-2395
Phone: (503) 655-9470
Fax: (503) 557-8134

Dove Adoptions International, Inc.
3735 SE Martins
Portland, OR 97202
Phone: (503) 774-7210
Fax: (503) 771-7893
E-mail: dove@adoptions.net
Web site: www.adoptions.net
− Intercountry Program
− Child Placement

Families Are Forever
4114 NE Fremont Street
Portland, OR 97212

Phone: (503) 282-7652
Fax: (503) 282-2582
E-mail: info@allgodschildren.org

Holt International Children's Services
9320 SW Barbur Boulevard,
Suite 220
Portland, OR 97266
Phone: (503) 244-2940
Fax: (541) 683-6175
E-mail: info@holtintl.org
Web site: www.holtintl.org
− Intercountry Program
− Child Placement

Journeys of the Heart Adoption Services
P.O. Box 39
Hillsboro, OR 97123
Phone: (503) 681-3075
Fax: (503) 640-5834
E-mail: info@journeysoftheheart.
net
Web site: www.
journeysoftheheart.net
− Intercountry Program
− Child Placement

LDS Family Services
7410 SW Beveland Street
Tigard, OR 97223-8658
Phone: (503) 620-1191
Fax: (503) 620-3940
E-mail: fam-or@ldschurch.org

Lutheran Community Services Northwest
605 SE 39th Avenue
Portland, OR 97214
Phone: (503) 231-7480
Fax: (503) 236-8815
Web site: www.lcsnw.org

New Hope Child & Family Agency
4370 NE Halsey Street, Suite 215
Portland, OR 97213
Phone: (503) 282-6726
Toll-Free: (800) 228-3150

Northwest Adoptions and Family Services
P.O. Box 5724
Salem, OR 97304
Phone: (503) 581-6652
Fax: (503) 585-3109
E-mail: nwadoptions@earthlink.
net
− Intercountry Program
− Child Placement

Open Adoption & Family Services, Inc.
5200 SW Macadam Avenue,
Suite 250
Portland, OR 97201
Phone: (503) 226-4870
Fax: (503) 226-4890
Toll-Free: (800) 722-1115
E-mail: information@openadopt.
org

Orphans Overseas
14986 NW Cornell Road
Portland, OR 97229
Phone: (503) 297-2006
Fax: (503) 533-5836
E-mail: info@orphansoverseas.
org
Web site: www.
orphansoverseas.org
− Intercountry Program
− Child Placement

Plan Loving Adoptions Now (PLAN), Inc.
P.O. Box 667
203 East 3rd Street, 2nd Floor
McMinnville, OR 97128
Phone: (503) 472-8452
Fax: (503) 472-0665
E-mail: info@planloving
adoptions.org
Web site: www.
planlovingadoptions.org
− Intercountry Program
− Child Placement

Tree of Life Adoption Center
9498 SW Barbur Boulevard,
Suite 304
Portland, OR 97219
Phone: (503) 244-7374
E-mail: info@toladopt.org
Web site: www.toladopt.org
– Intercountry Program
– Child Placement

Birth Family and Search Support Groups

A.N.S.R.S., Inc.
9203 SW Cree Circle
Tualatin, OR 97062-9046

Albertina Kerr Center for Children
722 NE 162nd
Portland, OR 97230
Phone: (503) 255-4205
Fax: (503) 255-5095
E-mail: info@albertinakerr.org
Web site: www.albertinakerr.org

Family Ties
4537 Souza Street
Eugene, OR 97402

Northwest Adoptive Families Association
P.O. Box 25355
Portland, OR 97225-0355
Phone: (503) 234-1356

O.A.R.A.
715 North 10
Springfield, OR 97477

Oregon Adoptive Rights Association
P.O. Box 882
Portland, OR 97202
Phone: (503) 235-3669
Web site: www.oara.org

Relative Research
Adoption Search and Support Group
Grant Pass, OR

Southern Oregon Adoptive Rights
1605 SW K Street
Grants Pass, OR 97526-2638

Southern Oregon Adoptive Rights
1076 Queens Branch Road
Rogue River, OR 97537

State Adoption Exchange/ Photolisting of Children Waiting For Adoption

ACT (Adopting Minority Children) for Children Today
State Office for Services to Children and Families
Building 400
1425 NE Irving
Portland, OR 97232
Phone: (503) 222-9661
Web site: http://adoptions.scf.hr.state.or.us/adopt.htm

State Adoption Specialist/Manager

Oregon Department of Human Services
State Adoption Specialist/Manager
Kathy Ledesman,
500 Summer Street, NE
Salem, OR 97310
Phone: (503) 945-5677
Fax: (503) 945-6969
E-mail: kathy.ledesma@state.or.us
Web site: www.scf.hr.state.or.us/adoption/index.htm

State Foster Care Specialist/Manager

Oregon Department of Human Services
Kevin George
500 Summer Street NE E77
Salem, OR 97310-1069
Phone: (503) 945-5987
Fax: (503) 945-6969
Toll-Free: (800) 331-0503
E-mail: kevin.george@state.or.us
Web site: www.dhs.state.or.us/foster/index.htm

State Interstate Compact on the Placement of Children (ICPC) Administrator

Oregon Department of Human Services
Harry Gilmore
500 Summer Street NE, E-70
Salem, OR 97310-1017
Phone: (503) 945-6685
E-mail: Harry.Gilmore@state.or.us
Web site: www./dhs.state.or.us/policy/childwelfare/manual_I/I-6342,htm

State Licensing Specialist

Oregon Department of Human Services
State Office for Services to Children and Families
500 Summer Street NE,
E-73
Salem, OR 97310-1017
Phone: (503) 947-5208
E-mail: Stephanie.Jernstedt@state.or.us

Christian Community Placement Center
P.O. Box 7361
Salem, OR 77303
Phone: (503) 588-5647

Oregon's Voluntary Adoption Registry

Oregon State Office for Services to Children and Families
HRB 2nd Floor South
500 Summer Street NE
Salem, OR 97310-1017
Phone: (503) 945-6643
E-mail: janice.pitts@state.or.us
Web site: www.scf.hr.state.or.us/ar/index.htm

Statewide Adoption Recruitment Line

Oregon Statewide Adoption Recruitment Line
Toll-Free: (800) 331-0503

Statewide Foster Care Recruitment Line

Oregon Statewide Foster Care Recruitment Line
Toll-Free: (800) 331-0503

State Complaints Office

Governor's Advocacy
Ombudsman Office
500 Summer Street, NE, 4th Floor
Salem, OR 97301
Phone: (800) 442-5238

Little People of America Adoption Committee
5289 NE Elam Young Parkway
Suite F – 700
Hillsboro, OR 97124
Phone: (503) 846-1562
Fax: (503) 846-1590
Toll-Free: (888) LPA-2001
E-mail: info@lpaonline.org
Web site: www.lpaonline.org/lpa_adoptions.html

National Indian Child Welfare Association
5100 SW Macadam Avenue,
Suite 300
Portland, OR 97239
Phone: (503) 222-4044

Fax: (503) 222-4007
E-mail: info@nicwa.org
Web site: www.nicwa.org

National Indian Children's Alliance
National Indian Child Welfare Association
5100 SW Macadam Avenue,
Suite 300
Portland, OR 97201
Phone: (503) 222-4044
Fax: (503) 222-4007
E-mail: info@nicwa.org
Web site: www.nicwa.org/services/initiatives/alliance/index.asp

Oregon Department of Human Services
State Office for Services to Children and Families
500 Summer Street NE E62
Salem, OR 97301-1067
Phone: (503) 945-5651
Phone: (503) 399-5152
Fax: (503) 581-6198
Web site: www.cwporegon.com

PENNSYLVANIA

Adoptive/Foster Family Support Groups

AASK Midwest
1020 Mainsville Road
Shippensburg, PA 17257
Phone: (717) 532-2560
Fax: (717) 532-3423

Adoption ARC
4701 Pine Street, #J7
Philadelphia, PA 19143-1816
Phone: (215) 748-1441
Fax: (215) 842-9881

Adoption Connection, Inc.
709 Third Avenue
New Brighton, PA 15066
Phone: (724) 846-2615
Fax: (724) 846-8358

Adoption Group of Clinton County
One Merlyn Drive
Mill Hall, PA 17751
Phone: (717) 748-8283

Adoption Resource Center
4701 Pine Street, #J7
Philadelphia, PA 19143-1816
Phone: (215) 748-1441
Fax: (215) 842-9881
E-mail: taralaw@aol.com

Adoption Support Group
452 South Roberts Road
Rosemont, PA 19010
Phone: (610) 525-5400
Web site: www.pcv.org

Adoption Unlimited, Inc
2148 Embassy Drive, Suite 121
Lancaster, PA 17603
Phone: (717) 431-2021
Fax: (717) 399-0093
E-mail: adoptionunlimited@paonline.com
Web site: www.adoptionunlimited.org

Adoption World
820 South 4th Street,
2nd Floor
Philadelphia, PA 19147
Phone: (215) 336-5135
Fax: (215) 271-1361
E-mail: adoption@adoptionworld.org
Web site: www.adoptionworld.org

Adoption, A Loving Option
480 Chestnut Lane
York, PA 17403

Adoptive Families Together
2655 Timberglen Drive
Wexford, PA 15090
Phone: (724) 935-4757

Adoptive Families Together
228 Monks Road
Valencia, PA 16059
Phone: (724) 352-5935

Adoptive Mothers Support Group
2868 Route 212
Coopersburg, PA 18036-9681
Phone: (610) 749-0948
E-mail: rockepa@aol.com

Adoptive Parents Network
6339 Woodbine Avenue
Philadelphia, PA 19151
Phone: (215) 878-7102
E-mail: adoptionsupportgroup@
angelfire.com
Web site: www.homestead.com/
overbrookfams/adoptionsupport.
html

Adoptive Parents Together
520 East Lancaster Avenue
Downingtown, PA 19335
Phone: (610) 873-1005
Fax: (610) 873-3317

After Adoption and Parenting Services for Families
Alden Park Manor, A202
5500 Wissahickon Avenue
Philadelphia, PA 19144
Phone: (215) 844-1312

Apple Corps
c/o Children's Aid Home
574 East Main Street
Somerset, PA 15501
Phone: (814) 443-1637
Fax: (814) 445-8481
Web site: www.cahprogram.org

Association of Puerto Ricans on the March
445-447 West Laray Street
Philadelphia, PA 19104
Phone: (215) 329-9580
Fax: (215) 329-4017

CCDCYF Post Adoption Services Group
601 Westtown Road, #310
West Chester, PA 19380-0990
Phone: (610) 344-5873
Fax: (610) 344-5858

Cambria Co CYS
401 Candlelight Drive, Suite 110
Ebensburg, PA 15931

Catholic Charities
P.O. Box 3551
4800 Union Depot Road
Harrisburg, PA 17105
Phone: (717) 657-4804

Catholic Charities of Greensburg
711 East Pittsburgh Street
Greensburg, PA 15601
Phone: (724) 837-1840

Catholic Social Services Adoptive Mother Club
227 North 18th Street
Philadelphia, PA 19107
Phone: (215) 854-7050

Chester County Post Adoption Services
Government Service Center
601 Westtown Road, Suite 310
West Chester, PA 19380-0990
Phone: (610) 344-5890
Fax: (610) 344-5858
Toll-Free: (800) 692-1100
E-mail: kboyd@chesco.org
Web site: www.chesco.org/cyf/
placemen.html

Children's and Home Adoptive Parents
142 Woodside Drive
Washington, PA 15301
Phone: (724) 228-7963

Common Sense Adoption Service
5021 E. Trindle Road, #300
Mechanicsburg, PA 17050-3622
Phone: (717) 766-6449
Fax: (717) 766-8015
Toll-Free: (800) 445-2444
E-mail: echick@csas-swan.org
Web site: www.csas-swan.org

Concerned Adoptive Parents
1110 Daniel Davis Lane
West Chester, PA 19382
Phone: (610) 793-2615

Council on Adoptable Children of Chester County
712 North Walnut Street
West Chester, PA 19380
Phone: (610) 344-5872

Council on Adoptable Children of Southwestern Pennsylvania and North American Council on Adoptable Children State Representative
224 S. Aiken Avenue
Pittsburgh, PA 15206
Phone: (412) 471-8722
Fax: (412) 471 4861
E-mail: mishand408@aol.com

Crawford County Foster Parent Association
414 Venango Avenue
Cambridge Springs, PA 16403
Phone: (814) 398-2901

Families All Together in Their Hopes
14 Gamewood Road
Levittown (Philadelphia), PA 19057
Phone: (215) 949-3893
Phone: (267) 391-6229
E-mail: faithfamilies@verizon.net
Web site: http://mysite.verizon.
net/vze7mzpe/index.html

Families Like Ours
2239 Hampton Street
Pittsburgh, PA 15218
Phone: (412) 242-8022

Families Like Ours
9018 East Willow Grove Avenue
Wyndmoor, PA 19038
Phone: (717) 233-1380

Families Like Ours
2239 Hampton Street
Pittsburgh, PA 15218
Phone: (412) 242-8022

Families Together
731 Apollo Lane
Rochester, PA 15074
Phone: (724) 774-7260

Families thru Adoption
103 Channel Drive
Carlisle, PA 17013

Families thru Adoption
3410 Schoolhouse Lane
Harrisburg, PA 17109

Families w/Russian Ukranian Adoptions
80 Roberts Road
Newtown Square, PA 19073-2012

Families with Children from China
3209 Arapahoe Road
Pittsburgh, PA 15241
Phone: (412) 835-4834

Families with Children from China
20 Garnet Circle
Conshohocken, PA 19428
Phone: (610) 941-6738

Families with Children from China Delaware Valley
P.O. Box 633
Berwyn, PA 19312
Phone: (610) 296-9140
E-mail: delvalfcc@aol.com

Families with Children from China Delaware Valley
7234 Sprague Street
Philadelphia, PA 19119-1701
Phone: (215) 248-3629

Family Options
6513 Meadow Street
Pittsburgh, PA 15206

Family Support Group
1733 Locust Road
Sewickley, PA 15143
Phone: (412) 366-7113
E-mail: marleenk@icubed.com

Finally Families
12 Hilloch Lane
Chadds Ford, PA 19317
Phone: (610) 358-5359

Fireside Foster Parent Group
320 Union Street
Hatfield, PA 19940
Phone: (215) 855-5128

Forever Families Adoptive Support Group
216 N Reading Avenue
Boyestown, PA 19512
Phone: (610) 367-1693

Foster Care and Adoption Matters
Phone: (215) 247-8397

Foster To Adopt Families
One South Home Avenue, N.E.
Topton, PA 19562
Phone: (610) 682-1504

Friends of Love the Children
450 Donalyn Lane
Berwyn, PA 19312
Phone: (610) 296-0469

From Russia With Love
26 Renne Circle
Richboro, PA 18954
Phone: (215) 322-6878

Gathering International Families Together (GIFT)
358 Maxwell Drive
Quarryville, PA 17566
Phone: (717) 786-7658
E-mail: giftgroup@att.net
Web site: http://communities.msn.com/GIFTTS

Indiana/Armstrong Support Group
RD #1, Box 11
Strongstown, PA 15957
Phone: (814) 749-8156

International Adoption Center
7401 Old York Road
Elkins Park, PA 19027
Phone: (215) 782-1191
Fax: (215) 782-1193
E-mail: ADOPTLAW@aol.com

John Strait & Amy Blackmond
1017 North Sheridan Avenue
Pittsburgh, PA 15206
Phone: (412) 363-5693

Keystone Adoptive Families
1006 Valley View Boulevard
Altoona, PA 16602
Phone: (814) 943-4767

LCFS/Post Adoption Support System
1256 Easton Road
Roslyn, PA 19001
Phone: (215) 881-6800

Lehigh Valley Adoptive Parents Group
1710 Monroe Street
Bethlehem, PA 18017-6439
Phone: (215) 896-1549

Living Bridges Support Group
Phone: (610) 649-7904
E-mail: mscribe@aol.com

Love the Children Support Group
15 Zelie Drive
Zelienople, PA 16063
Phone: (724) 452-7897

Loving Adoptive Families-Exchange (LAF)
1130 Kolbe Lane
West Chester, PA 19382
Phone: (610) 455-1458

Lutheran Social Services of Western Pennsylvania
1011 Old Salem Road, #107
Greensburg, PA 15601
Phone: (412) 521-3631
Fax: (724) 836-5873

McKean County Support Group
RD 2, Box 313A
Kane, PA 16735
Phone: (814) 945-6340

Mission Adoption
538 Dendron Drive
Coraopolis, PA 15108
Phone: (412) 859-3478
E-mail: kelrus@aol.com

Mothers of Adopted Children
2903 Tanglewood Lane
Norristown, PA 19403-3857
Phone: (610) 584-1996

National Adoption Center
1500 Walnut Street, Suite 701
Philadelphia, PA 19102
Phone: (215) 735-9988
E-mail: nac@adopt.org
Web site: www.adopt.org

One Church, One Child – Central Region
2747 Reel Street
Harrisburg, PA 17110
Phone: (717) 234-9559

One Church, One Child – Northeast Region
9 South 9th Street
Reading, PA 19602
Phone: (610) 374-4833
Fax: (610) 374-4581
E-mail: tinikt@cs.com

One Church, One Child of Pennsylvania
9 South Nine Street
Reading, PA 19602
Phone: (610) 374-4833
Fax: (610) 374-4581
Toll-Free: (800) 437-0268
E-mail: ococinpa@cs.com

One Church, One Child – Northwest Region
2624 German Street
Erie, PA 16504
Phone: (814) 866-4535

Our Children
482 Pinewood Road
Philadelphia, PA 19116
Phone: (215) 542-5955
PACO/Lawrence County
Road 1, Box 295
New Castle, PA 16101

Parent Advocate of Adoptive Children
2220 Gatesmille Drive
Erie, PA 16510
Phone: (814) 825-4656

Parent Network
217 North Wade
Washington, PA 15301
Phone: (714) 222-1766

Parent Network for the Post-Institutionalized Child
217 N. Wade
Washington, PA 15301
Phone: (724) 222-6009

Parents Adoption Group of Erie
Family Services of Northwestern PA
5100 Peach Street
Erie, PA 16509
Phone: (814) 866-4546
Fax: (814) 864-2677
E-mail: susanf@familyservices erie.org
Web site: www. familyserviceserie.org

Parents Advocating for Adopted Children
524 W Eaglewood Drive
Erie, PA 16511-2366
Phone: (814) 899-0123

Parents Involved Network (PIN)
135 Long Lane, 3rd Floor
Upper Darby, PA 19083
Phone: (610) 713-9405
Toll-Free: (800) 688-4226

Parents and Adopted Children's Organization
RE #1, Box 408N
New Castle, PA 16101
Phone: (724) 654-2242

Parents and Adopted Children's Organization of Lawrence County
4253 Ellwood Road
New Castle, PA 16101
Phone: (724) 652-4198

Parents and Adopted Children's Organization of Washington County
551 McCrea Avenue
Donora, PA 15033
Phone: (724) 379-5716

Parents of Adopted International Children
602 Tyson Avenue
Philadelphia, PA 19111

Parents of International Adopted Children
1184 Jamie-Lynn Drive
Downington, PA 19335
Phone: (610) 941-6738

Philadelphia Family Pride
P.O. Box 25223
Philadelphia, PA 19119
Phone: (215) 844-3360
E-mail: phillyfamilypride@hotmail. com
Web site: www.phillyfamilypride. org

Philadelphia State Foster Parent Association
2458 Rhodes Road
Gilbertsville, PA 19525
Phone: (610) 327-2444
Fax: (610) 327-3824

Pittsburgh Adoption Support Group
105 Church Lane
Pittsburgh, PA 15238

Phone: (412) 767-4250
E-mail: pghadoptsuprtgr@webtv.net

P.A.S.S. (Post Permanency and Adoption Support System)
348 East Walnut Lane
Philadelphia, PA 19144
Phone: (215) 849-8815 ext. 116
Fax: (215) 849-8957
E-mail: JApple@bethanna.org

Project STAR
2310 Seventh Avenue
Beaver Falls, PA 15010
Phone: (724) 847-2330
Fax: (724) 847-7895

Project STAR
6301 Northumberland Street
Pittsburgh, PA 15217
Phone: (412) 244-3055
Fax: (412) 242-7414
E-mail: mze@the-institue.org

Proud Parents of Golden Cradle
117 Vernon Lane
Media, PA 19063

SA Parents of Delaware Valley
2317 Naudain Street
Philadelphia, PA 19146
Phone: (215) 545-5323

Single Adoptive Parents of Delaware Valley
2239 Strahle Street, 2nd Floor
Philadelphia, PA 19152
Phone: (215) 745-2855

Single Adoptive Parents of Delaware Valley
40 Aberdale Road
Bala-Cynwyd, PA 19004
Phone: (610) 617-1197

Single Adoptive Parents of Delaware Valley
1415 Arline Avenue
Roslyn, PA 19001
Phone: (215) 657-7263

Some Families (Society of Multi-ethnic Families)
1798 Unionville Lenape Road
West Chester, PA 19382
Phone: (610) 793-1533

St. Jude's Mothers Club
132 South Wells Avenue
Glenolden, PA 19036
Phone: (610) 532-6591

Stars of David
702 N. 22nd Street
Allentown, PA 18104

Stars of David International, Inc.
Central Pennsylvania Chapter
Jewish Family Service of Harrisburg
3333 North Front Street
Harrisburg, PA 17110
Phone: (717) 233-1681
Fax: (717) 234-8258
E-mail: starsdavid@aol.com
Web site: www.starsofdavid.org

State College Parent Group
149 Meadow Lane
State College, PA 16801
Phone: (814) 237-5568

Support Group for Parents of Children with/ADD
310 North Matlack Street
West Chester, PA 15380
Phone: (610) 431-9508

Support Group of Greene County
203 Center Avenue
Carmichaels, PA 15320
Phone: (724) 966-8512

Tabor Adoptive Parents, Inc.
104 Hollow Road
Levittown, PA 19056
Phone: (215) 943-3134

Taplink and North American Council on Adoptable Children Representative
478 Moyers Road
Harleysville, PA 19438-2302
Phone: (215) 256-0669
Fax: (215) 256-0669
E-mail: taplink@hotmail.com
Web site: www.taplink.org

The Apple Corps
P.O. Box 1195
Somerset, PA 15501
Phone: (814) 443-1637
Fax: (814) 445-8481

Three Rivers Adoption Council
224 South Aiken Avenue
Pittsburgh, PA 15206
Phone: (412) 361-4419
Fax: (412) 271-4861
E-mail: sanderson@3riversadopt.org

Three Rivers Families with Children from China
148 Sunset Drive
Pittsburgh, PA 15235
Phone: (412) 829-2691

Together as Adoptive Parents, Inc.
478 Moyers Road
Harleysville, PA 19438-2302
Phone: (215) 256-0669
Fax: (215) 256-0669
After hours: (215) 256-6438
E-mail: taplink@comcast.net
Web site: www.taplink.org

Transcultural Adoptive Families
365 Kane Blvd
Pittsburgh, PA 15243
Phone: (412) 429-1775
E-mail: mmneary@aol.com

Tressler Lutheran Services/ Korean Connection
836 South George Street
York, PA 17403
Phone: (717) 845-9113

Welcome House Adoptive Parents
921 East Hemlock Street
Palmyra, PA 17078
Phone: (717) 838-5577

Welcome House Parent Association
520 Dublin Road
Perkasie, PA 18944
E-mail: WHParentAssociation@pearl-s-buck.org
E-mail: WHParentAssociation@yahoo.com

Women's Christian Alliance, Inc.
1610-1616 North Broad Street
Philadelphia, PA 00001-9121

Licensed Private Adoption Agencies

A Brave Choice
1011 Cedargrove Road
Wynnewood, PA 19096
Phone: (610) 642-7182

A Field of Dreams Adoption Services, Inc.
3208 Benner Pike Village, Suite 200
Bellefonte, PA 16823
Phone: (814) 355-4310
Fax: (814) 355-4393
Toll-Free: (877) 355-4310
E-mail: info@felidofdreams.com
Web site: www.afieldofdreams.com

A Second Chance, Inc.
204 North Highland Avenue
Pittsburgh, PA 15206
Phone: (412) 665-2300
Fax: (412) 242-5229
E-mail: valdab@asecondchance-kinship.com
Web site: www.asecondchance-kinship.com

A Second Change Licensed Adoption Agency, Ltd.
1074 Chelsea Way
Collegeville, PA 19426
Phone: (215) 412-2966

AAA Transitions Adoption Agency
355 West Lancaster Avenue
Haverford, PA 19041
Phone: (610) 642-4155
E-mail: transadopt@att.net

Absolute Love Adoptions (ALA)
412 Main Street, Suite 3
Irwin, PA 15642
Phone: (742) 861-8300
Fax: (724) 861-8311
Toll-Free: (800) 451-3910
E-mail: cparkhill@earthlink.net
Web site: www.absoluteloveadoptions.org

Adelphoi Village, Inc.
1003 Village Way
Latrobe, PA 15650
Phone: (724) 520-1111
E-mail: robink@adelphoivillage.org
Web site: www.hso.blairco.org/Adelphoi.html

Adopt Abroad, Inc.
1262 Wood Lane #205
Langhorne, PA 19047
Phone: (215) 702-0561
Fax: (973) 744-4760
E-mail: info@adopt-abroad.com
Web site: www.adopt-abraod.com

Adopt America Network
1020 Manesville Road
Shippensburg, PA 17257
Phone: (717) 532-9005
Fax: (717) 532-3423

Adoption ARC, Inc.
4701 Pine Street, J-7
Philadelphia, PA 19143

Phone: (215) 844-1082
Fax: (215) 842-9881
Toll-Free: (800) 884-4004
E-mail: taralaw@aol.com
Web site: www.adoptionarc.com

Adoption Connection, Inc.
709 Third Avenue
New Brighton, PA 15066
Phone: (724) 846-2615

Adoption Home Study Associates of Chester County, Inc.
1708 Yardley Drive
West Chester, PA 19380
Phone: (610) 429-1001
Fax: (610) 429-1001
E-mail: AHSACC1@AOL.COM

Adoption Horizons
899 Petersburg Road
Carlisle, PA 17103
Phone: (717) 249-8850

Adoption House, Inc.
527 Swede Street
Norristown, PA 19407
Phone: (215) 523-9234
Fax: (215) 523-9235
E-mail: htenenbaum@adoptionhouse.org
Web site: www.adoptionhouse.org

Adoption Resource Center, Inc.
4701 Pine Street
Philadelphia, PA 19143
Phone: (215) 844-1082
E-mail: taralaw@aol.com
Web site: www.adoptionarc.com

Adoption Services, Inc.
28 Central Boulevard
Camp Hill, PA 17011
Phone: (717) 737-3960
Fax: (717) 731-0517
E-mail: mail@adoptionservices.org
Web site: www.adoptionservices.org

Adoption Services, Inc.
28 Central Boulevard
Camp Hill, PA 17011
Phone: (717) 737-3960
E-mail: mail@adoptionservices.
org
Web site: www.
adoptionservices.org

Adoption Unlimited, Inc.
2148 Embassy Drive, Suite 121
Lancaster, PA 17603
Phone: (717) 431-2021
Fax: (717) 399-0093
Web site: www.
adoptionunlimited.org

Adoption by Choice
2503 West 15th Street, Suite 4
Erie, PA 16505
Phone: (814) 836-9887

Adoptions Forever, Inc.
509 Shrathmore Road
Havertown, PA 19083
Phone: (610) 853-2635
Fax: (610) 853-4576
E-mail: Adoptionsforever@
yahoo.com
Web site: www.adoptions
forever.org

**Adoptions From The Heart,
Inc.**
30-31 Hampstead Circle
Wynnewood, PA 10096
Phone: (610) 642-7200
Fax: (610) 642) 7938
E-mail: adoption@adoptions
fromtheheart.org
Web site: www.
adoptionsfromtheheart.org
— Intercountry Program
— Child Placement

**Adoptions From The Heart,
Inc.**
9 Claremont Drive
Greensburg, PA 15601
Phone: (724) 853-6633

E-mail: adoption@adoptions
fromtheheart.org
Web site: www.
adoptionsfromtheheart.org

**Adoptions From The Heart,
Inc.**
800 Main Street, Suite 101
Hellertown, PA 18055
Phone: (610) 838-9240
E-mail: adoption@adoptionsfrom
theheart.org
Web site: www.
adoptionsfromtheheart.org

**Adoptions From The Heart,
Inc.**
4331 North Point Street
Harrisburg, PA 17110
Phone: (717) 232-1787
E-mail: adoption@adoptionsfrom
theheart.org
Web site: www.
adoptionsfromtheheart.org
— Intercountry Program
— Child Placement

**Adoptions From The Heart,
Inc.**
1525 Oregon Pike Commons,
Suite 401-402
Lancaster, PA 17601
Phone: (717) 399-7766
E-mail: adoption@adoptionsfrom
theheart.org
Web site: www.
adoptionsfromtheheart.org
— Intercountry Program
— Child Placement

**Adoptions From The Heart,
Inc.**
2212 Union Boulevard
Allentown, PA 18109
Phone: (610) 838-9240
Web site: www.
adoptionsfromtheheart.org
— Intercountry Program
— Child Placement

Adoptions From the Heart
4331 North Front Street
Harrisburg, PA 17110
Phone: (717) 232-1787
E-mail: mrich@afth.org
— Intercountry Program
— Child Placement

Adoptions International, Inc.
601 South 10th Street
Philadelphia, PA 19147
Phone: (215) 238-9057
Fax: (215) 592-0465
E-mail: HWall334@aol.com
Web site: www.adoptionsintl.org
— Intercountry Program
— Child Placement

**American Adoptions Abroad,
Inc.**
Chadds Ford Professional Center
6 Dickinson Drive
Chadds Ford, PA 19317
Phone: (610) 361-8106
Fax: (610) 361-8107
Web site: www.
americanadoptionsabroad.com

American Friends of Children
619 Gawain Road
Plymouth Meeting, PA 19464
Phone: (610) 828-8166

**Asociacion Puertorriquenos
en Marcha**
445-447 Luray Street
Philadelphia, PA 19122
Phone: (215) 235-6788
Fax: (215) 932-9450
E-mail: misierra@earthlink.net
Web site: www.apm-phila.org
— Intercountry Program
— Child Placement

BASES
4300 Monument Road
Philadelphia, PA 19131
Phone: (215) 877-1925
Fax: (215) 877-1942

Bair Foundation of Pennsylvania, Inc.
3755 Library Road
Pittsburgh, PA 15234-2266
Phone: (412) 341-6850
Toll-Free: (800) 543-7058
Web site: www.wordfm.com/
AdvTpt.Bair.html

Bair Foundation of Pennsylvania, Inc.
12 Oaks Center
1801 Oberlin Road
Middletown, PA 17057
Phone: (717) 985-6450
E-mail: info@bair.org
Web site: www.the-plaza.com/bair/

Best Nest, Inc.
1709 Washington Avenue
Philadelphia, PA 19146
Phone: (215) 546-8060
Fax: (215) 546-8906
Web site: www.bestnet.org

Best Nest, Inc.
325 Market Street
Williamsport, PA 17701
Phone: (570) 321-1969
Fax: (570) 321-1980

Bethanna, Inc.
1030 Second Street Pike
Southampton, PA 18966
Phone: (215) 355-6500
Fax: (215) 355-8847
E-mail: kcosmas@bethanna.org
Web site: www.bethanna.org

Bethany Christian Services, Inc.
694 Lincoln Avenue
Pittsburgh, PA 152023421
Phone: (412) 734-2662
Fax: (412) 734-2110
E-mail: bcspittsburgh@bethany.org
Web site: www.bethany.org

Black Adoption Services
307 4th Street, Suite 710
Pittsburgh, PA 15222
Phone: (412) 471-8722
Fax: (412) 471-4861
E-mail: jwilson@3riversadopt.org
Web site: www.3riversadopt.org

Carson Valley School
Diocese of Allentown
6700 Germantown Avenue
Philadelphia, PA 19119
Phone: (215) 849-5505
E-mail: mharris@carsonvalley.org

Catholic Charities Counseling and Adoption Services, Inc.
90 Beaver Drive, Suite 111B
Dubois, PA 15801-2424
Phone: (814) 371-4717
E-mail: mattim@clearnet.net

Catholic Charities Counseling and Adoption Services, Inc.
786 East State Street
Sharon, PA 16146
Phone: (724) 346-4142
E-mail: cccas@infonline.net

Catholic Social Services
227 North Eighteenth Street
Philadelphia, PA 19103
Phone: (215) 854-7050
Fax: (215) 854-7100
E-mail: mmerman@chs-adphila.org
Web site: www.adoption-phl.org

Cherubs for Us
494 Regionald Lane
Collegeville, PA 19426
Phone: (610) 489-8590

Child and Home Study Associates, Inc.
1029 North Providence Road
Media, PA 19063
Phone: (610) 565-1544
Fax: (610) 565-1567
E-mail: chsadopt@aol.com

Web site: www.chsadoptions.org
– Intercountry Program
– Home Study

Child to Family Connections, Inc.
19394 Jamie Road
Saegertown, PA 16433
Phone: (814) 763-5826
Fax: (814) 763-2064

Children of the Light Mission, Inc.
5070 Parkside Avenue, Suite 1420
Philadelphia, PA 19131
Phone: (215) 473-5300

Children's Aid Society
1314 DeKalb Street
Norristown, PA 19401
Phone: (610) 279-2755
Fax: (610) 272-5447
Toll-Free: (800) 279-2756
E-mail: lgreen@childrensaid.net;
mphilips@childrensaid.net
Web site: www.childrensaid.net
– Intercountry Program
– Home Study

Children's Choice, Inc.
3948 West Branch Highway
Lewisburg, PA 17837
Phone: (570) 522-1030
Fax: (717) 230-9020
Toll-Free: (800) 355-1175
E-mail: cclewis@guidescape.net
Web site: www.childrenschoice.org

Children's Choice, Inc.
International Plaza II, Suite 325
Philadelphia, PA 19113
Phone: (215) 521-6270
Fax: (610) 521-6266
Toll-Free: (800) 355-1175
E-mail: chichoice@aol.com
Web site: www.childrenschoice.org

Children's Home Society of New Jersey, Inc.
771 North Pennsylvania Avenue
Morrisville, PA 19067
Phone: (215) 736-8550
Web site: www.chsofnj.org

Children's Home of Pittsburgh, Inc.
5618 Kentucky Ave
Pittsburgh, PA 15232
Phone: (412) 441-4884
Fax: (412) 441-0167

Children's Home of York, Inc.
77 Shoehouse Road
York, PA 17406
Phone: (717) 755-1033
Fax: (717) 840-3791
Web site: www.choyork.org

Children's Service Center of Wyoming Valley, Inc.
335 South Franklin Street
Wilkes-Barre, PA 18702
Phone: (570) 825-6425
Fax: (570) 829-3337
Toll-Free: (877) 433-5112
E-mail: cscwv@cscwv.org
Web site: www.cscwv.org

Children's Services, Inc.
1315 Walnut Street, 3rd Floor
Philadelphia, PA 19107-4769
Phone: (215) 546-3503
Fax: (215) 546-7977
E-mail: childphi@bellatlantic.net

Choices, Inc.
3526 Cottman Avenue
Philadelphia, PA 19149
Phone: (937) 264-0084
Fax: (937) 264-0095
E-mail: jan@choicesinc.net

Church of the Brethren Youth Services
1417 Oregon Road
Leola, PA 17540
Phone: (717) 656-6580
Fax: (717) 656-3056

E-mail: jenhostetter@cobys.net
Web site: www.cobys.net

Common Sense Adoption Services, Inc.
5021 East Trindle Road
Mechanicsburg, PA 17050-3622
Phone: (717) 766-6449
Fax: (717) 766-8015
Toll-Free: (800) 445-2444
E-mail: echick@csas-swan.org
Web site: www.csas-swan.org
– Intercountry Program
– Child Placement

Community Adoption Services of Heavenly Vision Ministries
6513 Meadow Street
Pittsburgh, PA 15206
Phone: (412) 661-4774

CONCERN
One West Main Street
Fleetwood, PA 19522
Phone: (610) 944-0445
Fax: (610) 944-1195
Web site: www.concern4kids.org

Council of Spanish Speaking Organization, Inc.
705-09 North Franklin Street
Philadelphia, PA 19123
Phone: (215) 627-3100
Fax: (215) 627-7440
Web site: www.elconcilio.net

Covenant Family Resources
743 Roy Road
King of Prussia, PA 19406
Phone: (610) 354-0555
E-mail: tburke@inti4.com

Crawford Care Management
22 East Union Street
Wilkes Barre, PA 18701
Phone: (570) 825-4482

Delta Community Supports, Inc.
2210 Mt. Carmel Avenue, Suite 105
Glenside, PA 19038
Phone: (215) 887-6300

Diakon Adoption Services
Diakon Lutheran Social Ministries
1 South Home Avenue
Topton, PA 19562-1317
Phone: (610) 682-1504
Fax: (610) 682-1582
Toll-Free: (888) 582-2230
E-mail: roachk@diakon.org
Web site: www.diakon.org/adoption

Eckels Adoption Agency, Inc.
994 Vallamont Drive
Williamsport, PA 17701
Phone: (570) 323-2520
Fax: (570) 323-2520
E-mail: eckels@chilitech.net

European Adoption Services, Inc.
7712 Dorcas Street
Philadelphia, PA 19111
Phone: (215) 942-4970

Every Child, Inc.
East Liberty Station
6401 Penn Avenue, Suite 300
Pittsburgh, PA 15206
Phone: (412) 421-8288
Fax: (412) 665-0755
E-mail: sdavus@everychildinc.org
Web site: www.everychildinc.org

Families Across Boundaries, Inc.
242 Hucklebarry Court
Wexford, PA 15090
Phone: (724) 940-0030
Fax: (412) 536-1290
E-mail: jourini1@marie.laroche.edu

Families Caring for Children, Inc.
96 Front Street
Nanticoke, PA 18634
Phone: (570) 735-9082
E-mail: jeanmbarn@aol.com

Families International
Adoption Agency, Inc.
P.O. Box 81964
1205 Farragut Street
Pittsburgh, PA 15206
Phone: (412) 362-6630
Web site: www.families-
international.com

Families United Network, Inc.
302 Brinton Avenue
Trafford, PA 15085
Phone: (412) 373-2353
E-mail: trafford@adelphia.net

Families United Network, Inc.
204-C Mumper Lane
Dillsburg, PA 17019
Phone: (717) 502-1576
Fax: (717) 367-3424
E-mail: fundburg@ptd.net

Families United Network, Inc.
406 South Angle Street
Mt. Joy, PA 17622
Phone: (717) 367-9798

Family Adoption Center
960 Penn Avenue, Suite 600
Pittsburgh, PA 15222
Phone: (412) 288-2138
Fax: (412) 288-9036
E-mail: adoption@fhcinc.org
Web site: www.fhcinc.org
– Intercountry Program
– Child Placement

Family Care Services, Inc.
4385 Edenville Road
Chambersburg, PA 15222
Phone: (717) 263-2285
E-mail: cruthrauff@familycarese
rvices.org

Family Hope Connection
– Jewish Family and Children's
Service, Inc.
5743 Bartlett Street
Pittsburgh, PA 15217
Phone: (412) 422-7200
Fax: (412) 422-1162

E-mail: fhcadopt@jfcspgh.org
Web site: www.fhcadopt.org

Family Pathways
316 North Main Street
Butler, PA 16001
Phone: (724) 284-9440

Family Service, Inc.
630 Janet Avenue
Lancaster, PA 17601
Phone: (717) 397-5241
E-mail: cgrill@fslancaster.org
Web site: www.fslancaster.org
– Intercountry Program
– Child Placement

Family Services and Children's
Aid Society of Venango County
716 East Second Street
Oil City, PA 16301
Phone: (814) 677-4005
Fax: (814) 677-6159
E-mail: Janet@usachoice.net

Family Services of Northwest-
ern Pennsylvania, Inc.
5100 Peach Street
Erie, PA 16509
Phone: (814) 866-4500
Fax: (814) 864-2677
E-mail: susanf@familyservices
erie.org
Web site: www.
familyserviceserie.org

Family Services of Western
Pennsylvania
3230 William Pitt Way
Pittsburgh, PA 15238
Phone: (412) 820-2050
Fax: (412) 820-2060
Toll-Free: (888) 222-4200
E-mail: fswp@fswp.org
Web site: www.fswp.org

First Steps International
Adoption, Inc.
RR 2 Box 38
Hawley, PA 18428
Phone: (570) 226-9186

Friends Association for the
Care and Protection of Children
P.O. Box 439
206 North Church Street
West Chester, PA 19381
Phone: (610) 431-3598
Fax: (610) 431-9768
Web site: www.friendsassoc.org

Friendship House, Inc.
1561 Medical Drive
Pottstown, PA 19464
Phone: (610) 327-2200
E-mail: fhpottstown@friendshiph
ousepa.org

Friendship House, Inc.
633 Rittenhouse Street, Suite C14
Philadelphia, PA 19144
Phone: (215) 438-6665
Fax: (215) 438-5320

Friendship House-Adoption,
Inc.
1509 Maple Street
Scranton, PA 18505
Phone: (570) 420-4577

Genesis of Pittsburgh, Inc.
185 Dakota Street
Pittsburgh, PA 15202
Phone: (412) 766-2693
E-mail: carole@genesispgh.org
Web site: http://trfn.clpgh.
org/genesis

Hempfield Counseling
Associates, Inc.
251 Wiconisco Street
Harrisburg, PA 17110
Phone: (717) 221-8004

ILB Adoption Agency, Inc.
734 Melbourne Street
Pittsburgh, PA 15217
Phone: (412) 521-2413

Institute for Human Resources
& Services, Inc.
Pierce Office Center
250 Pierce Street, Suite 301
Kingston, PA 18704

Phone: (570) 288-9386
Fax: (570) 288-9112

International adoption Center and Legal Aid Department
7401 Old York Road
Elkins Park, PA 19027
Phone: (215) 782-1191
Fax: (215) 782-1193
E-mail: director@adoptionlaw.org
Web site: www.adoptlaw.org

International Assistance Group, Inc.
531 Fifth Street
Oakmont, PA 15139
Phone: (412) 781-6470
Fax: (412) 828-5876
Toll-Free: (800) 720-7384
E-mail: info@iagadoptions.org
Web site: www.iagadoptions.org
– Intercountry Program
– Child Placement

International Families Adoption Agency
518 South 12th Street
Philadelphia, PA 19147
Phone: (215) 735-7171
Fax: (215) 545-3563
E-mail: intlfam@earthlink.net
Web site: www.4adoption.com
– Intercountry Program
– Child Placement

Jewish Family & Children's Service
10125 Veree Road, Suite 200
Philadelphia, PA 19116
Phone: (215) 698-9950
Fax: (215) 698-2148

Jewish Family Service
3333 North Front Street
Harrisburg, PA 17110
Phone: (717) 233-1681
Fax: (717) 234-8258

Jewish Family and Children's Service
5743 Barlett Street
Pittsburgh, PA 15217
Phone: (412) 428-7200
Fax: (412) 422-1162
E-mail: fhcadopt@jfcspgh.org
Web site: www.fhcadopt.org

Juvenile Justice Center, Inc.
100 West Coulter Street
Philadelphia, PA 19144
Phone: (215) 849-2112
Fax: (215) 849-0393
Web site: www.juvenilejustice.org

KidsPeace National Centers, Inc.
760 Corporate Circle,
Suite 600
New Cumberland, PA 17070
Phone: (717) 770-7364
Fax: (570) 271-1147
Toll-Free: (800) 854-3123
E-mail: admissions@kidspeace.org
Web site: www.kidspeace.org

KidsPeace National Centers, Inc.
1965 Lycoming Creek Road
Williamsport, PA 17701
Toll-Free: (800) 854-3123
E-mail: fostercare@kidspeace.org
Web site: www.kidspeace.org

KidsPeace National Centers, Inc.
930 Meadow Avenue
Scranton, PA 18505
Toll-Free: (800) 551-2235
E-mail: fostercare@kidspeace.org
Web site: www.kidspeace.org

La Vida International Adoption Agency, Inc.
150 South Warner Road, Suite 144
King of Prussia, PA 19406

Phone: (610) 688-8008
Fax: (610) 688-8028
E-mail: info@lavida.org
Web site: www.lavida.org
– Intercountry Program
– Child Placement

Living Hope Adoption Agency, Inc.
3205 Meetinghouse Road
Telford, PA 18969
Phone: (215) 721-8880
Toll-Free: (888) 886-8086
E-mail: information@livinghopeadoption.org
Web site: www.livinghopeadoption.org
– Intercountry Program
– Child Placement

Love the Children, Inc.
221 West Broad Street
Quakertown, PA 18951
Phone: (215) 536-4180
E-mail: cecelia@lovethechildren.com
Web site: www.lovethechildren.com
– Intercountry Program
– Child Placement

Lutheran Children & Family Services
1256 Easton Road
Roslyn, PA 19001
Phone: (215) 881-6800
Fax: (215) 884-3110
Toll-Free: (877) 700-5237
E-mail: kellim@lcfsinpa.org
Web site: www.lcfsinpa.org
– Intercountry Program
– Child Placement

Lutheran Home at Topton
1 South Home Avenue
Topton, PA 19562
Phone: (610) 682-1504
Fax: (610) 682-1582
Web site: www.diakon.org

Lutheran Service Society of Western Pennsylvania
1011 Old Salem Road, Suite 107
Greensburg, PA 15601
Phone: (724) 837-9385
Fax: (724) 836-5873
Web site: www.lsswpa.org

Madison Adoption Associates
2414 Blueball Avenue
Boothwyn, PA 19061
Phone: (215) 459-0454
Web site: www.
madisonadoption.org

Main Street Adoption Service, Inc.
620 Skyview Drive
York, PA 17402
Phone: (717) 845-4730
E-mail: info@mainstreet.com
Web site: www.
mainstreetadoption.com

Methodist Family Services of Philadelphia
4300 Monument Road
Philadelphia, PA 19131
Phone: (215) 877-1925
E-mail: cdunlap@methodist
services.org

Mountain Family Center for Human Services of PA, Inc.
449 Lincoln Highway East
Chambersburg, PA 17021
Phone: (717) 263-7295
E-mail: rpalmer@nhsonline.org

Muncy Program Office
276 Asher Manor Drive
Muncy, PA 17756
Phone: (570) 546-5165
E-mail: vickie@families4kids.org

New Beginnings Family and Children's Services
8 Pennsylvania Avenue
Matamoras, PA 18336
Phone: (516) 747-2204
Fax: (570) 491-2505
E-mail: newbeginn@aol.com

Web site: www.new-beginnings.
org

New Foundations, Inc.
1341 North Delaware Avenue
5th Street
Philadelphia, PA 19125
Phone: (215) 203-8733
Fax: (215) 203-8184
E-mail: jstover@nfi4kids.org

New Life Urban Ministries
712 Hawkins Avenue
Bradford, PA 15104
Phone: (412) 351-4077

Northeast Treatment Center
493 North 5th Street, Suite A
Philadelphia, PA 19123
Phone: (215) 574-9500

Northern Home for Children and Family Services
5301 Ridge Avenue
Philadelphia, PA 19128
Phone: (215) 482-1423
Fax: (215) 508-1114
E-mail: striumph@nhcfs.org

One Another Adoption Program
50 East Market Street
Hellam, PA 17406
Phone: (717) 600-2059
Fax: (717) 840-0014
E-mail: oneanotheradopt@
aol.com
– Intercountry Program
– Child Placement

Open Door Children and Youth Services, Inc.
606 Court Street, Suite 404
Reading, PA 19601
Phone: (610) 372-2200
E-mail: kids@opendoorcys.com
Web site: www.opendoorcys.com

PAACT
703 North Market Street
Liverpool, PA 17045
Phone: (717) 444-3629

PSI Services II, Inc.
714 Market Street, Suite 233
Philadelphia, PA 19106
Phone: (215) 238-5008
Fax: (215) 238-1944
E-mail: psiphilly@psifamilyserv
ices.com

PERL, Inc. for Families and Children (PERL/ Effective Resources and Linkages)
New Covenant Campus, Elders
Hall, Suite 104
7500 Germantown Avenue
Philadelphia, PA 19119
Phone: (215) 849-8072
Toll-Free: (877) 849-6600
E-mail: perl.inc@verizon.net
Web site: www.perlink.org

Pinebrook Services for Children & Youth, Inc.
402 North Fulton Street
Allentown, PA 18102-2002
Phone: (610) 432-3919
E-mail: childrenandyouth@
pinebrookservices.org
Web site: www.
pinebrookservices.org

Plan-It For Kids PC, Inc.
501 Main Street
Berlin, PA 15530
Phone: (814) 267-3182
Fax: (814) 267-4340
Toll-Free: (888) 810-5727
E-mail: carol@plan-itforkids.org
Web site: www.plan-itforkids.org
– Intercountry Program
– Child Placement

Presbyterian Children's Village
6517 Chester Avenue
Philadelphia, PA 19142
Phone: (215) 878-2480
E-mail: EBraham@pcv.org
Web site: www.pcv.org

Presbyterian Children's
Village Services
452 South Roberts Road
Rosemont, PA 19010
Phone: (610) 525-5400
E-mail: village@pcv.org
Web site: www.pcv.org

Pressley Ridge Adoption
Services
2611 Stayton Street
Pittsburgh, PA 15212-2759
Phone: (412) 442-4610
Fax: (412) 442-2958
E-mail: jd03@mail.pressleyridge.
org
Web site: www.pressleyridge.org

Professional Family Care
Services, Inc.
937 Menoher Boulevard
Johnstown, PA 15905
Phone: (814) 255-9559
E-mail: lpgruca@floodcity.net

Project Oz Adoptions, Inc.
378 Chestnut Street
Meadville, PA 16335
Phone: (814) 333-4201
Fax: (814) 333-8479
Toll-Free: (866) 236-7869
Web site: www.projectoz.com

Project STAR
6301 Northumberland Street
Pittsburgh, PA 15217
Phone: (412) 244-3066
E-mail: mze@the-institute.org
Web site: www.amazingkids.org

Project Star/Beaver County
2310 Seventh Avenue
Beaver Falls, PA 15010
Phone: (724) 847-2330

REJOICE, Inc.
2200 West Hamilton Street
Allentown, PA 18104
Phone: (610) 439-1990
Fax: (717) 221-0843
E-mail: rejoicekids@mindspring.
com

Rainbow Project
120 Charles Street
Pittsburgh, PA 15238
Phone: (412) 782-4457

Rejoice, Inc.
1800 State Street
Harrisburg, PA 17103-1551
Phone: (717) 221-0722

Salvation Army
344 North 7th Street
Allentown, PA 18102
Phone: (610) 821-7706
Fax: (610) 821-8121
E-mail: sacs@enter.net

Sanctuary House of
Chambersburg, Inc.
868 Lincoln Way West
Chambersburg, PA 17201
Phone: (717) 774-5865
E-mail: reneejc1958@innernet.net

Southern Latitudes Adoption
Services
1158 York Road
Warminster, PA 18974
Phone: (215) 343-8500
Fax: (215) 343-8517
E-mail: henrydeni@comcast.net
Web site: www.southernlatitude
sadoptions.com

Spectrum Family Network
Adoption Services
221 Penn Avenue
Pittsburgh, PA 15221
Phone: (412) 342-2300
E-mail:
hlipinski@spectrumfamily.net

St. Joseph's Center
2010 Adams Avenue
Scranton, PA 18509
Phone: (570) 342-8379
Fax: (570) 963-1298
Toll-Free: (800) 786-6346
E-mail: wecare@stjosephs
center.org
Web site: www.stjosephs
center.org

Tabor Children's Services, Inc.
601 New Britain Road
Doylestown, PA 18901-4248
Phone: (215) 348-4071
Fax: (215) 348-9261
Web site: www.tabor.org

Tabor Children's Services, Inc.
57 East Armat Street
Philadelphia, PA 18901
Phone: (215) 842-4800
Fax: (215) 348-9261
E-mail: aburrows@tabor.org
Web site: www.tabor.org

The International Center
Adoption Center
7401 Old York Road
Elkins Park, PA 19027

Three Rivers Adoption Coun-
cil/Black Adoption Services
307 4th Avenue, Suite 310
Pittsburgh, PA 15222
Phone: (412) 471-8722
Fax: (412) 471-4861
E-mail: beclement@3riversadopt.
org
Web site: www.3riversadopt.org
– Intercountry Program
– Child Placement

Three Rivers American Indian
Center
120 Charles Street
Pittsburgh, PA 15328
Phone: (412) 782-4457
Fax: (412) 767-4808
E-mail: mgold1008@aol.com

Transitions Adoption Agency,
Inc.
355 Lancaster Avenue
Haverford, PA 19041
Phone: (610) 642-4155
Fax: (610) 642-4187
E-mail: transadopt@att.net

Tressler Lutheran Services
960 Century Drive
Mechanicsburg, PA 17055
Phone: (717) 795-0300
Fax: (717) 852-8439

Try-Again Homes, Inc.
P.O. Box 1228
365 Jefferson Avenue
Washington, PA 15301
Phone: (724) 225-0510

Volunteers of America of Pennsylvania, Inc.
130 East Division Street
Wilkes-Barre, PA 18702
Phone: (570) 825-5261
E-mail: mandrews@voapa.org
Web site: www.voapa.org

Volunteers of America of Pennsylvania, Inc.
511 North Broad Street, Suite 501
Philadelphia, PA 19123
Phone: (215) 925-2620
E-mail: mandrews@voapa.org
Web site: www.voapa.org

Welcome House Adoption Program (of Pearl S. Buck International)
520 Dublin Road
Perksaie, PA 18944-3000
Phone: (215) 249-0100
Fax: (215) 249-9657
Toll-Free: (800) 220-2825
E-mail: info@pearl-s-buck.org
Web site: www.pearlsbuck.org
– Intercountry Program
– Child Placement

Welcome House Adoption Program (of Pearl S. Buck International)
2912 Talley Carey Road
Allison Park, PA 15101
Phone: (412) 492-8730
Fax: (412) 492-8731
E-mail: cparkhill@pearl-s-buck.org
– Intercountry Program
– Child Placement

Women's Christian Alliance, Inc.
1722-42 Cecil B. Moore Avenue
Philadelphia, PA 19121-3405
Phone: (215) 236-9911

Fax: (215) 236-9808
Web site: www.wcafamily.org

Youth Services, Inc.
410 North 34th Street
Philadelphia, PA 19104
Phone: (215) 222-3262
E-mail: info@ysiphila.org
Web site: www.ysiphila.org

Pennsylvania Adoption Exchange (PAE)
99 South Cameron Street
P.O. Box 1443
Harrisburg, PA 17105-1443
Phone: (717) 772-7011
Fax: (717) 214-3784
Toll-Free: (800) 227-0225
E-mail: klollo@state.pa.us
Web site: www.adoptpakids.org

Statewide Adoption Network's (SWAN) Prime Contractor
99 South Cameron Street
P.O. Box 1443
Harrisburg, PA 17105-1443
Phone: (717) 236-8490
Fax: (717) 236-8510
Toll-Free: (888) 793-2512
E-mail: information@diakon-swan.org
Web site: www.diakon-swan.org

State Adoption Specialist/Manager/ Foster Care Specialist

Pennsylvania Department of Public Welfare
Cathy Utz
P.O. Box 2675
7th and Forster Streets
Harrisburg, PA 17105-2675
Phone: (717) 705-2912
Fax: (717) 705-0364
E-mail: cutz@state.pa.us
Web site: www.dpw.state.pa.us/
Child/AdoptionFosterCare/0036
70363.htm

State Interstate Compact on the Placement of Children (ICPC) Administrator

Pennsylvania Department of Public Welfare
P.O. Box 2675
Harrisburg, PA 17105-2675
Phone: (717) 772-7016
E-mail: warlewis@state.pa.us

State Licensing Specialist

Pennsylvania Department of Public Welfare
Kimberly Hunter
P.O. Box 2675
Harrisburg, PA 17105-2675
Phone: (717) 705-2908
Fax: (717) 705-0364
E-mail: kihunter@state.pa.us
Web site: www.dpw.state.pa.us/
adoptakids/paeagencylist2.asp

State Reunion Registry

Adoption Medical History Registry
99 South Cameron Street
P.O. Box 1141
Harrisburg, PA 17105-1441
Phone: (717) 772-7011
Toll-Free: (800) 227-0225
E-mail: klollo@state.pa.us
Web site: www.dpw.state.pa.us/
adoptpakids/paemedicalhist.asp

Training

National Adoption Center
1500 Walnut Street, Suite 701
Philadelphia, PA 19102
Toll-Free: (800) TO-ADOPT
E-mail: nac@nationaladoption
center.org
Web site: www.
nationaladoptioncenter.org

Birth Families and Support Groups

Adoption Forum, Inc.
P.O. Box 814
Emmaus, PA 18049
Phone: (215) 238-1116
E-mail: infor@adoptionforum.org

Adoption Healing, Family Services of Western Pennsylvania
6401 Penn Avenue,
2nd Floor
Pittsburgh, PA 15206
Phone: (412) 661-1670
Fax: (412) 661-1820
E-mail: trunzoa@fswp.org

Berks County Branch of
Adoption Forum
21 Northridge Drive West
Mohnton, PA 19540-1239
Phone: (610) 777-9742

Bucks County Chapter of
Adoption Forum and PACFOA
20 Runnemede V2
New Hope, PA 18938
Phone: (215) 862-2695
E-mail: Alovett215@aol.com

Lost Loved Ones
621 W. Crawford Street
Edensburg, PA 115931
Phone: (814) 472-7525

Open Line Adoption Connection
817 East Third Street
Oil City, PA 16301
Phone: (814) 677-7850

Origins
Box 1032
Hawley, PA 18428
Phone: (717) 775-9729

PA Adoption Connection of
Western PA
898 High Point Road
Fort Hill, PA 15540
Phone: (814) 395-3938
E-mail: Gshay@aol.com

Parents/Adoptees Support
Together (PAST)
8130 Hawthorne Drive
Erie, PA 16509
Phone: (814) 899-1493
E-mail: BHAKEL@aol.com

PUERTO RICO

Adoptive/Foster Family Support Groups

Grupo de Padres Adoptivos de
Caguas and North American
Council on Adoptable Children
Representative
P.O. Box 6523
Caguas, PR 00926
Phone: (787) 258-0195

Attorney Referral Service

Puerto Rico Bar Association
P.O. Box 1900
San Juan, PR 00902
Phone: (787) 721-3358
Fax: (787) 725-0330

Licensed Private Adoption Agencies

Adoption Service of the
Caribbean, Inc.
Colinas Alturas de Mayaguez
Calle Cerro La Santa No. 2046
Mayaguez, PR 00680
Phone: (787) 265-8707

Hogar Cuna San Cristobal
P.O. Box 9407
Caguas, PR 00726
Phone: (787) 747-9488

Regional/District Public Agencies

Puerto Rico Department
of the Families
P.O. Box 15091
San Juan, PR 00912
Phone: (787) 724-0771
Fax: (787) 724-0767

State Adoption Specialist/Manager

Puerto Rico Administration
of Children and Families
Elizabeth Diaz-Rivera
P.O. Box 194090
San Juan, PR 00959-4090
Phone: (787) 724-5030
Fax: (787) 721-2245
E-mail: cnazario@yahoo.com

State Foster Care Specialist/Manager

Puerto Rico Administration
for Children and Families
Ines B. Lajara
P.O. Box 15091
San Juan, PR 00902
Phone: (787) 725-5443
Fax: (787) 725-0051

State Licensing Specialist

Puerto Rico Department of the
Families
Hon. Angie Varela Llavon
P.O. Box 11398
Santurce, PR 00910
Phone: (787) 723-1223
Fax: (787) 723-1223

RHODE ISLAND

Adoptive/Foster Family Support Groups

AFT/Parents Support Network
of Rhode Island
400 Warwick Avenue, Suite 12
Warwick, RI 02888
Phone: (401) 461-6855
E-mail: cathyciano@aol.com

Adoption Rhode Island and North American Council on Adoptable Children Representative
500 Prospect Street
Pawtucket, RI 02860
Phone: (401) 724-1910
Fax: (401) 724-1910
E-mail: adoptionri@ids.net
Web site: www.adoptionri.org

Adoptive Families in Action
P.O. Box 20008
Cranston, RI 02920
Phone: (401) 944-2342
E-mail: adoptivefamilies@juno.com
Web site: http://groups.yahoo.com/group/AFiA

Children's Friends and Service – ASAP Program
153 Summer Street
Providence, RI 02903
Phone: (401) 331-2900
Fax: (401) 331-3285
Web site: www.cfsri.org

Cindy Simpson
277 High Street
Westerly, RI 02891
Phone: (401) 348-3010
Fax: (401) 724-9443
E-mail: cynsimp@att.net
Web site: www.adoptionri.org

Foster and Adoptive Families of Rhode Island
P.O. Box 629
West Kingston, RI 02892
Phone: (401) 783-5864

Jewish Family Services Adoptive Parent Support Group
229 Waterman Street
Providence, RI 02906
Phone: (401) 331-1244
Fax: (401) 331-5772
E-mail: johnjfs@conversent.net

Stars of David International, Inc.
Providence Chapter
33 Edward Avenue
Rumford, RI 02916-3304
Phone: (401) 431-0728
E-mail: starsdavid@aol.com
Web site: www.starsofdavid.org

Licensed Private Adoption Agencies

Adoption Network, Ltd.
P.O. Box 195
Wakefield, RI 02880-0195
Phone: (401) 788-9118
Toll-Free: (800) 285-0450
Web site: www.adoptionnetworkltd.com

Children's Friend and Service
153 Summer Street
Providence, RI 02903
Phone: (401) 331-2900
Web site: www.childresnfriendsri.org

Communities for People
221 Waterman Street
Providence, RI 02906
Phone: (401) 273-7103

Gift of Life, Inc.
1053 Park Avenue
Cranston, RI 02910
Phone: (401) 943-6484
Fax: (401) 943-6806
Web site: www.giftoflife.cc
– Intercountry Program
– Child Placement

International Adoptions, Inc.
726 Front Street
Woonsocket, RI 02895
Phone: (401) 767-2300

Jewish Family Services/ Adoption Options
229 Waterman Street
Providence, RI 02906
Phone: (401) 331-5437
E-mail: jfs@conversent.net

Links to Adoption
P.O. Box 4824
Rumford, RI 02914
Phone: (401) 434-1353

Little Treasures Adoption Services
P.O. Box 255
Cranston, RI 02920
Phone: (401) 822-4735
Fax: (401) 826-8574
Web site: www.littletreasuresadopt.org
– Intercountry Program
– Child Placement

Lutheran Social Services
Rhode Island Adoption Program
116 Rolfe Street
Cranston, RI 02910
Phone: (401) 785-0015
Fax: (401) 785-0599
Toll-Free: (800) 286-9889
E-mail: LSSRIAdopt@aol.com
Web site: www.adoptlss.org
– Intercountry Program
– Child Placement

Urban League of Rhode Island, Inc.
Minority Recruitment and Child Placement Program
246 Prairie Avenue
Providence, RI 02905
Phone: (401) 351-5000

Birth Family and Search Support Groups

Yesterday's Children
77 Homer Street
Providence, RI 02903

State Adoption Exchange/ Photolisting of Children Waiting For Adoption

Adopt Rhode Island
500 Prospect Street
Pawtucket, RI 02860
Phone: (401) 724-1910
E-mail: adoptionri@ids.net
Web site: www.adoptionri.org

State Adoption Specialist/Manager

Rhode Island Department of Children, Youth and Families
Maureen Robbins
101 Friendship Street, 3rd Floor
Providence, RI 02903
Phone: (401) 528-3799
Fax: (401) 528-3870
E-mail: maureen.robbins@dcyf.ri.gov
Web site: www.dcyf.or.gov/adoption.htm

State Foster Care Specialist/Manager

Rhode Island Department of Children, Youth and Families
Lee Sperduti
101 Friendship Street, 4th Floor
Providence, RI 02903
Phone: (401) 528-3605
Fax: (401) 528-3650
E-mail: lee.sperduti@dcyf.ri.gov
Web site: www.dcyf.ri.gov/foster.htm

State Interstate Compact on the Placement of Children (ICPC) Administrator

Rhode Island Department of Children, Youth and Families
530 Wood Street
Bristol, RI 02809
Phone: (401) 254-7077
Fax: (401) 254-7099
E-mail: Everett.thornton.@dcyf.ri.gov

State Licensing Specialist

Rhode Island Department for Children, Youth and Families
Lee Ann Sperduti
101 Friendship Street
Providence, RI 02903
Phone: (401) 528-3605
Fax: (401) 528-3950
E-mail: sperdul@dcyf.state.ri.us
Web site: www.dcyf.state.ri.us

State Reunion Registry

State of Rhode Island and Providence Plantations
Family Court, Juvenile Division
One Dorrance Plaza
Providence, RI 02903
Phone: (401) 458-3290

State Complaints Office

Office of the Child Advocate
272 West Exchange Street, Suite 301
Providence, RI 02903
Phone: (401) 222-6650

SOUTH CAROLINA

Adoptive/Foster Family Support Groups

Anderson County Foster Parent Association
1415 Hilltop Drive
Anderson, SC 29621
Phone: (864) 226-0122
After hours: (864) 226-0122
E-mail: dmagaha@anmed.com

Berkeley County Foster/Adoptive Parents Association
411 Rick Way
Bonneau, SC 29431
Phone: (843) 565-3855
Fax: (843) 565-4944
E-mail: gaskinse@homexpressway.net
– Information/Referral

Carl Brown
124 Gleen Jacobs Road
Elgin, SC 29045
Phone: (803) 865-2020

Center for Child and Family Studies
Post-Legal Adoption Education and Training
University of South Carolina
Columbia, SC 29208
Phone: (803) 777-9408

Children Unlimited of Family Service Center
1825 Gadsden Street
Columbia, SC 29201
Fax: (803) 765-0284
Toll-Free: (800) 822-0877
E-mail: info@children-unlimited.org
Web site: www.children-umlimited.org

Dillion County Foster Parents Association
P.O. Box 1135
Lake View, SC 29563
Phone: (803) 759-9913

Fairfield County Foster Parents Association
545 Bundrick Road
Winnsboro, SC 29180
Phone: (803) 635-5594
Fax: (803) 635-1721
After hours: (803) 635-3939

Hampton County Foster Parents Association
P.O. Box 1366
Varnville, SC 29924
Phone: (803) 943-9191
Fax: (803) 943-9191
After hours: (803) 943-3614
E-mail: marymorris39@hotmail.com

Horry County Foster Parents Association
8872 Spring Branch Road
Nichols, SC 29581
Phone: (843) 692-1901
After hours: (843) 392-3968
E-mail: Michael.Stewart3@hcahealthcare.com

Kershaw County Foster Parents Association
50 Nature Lane
Elgin, SC 29045
Phone: (803) 408-0686
E-mail: kcfpa2001@yahoo.com

SEE US
P.O. Box 1453
Greenville, SC 29602-1453
Phone: (864) 269-9324

Single Adoptive Parents of South Carolina
P.O. Box 417
Norway, SC 29113-0417
Phone: (803) 263-4502
E-mail: jaykirk@earthlink.net

South Carolina Council on Adoptable Children
2005 Hampton Street, Suite F
Columbia, SC 29204
Phone: (803) 865-1949
Fax: (803) 256-2767
E-mail: schildren@sc.rr.com

South Carolina Foster/ Adoptive Parent Association
P.O. Box 39
Elgin, SC 29045
Phone: (803) 865-2020
Fax: (803) 865-2020
After hours: (803) 788-1149
E-mail: cbrown39@aol.com

Licensed Private Adoption Agencies

A Chosen Child Adoption Services
975 Bacons Bridge Road, Suite 148
Summerville, SC 29485
Phone: (843) 851-4004
Fax: (843) 851-4004
E-mail: AChosenChild@sc.rr.com
Web site: www.
ACCAdoptionServices.com
– Intercountry Program
– Child Placement

A Vision of Hope Adoption Agency
1797 Blue Ridge Boulevard
Seneca, SC 29672
Phone: (864) 882-8835

A Loving Choice International, Inc.
209 North Main Street, #103
Greenville, SC 29601
Phone: (864) 235-7221
E-mail: brendabakeradopt@aol.com
Web site: www.alovingchoiceinternational.org
– Intercountry Program
– Child Placement

A Vision of Hope Adoption Agency
1797 Blue Ridge Boulevard
Seneca, SC 29672
Phone: (864) 882-8835

Adoption Advocacy
150 Executive Center
P.O. Box 110
Greenville, SC 29615
Phone: (864) 329-8587
– Home Study Services
– Supervision for Domestic/ International and Special Needs Children

Adoption Center of South Carolina
P.O. Box 5961
Columbia, SC 29250
Phone: (803) 771-2272

All Kids are Special
905 Hayne Avenue
Aiken, SC 29801
Phone: (803) 641-4614

Bethany Christian Services
2141 B Hoffmeyer Road
Florence, SC 29501-4077
Phone: (843) 629-1177
Fax: (843) 629-1177
Toll-Free: (800) 922-0682

E-mail: bcsflorence@bethany.org
Web site: www.bethany.org
– Intercountry Program
– Child Placement

Bethany Christian Services
414 Center Street
West Columbia, SC 29169
Phone: (803) 796-9332
Fax: (803) 796-2992
Toll-Free: (800) 922-0682
E-mail: bcscolumbia@bethany.org
Web site: www.bethany.org

Bethany Christian Services
4605-C Oleander Drive
Myrtle Beach, SC 29577
Phone: (843) 839-5433
Fax: (843) 903-2629
Toll-Free: (800) 922-0682
E-mail: bcsmyrtlebch@bethany.org
Web site: www.bethany.org
– Intercountry Program
– Child Placement

Bethany Christian Services
620 East Washington Street
Greenville, SC 29601-2995
Phone: (864) 235-2273
Fax: (864) 233-6641
Toll-Free: (800) 922-0682
E-mail: bcsgreenville@bethany.org
Web site: www.bethany.org
– Intercountry Program
– Child Placement

Carolina Adoption Services
106 Chadwick Drive
Charleston, SC 29407
Phone: (843) 766-1120
Fax: (843) 766-0341
E-mail: mail@jsommers.com

Carolina Hope Christian Adoption, Inc.
819 E. North Street
Greenville, SC 29601
Phone: (864) 268-0570
Fax: (864) 370-0036
E-mail: cadopt@aol.com

Web site: www.
carolinahopeadoption.org
– Intercountry Program
– Child Placement

Catholic Charities Diocese of Charleston
1662 Ingram Road
Charleston, SC 29407
Phone: (843) 402-9115
Web site: www.catholiccharities.
org

Child of the Heart
1156 Bowman Road, Suite 200
Mt. Pleasant, SC 29464
Phone: (803) 881-2973
Fax: (843) 416-1097
– Intercountry Program
– Child Placement

Children Unlimited, Inc.
1825 Gadsden Street
Columbia, SC 29201
Phone: (803) 799-8311
Fax: (803) 765-0284
Toll-Free: (800) 822-0877
E-mail: info@children-unlimited.
org
Web site: www.children-
unlimited.org

Christian Family Services, Inc.
2166 Gold Hill Road
Fort Mill, SC 29708-9351
Phone: (803) 548-6030
Fax: (803) 547-3291
Toll-Free: (800) 489-6030
E-mail: christianfam@comporium.
net
Web site: www.
christianfamilyservices.org

Christian World Adoption, Inc.
111 Ashley Avenue
Charleston, SC 29401
Phone: (843) 722-6343
Fax: (803) 722-1616
Web site: www.cwa.org
– Intercountry Program
– Child Placement

Epworth Children's Home
P.O. Box 50466
2900 Millwood Avenue
Columbia, SC 29250
Phone: (803) 256-7394
Fax: (803) 212-4798
Web site: www.
epworthchildrenshome.org

Lutheran Family Services in the Carolinas
1440 Broad River Road
Columbia, SC 29210
Phone: (803) 622-0470
E-mail: dbuchman@sc.rr.com
Web site: www.lfscarolinas.org

Reid House
169 Saint Phillip Street
Charleston, SC 29413
Phone: (843) 723-7138
Fax: (843) 722-8797
Toll-Free: (888) 651-3240
E-mail: ariley@reid-house.com
Web site: www.reid-house.com

Small World Ministries, Inc.
349 Blake Dairy Road
Belton, SC 29527
Phone: (864) 338-4673

Southeastern Children's Home, Inc.
155 Children's Way
Duncan, SC 29334
Phone: (803) 439-0259

Special Link
1201 Haywood Road
Greenville, SC 29615
Phone: (864) 233-4872
Fax: (864) 233-0903
E-mail: speclink@infionline.net
Web site: www.special-link.org

Worldwide Adoption Services
187 North Church Street, Suite 436
Spartanburg, SC 29304
Phone: (864) 583-6981
Fax: (864) 583-0150
E-mail: info@worldwideadoption.
org

Web site: www.worldwide
adoption.org
– Intercountry Program
– Child Placement

Birth Family and Search Support Groups

A.A.L.M Triad
1725 Atascadero Drive
Columbia, SC 29206
Phone: (803) 787-3778

Adoptees and Birthparents in Search
8137 Ramsgate Road
North Charleston, SC 29406

Adoption Search for Life
303 Brighton Road
Anderson, SC 29621
Phone: (864) 287-4328

Adoption and Family Reunion Center
P.O. Box 103
Pacolet, SC 29373

Circles
5842 Ellisor Street
Columbia, SC 29212
Phone: (808) 407-1900
E-mail: circles@sc.rr.com

State Adoption Exchange/ Photolisting of Children Waiting For Adoption

Linking Children with Families
P.O. Box 1520
Columbia, SC 29202-1520
Toll-Free: (888) 227-3487
Web site: www.state.sc.us/dss/
adoption/intro.htm

Southeastern Exchange of the United States SEEUS
P.O. Box 1453
Greenville, SC 29602-1453
Phone: (864) 242-0460
Fax: (864) 242-8176
Web site: www.sc-adopt.org/
seeus/

State Adoption Specialist/Manager

South Carolina Department of
Social Services
Carolyn Orf
1535 Confederate Avenue
Columbia, SC 29202
Phone: (803) 898-7707
Fax: (803) 898-7792
Toll-Free: (800) 922-2504
E-mail: corf@dss.state.sc.us
Web site: www.state.sc.us/dss/
adoption/index.html

South Carolina Division of
Human Services
Human Services/Foster
Care-Adoption
Carolyn Orf
1535 Confederate Avenue
Columbia, SC 29201
Phone: (803) 898-7707
Fax: (803) 898-7792
E-mail: corf@dss.state.sc.us
Web site: www.state.sc.us/dss/
foster/index.html

State Interstate Compact on the Placement of Children (ICPC) Administrator

South Carolina Department of
Social Services
P.O. Box 1520
Columbia, SC 29202-1520
Phone: (803) 898-7360
E-mail: Mwilliams1@dss.state.
sc.us

State Reunion Registry

Adoption Reunion Registry
South Carolina Department of
Social Services
P.O. Box 1520
Columbia, SC 29202-1520
Phone: (803) 898-7570
Toll-Free: (800) 922-2504

State Adoption Exchange

Southeastern Exchange of the
United States
P.O. Box 1453
Greenville, SC 29202-1453
Phone: (864) 242-0460
Fax: (864) 242-8176
Web site: www.sc-adopt.org/
seeus/

State Photolisting of Children Waiting for Adoption

Linking Children with Families
2005 Hampton Street, Suite F
Columbia, SC 29204
Toll-Free: (888) 227-3487
E-mail: Gail-coac@sc.rr.com
Web site: www.sc-adoptorg/
intropics/htm

SOUTH DAKOTA

Adoptive/Foster Family Support Groups

Adoptive Family Connection of
South Dakota
P.O. Box 1749
Sioux Falls, SD 57101
Phone: (605) 334-6004
Fax: (605) 335-2776
Web site: www.adoptionsupport-
sd.org

Families Through Adoption
Box 90148
Sioux Falls, SD 57109
Phone: (605) 371-1404

Family Support Online
P.O. Box 1749
Sioux Falls, SD 57101
Phone: (605) 335-2776
E-mail: hines@chssd.org
Web site: www.chssd.org

Parents of Adopted Children
40559 273rd Street
Parkston, SD 57366

Phone: (605) 782-0782
E-mail: colleen.globke@k12sd.us
Web site: www.pacsd.org

Licensed Private Adoption Agencies

Bethany Christian Services,
Inc.
625 South Minnesota Avenue,
Suite 103
Sioux Falls, SD 57104
Phone: (605) 336-6999
Fax: (605) 330-0820
E-mail: bcssiouxfalls@bethany.org
Web site: www.bethany.org

Bethany Christian Services,
Inc.
2525 West Main Street, #309
Rapid City, SD 57702-2443
Phone: (605) 343-7196
Web site: www.bethany.org

Catholic Family Services, Inc.
Catholic Diocese of Sioux Falls
523 North Duluth Avenue
Sioux Falls, SD 57104-2714
Phone: (605) 988-3775
Fax: (605) 988-3747
Toll-Free: (800) 700-7867
E-mail: hvdbrink@sfcatholic.org
Web site: www.diocese-of-sioux-
falls.org

Catholic Family Services, Inc.
310 15th Avenue NE
Aberdeen, SD 57404
Phone: (605) 226-1304

Catholic Social Services
918 Fifth Street
Rapid City, SD 57701-3798
Phone: (605) 348-6086
E-mail: css@rapidnet.com
Web site: www.catholic-social-
services.net

Child Protection Program
P.O. Box 509
Agency Village, SD 57262-9802
Phone: (605) 698-3992

Children's Home Society
P.O. Box 1749
Sioux Falls, SD 57101-1749
Phone: (605) 334-3431

LDS Family Services, Inc.
2525 West Main Street, Suite 310
Rapid City, SD 57702-2443
Phone: (605) 342-3500
E-mail: jklinge@lsssd.org
Web site: www.lsssd.org

Lutheran Social Services of South Dakota
600 West 12th Street
Sioux Falls, SD 57104
Phone: (605) 336-3347
Fax: (605) 336-9141
E-mail: jklinge@lsssd.org
Web site: www.lsssd.org

Lutheran Social Services, Inc.
705 East 41st Street, Suite 200
Sioux Falls, SD 57105-6048
Phone: (605) 357-0100
Fax: (605) 357-0140
Toll-Free: (800) 568-2401

Lutheran Social Services, Inc.
1424 9th Avenue SE, Suite 7
Watertown, SD 57201
Phone: (605) 882-2740

New Horizons Adoption Agency
510 West 10th Street
Sioux Falls, SD 57104-3619
Phone: (605) 332-0310
E-mail: nhaa@means.net
Web site: www.nhadoptionagency.com
– Intercountry Program
– Child Placement

Sisseton Wahpeton Dakota Nation
P.O. Box 509
Agency Village, SD 57262
Phone: (605) 698-3992

Yankton Sioux Tribal Social Services
P.O. Box 248
Marty, SD 57361-0248
Phone: (605) 384-3804

Birth Family and Search Support Groups

Concerned United Birth parents (CUB)
41004 259 Street
Mitchell, SD 57301
Phone: (605) 966-6691
Web site: www.cubirthparents.org

State Adoption Exchange/ Photolisting of Children Waiting For Adoption

South Dakota's Waiting Children
700 Governor's Drive
Kneip Building
Pierre, SD 87501-2291
Phone: (605) 773-3227
E-mail: cps@dss.state.sd.us
Web site: www.state.sd.us/social/cps/Adoption/Children/htm

State Adoption Specialist/Manager

South Dakota Department of Social Services
Patricia Reiss
700 Governor's Drive
Richard F. Kneip Building
Pierre, SD 57501-2291
Phone: (605) 773-3227
Fax: (605) 773-6834
E-mail: patricia.reiss@state.sd.us
Web site: www.state.sd.us/social/cps/adoption/index.htm

State Foster Care Specialist/Manager

South Dakota Department of Social Services
Child Protection Services
Duane E. Jenner
700 Governors Drive
Kneip Building
Pierre, SD 57501-2291
Phone: (605) 773-3227
Fax: (605) 773-6834
E-mail: duane.jenner@state.sd.us
Web site: www.state.sd.us/social/cps/Fostercare/process/htm

State Interstate Compact on the Placement of Children (ICPC) Administrator

South Dakota Department of Social Services
Child Protection Services
Kneip Building
700 Governor's Drive
Pierre, SD 57501-2291
Phone: (605) 773-3227
Fax: (605) 773-6834
E-mail: Virgena.Wieselen@state.sd.us

State Licensing Specialist

South Dakota Department of Social Services
Child Protection Services
David Hanson
700 Governor's Drive
Kneip Building
Pierre, SD 57501-2291
Phone: (605) 773-3227
Fax: (605) 773-6834
E-mail: david.hanson@state.sd.us
Web site: www.state.sd.us/social/cps/services/licensing.htm

TENNESSEE

Adoptive/Foster Family Support Groups

Carroll County Foster Parents Association
40 Foust Lane
Hollow Rock, TN 38242
Phone: (731) 986-5316
E-mail: bettyh@aencas.net

Council on Adoptable Children and North American Council on Adoptable Children State Representative
7630 Luscomb Drive
Knoxville, TN 37919
Phone: (423) 693-8001

Inter-National Adoption Alliance
PMB 154
2441 Q Old Fort Parkway
Murfreesboro, TN 37128
Phone: (615) 890-3507
Fax: (615) 890-3507
E-mail: Interadopt@comcast.net
Web site: www.i-a-a.org

Johnson County Foster Adoptive Care Association
399 Mill Creek Road
Mountain City, TN 37683
Phone: (423) 727-4925
E-mail: patsy.napier@state.tn.us

Knoxville Council on Adoptable Children
1818 Andy Halt Drive
Knoxville, TN 37916
Phone: (865) 693-3053
Fax: (865) 974-2000
E-mail: jvdwiele@utk.edu

Mid-South Families Through Adoption
6151 Ashley Road
Arlington, TN 38002

Moms Alive
216 Oakdale Drive
White House, TN 37188
Phone: (615) 672-3011

Mountain Region Adoption Support Group
4428 Fieldstone Drive
Kingsport, TN 37664
Phone: (423) 523-7206

North American Council on Adoptable Children Representative
27 Windhaven Lane
Oak Ridge, TN 37830
Phone: (423) 482-5264

Ours of Middle Tennessee
3557 Bethlehem Road
Springfield, TN 37172
Phone: (615) 643-3426

Parents By Choice
843 West Raines Road
Memphis, TN 38126
Phone: (901) 289-9627
Phone: (901) 789-4722
Fax: (901) 789-9376
E-mail: roberta_wilburn@loc.edu

Licensed Private Adoption Agencies

A Child's Dream
1346 Quai Valley Trail
Apison, TN 37302-9533
Phone: (423) 236-4509
Fax: (423) 236-4546
E-mail: GKWOLFER@aol.com
Web site: www.AChildsDream.org

Adoption Consultants In Tennessee, Inc.
8921 Shallowford Road
Knoxville, TN 37923
Phone: (865) 769-9441
Fax: (865) 769-9442

Adoption Counseling Services
2185 Wickersham Lane
Germantown, TN 38139
Phone: (901) 753-9089
E-mail: ESRardin@aol.com
Web site: www.adoptionandyou.com

Adoption Home Studies and Social Services
909 Oak Street
Chattanooga, TN 37403
Phone: (423) 802-6367
Fax: (423) 266-8707

Adoption Place, Inc.
505 Oak Forest Circle
Antioch, TN 37013
Phone: (615) 399-2841

Adoption Promises
P.O. Box 253
Huntingdon, TN 38344
Phone: (731) 986-2001
Fax: (731) 989-2971
E-mail: joanne@adoptionpromises.com
Web site: www.adoptionpromises.com

Associated Catholic Charities of East Tennessee, Inc.
119 Dameron Avenue
Knoxville, TN 37917
Phone: (423) 971-3560
Fax: (423) 971-3575

Associated Catholic Charities of the Diocese of Memphis, TN, Inc.
3060 Baskin Street
Memphis, TN 38127-7799
Phone: (901) 354-6300
Fax: (901) 354-6343
Web site: www.cathchar.org

Association for Guidance, Aid, Placement and Empathy (AGAPE)
4555 Trousdale Drive
Nashville, TN 37204-4513

Phone: (615) 781-3000
E-mail: jrister@agapenashville.org

**Association for Guidance,
Aid, Placement and Empathy
(AGAPE) Child and Family
Services**
P.O. Box 11411
111 Racine Street
Memphis, TN 38111
Phone: (901) 323-3600
Fax: (901) 323-3640
Web site: www.agapemeanslove.
org

Bethany Christian Services
400 South Germantown Road
Chattanooga, TN 37411
Phone: (423) 622-7360
Fax: (423) 622-9085
Toll-Free: (800) 765-7335
E-mail: bcschattanooga@
bethany.org
Web site: www.bethany.org/
chattanooga/

Bethany Christian Services
Mid-South Christian Services
1044 Brookfield Road, Suite 102
Memphis, TN 38119
Phone: (901) 818-9996
Fax: (901) 761-9350
Toll-Free: (800) 972-8887
E-mail: dbrower@bethany.org
Web site: www.bethany.org

Bethany Christian Services
5816 Kingston Pike
Knoxville, TN 37919-6341
Phone: (865) 588-5283
Toll-Free: (800) 765-7335
E-mail: bcsknoxville@bethany.
org
Web site: www.bethany.org/
knoxville

**Catholic Charities of East
Tennessee**
119 Dameron Avenue
Knoxville, TN 37917
Phone: (865) 524-9896

Fax: (865) 971-3575
Toll-Free: (877) 990-4673
E-mail: sandi@etcatholiccharit
ies.com
Web site: www.cctenn.org

**Catholic Charities of
Tennessee**
30 White Bridge Road
Nashville, TN 37205
Phone: (615) 352-3087
Fax: (615) 352-8591
E-mail: dthomas1@cctenn.org
Web site: www.cctenn.org

**Chattanooga Family Service
Center**
6314 East Brainerd Road
Chattanooga, TN 37421-3999
Phone: (423) 855-4682
Fax: (432) 517-0021

Child and Family Services, Inc.
901 East Summit Hill Drive
Knoxville, TN 37915
Phone: (423) 524-7483
Fax: (865) 524-4790
Web site: www.child-family.org

Child and Family Services, Inc.
201 North Royal Street, Suite B
Jackson, TN 38301-3661
Phone: (615) 422-1107
Fax: (615) 422-2191
E-mail: cfs@aeneas.net

Children's Hope International
7003 Chadwick Drive, Suite 350
Brentwood, TN 37027
Phone: (615) 309-8109
Fax: (615) 309-8483
E-mail: Brenda@childrens
HopeInt.org
Web site: www.
childrensHopeInt.org

**Christian Children's Home of
Tennessee**
9399 Middlebrooke Pike
P.O. Box 30492
Knoxville, TN 37930-0492

Phone: (865) 357-7949
Fax: (865) 357-5218
E-mail: cchtknox@knology.net

**Christian Children's Homes of
Tennessee**
Main Office
P.O. Box 285
2600 State Line Road
Elizabethton, TN 37644-0285
Phone: (423) 542-4245
Fax: (423) 542-4369
E-mail: cchtn@chartertn.net
Web site: www.cch-tn.org

**Church of God Home for
Children**
P.O. Box 4391
449 McCarn Circle
Sevierville, TN 37864
Phone: (423) 453-4644
Fax: (423) 453-8812

Crossroads Counseling Center
620 West 5th Street
Morristown, TN 37814
Phone: (423) 581-5342
Fax: (423) 581-8650

**Exceptional Needs Care
Management Agency, Inc.**
2755 Colony Park, Suite 7
Memphis, TN 38118
Phone: (901) 360-0194
Fax: (901) 947-9707

**Family and Children's Services
of Chattanooga, Inc.**
300 East 8th Street
Chattanooga, TN 37403
Phone: (423) 755-2800
Fax: (423) 755-2758
Web site: www.fcschatt.org

**Family and Children's
Services-Center for Adoption**
1210 Foster Avenue
Nashville, TN 37243
Phone: (615) 253-3289
Fax: (615) 253-3326
Toll-Free: (800) 807-3228

Frontier Health/Traces
2001 Stonebrook Place
Kingsport, TN 37660
Phone: (424) 224-1067
Fax: (423) 224-1095

Global Village International Adoptions
P.O. Box 154
2441 Q Old Fort Parkway
Murfreesboro, TN 37128
Phone: (615) 890-3507
Web site: www.
globalvillageadopt.org
– Intercountry Program
– Child Placement

Greater Chattanooga Christian Services and Children's Home
744 McCallie Avenue, Suite 329
Chattanooga, TN 37403
Phone: (423) 756-0281
Fax: (423) 265-7326
E-mail: GCCS2002@netzero.com
Web site: www.chattanooga
christianservices.org

Happy Haven Homes, Inc.
2311 Wakefield Drive
Cookeville, TN 38501
Phone: (931) 526-2052
Fax: (931) 372-8837

Harmony Adoptions of Tennessee, Inc.
311 High Street
Maryville, TN 37804
Phone: (865) 982-5225
Fax: (865) 982-5950
E-mail: pfrye@harmony.cc
Web site: www.harmony.cc

Heaven Sent Children, Inc.
307 North Walnut Street
Murfreesboro, TN 37133-2514
Phone: (615) 898-0803
Fax: (615) 898-1990
E-mail: hscangels@bellsouth.net
Web site: www.
heavensentchildren.com
– Intercountry Program
– Child Placement

Holston United Methodist Home for Children, Inc.
P.O. Box 188
404 Holston Drive
Greeneville, TN 37744
Phone: (423) 638-4171
Fax: (423) 638-7171
Toll-Free: (800) 628-2986
Web site: www.usit.net/children
– Intercountry Program
– Child Placement

International Assistance and Adoption Project
1210-G Taft Highway
Signal Mountain, TN 37377
Phone: (423) 886-6986
Fax: (208) 692-8805
E-mail: iaap@iaapadoption.com
Web site: www.iaapadoption.com

International Mission of Hope
P.O. Box 154
2441 – Q Old Fort Pkwy
Murfreesboro, TN 37128
Phone: (615) 890-3507
Web site: www.imhadopt.org

Jewish Family Service, Inc.
6560 Poplar Avenue
Memphis, TN 38138
Phone: (901) 767-8511
Fax: (901) 763-2348

Knoxville Family Service Center
9915 D Kingston Pike
Knoxville, TN 37992
Phone: (865) 633-9844

Life Choices, Inc.
2235 Covington Pike, Suite 14
Memphis, TN 38128
Phone: (901) 388-1172
Fax: (901) 388-1225
E-mail: lchoices@bellsouth.net
Web site: www.life-choices.org

Life Choices, Inc.
3297 Park Avenue
Memphis, TN 38111
Phone: (901) 323-5433
Fax: (901) 388-1225

Memphis Family Service Center
2969 South Mendenhall
Memphis, TN 38115
Phone: (901) 363-1189
Fax: (901) 363-1180

Mercy Ministries, Inc.
P.O. Box 111060
15328 Old Hickory Boulevard
Nashville, TN 37222-1060
Phone: (615) 831-6987
Fax: (615) 315-9749
Web site: www.mercyministries.
com

Mid-Cumberland Children's Services, Inc.
106 North Mountain Street
Smithville, TN 37166
Phone: (615) 597-7134

Mid-South Christian Services
1044 Brookfield Road, Suite 102
Memphis, TN 38119
Phone: (901) 818-9996
Fax: (901) 761-9350
E-mail: dbrower@bethany.org
Web site: www.bethany.org

Miriam's Promise
37 Rutledge Street
Nashville, TN 37210
Phone: (615) 292-3500
Fax: (615) 292-0368
Toll-Free: (800) 320-1506
E-mail: info@miriamspromise.org
Web site: www.miriamspromise.
org
– Intercountry Program
– Child Placement

Northeast Region Adoption
2514 ½ Wesley Street
Johnson City, TN 37601
Phone: (423) 282-7044
Fax: (423) 282-7046

Omni Visions
2723 Berrywood Drive
Nashville, TN 37214
Phone: (615) 460-7051

Fax: (615) 460-7057
Toll-Free: (888) 742-3905
Web site: www.omnivisions.com

Porter-Leath Children's Center
868 North Manassas Street
Memphis, TN 38107-2516
Phone: (901) 577-2500
Fax: (901) 577-2506
E-mail: porterleath@porter-leath.
org
Web site: www.porter-leath.org

Small World Agency
401 Bonnaspring Drive
Hermitage, TN 37076
Phone: (615) 883-4372
Fax: (615) 885-7582
Toll-Free: (800) 544-5083
E-mail: Julie@swa.net
Web site: www.swa.net
– Intercountry Program
– Child Placement

Smoky Mountain Children's Home
P.O. Box 4391
449 McCarn Circle
Sevierville, TN 37864-4391
Phone: (865) 453-4644
Fax: (865) 453-8812

Tennessee Baptist Children's Homes, Inc.
P.O. Box 2206
Brentwood, TN 37024-2206
Phone: (615) 376-3140
Fax: (615) 371-1866
Toll-Free: (800) 624-8591
E-mail: office@tbch4kids.org
Web site: www.tbch4kids.org

Tennessee Children's Home
P.O. Box 10
Main Street
Spring Hill, TN 37174
Phone: (931) 486-2274
Fax: (615) 307-2300

Tennessee Children's Home-East
P.O. Box 7347
Knoxville, TN 37921
Phone: (865) 584-0841
Fax: (865) 588-6560
E-mail: etcs@usit.net

Tennessee Department of Children's Services
Southeast Region
1501 Riverside Drive, Suite 105
Chattanooga, TN 37406
Phone: (423) 493-5949

The Villages, Inc.
652 North Girl School Road
Indianapolis, TN 46214
Phone: (317) 273-7575
Fax: (317) 273-7565
Toll-Free: (800) 874-6880
Web site: www.villages.org

The Villages, Inc.
1522 SE Riverside Drive
Evansville, TN 47713
Phone: (812) 434-2956
Fax: (812) 434-2966
Web site: http://villages.org

Tri-Cities Family Service Center
P.O. Box 3768
215 East Springbrook Drive, Suite 1
Johnson City, TN 37602-3768
Phone: (423) 952-2290
Fax: (423) 952-2293

Williams International Adoptions, Inc.
5100 Stage Road, Suite A
Memphis, TN 38134
Phone: (901) 373-6003
Fax: (901) 373-0130
Web site: www.
williamsinternational.org
– Intercountry Program
– Child Placement

Birth Family and Search Support Groups

Group for Openness in Adoption
518 General George Patton Road
Nashville, TN 37221
Phone: (615) 646-8116

ROOTS
304 Arbuts Lane
Knoxville, TN 37919
Phone: (423) 573-1344

State Adoption Exchange/ Photolisting of Children Waiting For Adoption

Resource Exchange for Adoptable Children in Tennessee (REACT)
1210 Foster Avenue
Nashville, TN 37243
Phone: (615) 321-3867
Web site: www.state.tn.us/youth/adoption/react.htm

State Adoption Specialist/ Manager /Foster Care Specialist/Manager

Tennessee Department of Children's Services
Mattie Satterfield
Cordell Hull Building, 8th Floor
436 Sixth Avenue North
Nashville, TN 37243-1290
Phone: (615) 532-5637
Fax: (615) 532-6495
E-mail: mattie.satterfield@state.tn.us
Web site: www.state.tn.us/youth/adoption/foster/index.htm.

Tennessee Department of
Children's Services
Cordell Hull Building, 8th Floor
436 Sixth Avenue North
Nashville, TN 37243-1290
Phone: (615) 741-9206
Fax: (615) 532-6495
E-mail: william.mcsurdy@state.
tn.us
Web site: www.state.tn.us/
youth/children/foster/index.htm

**State Interstate Compact on
the Placement of Children
(ICPC) Administrator**

Tennessee Department of
Children's Services
Cordell Hull Building, 7th Floor
436 Sixth Avenue North
Nashville, TN 37243-1290
Phone: (615) 532-5618
Fax: (615) 532-5618
E-mail: Cheri.Stewart@state.
tn.us

State Licensing Specialist

Tennessee Department of
Children's Services
Jerry Hughett
Cordell Hull Building, 7th Floor
436 Sixth Avenue North
Nashville, TN 37243-1290
Phone: (615) 532-5598
E-mail: jerry.hughett@state.tn.us
Web site: www.state.tn.us/youth/
adoption/agencies/index.htm

State Reunion Registry

Advanced Notice Registry
Tennessee Department of
Children's Services
Post Adoption Services
436 Sixth Avenue North
Nashville, TN 37243-1290
Phone: (615) 532-5637
Web site: www.state.
tn.us/youth/children/special/
advancednotice.htm

TEXAS

**Adoptive/Foster Family
Support Groups**

Adopt 2000
4550 Post Oak Place, Suite 100
Houston, TX 77027
Phone: (713) 333-2232
Fax: (713) 333-2220
After hours: (713) 690-6830
E-mail: lglaze@adopt2000
houston.org
Web site: www.
adopt2000houston.org

Adopting Children Together
P.O. Box 120966
Arlington, TX 76012
Phone: (817) 265-1382
Fax: (817) 277-2176

Bennett Chapel Support Group
P.O. Box 1147
Center, TX 75935
Phone: (936) 598-5509
E-mail: rmartin@bcministry.org
Web site: www.bcministry.org

Bruce Edwards
732 Rittiman
Terrell Hills, TX 78209
Phone: (210) 639-0779
Fax: (210) 826-6847
E-mail: bedwards@grandecom.net

Casa De Esperanza
Box 66581
Houston, TX 77266
Phone: (713) 529-0639

Center for Children and
Families
1004 North Big Spring, Suite 325
Midland, TX 79701-3383
Fax: (915) 570-4069
Toll-Free: (800) 898-0459

Circle of Hope
c/o Hope Cottage
4209 McKinney
Dallas, TX 75205
Phone: (214) 526-8721

Council on Adoptable Children
P.O. Box 1554
4606 Log Cradle
Houston, TX 77251
Phone: (713) 466-0745

Council on Adoptable Children
of Austin
6600 Bradley Drive
Austin, TX 78723
Phone: (512) 928-0702

Council on Adoptable Children
of Houston
Rural Route 14
P.O. Box 177F
Edinburg, TX 78539
Phone: (281) 452-1599

Council on Adoptable Children
of Texas
S/B RR 14
P.O. Box 177F
Edinburg, TX 78539
Phone: (956) 381-2177
Fax: (956) 381-2177
E-mail: cflores@panam.edu

Dallas Minority Adoption
Council
6433 Autumn Wood Trail
Dallas, TX 75232
Phone: (214) 317-2384

Dallas Minority Adoption
Council
P.O. Box 764058
Dallas, TX 75376-4058
Phone: (214) 371-5280
Fax: (214) 820-2263

El Concilio de Padres de Ni-os
1712 Gardenia
McAllen, TX 78501

El Paso Adoptive Parents
10416 Mandy Way
El Paso, TX 79927
Phone: (915) 859-1520
After hours: (915) 859-1520

El Paso Area Foster and Adoptive Parent Association
10409 Bywood Drive
El Paso, TX 79935
Phone: (915) 598-5891
Fax: (915) 566-8883

Family Counseling Services
1635 NE Loop 410, #501
San Antonio, TX 78209
Phone: (210) 821-5980

Family Services of El Paso
— Post Adoption
2930 North Stanton
El Paso, TX 79902
Phone: (915) 544-4523
Fax: (915) 544-4368

Foster Parents for Foster Children of Tarrant County
1218 Vera Lane
Kennedale, TX 76060
Phone: (817) 561-4767
Fax: (817) 561-6239

Foster and Adoptive Parents of North Texas
9368 Hunters Creek
Dallas, TX 75243
Phone: (214) 345-7196
Fax: (214) 345-5933
E-mail: pattally@texashealth.org

Houston Council on Adoptable Children
207 Lakeside Drive
Channelview, TX 77530
Phone: (281) 866-0540

Life Matters
6025 North Central Expressway, #3040
Dallas, TX 75205
Phone: (214) 361-0055

Miracle Kids Adoption Support Group
8887 Buena Park
El Paso, TX 79907
Phone: (915) 858-0298
Fax: (915) 858-5056
After hours: (915) 820-2572

Reach of Texas Minority Parent Group
11239 Lera
Houston, TX 77016
Phone: (281) 442-3988

S.A.F.E.T. Net (Sharing Adoptive Family Experience Through Networking)
2660 Evans Avenue, Room 208
Fort Worth, TX 76104
Phone: (817) 923-4441
E-mail: ococdfw@aol.com
Web site: www.ococdfw.org

San Antonio Council on Adoptable Children
732 Rittiman Road
San Antonio, TX 78209
Phone: (210) 639-0779
Fax: (210) 826-6847
After hours: (210) 639-0779
E-mail: bedwards@grandecom.net

Texas Baptist Home
629 Farley Street
Waxahachie, TX 75168
Phone: (972) 937-1321
E-mail: dawnt@tbhc.org
Web site: www. texasbaptisthome.org

The Children's Shelter
2939 West Woodlawn Avenue
San Antonio, TX 78228
Phone: (210) 212-2558
E-mail: efloyd@chshel.org
Web site: www.childrensshelter.org

West Side Foster Parent Association
711 Woodcastle Bend
Houston, TX 77094
Phone: (281) 646-0711
Fax: (713) 443-5327
E-mail: Swepickles@aol.com

Licensed Private Adoption Agencies

A Cradle of Hope
311 North Market Street, Suite 300
Dallas, TX 75202
Phone: (214) 747-4500
— Intercountry Program
— Child Placement

AAA-Alamo Adoption Agency
P.O. Box 781
Adkins, TX 78101-0781
Phone: (210) 967-5337

ABC Adoption Agency, Inc.
417 San Pedro Avenue
San Antonio, TX 78212
Phone: (210) 227-7820
Fax: (210) 227-7820

Abrazo Adoption Associates
10010 San Pedro
San Antonio, TX 78216
Phone: (210) 342-5683
Toll-Free: (800) 454-5683
Web site: www.abrazo.org

Adoption Access
8330 Meadow Road, Suite 222
Dallas, TX 75231
Phone: (214) 750-4847
Fax: (214) 750-1970
Toll-Free: (800) 373-3484
E-mail: admin@adoptionaccess.com
Web site: www.adoptionaccess.com
— Intercountry Program
— Adoptive Parent/Family Preparation
— Agency Able to Place Children with United States Citizens Living Abroad
— Child Placement
— Information/Referral

Adoption Advisory, Inc.
3607 Fairmount
Dallas, TX 75219
Phone: (214) 520-0004
Web site: www.adoptadvisory.
com

Adoption Advocates, Inc.
1505 West 6th Street
Austin, TX 78703
Phone: (512) 477-1122
Toll-Free: (800) 966-HOPE (4673)
E-mail: Info@Adoption
Advocates.net
Web site: www.adoptiona
dvocates.net/index.html

Adoption Affiliates, Inc.
215 West Olmos Drive
San Antonio, TX 78212
Phone: (210) 824-9939
Fax: (210) 824-9977
Toll-Free: (800) 270-6757
E-mail: januscouve@aol.com

Adoption Alliance
7303 Blanco Road
San Antonio, TX 78216
Phone: (210) 349-3991

Adoption Angels, Inc.
118 Broadway, Suite 517
San Antonio, TX 78205
Phone: (210) 227-2229
Fax: (210) 227-2241
E-mail: lore@adoptionangels.com
Web site: www.adoptionangels.
com

Adoption As An Option
12611 Kingsride Lane
Houston, TX 77024
Phone: (713) 468-1053

Adoption Family Service
5408 Arapaho Road
Dallas, TX 75248
Phone: (972) 437-6991
Fax: (972) 437-1988
Toll-Free: (800) 437-6991
Web site: www.jssdallas.org

Adoption Information and Counseling
2020 Southwest Freeway, Suite 3
Houston, TX 77098
Phone: (713) 529-4341
Web site: www.adoptquest.com

Adoption Resource Consultants
P.O. Box 1224
Richardson, TX 75083
Phone: (972) 517-4119
Fax: (972) 423-1297
– Intercountry Program
– Child Placement

Adoption Services Associates
5370 Prue Road
San Antonio, TX 78240
Phone: (210) 699-6094
Fax: (210) 691-8836
Toll-Free: (800) 648-1807
E-mail: adopt@adoptionservices
associates.org
Web site: www.adoptionservices
associates.org

Adoption Services Worldwide, Inc.
7300 Blanco Road, Suite 206
San Antonio, TX 78216
Phone: (210) 342-0444
Fax: (210) 342-0710
E-mail: babyasa@aol.com
Web site: www.babyasw.com
– Intercountry Program
– Child Placement

Adoption Services, Inc.
3500 Overton Park West
Fort Worth, TX 76109
Phone: (817) 921-0718
Fax: (817) 924-4771
E-mail: adoptsvc@flash.net

Adoption-A Gift of Love
P.O. Box 50384
Denton, TX 76206
Phone: (940) 243-0749
Fax: (940) 380-9084
E-mail: agol@charter.net
Web site: www.adoption-agol.
org

– Intercountry Program
– Child Placement

Adoptionpros
1110 Kingwood Drive, Suite 200L
Kingwood, TX 77339
Toll-Free: (800) 419-0289
E-mail: adoptpros@aol.com
Web site: www.adoptionpros.
com

Adoptions International, Inc.
7475 Skillman Street, Suite D-107
Dallas, TX 75231
Phone: (214) 342-8388
Fax: (214) 341-6004
E-mail: adopt@adoptmeinterna
tional.org
Web site: www.
adoptmeinternational.org
– Intercountry Program
– Child Placement

Alternatives In Motion
20619 Aldine Westfield Road
Humble, TX 77338
Phone: (713) 821-6508

Andrel Adoptions
3908 Manchaca Road
Austin, TX 78704
Phone: (512) 448-4605
Fax: (512) 448-1905
E-mail: vikaa49@aol.com

Angel Adoptions of the Heart
5311 Kirby, Suite 101
Houston, TX 77005
Phone: (713) 523-2273
E-mail: angeladoptions@pdq.net

Buckner Adoption and Maternity Services
5200 South Buckner Boulevard
Dallas, TX 75227
Phone: (214) 319-3426
E-mail: domesticadoption@
buckner.org
Web site: www.buckner.org

Buckner International Adoption
4830 Samuell Boulevard
Dallas, TX 75228
Phone: (214) 381-1552
Toll-Free: (866) 236-7823
E-mail: internationaladoption@buckner.org
Web site: www.bucknerinternationaladoption.org
– Intercountry Program
– Child Placement

Caring Choices, Inc.
11601 Katy Freeway, Suite 109
Houston, TX 77079
Phone: (281) 920-4300

Catholic Counseling Services
P.O. Box 190507
Dallas, TX 75219-0507
Phone: (214) 526-2772
Fax: (214) 526-2941
Web site: www.catholiccharitiesdal.org

Catholic Family Service
P.O. Box 15127
Amarillo, TX 79105
Phone: (806) 376-4571
Fax: (806) 345-7947
E-mail: cfs@catholicfamilyservice.org
Web site: www.catholicfamilyservice.org

Catholic Social Services of Laredo
P.O. Box 3305
Laredo, TX 78044
Phone: (210) 722-2443

Child Placement Center of Texas
2212 Sunny Lane
Killeen, TX 75641
Phone: (817) 690-5959
Web site: www.childplacementcenter.com

Children and Family Institute
5787 South Hampton Road, Suite 360
Dallas, TX 75232
Phone: (214) 337-9979
Fax: (214) 337-9944
E-mail: cfi@cfiadopt.org
Web site: www.cfiadopt.org

Children's Home of Lubbock
P.O. Box 2824
Lubbock, TX 79408
Phone: (806) 762-0481
E-mail: info@childshome.org
Web site: www.childshome.org

Chosen Heritage – Christian Adoptions
606 West Wheatland Road, Suite 107
Duncanville, TX 75116
Phone: (972) 296-5111
E-mail: ChosenHeritage1987@yahoo.com

Christian Homes
1202 Estates Drive
P.O. Box 270
Abilene, TX 79604
Phone: (915) 677-2205
Fax: (915) 677-0332
Toll-Free: (800) 592-4725
E-mail: attention@christianhomes.com
Web site: www.christianhomes.com
– Intercountry Program
– Child Placement

Christian Services of the Southwest
6320 LBJ Freeway, Suite 122
Dallas, TX 75240
Phone: (972) 960-9981
Fax: (972) 960-0062
Web site: www.christianservices-sw.org

Counsel for Adoption Resources
1201 South W.S. Young Drive, Suite F
Killeen, TX 76541
Phone: (254) 690-2223

Cradle of Life Adoption Agency
245 North Fourth Street
Beaumont, TX 77701
Phone: (409) 832-3000
Fax: (409) 833-3935
Toll-Free: (800) 456-8001

DePelchin Children's Center
4950 Memorial Drive
Houston, TX 77007
Phone: (713) 730-2335
Fax: (713) 802-6307
Toll-Free: (888) 730-2335
E-mail: info@depelchin.org
Web site: www.depelchin.org

El Paso Adoption Services
905 Noble
El Paso, TX 79902
Phone: (915) 542-1086
Fax: (915) 544-7080

El Paso Center for Children
3700 Altura Boulevard
El Paso, TX 79930
Phone: (915) 565-8361

Gladney Center for Adoption
6300 John Ryan Drive
Fort Worth, TX 76132-4122
Phone: (817) 922-6000
Fax: (817) 922-5955
Toll-Free: (800) 452-3639
E-mail: info@gladney.org
Web site: www.adoptionsbygladney.com
– Intercountry Program
– Child Placement

Great Wall China Adoption
248 Addie Roy Road, A102
Austin, TX 78746
Phone: (512) 323-9595
Fax: (512) 323-9599
E-mail: info@gwcadopt.org
Web site: www.gwcadopt.org
– Intercountry Program
– Child Placement

Harrah's Adoption International Mission (AIM)
6700 Woodlands Parkway, #230-306
Spring, TX 77382
Phone: (281) 465-9990
Phone: (281) 465-9991
Fax: (281) 465-9992
E-mail: office@hfsadopt.com
Web site: www.hfsadopt.com

High Plains Children's Home
P.O. Box 7448
Amarillo, TX 79109
Phone: (806) 622-2272

Homes of Saint Mark
3000 Richmond Avenue, Suite 570
Houston, TX 77098
Phone: (713) 522-2800
Fax: (713) 522-3769

Hope Cottage, Inc.
4209 McKinney Avenue, Suite 200
Dallas, TX 75205
Phone: (214) 526-8721
E-mail: adoption@hopecottage.org
Web site: www.hopecottage.org
– Intercountry Program
– Child Placement

Hope International
311 North Market Street, Suite 300
Dallas, TX 75202
Phone: (214) 672-9399
Fax: (214) 939-3001
E-mail: srice@hopeadoption.org
Web site: www.hopeadoption.org
– Intercountry Program
– Child Placement

Inheritance Adoptions
P.O. Box 2563
Wichita Falls, TX 76307
Phone: (817) 322-3678
E-mail: adopt@wf.net
Web site: www.inheritanceadoptions.org

International Child Placing Agency
P.O. Box 112
Los Fresnos, TX 78566
Phone: (210) 233-5705

J&B Kids, Inc. Placing Agency
4062 Street Highway 72 West
Yorktown, TX 78164
Phone: (361) 564-9780
Fax: (361) 564-2898
E-mail: dgbtfamily@aol.com

LDS Social Services-Texas
1100 West Jackson Road
Carrollton, TX 75006
Phone: (972) 242-2182

Lena Pope Home, Inc.
3131 Sanguinet Street
Fort Worth, TX 76107
Phone: (817) 731-8681
Fax: (817) 731-9858
E-mail: vgriffin@lenapopehome.org
Web site: www.lenapopehome.org

Los Ninos International Adoption Center
2408 Timberloch Place, Suite D1
The Woodlands, TX 77380
Phone: (281) 363-2892
Fax: (281) 297-4191
E-mail: jerichsen@LosNinos.org
Web site: www.losninos.org
– Intercountry Program
– Child Placement

Loving Alternatives Adoptions
P.O. Box 131466
Tyler, TX 75713
Phone: (903) 581-7720

Lutheran Social Services of the South, Inc.
P.O. Box 140767
8305 Cross Park Drive
Austin, TX 78765
Phone: (512) 459-1000
Fax: (512) 452-6855
Toll-Free: (800) 938-5777
E-mail: konnie@lsss.org
Web site: www.lsss.org
– Intercountry Program
– Child Placement

Marywood Children and Family Services
510 West 26th Street
Austin, TX 78705
Phone: (512) 472-9251
Fax: (512) 472-4829
Toll-Free: (800) 251-5433
Web site: www.marywood.org

Methodist Children's Home
1111 Herring Avenue
Waco, TX 76708
Phone: (254) 753-0181
Fax: (254) 750-1300
Web site: www.methodistchildrenshome.org

New Life Children's Services
19911 State Hwy 249
Houston, TX 77070
Phone: (281) 955-1001
Fax: (281) 955-0114
Toll-Free: (800) 432-9124
Web site: www.newlifeadopt.com
– Intercountry Program
– Child Placement

Read Adoption Agency, Inc.
1011 North Mesa
El Paso, TX 79902
Phone: (915) 533-3697

Smithlawn Home
P.O. Box 6451
Lubbock, TX 79413
Phone: (806) 745-2574

Spaulding for Children
8552 Katie Freeway, Suite 300
Houston, TX 77027
Phone: (713) 681-6991
Fax: (713) 681-9089
Toll-Free: (800) 460-6298
E-mail: tlandry@spauldingforchi
ldren.org
Web site: www.
spauldingforchildren.org

Texas Cradle Society
6487 Whitby Road
San Antonio, TX 78240
Phone: (210) 696-2410
E-mail: mcdonald@mmhome.org
Web site: www.mmhome.org

Unity Children's Home
12027 Blue Mountain
Houston, TX 77067
Phone: (713) 537-6148

**Birth Family and Search
Support Groups**

Adoption Knowledge and
Affiliates
P.O. Box 4082
Austin, TX 78765
Phone: (512) 442-8252

Adoption Search and Support
P.O. Box 371
Pasadena, TX 77501
Phone: (713) 477-0491

Council on Adoptable Children
of Texas, El Concilio
1712 Gardenia
McAllen, TX 78501

Love, Roots Wings
10432 Achilles
El Paso, TX 79924
Phone: (915) 821-7253

Marywood Search Support
Group
510 W. 26th Street
Austin, TX 78705
Phone: (512) 472-9251

Orphan Voyage
1305 Augustine Court
College Station, TX 77840
Phone: (409) 764-7157

Orphan Voyage of Houston
5811 Southminster
Houston, TX 77035
Phone: (713) 723-1762

Searchline of Texas
1516 Old Orchard
Irving, TX 75061
Phone: (214) 445-7005

Triad Support Group
4208 Roxbury
El Paso, TX 79922

**State Adoption Exchange/
Photolisting of Children
Waiting For Adoption**

Texas Adoption Resource
Exchange (TARE)
Texas Department of Protective
and Regulatory Services
P.O. Box 149030, M.C. E-5557
701 West 51st Street
Austin, TX 78714-9030
Toll-Free: (800) 233-3405
Web site: www.adoptchildren.
org

**State Adoption
Specialist/Manager**

Department of Family and
Protective Services
Janis Brown
P.O. Box 149030
Austin, TX 78714-9030
Phone: (512) 438-3412
Fax: (512) 438-3312
E-mail: janis.brown@dfps.state.
tx.us

**State Foster Care
Specialist/Manager**

Department of Family and
Protective Services
Janis Brown
P.O. Box 149030, Mail Code E-558
701 West 51st Street
Austin, TX 78714-9030
Phone: (512) 438-3412
Fax: (512) 438-3782
E-mail: janis.brown@dfps.state.
tx.us
Web site: www.tdprs.state.tx.us/
Adoption_and_Foster_Care/
About_Foster_Care/default.asp

**State Interstate Compact on
the Placement of Children
(ICPC) Administrator**

Department of Family and
Protective Services
P.O. Box 149030
701 West 51st Street
Austin, TX 78714-9030
Phone: (512) 834-4474
Fax: (512) 339-5815
E-mail: carolyn.thompson@dfps.
state.tx.us

State Licensing Specialist

Department of Family and
Protective Services
Char Bateman
P.O. Box 149030
E-557
Austin, TX 78714-9030
Phone: (512) 438-3269
Fax: (512) 438-3782
E-mail: Char.bateman@dfps.
state.tx.us

State Reunion Registry

Central Adoption Registry
P.O. Box 140123
Austin, TX 787140123
Phone: (512) 458-7388
Web site: www.tdh.state.tx.us/
bvs/car/car.htm

Statewide Adoption Recruitment Line

Texas Statewide Adoption Recruitment Line
Toll-Free: (800) 233-3405

UTAH

Adoptive/Foster Family Support Groups

A Child's Dream
3600 South Market Street
West Valley City, UT 84119
Toll-Free: (800) 247-8280

Adopted Kids Association
785 East 500 South
Manti, UT 84642
Phone: (801) 835-2281

Adoptive Parent Support Group of Utah
645 East 4500 South
Salt Lake City, UT 84165
Phone: (801) 264-7500

African American Awareness
1139 North 1165 West
Orem, UT 84057
Phone: (801) 224-4982

An Act of Love
9561 South
700 East, Suite 101
Sandy, UT 84094
Phone: (801) 572-1696

Around the World Adoptions
756 West
1150 South
Provo, UT 84601
Phone: (801) 371-0968

Catholic Community Services Parent Support Group-Waiting Families
2570 West 1700 South
Salt Lake City, UT 84104
Phone: (801) 977-9119
Fax: (801) 977-8227
E-mail: mstclaire@ccsutah.org

Families for African-American Awareness
5131 West Parr Drive
West Jordan, UT 84088
Phone: (801) 280-3260
Web site: www.ffaaa.org

Families for Children and North American Council on Adoptable Children State Representative
1219 Windsor Street
Salt Lake City, UT 84105
Phone: (801) 487-3916
Web site: www.nacac.org

Families for Children from Cambodia
10468 South 465 East
Sandy, UT 84070
Phone: (801) 576-1501

Families for Children from Bolivia and Peru
1236 North 150 West
American Fork, UT 84003
Phone: (801) 756-5656

Families for Children from China
13848 South Timoney Road
Draper, UT 84020
Phone: (801) 756-8875

Families for Children from Columbia
785 Chesapeake Bay
Murray, UT 84107
Phone: (801) 266-4911

Families for Children from East India
542 East 100 South
Kaysville, UT 84037
Phone: (801) 547-0852

Families for Children from Guatemala
P.O. Box 521192
Salt Lake City, UT 84152
Phone: (801) 254-4011

Families for Children from Kazakstan
2739 East Sommet Drive
Salt Lake City, UT 84117
Phone: (801) 224-0607

Families for Children from Korea
9239 South Judd Lane
West Jordan, UT 84088
Phone: (801) 280-6559

Families for Children from Romania
484 East Mountainville Drive
Alpine, UT 84004
Phone: (801) 492-1140

Hand in Hand Adoption Agency
3087 South Lavell Lane
Salt Lake City, UT 84106

Karen Robinson-Richman
P.O. Box 966
Bountiful, UT 84011-0966
Phone: (801) 294-5890

LDS Family Services/Families Supporting Adoption
1525 Lincoln Avenue
Ogden, UT 84404
Phone: (801) 787-2727

Noah's Ark Adoptions
399 East 3575 North
North Ogden, UT 84414
Phone: (801) 782-5344

Parents for Attachment (PFA)
603 West 3750 North
Pleasant View, UT 84414
Phone: (801) 782-2727

Russian Parent Support Group
874 East Alpine Drive
Alpine, UT 84004
Phone: (801) 756-8875

Utah Foster Care Foundation
Salt Lake Valley-Salt Lake Office
136 East South Temple, Suite 960
Salt Lake City, UT 84111
Phone: (801) 303-4060

Fax: (801) 994-5206
Toll-Free: (877) 505 KIDS
E-mail: nikki@utahfostercare.org
Web site: www.utahfostercare.
org

Licensed Private
Adoption Agencies

A Act of Love/Alternative Options and Services for Children
9561 South 700 East, Suite 101
Sandy, UT 84070
Phone: (801) 572-1696
Fax: (801) 572-9303
Web site: www.
aactofloveadoptions.com
– Intercountry Program
– Home Study

A TLC Adoption
316 West 850 Street
Layton, UT 84041
Phone: (801) 444-4978
Fax: (801) 798-9355

Adopt an Angel
3615 West 1987 South
Salt Lake City, UT 84104
Phone: (801) 537-1622
Fax: (801) 359-6873
E-mail: adoptangel@worldnet.
att.net
Web site: www.adoptangel.org

Adoption Center of Choice, Inc.
241 West 520 North
Orem, UT 84057
Phone: (801) 224-2440
Fax: (801) 224-1899

Catholic Community Services of Utah
2570 West 1700 South
Salt Lake City, UT 84104
Phone: (801) 977-9119
Fax: (801) 977-8227
Web site: www.ccsutah.org

Children of Peace
715 East 3900 South, Suite 203
Salt Lake City, UT 84107-2182
Phone: (801) 263-2111
Fax: (801) 262-2259

Children's Aid Society of Utah
652 26th Street
Ogden, UT 84401
Phone: (801) 393-8671
Fax: (801) 394-3324
E-mail: info@casadoption.org
Web site: www.casadoption.org
– Intercountry Program
– Child Placement

Children's House International
1236 North 150 West
American Fork, UT 84003
Phone: (801) 756-0587
Fax: (801) 763-8384
Web site: www.adopting.com/chi

Children's House International
1053 North 1390 West
Layton, UT 84041
Phone: (208) 667-1898

Children's Service Society of Utah
124 South 400 East, Suite 400
Salt Lake City, UT 84111
Phone: (801) 355-7444
Fax: (801) 355-7453
Toll-Free: (800) 839-7444
E-mail: beth@cssutah.org
Web site: www.cssutah.org

Families for Children
P.O. Box 521192
Salt Lake City, UT 84152-1192
Phone: (801) 467-3413

LDS Family Services – Salt Lake City
132 South State Street, Suite 300
Salt Lake City, UT 84111
Phone: (801) 240-6500
Fax: (801) 2405508
Toll-Free: (800) 453-3860 ext 6521

E-mail: WatsonMG@ldschurg.org
Web site: www.
ldsfamilyservices.org

LDS Family Services
10 East South Temple, Suite 1250
Salt Lake City, UT 84111
Phone: (801) 248-6500
E-mail: fam-ut-
farmington@ldschurch.org

LDS Family Services
55 West 100 North
Richfield, UT 84701
Fax: (435) 596-8769
Toll-Free: (800) 994-8992
E-mail: fam-ut-
richfield@ldschurch.org

LDS Family Services
2202 North Main Street, Suite 301
Cedar City, UT 84720-9790
Phone: (435) 586-4479
Fax: (435) 865-2202

LDS Family Services
433 South 500 East
American Fork, UT 84003
Phone: (801) 216-8000
Fax: (801) 216-8001
Web site: www.providentliving.
org

LDS Family Services
2480 East Redcliff Drive
St. George, UT 84790
Phone: (435) 673-6446

LDS Family Services
4250 West 5415 South, Third Floor
Kearns, UT 84118
Phone: (801) 969-4181
Fax: (801) 969-1291
Toll-Free: (800) 537-2229
E-mail: fam-ut-
kearns@ldschurch.org
Web site: www.itsaboutlove.com

LDS Family Services
625 East
8400 South
Sandy, UT 84070
Phone: (801) 566-2556
Fax: (801) 566-2639
E-mail: fam-ut-sandy@ldschurch.org
Web site: www.itsaboutlove.com

LDS Family Services
P.O. Box 817
Richfield, UT 84701
Phone: (435) 896-6446
Fax: (435) 896-8769
Toll-Free: (800) 994-3992
E-mail: fam-ut-richfield@ldschurch.org

LDS Family Services
1525 Lincoln Avenue
Ogden, UT 84404
Phone: (801) 621-6510

LDS Family Services
294 East
100 South
Price, UT 84501
Phone: (435) 637-2991

LDS Family Services
95 West, 100 South, Suite 340
Logan, UT 84321
Phone: (435) 752-5302

LDS Family Services
1190 North
900 East
Provo, UT 84604
Phone: (801) 378-7620

Legacy International Adoptions, LLC
3198 Hampton Court
Salt Lake City, UT 84124
Phone: (801) 278-3066

Wasatch International Adoptions
3725 Washington Boulevard,
Suite 9
Ogden, UT 84403

Phone: (801) 334-8683
Fax: (801) 334-0988
E-mail: info@wiaa.org
Web site: www.wiaa.org

West Sands Adoptions
461 East 2780 North
Provo, UT 84604
Phone: (801) 377-4379
Fax: (801) 377-8627
E-mail: wes@adoptionnet.org
Web site: www.westsandsadoption.org
– Intercountry Program
– Child Placement

Birth Family and Search Support Groups

Adoption Connection of Utah
1349 Mariposa Avenue
Salt Lake City, UT 84106

Heart to Heart Adoption, Inc.
9669 South 700 East
Sandy, UT 84070
Phone: (801) 563-1000
Fax: (801 563-9899
Toll-Free: (877) 62 HEART
E-mail: Lnanna911@aol.com
Web site: www.hearttoheartadoptions.net

LAMB
672 East
2025 South
Bountiful, UT 84010

State Adoption Exchange/ Photolisting of Children Waiting For Adoption

The Adoption Exchange
Utah Office
302 West 5400 South, Suite 208
Murray, UT 84107
Phone: (801) 265-0444
Fax: (801) 412-0202
Toll-Free: (866) 872-7212
E-mail: ks@adoptex.org
Web site: www.utdcfsadopt.org/index.html

State Adoption Specialist/Manager

Utah Department of Human Services
Division of Child and Family Services
Marty Shannon
P.O. Box 45500
120 North, 200 West, Suite 225
Salt Lake City, UT 84103
Phone: (801) 538-3913
Fax: (801) 538-3993
E-mail: mshannon@utah.gov
Web site: www.hsdcfs.utah.gov/dopotion.htm

State Foster Care Specialist/Manager

Utah Department of Human Services
Division of Child and Family Services
120 North 200 West, Suite 225
Salt Lake City, UT 84145-0500
Phone: (801) 538-4316
Fax: (801) 538-3993
E-mail: angelakhairallah@utah.gov

State Interstate Compact on the Placement of Children (ICPC) Administrator

Utah State Division of Child and Family Services
Division of Children and Family Services
P.O. Box 45500
120 North, 200 West
Salt Lake City, UT 84145-7107
Phone: (801) 538-4100
Fax: (801) 539-3993
E-mail: mrchapman@utah.gov
Web site: www.dcfs.utah.gov

State Licensing Specialist

Utah Department of Human Services
Office of Licensing
Janice P. Knaphus

120 North, 200 West, #303
Salt Lake City, UT 84103
Phone: (801) 538-4242
Fax: (801) 538-4553
E-mail: jknphus@utah.gov
Web site: www.hslic.utah.gov

State Reunion Registry

Mutual Consent Voluntary
Adoption Registry
Utah Bureau of Vital Statistics
P.O. Box 16700
Salt Lake City, UT 84116-0700
Phone: (801) 538-6843
E-mail: mmuirbro@utah.gov
Web site: www.health.utah.
gov/vitalrecords/silver

VERMONT

Adoptive/Foster Family Support Groups

Casey Family Services
7 Palmer Court
White River Junction, VT
05001-3323
Phone: (802) 649-1400
Fax: (802) 649-2351
Toll-Free: (800) 607-1400
Web site: www.
caseyfamilyservices.org

Grandparents as Parents
76 Glen Road
Lund Family Center
Burlington, VT 05401
Phone: (801) 864-7467
E-mail: adoption@lundfamilyce
nter.org
Web site: www.lundfamilycenter.
org

Institute for Adoption Informa-
tion
P.O. Box 4405
Bennington, VT 05201
Phone: (802) 442-7135
E-mail: kcreedy@adoptionInform
ationinstitute.org

Web site: www.adoptioninformat
ioninstitute.org

Licensed Private Adoption Agencies

Acorn Adoption Inc.
278 Pearl Street
Burlington, VT 05401-8558
Phone: (802) 865-3898
E-mail: acornadoption@msn.com
Web site: www.acornadoption.org
– Intercountry Program
– Child Placement

Adoption Advocates, Inc.
521 Webster Road
Shelburne, VT 05482-6513
Phone: (802) 985-8289
– Intercountry Program
– Child Placement

Angels' Haven Outreach
P.O. Box 53
Monkton, VT 05469
Phone: (802) 453-5450
E-mail: sherry@angels-haven.com
Web site: www.angels-haven.com
– Intercountry Program
– Child Placement

Casey Family Services
160 Palmer Court
White River Junction, VT 05001-
3323
Phone: (802) 649-1400
Fax: (802) 649-2351
Toll-Free: (800) 607-1400
Web site: www.
caseyfamilyservices.org

Friends in Adoption
P.O. Box 1228
44 South Street
Middletown Springs, VT 05757-
1228
Phone: (802) 235-2373
Fax: (802) 235-2311
E-mail: fia@vermontel.net
Web site: www.
friendsinadoption.net

– Intercountry Program
– Child Placement

Friends in Adoption
431 Pine Street, #7
Burlington, VT 05401-4726
Phone: (802) 865-9886
E-mail: fia@vermontel.com
Web site: www.
friendsinadoption.org

Lund Family Center
P.O. Box 4009
76 Glen Road
Burlington, VT 05406-4009
Phone: (802) 864-7467
Fax: (802) 864-1619
Toll-Free: (800) 639-1741
E-mail: adoption@lundfamilyce
nter.org
Web site: www.lundfamilycenter.
org

Vermont Catholic Charities
351 North Avenue
Burlington, VT 05401-2921
Phone: (802) 658-6110, Ext. 312
Fax: (802) 860-0451
E-mail: charities@vermont
catholic.org

Vermont Catholic Charities
24 ½ Center Street
Rutland, VT 05701
Phone: (802) 773-3379
Web site: www.vermontcatholic.
org/vcc/vcc.html

Vermont Children's Aid Society
P.O. Box 127
79 Weaver Street
Winooski, VT 05404
Phone: (802) 655-0006
Fax: (802) 655-0073
Toll-Free: (800) 479-0015
E-mail: mainadmn@vtcas.org
Web site: www.vtcas.org
– Intercountry Program
– Child Placement

Vermont Children's Aid
Society
32 Pleasant Street
Woodstock, VT 05091
Phone: (802) 457-3084
Fax: (802) 457-3086
E-mail: vtcaswdstk@aol.com
Web site: www.vtcas.org
– Intercountry Program
– Child Placement

Wide Horizons For Children
(WHFC)
P.O. Box 53
Monkton, VT 05469
Phone: (802) 453-2581
E-mail: info@whfc.org
Web site: www.whfc.org

**Local/Regional Offices
of the State (Public)
Adoption Agency**

Vermont Department of Social
and Rehabilitation Services
255 North Main Street, Suite 7
Barre, VT 05641
Phone: (802) 479-4260
Fax: (802) 476-1660

**Birth Family and Search
Support Groups**

Adoption Alliance of Vermont
17 Hopkins Street
Rutland, VT 05701
Phone: (802) 773-7078

Adoption Alliance of Vermont
107 Twin Oaks
South Burlington, VT 05403
Phone: (802) 863-1727

Adoption Search/Support
Network
RR 1, Box 83
East Calais, VT 05650
Phone: (802) 456-8850

Beacon of Vermont
P.O. Box 152
Bakersfield, VT 05441-0152
Phone: (802) 758-2369

Institute for Adoption
Information
P.O. Box 4405
Bennington, VT 05201
Phone: (802) 442-7135
E-mail: kcreddy@adoptioninform
ationinstitute.org
Web site: www.adoptioninformat
ioninstitute.org

Lund Family Center
P.O. Box 4009
76 Glen Road
Burlington, VT 05406-4009
Phone: (802) 864-7467
Fax: (802) 864-1619
Toll-Free: (800) 639-1741
E-mail: adoption@lundfamily
center.org
Web site: www.lundfamilycenter.
org

**State Adoption Exchange/
Photolisting of Children
Waiting For Adoption**

Vermont's Waiting Children
130 South Main Street
Waterbury, VT 05671
Phone: (802) 241-2122
Web site: www.projectfamily.
state.vt.us/child_meet_kids_
html

**State Adoption
Specialist/Manager**

Vermont Department of Social
and Rehabilitation Services
Diane Dexter
103 South Main Street
Waterbury, VT 05671
Phone: (802) 241-2142
Fax: (802) 241-2407
E-mail: ddexter@srs.state.vt.us
Web site: www.Path.state.vt.us/
cwj/adoption/

**State Foster Care
Specialist/Manager**

Vermont Department of Social
and Rehabilitation Services
Shaun Donahue
103 South Main Street
Osgood Bldg, 3rd Floor
Waterbury, VT 05671-2401
Phone: (802) 241-2259
Fax: (802) 241-2407
Toll-Free: (800) 746-7000
E-mail: sdonahue@srs.state.vt.us
Web site: www.path.state.vt.us/
csj/PINS.html

**State Interstate Compact on
the Placement of Children
(ICPC) Administrator**

Vermont Department of Social
and Rehabilitation Services
103 South Main Street
Waterbury, VT 05671-2401
Phone: (802) 241-2131
E-mail: mbryce@srs.state.vit.us
Web site: www.state.vt.us/srs/

State Licensing Specialist

Vermont Department of Social
and Rehabilitation Services
Lucy Abair
103 South Main Street
Waterbury, VT 05671
Phone: (802) 241-2159
E-mail: lucy@srs.state.vt.us
Web site: www.state.vt.us/srs/
adoption/agencies.html

State Reunion Registry

Vermont Adoption Registry
103 South Main Street
Waterbury, VT 05671
Phone: (802) 241-2122
E-mail: lkutner@srs.state.vt.us
Web site: www.state.vt.us/srs/
adoption/registry.html

VIRGIN ISLANDS

Adoptive/Foster Family Support Groups

Lutheran Social Services of the Virgin Islands
24-27 Hospital Street
Fredrikstad, St. Croix, VI 00841-0866
Phone: (340) 772-4099
E-mail: lssvi@viaccess.net
Web site: www.lanadopt.org

Attorney Referral Service

Virgin Islands Bar Association
P.O. Box 4108
Christiansted, St. Croix, VI 00822
Phone: (340) 778-7497
TDD: (340) 773-5060

Local/Regional Offices of the State (Public) Adoption Agency

Department of Human Services
1303 Hospital Ground
Building A-Knud Hansen Complex
St. Thomas, VI 00802
Phone: (340) 774-4393, ext. 4243
Fax: (340) 774-0082
E-mail: erahming@hotmail.com

Regional/District Public Agencies

Division of Children, Youth and Families Anna's Hope
Christiansted, St. Croix, VI 00820
Phone: (340) 773-5303

State Adoption Specialist/Manager

Department of Human Services
Etta L. Rahming
1303 Hospital Ground
Building A-Knud Hansen Complex
St. Thomas, VI 00802
Phone: (340) 774-4393, ext. 4243

Fax: (340) 774-0082
E-mail: erahming@hotmail.com

State Foster Care Specialist/Manager

St. Thomas Department of Human Services
Division of Children, Youth and Families
Etta L. Rahming
1303 Hospital Ground, Building A
Knud Hansen Complex
St. Thomas, VI 00802
Phone: (340) 774-0930
Fax: (340) 774-0082
TDD: (340) 774-3466
E-mail: erahming@hotmail.com

State Interstate Compact on the Placement of Children (ICPC) Administrator

Program Development and Evaluation
Virgin Islands Department of Human Services
1303 Hospital Building A
Knud Hansen Complex
Charlotte Amalie, St. Thomas, VI 00802
Phone: (340) 774-0930
TDD: (340) 774-3466

State Licensing Specialist

Department of Human Services
1303 Hospital Ground Building A
Knud Hansen Complex
St. Thomas, VI 00802
Phone: (340) 774-4390
TDD: (340) 774-3466

Department of Human Services
1303 Hospital Building A
Knud Hansen Complex
Charlotte Amalie, St. Thomas, VI 00802
Phone: (340) 774-0930
TDD: (340) 774-3466

VIRGINIA

Adoptive/Foster Family Support Groups

Adoption Attachment Partners
8990-A Fern Park Drive
Burke, VA 22015
Phone: (703) 658-7103
Fax: (703) 658-7105

Adoption Support Adoption Preservation (ASAP)
P.O. Box 981
Glen Allen, VA 23060
Phone: (804) 553-8940
Fax: (804) 355-4157

Adoptive Families of the Fauquier Area (AFFA)
7129 Auburn Mill Road
Warrenton, VA 20187
Phone: (540) 347-7279
E-mail: laurahenson@verizon.net
Web site: www.affa.web.com

Adoptive/Kinship Parent Group of Southwestern Virginia
820 Campbell Avenue SW
Roanoke, VA 24016
Phone: (540) 344-2748
E-mail: Marge_savage@cccofvirginia
Web site: www.cccovirginia.org

Army New Parent Support Program
1231 Mahone Avenue
Fort Lee, VA 23801
Phone: (804) 734-6388

Association of Single Adoptive Families
2624 Chatham Woods Drive
Richmond, VA 23233
Phone: (804) 360-5788

Blue Ridge Adoption Group
103 Union Street
Salem, VA 24153

Braley and Thompson
2965 Colonnade Drive, Suite 130
Roanoke, VA 24018
Phone: (540) 989-7175
Fax: (540) 989-9141
Toll-Free: 1-800 969-6603

Braley and Thompson, Inc.
517 Leesville Road, Suite 202
Lynchburg, VA 24502
Phone: (434) 851-6088

Center for Adoption Support
and Education, Inc. (C.A.S.E.)
8505 Arlington Boulevard, Suite
420
Fairfax., VA 22031
Phone: (703) 573-3701
Fax: (703) 573-3704
E-mail: vsdrsfopy@adoptionsup
port.org
Web site: www.adoptionsupport.
org

The Center for Adoption
Support and Education, Inc.
(C.A.S.E.)
500 West Annandale Road
Falls Church, VA 22046
Phone: (703) 533-7950
Web site: www.adoptionsupport.
org

Diane Hendel
227 North Evergreen Street
Arlington, VA 22203
Phone: (703) 525-8620

Elmy Martinez
P.O. Box 5871
Springfield, VA 22150
Phone: (703) 866-4236
Fax: (703) 866-5888
E-mail: elmyemartinez@aol.com

Families Through Adoption
914 Greensboro Avenue
Virginia Beach, VA 23451
Phone: (757) 422-3932

Families for Russian and
Ukrainian Adoptions
P.O. Box 2944
Merrifield, VA 22116
Phone: (703) 560-6184
Fax: (413) 480-8257
Web site: www.frua.org

Fetal Alcohol Syndrome Sup-
port Group
John Randolph Hospital
Hopewell, VA 23380
Toll-Free: (800) 562-5682

Fostering Adoptive Families
1924 Arlington Boulevard, Suite
102
Charlottesville, VA 22901
Phone: (434) 979-9631
E-mail: datre@mindspring.com

Friends of Children's Services
5294 Lyngate Court
Burke, VA 22015
Phone: (703) 425-0100
Fax: (703) 425-2886
E-mail: lcullen@ccda.net
Web site: www.ccda.net/
children's_services.html

Hampton Roads Foster/Adop-
tive Family
1625 Tallwood Court
Norfolk, VA 23518
Phone: (747) 583-3411
E-mail: JOANVERE@COX.NET
Web site: www.members.cox.
net.hrchildren/kids/htm

Joint Council on International
Children's Services
1403 King Street, Suite 101
Alexandria, VA 22314
Phone: (703) 535-8045
Web site: www.jcics.org

Korean Focus (KF)
1906 Sword Lane
Alexandria, VA 22308
Phone: (703) 799-0591
E-mail: info@koreanfocus.org
Web site: www.koreanfocus.org

Lineages
2660 Petersborough Street
Herndon, VA 20171
Phone: (703) 715-1129
E-mail: scribblesbyShannon@
yahoo.com

North American Council on
Adoptable Children Represen-
tative
2904 Pineville Road
McGaheysville, VA 22840
Phone: (540) 289-9535
E-mail: info@nacac.org
Web site: www.nacac.org

North American Council on
Adoptable Children State
Representative
400 Farmer Street
Petersburg, VA 23804
Phone: (757) 861-4720
E-mail: info@nacac.org
Web site: www.nacac.org

Petersburg Area Adoptive
Association
5112 Front Drive
Petersburg, VA 23803
Phone: (804) 833-0924
Fax: (804) 355-4157

RESOLVE of Washington Met-
ropolitan Area, Inc.
P.O. Box 3423
Merrifield, VA 22116-3423
Phone: (202) 362-5555

Virginia One Church, One Child
1214 West Graham Road, Suite 2
Richmond, VA 23220
Phone: (804) 527-2172
Fax: (804) 329-3960

**Licensed Private
Adoption Agencies**

ABC Adoption Services
4725 Garst Mill Road
Roanoke, VA 24018
Phone: (540) 989-2845

E-mail: adoptabc@aol.com
– Intercountry Program
– Child Placement

Adoption Center of Washington, Inc.
100 Daingerfield Road, Suite 101
Alexandria, VA 22314
Phone: (703) 549-7774
Fax: (703) 549-7778
Toll-Free: (800) 452-3878
E-mail: linda@adoptioncenter.com
Web site: www.adoptioncenter.com
– Intercountry Program
– Child Placement

Adoption Connections
462 Herndon Parkway, Suite 206
Herndon, VA 20170-5235
Phone: (703) 464-5134
E-mail: PerkinsNP@aol.com
Web site: www.adoptionconnections.org

Adoption Options/Jewish Social Service Agency, Inc.
3018 Javier Road
Fairfax, VA 22031
Phone: (703) 204-9592
E-mail: blutton@jssa.org
Web site: www.jssa.org

Adoption Service Information Agency, Inc. (ASIA)
1305 North Jackson Street
Arlington, VA 22201
Phone: (703) 312-0263
E-mail: gsnaider@asia-adopt.org
Web site: www.asia-adopt.org
– Intercountry Program
– Child Placement

Adoption with Love
6718 Patterson Avenue
Richmond, VA 23226
Phone: (804) 282-5644
Fax: (804) 285-0006
E-mail: adoption@jfsrichmond.org
Web site: www.jfsrichmond.org

Adoptions From the Heart, Inc.
P.O. Box 16255
Chesapeake, VA 23328
Phone: (757) 546-3874
Web site: www.adoptionsfromtheheart.org
– Intercountry Program
– Child Placement

AUTUMN Adoptions, Inc.
6204 Old Franconia Road, Suite B
Alexandria, VA 22310
Phone: (703) 541-0697
Fax: (703) 922-4700
E-mail: autumnadoptions@msn.com
Web site: autunmadoptions.org

Autumn Adoptions, Inc
6707 Royal Thomas Way
Alexandria, VA 22315
Phone: (703) 541-2875
E-mail: autumnadoptions@msn.com

Barker Foundation
2955 Monticello Drive
Falls Church, VA 22042
Phone: (703) 536-1827
Fax: (301) 229-0074
Toll-Free: (800) 673-8489
E-mail: info@barkerfoundation.org
Web site: www.barkerfoundation.org

Bethany Christian Services, Inc.
10378-B Democracy Lane
Fairfax, VA 220302522
Phone: (703) 385-5440
Fax: (703) 385-5443
E-mail: bcsfairfax@bethany.org
Web site: www.bethany.org

Bethany Christian Services, Inc.
287 Independence Boulevard, Suite 241
Virginia Beach, VA 23462-2956
Phone: (757) 499-9367

Fax: (757) 518-8356
Web site: www.bethany.org

Bethany Christian Services, Inc.
1924 Arlington Boulevard, Suite 101
Charlottesville, VA 22903
Phone: (434) 979-9631
Fax: (804) 979-3061
E-mail: bcscharlottesville@bethany.org
Web site: www.bethany.org
– Intercountry Program
– Child Placement

Bethany Christian Services, Inc.
910 Little Page Street, Suite A
Fredericksburg, VA 22401
Phone: (540) 373-5165
Fax: (540) 373-6463
E-mail: bcsfredericksburg@bethany.org
Web site: www.bethany.org
– Intercountry Program
– Child Placement

Catholic Charities of Hampton Roads, Inc.
Churchland and Professional Center
3804 Poplar Hill Road, Suite A
Chesapeake, VA 23321
Phone: (757) 484-0703
Web site: www.cc-hr.org

Catholic Charities of Hampton Roads, Inc.
Windsor West Professional Center
12829-A Jefferson Avenue, Suite 101
Newport News, VA 23602
Phone: (757) 875-0060
Fax: (757) 877-7883
Toll-Free: (800) CARE-002
E-mail: dmason@cc-hr.org
Web site: www.cc-hr.org

Catholic Charities of Hampton Roads, Inc.
4855 Princess Anne Road
Virginia Beach, VA 23462-4446
Phone: (757) 467-7707
Fax: (757) 495-3206
Toll-Free: (800) CARE-002
E-mail: dmason@cc-hr.org
Web site: www.cc-hr.org

Catholic Charities of the Diocese of Arlington, Inc.
200 North Glebe Road
Arlington, VA 22203
Phone: (703) 841-3830
Fax: (703) 841-3840
E-mail: pmudd@ccda.net
Web site: www.ccda.net

Catholic Church of Hampton Roads, Inc.
1315 Jamestown Road, Suite 202
Williamsburg, VA 23185
Phone: (757) 253-2847
Web site: www.cc-hr.org

Children's Home Society of Virginia, Inc.
4200 Fitzhugh Avenue
Richmond, VA 23230
Phone: (804) 353-0191
Web site: www.chsva.org

Children's Home Society of Virginia, Inc.
1620 Fifth Street SW
Roanoke, VA 24016
Phone: (540) 344-9281
Fax: (540) 342-3253
Toll-Free: (800) 625-2445 (in Virginia)
E-mail: mcgraws@chsva.org
Web site: www.chsva.org
– Intercountry Program
– Home Study

Children's Home Society of Virginia, Inc.
2400 Fall Hill Avenue, Suite 238
Fredericksburg, VA 22401

Phone: (540) 899-3441
Web site: www.chsva.org

Children's Home Society of Virginia, Inc.
12584 Darby Brooke Court
Woodbridge, VA 22192
Phone: (703) 492-0463
E-mail: csvwb@csv-inc.com

Children's Services of Virginia, Inc.
P.O. Box 2867
311 Airport Road
Winchester, VA 22602
Phone: (540) 667-0116
Fax: (540) 660-0174
Web site: www.childrensservicesofva.com

Children's Services of Virginia, Inc.
7547 Presidential Lane
Manassas, VA 22110
Phone: (703) 331-0075
Fax: (703) 331-0078
E-mail: csva@erols.com
Web site: www.childrensservicesofva.com

Children's Services of Virginia, Inc.
Harrisonburg Branch Office
P.O. Box 177
Harrisonburg, VA 22803
Phone: (540) 801-0900
Fax: (540) 801-0886
Web site: www.childrensservicesofva.com

Commonwealth Catholic Charities, Inc.
P.O. Box 6565
1512 Willow Lawn Drive
Richmond, VA 23230-0565
Phone: (804) 285-5900
Fax: (804) 285-9130
Toll-Free: (800) 974-4494
E-mail: agency@cccofvirginia.org
Web site: www.cccofvirginia.org

– Intercountry Program
– Child Placement

Coordinators/2, Inc.
1617 Monument Avenue, Suite 301
Richmond, VA 23220
Phone: (804) 266-2694
Fax: (804) 355-1001
Toll-Free: (800) 690-4206
E-mail: info@c2adopt.org
Web site: www.c2adopt.org
– Intercountry Program
– Child Placement

Cradle of Hope Adoption Center, Inc.
4084 University Drive, Suite 204
Fairfax, VA 22030
Phone: (703) 352-4806
E-mail: lindacradle@aol.com

Datz Foundation
311 Maple Avenue West, Suite E
Vienna, VA 22180
Phone: (703) 242-8800
Fax: (703) 242-8804
E-mail: markeckman@hotmail.com
Web site: www.datzfound.com
– Intercountry Program
– Child Placement

DePaul Family Services, Inc.
5650 Hollins Road
Roanoke, VA 24019
Phone: (540) 265-8923
E-mail: info@depaulfamilyservices.org
Web site: www.depaulfamilyservices.org

DePaul Family Services, Inc.
440 Premier Circle
Charlottesville, VA 22901
Phone: (434) 977-9847
E-mail: info@depaulfamilyservices.org
Web site: www.depaulfamilyservices.org

Families United Through Adoption
102 Lide Place
Charlottesville, VA 22902
Phone: (434) 923-8253
E-mail: cwalker@cstone.net

Family Life Services
P.O. Box 4199
124 Liberty Mountain Drive
Lynchburg, VA 24502
Phone: (434) 845-5336
Fax: (434) 845-3486
E-mail: familylifeservices@juno.com
Web site: www.godparent.org

Forever Families Adoption Services, Inc.
9 North Third Street, Suite 100, #3
Warrenton, VA 20186
Phone: (540) 341-4679
E-mail: bslaton@foreverfamiliesadoption.org

Frost International Adoptions, Inc.
6348 Lakeview Drive
Falls Church, VA 22041
Phone: (703) 671-3711
Fax: (703) 671-0355
Toll-Free: (888) 823-2090
E-mail: Thogan@Frostadopt.org
Web site: www.frostadopt.org

Holston United Methodist Home for Children, Inc.
115 East Main Street
Abingdon, VA 24210
Phone: (276) 628-1023
E-mail: fsc-abingdon@holstonhome.org
Web site: www.holstonhome.org

Holy Cross Child Placement Agency, Inc.
400 South Washington Street
Alexandria, VA 22314
Phone: (703) 356-8824

Jewish Family Service of Tidewater, Inc.
United Jewish Community Center of the Virginia Peninsula
2700 Spring Road
Newport News, VA 23606
Phone: (757) 489-3111

Jewish Family Service of Tidewater, Inc.
James Building #18
6325 North Center Drive, Suite 203
Norfolk, VA 23606
Phone: (757) 459-4640
Fax: (757) 459-4643
E-mail: jfsvb@exis.net
Web site: www.jfshamptonroads.org

Jewish Family Services
6718 Patterson Avenue
Richmond, VA 23226
Phone: (804) 282-5644, Ext. 23
Fax: (804) 285-0006
E-mail: adoption@jfsrichmond.org

L.D.S. Family Services of Virginia, Inc.
8110 Virginia Pine Court
Richmond, VA 23237
Phone: (804) 743-0727
Fax: (804) 743-8729
Toll-Free: (877) 678-4663
E-mail: fam-va@ldschurch.org
Web site: www.itsaboutlove.org

Loving Families, Inc.
101 South Whiting Street, Suite 212
Alexandria, VA 22304
Phone: (703) 370-7140
E-mail: LovingFam@aol.com
Web site: www.alovingfamily.org
– Intercountry Program
– Child Placement

Lutheran Family Services of Virginia
2000 West Club Lane, Suite B
Richmond, VA 23226
Phone: (804) 288-0122
Toll-Free: (800) 359-3834
E-mail: kjones@lfsva.org
Web site: www.lfsva.org
– Intercountry Program
– Child Placement

Lutheran Social Services of the National Capital Area, Inc.
9506-A Lee Highway
Fairfax, VA 22031
Phone: (703) 273-0303
E-mail: hadzibajrick@lssnca.org
Web site: www.lssnca.org
– Intercountry Program
– Child Placement

Mother Goose Adoptions
43900 Frugality Court, Suite 101-B
Ashburn, VA 20147
Phone: (703) 729-3086
Fax: (703) 729-6718
E-mail: info@mothergooseadoptions.com
Web site: www.mothergooseadoptions.com

New Family Foundation
11350 Random Hills Road, Suite 600
Fairfax, VA 22030
Phone: (703) 273-5960

People Places of Charlottesville
1002 East Jefferson Street
Charlottesville, VA 22905
Phone: (434) 979-0335
E-mail: dmoore@peopleplaces.org
Web site: www.peopleplaces.org

Phillips Program
2010 Braddock Road
Annandale, VA 22003
Phone: (703) 941-3471
Web site: www.phillipsprogram.org

Rainbow Christian Services
6004 Artemus Road
Gainesville, VA 20156
Phone: (703) 754-8516
Fax: (703) 754-2809
Web site: www.manassaschurch.
org/rainbow/

SFI Adoption Services, L.C.
124 Amherst Street
Winchester, VA 22601
Phone: (540) 542-0406

Shore Adoption Services, Inc.
113 Holly Crescent, Suite 102
Virginia Beach, VA 23451
Phone: (757) 422-6361
E-mail: info@shoreadoptionser
vices.org
Web site: www.
shoreadoptionservices.org

**United Methodist Family
Services of Virginia, Inc.**
6335 Little River Turnpike
Alexandria, VA 22312
Phone: (703) 941-9008
Fax: (703) 750-0621
E-mail: northva@umfs.org
Web site: www.umfs.org

**United Methodist Family
Services of Virginia, Inc.**
715 Baker Road, Suite 201
Virginia Beach, VA 23462
Phone: (757) 490-9791
Fax: (757) 490-0159
E-mail: tidewater@umfs.org
Web site: www.umfs.org

**United Methodist Family
Services of Virginia, Inc.**
3900 West Broad Street
Richmond, VA 23230
Phone: (804) 353-4461
Fax: (804) 355-2334
E-mail: info@umfs.org
Web site: www.umfs.org

**Virginia Baptist Children's
Home and Family Services**
700 East Belt Boulevard
Richmond, VA 23224
Phone: (804) 231-4466
E-mail: stephenr@vbchfs.org
Web site: www.vbchfs.org

**Virginia Baptist Children's
Home and Family Services**
P.O. Box 8498
2828 Emerywood Parkway
Richmond, VA 23226
Phone: (804) 545-1200
Fax: (804) 545-12-1
E-mail: vbchrs@msn.com
Web site: www.vbchfs.org

**Welcome House Adoption
Program (of Pearl S. Buck
International)**
9412 Michelle Place
Richmond, VA 23229
Phone: (804) 740-7311
Fax: (804) 740-8038
E-mail: jt664@aol.com
Web site: www.pearl-s-buck.org
– Intercountry Program
– Child Placement

**Birth Family and Search
Support Groups**

**Adoptee Liberty Movement
Association (ALMA)**
c/o Marie Anderson, Coordinator
10321 Capilano Place
Richmond, VA 232336806
Phone: (804) 750-2975
Fax: (804) 750-1412

**Adoptees and Natural Parents
Organization**
949 Lacon Drive
Newport News, VA 23602

**Adoptees and Natural Parents
Organization**
949 Lacon Drive
Newport News, VA 23602

Adult Adoptees in Search
P.O. Box 203
Ferrum, VA 240880203

Bond Between Us
7B Loudoun Street
Leesburg, VA
Phone: (703) 777-1657

**Catholic Charities of the
Diocese of Arlington**
Birthparent Support Group
5294 Lyngate Court
Burke, VA 22015
Phone: (703) 425-0100
Fax: (703) 425-2886
Toll-Free: (800) 227-3002
Web site: www.ccda.net/
children's_services.html

Lineages
2660 Petersborough Street
Herndon, VA 20171
Phone: (703) 715-1129
E-mail: scribblesby
Shannon@yahoo.com

Metro Reunion Registry
An International Registry
6439 Woodridge Road
Alexandria, VA 223121336
E-mail: metro.
reunionregistry@verizon.net
Web site: www.
MetroReunionRegistry.org

**Parents and Adoptees in
Search**
3932 Durette Drive
Richmond, VA 23237

**State Adoption Exchange/
Photolisting of Children
Waiting For Adoption**

**Adoption Resource Exchange
of Virginia (AREVA)**
Virginia Department of Social
Services
7 North 8th Street, Fourth Floor
Richmond, VA 23219
Phone: (804) 726-7524

Fax: (804) 726-7499
Toll-Free: (800) 362-3678
E-mail: srd900@dss.state.va.us
Web site: www.adoptuskids.
org/states/va
– Intercountry Program
– Education/Preparation
– Information/Referral

State Adoption Specialist/Manager

Virginia Department Of Social Services
Brenda Kerr
7 North 8th Street
Richmond, VA 23219
Phone: (804) 726-7530
Fax: (804) 726-7499
Toll-Free: (888) 821-HOPE (4673)
E-mail: brenda.kerr@dss.state.
virginia.gov
Web site: www.dss.state.va.
us/family/adoption. html

State Foster Care Specialist/Manager

Virginia Department of Social Services
Division of Family Services
Therese Wolf
730 East Broad Street
Richmond, VA 23219-1849
Phone: (804) 726-7522
Fax: (804) 726-7499
E-mail: therese.wolf@dss.state.
virginia.gov
Web site: www.dss.state.va.us/
family/fostercare.html

State Interstate Compact on the Placement of Children (ICPC) Administrator

Virginia Department of Social Services
Division of Social Services
7 North 8th Street
Richmond, VA 23219-3301
Phone: (804) 726-7581

E-mail: RoseMarie.Keith@dss.
virginia.dss
Web site: www.dss.state.va.us/
family/interstate.html

State Licensing Specialist

Virginia Department of Social Services
Division of Family Services
Carolynne Stevens
7 North 8th Street
Richmond, VA 23219-3301
Phone: (804) 726-7156
Web site: www.dss.state.va.us/
facility/childplace.html

Statewide Adoption Recruitment Line

Virginia Statewide Adoption Recruitment Line
Toll-Free: (800) 362-3678

National Advocacy Organizations Based in Virginia

National Council For Adoption
225 North Washington Street
Alexandria, VA 22314-2561
Phone: (703) 299-6633
Fax: (703) 299-6004
E-mail: ncfa@adoptioncouncil.org
Web site: www.adoptioncouncil.
org

Military Family Resource-Center
CS4, Suite 302, Room 309
1745 Jefferson Davis Hwy
Arlington, VA 22202-3424
Phone: (703) 602-4964
Phone: 332-4964
Phone: (202) 628-8787
Fax: (703) 602-0189
Fax: 332-0189
E-mail: mfrcrequest@caliber.com
Web site: www.mfrc-dodqol.org

Foundations

Freddie Mac Foundation
8250 Jones Branch Drive
Mailstop A40
McLean, VA 22102
Phone: (703) 918-8888
Fax: (703) 918-8895
E-mail: freddiemac_foundation@
freddiemac.com
Web site: www.
freddiemacfoundation.org

Orphan Foundation of America
Tall Oaks Village Center
12020-D North Shore Drive
Reston, VA 20190-4977
Phone: (571) 203-0270
Fax: (571) 203-0273
E-mail: help@orphan.org
Web site: www.orphan.org

Not-for-profit/Nonprofit

American Counseling Association
5999 Stevenson Avenue
Alexandria, VA 22304
Phone: (703) 823-0252
Fax: (800) 473-2329
TDD: (703) 823-6862
Toll-Free: (800) 347-6647
Web site: www.counseling.org

American Foster Care Resources, Inc.
P.O. Box 271
King George, VA 22485
Phone: (540) 775-7410
Fax: (540) 775-3271
E-mail: afcr@afcr.com
Web site: www.afcr.com

Federation of Families for Children's Mental Health
1101 King Street, Suite 420
Alexandria, VA 22314
Phone: (703) 684-7710
Fax: (703) 836-1040
E-mail: ffcmh@ffcmh.org
Web site: www.ffcmh.org

Joint Council on International
Children's Services
117 S. Saint Asagh Street
Alexandria, VA 22314
Phone: (703) 535-8045
Fax: (703) 535-8049
E-mail: jcics@jcics.org
Web site: www.jcics.org

National Council For Adoption
225 North Washington Street
Alexandria, VA 22314-2561
Phone: (703) 299-6633
Fax: (703) 299-6004
E-mail: ncfa@adoptioncouncil.org
Web site: www.adoptioncouncil.
org

National Association of Children's Hospitals and Related
Institutions
401 Wythe Street
Alexandria, VA 22314
Phone: (703) 684-1355
Fax: (703) 684-1589
E-mail: mbrsvcs@nachri.org
Web site: www.
childrenshospitals.net/

Korean Focus for Adoptive
Families
1906 Sword Lane
Alexandria, VA 22308
E-mail: info@koreanfocus.org
Web site: www.koreanfocus.org

Military Family Resource
Center
CS4, Suite 302, Room 309
1745 Jefferson Davis Hwy
Arlington, VA 22202-3424
Phone: (703) 602-4964
Phone: 332-4964
Phone: (202) 628-8787
Fax: (703) 602-0189
Fax: 332-0189
E-mail: mfrcrequest@caliber.com
Web site: www.mfrc-dodqol.org

National Mental Health
Association
2001 North Beauregard Street,
12th Floor
Alexandria, VA 22311
Phone: (703) 684-7722
Fax: (703) 684-5968
TTY: (800) 433-5959
Toll-Free: (800) 969-6642
E-mail: nmhainfo@aol.com
Web site: www.nmha.org

Training

American Foster Care
Resources, Inc.
P.O. Box 271
King George, VA 22485
Phone: (540) 775-7410
Fax: (540) 775-3271
E-mail: afcr@afcr.com
Web site: www.afcr.com

Center for Adoption Support
and Education, Inc. (C.A.S.E.)
500 W. Annandale Road, Suite
200A
Falls Church, VA 22046
Phone: (703) 533-7950
Fax: (703) 533-8573
Web site: www.adoptionsupport.
org

National Child Care
Information Center
243 Church Street, NW, 2nd Floor
Vienna, VA 22180
Fax: (800) 716-2242
TTY: (800) 516-2242
Toll-Free: (800) 616-2242
Web site: http://nccic.org

**Licensed Private
Adoption Agencies for
Intercountry Adoptions**

America World Adoption
Association
6723 Whittier Avenue, Suite 406
McLean, VA 22101
Phone: (703) 356-8447

Toll-Free: (800) 429-3369
E-mail: info@awaa.org
Web site: www.awaa.org

WASHINGTON

**Adoptive/Foster Family
Support Groups**

Aberdeen Parent Support Group
755 Wenzel Slough Road
Elma, WA 98541

Adoption Resource Center of
Children's Home Society
2323 North Discovery Place
Spokane Valley, WA 99216
Phone: (509) 747-4174
Fax: (509) 838-3847
E-mail: WayneR@chs-wa.org

Adoptive Families Group
201 South 34th Street
Tacoma, WA 98408
Phone: (253) 472-3355

Adoptive Families United
1537 Northeast 92nd Street
Seattle, WA 98115
Phone: (206) 527-0425

Adoptive Families of South
Puget Sound
10106 63rd Avenue, Court E
Puyallup, WA 98373
Phone: (253) 565-6493

Adoptive Parent Group
Bellingham, WA 09225
Phone: (206) 733-5800

Advocates for Single Adoptive
Parents
11634 SE 49th Street
Bellevue, WA 98006
Phone: (425) 644-4761

Advocates for Single Adoptive
Parents – NW
5706 NE 204th Street
Kenmore, WA 98028
Phone: (425) 485-6770

Becoming Adoptive Parents – CEAS
10021 Holman Road
Seattle, WA 98177
Phone: (206) 789-0883
E-mail: info@ceaseattle.org
Web site: www.ceaseattle.org

FAS Family Resource Institute
P.O. Box 2525
Lynnwood, WA 98036
Phone: (253) 531-2878
Fax: (253) 531-2668
E-mail: vicfas@hotmail.com
Web site: http://
fetalalcoholsyndrome.org

Families Like Ours, Inc.
P.O. Box 3137
Renton, WA 98056-3137
Phone: (425) 795-7911
Fax: (425) 671-0856
E-mail: david@familieslikeours.
org
Web site: www.familieslikeours.
org

Families with Children Adopted from Bulgaria
7933 Northeast 124th Street
Kirkland, WA 98034
Phone: (425) 823-8018
Web site: http://groups.yahoo.
com/group/FaCAB1

Fast Friends Family Support Group
151 Conners Road
Camano Island, WA 98282
Phone: (425) 870-4749
Fax: (360) 387-7357
E-mail: cope@camano.net
E-mail: FASDSupport@aol.com

Friends in Adoption
1717 F Court Southwest
Auburn, WA 98002
Phone: (253) 939-5664

Friends in Adoption Support Group
P.O. Box 659
Auburn, WA 98071-0659

GASP – for Adolescent Adoptees
P.O. Box 24
Duvall, WA 98019
Phone: (206) 788-1710

Goldendale Adoptive Parent Group (GAPA)
490 Pine Street Extension
Goldendale, WA 98620
Phone: (509) 773-5737
E-mail: aliced@gorge.net

Guatemalan North American Adoptive Families
2810 1st Avenue North
Seattle, WA 98109
Phone: (206) 285-6254

Jefferson County Adoption Group
132 35th Street
Port Townsend, WA 98368
Phone: (360) 385-5335

Kitsap Adoption Group
5219 Northeast Falcon Ridge Lane
Poulsbo, WA 98370
Phone: (360) 697-2997

Korean Identity Development Society
8315 Lake City Way Northeast, #120
Seattle, WA 98115
Phone: (206) 340-0937

Los Ninos de Colombia
129 Northwest 50th
Seattle, WA 98107
Phone: (206) 827-7152

MT State Foster and Adoption
P.O. Box 169
Colton, WA 99113
Phone: (509) 229-3279

Northend/Eastside Parents Group
10622 Northeast 123rd Street
Kirkland, WA 98034

Northwest Family and Children Services
1303 South 2nd Street
Mt. Vernon, WA 98273
Phone: (360) 336-5244

Omak Parents Support Group
P.O. Box 1065
Omak, WA 98841

One Church, One Child
6419 Martin Luther King Jr. Way
Seattle, WA 98118-3149
Phone: (206) 760-3456
Fax: (206) 760-5678
E-mail: gwendolyn@ococujima.
org
Web site: www.ococujima.org

PRIDE: Native American Adoptive Parents
P.O. Box 24
Duvall, WA 98019
Phone: (206) 788-1710

Parents of Adopted Children
112 Grant Street
Port Angeles, WA 98362
Phone: (206) 452-4757

Precious Connections
9185 Spargur Loop Road
Bainbridge Island, WA 98110
Phone: (206) 340-0937

Program for Early Parent Support
4649 Sunnyside Avenue North, #324
Seattle, WA 98103
Phone: (206) 547-8570

RESOLVE of Washington State
P.O. Box 31231
Seattle, WA 98103
Phone: (206) 524-7257

SSAFE
5581 – 2nd Avenue
Fendale, WA 98248
Phone: (206) 384-0629

San Juan Island Support
Group
P.O. Box 267
Eastsound, WA 98245

Sharing Activities Regarding
India
2031 – 216th Place Northeast
Sammamish, WA 98053
Phone: (425) 868-6259

South Whidbey Island Support
Group
2140 East Milman Road
Langley, WA 98260

Stars of David
7212 – 54th Avenue South
Seattle, WA 98118
Phone: (206) 364-8270

Support Group for Gay &
Lesbian Parents
CHS of WA
3300 NE 65th Street
Seattle, WA 98115
Phone: (206) 695-3200
Fax: (206) 695-3201

Touched by Adoption
405 Denny Building
Walla Walla, WA 99362
Phone: (509) 529-2130

Unlimited Parents
840 North Broadway MSN 31-10
Everett, WA 98201
Phone: (206) 339-4817

Washington Adoption
Resource Exchange
600 Stewart Street, Suite 1313
Seattle, WE 98101
Phone: (206) 441-6822
Fax: (206) 441-7281
Toll-Free: (800) 927-9411
E-mail: ware@nwresource.org

Web site: www.nwresource.
org/af_ware.htm

Yakima Parent Support Group
404 South 37th Avenue
Yakima, WA 98902

**Licensed Private
Adoption Agencies**

A Child's Dream
P.O. Box 680
Poulsbo, WA 98370
Phone: (360) 589-6533
Fax: (360) 598-6729
Toll-Free: (800) 247-8280
E-mail: amadoption@comcast.
net
Web site: www.achildsdream.org
– Intercountry Program
– Home Study

Adoption Advocates Interna-
tional
401 East Front Street
Port Angeles, WA 98362
Phone: (360) 452-4777
Fax: (360) 452-1107
E-mail: merrily@adoptionadvoc
ates.org
Web site: www.
adoptionadvocates.org
– Intercountry Program
– Child Placement

Americans Adopting Orphans
12345 Lake City Way NE,
#2001
Seattle, WA 98125
Phone: (206) 524-5437
Fax: (206) 527-2001
E-mail: aao@orphans.com
Web site: www.orphans.com

Bethany Christian Services
19936 Ballinger Way NE, Suite D
Seattle, WA 98155
Phone: (206) 367-4604
Fax: (206) 367-1860
Toll-Free: (800) 733-4604
E-mail: bcseattle@bethany.org
Web site: www.bethany.org

Catholic Children and Family
Services of Walla Walla
Drumheller Building, Suite 33
Walla Walla, WA 99362
Phone: (509) 525-0572
Fax: (509) 525-0576
E-mail: wwcounseling@dioceseo
fspokane.org
Web site: http://www.ccfs-
walla2.org

Catholic Children's Services of
Northwest Washington
1133 Railroad Avenue, Suite 100
Bellingham, WA 98226
Phone: (360) 733-5800

Catholic Community Services
100 23rd Avenue South
Seattle, WA 98144
Phone: (206) 328-5921
Fax: (206) 328-5909
E-mail: carolr@ccsww.org
– Intercountry Program
– Child Placement

Catholic Family and Child
Service
1023 Riverside Avenue
Spokane, WA 99201
Phone: (509) 358-4260

Catholic Family and Child
Service of Wenatchee
23 South Wenatchee, #320
Wenatchee, WA 98801-2264
Phone: (509) 662-6761
Fax: (509) 663-3182
Toll-Free: (800) 261-1094
E-mail: STryon@cfcs.net.

Catholic Family and Child
Service of Yakima
5301-C Tieton Drive
Yakima, WA 98908
Phone: (509) 965-7100
Fax: (509) 966-9750
Toll-Free: (800) 246-2962
E-mail: csampson-
kruse@cfcsyakima.org
Web site: www.cfcsyakima.org

Catholic Family and Child
Services
2139 Van Giesen
Richland, WA 99352
Phone: (509) 946-4645
Fax: (509) 943-2068

Children's Home Society of
Washington
Regional Headquarters
P.O. Box 15190
3300 NE 65th Street
Seattle, WA 98115-0190
Phone: (206) 695-3200
E-mail: chswa@chs-wa.org
Web site: www.chs-wa.org

Children's Home Society of
Washington, Southeast Area
1014 Walla Walla Avenue
Wenatchee, WA 98801-1523
Phone: (509) 663-0034
E-mail: chswa@chs-wa.org
Web site: www.chs-wa.org

Children's Home Society of
Washington, Southwest Area
309 West 12th Street
Vancouver, WA 98666
Phone: (360) 695-1325
E-mail: chswa@chs-wa.org
Web site: www.chs-wa.org

Children's Home Society of
Washington, West Central
Area
201 South 34th
Tacoma, WA 98408
Phone: (253) 472-3355
E-mail: chswa@chs-wa.org
Web site: www.chs-wa.org

Children's Hope International
(CHI)
1495 NW Gilman Boulevard,
Suite #4
Issaquah, WA 98027
Phone: (425) 391-9150
E-mail: Linda@childrenshope.com
Web site: www.childrenshope.
com

Children's House International
P.O. Box 1829
Ferndale, WA 98248
Phone: (360) 380-5370
Fax: (360) 383-0640
E-mail: chi4adopt@aol.com
Web site: www.childrenshouse
international.com
– Intercountry Program
– Child Placement

Christian Family Adoptions
P.O. Box 87636
Vancouver, WA 98687
Phone: (503) 232-1211
Phone: (360) 892-1572
E-mail: mail@christianfamilyado
ptions.org
Web site: www.
christianfamilyadoptions.org

Faith International Adoptions
535 East Dock Street, Suite 103
Tacoma, WA 98402
Phone: (253) 383-1928
Fax: (253) 572-6662
E-mail: faith@faithadodopt.org
Web site: www.faithadopt.org
– Intercountry Program
– Child Placement

LDS Family Services, Inc.
200 North Mullon, Suite 222
Spokane, WA 99206
Phone: (801) 752-5302

Lutheran Community Services
North West
433 Minor Avenue North
Seattle, WA 98109
Phone: (206) 694-5700
E-mail: lssnw@aol.com
Web site: www.lcsnw.org

Lutheran Social Services of
Washington, Southeast Area
3321 Kennewick Ave
Kennewick, WA 99336
Phone: (509) 735-6446

Medina Children's Services
123 16th Avenue
Seattle, WA 98122
Phone: (206) 260-1700
Fax: (206) 260-1777
Toll-Free: (800) 239-9238
E-mail: info@medinachild.org
Web site: www.medinachild.org

New Hope Child and Family
Agency
19304 King's Garden Drive North
Seattle, WA 98133
Phone: (206) 363-1800
Fax: (206) 363-0318
E-mail: info@newhopekids.org
Web site: www.newhopekids.org
– Intercountry Program
– Child Placement

New Hope Children and Family
Agency
2611 NE 125th Street, Suite 146
Seattle, WA 98125
Phone: (509) 926-6581

World Association for Children
and Parents (WACAP)
P.O. Box 88948
Seattle, WA 98138
Phone: (206) 575-4550
Fax: (206) 575-4148
E-mail: wacap@wacap.org
Web site: www.wacap.org
– Intercountry Program
– Child Placement

**Birth Family and Search
Support Groups**

Adoption Resource Center of
Children's Home Society of
Washington
Northwest Branch
3300 Northeast 65th Street
Seattle, WA 98115
Phone: (206) 524-6020
E-mail: chswa@chs-wa.org
Web site: www.chs-wa.org

Adoption Search and
Reconciliation
14320 SE 170
Renon, WA 98058
E-mail: shea@oz..net

Concerned United
Birthparents
10014 Northeast 35th Street
Vancouver, WA 98662

Confidential Intermediary
Services
625 East Paradise Road
Spangle, WA 99031
Phone: (509) 448-3740
Fax: (509) 448-0967
E-mail: SamsSearch@msn.com
Web site: www.Sams.
Search.com

Open Arms
6816-135 Court, NE
Redmond, WA 98052

Washington Adoptees
Rights Movement (WARM)
5950 Sixth Avenue South,
Suite 107
Seattle, WA 98108-2317
Phone: (206) 767-9510
E-mail: warm@wolfenet.com
Web site: www.warmsearch.org

**State Adoption Exchange/
Photolisting of Children
Waiting For Adoption**

Northwest Adoption
Exchange
600 Stewart Street, Suite 1313
Seattle, WA 98101
Phone: (206) 441-6822
Fax: (206) 441-7281
Toll-Free: (800) 927-9411
E-mail: ware@nwresource.org

**State Adoption
Specialist/Manager**

Washington Department of
Social and Health Services
Division of Children and Family
Services
Pam Kramer
P.O. Box 45713
1115 Washington Street, SE
Olympia, WA 98504
Phone: (360) 902-7968
Fax: (360) 902-7904
E-mail: caip300@dshs.wa.gov
Web site: www1.dshs.wa.gov/
ca/adopt/intro.asp

**State Foster Care
Specialist/Manager**

Washington Department of
Social and Health Services
Division of Children & Family
Services
Deanna Bedell
P.O. Box 45710
14th & Jefferson OB-2
Olympia, WA 98504
Phone: (360) 902-7986
Fax: (360) 902-7903
Web site: www1.dshs.wa.gov/
ca/fosterparent/index/asp

**State Interstate Compact on
the Placement of Children
(ICPC) Administrator**

Washington Department of
Social and Health Services
Children's Administration
P.O. Box 45711
Olympia, WA 98504-5710
Phone: (360) 902-7984
Fax: (360) 902-7903

State Licensing Specialist

Washington Department of
Social and Health Services
Division of Licensed Resources
Susan Muggoch
P.O. Box 45700
Olympia, WA 98504
Phone: (360) 902-8009

WEST VIRGINIA

**Adoptive/Foster Family
Support Groups**

Errands of Mercy
305 Jasper Drive
Beckley, WV 26801
Phone: (304) 237-6183
E-mail: rns/@ureach.com
Web site: www.errandsofmercy.
org

Guatemala Adoptive Family
Association of WV
P.O. Box 673
Charleston, WV 25323
E-mail: cstump@swartzstump.
com

Parents Adopting and Learning to Support
301 High Street
Belington, WV 26250
Phone: (304) 823-3015

**Licensed Private
Adoption Agencies**

Adoption Services, Inc.
Route 1, Box 675
Berkley Springs, WV 25411
Phone: (717) 737-3960
Fax: (717) 731-0157
Toll-Free: (800) 943-0400
E-mail: mail@adoptionservices.
org
Web site: www.
adoptionservices.org

Bailey and Thompson, Inc.
P.O. Box 1396
St. Albans, WV 25177
Phone: (304) 722-1704

Burlington United Methodist Family Services
Box 346A, Route 3
Grafton, WV 26354
Phone: (304) 265-1338
Fax: (304) 757-9136
Toll-Free: (800) 296-6144
Web site: www.bumfs.org
– Intercountry Program
– Child Placement

Burlington United Methodist Family Services
Box 3122, Route 3
Keyser, WV 26726
Phone: (304) 788-2342
Fax: (304) 788-2409
E-mail: janice@bumfs.org
Web site: www.bumfs.org
– Intercountry Program
– Child Placement

Burlington United Methodist Family Services
P.O. Box 370
Scott Depot, WV 25560-0370
Phone: (304) 757-9127
Fax: (304) 757-9136
E-mail: donna@bumfs.org
Web site: www.bumfs.org

Childplace, Inc.
5101 Chesterfield Avenue SE
Charleston, WV 25304
Phone: (304) 757-0763
E-mail: nathans@childplace.org
Web site: www.childplace.org

Children's Home Society of West Virginia
165 Scott Avenue, Suite 106
Morgantown, WV 26508
Phone: (304) 284-0992
E-mail: dneighbors@adelphia.net
Web site: www.childhswv.org

Children's Home Society of West Virginia
815 West King Street, Suite 200
Martinsburg, WV 25401
Phone: (304) 264-0225

Children's Home Society of West Virginia
1145 Greenbrier Street
Charleston, WV 25311
Phone: (304) 345-3894
Fax: (304) 345-3899
E-mail: ARCCHS@childhswv.org
Web site: www.childhswv.org

Children's Home Society of West Virginia
P.O. Box 5533
1805 Honaker Avenue
Princeton, WV 24740
Phone: (304) 431-2424
E-mail: childrenshomesociety@childhswv.org
Web site: www.childhswv.org

Birth Family and Search Support Groups

Legacies
826 Honaker Lane
Charleston, WV 25312

State Adoption Exchange/ Photolisting of Children Waiting For Adoption

West Virginia Adoption Resource Network
Office of Social Services
350 Capitol Street, Room 691
Charleston, WV 25301
Phone: (304) 558-2891
Fax: (304) 558-4563
Web site: www.wvdhhr.org/oss/adoption/

State Adoption Specialist/Manager

West Virginia Department of Health and Human Resources
Children and Adult Services
Laura Lou Harbert
Office of Social Services
350 Capitol Street, Room 691
Charleston, WV 25301
Phone: (304) 558-4303
Fax: (304) 558-7980
E-mail: lauraharbert@wvdhhr.org
Web site: www.wvdhhr.org/oss/children/adoption.htm

State Foster Care Specialist/Manager

West Virginia Department of Health and Human Resources
Office of Social Services
Christina Bertelli
350 Capitol Street, Room 691
Charleston, WV 25301-3704
Phone: (304) 558-3290
Fax: (304) 558-4563
E-mail: cbertelli@wvdhhr.org
Web site: www.wvdhhr.org/bcf/children_adult/foster/

State Interstate Compact on the Placement of Children (ICPC) Administrator

West Virginia Department of Health and Human Resources
Office of Social Services
350 Capitol Street, Room 691
Charleston, WV 25301-3704
Phone: (304) 558-1260
Phone: (304) 558-3431
Fax: (304) 558-4563
E-mail: nchalhoub@wvdhhr.org
E-mail: suehage@wvdhhr.org

State Licensing Specialist

West Virginia Department of Health and Human Resources
Kathie King
350 Capitol Street,Room 691
Charleston, WV 25301
Phone: (304) 558-8839
Fax: (304) 558-4563
E-mail: kking@wvdhhr.org

WISCONSIN

Adoptive/Foster Family Support Groups

Adoption Adventure
920 12th Avenue West
Ashland, WI 54806
Phone: (715) 682-9070
E-mail: kswanson@ncis.net

Adoption Adventure Support Group
P.O. Box 577
137 East Tyler Avenue
Mellen, WI 54546
Phone: (715) 274-4343

Adoption Resource Network
4511 Woodridge Drive
Eau Claire, WI 54701
Phone: (715) 835-6695

Adoption is Forever
3305 West Justin Street
Appleton, WI 54914
Phone: (920) 734-1153
E-mail: JM11654@aol.com

Adoptive Families of Greater Milwaukee
6358 West Arch Avenue
Brown Deer, WI 53223
Phone: (414) 355-3970

Adoptive Families of Wisconsin
P.O. Box 575, Route 3
North 12652, Highway M
Galesville, WI 54630
Phone: (608) 582-4254

Adoptive Family Connections of Greater Milwaukee
15385 West Glenora Court
New Berlin, WI 53151
Phone: (262) 860-0940
E-mail: ahale@wi.rr.com

Adoptive Moms Discussion Group
Jewish Community Center
6255 North Santa Monica Boulevard
Whitefish Bay, WI 53217
Phone: (414) 964-4444

Adoptive Moms and Foster Moms
206 South University Avenue
Beaver Dam, WI 53916
Phone: (414) 885-6903
E-mail: syaroch@hotmail.com

Adoptive Parent Group of Southern Wisconsin
1408 Vilas Avenue
Madison, WI 53711
Phone: (608) 251-0736
Fax: (608) 251-6856
E-mail: Mauri@aol.com

Adoptive and Foster Families Support Group
North 348, Highway 89
Columbus, WI 53925
Phone: (920) 623-3551

Birthparent Support Group
3200 West Highland Boulevard
Milwaukee, WI 53208
Phone: (414) 342-7175

Breaking the Silence
N 2764 Alexander Lake Road
Merrill, WI 54452-9362

C.H.A.D.D. of Southeast Wisconsin
P.O. Box 1477
Milwaukee, WI 53201-1477
Phone: (414) 299-9442

Catholic Charities – Diocese of La Crosse
Post Adoption Resource Center (P.A.R.C.)
128 South Sixth Street
La Crosse, WI 54601-0266
Phone: (608) 782-0710
Toll-Free: (888) 212-4357
E-mail: info@catholiccharitiesl ax.org
Web site: www. catholiccharitieslax.org

Central Wisconsin Support Group
P.O. Box 451
Colby, WI 54421
Phone: (715) 223-4581
E-mail: magnus2@verizon.net

Cindy Hodgeman
869 North Cates Road
Belleville, WI 53508-9539
Phone: (414) 462-8193

Community Adoption Center (CAC)
3701 Kadow Street
Manitowoc, WI 542220
Phone: (920) 682-9211
Fax: (920) 682-8611
Toll-Free: (800) 236-7863
E-mail: Communityadoption.com

FUSE Families United of Southeast Wisconsin
141 Northwest Barstow, #209
Waukesha, WI 53188
Phone: (414) 521-5109

Families United Through Adoption (FUTA)
297 Saint Augustine Road
Colgate, WI 53017
Phone: (414) 628-4559

Families from Colombia
718 Marcks Lane
Luxemburg, WI 54217
Phone: (920) 845-2075

Families of Russian and
Ukrainian Adoptions
1449 Hilltop View Court
Hubertus, WI 53044-9436
Phone: (414) 297-9000
Fax: (414) 423-1481
Web site: www.frua.org

Families with Children from
China
21150 Stratford Court
Brookfield, WI 53045
Phone: (414) 784-4404

Family Services of Northeast
Wisconsin
300 Crooks Street
Green Bay, WI 54301
Phone: (920) 436-4360
Fax: (920) 432-5966
Toll-Free: (800) 998-9609
E-mail: postadoption@familyserv
icesnew.org
Web site: www.
familyservicesnew.org/
fcguidanceserv.html

Fox Valley Friends in Adoption
N 1611 Prairie View Drive
Greenville, WI 54942
Phone: (920) 757-6149

Friends of Adoption
1702 Old A Road
Spooner, WI 54801
Phone: (715) 468-2881

HOPE
2218 Inverness Drive
Waukesha, WI 53186
Phone: (414) 548-3574
Fax: (262) 548-3589
E-mail: freddy@pitnet.net

Heart Holders
2637 Pennwall Circle
Fitchburg, WI 53711
Phone: (608) 274-7967

Infertility Support Group
113 South Franklin Street
Janesville, WI 53545-3812

Interracial Families Network/
Family Enhancement
2120 Fordem Avenue
Madison, WI 53704
Phone: (608) 231-1490

Just in Time for Dads/KAY
Foundation
P.O. Box 46160
Madison, WI 53744
Phone: (608) 273-2888
Fax: (608) 273-2876
Web site: www.kayfoundation.
org

Lakeshore Adoptive Families
1460 Iris Drive
Manitowoc, WI 54220
Phone: (920) 682-1647

MUMS National Parent to
Parent Network
150 Custer Court
Green Bay, WI 54301
Phone: (920) 336-5333

Milagros de Guatemala
Madison, WI
Phone: (608) 833-4211
E-mail: laduruss@yahoo.com
Web site: www.madison.com/
communities/mdguate

Mothercare
4803 West Burleigh
Milwaukee, WI 53210
Phone: (414) 449-2868

NAMASTE
546 Black Earth Court
Wales, WI 53813
Phone: (262) 968-4564
E-mail: Reinbold@execpc.com

NICA Parent Group
2809 North 56th Street
Milwaukee, WI 53210
Phone: (414) 445-5088

National Foster Parent
Association, Inc.
2706 Badger Lane
Madison, WI 53713
Phone: (608) 774-9111

Ours Through Adoption of
Northeast Wisconsin
Phone: (920) 435-2626
Web site: www.geocities.com/
oursadopt

Post Adopt On-Line Support
Group
206 South University Avenue
Beaver Dam, WI 53916
Phone: (920) 885-6903
E-mail: syaroch@hotmail.com
Web site: www.geocities.com/
syaroch.geo

Post Adoptive Resource
Project
7800 South Butterfly Road
Beloit, WI 53511
Phone: (608) 365-9554

RESOLVE of Northern
Wisconsin
1028 9th Street
Menasha, WI 54952
Phone: (414) 722-5021

RESOLVE of SE Wisconsin
P.O. Box 13842
Wauwatosa, WI 53213-0842
Phone: (414) 521-4590

Racine Support Group
618 Monroe Avenue
Racine, WI 53405

Search
908 North Superior Street
Appleton, WI 54911
Phone: (920) 739-7444
E-mail: jkbogie3@aol.com

SideKicks
11672 Mascot Avenue
Cashton, WI 54619
Phone: (608) 654-7607
Fax: (608) 269-1850
E-mail: tabby37@elroynet.com

Special Needs Adoptive
Parents Support of
Southeastern Wisconsin
357 Juniper Court
Grafton, WI 53024
Phone: (262) 376-0259
E-mail: beloin@execpc.com
Web site: www.4snaps.com

Support Group for Foster and
Adoptive Parents
6763 Hand Hill Drive
Dodgeville, WI 53533
Toll-Free: (888) 485-7385

Support Group for Foster and
Adoptive Parents
3577 High Point Road
Madison, WI 53744
Fax: (608) 821-3125

Support Group for Foster and
Adoptive Parents
2507 Sunshine Lane
Beloit, WI 53511-2254

Transracial Adoptive Family
Network
1801 North 49th Street
Milwaukee, WI 53208
Phone: (414) 784-0504

Transracial Families of
Milwaukee (TFM)
Doug H. of TFM
P.O. Box 370961
Milwaukee, WI 53237-2061
Phone: (414) 486-7553
E-mail: transracialfamiliesmilw@
hotmail.com

Uniquely Ours Support Group
W3839 Little Prairie Road
East Troy, WI 53120

Phone: (262) 642-7975
E-mail: Adoptmom8@netwurx.
net

United Family Organization
909 River Street
Rhinelander, WI 54501
Phone: (715) 362-5846

United Foster Parent Association of Greater Milwaukee, Inc.
12828 Woods Road
Muskego, WI 53150
Phone: (414) 525-1163

United States Chilean
Adoptive Families
1239 East Broadway Street
Waukesha, WI 53186
Phone: (262) 547-0671

Voices United
2333 North 60th Street
Wauwatosa, WI 53210

Voices United, Inc.
2645 South 30th Street
Milwaukee, WI 53215
Phone: (414) 645-9656
E-mail: joeandkia@aol.com
Web site: voices-united.org

Waiting to Adopt Support
Group
680 Wolcott Street
West Bend, WI 53090
Phone: (414) 334-0424
E-mail: dmiske@hnet.net

Wausau Area Adoptive Par-
ents Support Group
9407 Cedar Park
Rothschild, WI 54474
Phone: (715) 359-4857

Wisconsin Association of
Single Adoptive Parents
4520 North Bartlett Avenue
Shorewood, WI 53211-1509
Phone: (414) 962-9342

Wisconsin Association of
Single Adoptive Parents
3634 North 99th Street
Milwaukee, WI 53222

Wisconsin Attachment
Resource Network
P.O. Box 236
Dousman, WI 53118
Phone: (262) 965-5170
E-mail: ruder@w-a-r-n.com
Web site: www.w-a-r-n.com

Wisconsin Family Ties
16 North Carroll Street, #640
Madison, WI 53703
Phone: (608) 267-6888
E-mail: info@wifamilyties.org
Web site: www.wifamilyties.org

Wisconsin Federation of Fos-
ter Parent Association, Inc.
7057 South Lasch Lane
Lake Nebagamon, WI 54849
Phone: (715) 374-2180
Fax: (715) 374-2137
E-mail: varankin@discover-net.
net

Wisconsin Foster Adoptive
Parent Association
901 7th Street
Menasha, WI 54952
Phone: (920) 725-4450
After hours: (920) 725-4450
E-mail: coenenhome12@new.
rr.com

Wisconsin Foster and
Adoptive Parents Association,
Inc. (WFAPA)
North 98 West 15725 Shagbark
Road
Germantown, WI 53022
Phone: (262) 251-4412
Fax: (262) 251-2167
E-mail: adopt12@aol.com
Web site: www.wfapa.org

Wisconsin Open Door Society
2841 North Stowell Avenue
Milwaukee, WI 53211
Phone: (414) 963-0273

Wisconsin Single Adoptive
Parents
127 St. Louis Drive
Prairie Du Chien, WI 53821
Phone: (608) 326-6657

Wisconsin Single Parents of
Adopted Children
403 Vilas Avenue
Nekoosa, WI 54457
Phone: (715) 886-5572

Wisconsin Single Parents of
Adopted Children
810 Richards Street
Watertown, WI 53094
Phone: (920) 262-2540

**Licensed Private
Adoption Agencies**

Adoption Advocates, Inc.
2713 International Lane, Suite
119
Madison, WI 53704
Phone: (608) 246-2844
Fax: (608) 246-2875
– Intercountry Program
– Child Placement

Adoption Choice
924 East Juneau Avenue, Suite
410
Milwaukee, WI 53202-2748
Phone: (414) 276-3262
Fax: (414) 276-2644
Toll-Free: (800) 255-6305
E-mail: adoptionchoice@aol.com
Web site: www.adoption.com/
adoptionchoice
– Intercountry Program
– Child Placement

Adoption Option
1804 Chapman Drive
Waukesha, WI 53189
Phone: (262) 544-4278

Adoption Services, Inc.
2439 South Oneida Street
Appleton, WI 54915
Phone: (920) 735-6750
E-mail: adoptionserv@milwpc.
com
Web site: www.
adoptionservicesinc.com
– Intercountry Program
– Child Placement

Adoption Services, Inc.
2314 North Grandview Boulevard,
Suite 300
Waukesha, WI 53188
Phone: (262) 513-0443
E-mail: adoptionserv@milwpc.com
Web site: www.
adoptionservicesinc.com
– Intercountry Program
– Child Placement

Adoptions of Wisconsin
434 South Yellowstone Drive
Madison, WI 53719
Phone: (608) 821-8220

Bethany Christian Services of
Wisconsin
2312 North Grandview Boulevard,
Suite 207
Waukesha, WI 53188-1606
Phone: (262) 547-6557
Fax: (414) 547-3644
Toll-Free: (800) 238-4269
E-mail: info@bethany.org
Web site: www.bethany.org
– Intercountry Program
– Child Placement

Catholic Charities of the
Diocese of La Crosse, Inc.
(Friends of Adoption: Post
Adoption Resource Center)
1416 Cumming Avenue
Superior, WI 54880
Phone: (715) 394-6617
Fax: (715) 394-5951
Toll-Free: (888) 831-8446
E-mail: phawkins@catholic
chartieslax.com

Web site: www.friendsof
adoption.org

Catholic Charities – Madison
3577 Highpoint Road
Madison, WI 53719
Phone: (608) 821-3100

Catholic Charities of the
Archdiocese of Milwaukee
2021 North 60th Street
Milwaukee, WI 53208
Phone: (414) 771-2881
Fax: (414) 771-1674
E-mail: pwenddt@ccmke.org
Web site: www.ccmke.org

Catholic Charities, Inc.
P.O. Box 266
128 South 6th Street
LaCrosse, WI 54602-0266
Phone: (608) 782-0704
E-mail: info@catholiccharities
lax.org
Web site: www.catholic
charitieslax.org

Catholic Social Services
– Green Bay
P.O. Box 23825
Green Bay, WI 54305-3825
Phone: (920) 437-6541
E-mail: diocmail@gbdioc.org
Web site: www.gbdioc.org

Center for Child and Family
Services, Inc.
6427 West Capitol Drive
Milwaukee, WI 53216
Phone: (414) 442-4702

Children and Families First,
Inc.
583 D'Onofrio Drive, Suite 220
Madison, WI 53719
Phone: (608) 826-0498
E-mail: info@cffwi.org
Web site: www.cffwi.org
– Intercountry Program
– Child Placement

Children's Service Society of Wisconsin
1212 South 70th Street
West Allis, WI 53214
Phone: (414) 453-1400
Fax: (414) 453-3389
Toll-Free: (800) 653-2779
Web site: www.cssw.org
– Intercountry Program
– Child Placement

Community Adoption Center
3701 Kadow Street
Manitowoc, WI 54220
Phone: (920) 682-9211
Fax: (920) 682-8611

Crossroads Adoption Services
911 Fourth Street, Suite 214
Hudson, WI 54016
Phone: (715) 386-5550
Fax: (715) 386-5670
E-mail: xroadswi@pressenter.com
Web site: www.crossroadsadoption.com
– Intercountry Program
– Child Placement

Evangelical Child and Family Agency
District Office
1617 South 124th Street
New Berlin, WI 53151
Phone: (262) 789-1881
Fax: (262) 789-1887
Toll-Free: (800) 686-3232
E-mail: ecfawisc@aol.com
Web site: www.ecfawisc.org
– Intercountry Program
– Home Study

LDS Social Services
1711 University Avenue
Madison, WI 53705

Lifelink Adoption Services
4435 North Calhoun Road
Milwaukee, WI 53005
Phone: (262) 781-7781
Fax: (262) 781-7781

Web site: www.lifelinkadoption.org
– Intercountry Program
– Child Placement

Lifelink Adoption Services
1130 West Marquette Street
Appleton, WI 54914-2312
Phone: (920) 882-8450
Fax: (920) 882-8450
Web site: www.lifelinkadoption.org
– Intercountry Program
– Child Placement

Lutheran Counseling and Family Services
P.O. Box 13367
3800 North Mayfair Road
Wauwatosa, WI 53222
Phone: (414) 536-8333
E-mail: lcfsadoption@bizwi.rr.com
Web site: www.lcfswi.org

Lutheran Social Services of Wisconsin and Upper Michigan
647 West Virginia Street, Suite 300
Milwaukee, WI 53204-1535
Phone: (414) 281-4400
Fax: (414) 325-3124
E-mail: info @lsswis.org
Web site: http://lsswis.org
– Intercountry Program
– Child Placement

PATH, Inc.
516 2nd Street, Suite 209
Hudson, WI 54016-1591
Phone: (715) 386-1547

Pauquette Children's Services, Inc.
P.O. Box 162
315 West Conant Street
Portage, WI 53901-0162
Phone: (608) 742-8004
Fax: (608) 742-7937
E-mail: adopt@palacenet.net
Web site: www.adoptpas.com

Special Beginnings Adoption Services
275 Regency Court, Suite 104
Brookfield, WI 53045
Phone: (262) 432-1055
Toll-Free: (800) 481-3611
E-mail: specialbeginnings@voa.org

Special Children, Inc.
15285 Watertown Plank Road, Suite 3
Elm Grove, WI 53122
Phone: (262) 821-2125
Fax: (262) 821-2157
E-mail: spchild@execpc.com
– Intercountry Program
– Child Placement

Sunshine International Adoption, Inc.
910 Elm Grove Road, Suite 34
Elm Grove, WI 53122
Phone: (262) 796-9898

Van Dyke, Inc.
1224 Weeden Creek Road, Suite 4
Sheboygan, WI 53081-8225
Phone: (920) 452-5358
Fax: (920) 452-5515
E-mail: raa@execpc.com
Web site: www.execpc.com/romanian_adoption_assistance/
– Intercountry Program
– Child Placement

Birth Family and Search Support Groups

Adoption Roots Traced
N5080 17th Avenue
Mauston, WI 53948

Birthparent Forum
2314 North Grandview Boulevard, Suite 300
Waukesha, WI 53188
Phone: (262) 513-0443
Fax: (262) 513-6756
Toll-Free: (888) 686-0443
E-mail: info@birthparentforum.org

Common Bonds
ISC
280 D North Campbell Road
Oshkosh, WI 54901

Opens Ends of Adoption
1219 Hobart Drive
Green Bay, WI 54305-0875

State Adoption Exchange/ Photolisting of Children Waiting For Adoption

Adoption Resources of Wisconsin
6682 West Greenfield Avenue, Suite 310
Milwaukee, WI 53214
Phone: (414) 475-1246
Fax: (414) 475-7007
Toll-Free: (800) 762-8063
E-mail: info@wiadopt.org
Web site: www.wiadopt.org/ AdoptionResourcesofWisconsin. aspx

State Adoption Specialist/Manager

Wisconsin Department of Health and Family Services
Division of Child and Family Services
Dale Langer
1 West Wilson
Madison, WI 53708-8916
Phone: (608) 266-3595
Fax: (608) 264-6750
E-mail: langedw@dhfs/state/ wi.us
Web site: www.dhfs.state.wi.us/ children/adoption/index.htm

State Foster Care Specialist/Manager

Wisconsin Department of Health and Family Services
Division of Children and Family Services
Connie Klick

P.O. Box 8916
1 West Wilson
Madison, WI 53708-8916
Phone: (608) 266-1489
Fax: (608) 264-6750
E-mail: klickel@dhfs.state.wi.us
Web site: www.dhfs.wisconsin. gov/children/foster

State Interstate Compact on the Placement of Children (ICPC) Administrator

Wisconsin Division of Children and Family Services
Office of Children and Family Services
P.O. Box 8916
Madison, WI 53708-8916
Phone: (608) 266-1489
Fax: (608) 264-6750
E-mail: klickel@dhfs.state.wi.us

State Licensing Specialist

Wisconsin Department of Health and Family Services
Bureau of Regulation and Licensing
P.O. Box 8916
Madison, WI 53708-8916
Phone: (608) 266-0415
Fax: (608) 267-7252
E-mail: deessh@dhfs.state.wi.us
Web site: www.dhfs.state.wi.us/ licensing.htm

WYOMING

Adoptive/Foster Family Support Groups

Northern Wyoming Adoptive Parents and North American Council on Adoptable Children State Representative
P.O. Box 788
Basin, WY 82410
Phone: (307) 568-2729
E-mail: ikftate@hotmail.com

Wyoming Children's Society
P.O. Box 105
Cheyenne, WY 82003
Phone: (307) 632-7619
Fax: (307) 632-3056
Toll-Free: (800) 584-9384
E-mail: wyomingcs@wyomingcs. org
Web site: www.wyomingcs.org
– Intercountry Program
– Child Placement

Adoption Agencies

A.D.O.P.T.
7860 Chukar Drive
Gillette, WY 82716
Phone: (307) 687-7147
Fax: (307) 682-4157

Adoption in the Teton
P.O. Box 3774
Jackson, WY 83001
Phone: (307) 733-5680

Casey Family Program
130 Hobbs Avenue
Cheyenne, WY 82009
Phone: (307) 638-2564
Fax: (307) 632-5251

Catholic Charities of Wyoming, Inc
P.O. Box 1468
Cheyenne, WY 82003
Phone: (307) 638-1530
Fax: (307) 637-7936
Toll-Free: (800) 788-4606
E-mail: betsy@dioceseof cheyenne.org
Web site: www. dioceseofcheyenne.org/catholic_ social_services_htm

Focus on Children, Inc.
405 Sage Street
Cokeville, WY 83114
Phone: (307) 279-3434
Fax: (307) 279-3444
E-mail: thorns@allwest.net
Web site: www.focus-on-children.com
– Intercountry Program
– Child Placement

Global Adoption Services, Inc.
50 East Loucks Street, Suite 205
Sheridan, WY 82801
Phone: (307) 674-6606
Fax: (307) 672-7605
E-mail: Wyoming@adoptglobal.org
Web site: www.adoptglobal.org
– Intercountry Program
– Child Placement

LDS Family Services, Inc.
1898 Fort Road, #16A
Sheridan, WY 82801-8320
Phone: (307) 637-5364
Fax: (307) 638-7422
Toll-Free: (800) 537-2229

Wyoming Children's Society
314 21st Street
Cheyenne, WY 82001-3721
Phone: (307) 632-7619
Fax: (307) 632-3056
Toll-Free: (800) 584-9384
E-mail: wyomingcs@wyomingcs.org
Web site: www.wyomingcs.org

Wyoming Parenting Society
P.O. Box 3774
Jackson, WY 83001
Phone: (307) 733-3998
Fax: (307) 734-5754
E-mail: kingwill@blissnet.com
– Intercountry Program
– Child Placement

State Adoption Exchange/ Photolisting of Children Waiting For Adoption

Wyoming Children Available for Adoption
2300 Capitol Avenue
Cheyenne, WY 82002
E-mail: mclift@missc.state.wy.us
Web site: http://dfsweb.state.wy.us/childsvc/updates/adoption/tocadp.htm

Wyoming Department of Family Services Hathaway Building
Maureen Clifton
2300 Capitol Avenue, 3rd Floor
Cheyenne, WY 82002-0490
Phone: (307) 777-3570
Fax: (307) 777-3693
E-mail: mclift@state.wy.us
Web site: http://dfsweb.state.wy.us

State Interstate Compact on the Placement of Children (ICPC) Administrator

Wyoming Department of Family Services Hathaway Building
2300 Capitol Avenue,
3rd Floor, Room 376
Cheyenne, WY 82002-0490
Phone: (307) 777-3570
Fax: (307) 777-3693
E-mail: mclift@state.wy.us
Web site: www.dfsweb.state.wy.us/adoption.html

Wyoming Department of Family Services
130 Hobbs Avenue
Cheyenne, WY 82002-0490
Phone: (307) 777-6081
Fax: (307) 777-3693
E-mail: svajda@state.wy.us

State Adoption Specialist/Manager

Wyoming Department of Family Services Hathaway Building
Maureen Clifton
2300 Capitol Avenue, 3rd Floor, Room 376
Cheyenne, WY 82002-0490
Phone: (307) 777-3570
Fax: (307) 777-3693
E-mail: mclift@state.wy.us
Web site: www.dfsweb.state.wy.us/childsvc/certlist.htm

State Confidential Intermediary Service

Wyoming Confidential Adoption Intermediary Services
2300 Capitol Avenue
Cheyenne, WY 82002-0710
Phone: (307) 777-3570
Fax: (307) 777-3693

State Foster Care Specialist/Manager

State Complaints Office
Maureen Clifton
Wyoming Dept. of Family Services
2300 Capitol Ave.
Cheyenne, WY 82002-0490
Phone: (307) 777-3570
Fax: (307) 777-3693
E-mail: mclift.@state.wy.us

Index

A

Accutane (isotretinoin), affecting infants, 378
Acquired Immune Deficiency Syndrome (AIDS), 366–67
Active registries, 116–17
Adoptee Search Center, 112–13, 117
Adoptees Liberty Movement Association (ALMA), 116
Adopting
choosing kind of child, 6
eligibility for, 4–5
reasons for wanting children and, 8–10
where to begin, 5–6
Adoption
accepting parenthood through, 7–10
finalizing, 398–99. *See also specific states*
historical perspective, 76–77
Adoption agency. *See also* Agency adoption; Private agencies
defined, 12
international adoptions, 156–57, 158–60
investigating reputations of, 31
overview of, 12–13
purpose of, 12–13
representing adoptive parents, 25
representing birth parents, 12–13, 25
screening process of, 26
traditional adoption, 16–18
turning you down, 26
types of, 12
Adoption and Safe Families Act (ASFA), 263
Adoption consent requirements, 394, 397–98. *See also specific states*
Adoption hearing, notice of, 35–36, 395–96. *See also specific states*
Adoption organizations. *See* Appendix B
Adoption petition (complaint), 35,
396–97. *See also specific states*
Adoption petition/hearing. *See also specific states*
Adoption Taxpayer Identification Number, 214
Adoptive parents
qualities birth mothers look for in, 80
rights of, 26–27
Advertising. *See also* Birth mother, finding
for facilitated agency adoption, 18
how long to run, 68
for independent adoptions, 33, 61–68
on Internet, 69
legalities of, 394.
See also specific states
sample ads, 65–66
for transracial adoption, 298–99
what to include in, 61–65
where to place, 66–68

673